PSYCHIATRIC DISABILITY

Clinical, Legal, and
Administrative Dimensions

PSYCHIATRIC DISABILITY

CLINICAL, LEGAL, AND ADMINISTRATIVE DIMENSIONS

Edited by
Arthur T. Meyerson, M.D.
Theodora Fine, M.A.

American
Psychiatric
Press, Inc.

1400 K Street, N.W.
Washington, D.C. 20005

Library of Congress Cataloging-in-Publication Data

Psychiatric disability

Includes bibliographies and index.
1. Psychiatric disability evaluation—United States.
2. Mental illness—United States—Epidemiology.
3. Social security—United States.   4. Mentally ill—
Rehabilitation—United States.   I. Meyerson, Arthur T.,
1936–   . II. Fine, Theodora, 1949–   . [DNLM:
1. Disability Evaluation.   2. Insurance, Psychiatric—
United States.   3. Mental Disorders—occurrence—
United States.   4. Mental Disorders—rehabilitation.
5. Mental Health Services—United States.   WM 30 P9725]
RC470.P79   1987   616.89′075   87-1069
ISBN 0-88048-210-9

CONTENTS

CONTRIBUTORS

William A. Anthony, Ph.D.
Director, Center for Rehabilitation Research and Training in Mental Health, Boston University, Boston, Massachusetts

Leona L. Bachrach, Ph. D.
Research Professor of Psychiatry, Maryland Psychiatric Research Center, University of Maryland School of Medicine, Baltimore, Maryland

Bertram Black, M.S.W.
Professor (Rehabilitation), Department of Psychiatry, Albert Einstein College of Medicine, Bronx, New York

Gayla A. Blackwell, R.N., M.S.W.
Chief, Behavioral Rehabilitation Program, Brentwood VA Medical Center, Los Angeles, California

Carroll M. Brodsky, M.D., Ph.D.
Professor of Psychiatry, University of California, San Francisco Medical Center, San Francisco, California

Robert N. Butler, M.D.
Chairman and Professor, Department of Geriatrics and Adult Development, Mt. Sinai Medical Center, New York, New York

Mikal R. Cohen, Ph.D.
Director of Training of the Center for Rehabilitation Research and Training in Mental Health, Boston University, Boston, Massachusetts

Murray J. Cohen, M.D.
Associate Psychiatrist and Chief of Psychiatric Outpatient Department, Lenox Hill Hospital, New York, New York

Mary P. Crosby
Assistant Director, American Academy of Child Psychiatry, Washington, D.C.

Ronald J. Diamond, M.D.
Associate Professor of Psychiatry, University of Wisconsin Medical School; and Medical Director, Mobile Community Treatment Program, Dane County Mental Health Center, Madison, Wisconsin

Patricia Dilley, J.D.
Staff Director, Subcommittee on Social Security, Committee on Ways and Means, U.S. House of Representatives, Washington, D.C.

Robert M. Factor, M.D., Ph.D.
Assistant Professor of Psychiatry and Director of Psychiatric Residency Training, University of Wisconsin Medical School; and Medical Director, Emergency Services Unit, Dane County Mental Health Center, Madison, Wisconsin

Marianne D. Farkas, Sc.D.
Associate Director of Training, Center for Psychiatric Rehabilitation, Boston University, Boston, Massachusetts

Theodora Fine, M.A.
Assistant Director, Office of Research, American Psychiatric Association, Washington, D.C.

Eric J. Fischer, J.D.
Supervising Attorney, Community Legal Services, Inc., Philadelphia, Pennsylvania

Roland M. Gallagher, M.D.
Associate Professor of Psychiatry and Family Practice, University of Vermont College of Medicine, Burlington, Vermont

Martin Gittelman, Ph.D.
Faculty, New York College of Medicine, Lincoln Hospital, Bronx, New York

Howard H. Goldman, M.D., Ph.D.
Associate Professor of Mental Health Policy Studies, Department of Psychiatry, University of Maryland Medical School, Baltimore, Maryland

Ernest M. Gruenberg, M.D., Dr.P.H.
Consultant, Bethesda, Maryland

John M. Hamilton, M.D.
Private practice of psychiatry; and Social Security Administration Quality Assurance Consultant, Baltimore, Maryland

Raymond F. Hanbury, Jr., Ph.D.
Director of Clinical Services, Narcotics Rehabilitation Center; and Assistant Professor, Department of Psychiatry, Mt. Sinai Hospital and School of Medicine, New York, New York

John Heinz
U.S. Senator, Republican of Pennsylvania; and Ranking Minority Member, Senate Special Committee on Aging, Washington, D.C.

Harvey E. Jacobs, Ph.D.
Assistant Research Psychologist, UCLA School of Medicine, Los Angeles, California

Charles A. Kaufmann, M.D.
Assistant Professor of Clinical Psychiatry, College of Physicians and Surgeons, Columbia University, New York, New York

Cille Kennedy, Ph.D.
Director of Research and Training, Social Security Disability Evaluation Study, American Psychiatric Association, Washington, D.C.

James Krajeski, M.D.
Regional Medical Advisor, Social Security Administration, San Francisco, California

H. Richard Lamb, M.D.
Professor of Psychiatry, University of Southern California School of Medicine, Los Angeles, California

Juliet C. Lesser, Ph.D.
Psychologist, Bronx VA Medical Center, Bronx, New York

Robert Paul Liberman, M.D.
Professor of Psychiatry, UCLA School of Medicine, Los Angeles, California

John O. Lipkin, M.D.
Associate Director for Psychiatry, Mental Health and Behavioral Sciences Service, Veterans Administration Central Office, Washington, D.C.

Melvin Lipsett, M.D.
Private practice of psychiatry, San Francisco, California; and member, American Psychiatric Association Task Force on SSI/SSDI and Joint Commission on Government Relations, Washington, D.C.

Ronald W. Manderscheid, Ph.D.
Chief, Survey and Reports Branch, National Institute of Mental Health, Rockville, Maryland

H. Keith Massel, Ph.D.
Assistant Research Psychologist, UCLA School of Medicine, Los Angeles, California

Arthur T. Meyerson, M.D.
Professor of Clinical Psychiatry, and Vice-Chairman of Psychiatry, Mt. Sinai School of Medicine, New York, New York

Richard C. Mohs, Ph.D.
Psychologist, Bronx VA Medical Center, Bronx, New York; and Associate Professor, Department of Psychiatry, Mt. Sinai School of Medicine, New York, New York

J.J. Pickle
U.S. Representative, Democrat of Texas; member, House Ways and Means Committee; and Chairman, Subcommittee on Oversight, Washington, D.C.

Nancy C.A. Roeske, M.D.
Dr. Roeske, who died on April 21, 1986, was the liaison of the American Psychiatric Association to the Consortium on Child Mental Health and served on a variety of components of the APA governance structure.

Leonard S. Rubenstein, J.D.
Legal Director, Mental Health Law Project, Washington, D.C.

Irvin D. Rutman, Ph.D.
Director, Matrix Research Institute, Philadelphia, Pennsylvania

Alan Simpson, Ph.D.
Chief, Vocational Restoration Program, Brentwood VA Medical Center, Los Angeles, California

Leonard I. Stein, M.D.
Professor of Psychiatry, University of Wisconsin Medical School; and Medical Director, Dane County Mental Health Center, Madison, Wisconsin

Frances Stewart, M.D.
Professor of Psychiatry, University of Vermont, Burlington, Vermont

Daniel R. Weinberger, M.D.
Chief, Clinical Neuropsychiatry and Neurobehavior Section, Neuropsychiatry Branch, National Institute of Mental Health Intramural Research Program, Washington, D.C.

Jane Bloom Yohalem, J.D.
Former Director of Children's Programs, Mental Health Law Project, Washington, D.C.

Foreword 1

One of the highlights of my 20 years in Congress was the passage, after almost 2 years of effort by many members of the Committee on Ways and Means and of the Senate, of the 1984 Social Security Disability Benefits Reform Act. I know of few issues that have stirred the indignation of members of Congress of all political persuasions as the campaign in 1981–1983 to terminate disability benefits for hundreds of thousands of disabled people, particularly mentally disabled people.

It is a great pleasure to introduce this study of an extremely important, but all too often neglected area: psychiatric disability and the public policy response to it. The entire process of diagnosing and treating a mental impairment, and determining its effect on a person's ability to work, is very complex and difficult, and it is crucial that innovative research in this area be supported and made available to policy makers, professionals, and the public. I believe this volume will contribute substantially to our understanding of many current issues in this exciting field, and will promote better policy making in the future.

Of all the reforms mandated by the comprehensive disability legislation enacted in 1984, one of the most significant is the overhaul of the standards used to evaluate mental disabilities. These changes, which were initiated as a result of compelling evidence that the standards for reviewing mental impairments were antiquated, unfair, and unrealistic, are wide ranging and will likely affect the disability program for years to come. The new rules, which were authorized in broad purpose by the Congress and developed in detail by an advisory panel of psychiatric experts, are finally in place. It will take the energy and initiative of all participants in the disability adjudication process—treating professionals, claimants' lawyers and advocates, and the Social Security Administration—to assure that these new standards work in assuring that the mentally impaired receive balanced, reasonable, and fair decisions. I also expect the Congress and, in particular, the Committee on Ways and Means which has a long history of interest and activity in the disability area, to continue close oversight of the adjudicative process to guarantee that the new standards are operating as we intended and to assess their impact on the program as a whole.

The identification and assessment of mental disorders, and the evaluation of a mentally impaired individual's ability to function in the competitive workplace, is an area that will continue to witness considerable change and innovation in the coming years. As a society, we must strive to keep the principal mechanism we have for protecting the mentally disabled from financial ruin, and, at the same time, keep the Social Security Disability Insurance and Supplemental Security Income programs up to date with these changes. People with mental disorders are a particularly vulnerable group, and we must ensure that the programs designed to serve them are compassionate and effective. The real challenge for the future is twofold: to assure that state-of-the-art knowledge and research are incorporated into the mental disability adjudication rules and procedures; and to develop new approaches to psychiatric treatment and rehabilitation that improve the ability of the mentally disabled to overcome their impairments and to live and work independently. The present book is an important contribution toward this end, and should be welcomed by all concerned in this field.

Congressman J.J. Pickle (D-Texas)
Chairman, Subcommittee on Oversight
Former Chairman, Social Security Subcommittee
Committee on Ways and Means
U.S. House of Representatives

Foreword 2

J ust two years ago, Congress struggled with a Social Security disability program in a state of near anarchy. We confronted an unprecedented revolt of both states and courts against the Social Security Administration (SSA) in its management of the continuing eligibility reviews.

At the heart of this national crisis were alarming accounts of severely disabled individuals being terminated from the program rolls under an inflexible, inhuman review process. As established in testimony before the Senate Special Committee on Aging, of which I am the Chairman, individuals with mental impairments were particularly vulnerable. Many lost their benefits based solely upon their ability to feed a pet, watch television, or visit relatives, notwithstanding clear medical evidence demonstrating severe mental impairment, and inability to work.

Congress responded to these abuses and the extremely negative climate within the SSA with the Social Security Disability Benefits Reform Act (Public Law 98-460). Signed into law on October 9, 1984, the act both placed a moratorium on all reviews of the mentally impaired until implementation of a new standard for such persons, and required the development of a new standard requiring the demonstration of medical improvement before someone could be removed from the SSDI rolls.

New standards for evaluating disabilities caused by mental impairments resulted in large part from the work of many of the contributors to this volume. Published in late summer, 1985, these rules established an increased number of medically appropriate categories for mental disorders and new standards for medical evidence. Disability reviews began again in January, 1986, with the new law and many more protective regulations in place.

This text, developed since the new regulations were formulated, defines the population of severely mentally ill and outlines the rehabilitative options for getting these individuals back into the real world. Its authors combine a detailed evaluation of the Social Security disability program with a walk through the system's administrative and legal frameworks, and advice on how to make it work for the beneficiary. The sum product is a comprehensive overview of psychiatric disability: an excellent resource for doctors, teachers, and members of the legal profession.

The ultimate goal of the Social Security disability program is the rehabilitation of the chronically ill—including the chronically mentally ill. One certainty is that the Senate Special Committee on Aging will continue to monitor the treatment of mentally disabled Americans on the disability insurance rolls to assure they receive the assistance the law intends.

Senator John Heinz (R-Pennsylvania)
Chairman, Senate Special Committee on Aging
United States Senate

Introduction

Arthur T. Meyerson, M.D.
Theodora Fine, M.A.

This volume, intended to bring together clinical, administrative, and legal issues relating to psychiatric disability, is a comprehensive textbook which focuses on converging and diverging definitions of, programmatic approaches to, and benefit programs for, the psychiatrically disabled. Intended as a sourcebook, it provides extensive textual and bibliographic material about:

- epidemiology and clinical pathology of psychiatric disability;
- clinical issues arising in specific disorders and populations;
- approaches to programs for the psychiatrically disabled;
- training models for psychiatrists and rehabilitation workers;
- specific guides for the conduct of psychiatric evaluations required by Social Security, Veterans' Administration, and workers' compensation programs; and
- administrative and legal processes which underlie major disability programs.

In Webster's New Collegiate Dictionary, disability is defined within entitlement programs as a simple linear function—an "inability to pursue an occupation because of physical or mental impairment." While this approach offers the appeal of simple logic, John Strauss (1974, 1977) and others have advocated substantially more complex models of understanding mental illness and functional capacity which more accurately reflect the reality of psychiatric disability. To date, this divergence of definition has yet to be resolved.

Several of the chapters, dealing with the history, administrative process, and clinical evaluation within specific entitlement programs, reflect the simple linear model. These chapters are intended to enable clinicians working in the field to better understand and function within the restricted models used by specific entitlement programs. In contrast, many of the other chapters encompass more holistic (albeit more complex) approaches, reflecting the scientific evolution of the psychiatric disability field. Further, because of this

divergence in definition, determinations of the incidence and prevalence of psychiatric disability vary. However, there is agreement both
within psychiatry and among public policy makers that psychiatric
disability is a major public health concern.

The book is divided into sections dealing with epidemiology and
clinical pathology, psychiatric rehabilitation, and administrative and
legal issues.

The first section's overview describes the epidemiology and clinical pathology of psychiatric impairment, walking the reader through
biologic and sociologic–environmental determinants of psychiatric
disability. The section on clinical issues explores a variety of populations, based both on diagnostic category (schizophrenia, substance
abuse disorder, severe physical illness) and on social characteristics
(homelessness, aging, childhood).

The section on psychiatric rehabilitation examines the complex
constellation of services and practices which has as its goal the
prevention, reduction, or resolution of psychiatric disability. An overview of the state of the art is provided. The use of skills training in the
conduct of rehabilitation is examined, and training models for rehabilitation workers and psychiatrists are presented.

The sections on legal and administrative issues provide a practical guide to the development and conduct of psychiatric evaluations
under the Social Security Disability Insurance (SSDI), workers' compensation, and Veterans' Administration disability programs. They
further examine incentives and disincentives of disability programs
as they affect the rehabilitation of the chronically mentally ill. A
review of the state of psychiatric rehabilitation in western Europe
provides a cross-cultural perspective. In the section on judicial perspectives, authorities within Congress and the executive branch review the legislature and regulatory history of the SSDI program,
providing insight into the inner workings of public policy decision
making as it bears on the psychiatrically disabled, and presaging
possible future program directions. The past, current, and future role
of the courts as interpreters and catalysts for change of federal disability programs is carefully examined by attorneys with expertise
and involvement in the significant psychiatric disability litigation.

The contributors, from a multiplicity of disciplines, cover the
complex of factors affecting the psychiatrically disabled. At the same
time, they highlight the need for educated and committed professionals to become more involved in working with the mentally disabled. The editors intend this book to both educate and challenge its
readers to become so involved.

REFERENCES

Strauss JS, Carpenter WT: The prediction of outcome in schizophrenia II: Relationships between predictors and outcome variables. Arch Gen Psychiatry 31:37-42,
1974
Strauss JS, Carpenter WT: Prediction of outcome in schizophrenia III. Arch Gen
Psychiatry 34:159-163, 1977

EPIDEMIOLOGY AND CLINICAL PATHOLOGY: OVERVIEW

1

A Lexicology for the Consequences of Mental Disorders

Cille Kennedy, Ph.D.
Ernest M. Gruenberg, M.D., Dr.P.H.

Disease and injury can limit the victim's life. These limitations occur at three levels which are fundamentally different, but rarely sharply distinguished from each other in the literature. What makes matters worse is that it is common to use the same terms to describe the three different levels of limitation. This chapter presents a framework which distinguishes the different levels of experience at which a person's life can become limited as a consequence of disease or injury. We focus particularly upon the consequences of disturbances in mental function. The chapter then offers a paradigm, developed by the World Health Organization (1980), which places these limitations into one of three conceptual levels, helping to avoid ambiguity and misunderstanding among those exchanging information about mentally disordered people. Finally, the chapter addresses the diversity of terminology utilized in the field. Of particular interest is the variety of meaning given to the word *disability*.

We need an explicit framework in which to anchor our terminology. This need becomes especially clear when we consider the interactions among clinicians, administrators, and the legal system in making decisions about the eligibility of mentally disordered people seeking disability benefits. The problems surrounding the adjudication of claims in the Social Security Administration's (SSA) disability programs offer a good example of the difficulty.

In its regulations and program manuals, the SSA has established an administrative procedure to determine the disability status of claimants, based in its interpretation of what Congress meant by "disability" under Titles II and XVI of the Social Security Act. Determining that disability status should be based on review of both medical and nonmedical factors alike, SSA has constructed a procedure through which both are evaluated. The review is based upon detailed medical evidence submitted by the claimant's physician(s) and other acceptable (as identified by the SSA) sources. Unfortunately, the SSA adjudicator and the practicing medical clinician generally do not share a common definition of disability. For the clinician, disability is but one of a number of criteria which establish a patient's diagnosis. The American Psychiatric Association's *Diagnostic and Statistical Manual of Mental Disorders, Third Edition* (*DSM-III;* 1980) requires the presence of disability in order to establish the presence of some disorders. Thus, for many clinicians, once a diagnosis is established, a patient's "disability" is *de facto.* Beyond a statement regarding diagnosis, detailed information of a patient's disability seems redundant, and often is not provided to SSA adjudicators.

In contrast, SSA regulations and procedures manuals do not utilize the concept of diagnosis in the same way. Diagnosis is but one part of the medical evidence required to establish evidence of a disability. Clinicians, then, often do not understand why their patients are not awarded disability benefits because, as they see it, the existence of a diagnosis establishes the very presence of a disability.

Thus, the difference between the use of the term disability by clinicians and the SSA leads to an inappropriate or inadequate sharing of knowledge about the status of many mentally disordered people, to their serious detriment.

THREE LEVELS AT WHICH LIFE CAN BECOME LIMITED

A person's life can be limited at three different levels. In brief, the first limits the function of a body organ or part; the second limits a person's actions in specific situations; and the third limits a person's participation in important social institutions.

Organ Functions

The function of a single organ or limb, or a part thereof, can be limited by that part's absence, injury, or disease. For instance, eye damage or the loss or absence of an eye causes blindness; damage to auditory structures can cause deafness. Spinal cord injury causes paraplegia. Many specific mental functions can be limited. For example, Alzheimer's disease can produce loss of memory and of other cognitive functions. The organ damage may be present at birth or occur at any stage of life. The absence, injury, or disease of a body part is the fact which *may* limit life activity. However, the same defect of the organ or body part in two given individuals may limit them in very different ways.

Person's Actions

The second level at which life can be limited is when a person is acting in a specific situation. Limited function of an organ or organ system may affect a person's capacity to function in particular settings or to perform particular tasks. For example, people with impaired leg function may be restricted in their ability to move freely from place to place; mobility is limited. The blind cannot read; the deaf cannot converse.

Person's Social Participation

The third level of life which may be limited is the ability to participate in important social activities which make for a "normal" life. This refers to the ordinary ebb and flow of daily home and family life: going to school, engaging in work, shopping, recreation, dating and courting, sexuality, etc. Limitations at this level *result* in social disadvantage. The resulting social disadvantages include failure to develop friendships, not being included in the plans of others, social isolation, and the like.

Other factors external to the individual also affect the extent to which a person's social activities may be limited. Social practices and attitudes may further limit the social participation of a person whose activities are diminished. For example, those limited in their mobility are not often invited to attend dances which in turn deprives them of participation in such social activities, thereby limiting their social world.

WAYS OF REDUCING THESE LIMITATIONS

Limitations at each of the three levels of function may be reduced. The most fundamental is to cure the disease which is causing the organ impairment, as with some forms of encephalitis. Partial correction or cure at the organ level represents the next most basic approach. These are dependent upon the state of medical knowledge and technology.

Prostheses can reduce physical limitations at both the level of the organ and at that of the person's activity (e.g., eyeglasses, leg braces, false teeth, hearing aids, artificial limbs, etc.). These prostheses either correct or replace the function of the organ or body part. These compensatory mechanisms enable the person to make actions otherwise impossible. For instance, wheelchairs and ramps can extend the range of movement in the physical environment for amputees and paraplegics. Closed-caption television, sign language, and lip-reading can assist those whose limitation in hearing affects their ability to communicate. Braille, reading services, seeing-eye dogs, and canes reduce some of the limitations of activity created by blindness.

These prosthetic devices or other compensatory mechanisms do not eliminate the limited organ functioning. They simply reduce the effect of the limitation on the person's actions.

At the third level, reduction of limitations of social participation may be accomplished through changes in social practice, policy, education, or legislation. For example, federal legislation now requires buildings constructed with federal funds to be accessible to all. As a result, these buildings are constructed with ramps and barrier-free restrooms. People whose mobility has been improved by these changes have increased the social advantages available to them.

Reducing social disadvantage is not solely a matter of gadgetry. It is also a matter of social attitudes and culture. The person of limited mobility, of limited vision, of limited hearing or speech can be welcomed by, benefit from, and contribute to schools, work sites, recreational and cultural events to a greater extent if other participants are unprejudiced and willing to help. These attitudes and courtesies can make a substantial difference in social participation. Asking for help, accepting help, and describing the help needed without making the helper uncomfortable is a challenge to the person with limited action potential. Attitudinal adaptation on the part of the "disabled" therefore is also useful.

LIMITATIONS OF MENTAL FUNCTIONING AND REPERCUSSIONS

Mental disorders impose limitation at all three levels. One example is suggested by Alzheimer's disease, which causes loss of memory and of other cognitive functions. A schizophrenic who hallucinates suffers a functional loss of contact with reality. These are examples of functional limitations at the organ level based on mental disorders.

At the level of activity or action, the Alzheimer's patient might not be able to carry out a coherent conversation. He or she might be able to compensate by participating in a superficial way, and using such pre-stored responses as, "It's a lovely day, isn't it." Such a person might invite a friend to dinner, then forget having called, and phone the friend six more times with the same invitation. The schizophrenic's ability to communicate might be limited by the loss of reality-testing capacity. She or he might interrupt conversations to respond to hallucinated voices. These are examples of functional limitations at the level of the person in action.

Limitations in participation in society often occur because of the stigma attached to mental disorders. People qualified for jobs are not hired because of a history of psychiatric hospitalizations. Former mental patients are excluded from group living, in certain neighborhoods, by zoning ordinances enacted to keep them out. It is estimated that for every community residential program which is established, another is successfully blocked (Piasecki 1975). Friends of Alzheimer's patients become annoyed with the forgetfulness and stop initiating social contact. Such social network withdrawal places the patient at a social disadvantage; resources are reduced and new ones are difficult to develop. In each of these instances, individuals systematically are placed at a disadvantage by their inability to participate in society, whether in the work setting, the neighborhood, or other settings.

Professional discussion of the process of reducing limitations on social participation are labeled *normalization* in the literature on mental retardation (Wolfensberger 1970), and either *social integration* or *community integration* in the mental health literature (Segal and Aviram, 1978).

THE WORLD HEALTH ORGANIZATION DRAFT CLASSIFICATION

In an attempt to provide a classification system for the sequelae or consequences of disorder, disease, or injury, the World Health Organization (WHO) developed a draft supplement to the *International Classification of Diseases, Ninth Revision* (World Health Organization 1978). It classifies dysfunctions into those that occur in the same three levels of life which may be affected adversely by a disease or disorder: impaired functions of an organ, "disabled" activities of a person in a specific situation, and "handicapped" participation in society. The WHO labels these levels of dysfunction as impairment, disability, and handicap.

These are unfortunate choices as all three terms have widespread usage to refer to the other two levels. *Handicap* is often used as an euphemism for a fixed deficit of a limb, of intelligence, or of vision. Confining our usage of each term to the specific level, as we do in this chapter, requires some effort and thought. The effort and thought expended, however, are repaid as one finds that issues which previously seemed thorny and tangled become much more readily understandable and manageable.

Impairment—an impairment is a limitation due to a defect in an organ's functioning. Impairment can be produced by a disorder or by trauma. In other words, defective or absent organs or body parts can result in a distorted or defective function, termed an impairment.

Disability—disabilities occur at the level of the person's actions in specific situations. The limitation of activity produced by an impairment, thus, is termed disability. Disabilities in personal self-care, such as dressing, grooming, excretory control, getting to bed, and eating, are grouped together by WHO. Occupational disabilities form another group. Disabilities of social interaction form another. Gruenberg (1982) groups disabilities into loss of control of socially unacceptable impulses, and loss of self-care, work, and recreational activities.

There are three aspects of disability which bear attention. First, the same impairment may lead to different degrees of disability in different people. One person with paraplegia spins vigorously down the streets and long corridors in her wheelchair and flips the wheelchair easily into the back seat of her car, while her older, less vigorous friend pushes through the same route more slowly and with more fatigue. The greater limitation of ability in the older paraplegic is not due to extra impairment, but rather to fewer energy reserves with which to overcome the impairment. While both are fully independent, live alone, and go to work daily, this independence would end if either suffered a fractured arm, foreclosing the use of a wheelchair. Both would become seriously disabled, essentially bed-bound, until the arm was restored to full strength. The second issue to be aware of, thus, is that a combination of two impairments can produce a disability of greater severity than their simple sum. The third is that a particular disability can be the result of different impairments in different organ systems. For example, inability to read may be caused by blindness, by severe cognitive deficit, or delirium. One person cannot walk because of a broken ankle, another because of a spinal cord injury, and yet a third because he or she has only one leg. In addition, disabilities are manifested when the individual interacts with the physical and social environment. The severity of disability can be reduced not only by the individual's efforts to compensate, but also by the environment's adaptability.

Handicap—handicap is a disadvantage to or limitation in social participation. The WHO manual does not try to classify the varieties of social disadvantages. Instead it suggests a six-dimensional profile of the competencies needed for full social participation. These dimensions of competence, called "survival roles," include orientation in place, physical independence, mobility in space, occupational engagement (both at work and play), social integration, and economic self-sufficiency. Disadvantages or limitations in these competencies may be barriers to full participation in society. Stigma or prejudice sometimes further limits participation for the physically and mentally handicapped.

THE USES AND DEFINITIONS OF ESSENTIAL TERMS

Different definitions of disability have been developed and used to determine if people should qualify for special benefits or services, or be excused from obligations (e.g., military service, exemption from ordinary school or work). Several chapters in this volume illustrate some of these differences, especially differences among federal programs. The Veterans' Administration has one set of criteria, workers' compensation programs another, and the Social Security Administration, a third. Access to services and programs for chronically mentally ill adults depends on another use of the term disability. The remainder of this chapter identifies similarities and differences among the uses of the term in different settings.

Social Security Administration Programs

In their chapters, Eric Fischer, Patricia Dilley, and John Hamilton give an overview of the Social Security Administration's (SSA) two disability programs, Social Security Disability Insurance (SSDI) and Supplemental Security Income (SSI). The two programs are based on the same statutory definition of disability—the most strict of all vocational disability standards. Patricia Dilley's chapter provides a rich review of the development of SSA disability legislation, Hamilton's, an analysis of the regulatory issues surrounding the programs, and Fischer's describes the administrative procedures used in making a disability determination. Therefore, we limit our comments to a comparison of SSA's use of the term with that of the WHO paradigm.

Section 223(d)(1) of the Social Security Act states that "the term 'disability' means the inability to engage in any substantial gainful activity by reason of any medically determinable physical or mental impairment(s) which can be expected to result in death or which has lasted or can be expected to last for a continuous period of not less than 12 months" (SSA 1985a). This definition is consistent with the WHO classification of impairment as the basis for disability. Moreover, the statute further states that "impairments are the result of anatomical, physiological or psychological abnormalities," also consistent with the WHO paradigm. In its regulations and operations manuals, Program Operations Manual System (POMS), the SSA defines "substantial gainful activity" (SGA) as competitive work, and is only concerned with disabilities which are related to paid work.

The SSA definition of disability encompasses two domains: medical and nonmedical. Among the nonmedical aspects are the claimant's age, education, and prior work experience, and the types of jobs that exist in the national economy. The SSA is concerned with the handicapping features of a person's age or the number of appropriate jobs for a claimant in the region where the claimant lives. The SSA recognizes that an older individual is less likely to be able to get a job. However, in the case of younger persons for whom suitable jobs exist in sufficient numbers in the economy, the SSA disregards whether or not the person, in reality, would be hired. These types of nonmedical assessment, perhaps seen as an assessment of the claimant's handicaps under the WHO paradigm, are conducted by the nonmedical members of the review team.

While the SSA admits that impairment exists along a continuum of severity, the statute does not permit partial or temporary payments. Claims adjudications are substantially more cut and dried: The person is or is not disabled under the statutory definition and is or is not eligible for benefits on that basis alone.

Workers' Compensation Programs
Worker-compensation programs, described in Carroll Brodsky's chapter, pay benefits to those found to be disabled as defined by their inability to work. Disability benefits are paid to cover medical care, temporary wage replacements, rehabilitation, and for permanent wage compensation.

Because worker-compensation programs pay for partial, as well as total disability, physicians are required to provide both qualitative and quantitative information about the degree of disability. In order to do this, many worker-compensation programs rely on such standards as the American Medical Association's *Guides to the Evaluation of Permanent Impairment* (AMA 1984). The AMA *Guides* was developed to provide clinically sound criteria for rating impairment. It is used by physicians, attorneys, and adjudicators to assess individuals seeking disability benefits from agencies and programs.

The *Guides* attempts to follow the WHO classification system although the conceptual delineation among impairment, disability, and handicap is somewhat indistinct in the area of mental impairment. The absence of a precise definition is exacerbated by the *Guides'* glossary which does not follow the WHO system and to which the reader is referred. The *Guides* contains a table which lists degrees of impairment along three dimensions for mental disorder. The first is mental status, containing six subcategories: intelligence, thinking, perception, judgment, affect, and behavior. The two other dimensions are disabilities: activities of daily living and rehabilitation or treatment potential. By combining ratings in each of these categories, the collective, or whole-person impairment rating is achieved.

This process indicates that no distinction is made between impairments and disabilities as in the WHO tradition. Most notably, activities of daily living and rehabilitation potential are seen as classes of impairment which combine to establish the whole-person impairment rating. In the WHO nomenclature, activities of daily living are but one kind of disability; rehabilitation or treatment potential, however, is not a loss of organ level function. In practice, the *Guides* uses *impairment* to refer to both impairments and disabilities.

Veterans' Administration Disability Programs
As Fischer and Lipkin note in their chapters, there are two broad Veterans' Administration (VA) disability programs. The difference between the two is based on whether or not the disability is service-connected. Fischer does not define the term directly but states that disability results from personal injury or disease. It is evident that the VA views disability as a limit on the claimant's earning capacity. In other words, disability is linked directly to the ability to work.

For service-connected disabilities, the VA differs from the SSA's all-or-nothing definition of ability to work. The VA has a schedule of compensation ranging from a minimum of 10 percent, for partial disability, to 100 percent for total disability. For the nonservice-connected program, disabilities in the VA and the SSA are alike in that benefits are only given to those found to be totally disabled. To reiterate, both the VA and the SSA consider *only* disability for work as the criterion for benefits in their programs. None of the other areas of disability noted earlier in this chapter—self-care, recreation, or control of socially unacceptable, troublesome impulses—are sufficient as entitlement criteria under these two programs.

Programs for the Chronically Mentally Ill Adult

In Goldman and Manderscheid's chapter on epidemiology, identification of the chronic and disabled mentally ill population is based on diagnosis, disability, and duration. The authors define the term disability as the functional limitations of the person in action. This is consistent with the WHO classification. The areas of activities which they list as potentially limited are consistent with the areas of disability described by Gruenberg (1982).

One might infer, erroneously, that disorders lead to disabilities. But, as the WHO nomenclature states, disorders do not lead to disabilities; impairments do. Identifying particular clusters of impairment leads to the diagnosis of a particular disorder. Since *DSM-III-R* criteria define some disorders as equivalent to symptoms which are also impairments, confusion can arise, as in the case of some phobias.

In Goldman and Manderscheid's description of the medical aspects of the SSA's process for determining claimant disability status, they identify four areas of functional limitation which are to be assessed. Three of those areas can be disabling, and the fourth impairing, if we apply WHO definitions. The three areas that can be termed disabling are activities of daily living, social functioning, and function in the work setting. Concentration and task persistence are organ-level functions that become impaired. While the SSA's definition of disability only relates to the inability to work, the SSA does assess other areas of disability, as described by Goldman and Manderscheid, as evidence that work disability is present.

SUMMARY

With the growing interest in disability as a consequence of mental disorders, we need a common language understood by all professions. This chapter discusses three levels at which a person's life can be limited by mental disorder. The nomenclature described is offered as a step toward a unified set of definitions of the consequences of mental disorders which can be used by clinical, legal, and administrative professionals.

In discussing the term disability, it becomes clear how diversely the word is applied. Our comparison of these usages is intended to highlight the differences and to help the readers of this volume avoid the assumption that the word means the same thing in the different contexts encountered throughout this volume. Our description of the WHO classification is intended to communicate a common framework and nomenclature for this volume.

REFERENCES

American Medical Association: Guides to the Evaluation of Permanent Impairment, second edition. Chicago, American Medical Association, 1984

American Psychiatric Association: Diagnostic and Statistical Manual of Mental Disorders, third edition (DSM-III). Washington, DC, American Psychiatric Association, 1980

Gruenberg EM: Social breakdown in young adults: keeping crises from becoming chronic. New Directions for Mental Health Services 14:43-50, 1982

Piasecki JR: Community response to residential services for the psycho-socially disabled: preliminary results of a national survey. Paper presented at the First Annual Conference of the International Association of Psycho-Social Rehabilitation Services. Available from Horizon House, Philadelphia, 1975

Segal SP, Aviram U: The Mentally Ill in Community-Based Sheltered Care: A Study of Community Care and Social Integration. New York, John Wiley & Sons, 1978

Social Security Administration: Program Operations Manual System; Sections 00401.015-00401.225 (SSA Pub. No. 68-0400401) Baltimore, SSA, 1968-current, Washington, DC

Social Security Administration: Compilation of the Social Security Laws: Including the Social Security Act, as Amended and Related Enactments through January 1, 1985 (45-631 0). Washington, DC, U.S. Government Printing Office, 1985a

Social Security Administration: Federal Old-Age, Survivors and Disability Insurance: Listings of Impairments—Mental Disorders; Final Rule. Federal Register, 20CFR Part 404 (reg. No. 4) 50 (167), 35038-35070, 1985b

Wolfensberger W: The principle of normalization and its implications to psychiatric services. Am J Psychiatry 127:291-297, 1970

World Health Organization: The International Classification of Diseases (9th revision) Geneva, WHO, 1978

World Health Organization: International Classification of Impairments, Disabilities and Handicaps. Geneva, WHO, 1980

2

The Epidemiology of Psychiatric Disability

Howard H. Goldman, M.D., Ph.D.
Ronald W. Manderscheid, Ph.D.

Diagnosis, disability, and duration are three dimensions used to define and enumerate the chronically mentally ill (Goldman et al. 1981). Of these dimensions, disability is the key to understanding the functional limitations of this population. Disability is also the most complicated aspect of chronicity to define. The National Plan for the Chronically Mentally Ill (1980) suggested the following definition for its target population:

> The chronically mentally ill population encompasses persons who suffer certain mental or emotional disorders (organic brain syndrome, schizophrenia, recurrent depressive and manic-depressive disorders, and paranoid and other psychoses, plus other disorders that may become chronic) that erode or prevent the development of their functional capacities in relation to three or more primary aspects of daily life—personal hygiene and self-care, self-direction, interpersonal relationships, social transactions, learning, and recreation—and that erode or prevent the development of their economic self-sufficiency.
>
> Most such individuals have required institutional care of extended duration, including intermediate-term hospitalization (90 days to 365 days in a single year), long-term hospitalization (one year or longer in the preceding five years), or nursing home placement because of a diagnosed mental condition or a diagnosis of senility without psychosis. (p. 3)

13

This definition operationalizes disability in terms of functional incapacities in activities of daily living, economic self-sufficiency, or length of stay in residential facilities. Data on some of these measures of disability are difficult to obtain and remain a challenge to research.

After reviewing definitions and the basic epidemiology of chronic mental disorder, this chapter describes data on mental disability in the community, and concludes with an estimate of the direct costs, burden, and impact of chronic psychiatric disability in the United States.

DEFINING DISABILITY

The concept of functional incapacity is central to most definitions of disability. For example, Minkoff (1979) defines disability in terms of "partial or total impairment of instrumental (usually vocational or homemaking) role performance." Public Law 95-605 defines disability as a condition that "results in substantial functional limitations in three or more of the following areas of major life activity: (i) self-care, (ii) receptive and expressive language, (iii) learning, (iv) mobility, (v) self-direction, (vi) capacity for independent living, and (vii) economic self-sufficiency." The statutory definition of disability for programs of the Social Security Administration (SSA) refers to "a medically determinable impairment which has lasted or can be expected to last for a continuous period of not less than 12 months . . . " which results in an inability to perform "substantial gainful activity." The major problem with all of these definitions of disability is operationalizing them and finding objective measures of such functional limitations. Similar vocational criteria are commonly used in the definitions of disability in a variety of community surveys, such as those to which we will refer below. In addition, chronic disability may also be inferred from extended stays in hospitals or other supervised residential arrangements.

Until recently, the Social Security Administration often operationalized its definition of disability in terms of functional limitations in activities of daily living and social functioning alone. Moreover, its evaluation process often emphasized the severity of symptomatology as a measure of functional impairment, although the research evidence fails to establish a strong connection between signs and symptoms, and the ability to perform work or other substantial gainful activity (Anthony and Jansen 1984). Recent changes in Social Security Administration regulations undertaken to define and operationalize impairment due to mental disorders address some of these basic definitional problems. Details of these changes are discussed below.

The new mental disability standards developed by the Social Security Administration in 1985 (*Federal Register*) operationalized disability through four general criteria described in paragraphs B1 through B4 of the "listings of mental impairment," (descriptions of restrictions of activities of daily living, social functioning, concentration and task persistence, and ability to tolerate increased mental demands associated with competitive work). The following material taken from the new federal regulations on impairments due to mental disorders describes the definition of disability and functional impairment. The listings for mental disorders are so constructed that an individual meeting the criteria could not reasonably be expected to engage in gainful work activity. "Meeting or equaling the criteria of the listings" means that the mental disorder would be sufficiently severe, in and of itself, to result in: (a) an inability to perform routine, repetitive tasks on a sustained basis (six to eight hours per day) without excessive supervision, and (b) an inability to interact in an acceptable manner with co-workers, supervisors, or the public in a normal work setting.

ASSESSING SEVERITY

For mental disorders, disability is assessed by the Social Security Administration in terms of the functional limitations imposed by the impairment. Functional limitations are evaluated using the criteria in paragraph B of the listings for mental disorders. Four areas are considered:

1. *Activities of daily living* include adaptive activities such as cleaning, shopping, cooking, taking public transportation, paying bills, maintaining a residence, caring appropriately for one's grooming and hygiene, using telephones and directories, using a post office, etc. In the context of the individual's overall situation, the quality of these activities is judged by their independence, appropriateness, and effectiveness. It is necessary to define the extent to which the individual is capable of initiating and sustaining participation in activities independent of supervision or direction.

2. *Social functioning* refers to an individual's capacity to interact appropriately and effectively with other individuals. Social functioning includes the ability to get along with others (e.g., family members, neighbors, grocery clerks, landlords, bus drivers, etc.). Impaired social functioning may be demonstrated by a history of altercations, evictions, firings, fear of strangers, avoidance of interpersonal relationships, social isolation, etc. Strength in social functioning may be documented by an individual's ability to initiate social contacts with others, communicate clearly with others, interact and actively participate in group activities, etc. Cooperative behaviors, consideration for others, awareness of others' feelings, and social functioning in work situations may involve interactions with the public, responding appropriately to supervisors or others in positions of authority, or cooperative behaviors involving co-workers.

3. *Concentration, task persistence, and pace* refer to the ability to sustain focused attention sufficiently long to permit the completion

of tasks commonly found in work settings. In activities of daily living, concentration may be reflected in terms of ability to follow and understand simple story lines or news items on television or radio, ability to complete tasks associated with everyday household routines, etc. Major deficiencies in concentration and task persistence are best observed in work and worklike settings, but can often be assessed through direct psychiatric examination and/or psychological testing. Concentration is assessed on mental status examinations by tasks such as having the individual subtract serial 7s from 100. Psychological tests of intelligence or memory assess concentration through tasks requiring short-term memory or through tasks that must be completed within established time limits. In work evaluations, concentration is assessed through such tasks as filing index cards, locating telephone numbers, or disassembling and reassembling objects. Strengths and weaknesses in areas of concentration, persistence, and pace can be discussed in terms of frequency of errors, time it takes to complete the task, and extent to which assistance is required to complete the task.

4. *Deterioration or decompensation* in work or worklike situations refers to repeated failure to adapt to stressful circumstances which cause the individual either to withdraw from that situation and/or to experience exacerbation of signs and symptoms (i.e., decompensation), with an accompanying difficulty in maintaining activities of daily living, social relationships, and/or maintaining concentration and task persistence (i.e., deterioration). Stresses common to the work environment include decisions, attendance, schedules, completing tasks, interactions with supervisors, interactions with peers, and so forth.

ESTIMATING PREVALENCE

When Goldman et al. (1981) prepared estimates for the National Plan for the Chronically Mentally Ill, three major sources of national data were available on chronic mental disability in the community: the Bureau of the Census (Survey of Income and Education in 1976), the Social Security Administration (Survey of Disabled Adults in 1966), and a 1973 Comprehensive Needs Assessment Study, conducted by the Urban Institute, for the Department of Health and Human Services. These studies indicated that between 350,000 and 800,000 individuals are severely disabled by emotional disorder in the community, and perhaps an additional 700,000 persons 3 years of age or older (2.5 percent of a total of 28 million disabled) have an "activity limitation" due to severe mental disturbance. A total of 350,000 individuals between the ages of 18 to 64 have some work disability (including total disability) secondary to severe emotional disturbance (Bureau of the Census, 1979). Extrapolations from the Urban Institute (1975) study indicate that approximately 800,000 individuals in the community have a severe mental disability, and 700,000 more are moderately or partially disabled.

Recently, these estimates have been supplemented (or corroborated) by data from several other surveys. Most important among them is the 1978 Social Security Administration Survey of Disability and Work. In research reviewed in more detail below, Ashbaugh and his colleagues (1983) found that there were approximately 1.07 million Americans living in households who consider themselves disabled by mental disorders. In addition, preliminary 1984 estimates are available for the number of adults, aged 18–64, who are recipients of Supplemental Security Income (SSI) and/or Social Security Disability Insurance (SSDI) benefits for reasons of disabling mental illness. In 1984, about 827,000 chronically mentally ill adults were receiving these payments. Of this number, about 408,000 were recipients of SSI; 381,000, recipients of SSDI; and 38,000, recipients of both types of payment. For SSI, these numbers show that chronically mentally ill adults represented about 18 percent of all adult disabled SSI recipients; for SSDI, about 14 percent of the total adult SSDI population. Generally, one must assume that these numbers represent conservative estimates of the chronically mentally ill population between ages 18 and 64, and undoubtedly reflect the most disabled members of this population.

DEMOGRAPHY OF DISABILITY

The following section is adapted directly from Ashbaugh et al. (1983). The reader is referred to that source for more details on survey procedures.

The Survey of Disability and Work was administered from July 1978 to September 1978, with a survey sample drawn from two frames. The first frame was a general population frame of noninstitutionalized persons in the continental United States, aged 18–64 as of June 1978. The second frame consisted of about 1.8 million persons obtained from the Social Security Administration's Master Beneficiary Record. About 1.67 million of these persons represented Social Security disability beneficiaries. The remaining .13 million represented persons who had applied for benefits but had been denied.

Definitions

Ashbaugh and his colleagues (1983) counted as "chronically mentally ill" those persons who reported themselves to be "limited in the kind or amount of work or housework" they could do (disability criterion), who had been so or expected to be so for a period of at least 12 months (duration criterion), mainly because of mental illness or a chronic nervous disorder (diagnostic criterion). It should be noted that while these criteria may be the best measures of the dimensions of disability, duration, and diagnosis obtainable from the survey, they do not constitute complete measures of their respective dimensions.

The disability criterion is narrowly defined to include limitations only in the kind or amount of work or housework a person can do. It does not reflect other serious functional and social impairments manifested in the inability or limited ability to manage one's finances, to cook, to socialize, or to engage in other routine activities of daily living. In addition, the survey is totally dependent upon self-reports, and some evidence exists that people with a diagnosis of schizophrenia tend to underreport the extent to which they have impairments in social functioning (Weissman et al. 1978).

The duration criterion is rigidly defined to include only those persons who reported being disabled at the time of the interview and who had been so or were expected to be so for a period of at least 12 months. Generally speaking, a chronic disability, particularly a chronic mental illness, characteristically includes periods of apparent wellness with intermittent periods of acute illness. This criterion, then, would not include as "chronic" those persons in a period of temporary wellness at the time of the survey.

The validity of the diagnosis criterion is open to question since it relies on respondent self-assessments and disclosures. Self-reports of mental illness as part of community surveys have alternatively been found to lead to underestimates (Trussell et al. 1956) and overestimates of psychiatric disorders relative to clinical evaluations (Link and Dohrenwend 1980).

Lending strength to the respondents' self-diagnosis is the fact that over 95 percent of the persons classified as chronically disabled for reasons of mental illness stated that they had talked to a doctor about their mental or chronic nervous trouble. Similarly, over 95 percent of the persons classified as chronically disabled for reasons of mental illness identified their mental illness or nervous or emotional problem as a condition that a doctor had told them about.

Since the survey samples are limited to adults residing in households, the estimates apply only to one segment of the chronically mentally ill population, that is, to persons aged 20–64 who live in a house, apartment, or room intended for occupancy as a separate living quarter. The estimates do not apply to children, adolescents, or elderly persons nor to adults residing in group quarters such as boarding homes, dormitories, and other such living arrangements containing five or more persons unrelated to the person in charge. Finally, they do not apply to persons living in institutional settings, such as mental health facilities and nursing homes.

FINDINGS

According to the survey estimates, the prevalence of chronic mental illness in U.S. households was approximately 9 per 1,000 population in 1978, or about 1.07 million adults between the ages of 20 and 64.

Further investigation showed that the proportion of females in the chronically mentally ill population was higher than the proportion of females in the population disabled for other reasons or in the nondisabled population. Respectively, percentages were 63 percent, 52 percent, and 50 percent. These findings suggest that when disability and chronicity were taken into account, females were more likely than males to meet the criteria for chronic mental illness.

The survey also shows that the proportion of persons having a disability increases with age. This holds for those persons disabled for reasons of mental illness, as well as for those disabled for other reasons. The percentage of household residents aged 55–64 was significantly larger in the disabled population than in the nondisabled population, and the percentage of residents aged 20–24 was significantly smaller in the disabled populations than in the nondisabled population. This is not surprising, since disability generally increases with age. Respective percentages of chronically mentally ill adults by age group were as follows: 5 percent (20–24); 15 percent (25–34); 18 percent (35–44); 25 percent (45–54); 36 percent (55–64).

In terms of marital status, the 1978 survey found that the chronically mentally ill were much less likely to be married, and much more likely to be single (having never married) than individuals who were disabled for reasons other than mental illness or who were not disabled. The survey also found that the percentage of household residents who were widowed, divorced, or separated among the chronically mentally ill population was higher than among the other disabled or nondisabled populations. Among the chronically mentally ill, 59 percent were married; 27 percent widowed, separated, or divorced; and 13 percent single (never married).

In terms of race, the survey provided some indication that the population of household residents who are black is greater among the disabled population than among the nondisabled population. Percentages of blacks were 13 percent, 15 percent, and 10 percent, respectively, for chronically mentally ill adults, other disabled adults, and nondisabled adults between the ages of 20 and 64.

Generally, findings from this survey suggest that chronically mentally ill adults between the ages of 20 and 64 are more likely to be female, older, not currently married, and black when compared with the nondisabled population. These age and race characteristics are similar to those for the population disabled for other reasons. Sex and marital status characteristics differ between these two disability populations.

COST OF DISABILITY

Chronic mental disability is not only prevalent, painful, and emotionally burdensome, it is also very expensive. The indirect cost of chronic disability is not known, but the direct cost of services in 1980 has been estimated at $7.4 billion, 43 percent of the total direct costs for mental disorders (excluding substance abuse and developmental disabilities) (Goldman and Frank 1985). In addition, 1980 Social

Security disability payments were conservatively estimated to amount to more than $1.87 billion per year (Frank and Kamlet 1985).

Of the $7.4 billion, the largest investment by far is in institutional and hospital care. There is a suggestion that "real" resources for the care of the chronically mentally ill population in the community have declined while need has continued to rise. The ultimate economic question is what is the optimal investment—in terms of the level and types of resources—and what mechanisms should be used to finance the system of care.

Informed policy requires an appreciation of the prevalence, demography, and cost of psychiatric disability. The data are incomplete, but suggest that the problem is large, expensive, and getting larger (Kramer 1985). Effective clinical and public health interventions are critical to reverse the trend. In the interim, public policy must be focused on holding the line against a mismatch of needs and resources.

REFERENCES

Anthony WA, Jansen MA: Predicting the vocational capacity of the chronically mentally ill. Am Psychol 39:537-544, 1984

Ashbaugh JW, Leaf PJ, Manderscheid RW et al: Estimates of the size and selected characteristics of the adult chronically mentally ill population in U.S. households, in Research in Community and Mental Health. Edited by Greenley JR. Greenwich, CT, JAI Press, 1983

Bureau of the Census: Survey of Income and Education, Digest of Data on Persons With Disabilities. Washington, DC, Department of Health, Education and Welfare, 1979

Federal Register: Federal Old-Age, Survivors, and Disability Insurance; Listing of Impairments—Mental Disorders; Final Rule, 50(167):35038–35070. Washington, DC, U.S. Government Printing Office, 1985

Frank RG, Kamlet MS: Direct costs and expenditures for mental health in the United States, 1980. Hosp Community Psychiatry 36:165–168, 1985.

Goldman HH, Frank RA: Evaluating the costs of chronic disability. Paper presented at the meeting on Economics of Disability, Washington, DC, April 9, 1985

Goldman HH, Gattozzi AA, Taube CA: Defining and counting the chronically mentally ill. Hosp Community Psychiatry 32:21–27, 1981

Kramer M: The changing institutional scene in the United States, in The Chronically Mentally Ill. Edited by Sluss-Radebaugh T, Gruenberg EM, Kramer M. et al. Johns Hopkins School of Hygiene and Public Health (mimeo), 1985

Link B, Dohrenwend BP: Formulation of hypotheses about the ratio of untreated disorders in adults in the United States, in Mental Illness in the United States. Edited by Dohrenwend BP, et al. New York, Praeger, 1980

Minkoff K: A map of chronic mental patients, in The Chronic Mental Patient. Edited by Talbott JA. Washington, DC, American Psychiatric Association, 1979

National Plan for the Chronically Mentally Ill: Final draft report to the Secretary of Health and Human Services. Washington, DC, U.S. Government Printing Office, 1980

Social Security Administration: Survey of Disabled Adults. Washington, DC, Dept. of HEW, 1966

Social Security Administration: Survey of Disability and Work. Washington, DC, Dept. of HHS, 1978

Trussell RE, Elinsen J, Levin ML: Comparisons of various methods of estimating the prevalence of chronic disease in a community—the Hunterdon County study. Am J Public Health 46:173–182, 1956

Urban Institute: Report of the Comprehensive Service Needs Study, Department of Health, Education and Welfare, Washington, DC, 1975

Weissman MM, Prusoff BA, Thompson DW, et al: Social adjustment by self-report in a community sample and in psychiatric outpatients. J Nerv Ment Dis 166:317–326, 1978

3

The Neurobiological Basis of Psychiatric Disability

Charles A. Kaufmann, M.D.
Daniel R. Weinberger, M.D.

Disability may be defined as a functional limitation, imposed by disease, on capacities necessary for independent living and economic self-sufficiency. These capacities have been specified by statute, and include mobility, receptive and expressive language, learning, self-care, and self-direction (P.L. 95-602 1978). We are accustomed to thinking of incapacities in mobility and language, in patients with neurologic conditions such as stroke or multiple sclerosis, and of incapacity in learning, in patients with retardation or developmental disorders. Many patients with psychiatric illnesses, however, are equally limited, especially in their capacities for self-care and self-direction. For some, the limitation is so severe as to preclude life outside the hospital. For others, community tenure is possible, but only with considerable support.

Psychiatric illness ranks fifth among major disease categories contributing to limitations in activity (Kottke et al. 1982). An estimated 900,000 chronically mentally ill individuals reside in institutions. An additional 350,000–800,000 severely disabled and 700,000 moderately disabled individuals reside in the community (Goldman 1984), of whom 550,000 receive Supplemental Security Income payments (Anderson 1982). Clearly, chronic psychiatric illness represents a major public health problem.

23

Symptoms that contribute to disability may be broadly classified as either excesses or deficits. Thus, a patient with multiple sclerosis may be unable to walk because of excessive motor tone (spasticity) or because of inadequate motor function (paresis). In discussing neurologic disability, such as that which accompanies multiple sclerosis, we can go beyond relating functional impairment to specific neurologic symptoms by providing neuroanatomic localization for these symptoms (e.g., attributing paraparesis to myelitis), by understanding their pathogenesis, and by considering rehabilitation approaches aimed either at the patient (e.g., corticosteroids and physical therapy) or at the patient's surroundings (e.g., ramps).

Similarly, the psychiatric patient may be incapacitated by excessive expressions of personal distress, of inappropriate affect, of incoherent speech, of bizarre and threatening behavior, or by deficient cognitive, social, and instrumental functioning (Paul 1969). Psychiatric (especially pharmacologic) treatment has often focused on suppressing excesses. Reduction of excess symptomatology, per se, however, may not affect the long-term prognosis of major psychiatric disorders (Scarpiti et al. 1964; Pritchard 1967). Rather, it has become increasingly apparent that outcome (and residual disability) may be more highly correlated with deficit symptoms (Crow et al. 1982; Tsuang 1982). We must focus, therefore, on these latter symptoms, if we are to better understand the neurobiological basis of psychiatric disability.

In the discussion of psychiatric disability which follows, with neurologic disability as our model, we will not only highlight phenomenologic features (primarily deficit symptoms and neuropsychologic impairment) which are associated with ongoing disability, but propose anatomic localization for these features and relate them to underlying pathogenic (neurochemical, neuroradiological, and neurophysiological) changes, and treatment response. Moreover, we hope to consider the implications of these findings for rehabilitation efforts directed both at changing the individual (through pharmacotherapy or skill acquisition) and at developing resources in the environment (Anthony et al. 1984). While the discussion will focus on deficit states in three major psychiatric disorders—schizophrenia, alcoholism, and bipolar disorder—we hope to emphasize commonalities which cut across traditional diagnostic categories.

SCHIZOPHRENIC DEMENTIA

Phenomenology
Schizophrenic dementia refers not to a single disease, but to a group of psychiatric disorders characterized by psychosis, chronic deterioration (over 50 percent of patients are unable to work—Wistedt 1981; Westermeyer et al., in submission), and early onset (the latter two features accounting for the alternative name, dementia praecox).

Early theoreticians, such as Bleuler, recognized the distinction between accessory symptoms (delusions, hallucinations, and catatonic symptoms) and fundamental symptoms (dissociation of thinking, weakening of the will, withdrawal, ambivalence, and affective flattening) in schizophrenia (Bleuler 1950). Current theoreticians, such as Crow, have reiterated this distinction, referring to positive (accessory) and negative (fundamental) symptoms respectively (Crow 1980). Despite similarities in language, Bleuler's and Crow's concepts differ. Bleuler, as an adherent to Wundt's association psychology, believed that dissociation of thinking was the primary disturbance in schizophrenia and that this disturbance allowed the emergence of other secondary symptoms. His notion is also compatible with Hughlings Jackson's view of hierarchical nervous system in which positive symptoms reflect lower centers' release from inhibition from higher centers, while negative symptoms reflect pathology in those higher centers (Hughlings-Jackson 1984). Crow, on the other hand, has suggested that positive and negative symptoms may develop independent of one another (Berrios 1985).

In the discussion of pathogenesis to follow, we shall adopt a Jacksonian model. Nevertheless, from a strictly phenomenologic standpoint, accessory and positive symptoms and fundamental and negative symptoms are similar and essentially refer to the excess and deficit symptoms discussed earlier.

Positive symptoms are characteristic of, but not specific to schizophrenia. Patients with other psychiatric disorders, such as manic depressive illness, often manifest persecutory delusions, auditory hallucinations, and catatonic symptoms (Pope and Lipinski 1978). Moreover, positive symptoms may be episodic (Strauss and Carpenter 1974; Zubin and Spring 1977; Crow 1980; Zubin et al. 1983) and as such, may be more appropriately understood as state and not trait markers. Finally, positive symptoms, at least those which occur acutely (during an index hospitalization), appear to lack prognostic value (Strauss and Carpenter 1974; Brockington et al. 1978; Bland and Orn 1980), although there is some evidence to suggest that positive symptoms which occur subacutely (for example, two or more years after discharge) may predict later poor role functioning (Pogue-Geile and Harrow 1985).

In contrast, negative symptoms appear to be more specific to schizophrenia (although other psychiatric patients, for example those with psychotic depression, may manifest negative symptoms to a limited degree (Pogue-Geile and Harrow 1984)). Unlike positive symptoms, negative symptoms appear to be persistent or to progress over time (Strauss and Carpenter 1974; Crow 1980; Pfohl and Winokur 1982), although they may remit somewhat, especially following an acute episode in younger patients (Pogue-Geile and Harrow 1985). Furthermore, negative symptoms may predict poor outcome (including residual symptoms, more frequent hospitalizations, and poorer instrumental work functioning) (Crow 1982; Tsuang 1982; Pogue-Geile and Harrow 1985).

In addition to positive and negative symptoms, schizophrenic patients often manifest minor ("soft") neurological signs (Rochford et al. 1970; Tucker et al. 1975; Quitkin et al. 1976), nonspecific indicators of brain damage (Kennard 1960), and cognitive impairment (Lilliston 1973; Heaton et al. 1978), also suggestive of organic brain dysfunction. Cognitive abnormalities which have been reported include impairments on the Wechsler Adult Intelligence Scale (Watson 1965; de Wolfe et al. 1971), Bender Gestalt Test (Bernstein 1963; Orme et al. 1964), Halstead–Reitan Battery (de Wolfe et al. 1971; Watson 1971), and Graham and Kendall Memory for Design Test (Lilliston 1970). There is some evidence that neurological soft signs and cognitive impairment coexist (Mosher et al. 1971; Quitkin et al. 1976), and that cognitive impairment occurs more frequently in patients with predominantly negative symptoms (Johnstone et al. 1978a), suggesting that these abnormalities may result from a common underlying organic process. Nonetheless, this matter is not fully resolved (see Kolakowska et al. 1985). Cognitive impairments may remain stable over 8–14 years follow-up (Ginett and Moran 1964; Hamlin 1969) or may progress (Haywood and Moelis 1963; Smith 1964). Specific impairments at index hospitalization, such as memory deficits without clouding of consciousness, have been associated with poor long-term outcome (Tsuang 1982).

Pathogenesis

Neurochemistry
Positive and negative symptoms may be distinguished further on the basis of pathogenesis. Pharmacological and neurochemical data suggest that positive symptoms may be associated with increased dopamine agonist amphetamine (Randrup and Munkvard 1970) is known to induce an organic syndrome (associated with hallucinations and paranoid delusions) in normal individuals (Ellinwood 1967) and to exacerbate selectively positive symptoms in schizophrenic patients (Angrist et al. 1980). Conversely, dopamine antagonists, like neuroleptics, reverse the symptoms of amphetamine psychosis (Angrist et al. 1974) and have a relatively selective beneficial effect on positive symptoms (Johnstone et al. 1986b). This "dopamine hypothesis" of positive symptoms finds neurochemical support in studies of cerebrospinal fluid (CSF) and plasma monoamines and their metabolites. We have recently found a direct correlation between positive symptom score, assessed by the Brief Psychiatric Rating Scale, and CSF dopamine metabolites such as dihydroxyphenylacetic acid (DOPAC) ($r = 0.52, p < 0.05$) and homovanillic acid (HVA) ($r = 0.47, p < 0.01$) in neuroleptic-free schizophrenic patients (Kaufmann et al., in submission). Other authors have noted similar

correlations between positive symptoms and plasma HVA (Pickar et al. 1984; Davis et al. 1985). As positive symptoms are not specific to schizophrenia, it is not surprising that there have been reports of increased CSF HVA accumulation in patients with a variety of diagnoses but with shared positive symptomatology (van Praag and Korf 1975). Moreover, as positive symptoms are episodic (state) variables and not persistent (trait) variables, it is also not surprising that several studies have failed to find differences in CSF HVA between schizophrenic patients and other diagnostic groups (Bowers et al. 1969; Shopsin et al. 1973; Post et al. 1975).

In contrast to positive symptoms, negative symptoms may be associated with decreased activity in (possibly different) dopaminergic pathways. There have been reports of an inverse correlation between negative symptoms and CSF HVA (Lindstrom 1985). In addition, we have noted decreased concentrations of dopamine sulfate, an independent index of dopamine function, in the CSF of schizophrenic patients compared with neurologic controls (Kaufmann et al., in submission). As noted previously, negative symptoms are associated with poor outcome. We might also expect, therefore, that diminished CSF HVA would be associated with poor prognosis; and this, in fact, has been observed (Bowers 1974).

Clinical and preclinical data lend further support to the association between negative symptoms and diminished dopamine function. Negative symptoms are phenomenologically similar to the apathy and impaired concept formation seen in Parkinson's disease (Javoy-Agid and Agid 1980) and to the lack of spontaneity and goal-directedness seen in neuroleptic-induced akinesia (Klein et al. 1980); Parkinson's disease and akinesia are idiopathic and iatrogenic dopamine-deficiency disorders. Furthermore, negative symptoms are associated with cognitive impairments in patients, for example, inability to perform the Wisconsin Card Sort (Malmo 1974), which resemble cognitive impairments in primates (e.g., inability to perform delayed-response tasks) that have been depleted of cortical dopamine (Brozoski et al. 1979). To recapitulate, negative symptoms may be relatively persistent trait markers which are mediated by diminished dopamine activity, while positive symptoms may be intermittent state markers which are mediated by enhanced dopamine activity.

That the symptoms of schizophrenia might result from both decreased and increased dopamine function seems paradoxical, particularly if one considers that negative and positive symptoms can coexist. This apparent paradox may be resolved if we recall that dopamine is utilized as a neurotransmitter in several brain pathways (projecting to both cerebral cortex and subcortical nuclei), and if we adopt an hierarchical Jacksonian model: Depletion of cortical dopamine results in persistent negative symptoms and in disinhibition of subcortical dopaminergic pathways (the schizophrenic diathesis). This disinhibition, in turn, results in vulnerability to intermittent (stress-induced) increases in subcortical dopamine neurotransmission, and positive symptoms. This model is compatible with both stress and diathesis elements in the pathogenesis of schizophrenia (Zubin 1980). It accounts for the inverse correlation between negative symptoms and CSF HVA, as CSF HVA in primates correlates with prefrontal cortical dopamine activity (Elsworth et al. 1983). It finds experimental support in the observation that destruction of mesocortical dopamine afferents to the prefrontal cortex produces increased subcortical (mesolimbic) dopamine activity in rodents (Pycock 1980). While this model suggests that selective damage to the prefrontal cortex may underlie the symptoms of schizophrenia, other data implicate more diffuse damage to the brain. CSF neurochemistry, an indirect window on brain function, provides little help in choosing between these alternatives. Other neuroradiologic and neurophysiologic windows are needed.

Neuroradiology
Neuroradiologic studies of schizophrenia, dating back to 1927 and initially utilizing pneumoencephalography (PEG), more recently have employed computerized axial tomography (CT scan). Most reports have suggested central (that is, subcortical) atrophy, although some reports have suggested selective atrophy of the prefrontal cortex. Over 30 PEG studies have described abnormalities, especially lateral ventricular enlargement, in 25 to 70 percent of chronic schizophrenic patients (Weinberger et al. 1979). Similarly, over 25 CT scan studies have described lateral ventricular enlargement (Johnstone et al. 1976) in 20 to 50 percent of chronic schizophrenic patients, while 20 studies have described cortical atrophy (Shelton et al., in submission). Lateral ventricular enlargement seen with PEG has been associated with personality and intellectual disintegration (Haug 1962), while ventricular enlargement on CT scan has been associated with negative symptomatology (Andreasen et al. 1982; Pearlson et al. 1984; Pearlson et al. 1985; Williams et al. 1985) and cognitive impairment (Johnstone et al. 1976; Johnstone et al. 1978a; Donnelly et al. 1980; Golden et al. 1980; Golden et al. 1982). Like negative symptoms, neuroradiologic abnormalities appear to be static (Lemke 1939; Weinberger et al. 1982), or may progress minimally (Haug 1962). As both negative symptoms and cognitive impairment have been associated with poor outcome, it is not surprising that lateral ventricular enlargement independently predicts poor outcome (DeLisi et al. 1983; Williams et al. 1985) with unremitting clinical (positive and negative) symptoms, impaired social functioning, and persistent unemployment (Seidman 1983; Pearlson et al. 1984; Pearlson et al. 1985).

Neuroradiological and neurochemical abnormalities in schizophrenia may be related. Thus, there have been several reports of diminished CSF HVA in patients with enlarged lateral ventricles

(Nyback et al. 1983; van Kammen et al. 1983) or cortical atrophy (van Kammen et al. 1983). We have recently found a 40-percent reduction in CSF HVA and a 55-percent reduction in CSF DOPAC in patients with cortical atrophy (Kaufmann et al., in submission), and have preliminary evidence that these dopamine metabolites are affected primarily by prefrontal rather than generalized cortical atrophy (Kaufmann and Weinberger, unpublished observations 1985). Once again, this is not surprising given the association of CT abnormalities with negative symptoms, and of negative symptoms with reduced CSF HVA.

Neurophysiology
Neurophysiologic approaches to schizophrenia include electroencephalography (EEG), positron emission tomography (PET scan), and regional cerebral blood flow (rCBF); EEG and related techniques (such as evoked potentials) have been employed in hundreds of studies of schizophrenic patients (Itil 1977; Seidman 1983). Approximately 25 percent of patients (especially those with predominantly negative symptoms) have demonstrated abnormalities, including diffuse delta (0 to 3.5 Hz) slowing (Mirsky 1969; Fenton et al. 1980; Stevens and Livermore 1982). Tomographic refinements of EEG, such as brain electrical activity mapping (BEAM), have localized this slowing to frontal regions bilaterally (Buchsbaum et al. 1982a; Morihisa et al. 1983).

   PET scan and rCBF studies rely on the correlations among local metabolism (that is, glucose and oxygen consumption), regional blood flow, and function in the brain (Sokoloff 1977). As with BEAM, PET scan studies suggest prefrontal dysfunction (specifically, lower utilization of the glucose analog, deoxyglucose) in chronic schizophrenic patients (Farkas et al. 1980; Buchsbaum et al. 1982b). Likewise, rCBF studies also suggest prefrontal dysfunction ("hypofrontality," that is, lower blood flow or reversal of the usual rostral–caudal blood flow gradient) in chronic schizophrenic patients both at rest (Ingvar et al. 1976) and in response to cognitive stimuli. In fact, we have observed that schizophrenic patients fail to increase frontal blood flow (and by implication, neuronal metabolism) in response to cognitive tasks, like the Wisconsin Card Sort, that ordinarily activate frontal flow in normals (Weinberger et al. 1985). Frontal blood flow deficits appear most pronounced in older patients (Ingvar and Franzen 1974; Mubrin et al. 1982) with predominantly negative symptoms; such deficits are also associated with cognitive impairment (the lower the CBF to prefrontal cortex, the worse the performance on the Wisconsin Card Sort) (Weinberger et al. 1985). Reductions in prefrontal CBF have not been observed in acute, never-medicated schizophrenic patients (Sheppard et al. 1983) or in younger patients specifically screened for organicity (Gur et al. 1985). While PET scan and rCBF abnormalities have not been related to

prognosis, EEG abnormalities have. Specifically, so-called hypersta-
ble EEG records, characterized by slowing and poor response to
(light) stimulation, have been associated with poor prognosis (Pincus
and Tucker 1978).

The neurophysiologic abnormalities reviewed here may not be
unrelated. As mean EEG frequency may correlate with cerebral blood
flow (Ingvar et al. 1976), the frontal slowing noted with BEAM may
correspond to the hypofrontality noted with PET scan and rCBF.
Furthermore, just as neuroradiological abnormalities may be associated with neurochemical abnormalities, so may they be associated
with neurophysiological abnormalities in schizophrenia. Thus, patients with CT scan evidence of frontal atrophy differ from patients
without atrophy in BEAM auditory and evoked potentials, especially
over the frontal lobes (Morihisa and McAnulty 1985). In addition,
patients with CT scan evidence of ventricular enlargement are particularly likely to show reduced frontal blood flow on rCBF (Berman
and Weinberger, unpublished data). Finally, while we have no clinical
data bearing on the relationship between neurochemical and neurophysiological abnormalities in schizophrenia, we might expect to
find decreased dopamine turnover (that is, decreased CSF HVA) in
patients with decreased prefrontal cortical activity. A direct correlation between dopamine activity and regional cerebral metabolism is
supported by preclinical evidence: The dopamine agonist apomorphine causes a dose-dependent increase in frontal cortex glucose
utilization in the rat (McCulloch et al. 1982).

Treatment Response
As noted above, positive symptoms of schizophrenia are particularly
responsive to neuroleptic treatment (National Institute of Mental
Health 1964; Johnstone et al. 1978b). This is understandable if we
consider such symptoms to reflect increased subcortical dopamine
activity, and if we consider chronic neuroleptic treatment to work by
decreasing mesolimbic dopamine activity (Pickar et al. 1984). In
contrast, negative symptoms may be less responsive to neuroleptic
treatment (Johnstone et al. 1978b), and may even be made worse by
such treatment (Sutter et al. 1966; Andrews 1973), although the matter is not fully resolved (Goldberg 1985). There is even evidence to
suggest that negative symptoms may respond to dopamine agonists
like amphetamine (Angrist et al. 1982) or dopamine precursors like
levodopa (Gerlach and Luhdorf 1975; Ogura et al. 1976; Brambilla et
al. 1979). Once again, this is understandable if we consider such
symptoms to reflect decreased cortical dopamine activity. In support
of this notion, we have recently found a direct correlation between
pretreatment CSF concentrations of HVA and DOPAC and response to
fixed-dose neuroleptic treatment: Patients with the lowest metabolite
concentrations benefitted least from six weeks of haloperidol therapy
(Kaufmann et al., in submission).

Cognitive impairments are associated with negative symptoms and, like negative symptoms, may not be responsive to neuroleptics (Depue et al. 1975; Goldberg 1985). Cognitive impairments are also associated with ventricular enlargement, and not surprisingly, this neuroradiologic abnormality predicts poor response to neuroleptics (Weinberger et al. 1980; Schulz et al. 1983; Smith et al. 1983; Luchins et al. 1984). Finally, there is growing evidence that neurophysiologic abnormalities such as frontal increases in EEG delta activity (Morihisa et al. 1983) and diminished prefrontal blood flow (with its associated impairment on the Wisconsin Card Sort) (Berman et al. 1986) may not be affected by neuroleptic treatment.

Summary

As suggested by the preceding discussion, some consistency can be found amidst the diversity of schizophrenia. Schizophrenic dementia appears to be a valid diagnostic construct in which phenomenology, pathogenesis, treatment response, and prognosis converge (Feinstein 1977). Negative symptoms, cognitive impairment, diminished cortical dopamine activity, subcortical and cortical atrophy, prefrontal physiologic dysfunction, and neuroleptic refractoriness characterize a population of patients with poor prognosis and persistent disability. Abnormalities in the structure and function of the prefrontal cortex may be particularly important in the pathogenesis of schizophrenia. These abnormalities may not only result directly in considerable incapacity, but indirectly may set the stage for stress-induced exacerbations of illness.

We shall have more to say about prefrontal cortical dysfunction and its bearing on rehabilitation. First, however, we shall touch briefly on two other disorders, alcoholic and bipolar dementia, which also are associated with chronic disability.

ALCOHOLIC DEMENTIA

Phenomenology

Progressive impairment in cognitive and social function is a frequent complication of chronic alcoholism. Cognitive deficits appear to fall along a continuum: Milder degrees of impairment correlate with the amount of alcohol consumed even by nonalcoholic social drinkers (Parker et al. 1983), while more severe deficits occur in alcoholics with long drinking histories and heavy consumption (Jones and Parsons 1971; Tartar and Parsons 1971; Horvath 1975). Dementia frequently is preceded by episodes of delirium tremens, Wernicke's encephalopathy, or head trauma.

Demented alcoholics frequently demonstrate soft neurological signs (Cox and Ludwig 1979). They are impaired in a number of cognitive capacities that implicate prefrontal cortical dysfunction: visuospatial abstracting (analyzing complex visual stimuli) (Jones and Parsons 1972), verbal abstracting (Parker et al. 1974), and concept formation and shifting (Tartar 1975). Wilkinson and Carlen (1980) have characterized these tasks as having a high problem-solving component. Impairments in abstracting ability, assessed by the Halstead–Reitan Battery categories test, may be comparable to that of brain-damaged controls (Jones and Parsons 1971) and again suggest dysfunction of the prefrontal cortex (Tartar 1975). Frontal lobe damage also may underlie the personality changes seen in chronic alcoholism, such as apathy and impaired judgment (Horvath 1975). Psychometric test performance may improve somewhat with abstinence (Carlen 1979). Nonetheless, some cognitive impairments are slow to recover (Long and McLachlan 1974; Berglund et al. 1977; Schau et al. 1980), and some, such as visuospatial abstracting or paired associate learning, may persist even after seven years of continuous sobriety (Brandt et al. 1983).

As in schizophrenia, cognitive impairment may have significant prognostic implications for alcoholism. Several authors have observed that the degree of cognitive dysfunction during treatment significantly predicts outcome, specifically relapse versus abstinence versus controlled drinking, at follow-up one to five years later (Berglund et al. 1977; Abbott and Gregson 1981). In one study of 100 consecutive demented alcoholics referred for treatment, 40 required admission to long-stay institutions, 14 showed significant improvement in cognitive functioning, and only 4 were able to achieve voluntary abstinence (Horvath 1975). Clearly, cognitive impairment is not only the result of prolonged alcohol consumption, but the cause of further cycles of abuse.

Pathogenesis
There have been no studies, to our knowledge, which have examined CSF neurochemistry in patients with alcoholic dementia. There have been, however, studies of patients with alcohol amnestic disorder (Korsakoff's psychosis), a disorder which is distinct from, but somewhat overlapping with, alcoholic dementia (Horvath 1975). The role of dopamine metabolism in the latter disorder is unclear (Martin et al. 1984), although it bears mentioning that pretreatment CSF HVA concentrations appear to predict response of a psychometric test (the Wechsler Memory Scale) to a two-week trial with the catecholamine agonist amphetamine (McEntee et al. 1983). Abnormalities in norepinephrine metabolism, on the other hand, may play a significant role in Korsakoff's psychosis, with patients demonstrating significantly lower CSF concentrations of the major norepinephrine metabolite, 3-methoxy-4-hydroxyphenylglycol (MHPG), than psychiatric controls (McEntee and Mair 1978). Perhaps patients with alcoholic dementia also manifest diminished norepinephrine turnover. There is indirect support for this hypothesis: The incidence of dementia among alcoholics (Horvath 1975), like the incidence of cognitive impairment

among nonhuman primates, increases with age. Moreover, cognitive decline in aged primates may be associated with prefrontal cortical noradrenergic deficits (Arnsten and Goldman–Rakic, in submission).

Neuroradiologic studies of alcoholic dementia have included both PEG and CT scan. PEG has revealed ventricular enlargement or cortical atrophy in 70 percent of chronic alcoholics, all under the age of 60 (Haug 1968; Brewer and Perrett 1971; Horvath 1975). CT scan abnormalities have also included ventricular enlargement and cortical, especially prefrontal, atrophy (Cala et al. 1978; Wilkinson and Carlen 1980; Kroll et al. 1980). These neuroradiologic findings complement postmortem findings of atrophy, especially of the dorsolateral prefrontal cortex, in alcoholics (Courville 1955). Neuroradiologic abnormalities and neuropsychologic impairments seem to be correlated (Brewer and Perrett 1971; Cala et al. 1978; Wilkinson and Carlen 1980), although the correlation does not predict more than 25 percent of the covariance (Sanchez-Craig and Wilkinson 1979); both may improve somewhat with prolonged abstinence (Carlen et al. 1978; Carlen 1979).

Neurophysiologic studies of alcoholic dementia have employed EEG, evoked potentials, and rCBF. Chronic alcoholics have been observed to have diffuse alpha slowing on EEG, an abnormality which may improve during the first month of abstinence (Carlen et al. 1977). Change in alpha frequency appears to be highly correlated with improvement on the Wechsler Memory Scale (Carlen 1979). No study, to our knowledge, has examined rCBF in alcoholic dementia, per se. Nonetheless, it should be recalled that the incidence of dementia among alcoholics increases with age and that studies of rCBF in alcoholism suggest a decrease in flow to the frontal cortex among older alcoholics, exceeding that of age-matched controls (Berglund and Ingvar 1976).

BIPOLAR DEMENTIA

Phenomenology
While authors since Kraepelin (1919) have stressed that bipolar disorder, unlike schizophrenia, is associated with a favorable outcome, more recently it has been suggested that this may not be entirely the case (Welner 1977). Longitudinal studies of bipolar illness have shown a progressive increase in the frequency of cycling and a decrease in well intervals between cycles, changes which occur despite pharmacotherapy and which appear to be related both to age and to the number of previous episodes (Goodwin and Jamison 1983). Manic patients do fare significantly better than schizophrenic patients, yet in a cohort of 100 patients followed for 30 to 40 years, 25 percent had incapacitating symptoms, 21 percent were unable to work, 19 percent had never married, and 12 percent had been chronically hospitalized (Tsuang et al. 1979). Detailed studies of biological markers in these

poor-prognosis bipolar patients are limited. Nonetheless, in light of the association in both schizophrenia and alcoholism between brain damage (assessed by neuropsychological, neurochemical, neuroradiological, and neurophysiological measures) and poor outcome, several observations are relevant.

Neuropsychological testing of bipolar patients, including tests of abstraction in the Halstead–Reitan Battery, has revealed impairments consistent with prefrontal dysfunction, in approximately 30 percent of patients, which exceed those in unipolar depressed patients and controls (Donnelly et al. 1972). These deficits are most apparent in older patients and persist despite clinical recovery (Friedman et al. 1977; Savard et al. 1980). Some reports implicate dysfunction of the nondominant hemisphere (Taylor et al. 1981). Like schizophrenic patients, manic patients may manifest soft neurological signs (Nasrallah et al. 1983), albeit less frequently (Rochford et al. 1970). Correlations between these phenomenological features and treatment response–prognosis are not available.

Pathogenesis
Several studies which have measured noradrenergic metabolites in bipolar illness have found decreased CSF MHPG, particularly in depressed patients, compared to controls (Post et al. 1973; Subrahmanyam 1975). Studies which have examined dopaminergic metabolites have reported diminished base-line and probenecid-induced HVA in the CSF of manic patients who have complied with bedrest (Sjostrom 1973; Banki 1977; Post and Goodwin 1978). Once again, associations with symptomatology and outcome are not available.

PEG studies of bipolar disorder have revealed ventricular enlargement in approximately 30 percent of patients (Nagy 1963). (Recall that approximately 30 percent of bipolar patients show cognitive impairment and that 25 percent are chronically disabled.) More recent CT-scan studies have replicated this finding: Mean lateral ventricle size may not differ between chronic bipolar and schizophrenic patients (Pearlson and Veroff 1981), with approximately 30 percent of either group showing ventricles two standard deviations larger than the control mean (Nasrallah et al. 1982). Correlations between ventricular enlargement and symptoms have not been explored. Correlations with outcome have been made, however, with large ventricles predicting chronicity, lower social competence, persistent unemployment, and overall "poor prognosis" (Nagy 1963; Pearlson et al. 1984; Pearlson et al. 1985).

EEG studies of bipolar disorder have revealed (among other findings) nonspecific slowing; contrary to expectation, however, this was associated with good treatment outcome (Taylor and Abrams 1981). PET-scan studies in patients with affective illness, like those in schizophrenic patients, suggest "hypofrontality" (Buchsbaum et al. 1983), although this is not a consistent finding (Baxter et al. 1985).

CBF studies of bipolar patients have demonstrated slightly reduced flow to the nondominant hemisphere (in accord with neuropsychological test results); however, they have not assessed regional differences (Rush et al. 1982).

Summary
Despite diagnostic differences, schizophrenia, alcoholism, and bipolar disorder share many similarities.

All three disorders may be associated with a dementia marked by neuropsychological test abnormalities and minor neurological abnormalities. The role of negative symptoms in schizophrenic dementia is established; their role in alcoholic and bipolar dementias needs

Table 1.

A Comparison of Schizophrenic, Alcoholic, and Bipolar Dementia*

	Schizophrenic	Alcoholic	Bipolar
Neurobiological marker			
Neuropsychological (HRB)			
impaired abstraction	+	+	+
Neurological			
soft signs	+	+	+
Neurochemical (CSF)			
decreased HVA, MHPG	+	+	+
Neuroradiological (PEG, CT)			
cortical atrophy	+	+	·
ventricular enlargement	+	+	+
Neurophysiological			
EEG—slowing	+	+	+
PET—hypofrontality	+	·	+
rCBF—decreased flow	+^	+^	+#
Treatment response			
Refractory	+	+	+
Prognosis			
Impaired functioning	+	+	+

* HRB: Halstead–Reitan Battery; CSF: cerebrospinal fluid; HVA: homovanillic acid; MHPG: 3-methoxy-4-hydroxyphenylglycol; PEG: pneumoencephalography; CT: computerized axial tomography; EEG: electroencephalography; PET: positron emission tomography; rCBF: regional cerebral blood flow

^ Prefrontal cortex
# Nondominant hemisphere

to be clarified. Schizophrenic, alcoholic, and bipolar dementias may be accompanied by alterations in dopamine and/or norepinephrine metabolism (Carlsson 1979), alterations which may be relevant to the function of the prefrontal cortex. All three disorders may be characterized by neuroradiological and neurophysiological changes which either implicate diffuse cerebral damage or selective impairment of the prefrontal cortex. In schizophrenia and alcoholism, these abnormalities may be associated with treatment failure. In schizophrenia, this includes neuroleptic unresponsiveness; in alcoholism it includes an inability to maintain sobriety. In all three disorders, these biological markers predict poor outcome, with ongoing impairments in cognitive, social, and instrumental functioning.

THE PREFRONTAL CORTEX IN PSYCHIATRIC DISABILITY

Neuroanatomic localization is a fundamental principle of neurologic and psychiatric practice. We have summarized several lines of evidence that suggest, but do not establish, a role for dysfunction of the prefrontal cortex in psychiatric disability. Nonetheless, prefrontal dysfunction has considerable heuristic value in understanding disability.

The prefrontal cortex, while phylogenetically recent, represents more than 25 percent of the cerebrum in man. It serves a synthetic function and, from a hierarchical perspective, represents the highest (and most "human") center of the nervous system. The prefrontal cortex receives a variety of inputs, related to the general drive state and internal needs of the individual and to the motivational significance of external stimuli in gratifying those needs. Its outputs, in turn, are cohesive behavioral programs aimed at obtaining those goals. Simple, habitual behavioral patterns can be performed without the prefrontal cortex; more complex, novel behaviors, especially those which are punctuated by long delays, cannot.

The prefrontal cortex can be divided, on the basis of connections and functions, into two components, lying dorsolaterally and ventromedially. The dorsolateral prefrontal cortex is involved in both prospective functions (such as anticipation, that is, preparing the individual for a range of possible environmental stimuli relevant to a goal) and retrospective functions (such as provisional memory, that is, allowing the individual to compare behaviors within a sequence to one another and to the original program). The ventromedial prefrontal cortex also is involved in two functions: suppressing interference (from irrelevant external stimuli or irrelevant internal drives and affects) and maintaining "cortical tone" (Luria 1973; Fuster 1980).

Lesions to the prefrontal cortex result in characteristic impairments in language/cognitive, social/affective, and instrumental functioning. Most of the negative and some of the positive symptoms to which we have already referred can be localized to the dorsolateral or ventromedial prefrontal cortex. Lesions to the anterior dorsolateral prefrontal cortex may affect the discourse aspect of language, governing the manner in which sentences are combined to construct an idea or story. This aspect may be especially disrupted in schizophrenia (Andreasen 1982), and may be the linguistic counterpart of the "dissociation of thinking" to which Bleuler referred. More extensive lesions to the dorsolateral prefrontal cortex may result in impoverished, nonspontaneous speech (that is, *alogia*, a frequently cited negative symptom). Furthermore, as dorsolateral lesions interfere with provisional memory, language loses primacy over behavior. The individual with such a lesion may very well be able to describe and intend to comply with a plan of action, but may be unable to compare his actions with this plan (Luria 1973). This may be the neuropsychological basis of "lack of insight," felt to be a major obstacle in the rehabilitation of the psychiatrically disabled (Stanton 1978).

Lesions to the ventromedial prefrontal cortex result in different cognitive disturbances, primarily in the ability to sustain attention and to suppress irrelevant stimuli. The analysis of complex stimuli suffers, as synthetic interpretations are replaced with fragmentary guesses based on irrelevant details. Such attentional deficits may underlie the characteristic "overinclusive" thought disorder of schizophrenia (Cameron 1964). This may be conceptualized as an excess, or positive, symptom and may be responsive to neuroleptic treatment (Chapman and Knowles 1964).

Damage to the prefrontal cortex also produces disorders in social and affective functioning. Dorsolateral lesions result in profound indifference and blunted affect, the "withdrawal" (or "autism") and "affective flattening" of Bleuler (Grafman et al., in submission).

Finally, lesions to the prefrontal cortex result in characteristic impairments in motor behavior and instrumental functioning. Dorsolateral lesions disrupt anticipation and, not surprisingly, affect the spontaneity and purposefulness of behavior. Severe lesions produce a syndrome in which behavior can be provoked, but is not initiated (that is, they produce "weakening of the will," as described by Bleuler). Ventromedial lesions, on the other hand, produce a syndrome in which behavioral programs are disrupted by imitative (echopraxic) actions or are replaced by familiar but irrelevant behaviors (stereotypes) (Luria 1973). Behavior can be said to be controlled, not by a superordinate goal, but by environmental stimuli. We submit that this is the neuropsychologic counterpart of psychotic "ambivalence," another of Bleuler's fundamental symptoms. In sum, dysfunction of the prefrontal cortex can be considered as the primary defect underlying impairments in self-care and self-direction which characterize the psychiatrically disabled.

REHABILITATION

As Anthony and associates (1984) have suggested, the two fundamental interventions of psychiatric rehabilitation are client skill development and environmental resource development. We might also include pharmacotherapy under the rubric of client development. What are the implications of the foregoing discussion for these interventions?

Regarding pharmacotherapy, neuroleptics are a mainstay in the treatment of the chronically psychotic patient. As indicated above, they are particularly effective against positive symptoms. As further indicated, they are less effective against negative symptoms and cognitive impairments, especially with prolonged use (Goldberg et al. 1967). This loss of efficacy may account for the considerable relapse rate (perhaps 30 percent within one year) among schizophrenic patients, a relapse rate which persists even when medication compliance is assured (Schooler et al. 1980). We have hypothesized that the relative refractoriness of negative symptoms to neuroleptic treatment is a result of their being mediated by diminished cortical dopamine activity. This hypothesis has clear implications for treatment. Schizophrenic (and other psychotic) patients who manifest predominantly negative symptoms warrant a reduction in neuroleptic dose, a trial of anticholinergic medication, or, possibly, the judicious administration of dopamine agonists (Carpenter et al. 1985).

Regarding skill development, both behavioral modification (Comes-Schwartz 1979) and systematic didactic approaches (Anthony et al. 1984) have been employed. Severely psychiatrically disabled clients have been taught problem-solving skills (Coche and Flick 1975; Siegel and Spivack 1976), social skills (Bellack et al. 1976; Jaffe and Carlson 1976; Finch and Wallace 1977; Eisler et al. 1978; Malm 1982), and vocational skills (Shean 1973). We might expect that clients with impairments in abstract reasoning (vide supra) would have difficulty in generalizing skills learned to novel contexts. This is, in fact, what has been observed. Thus, clients trained in role playing may improve in role playing, but not in social contact (Finch and Wallace 1977); similarly, clients taught occupational skills in the hospital setting may not be able to use those skills in the community (Anthony 1979). Impairments in skill generalization suggest that skills should be taught in a variety of situations and that support services may need to follow the client directly into the environment of need (Cohen 1983). We might also expect that specific approaches used to retrain neurologic patients with frontal lobe injuries (Craine 1982) would be useful in retraining psychiatric patients with prefrontal dysfunction. Such approaches might include the use of formalized algorithms (allowing stepwise solutions to complex tasks) and articulated feedback (overcoming deficits in "insight") (Carpenter et al. 1985).

Finally, regarding resource development, disabled patients with largely irreversible prefrontal dysfunction may require ongoing compensatory intervention, what Lindsley (1970) has called a "prosthetic environment." Impairments in anticipation and planning suggest the need for active case management (Lamb 1980) and aggressive outreach. Without these interventions, the mentally ill's lack of self-direction would deny them continuous access to the very treatment they need. In this regard, a recent follow-up study of schizophrenic patients discharged from the hospital is illuminating. Of the initial cohort, 55 percent were alive and residing in the community five to nine years after release. Of these, only 35 percent had ongoing psychiatric contact, despite the fact that 82 percent had significant residual symptoms, and over 50 percent were actively psychotic (Johnstone et al. 1984). Clearly, in the absence of specific measures aimed at ensuring patient contact, most patients had been lost to psychiatric follow-up, despite considerable disability.

Impairments in suppressing disruptive stimuli suggest the need for limiting stimulation by caretakers and care providers. A failure to control disruptive stimuli may have accounted for the high relapse rate among neuroleptic-free schizophrenic patients who returned to overinvolved families with high levels of expressed emotion (Vaughn and Leff 1976), or who received intensive social casework (Hogarty et al. 1974). Neuroleptics, as noted above, may reverse partially these deficits in filtering stimuli, allowing the patient to tolerate added environmental stimulation. Social withdrawal may reduce the stimuli themselves and, for that reason, may not be entirely undesirable (Falloon and Liberman 1983).

CONCLUSIONS

The psychiatrically disabled are a group of patients with varied diagnoses but a shared pathogenesis. They suffer from behavioral and cognitive deficits which are relatively irreversible and which are correlated with chronicity and poor outcome. Neuropsychological, neurological, neurochemical, neuroradiological, and neurophysiological features suggest a common underlying organic insult. Dysfunction of the prefrontal cortex may be particularly important in the development of disability. Despite considerable functional limitation, rehabilitation is possible, especially if pharmacotherapy is combined with skill acquisition, cognitive retraining, and environmental interventions. The goal of such rehabilitation should be restoration, not necessarily to "normality," but to a degree of independence and improved quality of life.

REFERENCES

Abbott MW, Gregson RAM: Cognitive dysfunction in the prediction of relapse in alcoholics. J Stud Alcohol 42:230-243, 1981

Anderson JR: Social Security and SSI benefits for the mentally disabled. Hosp Community Psychiatry 33:295-298, 1982

Andreasen NC: The relationship between schizophrenic language and the aphasias, in Schizophrenia as a Brain Disease. Edited by Henn FA, Nasrallah HA. New York, Oxford University Press, 1982, pp 99-111

Andreasen NC, Olsen SA, Dennert JW, et al: Ventricular enlargement in schizophrenia: relationship to positive and negative symptoms. Am J Psychiatry 139:297-302, 1982

Andrews WM: Long-acting tranquilizers and the amotivational syndrome in the treatment of schizophrenics, in Community Management of the Schizophrenic in Chemical Remission. Edited by King EH. Amsterdam, Excerpta Medica, 1973

Angrist B, Lee HK, Gershon S: The antagonism of amphetamine-induced symptomatology by a neuroleptic. Am J Psychiatry 131:817-819, 1974

Angrist B, Rotrosen J, Gershon S: Positive and negative symptoms in schizophrenia—differential response to amphetamine and neuroleptics. Psychopharmacology 72:17-19, 1980

Angrist B, Peselow E, Rubinstein M, et al: Partial improvement in negative schizophrenic symptoms with amphetamine. Psychopharmacology 78:128-130, 1982

Anthony WA: Principles of Psychiatric Rehabilitation. Baltimore, University Park Press, 1979

Anthony WA, Cohen MR, Cohen BF: Psychiatric rehabilitation, in The Chronic Mental Patient: Five Years Later. Edited by Talbott JA. Orlando, Florida, Grune & Stratton, 1984

Banki CM: Correlation between cerebrospinal fluid amine metabolites and psychomotor activity in affective disorders. J Neurochem 29:255-257, 1977

Baxter LR Jr, Phelps ME, Mazziotta JC, et al: Cerebral metabolic rates for glucose in mood disorders. Arch Gen Psychiatry 42:441-447, 1985

Bellack A, Hersen M, Turner S: Generalization effects of social skills training and chronic schizophrenia: an experimental analysis. Behav Res Ther 14:391-398, 1976

Berglund M, Ingvar DH: Cerebral blood flow and its regional distribution in alcoholism and Korsakoff's psychosis. J Stud Alcohol 37:586-597, 1976

Berglund M, Leijonquist H, Horlen M: Prognostic significance and reversibility of cerebral dysfunction in alcoholics. J Stud Alcohol 38:1761-1770, 1977

Berman KF, Zec RF, Weinberger DR: Physiological dysfunction of dorsolateral prefrontal cortex in schizophrenia, II: role of neuroleptic treatment, attention, and mental effort. Arch Gen Psychiatry 43:126-135, 1986

Bernstein IH: A comparison of schizophrenics and nonschizophrenics on two methods of administration of the Bender-Gestalt Test. Perceptual and Motor Skills 16:757-763, 1963

Berrios GE: Positive and negative symptoms and Jackson. Arch Gen Psychiatry 42:95-97, 1985

Bland RC, Orn H: Schizophrenia: Schneider's first rank symptoms and outcome. Br J Psychiatry 137:63-68, 1980

Bleuler E: Dementia Praecox or the Group of Schizophrenias. Translated by Zinkin J. New York, International Universities Press, 1950

Bowers MB Jr: Central dopamine turnover in schizophrenic syndromes. Arch Gen Psychiatry 31:50-54, 1974

Bowers MB Jr, Heninger GR, Gerbode FA: Cerebrospinal fluid 5-hydroxyindoleacetic acid and homovanillic acid in psychiatric patients. International Journal of Neuropharmacology 8:255-262, 1969

Brambilla F, Scarone S, Ponzano M, et al: Catecholaminergic drugs in chronic schizophrenia. Neuropsychobiology 5:185-200, 1979

Brandt J, Butters N, Ryan C, et al: Cognitive loss and recovery in long-term alcohol abusers. Arch Gen Psychiatry 40:435-442, 1983

Brewer C, Perret L: Brain damage due to alcohol consumption: an airencephalographic, psychometric and electroencephalographic study. Br J Addict 66:170-182, 1971

Brockington IF, Kendell RE, Leff JB: Definitions of schizophrenia: concordance and prediction of outcome. Psychol Med 8:387-398, 1978

Brozoski TJ, Brown RM, Rosvold HE, et al: Cognitive deficit caused by regional depletion of dopamine in prefrontal cortex of rhesus monkey. Science 205:929-932, 1979

Buchsbaum MS, Cappelletti J, Coppola R, et al: New methods to determine the CNS effects of antigeriatric compounds: EEG topography and glucose use. Drug Development Research 2:489-496, 1982a

Buchsbaum MS, Ingvar DH, Kessler R, et al: Cerebral glucography with positron tomography: use in normal subjects and patients with schizophrenia. Arch Gen Psychiatry 39:251-259, 1982b

Buchsbaum MS, Holcomb HH, DeLisi LE, et al: PET in schizophrenia and affective illness, in New Research Abstracts, 136th Annual Meeting of the American Psychiatric Association, New York, 1983

Cala LA, Jones B, Mastaglia FL, et al: Brain atrophy and intellectual impairment in heavy drinkers—a clinical psychometric and computed tomography study. Aust NZ J Med 8:147-153, 1978

Cameron NS: Experimental analysis of schizophrenic thinking, in Language and Thought in Schizophrenia. Edited by Kasanin JS. New York, W W Norton, 1964

Carlen PL: Reversible effects of chronic alcoholism on the human central nervous system: possible biological mechanisms, in Cerebral Deficits in Alcoholism. Edited by Wilkinson DA. Toronto, Addiction Research Foundation, 1979

Carlen PL, Blair RDG, Singh R, et al: Improvement from alcoholic organic brain syndrome: early EEG changes predict degree of psychologically and clinically assessed recovery. Can J Neurol Sci 4:224, 1977

Carlen PL, Wortzman G, Holgate RC, et al: Reversible cerebral atrophy in recently abstinent chronic alcoholics measured by computer tomography scans. Science 200:1076-1078, 1978

Carlsson A: The impact of catecholamine research in medical science and practice, in Catecholamines: Basic and Clinical Frontiers. Edited by Usdin E, Kopin IJ, Barchas J. New York, Pergamon Press, 1979

Carpenter WT Jr, Heinrichs DW, Alphs LD: Treatment of negative symptoms. Schizophr Bull 11:440-452, 1985

Chapman LJ, Knowles RR: The effects of phenothiazine on disordered thought in schizophrenia. Journal of Consulting Psychology 28:165-169, 1964

Coche E, Flick A: Problem solving training groups for hospitalized psychiatric patients. Psychology 91:19-29, 1975

Cohen BF, Ridley D, Cohen MR: Teaching skills to severely psychiatrically disabled persons, in Proceedings of the 1982 CSP Region 4 Conference. Edited by Marlowe H, Weinberg R. Tampa, Florida, University of South Florida, 1983

Comes-Schwartz B: Modification of schizophrenic behavior. Behav Modif 3:439-468, 1979

Courville CB: The Effects of Alcohol on the Nervous System of Man. Los Angeles, San Lucas Press, 1955

Cox SM, Ludwig AM: Neurological soft signs and psychopathology: incidence in diagnostic groups. Can J Psychiatry 24:668-673, 1979

Craine JF: The retraining of frontal lobe dysfunction, in Cognitive Rehabilitation: Conceptualization and Intervention. Edited by Trexler LE. New York, Plenum Press, 1982

Crow TJ: Molecular pathology of schizophrenia: more than one disease process? Br Med J 280:66-68, 1980

Crow TJ, Cross AJ, Johnstone EC: Two syndromes in schizophrenia and their pathogenesis, in Schizophrenia as a Brain Disease. Edited by Henn FA, Nasrallah HA. New York, Oxford University Press, 1982

Davis KL, Davidson M, Mohs RC, et al: Plasma homovanillic acid concentration and the severity of schizophrenic illness. Science 227:1601-1602, 1985

DeLisi LE, Schwartz CC, Targum SD, et al: Ventricular brain enlargement and outcome of acute schizophreniform disorder. Psychiatry Res 9:169-171, 1983

Depue RA, Dupicki MD, McCarthy T: Differential recovery of intellectual associational and physiological functioning in withdrawn and active schizophrenics. J Abnorm Psychol 84:325-330, 1975

de Wolfe AS, Barrell RP, Becker BC, et al: Intellectual deficit in chronic schizophrenia and brain damage. J Consult Clin Psychol 36:197-204, 1971

Donnelly E, Dent J, Murphy D, et al: Comparison of temporal lobe epileptics and affective disorders on the Halstead-Reitan test battery. J Clin Psychol 28:61-62, 1972

Donnelly EF, Weinberger DR, Waldman IN, et al: Cognitive impairment associated with morphological brain abnormalities on computed tomography in chronic schizophrenic patients. J Nerv Ment Dis 168:305-308, 1980

Eisler R, Blanchard E, Fitts H, et al: Social skills training with and without modeling for schizophrenics and non-psychotic hospitalized psychiatric patients. Behav Modi 2:147-172, 1978

Ellinwood EH: Amphetamine psychosis, I: description of the individuals and the process. J Nerv Ment Dis 144:274-283, 1967

Elsworth JD, Roth RH, Redmond DE Jr: Does HVA concentration in CSF or plasma reflect central dopamine function in primates? Prog Neuropsychopharmacol 125:Suppl 128, 1983

Falloon RH, Liberman RP: Interactions between drug and psychosocial therapy in schizophrenia. Schizophr Bull 9:543-554, 1983

Farkas T, Reivich M, Alavi A, et al: The application of 18F2-deoxy-2-fluoroglucose and positron emission tomography in the study of psychiatric conditions, in Cerebral Metabolism and Neural Function. Edited by Passonneau JV, Hawkins RA, Lust WD, et al. Baltimore, Williams & Wilkins, 1980

Feinstein AR: A critical overview of diagnosis in psychiatry, in Psychiatric Diagnosis. Edited by Rakoff VM, Stancer HL, Kedward HB. New York, Brunner/Mazel, 1977

Fenton GW, Fenwick PBC, Dollimore J: EEG spectral analysis in schizophrenia. Br J Psychiatry 136:445-455, 1980

Finch B, Wallace D: Successful interpersonal skills training with schizophrenic inpatients. J Consult Clin Psychol 45:885-890, 1977

Friedman M, Culver C, Ferrell R: On the safety of long-term treatment with lithium. Am J Psychiatry 134:1123-1126, 1977

Fuster JM: The Prefrontal Cortex: Anatomy, Physiology, and Neuropsychology of the Frontal Lobe. New York, Raven Press, 1980

Gerlach J, Luhdorf K: The effect of L-dopa on young patients with simple schizophrenia treated with neuroleptic drugs: a double-blind crossover trial with madopar and placebo. Psychopharmacologia 44:105-110, 1975

Ginett LE, Moran LJ: Stability of vocabulary performance by schizophrenics. Journal of Consulting Psychology 28:178-179, 1964

Goldberg SC: Negative and deficit symptoms in schizophrenia do respond to neuroleptics. Schizophr Bull 11:453-456, 1985

Goldberg SC, Schooler NR, Mattsson N: Paranoid and withdrawal symptoms in schizophrenia: differential symptom reduction over time. J Nerv Ment Dis 145:158-162, 1967

Golden CJ, Moses JA, Zelazowski R, et al: Cerebral ventricular size and neuropsychological impairment in young chronic schizophrenics measured by the standardized Luria-Nebraska Neuropsychological Battery. Arch Gen Psychiatry 37:619-623, 1980

Golden CJ, MacInnes WD, Ariel RN, et al: Cross-validation of the ability of the Luria-Nebraska Neuropsychological Battery to differentiate chronic schizophrenics with and without ventricular enlargement. J Consult Clin Psychol 50:87-95, 1982

Goldman HH: Epidemiology, in The Chronic Mental Patient: Five Years Later. Edited by Talbott JA. Orlando, Florida, Grune & Stratton, 1984

Goodwin FK, Jamison KR: The natural course of manic depressive illness, in Neurobiology of Mood Disorders. Edited by Post RM, Ballenger JC. Baltimore, Williams & Wilkins, 1983

Gur RE, Gur RC, Skolnick BE, et al: Brain function in psychiatric disorders. Arch Gen Psychiatry 42:329-334, 1985

Hamlin RM: The stability of intellectual function in chronic schizophrenia. J Nerv Ment Dis 149:496-503, 1969

Haug JO: Pneumoencephalographic studies in mental disease. Acta Psychiatr Scand 38 (Suppl 165): 1-104, 1962

Haug JO: Pneumoencephalographic evidence of brain damage in chronic alcoholics. Acta Psychiatr Scand (Suppl 204): 135-143, 1968

Haywood HC, Moelis I: Effect of symptom change on intellectual function in schizophrenia. Journal of Abnormal and Social Psychology 67:76-78, 1963

Heaton RK, Baade LE, Johnson KL: Neuropsychological test results associated with psychiatric disorders in adults. Psychol Bull 85:141-162, 1978

Hogarty GE, Goldberg SC, Schooler NR, et al: Drug and sociotherapy in the aftercare of schizophrenic patients, II: two-year relapse rates. Arch Gen Psychiatry 31:603-608, 1974

Horvath TB: Clinical spectrum and epidemiological features of alcoholic dementia, in Alcohol, Drugs and Brain Damage: Proceedings of a Symposium, Effects of Chronic Use of Alcohol and other Psychoactive Drugs on Cerebral Function. Edited by Rankin JG. Toronto, Alcoholism and Drug Addiction, 1975

Hughlings-Jackson J: Evolution and dissolution of the nervous system: lecture I. Br Med J 1:591-593, 1984

Ingvar DH, Franzen G: Abnormalities of cerebral blood flow distribution in patients with chronic schizophrenia. Acta Psychiatr Scand 50:425-462, 1974

Ingvar DH, Sjolund B, Ardo A: Correlation between dominant EEG frequency, cerebral oxygen uptake, and blood flow. Electroencephalogr Clin Neurophysiol 41:268-276, 1976

Itil TM: Qualitative and quantitative EEG findings in schizophrenia. Schizophr Bull 3:61-79, 1977

Jaffe P, Carlson P: Relative efficacy of modeling and instruction in eliciting social behavior from chronic psychiatric patients. J Consult Clin Psychol 44:200-209, 1976

Javoy-Agid F, Agid Y: Is the mesocortical dopamine system involved in Parkinson's disease? Neurology 30:1326-1330, 1980

Johnstone EC, Crow TJ, Frith CD, et al: Cerebral ventricular size and cognitive impairment in chronic schizophrenia. Lancet 2:924-926, 1976

Johnstone EC, Crow TJ, Frith CD: The dementia of dementia praecox. Acta Psychiatr Scand 57:305-324, 1978a

Johnstone EC, Crow TJ, Frith CD, et al: Mechanism of the antipsychotic effect in the treatment of acute schizophrenia. Lancet 1:848-851, 1978b

Johnstone EC, Owens DGC, Gold A, et al: Schizophrenic patients discharged from hospital—a follow-up study. Br J Psychiatry 145:586-590, 1984

Jones B, Parsons OA: Impaired abstracting ability in chronic alcoholics. Arch Gen Psychiatry 24:71-75, 1971

Jones B, Parsons OA: Specific versus generalized deficits of abstracting ability in chronic alcoholics. Arch Gen Psychiatry 26:380-384, 1972

Kennard MA: Value of equivocal signs in neurologic diagnosis. Neurology 10:753-764, 1960

Klein DF, Gittelman R, Quitkin A (Eds): Diagnosis and Drug Treatment of Psychiatric Disorders: Adults and Children. Baltimore, Williams & Wilkins, 1980

Kolakowska T, Williams AD, Jambor K, et al: Schizophrenia with good and poor outcome, III: neurological "soft" signs, cognitive impairment and their clinical significance. Br J Psychiatry 146:348-357, 1985

Kottke FJ, Lehmann JF, Stillwell GK: Preface, in Krusen's Handbook of Physical Medicine and Rehabilitation. Edited by Kottke FJ, Stillwell GK, Lehmann JF. Philadelphia, WB Saunders, 1982

Kraepelin E: Dementia Praecox and Paraphrenia. Translated by Barclay RM. Huntington, New York, Krieger Publishing, 1919

Kroll P, Seigel R, O'Neill B: Cerebral cortical atrophy in alcoholic men. J Clin Psychiatry 41:417-421, 1980

Lamb HR: Therapist-care manager: more than brokers of service. Hosp Community Psychiatry 31:762-764, 1980

Lemke R: Untersuchungen uber die social prognose der schizophrenie unter besonderer beruksichtisung des encephalographischen befundes. Archiv fur Psychiatrie 104:89-136, 1936

Lilliston L: Tests of cerebral damage and the process reactive dimenion. J Clin Psychol 26:180-181, 1970

Lilliston L: Schizophrenic symptomatology as a function of probability of cerebral damage. J Abnorm Psychol 82:377-381, 1973

Lindsley OR: Geriatric behavioral prosthetics, in New Thoughts on Old Age. Edited by Kastenbaum RJ. New York, Springer, 1970

Lindstrom LH: Low HVA and normal 5HIAA CSF levels in drug-free schizophrenic patients compared to healthy volunteers: correlations to symptomatology and family history. Psychiatry Res 14:265-273, 1985

Long JA, McLachlan JFC: Abstract reasoning and perceptual motor efficiency in alcoholics: impairment and reversibility. Quarterly Journal of Studies on Alcohol 35:1220-1229, 1974

Luchins DJ, Lewine RRJ, Meltzer HY: Lateral ventricular size, psychopathology, and medication response in the psychoses. Biol Psychiatry 19:29-44, 1984

Luria AR: The Working Brain: An Introduction to Neuropsychology. Translated by Haigh B. New York, Basic Books, 1973

Malm U: The influence of group therapy on schizophrenia. Acta Psychiatr Scand 65(Suppl 297):1-65, 1982

Malmo HP: On frontal lobe functions: psychiatric patient controls. Cortex 10:231-237, 1974

Martin PR, Weingartner H, Gordon EK, et al: Central nervous system catecholamine metabolism in Korsakoff's psychosis. Ann Neurol 15:184-187, 1984

McCulloch J, Savaki HE, McCulloch MC, et al: The distribution of alterations in energy metabolism in the rat brain produced by apomorphine. Brain Res 243:67-80, 1982

McEntee WJ, Mair RG: Memory impairment in Korsakoff's psychosis: a correlation with brain noradrenergic activity. Science 202:905-907, 1978

McEntee WJ, Mair RG, Langlais PJ: Cerebrospinal fluid monoamine metabolites in Korsakoff's disease: relationship to memory impairment and drug response, in Neurobiolgy of Cerebrospinal Fluid. Edited by Wood JR. New York, Plenum Press, 1983

Mirsky AF: Neuropsychological bases of schizophrenia. Ann Rev Psychol 20:321-348, 1969

Morihisa JM, Duffy FH, Wyatt RJ: Brain electrical activity mapping (BEAM) in schizophrenic patients. Arch Gen Psychiatry 40:719-728, 1983

Morihisa JM, McAnulty GB: Structure and function: brain electrical activity mapping and computed tomography in schizophrenia. Biol Psychiatry 20:3-19, 1985

Mosher L, Pollin W, Stabenau J: Identical twins discordant for schizophrenia. Arch Gen Psychiatry 24:422-430, 1971

Mubrin Z, Krezevic S, Koretic D, et al: Regional cerebral blood flow patterns in schizophrenic patients. rCBF Bulletin 3:43-46, 1982

Nagy K: Pneumoencephalographische befunde bei endogen psychosen. Nervenarzt 34:543-548, 1963

Nasrallah HA, McCalley-Whitters M, Jacoby CG: Cerebral ventricular enlargement in young manic males: a controlled CT study. J Affective Disord 4:15-19, 1982

Nasrallah HA, Tippin J, McCalley-Whitters M: Neurological soft signs in manic patients: a comparison with schizophrenic and control groups. J Affective Disord 5:45-50, 1983

National Institute of Mental Health, Psychopharmacology Service Center, Collaborative Study Group: Phenothiazine treatment in acute schizophrenia: effectiveness. Arch Gen Psychiatry 10:246-261, 1964

Nyback H, Berggren B-M, Hindmarsh T, et al: Cerebroventricular size and cerebrospinal fluid monoamine metabolites in schizophrenic patients and healthy volunteers. Psychiatry Res 9:301-308, 1983

Ogura C, Kishimoto A, Nakao T: Clinical effect of L-dopa on schizophrenia. Current Therapeutic Research, Clinical and Experimental 20:308-318, 1976

Orme JE, Lee D, Smith MR: Psychological assessments of brain damage and intellectual impairment in psychiatric patients. Br J Soc Clin Psychol 3:161-167, 1964

Parker ES, Alkana RL, Birnbaum IM, et al: Alcohol and the disruption of cognitive processes. Arch Gen Psychiatry 31:824-828, 174

Parker DA, Parker ES, Brody JA, et al: Alcohol use and cognitive loss among employed men and women. Am J Public Health 73:521-526, 1983

Paul GL: The chronic mental patient: current status—future directions. Psychol Bull 71:81-94, 1969

Pearlson CG, Garbacz DJ, Breakey WR, et al: Lateral ventricular enlargement associated with persistent unemployment and negative symptoms in both schizophrenia and bipolar disorder. Psychiatry Res 12:1-9, 1984

Pearlson CG, Garbacz DJ, Moberg PJ, et al: Symptomatic, familial, perinatal, and social correlates of computerized axial tomography (CAT) changes in schizophrenics and bipolars. J Nerv Ment Dis 173:42-50, 1985

Pearlson GD, Veroff AE: Computerized tomographic scan changes in manic-depressive illness. Lancet 2:470, 1981

Pfohl B, Winokur G: The evolution of symptoms in institutionalized hebrephrenic catatonic schizophrenia. Br J Psychiatry 141:567-572, 1982

Pickar D, Labarca R, Linnoila M, et al: Neuroleptic-induced decrease in plasma homovanillic acid and antipsychotic activity in schizophrenic patients. Science 225:954-957, 1984

Pincus JH, Tucker GJ: Behavioral Neurology, Third edition. New York, Oxford University Press, 1978

Pogue-Geile MF, Harrow M: Negative and positive symptoms in schizophrenia and depression: a followup. Schizophr Bull 10:371-387, 1984

Pogue-Geile MF, Harrow M: Negative symptoms in schizophrenia: their logitudinal course and prognostic importance. Schizophr Bull 11:427-439, 1985

Pope HG, Lipinski JF: Diagnosis in schizophrenia and manic-depressive illness: a reassessment of the specificity of "schizophrenic" symptoms in light of current research. Arch Gen Psychiatry 35:811-828, 1978

Post RM, Goodwin FK: Approaches to brain amines in psychiatric patients: a reevaluation of cerebrospinal fluid studies, in Handbook of Psychopharmacology. Edited by Iversen LL, Iversen SD, Snyder S. New York, Plenum Press, 1978

Post RM, Gordon EK, Goodwin FK, et al: Central norepinephrine metabolism in affective illness: MHPG in the cerebrospinal fluid. Science 9:1002-1003, 1973

Post RM, Fink E, Carpenter WT, et al: Cerebrospinal fluid amine metabolites in acute schizophrenia. Arch Gen Psychiatry 32:1063-1069, 1975

Pritchard M: Prognosis of schizophrenia before and after pharmacotherapy. Br J Psychiatry 113:1345-1359, 1967

Public Law 95-602: Rehabilitation, Comprehensive Services, and Developmental Disabilities Amendments of 1978. Washington, DC, U.S. Government Printing Office, 1978

Pycock CJ, Kerwin RW, Carter CJ: Effect of lesion of cortical dopamine terminals on subcortical dopamine in rats. Nature 286:74-77, 1980

Quitkin F, Rifkin A, Klein DF: Neurological soft signs in schizophrenia and character disorders: organicity in schizophrenia with premorbid asociality and emotionally unstable character disorders. Arch Gen Psychiatry 33:845-853, 1976

Randrup A, Munkvad I: Biochemical, anatomical and psychological investigations of stereotyped behavior induced by amphetamines, in Amphetamines and Related Compounds. Edited by Costa E, Garattini S. New York, Raven Press, 1970

Rochford JM, Detre T, Tucker GJ, et al: Neuropsychological impairments in functional psychiatric diseases. Arch Gen Psychiatry 22:114-119, 1970

Rush AJ, Schlesser MA, Stockey E, et al: Cerebral blood flow in depression and mania. Psychopharmacol Bull 18:6-8, 1982

Sanchez-Craig M, Wilkinson DA: Investigations of brain function in alcoholics: a methodological critique, in Cerebral Deficits in Alcoholism. Edited by Wilkinson DA. Toronto, Addiction Research Foundation, 1979

Savard RJ, Rey AC, Post RM: Halstead-Reitan category test in bipolar and unipolar affective disorders: relationship to age and phase of illness. J Nerv Ment Dis 168:297-304, 1980

Scarpiti FR, Lefton M, Dinitz S: Problems in a homecare study for schizophrenia. Arch Gen Psychiatry 10:143-154, 1964

Schau EJ, O'Leary MR, Chaney EF: Reversibility of cognitive deficit in alcoholics. J Stud Alcohol 41:733-740, 1980

Schooler NR, Levine JR, Brauzer D, et al: Prevention of relapse in schizophrenia: an evaluation of fluphenazine decanoate. Arch Gen Psychiatry 37:16-24, 1980

Schulz SC, Sinicrope P, Kinshore P, et al: Treatment response and ventricular enlargement in young schizophrenic patients. Schizophr Bull 19:510-512, 1983

Seidman LJ: Schizophrenia and brain dysfunction: an integration of recent neurodiagnostic findings. Psychol Bull 94:195-238, 1983

Shean G: An effective and self-supporting program of community living for chronic patients. Hosp Community Psychiatry 24:97-99, 1973

Sheppard G, Gruzelier J, Manchanda R, et al: 150 Positron emission tomography scanning in predominantly never treated acute schizophrenic patients. Lancet 2:1448-1452, 1983

Shopsin B, Wilk S, Gershon S: Collaborative psychopharmacologic studies exploring catecholamine metabolism in psychiatric disorders, in Frontiers in Catecholamine Research. Edited by Usdin E, Snyder S. New York, Pergamon Press, 1973

Siegel JM, Spivack G: Problem-solving therapy: the description of a new program for chronic psychiatric patients. Psychotherapy: Theory, Research and Practice 4:368-373, 1976

Sjostrom R: 5-Hydroxyindoleacetic acid and homovanillic acid in cerebrospinal fluid in manic-depressive psychosis and the effect of probenecid treatment. Eur J Clin Pharmacol 6:75-80, 1973

Smith A: Mental deterioration in chronic schizophrenia. J Nerv Ment Dis 139:479-487, 1964

Smith RC: Largen J, Calderon M, et al: CT scans and neuropsychological tests as predictors of clinical response in schizophrenics. Schizophr Bull 19:505-509, 1983

Sokoloff L: Relation between physiologic function and energy metabolism in the central nervous system. J Neurochem 29:13-26, 1977

Stanton AH: The significance of ego interpretive states in insight-directed psychotherapy (Harry Stack Sullivan Colloquium). Psychiatry 41:129-140, 1978

Stevens JR, Livermore A: Telemetered EEG in schizophrenia: spectral analysis during abnormal behavior episodes. J Neurol Neurosurg Psychiatry 45:385-395, 1982

Strauss JS, Carpenter WT: The prediction of outcome in schizophrenia, II: relationships between predictors and outcome variables. Arch Gen Psychiatry 31:37-42, 1974

Subrahmanyam S: Role of biogenic amines in certain pathological conditions. Brain Res 87:355-362, 1975

Sutter JM, Debrie ML, Scotto JC: Recherches sur les effets psychologiques de la fluphenazine dans les psychoses chroniques. Annales Medico-Psychologiques (Paris) 124:19-33, 1966

Tartar RE: Psychological deficit in chronic alcoholism: a review. Int J Addict 10:327-368, 1975

Tartar RE, Parsons OA: Conceptual shifting in chronic alcoholics. J Abnorm Psychol 77:71-75, 1971

Taylor MA, Abrams RC: Prediction of treatment response in mania. Arch Gen Psychiatry 38:800-803, 1981

Taylor MA, Redfield J, Abrams R: Neuropsychological dysfunction in schizophrenia and affective disease. Biol Psychiatry 16:467-478, 1981

Tsuang MT: Schizophrenic syndromes: the search for subgroups in schizophrenia with brain dysfunction, in Schizophrenia as a Brain Disease. Edited by Henn FA, Nasrallah HA. New York, Oxford University Press, 1982

Tsuang MT, Woolson RF, Fleming JA: Long-term outcome of major psychoses, I: schizophrenia and affective disorders compared with psychiatrically symptom-free surgical conditions. Arch Gen Psychiatry 39:1295-1301, 1979

Tucker GJ, Campion EW, Silberfarb PM: Sensorimotor functions and cognitive disturbance in psychiatric patients. Am J Psychiatry 132:17-21, 1975

van Kammen DP, Mann LS, Sternberg DE, et al: Dopamine beta-hydroxylase activity and homovanillic acid in spinal fluid of schizophrenics with brain atrophy. Science 220:974-977, 1983

van Praag HM, Korf J: Neuroleptics, catecholamines, and psychoses: a study of their intercorrelations. Am J Psychiatry 132:593-597, 1975

Vaughn CE, Leff JP: The influence of family and social factors on the course of psychiatric illness. Br J Psychiatry 129:125-137, 1976

Watson CG: WAIS profile patterns of hospitalized brain-damaged and schizophrenic patients. J Cosult Clin Psychol 21:294-295, 1965

Watson CG: Separation of brain-damaged from the patients by Reitan-Halstead pattern analysis: an unsuccessful replication. Psychol Rep 29:1343-1346, 1971

Weinberger DR, Torrey EF, Neophytides AN, et al: Lateral cerebral ventricular enlargement in chronic schizophrenia. Arch Gen Psychiatry 36:735-739, 1979

Weinberger DR, Bigelow LB, Kleinman JE, et al: Cerebral ventricular enlargement in chronic schizophrenia, an association with poor response to treatment. Arch Gen Psychiatry 37:111-113, 1980

Weinberger DR, DeLisi LE, Perman GP, et al: Computed tomography in schizophreniform disorder and other psychiatric disorders. Arch Gen Psychiatry 39:778-783, 1982

Weinberger DR, Berman KF, Zec RF: Physiological dysfunction of dorsolateral prefrontal cortex in schizophrenia, I: Regional cerebral blood flow (rCBF) evidence. Arch Gen Psychiatry 43:114-124, 1985

Welner A, Welner Z, Leonard MA: Bipolar manic-depressive disorder: a reassessment of course and outcome. Compr Psychiatry 18:327-332, 1977

Wilkinson DA, Carlen PL: Relation of neuropsychological test performance in alcoholics to brain morphology measured by computed tomography, in Advances in Experimental Medicine and Biology Series: Biological Effects of Alcohol. Edited by Begleiter H, Kissin B. New York, Plenum Press, 1980

Williams AO, Reveley MA, Kolakowska T, et al: Schizophrenia with good and poor outcome, II: cerebral ventricular size and its clinical significance. Br J Psychiatry 146:239-246, 1985

Wistedt B: Schizophrenia: a chronic disease. Acta Psychiatr Scand 63 (Suppl 291):9-19, 1981

Zubin J: Chronic schizophrenia from the standpoint of vulnerability, in Perspectives in Schizophrenia Research. Edited by Baxter C, Melnechuk T. New York, Elsevier, 1980

Zubin J, Spring B: Vulnerability—a new view of schizophrenia. J Abnorm Psychol 86:103-126, 1977

Zubin J, Magaziner J, Steinhauer SR: The metamorphosis of schizophrenia: from chronicity to vulnerability. Psychol Med 13:557-571, 1983

4

Factors Influencing Work-Related Disability

Carroll M. Brodsky, M.D., Ph.D.

Disability behavior can be puzzling if one does not understand the cultural, social, biological, and psychological components of the systems that determine decisions to seek employment, change employment, become formally unemployed, or to seek or to be assigned disability status. The professionals who evaluate claims of disability frequently are governed by work values and motivations which differ substantially from those of the subjects they are evaluating. Most of the health professionals believe that work is good and gratifying and that they will retire only when it is no longer feasible to continue working or when forced to halt work. Others in the work force may not share these attitudes toward work and some of them may be seen among disability clients.

There are many in our society who would not choose to work at any job available to them if they did not have to do so. There are many who cannot find a position offering a sufficiently substantial wage which makes a difference in living standard. Some make affirmative choices to avoid formal work-for-pay jobs, while others remain unemployed without making a decision to do so. Some are supported by relatives or by part-time jobs in the underground economy, while others have no sources of income at all.

Among the public and private channels providing financial and medical supports are the welfare system; federal, state, and private disability insurance plans; and unemployment insurance. Those who are needy may seek entry into one or more of these channels in order to avail themselves of whatever benefits society provides for eligible persons. Not all who enter those channels do so legitimately, and conversely, many who are entitled to benefits do not receive them.

In order to understand the social, cultural, and psychological forces operating in either those who have decided, consciously or unconsciously, that they will not stay in the work force and will claim disability, or those who have been excluded from the work force as disabled, one can study those who leave work in the absence of evident physical or mental impairment that would justify a claim of disability sufficient to preclude employment. We must come to understand how *social* impairments predispose to *psychosocial* disability (Ruesch and Brodsky 1968).

THE CULTURE OF WORK AND WORK VALUES

Work occupies a central role in the lives of most people, in terms of time and energy expended. For most, the jobs they hold influence where they live, their associations, their material possessions, and the attitudes they hold, including these directed toward themselves. "What do you do?" and "Where do you work?" are defining questions in some segments of society. Each culture tends to create and perpetuate its unique emphasis on what is important in life and what is worth working for and, thus, distinct, relatively stable national patterns of work values can be identified (Peck 1975).

Each society has its own work culture and, in some, that culture changes, shifting, for example, from emphasis on work to emphasis on leisure, from valuing the agricultural worker to idealizing high technology. In wartime, not working is perceived as unpatriotic, and those formerly precluded from work as disabled become "qualified" and desirable workers. In a society as complex as ours, with its diverse work settings, work roles, and rewards for work, it is difficult to describe a work culture applicable to our entire work life. Nonetheless, those seeking to understand the forces that make for disability in a given setting—a warehouse, a mental hospital, or an assembly line—must study the culture of that work organization in order to understand differences in the incidence of disability among those in that specific work place. We must study the individual worker's special place in that culture if we are to understand workers' differential reactions to the same work culture.

The proverbial "Puritan work ethic" in Western culture is based on four principles: (1) a person's duty is to work and to work hard; (2) success in work is evidence of personal worth; (3) the measure of success is money, property, and possessions; and (4) the way to success is by industry and thrift. As Yankelovich and Immerwahr (1984) found, the work ethic still has wide currency in contemporary America, but not all individuals in our society share these attitudes. The value attached to work and working are affected by a number of social factors.

Education, gender, and socioeconomic status have pervasive impact on work values. Educational attainment affects both intrinsic and extrinsic work values significantly, and educational selection is itself a consequence of already delineated work values. The more education, the more likely a person is to value the *intrinsic* rewards of work. Moreover, the more education, the greater the probability of *extrinsically* rewarding work. Job characteristics are also affected by higher levels of education: The more extensive the education, the more likely individuals are to enter occupations offering greater self-direction and intellectually rewarding content (Lindsay and Knox 1984). We must assume that work values are different for many of the approximately one-quarter of the high school population nationwide who do not graduate, thereby reducing their life chances greatly in terms of employment and all that it implies (Bloom 1984).

SOCIALIZATION FOR WORK

Developmental psychologists (Rice 1984) believe that socialization for work begins between the ages of 5 and 15, when a child begins to identify with a worker (usually a parent) and to acquire a concept of working and the basic habits of "industry"—organizing time, following through to a goal, and putting work ahead of play in appropriate situations. Between ages 15 and 25, most youths get experience in the world of work and identify themselves as "workers." For some, choosing a vocation or career is a decision-making process, while for others, no choice is made at all, and the youths take the first job they can get.

Appropriate parental and occupational role models often are lacking in areas in which unemployment is high and the level of available jobs and high-status, legitimate work is low. For those living in such areas, the American Dream seems unattainable through conventional, legitimate means. Many young people have difficulty finding and keeping jobs because they lack the "prework training"—the social skills of neatness, communication, hygiene, cooperation, punctuality, politeness, industriousness—that others learn in school and family settings. They see themselves as excluded from occupations or professions that might provide work satisfaction and adequate monetary rewards (Auletta 1982). They seek paid employment when they can find no other way to support themselves and tend to work episodically or seasonally when they run out of welfare, unemployment, or disability benefits or see means of getting extra money without losing those benefits. They find that one can survive with very little effort while free of the constraints of work.

The difficulties the "hardcore disadvantaged" have in making the transition from their subculture to the work culture was outlined by Gass (1970). Frustrating their efforts were such characteristics as poor motivation, underlying rebellion manifested by constant bend-ing and testing of rules, a tendency to "disappear" into illness when under stress, suspiciousness and hypersensitivity, and ambivalence about succeeding. The "hardcore disadvantaged," he observed, are not easy for employers to relate to and are prone to somatization in an attempt to solve difficult life and/or emotional problems.

THE WORKER IN A SYSTEM

Attempting to understand disability behavior requires a systems approach, an appreciation of the interrelationships of the worker's biological and psychological substrate with his or her physical and social environment. Although some workers become disabled as a result of a single event or trauma, many develop a perception of themselves as disabled long before they declare themselves as such. Some are uncertain of their capacity to cope with the physical or psychological requirements of a job even before they start working, while others, after taking a job, become convinced that it will exhaust them or harm them in some way and therefore start to observe themselves for signs of damage. Retrospective analysis would suggest that many workers are high-probability candidates for physical or psychological disability.

An insightful systems-approach study of the influence of Appalachian subcultural beliefs and expectations on disability behavior was presented by Horton (1984) and is a good illustration of the complex psychologic, biologic, and social factors interacting throughout the disability process. Work-related disability in the rural, lower-class West Virginia community she studied was not only inevitable among the males—not a question of "if" but "when"—but also inevitably accompanied increased age. All the men she interviewed (ages not provided) claimed incapacitating low back pain and had received disability compensation for an injury incurred on the job in one of the physically demanding industries—mining, lumbering, or glass manufacturing. Although their temporary disability benefits had terminated, they refused to enroll in vocational training programs, believing that a painful back was permanently and totally disabling and rendered them incapable of ever again performing any remunerative work. The entire community supported the view that such a man is neither expected nor required to work—he has been "honorably discharged" from the labor force.

There are, nonetheless, certain community criteria for the label of "deserving" disabled. A man must be "clean" (including his body, family, and house) and "nice" (be friendly and sober and attend church), must not be idle, and must obtain a medical certification of disability that validates the disabled role and qualifies him for disability compensation. Horton stressed the focal role of the man's wife in the process. She "vociferously" declares to one and all that her husband is disabled and deserving of compensation, not only for moral support but also because legitimated compensation claims are of major economic importance to family maintenance. Family stability and traditional sex-role behavior are core values in Appalachia, and a husband cannot be seen as "illegitimately" abdicating his role as breadwinner. In addition, the family needs a more reliable income than would or could be provided by a disabled husband's sporadic work at unskilled labor. The wife also handles the paperwork necessary for claims processing; the husband only signs the forms.

Other "gains" of this disability behavior are that the man's family acquires a dependable income, the community can rely on the behavior of a full-time, nondependent member, and the health care professions gain a permanent patient.

One approach, then, to the disability process is to consider the contributions of personal, work-related, and nonwork-related influences that interact while moving an individual along the health–illness continuum. The following review is necessarily brief and selective, and the reader need keep in mind that in practice or application, the three categories cannot be neatly segregated.

Personal Factors

Work as a shock
Anthropologists have used the concept of *culture shock* to describe the impact of some cultures on outsiders when first exposed to it. Some workers experience culture shock when they first start working or move to jobs for which previous school, family, or social experience have not prepared them, and thus are unable to make a normal transition into the work culture. For example, some entering regular employment for the first time cannot cope with that basic requirement that workers commit the time for which they are paid to the tasks assigned by the employer, as directed by supervisors. There are some who find it difficult to follow some of the simplest rules of work (e.g., arriving on time, leaving on time, taking breaks when scheduled and for no longer than scheduled). Some are unable to limit personal telephone calls during the working hours, or to limit absences to true emergencies. The successful transition from nonworker to worker also depends on an attitude of seriousness in producing desired outcomes for someone else and an ability to distinguish between instruction or criticism directed toward one's role performance and criticism of oneself. Some workers find instruction offensive and experience criticism as personally destructive. They cannot recognize their own errors and cannot accept supervision except in the form of praise. They feel badly treated when they are not praised frequently or when others are. Some workers who cannot adjust quit, while others stay on and struggle until some work-related event occurs that justifies their seeing themselves as disabled.

A job may be a shock in another sense to those whose individual expectations of a given career or organization, perhaps, were inaccurate; for example, regarding the value orientation or the status of the work organization, opportunities for further training and/or promotion, or continuing consumer demand for the product or service offered (Wanous 1977).

Job–personality fit

Specific job characteristics make temperamental demands of the worker, and, ideally, these demands are congruent with the personality makeup of the worker. Incongruities between personality and job demands increase the likelihood of job dissatisfaction and hence of leaving the job, by one means or another. During the entry process, a person's abilities but, less likely, his or her "needs," may have been assessed. As examples of job–personality fit, Trice and Roman (1971) cite several studies showing that individuals making the best adjustment to being a night watchman or to assembly-line work were those with low need for social interaction. They also found that high "suitability scores" between supervisors' management styles and workers' autonomy needs correlate positively with job satisfaction. Jobs requiring high levels of independent thinking and a variety of tasks and having promotions based on merit rather than seniority were more compatible with high risk-taking personalities.

Continual adaptation by a worker is necessary since both people and jobs change over time and because there is constant labor force "movement," through hirings, resignations, promotions, and firings (Wanous 1973). A match between a worker's needs and an organization's "reinforcers" results in job satisfaction and commitment, reducing voluntary turnover (Rhodes 1983).

Incompetence

Some workers lack technical or educational skills to do the job from the beginning, but are unaware of their deficiencies. Therefore, they blame the job and feel that they are being harassed by superiors and co-workers who are critical. Other workers, embodiments of the Peter Principle (Peter and Hull 1969), are promoted well beyond their competence. The consequences of job incompetence are interpersonal friction, frustrations, and disappointments that may find relief via socially sanctioned withdrawal from the job in the form of disability (Brodsky 1971b).

Burnout

Workers in the helping professions may be idealistic, committed, sensitive individuals motivated to do something good for other people and, by so doing, to find personal fulfillment. Certain of these workers describe themselves as being "burned out" when they become exasperated or disillusioned by being unable to effect change, by lack of autonomy, and by feeling stymied by the "system" (Farber 1983). Their goals may have been unrealistic or they may have romanticized or glorified their jobs, but the common denominator is that they lose their motivation and come to feel alienated. Burnout can be "instant" if one's expectations were grossly inflated and the work environment immediately stressful. More commonly, the process is insidious, and one "burns out" after repeated disappointments. Disability, then, may become a way out of a vicious cycle. Such reactions are seen not uncommonly in police and correctional officers, teachers, social workers, and others in "buffer" occupations (Brodsky 1977a).

Mental disorders
Some workers have overt psychiatric conditions, such as psychoses and addictions, that reduce their cognitive capacities or flexibility, affective stability, and control of their behavior, but who nonetheless work regularly in supportive environments if their conditions are controlled with medication. Substance abusers, those dependent on drugs or alcohol, find their jobs confusing or demanding when they are under the influence of such substances, and often are irritable and/or bored when they cannot use drugs and alcohol on the job.

Personality predisposition
Other workers, while not seeming to manifest overt psychiatric illness, are vulnerable when predispositions to such illness interact with aggravating experiences in the work environment. Chambers (1963) noted the presence of obsessive–compulsive traits in a larger number of his compensation cases, while Weighill (1983) found that persons with histrionic traits were overrepresented among individuals with *compensation neurosis*. Brodsky (1983) noted the presence of premorbid health preoccupation among his group of allergic and toxic patients. Enelow (1968) referred to "sociopaths," who used occupational injuries as a means to a guaranteed income and added that malingerers are found in this group. Ruesch (1948) recognized the contribution of an "infantile" personality to somatization.

Several investigators (Enelow 1968; Ford 1977–78; Fann and Sussex 1976; Henderson 1974; Nemiah 1963; Safilios-Rothschild 1970) have observed the presence of dependency conflicts in a group of "pseudo self-sufficient" and somewhat "rigid," responsible males, who characteristically went to work early to support their families of origin and worked industriously and faithfully for many years until some relatively minor work-related incident occurred in middle age and was seized upon as a socially acceptable excuse for "enforced" dependency on health care providers and spouses. Florence (1984) refers to this *inadequacy syndrome* in the context of chronic pain patients, and Ford (1977–78), terming this psychodynamic constellation the *Humpty–Dumpty syndrome*, also discussed the contributing role of underlying hostility and depression. Fann and Sussex (1976) recognized the effects of the aging process, in that some middle-aged males find physical aging hard to ignore and that their chosen life styles are apparently irreversible. Diminishing rewards from work (e.g., perhaps because a promotion puts him in a position of responsibility he cannot meet or exposes him to subordinates' anger and dependency or because a long-sought promotion is no longer within reach) may add further stress that contributes to finding emotional gain in the disabled role.

Age

Older workers in general are less likely to return to work following an occupational injury or illness (Root 1981), particularly if they are unskilled or semiskilled manual laborers in physically demanding jobs (Safilios-Rothschild 1970). Not only do social expectations about aging affect the perceived capacities and self-perceptions of older workers (Butler 1975), but an employer's personnel practices, seniority systems, and rate of technological change also may prevent older persons from returning to work even if they desire to do so. Occupational exemptions through disability, then, may seem the only feasible alternative, especially for an older, unskilled, physically impaired worker with limited opportunities (Brodsky, 1971a).

In reviewing the effects of age on occupational injuries, Root (1981) found that although the rate of injury decreases with age, the consequences of injury, specifically the rate of fatalities, the severity of injuries, and the rate of permanent disabilities, are highest among older workers. Powell (1973) observed that one explanation for the negative association between age and accidents is that older workers who are less physically capable of meeting job demands leave physically demanding and hazardous jobs.

Risk behavior

Certain jobs are widely understood to be physically risky, such as coal mining, law enforcement, structural iron work, and the chemical industry; while others (e.g., farming, school teaching, or working in a convenience store or gas station) may be less obviously so. If a worker takes a job he knows is dangerous, there must be some other aspects that compensate for the risk, whether higher wages, more fringe benefits, more convenient work hours, or enhanced occupational prestige (Vicusi 1983). Often, workers begin jobs without complete information regarding inherent risks or regarding the implications of the risk for their personal welfare. Some workers are unwilling to take a minor risk while others seem to take almost any risk.

At some point in certain workers, there appears to be a change in either their perception of the risk or their willingness to accept the consequences, which may be occasioned by personal injury, by a "near miss," or perhaps by nonwork events, such as becoming a parent or inheriting wealth. Willingness to take risks in general diminishes as people grow older. Not only, for example, are older workers less willing to sustain physical injuries and more likely to remove themselves from unsafe jobs (Powell 1973), but also, as Humple and Lyons (1983) note, older managers are more hesitant to make decisions that entail "economic risks." Individuals at or near the bottom of the occupational hierarchy have both more physically hazardous jobs (Graebner 1984; Robinson 1984) and fewer options in changing occupations (Nelkin and Brown 1984a, 1984b) and may subconsciously opt to "injury out" rather than to admit they are afraid of being hurt or are fatigued by continual concern about health risks.

Work–nonwork conflicts
Some workers who have not solved conflicts between the requirements of their jobs and their commitments to child care, personal education, or to other preferred careers such as acting or athletics come to feel harassed when they are forced to make a choice. Some welcome the conflict resolution provided by a minor physical or psychological work-related event and remain disabled long after they are declared healed.

Adaptation to change
Some workers cannot accept and/or adapt to change in the work place. They become upset when their desks or sections are moved or they resent new supervisors and resist any change in work assignments. They behave in a passive-aggressive manner or otherwise sabotage operations when policy changes are imposed on the work organization. They resent new types of workers (e.g., women or men in positions formerly held by the other sex). They find intolerable the work patterns of younger workers, their dress, their talk, and any differences in their work ethic.

Work-Related Factors

The following elements are seen frequently in cases of work-incurred injury or illness where the disability reaction seems excessive and prolonged (Brodsky 1977b).

The physical environment
  • Low pay
  • Boring, repetitive work with regular pressure to produce more physically
  • Work that is heavy and requires great physical strength and stamina in order to maintain the required level of production
  • Dangerous work
  • An uncomfortable or unhealthy physical environment: too hot, too cold, drafty, or without ventilation. Some workers cannot tolerate windowless offices while others believe air conditioning lowers the quality of the air. Some persons are concerned

about environments that are known to have chemical fumes, dusts, or tobacco smoke or grow anxious if they detect unfamiliar odors that suggest noxious substances are present. Workers are aware that noise can be harmful, and become concerned that it will affect them adversely.

The work organization
- Perceived inequity of pay and/or promotion
- Authoritarian supervisory style
- Poor communication between workers and management
- Lack of autonomy
- Salary or promotion dictated by favoritism or nepotism
- Management that permits or encourages sexual or social discrimination or harassment
- Practical joking and horseplay
- Frequent changes in organizational structure and chain of command
- Where the function of the organization is to serve as a social "buffer" between society and its unwanted (e.g., mental hospitals, prisons, and other organizations that serve difficult clients, in which workers feel unsupported by the public or by their own administrators) (Brodsky 1977b; Porter and Steers 1973; Yelin et al. 1980)

Nonwork Factors

Family relationships
There is both positive and negative "spillover" between family and work environments (Crouter 1984). Home situations can distract workers and make them hazards to others' safety or can otherwise predispose them to become disabled and remain in that state. To varying degrees, parents of a newborn child may feel the need to be with the child during its earliest, most needful time. Similarly, having a chronically ill family member who needs care may produce a role conflict that predisposes a worker to injury and then to prolongation of disability.

Workers with delinquent children or unfaithful spouses are apt to feel either that they are not being supported by their families and, therefore, resent work, or that they should spend more time at home in order to maintain better control. Workers whose spouses have retired because of mandatory retirement or because of disability seem inclined to consider retirement themselves. Sometimes the most convenient avenue to that retirement is Workers' Compensation disability (Brodsky 1971a).

Disability resulting from illness or injury exerts a significant effect upon the "well" members of a family, by producing a disequilibrium in customary role behavior, dominance patterns, affective communication, sexual activity, maintenance of discipline, home routines, and self-esteem. Following reorganization after a member of the family becomes disabled, a family may function as well or better than before the crisis or, in the process of reorganization, family roles and structures may change substantially. The dynamics of the new family equilibrium may affect and be affected by the outcome of the worker's disability, in that there may be gains to the spouse and other family members by encouraging the worker's dependency and ensuring continuation of the compensation benefits (Rickarby 1979). In some instances, the uninjured spouse may become the manager or spokesperson for the compensation claim. The uninjured spouse may find paid employment, if not already employed, or change from part-time to full-time employment. Child care or supervision may fall to the disabled spouse, thus providing a meaningful economic and familial role. Some disabled persons pursue activities such as selling cosmetics or cleaning products or making objects for sale. Frequently they do not consider these activities to be "paid work," even though they earn money from them.

The Disability System

Economic influences
Financial awards are contingent on documented residual disability. Economists who study Workers' Compensation programs have found that a 10 percent increase in benefits paid out produces a 14 percent increase in costs to the system (Price 1979). They explain that the difference is the result of the increased economic incentives to become and remain "disabled." It seems unlikely that in the microscopic world of the individual, a small increase in benefits is a conscious factor in becoming or remaining disabled. Nevertheless, these statistics show that differences in benefits do play a role in and become part of the system that affects the tendency to move into or stay in a disabled status. As more and more people label themselves "disabled," claims and awards under disability programs increase (Sunshine 1981). The meaning of the amount of disability payments changes as individuals evolve in the course of their own disability.
Based on cases I have reviewed, I would conclude that:

- At the time they become disabled, many injured workers are unaware of the benefits available to them. Some do not know that they are entitled to treatment and monetary payments. On the other hand, in certain occupations such as law enforcement (Vulcano et al. 1981) and air traffic control (Alexander 1980) the various effects of "job stress" and the range of compensation benefits are well known.

- The amount of the benefit payments becomes a consideration after workers rearrange their lives and can assess the meaning of the new financial situation, which they learn has actualities and potentialities. The actualities consist of their Workers' Compensation temporary disability benefits, private disability policies that they had purchased, and short-term and long-term disability benefits from employer-provided insurance supplementing Workers' Compensation benefits. Frequently, people who are buying homes or automobiles will include in their monthly payments a sum that purchases insurance that will make those payments in the event of death or disability. Generally, these disability payments are tax-free.

- The potentialities include Social Security benefits (SSDI, Medicare, and SSI) received when there is a permanent loss of earning capabilities, rehabilitation benefits, and possible gains from third-party law suits against the manufacturer of products or others who are not co-workers who contributed to the cause of the injury. If patients can obtain Workers' Compensation payments along with Social Security disability, then their income can be higher than the after-tax income would have been had they continued to work.

- As the economic actualities and potentialities change and crystalize at points in the evolution of the disability process, and as these are balanced against the benefits associated with returning to work, it seems reasonable to believe that the differences between the two must be considered among the factors determining the outcome of the disability.

Structural barriers
Several additional factors (Brodsky 1977a) evolving from the structure of the Workers' Compensation process may act and interact to perpetuate disability behavior, including the response of the work place and the health care system to the worker's initial report of injury or illness, and the worker's subsequent interaction with the employer, the insurance company, and other health care providers. Reactions implying that the worker's credibility is being questioned may well result in accentuation and perpetuation of the disability in order to "prove" his or her claims. Bureaucratic errors or omissions, whether in filing necessary paperwork, issuing compensation checks, or not returning phone calls, infuriate an injured worker. In addition, the actions of medical personnel, whether through comments such as, "You're lucky to be alive" or by performing invasive procedures, may reinforce a subjective conviction of an inability to work and result in the entrenchment of symptoms and self-image as disabled and unrehabilitable.

Companies may terminate the employment of an impaired worker because of concerns about possible reinjury or the worker's potential inability to perform satisfactorily. Thus, the individual released to return to work with no restriction may have no job to which to return. When claims are disputed, the compensation process is prolonged, often for several years, which may leave individuals in "limbo." They can neither return to work nor relinquish the symptoms of prolonged disability without jeopardizing the claim. Litigation itself fixes their symptoms and disability, and an adversarial relationship between employer and employee lowers the probability of a quick return to work.

Dansak (1973) has introduced the concept of "tertiary gains" of illness (i.e., the gain from a patient's illness to someone other than the patient), and Bokan et al. (1981) have pointed out how health care providers may obtain tertiary gain from patients' symptoms and disability, therefore unconsciously tending to prolong them.

Claimants may perceive themselves as hopelessly caught up in a large complex system that does not really care about them, and this breeds anger and resentments as well as a determination to fight for their "rights." In Ellard's (1970) view, they do not seek to be healed, but to be "justified."

Disability subculture
The disabled frequently develop subcultures of their own, both for social support and for exchange of information regarding the intricacies of the Workers' Compensation and Social Security systems. Conflicts about returning to work may be engendered or heightened when disabled workers find acceptance among groups of other disabled persons and when that group provides them with a sense of closeness, identity, and warmth that was not present in the work place or in the home. These subcultures value the disabled, see them as deprived and possibly downtrodden by society, and serve as a place to share information about resources for improving their conditions.

CONCLUSIONS
Futile are attempts to find a single or simple factor that explains why some workers become and remain disabled while others, seemingly suffering no lesser injury, either do not enter into a disability status or role or recover much earlier if they do become disabled. Just as an increase of 10 percent in benefits increases the disability payments by 14 percent, and therefore might be considered one of the elements, so must other facets of a subject's existence (both related and unrelated to the work place) be studied in order for us to gauge their weight. Although it is highly probable that as one factor is piled upon another, the greater weight will increase the probability of disability, nevertheless, this compounding, in itself, does not predict disability. In addition to the total weight, we must study the special configuration and interaction of the various elements as well as their duration

or period of incubation. Each disabled worker has a unique personal disability system, and we must understand that unique system before we can design more effective programs for prevention, treatment, rehabilitation, or retirement.

REFERENCES

Alexander RJ: "Burning out" verus "punching out." J Human Stress 37-41, 1980

Auletta K: The Underclass. New York, Random House, 1982

Beals RKL: Compensation and recovery from injury. Western J Med 140:233-237, 1984

Behan RC, Hirschfeld AH: The accident process, II: Toward more rational treatment of industrial injuries. JAMA 186:300-306, 1963

Behan RC, Hirschfeld AH: Disability without disease or accident. Arch Environ Health 12:655-659, 1966

Block AR, Boyer SL: The spouse's adjustment to chronic pain: cognitive and emotional factors. Social Sci Med 19:1313-1317, 1982

Bloom M: Configurations of Human Behavior. Life Span Development in Social Environments. New York, Macmillan, 1984

Bokan JA, Ries RK, Katon WJ: Tertiary gain and chronic pain. Pain 10:331-335, 1981

Boskoff A: Social failure in modern society: a reformulation and a tentative theoretical framework. Sociological Inquiry 52:89-105, 1982

Brill NA: The hard core. Psychiatr J Univ Ottawa 9:1-7, 1984

Brodsky CM: Compensation illness as a retirement channel. J Am Geriatr Soc 19:51-60, 1971a

Brodsky CM: Social psychiatric consequences of job incompetence. Compr Psychiatry 12:526-536, 1971b

Brodsky CM: The Harassed Worker. Lexington MA, Lexington Books, 1976

Brodsky CM: Genesis of a problem population, in Communication and Social Interaction. Edited by Ostwald PF. New York, Grune and Stratton, 1977a

Brodsky CM: Long-term work stress in teachers and prison guards. J Occup Med 19:133-138, 1977b

Brodsky CM: Psychological factors contributing to somatoform diseases attributed to the workplace. J Occup Med 25:459-464, 1983

Buchholz RA: An empirical study of contemporary beliefs about work in American society. J Appl Psychol 63:219-227, 1978

Butler RJ: Wage and injury rate response to shifting levels of workers' compensation, in Society and the Work Force: Incentives and Disincentives in Workers' Compensation. Edited by Worrall JD. Ithaca, NY, ILR Press, 1983

Butler RN: Why Survive? Being Old in America. New York, Harper and Row, 1975

Chambers WN: Emotional factors complicating industrial injuries. J Occup Med 5:568-574, 1963

Crouter AC: Spillover from family to work: the neglected side of the work-family interface. Human Relations 37:425-442, 1984

Dansak D: On the tertiary gain of illness. Compr Psychiatry 14:523-528, 1973

Dunnette MD, Arvey RD, Manas PA: Why do they leave? Personnel 50: 25-39, 1973

Eaton MW: Obstacles to the vocational rehabilitation of individuals receiving workers' compensation. Journal of Rehabilitation 45:59-63, 1979

Ellard J: Psychological reactions to compensable injury. Med J Aust 2:349-355, 1970

Enelow AJ: Industrial injuries: prediction and prevention of psychological complications. J Occup Med 10:683-687, 1968

Engel GL: The clinical application of the biopsychosocial model. Am J Psychiatry 137:535-544, 1980

Fann WE, Sussex JN: Late effects of early dependency need deprivation: the meal ticket syndrome. Br J Psychiatry 128:262-268, 1976

Farber BA (Ed): Stress and Burnout in the Human Service Professions. New York, Pergamon Press, 1983

Fielding JE: Corporate Health Management. Reading, MA, Addison-Wesley, 1984

Florence DW: Chronic pain in the medicolegal aspects of workers' compensation cases, in Disability. Edited by Carmi A, Chigier E, Schneider S. New York, Springer-Verlag, 1984

Ford CV: A type of disability neurosis: the Humpty Dumpty syndrome. Int J Psychiatry Med 8:285-294, 1977-1978

Ford CV: The Somatizing Disorders: Illness as a Way of Life. New York, Elsevier Science, 1983

Franklin PA: Impact of disability on the family structure. Soc Secur Bull 40:3-18, 1977

Gardell B: Psychological and social problems of industrial work in affluent societies. International Journal of Psychology 12:125-134, 1977

Gass GZ: Hardcore personality and industrial illnesses and accidents. Industrial Medicine and Surgery 39:33-37, 1970

Goode WJ: The projection of the inept American Sociology Review 32:5-19, 1957

Graebner W: Doing the world's unhealthy work: the fiction of free choice. Hastings Cent Rep 15:28-37, 1984

Henderson S: Care-eliciting behavior in man. J Nerv Ment Dis 159:172-181, 1974

Hirschfeld AH, Behan RD: The accident process, I: etiological consideration of industrial injuries. JAMA 186:193-199, 1963

Hirschfeld AH, Behan RD: The accident process, III: disability: acceptable and unacceptable. JAMA 197:85-89, 1966

Horton CF: Women have headaches, men have backaches: patterns of illness in an Appalachian community. Social Sci Med 19:647-654, 1984

Howards I, Brahm H, Nagi S: Disability: From Social Problem to Federal Program. New York, Praeger, 1980

Humple C, Lyons M: Management and the Older Workforce. Policies and Programs. New York, American Management Association, 1983

Lando ME, Coate MB, Kraus R: Disability benefit applications and the economy. Soc Secur Bull 42:3-10, 1979

Larson DL, Spreitzer EA: The disabled role, affluence, and the meaning of work. Journal of Rehabilitation 36:29-32, 1970

Leggo C: Resentment—an obstacle to recovery. Industrial Medicine and Surgery 22:241-245, 1953

Lindsay P, Knox WE: Continuity and change in work values among young adults: a longitudinal study. American Journal of Sociology 89:918-931, 1984

Miller H: Accident neurosis. Br Med J 1:919-925, 1961

Miller MF, Watkins C, Davis CL: Some attitudes commonly found in patients injured on the job. Industrial Medicine and Surgery 30 135-137, 1961

Mortimer JT, Lorence J: Work experience and occupational value socialization. American Journal of Sociology 84:1361-1385, 1979

Neff WS: Work and Human Behavior. Chicago, Aldine, 1977

Nelkin D, Brown MS: Observations on workers' perception of risk in the dangerous trades. Science, Technology and Human Values 9:3-10, 1984a

Nelkin D, Brown MS: Workers at Risk: Voices from the Workplace. Chicago, University of Chicago Press, 1984b

Nelson H, Fiedler FP: Welfare for the unemployed: the rise and fall of a social experiment. Human Organization 43:168-177, 1984

Nemiah JC: Psychological complications in industrial injuries. Arch Environ Health 1:481-486, 1963

Parker N: Accident Neurosis, in Modern Perspectives in the Psychiatric Aspects of Surgery. Edited by Howells JG. New York, Brunner/Mazel, 1976

Peck RF: Distinctive national patterns of career motivation. International Journal of Psychology 10:125-134, 1975

Peter LH, Hull R: The Peter Principle. New York, Random House, 1969

Porter LW, Steers RM: Organizational, work and personal factors in employee turnover and absenteeism. Psychol Bull 80:151-176, 1973

Powell P: Age and occupational change among coal miners. Occupational Psychology 47:37-49, 1973

Price DN: Workers' compensation program in the 1970's. Soc Secur Bull 42:3-24, 1979

Rhodes SR: Age-related differences in work attitudes and behavior: a review and conceptual analysis. Psychol Bull 93:328-367, 1983

Rice FP: The Adolescent: Development, Relationships and Culture, 4th edition. Boston, Allyn and Bacon, 1984

Rickarby GA: Compensation-neurosis and the psycho-social requirements of the family. Br J Med Psychol 52:333-338, 1979

Riordan T: Adding insult to injury. The Washington Monthly 13-22, March 1984

Robinson JC: Racial inequality and the probability of occupation-related injury or illness. Milbank Memorial Fund Quarterly 62:567-590, 1984

Root N: Injuries at work are fewer among older employees. Monthly Labor Review 104:3-34, 1981

Ruesch J: The infantile personality: the core problem of psychosomatic medicine. J Nerv Ment Dis 10:134-144, 1948

Ruesch J, Brodsky CM: The concept of social disability. Arch Gen Psychiatry 19:394-403, 1968

Safilios-Rothschild C: The Sociology and Social Psychology of Disability and Rehabilitation. New York, Random House, 1970

Schechter ES: Commitment to work and the self-perception of disability. Social Security Bulletin 44:22-37, 1981

Seres JL, Newman RI: Negative influences of the disability compensation system: perspectives for the clinician. Seminars in Neurology 3:360-369, 1983

Shands HC: Disability, psychosomatic disease, and psychoneurosis: the problem of differential disability. Psychother Psychosom 27:170-184, 1976-1977

Shanfield SB, Heiman EM, Cope DN, et al: Pain and the marital relationship: psychiatric distress. Pain 7:343-351, 1979

Shiekh K, Mattingly S: Employment rehabilitation: outcome and prediction. Am J Ind Med 5:383-393, 1984

Simons J, Slaiken KA: Crisis intervention on the job/in the office, in Crisis Intervention. A Handbook for Practice and Research. Boston, Allyn and Bacon, 1984

Stone DA: Diagnosis and the dole: the function of illness in American distributive politics. Journal of Health Politics, Policy, and Law 4:507-521, 1979

Strang JP: The chronic disability syndrome, in Evaluation and Treatment of Chronic Pain. Edited by Aronoff GM. Baltimore-Munich, Urban and Schwarzenberg, 1985

Strasser AL: Disability system needs definition. Occupational Health and Safety 52:57-58, 1983

Sunshine J: Disability payments stabilizing after era of accelerating growth. Monthly Labor Review 104:17-22, 1981

Terkel S: Working. New York, Random House, 1974

Trice HM, Roman PM: Occupational risk factors in mental health and the impact of role change experience, in Compensation in Psychiatric Disability and Rehabilitation. Edited by Leedy JL. Springfield IL, Charles C Thomas, 1971

Vicusi WK: Risk by Choice: Regulating Health and Safety in the Workplace. Cambridge, MA, Harvard University Press, 1983

Vulcano BA, Barnes GE, Breen LJ: The prevalence and predictors of psychosomatic symptoms and conditions among police officers, in Psychosomatic Medicine: Theoretical, Clinical and Transcultural Aspects. Edited by Krakowski AJ, Kimball CP. New York, Plenum Press, 1981

Wanous JP: Effects of a realistic job preview on job acceptance, job attitudes, and job survival. J Appl Psychol 58:327-332, 1973

Wanous JP: Organizational entry: newcomers moving from outside to inside. Psychol Bull 84:601-618, 1977

Warr P: Psychological effects of employment and unemployment. Psychol Medicine 12:7-11, 1982

Weighill VE: Compensation neurosis: a review of the literature. J Psychosom Res 27:97-104, 1983

Weijel JA: The influence of social security in an affluent society on illness behavior. Psychother Psychosom 23:272-282, 1974

Weinstein MR: The disability process: contributions of service agencies to client disability. Compr Psychiatry 10:398-405, 1969

Wiseman M: Workfare. Calif Journal 16:289-292, 1985

Worrall JD: Compensation costs, injury rates, and the labor market, in Safety and the Work Force: Incentives and Disincentives in Workers' Compensation. Edited by Worrall JD. Ithaca, NY, ILR Press, 1983

Yankelovich D, Immerwahr J: Putting the work ethic to work. Society 21:58-76, 1984

Yelin E, Nevitt M, Epstein W: Toward an epidemiology of work disability. Milbank Memorial Fund Quarterly 58:386-415, 1980

Section II

EPIDEMIOLOGY AND CLINICAL PATHOLOGY: CLINICAL ISSUES

5

Schizophrenia and Disability

Richard C. Mohs, Ph.D.
Juliet C. Lesser, Ph.D.

I t is generally recognized that certain forms of schizophrenia are associated with very high levels of disability. Emil Kraepelin, among others, emphasized particularly the deterioration of social, occupational, and mental functioning in patients with the disease he referred to as dementia praecox (Kraepelin 1971). The notion that schizophrenia is a disease leading to chronic disability is accepted widely enough so that the poor long-term outcome is often used as a criterion for validating diagnostic systems designed to distinguish schizophrenia from other psychiatric disorders (Brockington et al. 1978). In fact, some diagnostic systems, such as in the *Diagnostic and Statistical Manual of Mental Disorders, Third Edition, Revised (DSM-III-R)* (American Psychiatric Association 1987) and the one proposed by Feighner et al. (1972), require that a patient have a period of disability covering several months before the diagnosis of schizophrenia is made. Comparison of the Feighner system and *DSM-III-R* with other diagnostic systems indicates, however, that the chronicity requirement excludes many patients who would be diagnosed as schizophrenic by other widely used criteria and by most experienced psychiatrists (Overall and Hollister 1979). Furthermore, genetic studies indicate that a variety of conditions other than classical schizophrenia, including schizotypal personality disorder, some paranoid states, and some types of schizoaffective disorder, all tend to aggregate in biologically related individuals and thus share some genetic etiology (Kendler and Gruenberg 1984). This clustering of genetically related conditions, some of which are not always associated with very poor outcome, has given rise to the notion of the schizophrenia spectrum disorders (Kendler et al. 1984).

Clearly, any conclusions drawn about the disability associated with schizophrenia will depend on how the diagnosis of schizophrenia is made. At present, there are no biologic, etiologic, or other markers that can be used to validate the diagnosis of schizophrenia on a case-by-case basis. Rather, the diagnosis is based primarily on the appearance of characteristic signs and symptoms. The signs and symptoms required vary somewhat from one system to another. In addition, systems vary in the types of criteria used to exclude other psychiatric conditions, such as affective disorders, and in the extent to which patients must satisfy certain demographic criteria, such as age of onset. Comparative studies (Brockington et al. 1978) demonstrate that systems with broad inclusion and few exclusion criteria such as the New Haven Schizophrenia Index (Astrachan et al. 1972) may diagnose schizophrenia in five times as many patients as a system such as that of Feighner et al. (1972), which has very strict inclusion and exclusion criteria. Agreement between pairs of different diagnostic criteria varied from a low of 32 percent to a high of 83 percent in one comparative study of 10 diagnostic systems (Overall and Hollister 1979). Choice of any particular diagnostic system affects both the number and the type of patients who receive the diagnosis of schizophrenia.

The purpose of the present paper is not to argue for the validity of any one diagnostic system over others, but rather to review findings on the lifetime disability associated with the broad range of conditions that fall within the schizophrenia spectrum. There are at least three reasons for including a broad range of conditions in this review. As described below, most of the long-term follow-up studies examining aspects of disability in schizophrenics have used a rather broad definition of schizophrenia similar to the ones employed by Bleuler (1974) or in *DSM-II* (American Psychiatric Association 1968). Second, most diagnostic systems that define schizophrenia very narrowly require a specified period of disability before the diagnosis is made. To examine disability in patients already selected for their disability would not be particularly informative. Finally, as mentioned above, there is evidence from family and adoption studies that a variety of conditions in addition to narrowly defined schizophrenia share a common genetic load as to a predisposing factor. Unless specifically noted to the contrary then, all of the studies reviewed below include patients falling within a fairly broad definition of schizophrenia. In interpreting these studies, it should be kept in mind that many of the patients with little evidence of long-term disability would undoubtedly not be diagnosed as schizophrenic by some of the more restrictive diagnostic systems.

The disability associated with schizophrenia can be measured in a variety of different ways and no single best way has been agreed upon by most investigators. In fact, studies employing multiple measures of disability have generally found rather low correlations among those measures (Strauss and Carpenter 1977; Moller et al. 1982), suggesting that they are independently determined. This review concentrates on three primary measures of disability: persistent clinical symptoms, use of hospital and other treatment facilities, and occupational status. These three were selected because of their face validity and also because they are the most common measures used in long-term, follow-up studies. The last section of this paper reviews studies that have investigated clinical, biologic, and treatment factors that may predict long-term disability.

MEASURES OF DISABILITY

Clinical Condition

Long-term follow-up studies of schizophrenic patients are very difficult to complete, particularly in countries such as the United States which has a highly mobile population and no centralized system of health care. In some European countries, long-term follow-up studies are made more practical and, as a result, many of the most informative studies have been performed there. Table 1 presents a summary of the follow-up data on clinical conditions for five such studies. This table is not meant to be exhaustive, but does include enough of the large, well-documented follow-up studies so that general conclusions about the long-term outcome of schizophrenia can be drawn. Since there is no generally accepted system for categorizing clinical states longitudinally, the table presents results in terms of outcome categories used by the different investigators.

The first two studies, conducted in Switzerland, involved large numbers of patients diagnosed as schizophrenic by the rather broad Bleulerian criteria and followed patients for very long periods of time, with few dropouts. The study reported by Ciompi (1980a, 1980b) is essentially a study of old schizophrenics, since the outcome data represent only the 289 patients who survived for 37 years of follow-up. The original sample included 1,642 patients and the average age at follow-up for the surviving 289 was approximately 75.5 years. Bleuler's (1974) report includes all of the schizophrenics he treated for at least 20 years or until their deaths. Both studies found a wide range of outcomes. Between 22 to 27 percent of patients recovered completely; between 10 and 20 percent were chronically psychotic and severely ill; the remaining patients were less severely ill but never totally recovered. Similar findings emerged from the long-term follow-up study of schizophrenics conducted in Bonn, Germany, although the outcome categories used were different (Huber et al. 1980). Again, approximately 22 percent of patients recovered totally; of the remaining patients, 34.7 percent remained actively psychotic after 22 years, while 43.2 percent had primarily negative symptoms.

Two more recent studies listed in the table had shorter follow-up periods and generally tended to find fewer patients with total recovery. The study by Moller et al. (1982) was a follow-up of patients

Table 1.

Outcome Studies of Schizophrenia: Clinical Condition

Study	N	Sex	Follow-up Period	Clinical Outcome Categories	Percentage
Ciompi (1980a, b)	289	197M 92F	Mean = 37 yrs.	Recovery	26.6
				Mild end state	22.1
				Moderately severe end state	23.9
				Most severe end state	18.0
				Uncertain/not stabilized	9.4
Bleuler (1974)	208	?	20 yrs.	Recovered	22.2
				Stable, not recovered	33.3
				Episodic psychoses, not recovered	33.3
				Chronically, severely ill	10.8
Huber et. al. (1980)	502	209M 293F	Mean = 22.4 yrs.	Complete remission	22.1
				Noncharacteristic residual syndromes	43.2
				Characteristic residual syndromes	34.7
Moller et. al. (1982)	81	40M 51F	5–6 yrs.	No symptoms	10
				Mild symptoms	33
				Moderate symptoms	10
				Serious symptoms	13
				Major impairment	31
Kolakowska et al. (1985)	77	49M 28F	2–20 yrs.	Good, including some total remissions	32.5
				Intermediate, with residual symptoms	46.5
				Poor, some with continuous hospitalization	30

included in the International Pilot Study of Schizophrenia (World Health Organization 1973). After five to six years, only 10 percent of those patients were symptom-free, and 44 percent had either serious or major impairment. The study by Kolakowska et al. (1985) was a follow-up of patients who had participated in a clinical drug trial. Very few of these patients were in total remission 2 to 20 years after their initial episodes, and 30 percent had a poor clinical outcome. It is unlikely that the poorer outcomes found in these recent studies are due to their relatively short follow-up periods; most investigators (Bleuler 1974; Strauss and Carpenter 1977) agree that outcome over a 2–5-year period is highly predictive of outcome over longer periods of time. A more likely possibility is that the recent studies used more restrictive criteria for the diagnosis of schizophrenia. Thus, patients with better prognosis conditions, such as schizophreniform psychosis or schizoaffective disorder, were excluded more frequently. In any event, these studies all indicate that the great majority of schizo-phrenic patients have some lifelong disability and that there is a substantial core group of schizophrenics who remain psychotic and severely disabled throughout their lives.

Hospitalization and Treatment

Admission to hospital and use of other treatment facilities undoubt-edly is determined at least in part by factors other than a patient's clinical state. Availability of treatment facilities, a patient's financial situation, availability of other caregivers, and the nature of the pa-tient's disability will all affect the rate at which a patient utilizes medical services. Comparison of time spent in hospital with other measures of social and occupational disability in one study (Strauss and Carpenter 1977) indicated only very modest correlation among the various measures; in fact, time in hospital had a lower correlation with the other measures than did the social and occupational meas-ures with each other. Nevertheless, use of treatment facilities is at least a rough index of disability and is certainly some measure of the cost that schizophrenia places on the rest of society.

Table 2 presents long-term hospitalization data from three fol-low-up studies of schizophrenics. The first two are the same Swiss long-term studies described above. As might be expected from the wide variety of clinical outcomes described, these studies both found that patients varied substantially in their total duration of hospi-talization. Nearly half of the patients followed by Ciompi spent less than 1 year in the hospital, but 23 percent were hospitalized for over 20 years. Bleuler found that 10 percent of his schizophrenics were essentially permanent hospital residents, 25 percent were usually hospitalized at any one time, and over the entire follow-up period,

Table 2.

Outcome Studies of Schizophrenia: Hospitalization and Treatment

Study	N	Follow-up Period	Treatment Outcome Categories	Percentage
Ciompi (1980a, b)	289	Mean = 37 yrs.	1 yr. in hospital	47
			1–20 yrs. in hospital	30
			20 yrs. in hospital	23
Bleuler (1980)	208	20 yrs.	Averaged ⅓ of time, since diagnosis, in hospital	n.a.
Curson et al.	64	7 yrs.	No admissions to hospital, outpatient, or no treatment	37.5
			1–7 admissions	50
			8+ admissions	12.5

patients spent an average of one-third of their lives in the hospital. Clearly, the treatment cost and the loss of productive years were both very high for these two groups, containing a broad range of good- and poor-prognosis patients. The last study listed in Table 2 is a more recent study conducted in Great Britain at a time when frequent short hospitalizations and outpatient treatment were favored over long-term hospitalization (Curson et al. 1985). This change in treatment emphasis may have reduced the total time spent in hospital but, still, the intensity of treatment required by these patients was quite high. Nearly all required some treatment, over 60 percent were hospitalized at least once in 7 years, and 12.5 percent were hospitalized eight times or more.

Social and Occupational Status

That schizophrenia leads to a dramatic loss in the ability to work, to earn a living, and to be a productive member of society is indisputable, although the extent of this loss is difficult to measure precisely. It is well established that schizophrenia is associated with downward drift in both social and economic status. Children who are schizophrenic have lower social and economic status as adults than did their parents who were not schizophrenic (Huber et al. 1980).

Table 3 presents the long-term occupation status of schizophrenics as determined in two studies. The figure reported by Ciompi (1980a, 1980b) must be interpreted in light of the fact that these patients were quite old at follow-up (mean age = 75 years) and that these were only the survivors of a much larger cohort. As can be seen, 17 percent of these people were employed full time. This is less than would be expected for others of similar age (Ciompi 1980a). Furthermore, it is reported that 72 percent of this sample were definitely poor or dependent in their social relationships. The data presented by Huber et al. (1980) are more representative of the broad range of schizophrenics observed during their usual productive years. Al-

Table 3.

Outcome Studies of Schizophrenia: Occupational Status

Study	N	Follow-up Period	Treatment Outcome Categories	Percentage
Ciompi (1980a, b)	289	Mean = 37 yrs.	Employed full time	17
			Employed part time	34
			Unemployed	49
Huber et al. (1980)	502	Mean = 22.4 yrs.	Fully employed at premorbid level	38.6
			Limited ability to work	19.4
			Incapable of earning a living	16.5
			Incapable of any work	7.8

though nearly 40 percent of these patients were employed at their premorbid level, the premorbid adjustment, and hence occupational status of schizophrenics, is often poorer than nonschizophrenics (Gittelman-Klein and Klein 1969). Nearly 30 percent of the patients were capable of little or no work, while the remaining 17.6 percent were employed below their premorbid level. In summary, these results indicate that, although most schizophrenics are capable of some productive work and a sizable minority can work at their premobid level, on average, schizophrenics have a dramatically reduced capacity for productive work.

Mortality
In addition to its profound effects on the lives of its victims, schizophrenia is also associated with significant increases in mortality from some causes. Suicide, in particular, is much more likely in schizophrenics than in normals or in most other psychiatric groups. It has been estimated that as many as 10 percent of all schizophrenics may die due to suicide (Drake et al. 1985); young schizophrenics are particularly likely to die in this way. The rate of death due to all unnatural causes is increased in schizophrenics (Martin et al. 1985), as is the rate of death due to natural causes (Martin et al. 1985). Total mortality for schizophrenics in one study was over three times that expected based on population data (Martin et al. 1985). In addition to suicide, schizophrenics have higher than normal rates of death due to infectious disease, particularly tuberculosis, and illness due to respiratory disease (Ciompi 1980a). On average, then, schizophrenics have shorter, more violent, and certainly less productive lives than normal people.

PREDICTORS OF DISABILITY

Diagnostic and Symptomatic Factors
Apart from its characteristic age of onset (Huber et al. 1980) and its tendency to aggregate in biologically related individuals (Kety et al. 1975), there are no well-established predictors or risk factors for schizophrenia. The pathophysiology of schizophrenia is being investigated actively but, at the present time, there are no biologic measures characteristic of the disease. It has been speculated that schizophrenia, in fact, may be a collection of different diseases, each with its own etiology and course, or that it may be a single disease presenting with different degrees of severity in different individuals (Zubin et al. 1985). Both theories are attempts to explain the wide variety of symptoms and the wide range of different outcomes observed in schizophrenic patients. Whichever of these viewpoints is more correct, there is little doubt that it would be worthwhile to identify variables that could predict either good or poor outcome within the broad spectrum of schizophrenic patients.

Several studies have been done, in an attempt to determine which of the available diagnostic systems are better at identifying patients with a poor long-term prognosis. Systems such as *DSM-III* and the Feighner system, which require a six-month period of symptoms before the diagnosis of schizophrenia is made, tend to identify poor-prognosis patients more than other, less restrictive systems (Overall and Hollister 1979). However, this is a tautological form of validation and does not address the question of whether systems that rely on restricted classes of symptoms are more likely to identify poor-prognosis patients. The answer to this question is generally yes, although the predictive power of the more restrictive systems is not great. One large comparative study (Brockington et al. 1978; Kendell et al. 1979) of 10 diagnostic systems found that three systems—the Research Diagnostic Criteria (RDC; Spitzer et al. 1978), the criteria of Gabriel Langfeldt (1960), and the Flexible System with a threshold of six symptoms (Carpenter et al. 1973)—proved to be more restrictive and better as predictors of poor outcome than were the broader systems such as the New Haven Schizophrenia Index (Astrachan et al. 1972) or the *International Classification of Diseases (ICD)* criteria for codes 295 or 297 (World Health Organization 1965). A smaller study by Carpenter et al. (1973) found that the RDC defined a smaller group of schizophrenics than did *DSM-III*, but the smaller group had no worse prognosis. The range of outcome in the latter study was not great, however, and this fact probably reduced the likelihood of finding a predictor.

Other clinical factors which may help to differentiate good- and poor-prognosis patients include the presence of an affective syndrome, cognitive status, and premorbid adjustment. It is well established that the major affective disorders have a distinctly different prognosis and respond to different types of treatment than does narrowly defined schizophrenia (Pope and Lapinski 1978). What is not as clear, however, is whether those patients who have prominent affective symptoms as well as prominent schizophrenic symptoms have a different prognosis from narrowly defined schizophrenics. Several studies have now examined this question, and the answer is generally yes, although a few studies (e.g., Gift et al. 1980) find little difference between schizophrenics with and without affective symptoms. One comparison of schizoaffective patients with narrowly defined schizophrenics and with bipolar disorder patients found the long-term prognosis for schizoaffectives to be similar to that of the bipolars, while that for typical schizophrenics was worse (Tsuang et al. 1976). Similarly, one of the follow-up studies discussed above (Kolakowska et al. 1985), which included 62 schizophrenics and 15 schizoaffectives found that 20 of the schizophrenics, but none of the schizoaffectives, had a poor outcome after 2 to 20 years. Results of this type support the utility of including a separate category for schizoaffective patients in a diagnostic system and reserving the diagnosis of schizophrenia for patients without prominent affective symptoms (Spitzer et al. 1978).

Poor cognitive functioning and poor premorbid adjustment have also been associated with poor-prognosis schizophrenia in several studies. Schizophrenics who reported cognitive impairment at their first admission tended to have poorer social, occupational, and symptomatic outcomes 30 to 40 years later in the Iowa 500 sample (Tsuang 1982). In the study reported by Huber et al. (1980), schizophrenics with learning difficulties in elementary school had poorer outcome when followed up over 20 years after their first schizophrenic episode than did patients with no learning difficulties. These findings suggest the existence of some brain abnormality in poor-prognosis patients prior to the onset of overt psychotic symptoms. Findings on premorbid adjustment can be interpreted in a similar way, although it is worth noting that the assessment of premorbid adjustment must usually be done retrospectively, and these reports tend to be somewhat unreliable (Small et al. 1984). Nevertheless, both a retrospective (Gittelman-Klein and Klein 1969) and at least one prospective study (Ciompi 1980a) have found poor-outcome patients to have had poorer social adjustment prior to the onset of psychosis than have good-outcome schizophrenics. It is possible, then, that poor-outcome schizophrenics also have subtle signs of brain dysfunction well before they become psychotic. If this is true, it might be possible to develop premorbid biological or behavioral indicators of vulnerability to schizophrenia.

Biological and Treatment Factors
A very modest degree of progress had been made in an attempt to find biologic and treatment factors that are associated with poor outcome in schizophrenia. The biologic measures of most-current interest are complementary to some of the clinical measures, particularly cognitive impairment, discussed above. It has long been recognized that some schizophrenics have a greater than normal number of neurologic soft signs, which is suggestive of brain damage (Quitkin et al. 1976). The development of brain-imaging techniques such as the computerized tomographic scanner (CT scan) has made it possible to look, in a more direct way, for structural brain defects. Numerous studies have compared CT scans obtained from schizophrenics with those from normal controls and most (Johnstone et al. 1976; Weinberger et al. 1979) but not all (Jernigan et al. 1982), have found some proportion of schizophrenics who appear to have diffuse brain atrophy as measured by an increase in the ratio of ventricle size to brain size (VBR). Since it is also the case that larger ventricles are correlated with poor cognitive performance (Johnstone et al. 1976; Golden et al. 1980), it is reasonable to hypothesize that they would be more common in poor-outcome patients. If so, it may be that ventricular

enlargement is a true prognostic factor since some patients with first-episode schizophreniform disorder also have enlarged ventricles (Weinberger et al. 1982). Follow-up studies of such patients will be required to evaluate the prognostic value of ventricular enlargement.

Despite the fact that neuroleptic treatment is very effective in reducing schizophrenic symptoms and in preventing schizophrenic relapse (Davis 1975), the relationship of neuroleptic responsivity to the long-term course of schizophrenia is poorly understood. Neuroleptic drugs do not provide a permanent cure for schizophrenia but, even in comparison to other types of therapy, are very effective in helping to reduce symptoms, relapse rates, and numbers of hospitalizations (May et al. 1976). Long-term follow-up studies, however, have not found any obvious indication that neuroleptic treatment affects the overall remission rate among schizophrenics. The percentage of patients reaching complete remission currently appears to differ very little from the percentage observed in the preneuroleptic era (Bleuler 1974; Ciompi 1980a, 1980b). Further, the percentage of patients who remain chronically psychotic and very debilitated appears not to have changed. A different question is whether responsiveness to neuroleptics early in the course of a schizophrenic illness in any way is predictive of the long-term course of the illness. Few data are available to help answer this question because of the obvious difficulty in following patients for many years after careful assessment of their neuroleptic responsivity. Most studies that have followed schizophrenics longitudinally find that patients who recover quickly from their first episode and have a short initial hospitalization do better in the long run than do less treatment-responsive patients (Ciompi 1980a; Huber et al. 1980). This suggests that neuroleptic responsivity is correlated with long-term outcome but, because treatments were not standardized, and because of confounding with the natural history of the disease, no definitive conclusions can yet be drawn.

Other treatments in addition to neuroleptics have also been shown to lessen the short-term disability associated with schizophrenia. Most effective appears to be family therapy designed to reduce the amount of hostility directed by family members toward the patient and to improve family members' tolerance of and ability to manage schizophrenic symptoms. Among patients maintained on neuroleptics, family therapy is more effective than no therapy (Leff et al. 1985) or individual psychotherapy (Falloon et al. 1982) in preventing symptomatic exacerbation and rehospitalization in chronic schizophrenia. The importance of concomitant drug treatment for effective utilization of family therapy is demonstrated by studies showing that therapy only reduced symptomatology and relapse rate in patients who were maintained on adequate doses of neuroleptics (Goldstein et al. 1978; Hogarty et al. 1979). A combination of neuroleptic treatment plus family therapy seems to offer the best method currently available for reducing the short-term disability associated with schizophrenia.

CONCLUSIONS

The range of disability found among schizophrenics depends upon the criteria used to diagnose the disease. By most of the widely used diagnostic systems, schizophrenia is a disease with heterogeneous outcomes ranging from complete recovery to chronic and unremitting psychosis with extensive disability. The majority of schizophrenics identified by any diagnostic system have some lifelong disability as measured by incomplete remission of clinical symptoms, need for ongoing medical treatment, and/or inability to work and earn a living at their premorbid level. Given that an estimated 1 percent of the population in most countries meets some broad definition of schizophrenia (Robins et al. 1984), it is obvious that the costs of schizophrenia are very great, not only in terms of human suffering, but also in terms of lost productivity and use of medical resources. Narrow diagnostic systems that require specific psychotic symptoms before a patient is diagnosed as schizophrenic identify a group that is more disabled, on average, than do systems which use broader, less specific diagnostic criteria. Attempts to find other predictors of chronicity and disability have been only moderately successful. A concomitant affective syndrome is usually associated with better outcome whereas cognitive impairment is predictive of poorer outcome. Evidence of diffuse brain damage by CT scan and poor response to neuroleptic treatment are likely but, as yet, unproven predictors of poor outcome and chronic disability. Studies of these and other biologic factors may eventually provide useful predictors of clinical course and ultimately provide clues to the etiology of this disease.

REFERENCES

American Psychiatric Association: Diagnostic and Statistical Manual of Mental Disorders, second edition. Washington, DC, American Psychiatric Association, 1968

American Psychiatric Association: Diagnostic and Statistical Manual of Mental Disorders, third edition. Washington DC, American Psychiatric Association, 1980

American Psychiatric Association: Diagnostic and Statistical Manual of Mental Disorders, third edition, revised. Washington, DC, American Psychiatric Association, 1987

Astrachan BM, Harrow M, Adler D, et al: A checklist for the diagnosis of schizophrenia. Br J Psychiatry 121:529-539, 1972

Bleuler M: The long-term course of the schizophrenia psychoses. Psychol Medicine 4:244-254, 1974

Brockington IF, Kendell RE, Leff JP: Definitions of schizophrenia: concordance and prediction of outcome. Psychiatric Medicine 8:387-398, 1978

Carpenter WT, Strauss JS, Bartko JJ: Flexible system for the diagnosis of schizophrenia: report from the WHO international pilot study of schizophrenia. Science 182:1275-1278, 1973

Ciompi L: Catamnestiic long-term study on the course of life and aging of schizophrenics. Schizophr Bull 6:606-618, 1980a

Ciompi L: The natural history of schizophrenia in the long term. Br J Psychiatry 136:413-420, 1980b

Curson DA, Barnes TRE, Bamber RW, et al: Long-term depot maintenance of chronic schizophrenic outpatients: the seven year follow-up of the Medical Research Council fluphenazine/placebo trial I and II. Br J Psychiatry 146:464-480, 1985

Davis JM: Overview: maintenance therapy in psychiatry, I: schizophrenia. Am J Psychiatry 132:1237-1245, 1975

Drake RE, Gates C, Whitaker A, et al: Suicide among schizophrenics: a review. Compr Psychiatry 26:90-100, 1985

Falloon IRH, Boyd JL, McGill CW, et al: Family management in the prevention of exacerbations of schizophrenia. N Engl J Med 306:1437-1440, 1982

Feighner JP, Robins E, Guze SB, et al: Diagnostic criteria for use in psychiatric research. Arch Gen Psychiatry 26:57-63, 1972

Gift TE, Strauss JS, Kokes RF, et al: Schizophrenia affect and outcome. Am J Psychiatry 137:580-585, 1980

Gittelman-Klein R, Klein DF: Premorbid asocial adjustment and prognosis in schizophrenia. J Psychiatr Res 7:35-53, 1969

Golden CJ, Moses JA, Zelazowski R, et al: Cerebral ventricular size and neuropsychological impairment in young and chronic schizophrenics: measurements by the standardized Luria-Nebraska neuropsychological battery. Arch Gen Psychiatry 37:619-623, 1980

Goldstein MJ, Rodnick EH, Evans JR, et al: Drug and family therapy in the aftercare of acute schizophrenics. Arch Gen Psychiatry 35:1169-1177, 1978

Hogarty GE, Schooler NR, Ulrich R, et al: Fluphenazine and social therapy in the after care of schizophrenic patients. Arch Gen Psychiatry 36:1283-1294, 1979

Huber G, Gross G, Schuttler R, et al: Longitudinal studies of schizophrenic patients. Schizophr Bull 6:592-605, 1980

Jernigan TL, Zatz LM, Moses JA, et al: Computed tomography in schizophrenics and normal volunteers. Arch Gen Psychiatry 39:765-770, 1982

Johnstone EC, Crow TJ, Frith CD, et al: Cerebral ventricular size and cognitive impairment in chronic schizophrenia. Lancet 2:924-926, 1976

Kendell RE, Brockington IF, Leff JP: Prognostic implications of six alternative definitions of schizophrenia. Arch Gen Psychiatry 36:25-31, 1979

Kendler KS, Gruenberg AM: An independent analysis of the Danish adoption study of schizophrenia VI. Arch Gen Psychiatry 41:555-564, 1984

Kendler KS, Masterson KC, Ungaro R, et al: A family history study of schizophrenia related disorders. Am J Psychiatry 141:424-427, 1984

Kety SS, Rosenthal D, Wender PH, et al: Mental illness in the biological and adoptive families of adopted individuals who have become schizophrenic: a preliminary report based on psychiatric interviews, in Genetic Research in Psychiatry. Edited by Fieve R, Rosenthal D, Brill H. Baltimore, MD, Johns Hopkins University Press, 1975

Kolakowska T, Williams AO, Ardern M, et al: Schizophrenia with good and poor outcome I and II. Br J Psychiatry 146:229-246, 1985

Kraepelin E: Dementia Praecox and Paraphrenia. Translated by Barclay RM. Huntington, NY, Krieger, 1971

Langfeldt G: Diagnosis and prognosis of schizophrenia. Proc Royal Soc Med 53:1047-1051, 1960

Leff J, Kuipers L, Berkowitz R, et al: A controlled trial of social intervention in the families of schizophrenic patients: two year follow-up. Br J Psychiatry 146:594-600, 1985

Martin RL, Cloninger CR, Guze GB, et al: Mortality in a follow-up of 500 psychiatric outpatients I and II. Arch Gen Psychiatry 42:47-66, 1985

May PRA, Tuma H, Yale C, et al: Schizophrenia: a follow-up study of the results of treatment II. Arch Gen Psychiatry 33:481-486, 1976

Moller JH, Serssen DV, Werner-Elliot K, et al: Outcome of schizophrenic and similar paranoid psychoses. Schizophr Bull 8:99-108, 1982

Overall JE, Hollister LE: Comparative evaluation of research diagnostic criteria for schizophrenia. Arch Gen Psychiatry 36:1198-1205, 1979

Pope HG, Lapinski JF: Diagnosis of schizophrenia and manic-depressive illness. Arch Gen Psychiatry 35:811-828, 1978

Quitkin F, Rifkin A, Klein DF: Neurologic soft signs in schizophrenia and character disorders. Arch Gen Psychiatry 33:845-853, 1976

Robins LN, Helzer JE, Weissman MM, et al: Lifetime prevalence of specific psychiatric disorders in three sites. Arch Gen Psychiatry 41:949-958, 1984

Small NE, Mohs RC, Halperin R, et al: A study of the reliability of reported premorbid adjustment in schizophrenic patients. Biol Psychiatry 19:203-211, 1984

Spitzer RL, Endicott J, Robins E: Research diagnostic criteria. Arch Gen Psychiatry 35:773-782, 1978

Strauss JS, Carpenter WT: Prediction of outcome in schizophrenia, III. Arch Gen Psychiatry 35:773-782, 1977

Tsuang MT: Memory deficit and long-term outcome in schizophrenia: a preliminary study. Psychiatry Res 6:355-360, 1982

Tsuang MT, Dempsey M, Rauscher F: A study of "atypical schizophrenia." Arch Gen Psychiatry 33:1157-1160, 1976

Weinberger DR, Torrey EF, Neophytides AN, et al: Lateral cerebral ventricular enlargement in chronic schizophrenia. Arch Gen Psychiatry 36:735-739, 1979

Weinberger DR, DeLisi LE, Perman GP, et al: Computed tomography in schizophreniform disorder and other acute psychiatric disorders. Arch Gen Psychiatry 39:778-793, 1982

World Health Organization: International Classification of Diseases (vol 1). Geneva, WHO, 1973

Zubin J, Steinhauer SR, Day R, et al: Schizophrenia at the crossroads: a blueprint for the 80's. Compr Psychiatry 26:217-240, 1985

6

Psychiatric Disability and Substance Use Disorders

Murray J. Cohen, M.D.
Raymond F. Hanbury, Jr., Ph.D.

The combination of psychiatric disability and substance use results in a withdrawal of hundreds of thousands—perhaps millions—of people from the work force.

There is controversy regarding the specific pathogenesis of work inhibition: Does chronic, relentless, and severe substance use disorder (hereinafter, SUD) lead to psychiatric disability, or can significant psychiatric disability produce a SUD? Both can be true. Failure to understand the different pathogenetic possibilities often results in unrealistic therapeutic goals, inappropriate treatment planning, prejudicial treatment of the afflicted patient by social and governmental agencies, and unfair treatment reimbursement policies on the part of insurance companies.

Psychiatric disability arising from chronic SUD is more easily recognized. A significant percentage of substance abusers have severe psychiatric problems (Salzman 1981), which, by themselves can produce disability, and the SUD, in fact, may be an attempt to cope with and/or to treat their disturbance (Khantzian and Treece 1977; Wurmser 1978).

The *Diagnostic and Statistical Manual of Mental Disorders, Third Edition, Revised (DSM-III-R)* of the American Psychiatric Association (1987) lists SUD as a behavioral dysfunction which constitutes and indicates a primary mental disorder. No longer is the use of drugs and/or alcohol thought to be present only as a consequence of a different, primary mental disorder. SUD has been established as a primary illness. Nonetheless, it is still sometimes necessary to imply that a diagnosis other than SUD is primary. Some of these diagnostic issues might be directly related to the fact that the existing literature on SUD and psychiatric diagnosis is very scant.

BASIC CONCEPTS

Substance Use Disorder

One of the basic difficulties in approaching this subject involves the imprecision of the terms which define it. Concepts with differing meaning, such as *abuse, dependence, misuse,* and *addiction,* are often used interchangeably. In particular, the term addiction is ambiguous and has been criticized by many writers (Ludwig 1980; Adriani 1976). Ludwig writes that "addiction denotes a pattern of compulsive drug acquisition and use, combined with a heightened tendency for relapse after a period of abstinence, . . . and should not be viewed as equivalent to physical dependence, which can also be produced unwittingly in medically ill persons." Adriani (1976) writes, "the terms 'addiction' and 'habitation' are still used by some physicians interchangeably and, in most instances, incorrectly." He goes on to say that "the term . . . is invariably used by nonphysicians to indicate any abuse of drugs, irrespective of type. . . ."

The term addiction is a medically imprecise term without a clear definition, and, therefore, should probably be avoided whenever possible. To call a person "an addict" has become pejorative, with legal, moral, sociological and spiritual overtones and connotations. Thus, medical objectivity is often lost and the impact of medical intervention compromised. The most appropriate use of the word will be suggested later in this section, after more objective concepts and alternatives are reviewed.

In an attempt to resolve some of the confusion in nomenclature, to provide a method of labeling patients' drug use patterns in an objective, treatment-oriented manner, and to give health care providers a common language with which to communicate, in 1980 the American Psychiatric Association issued a new diagnostic nomenclature. The behavioral dysfunction which constitutes and indicates a mental disorder involving improper use of drugs is called a *substance use disorder* (SUD). This disorder includes two types: *substance abuse* and *substance dependence*. There are three diagnostic criteria required to establish the presence of substance abuse. They are: (1) pattern of pathological use; (2) impairment in social or occupational functioning due to substance use; and (3) a one-month minimum duration of disturbance. The pattern of pathological use is defined by any one of five characteristics: (1) inability to cut down or stop; (2) repeated efforts to control use through periods of temporary abstinence or restriction of use to certain times of day; (3) intoxication throughout the day; (4) frequent use of excessive quantities of the substance; (5) two or more overdoses with the same substance. One diagnostic criterion is required to establish the presence of substance dependence (for drugs other than alcohol or cannabis): tolerance or withdrawal.

Thus, two categories, one physiological (substance dependence), and one psychological (substance abuse), have been specified. Both conditions often are present in the same patient. Substance abuse may be present without substance dependence, although in most instances a person who abuses a drug is also dependent on it. However, it is not infrequent for substance dependence to be present without substance abuse. This is particularly important to bear in mind when treating patients for chronic painful conditions accompanied by iatrogenic drug dependence.

The term *psychological dependence* is no longer used; dependence now means *physical* dependence. The concept of psychological dependence, also called habituation or compulsive drug use (now, pattern of pathological use), is currently subsumed under the term substance abuse. The diagnosis of substance abuse also requires a specified duration as well as an objective demonstration of deterioration in the patient's life. The mere presence of pathological use (psychological dependence) or, for that matter, (physical) dependence, is *insufficient* as a basis for the determination that a patient is a drug abuser.

In addition, prescription misuse, occasional, experimental, or recreational use of intoxicants, as well as chronic use of narcotics for pain control—although all potentially dangerous and fraught with risk—do not, in and of themselves, justify a diagnosis of drug abuse, according to *DSM-III-R*.

The term addiction should only be used to indicate the morbid state of a patient who shows both substance abuse and dependence, and whose drug use also has become a central issue of life: a priority which dwarfs other responsibilities or commitments. The term carries with it an extremely poor prognosis, and should only be used when a patient's life is in such disarray from drug use that the outlook is extremely bleak.

Aspects of Disability

The concept of disability becomes murky when applied to the criminal and to those persons with what some call *volitional disorders* (i.e., obesity, drug addition, and alcoholism). Referring to these morbid states as volitional disorders undermines our ability to consider them pathogenetic of disability, and rejects explicitly one of the essential aspects of the diagnosis of substance abuse—the pattern of pathological use involving loss of control and compulsive behavior.

Even less volitional are the disorders involving substance dependence, where physiological changes, such as hepatic enzyme induction and neuroreceptor transformation, produce tolerance and altered homeostasis. Even the volitional nature of *beginning* misuse of substances can be challenged in many instances, given the genetically based constitutional factors involved in some cases of alcoholism, the self-medication involved in some cases of genetically determined major affective disorders, and the correlations found between SUD and certain types of personality disorders (Stabenou and Hesselblock 1984; Goodwin 1984; Mirin et al. 1984a, 1984b; Siever et al. 1983; Cloninger, 1978).

The etiologies of SUDs are numerous and the theories to explain its causation encompass the psychodynamic, behavioral, psychosocial, sociological, and neurobiological. Thus, differing views of SUD as disabling are understandable and quite common.

Evaluation of Disability
Disability benefits for SUD under the Social Security Disability Insurance (SSDI) program have been in effect since 1954; Supplemental Security Income (SSI) coverage was added in 1967 when Congress grafted SSI to the Social Security Act. Drug addiction and alcoholism frequently have been considered insufficient diagnoses alone to qualify a claimant for benefits. This dilemma was partially resolved by stipulating that any personality disorder or any antisocial pattern associated with psychosis, psychoneurosis, or organic disease, and correlated with sufficient loss of function, could be considered a disability (Lerner 1971). However, to demonstrate the point that SUD *per se* is still not fully accepted as a disability, we have only to look at the Listings of Impairments—the regulations stipulating what constitutes medical impairment under the SSI/SSDI programs—to determine whether such an individual would qualify for benefits.

Within the regulations' general listing of mental disorders, only one implicit reference to SUD may be found in the category of functional nonpsychotic disorders. It is described simply as "addictive dependence on alcohol or drugs" (Morton 1983). The SSI/SSDI program is based on the existence of a psychiatric condition which has precluded work and results in a substantial and persistent loss of function (Lerner 1971). Further, the American Medical Association established a series of practical guides for the rating of impairments used in the medical determination of disability. The section on mental and behavioral disorders does not allude to substance abuse (American Medical Association 1984). Since SUD certainly fulfills the criteria for disability, it is difficult to understand why more attention has not been given to this diagnostic category in either the SSA regulations or AMA guidelines.

EPIDEMIOLOGY OF SUD-INDUCED PSYCHIATRIC DISABILITY
There is little available data concerning the epidemiology of SUD-induced psychiatric disability, based in large part upon the following factors: the diagnosis of SUD is often made in a nonobjective and

inaccurate manner; the presence of SUD is often concealed by the patient because of its stigma; other psychiatric diagnoses often are given priority as primary (even when SUD is the primary diagnosis), to facilitate third-party reimbursement, admission to a hospital, eligibility for and continuation of disability insurance, etc; and the concept of psychiatric disability is difficult to prove. The following provides an understanding of the degree to which SUD-induced psychiatric disability may be manifest (Winick 1981; Gold 1984; Haglund and Schuckit 1977; Tennant et al. 1979; Bluestone et al. 1981; Trice 1979; Hanlon 1963; U.S. Department of Health, Education, and Welfare 1971; Cohen 1984b; Gleaton and Goren, 1985; Johnston et al. 1985):

- Over one-half million persons in the United States are dependent on heroin, of whom 20 percent are in prisons and 25 percent are in treatment;
- 2–3 percent of adults have used barbiturates illegally;
- There are over a quarter of a million barbiturate abusers;
- There are close to half a million persons who abuse nonmedically obtained tranquilizers;
- 13 million persons use marijuana, 3 million of them daily;
- Alcoholism is increasing, with greater per capita consumption and declining age of alcoholics;
- 20–50 percent of patients in a general hospital have alcohol and/or drug-related problems;
- The National Institute of Drug Abuse reports that in 1982, at a minimum: (a) 21.6 million Americans had tried cocaine; (b) 12 million had used it in the preceding year; (c) 4.2 million used it at least once a month;
- A 1982 report from the Centers for Disease Control revealed that: (a) 950 cocaine abusers per month were admitted to federally funded drug abuse programs in 1980 (triple the number in 1977); and (b) the number of emergency room admissions and deaths directly attributed to cocaine abuse sharply increased over five years;
- Of 150 consecutive, first-visit general medical admissions to a general hospital, 17 patients (11.3 percent) used psychoactive drugs or alcohol on a regular basis and considered it an abuse problem;
- 5–10 percent of persons in the labor market are estimated to be alcoholic, with the annual cost of alcohol abuse/dependence to American business estimated at over $15 billion;
- The Metropolitan Life Insurance Company estimates that on-the-job drug taking directly costs industry $85 billion a year from lost time, impaired productivity, and injury;
- The Department of Defense has said that drug–alcohol problems have "seriously impaired military capabilities."

In children and young adults:

- In 1982, the National Institute of Drug Abuse (NIDA) reported the following findings about drug use among children aged 14–15:

  1,000,000 using alcohol
  740,000 using cigarettes
  640,000 using marijuana
  100,000 using cocaine
  100,000 using amphetamines
  100,000 using sedative-tranquilizers

- Between 1973–1983, the United States showed the highest rate of drug abuse by children and young adults in the industrialized world;
- 62 percent of all young adults try illicit drugs before they finish high school, with 40 percent using drugs other than marijuana;
- From 1975 to 1984, the incidence of children smoking marijuana increased from 17 to 25 percent;
- Regarding marijuana use by high school seniors in 1984, as reported by the NIDA 1985 report, 55 percent used it at all, 40 percent used it in the past year, 25 percent used it in the past month, and 5 percent used it daily (down from 11 percent, 5 years earlier);
- 46 percent of high school seniors in 1984 used other illicit drugs, 28 percent used stimulants (up from 15 percent in 10 years), 16 percent used cocaine (up from 9 percent in 10 years), 26 percent used tranquilizer-sedatives, 19 percent used inhalants, at least 1.3 percent used heroin, and 10 percent used other opiates (NIDA 1985);
- Regarding use of alcohol by high school seniors in 1984 (NIDA, 1985), 93 percent used it at all, 67 percent used it during the prior month, 5 percent used it daily, and 39 percent used it in significant amounts (five or more drinks in a row) at least once in the prior two-week period.

We do know that less than half of a group of SUD patients studied showed a pattern of steady employment prior to the onset of their SUD (O'Donnell 1969). Another study revealed a 47.5 percent unemployment rate (Nurco and Lerner 1974). The latter study also found that the most frequent job classifications among those employed were service occupations (10.1 percent); clerical and sales (9 percent); and processing, machine trades, and bench work (12.2 percent). As to the reasons for leaving jobs prior to addiction, approximately half left of their own volition for "negative" reasons (personnel conflicts, drug use, incarceration, family problems), whereas approximately a third left voluntarily for positive reasons (better job, job training program, self-employment, or armed forces).

Cohen et al., studying the effects of alcoholism on productive activity in methadone-maintained persons, found that:

Psychiatric disability is not uncommon. Frank psychosis does not appear to be frequent, possibly because of the selection process or the effects of the neuroleptic action of methadone. However, severe characterological dysfunction in the form of borderline, antisocial, paranoid, infantile, explosive, and schizoid personality disorders may render many patients unable to function satisfactorily. . . . Chronic manifestations of sustained heroin or sedative abuse, such as organic brain disease, chronic renal disease, cardiac failure, or chronic ulcerative lymphostasis reduce the rehabilitative potential and functional activity of certain patients (Cohen et al. 1982).

RELATIONSHIP BETWEEN SUD AND DISABILITY

Clearly, a relationship exists between SUD and psychiatric disability. However, since many persons suffering with SUD are not disabled, SUD must be associated with a *severe functional impairment* to render the person disabled. The association can consist of disability from direct behavioral aspects of the SUD itself, from direct chemical aspects of the SUD itself, from other behavioral disturbances (psychiatric syndromes) which *stem from* the SUD, or from a primary psychiatric syndrome of which the SUD is but one part.

Mirin has concluded that, although difficult ". . . in the evaluation of substance abusers one must separate those character traits and behaviors which preceded the development of drug dependence from those which evolved in response to the need to survive in a drug-using subculture. At the same time, clinicians have become aware of the need to distinguish symptoms produced by drug intoxication or withdrawal from those which may stem from an underlying psychiatric disorder" (Mirin 1984).

Disability from Direct Behavioral Aspects of the SUD

Disability is most often related to the substance *abuse* aspect of SUD and usually involves personality pathology. Substance abuse involves a pattern of pathologic (compulsive) use which is extremely time consuming and often impedes the pursuit of other activities such as job, school, spouse, family, friends, conforming to the law. As a result, these areas are neglected and some or all of them gradually suffer considerably, with eventual exclusion of the individual from participation. Time is also lost in ways specific to the different substances (e.g., blackouts from alcohol, overdoses from opioids).

Impairment in social or occupational functioning may take the form of disturbed social relations, failure to meet important obligations, erratic and impulsive behavior, inappropriate expression of hostility, legal problems, or missing or functioning poorly at work or school (American Psychiatric Association 1980). Zinberg (1975) has concluded that heroin addicts show grossly abnormal personalities due to the loss of social and familial relationships, the hustling behavior required to procure drugs, and the "deviant label."

Youthful drug abusers are particularly vulnerable to developing disability from direct behavioral effects of SUD. Today's adolescents face a cornucopia of both licit and illicit drugs from which to choose and, being characteristically curious about their world, and convinced of their immortality, are willing to take more risks than adults. The drug experience itself, the lure of adult activities and status, and the influence of friends, all may contribute to the popularity of drug use among the young. It is assumed commonly that in addition to producing pleasurable euphoria, drugs provide adolescents with relief from distressing everyday realities and inner conflicts. Although the majority of adolescents initially use drugs to satisfy curiosity or a need for experimentation, some continue to do so because the drugs fulfill psychological needs at some level (Freud 1946). However, our focus will remain on the effects of the drug-using behavior.

Adolescence is a time when the young person must learn to develop and expand defense mechanisms which are required to deal with the vicissitudes and emotional turmoil of later life (Balter 1974). To develop these mechanisms, the youngster must experience, and master, a whole range of powerful affects: anxiety, depression, rage, guilt, hurt, disappointment, love, sexual desire, jealousy, frustration, humiliation. Preoccupation with and reliance on drug use, compounded by the psychotropic effects of the drugs themselves, inhibits a person's ability to "cope" with these emerging affects. The drug itself becomes a coping mechanism (Khantzian et al. 1974). Discontinuation of the drug(s) at a later stage in life leaves the individual psychologically naked and ill equipped to perform at a healthy, adaptive level. Deprived of the ability to cope, abstinence attempts may fail and result in chronic SUD, or some other psychiatric malady, any of which can potentially lead to disability.

Disability from Chemical Aspects of the SUD
While personality abnormalities usually result as direct sequelae of the substance abuse aspect of SUD, the substance *dependence* aspect usually causes disability through the production of a psychotic state, a depression, or an organic mental disorder. A distinction is made between the *acute* psychopathologic effects of any particular drug (many of which can precipitate psychopathology as direct chemical effects when used nonabusively and without dependence), and the psychopathologic effects of the *dependence* on a particular drug (i.e., the *SUD*-induced rather than the *drug*-induced psychopathology). This difference may often be difficult to establish, and the two may

overlap. However, attempts to distinguish them should be made for the purposes of both prognosis and treatment.

For example, an amphetamine psychosis (usually a toxic psychosis) may follow a single large dose in persons with or without SUD. However, more commonly a psychosis only occurs after chronic use, with abuse and dependence (Snyder 1972). An amphetamine-induced toxic psychosis usually abates rapidly, reveals organic features (disorientation, memory impairment) and does not involve compulsive behavior or fixed delusions. In contrast, the amphetamine-induced nontoxic psychosis (seen in SUD patients) may last for a long time, is also associated with organic features, and usually does manifest compulsive and delusional features (Uhde et al. 1982).

Schizophreniform psychoses have been precipitated by chronic abuse of and dependence on amphetamines, cocaine, sedative-hypnotics (during the withdrawal phase), and marijuana with high tetrahydrocannabinol content (Uhde et al. 1982). (Chronic opiate abuse/dependence is not associated with schizophreniform psychosis.) In each instance, the effect of the SUD merely may be to unmask or exacerbate underlying schizophrenia. Likewise, a patient undergoing methadone detoxification for opioid dependence may begin to manifest psychotic features due to the decreased neuroleptic effect of methadone on the underlying psychosis. Evidence for this explanation involves clinical experience as well as the dopamine receptor-blocking/prolactin-increasing effect of methadone (Kleber and Gold 1978; Tolis et al. 1978).

The relationship between depression and SUD is complex and will be explored in greater detail in the next sections. Chronic opiate use, while masking depressive symptoms in some, can precipitate them in others (Wikler 1952; Haertzen and Hooks 1969; Mirin et al. 1976). Chronic alcohol intoxication causes alcoholics to be more withdrawn, less self-confident, and more depressed (Mendelson and Mello 1966). Also, chronic use, with tolerance, of certain hypnotics and benzodiazepines seems to lead to or exacerbate depression in certain individuals. Vaillant (1981) considers the dysphoric effects of chronic intoxication to cast doubt on the significance and importance of etiological explanations of alcohol and drug use involving nonconstitutional factors.

Organic mental disorders are due usually to the direct chemical effect of the drug, and will not be delineated further in this chapter. However, such disorders may also result from tolerance and dependence produced by the SUD. Most often this occurs during the withdrawal phase of alcohol–tranquilizer–sedative-hypnotic use disorder in the form of delirium—usually an acute state and not ordinarily directly related to psychiatric disability. In addition to alcohol, barbiturates, nonbarbiturate hypnotics, and meprobamate, it is now known that a full withdrawal syndrome, including delirium, seizures, and hallucinosis, can occur as a result of benzodiazepine withdrawal, even after treatment in low-to-moderate doses (Winokur et al. 1980).

Disability from SUD-Induced Behavioral Disturbances

Paranoid disorders are not uncommon among persons with opioid use disorder, most particularly in those whose drug of choice is heroin and who live a "street life." The use of an illegal drug and the associated negative stigma—the need for the drug several times a day, the uncertain amount of heroin contained in the white powder, the constant threat of police intervention, the desperate pursuit of money, the relaxation (often disappearance) of superego controls, the terror created by fear of withdrawal, the high percentage (40–50 percent) of opioid use disorder patients with antisocial personality (20–25 percent with antisocial personality unaccompanied by any other psychiatric diagnosis besides SUD) (Rounsaville et al. 1982a; Woody et al. 1983), the need to manipulate and to protect against being manipulated, the omnipresent threat and fear of violence—all may contribute to a paranoid orientation.

Zinberg (1975) explains the dynamic development of such a condition by postulating that enforced social isolation and deviant status reduce input from external reality, undermine the ego's relative autonomy from the id, affect socially supported superego structures, and result in increased dependence on the environment for drugs and for remaining social relations, thereby weakening a person's autonomy from the environment and resulting in an ego regression. Pinsker (1983) describes a behavioral style, known as "street behavior," which resembles paranoid disorder: "This style . . . is characterized by self-centeredness, contempt for authority, exploitiveness, restlessness, and wariness. Much . . . time is spent 'hanging out,' talking about drugs. Personal responsibility is denied and . . . there may be a . . . quickness to take offense."

Wikler's conditioning theory (1980) attempts to explain opiate addiction, and may also explain compulsive disorders which develop as a result of linkage to injecting narcotics or using other drugs. Thus, some former heroin addicts, on "blocking" doses of methadone or naltrexone, will continue to inject water into their veins with unsterile syringes and will continue to display all the rituals of "shooting up." These "needle freaks" experience uncontrollable impulses to repeat past behaviors which resulted in "getting high"—some experiencing euphoria after the injection of a chemically inert substance. Recovered alcoholics not infrequently increase their consumption of nonalcoholic beverages, and Alcoholics Anonymous meetings are notorious for the number of coffee cups scattered about. Cocaine and sedative pill users in remission may still strive compulsively to obtain the substance of former abuse, only to throw it out or flush it down the toilet after they succeed.

Since obsessive thinking is usually an integral part of the substance abuse variety of SUD, it is not surprising that even during remission, and certainly during active illness, obsessional syndromes occur and persist. Not infrequently, experiences previously associated with drug or alcohol use, when reexperienced in the abstinent state, precipitate preoccupation with substance use. There have been instances reported where, after many years of successful rehabilitation-induced abstinence, the individual, after returning to a previous neighborhood, suddenly develops intense drug/alcohol cravings, exhibits drug-seeking behavior, and may even experience a subjective or objective abstinence syndrome—so-called pseudowithdrawal (Whitehead 1974). This phenomenon is also explained by conditioning theory (Childress et al. 1985).

Other stimuli—persons, affect states, smells, movies, conversational topics—all have the capacity to produce the experience of withdrawal, the reemergence of drug cravings and obsessional thinking, and a SUD relapse. For this reason, to facilitate and sustain a SUD remission, patients are told to sever relationships with other substance users, change neighborhoods, and abandon previous SUD-tainted habits. The residual and/or reemergent obsessional behavior and compulsiveness also explain the value of the self-help groups—Alcoholics Anonymous, Narcotics Anonymous, etc.—which substitute healthier, more adaptive obsessional-compulsive habits and techniques for those which continue an individual's susceptibility to SUD relapse (Emrick et al. 1977; Cohen 1984b). Finally, these factors, as well as the impulsiveness so common in the SUD patient, explain the value of using the orally effective, long-acting narcotic antagonist naltrexone (Trexan) to provide added insurance against relapse (O'Brien et al. 1974; O'Brien et al. 1984a).

Other anxiety disorders, including generalized anxiety disorder and panic disorder, are also associated with SUD. The etiological relationship is unclear; each probably can cause the other. The development of an anxiety or panic state resulting from SUD is of importance. Panic states may be caused by dysphoric marijuana reactions, paradoxical sedative-tranquilizer reactions, acute adverse stimulant reactions, and abstinence syndromes of varying types. SUD can cause, precipitate, or exacerbate anxiety and panic states. This relationship may be explained by anticipatory anxiety regarding procurement of more drug, concern over being discovered, stress and worry about deteriorating areas of one's life, legal difficulty, or, after abstinence (or stable maintenance), strong impulses to resume drug or alcohol use.

Gold et al. (1982a) suggest that the similarity between naturally occurring anxiety and panic states and opiate withdrawal may be explained by a common neural pathway involving noradrenergic hyperactivity from increased locus coeruleus activity. This would explain the efficacy of clonidine (Catapres), an alpha-two adrenergic agonist which decreases locus coeruleus activity, in both relieving narcotic abstinence manifestations (Gold and Pottash 1981) as well as naturally occurring anxiety and panic (Gold et al. 1980a).

Although usually mild, the protracted (secondary) abstinence syndrome not infrequently seen subsequent to opiate detoxification may be sufficiently severe to cause psychiatric disability. This syndrome can last up to six months or longer after detoxification, and consists of meiosis; mild decrease in pulse, blood pressure, and temperature; hyposensitivity of the cerebral respiratory center to CO_2; and increased urinary epinephrine excretion (Jasinski 1981). Patients complain of dysphoria, restlessness, insomnia, joint and bone pains, chills alternating with hot flushes, and opiate craving. It is thought that this syndrome may be responsible for many opiate SUD relapses. Patients suffering from protracted abstinence syndrome often feel too sick to work. The pathogenesis of the syndrome is not known. The effect of chronic opiate use on the endorphin system has been suggested as pathogenic (Gold et al. 1980b). Neither clonidine (Catapres) nor naltrexone (Trexan) is particularly effective in treating this condition, and for some individuals methadone maintenance is necessary. An abstinence syndrome following cessation of alcohol, sedative-hypnotics, and stimulant use generally includes depression (usually mild to moderate), but rarely causes disability and usually responds to antidepressant chemotherapy.

Disability may occur after many years of suffering from SUDs. Chronic alcoholics may develop an encephalopathy—Wernicke/Korsakoff's psychosis—involving an irreversible organic mental disorder. Chronic sedative-hypnotic abusers often suffer multiple overdoses. Eventually, the repeated cerebral hypoxia and microinfarctions may lead to chronic organic mental disorder (together with seizure disorder). Chronic stimulant abusers may develop an irreversible chronic schizophreniform paranoid psychosis. Certain reactions to hallucinogenic drugs (LSD, mescaline, psilocybin, tetrahydrocannabinol) may result in permanent psychotic states, usually in those predisposed by significant preexisting psychopathology. Phencyclidine (PCP) likewise can produce permanent psychosis.

As previously stated, the relationship between SUD and depression is unclear. Mirin et al. (1984a) concluded that "although depressive symptomatology appears to occur with greater than expected frequency in substance abusers, the precise causal relationship between these two clinical entities is often unclear. Certainly, drug and/or alcohol intoxication or withdrawal is frequently accompanied by alterations in mood. Conversely, many patients with affective illness . . . abuse drugs and/or alcohol in an attempt to alter undesirable mood states. . . . In many patients the exact chronology of symptom development is obscure."

Dakis and Gold (1984) mirror this view, stating, "the persistence of depressive symptoms in methadone patients is in fact very difficult to interpret. It is difficult to determine whether patients are some-what overmedicated and thus subject to depressant effects of meth-adone. Conversely, patients with some degree of opiate abstinence might experience depressive symptoms, particularly those associated with withdrawal such as insomnia, psychomotor agitation, irri-tability and anorexia. In addition, many of these patients concomi-tantly abuse other substances with strong mood-altering effect." A more detailed examination of the relationship between SUD and affective disorder is offered in the next section.

Since little is known definitively about the relationship between specific SUDs and specific behavioral abnormalities, McLellan et al. (1979) tried to elucidate the subject by studying the development of psychiatric disorder among 51 individuals who abused drugs contin-uously over six years. Repetitive stimulant abusers developed psy-chotic disorders (5 of 11), repetitive depressant abusers developed depressive disorders (8 of 14), and repetitive opioid abusers showed no change in psychopathology.

Disability from SUD Existing as a Component of Other Behavioral Disturbances

Rounsaville et al. (1983) studied 72 opiate addicts maintained on methadone (representing only 5 percent of eligible patients). The psychiatric diagnostic breakdown was as follows:

Psychosis (0)
Affective disorder (49%)
     major depression   15%
     minor depression   1%
     intermittent depression   11%
     cyclothymic personality   1%
     labile personality   21%
Anxiety disorder (6%)
     generalized anxiety disorder   3%
     phobic disorder   3%
Somatoform disorder (4%)
     somatization disorder   4%
Personality disorder (41%)
     antisocial personality   17%
     borderline personality   10%
     mixed personality   7%
     schizotypal personality   6%
     narcissistic personality   1%

Although the incidence of psychosis in narcotics addicts has often been reported as low (e.g., 2 percent, Pfeffer and Ruble 1948), it is possible that the zero incidence reported here reflects acceptance selection criteria as well as the neuroleptic effects of methadone

(Tolis et al. 1978). It is therefore useful to look at the psychopathology profile of 100 opiate addicts on methadone maintenance who were screened to eliminate those with psychosis. (The diagnoses are not mutually exclusive and are lifetime (Woody et al. 1983).)

Affective disorder (74%)	
major depressive disorder	43%
minor depressive disorder	7%
intermittent depressive disorder	7%
labile personality	9%
cyclothymic personality	10%
hypomanic disorder	19%
manic disorder	1%
bipolar II disorder	10%
Anxiety disorders (9%)	
general anxiety disorder	3%
panic disorder	0%
phobic disorder	4%
depressive-compulsive disorder	2%
Alcoholism (24%)	
Personality disorders (21%)	
schizotypal	6%
antisocial	15%
Other psychiatric disorders (1%)	

The authors conclude that "there is a high incidence and a wide range of psychiatric symptoms among drug abusers, which contributes [sic] in various ways to the drug taking and to the attendant adjustment problems. . . . Clinical observations suggest that some proportion of drug taking in almost all addicts is an attempt to self-medicate discomfort associated with life stress or psychiatric symptoms. However, there is reason to believe that this attempt at self-medication may account for a much greater proportion of drug taking in those addicts with clinically significant levels of psychiatric symptoms" (Woody et al. 1984).

O'Brien et al. (1984) conclude from these two studies that 80 percent of the patients had a lifetime history of psychiatric disorder other than opioid dependence, and 70 percent had a current psychiatric disorder. It is noteworthy to observe the consensual validation of certain diagnoses:

anxiety disorder	6% and 7%
antisocial personality disorder:	17% and 15%
schizotypal personality disorder:	6% and 6%
intermittent/minor depression:	12% and 14%
labile personality, versus labile personality plus hypomanic, manic, and bipolar II disorders:	21% and 28%

Indeed, the major area of disagreement involved major depression: 15 percent versus 43 percent (to be discussed later). The proportion of patients with antisocial personality disorder complements the findings of Mirin et al. (1984a), who discovered that, in a group of 160 nonpsychotic substance abusers, almost all patients diagnosed as having antisocial personality disorder were opiate abusers. Interestingly, the 24 percent alcoholism rate corresponds to that of another study, in which 625 methadone-maintained patients displayed a 25 percent alcoholism rate—17 percent active and 8 percent inactive (Stimmel et al. 1983). Recent experimental research documenting these interactions correlates with clinical observations in opiate addicts and may help explain the increased morbidity in alcoholics on methadone maintenance (Ho and Allen 1981; Kreek 1984). This points out the need for special treatment approaches with such patients (Gerston et al. 1977; Stimmel et al. 1978a). Along with alcoholism and polydrug abuse, the incidence and prevalence of psychiatric syndromes far exceed those found in the general population (Rounsaville et al. 1982a). It underscores the degree and significance of psychopathology and psychiatric disability seen in these persons as well as the need for psychiatric care, usually not available as part of a methadone-maintenance program. Verebey (1981) has suggested that much of the psychopathology may be explained by variations and alterations in endogenous opioids.

Attempts have been made to correlate specific classes of drugs with different personality types and symptom clusters, in an effort to understand the relationship between different types of SUDs and different psychiatric syndromes (Milkman and Frosch 1973). Khantzian et al. (1974) and Khantzian (1975) note that the choice of a particular abused drug is not serendipitous; rather, patients with SUD initially experiment with many different types of drug, and select the one with the distinctive psychoactive action preferred by that individual: ". . . one of the main appeals [of opiates] for narcotic addicts resides in their ability to relieve states of dysphoria associated with aggression, violent feelings, rage and associated depression. . . . Addicts obtain short-term relief from the anti-aggression, muting action of opiates, and it is on this basis that opiates are appealing. The same but more sustained effect of the long-acting opiate methadone accounts for its stabilizing and containing influences in the treatment of opiate addicts" (Khantzian 1985). Wurmser (1974) agrees with drug-choice specificity, emphasizing that "the importance of the effect of the drug in the inner life of these patients can perhaps be best explained as an artificial or surrogate defense against overwhelming affects. . . . Patients prefer those drugs which specifically help them cope with the affects that trouble them most." For example, clinical observation links cocaine use to persons who experience anergia, depletion, boredom, and emptiness.

The following represent examples of psychiatric syndromes which often include SUD as part of the clinical picture, the combination of which may lead to psychiatric disability. The general model, by no means proven, is that a primary psychiatric syndrome leads to sufficient dysphoria that SUD develops, which is ostensibly used by the patient to help cope with the painful affects involved. In some cases, the SUD then aggravates the severity of the primary disturbance, sometimes increasing the symptoms of the original disorder.

Patients with affective disease (excluding for the moment major depressive illness) are inclined toward stimulant abuse/dependence (Khantzian and Khantzian 1984; Gawin and Kleber 1984). Dysthymic disorder patients tend to abuse cocaine (Khantzian and Khantzian 1984), and some persons on methadone maintenance misuse or abuse amitriptyline (Elavil) (Cohen et al. 1978). Cyclothymic disorder patients also abuse cocaine (Khantzian and Khantzian 1984; Gawin and Kleber 1984) and, probably, amphetamines. Bipolar patients often abuse cocaine (Khantzian and Khantzian 1984; Gawin and Kleber 1984) and, while in the manic phase, they also have been found to abuse alcohol (Estroff et al. 1984). Cocaine is also abused by sufferers of the hyperactivity/attention deficit disorder/emotional lability syndrome (Khantzian and Khantzian 1984; Gawin and Kleber 1984). Khantzian (1974) has described the experiences of patients while using cocaine: They overcame their anergia, became mobilized, were better able to perform and interact, experienced heightened self-esteem, felt a calming effect, felt a reversal of their dysthymic mood cycle, and felt their hypomania augmented.

Persons predisposed to cocaine and amphetamine misuse are also probably at high risk to abuse other stimulants, namely methylphenidate (Ritalin), phenmetrazine (Preludin), diethylpropion (Tenuate), phenylpropanolamine (Dexatrim), and ephedrine. Cases have been reported of tranylcypromine (Parnate) abuse, which, because its chemical structure is similar to amphetamine, may act as a stimulant as well as an antidepressant. The abuse of this drug may be augmented by the fact that it is often used to treat cases of atypical depression manifesting as hysteroid dysphoria. The potential drug-abusive patient may be introduced to tranylcypromine in this fashion. It is known that even within recommended dose ranges, all monoamine oxidase inhibitors (MAOI) can precipitate an amphetamine-like picture, with hypomania and all of its concomitants. Because of the dangers inherent in using MAOI (Shopsin and Kline 1976), it is recommended that they be avoided in treating depression in the SUD population (Kleber and Gold 1978).

Generalized anxiety disorder patients often abuse sedative-hypnotic drugs (Mirin et al. 1984a; McLellan et al. 1979). Benzodiazepines are equally popular, especially diazepam (Valium) because of its lipophilia-induced rapid onset of action. Persons suffering from panic disorders may present with a withdrawn, depressant, or alcohol-abusing agoraphobic clinical picture. This is because these substances may be started during the anticipatory anxiety phase of the illness, and use may evolve to abuse/dependence (Mirin et al. 1984a; Quitkin et al. 1972; Mullaney and Trippett 1979).

SUD is not infrequently seen in association with somatoform disorders. These patients should be evaluated for SUD by inspection for stigmata of the disorder, communication with the patient's other physicians, communication with family members, and urine toxicologic screening. Somatization disorder (Briquet's syndrome) patients tend to have depressant and/or alcohol SUDs; those with secondary depression may have a concomitant stimulant SUD. Patients with psychogenic pain disorder (pain-prone disorder, chronic intractable benign pain syndrome) may have one (or more) of several types of SUDs. Depressants may be abused because of chronic anxiety, stimulants because of secondary depression (or primary depression—some clinicians believe chronic pain to be a paradigm of masked depression) (Blumer and Heilbron 1984), or opiates because of the need to reduce the pain-induced emotional suffering. Unfortunately, chronic opiate use can exacerbate pain, since chronic use of these drugs may lead to depression (Mirin et al. 1976), aggravating pain. Such opiate use also may reduce the pain threshold and cause recurrent withdrawal-induced dysphoria, further increasing pain.

Schooff et al. (1984) believe that there are two types of psychogenic pain disorder (PPD). The first includes patients with a healthy premorbid personality who functioned effectively, but who, subsequent to the onset of depression, begin "abusing drugs almost as though they were antidepressants, attempting to reinforce the denial of their feelings of anger, protest and despair." Patients in the second group have strong dependency needs, have a history of a troubled life, and appear headed toward overt psychiatric illness. Instead, they develop a pain-producing disorder, and "are attempting to suppress strong feelings of depression and anxiety and may have had guilty bouts of alcoholism or drug abuse followed by struggling periods of abstinence and increasing tension."

S. Cohen (1984a) believes that the pain of PPD may be reinforced and perpetuated by the retirement and compensation systems we employ. He states: "Many of [these] patients are dependent on narcotics or sedatives and tolerance to these drugs increases their drug-seeking behavior. . . . As many as half of the patients arrive at the office or clinic already dependent on a narcotic or sedative. . . . [These] patients should learn the difference between a handicap and a disability. A significant minority of our work force performs under substantial handicaps, including pain. The (PPD) patient believes that he is disabled. When he comes to the conclusion that he is only handicapped, his existence becomes much more bearable and rewarding."

It is essential to differentiate between those patients with PPD, who are at high risk for the development of SUD, and medical patients with organically based pain and iatrogenic opiate dependence.

The latter patients are not at high risk of SUD (Porter and Jick 1980), and may be undermedicated for pain (Parry 1984) based on physicians' "opiophobia." One of the chapter authors (Cohen 1986) has previously written:

> Although dependency does constitute an SUD, it does *not* imply . . . abuses, and it is the abusive aspects that constitute the hub of 'addiction.' Dependency alone, even chronic opiate dependency, may be a quite benign condition (when iatrogenically induced). It is the set (the user's personality and attitudes toward taking the drug) and the setting (the characteristics of the physical and social setting in which use occurs) that determine whether or not 'addiction' will occur. . . . In the case of medically ill patients with pain, even though they often receive enough narcotics to produce dependence, . . . the set and the setting are usually not pathogenic. In fact, these patients are quite different from those persons who will go on to develop opiate abuse. . . . But, of course, there *are* patients with chronic underlying painful organic illnesses who are, in addition (to being opioid dependent), opioid abusers.

Eleven guidelines are then offered to manage opiate dependence in chronic organically based pain patients.

Although there is no reliable literature on the subject, it is thought that persons with personality-constricting types of psychic organization would be predisposed to abuse hallucinogenic (psychotomimetic, psychedelic) drugs. These kinds of disorders would presumably include schizoid, schizotypal, dependent, compulsive, and passive-aggressive personality disorders, occupational or scholastic inhibition, borderline intellectual problems, and various types of adjustment disorder.

Beyond their abuse of diuretics and cathartics, bulimic patients also show as high as a 50 percent incidence of substance abuse, usually polysubstance abuse. In all likelihood this is because bulimics are significantly impulsive, suicidal, antisocial, anxious, depressed, guilty, interpersonally sensitive, somatically preoccupied, and psychotic (Casper et al. 1980; Garfinkel et al. 198; Halmi and Falk 1982). Possibly, bulimics are also drug abusers because their eating disorder is actually a manifestation of an underlying depressive or obsessive disorder.

The relationship between schizophrenia and SUD, in Salzman's view (1981), is "complex and confusing." It is virtually impossible, with the current degree of understanding, to know with certainty to what extent SUD exists as part of the schizophrenia picture. Other connections between the two have been described previously, but the true pathogenic connection remains unclear for a number of reasons: the accuracy and reliability of diagnosis of schizophrenia has been poor; the diagnosis changes over time; many types of drug use cause schizophreniform psychoses; some abused drugs have a neuroleptic action; schizophrenic drug addicts learn to hide their symptoms by developing a "pseudopsychopathy" (Salzman 1981, p. 758). In general, it appears that SUD is not a significant pathogenic concomitant to schizophrenia. In a study of 218 consecutive admissions to the psychiatric service of a general hospital, schizophrenia was underrepresented and character disorders overrepresented among moderate and heavy drug users. A comparison of the heavy drug users to the entire population of 218 (of which 118 had a history of drug use) showed that the ratio of character disorders to schizophrenics was 2.5 times greater in heavy drug users (Cohen and Klein 1974).

One type of SUD that does appear to be linked to the schizophrenia syndrome is abuse of antiparkinsonism drugs (Rubenstein 1978). In two British studies, the majority of hospitalized anticholinergic-abusing patients were schizophrenic. Most of the anticholinergic abuse occurred as part of a polysubstance abuse pattern (Cranshaw and Mullen 1984; Pullen et al. 1984).

There is a rich literature documenting and measuring the joint pressure of SUD and depression which will not be reviewed here (Kleber and Gold 1978; Mirin et al. 1976; Weissman et al. 1977; Mintz et al. 1979; Woody and Blaine 1979). However, as previously stated, the exact relationship between the two has remained elusive (Mirin et al. 1984a).

The high prevalence of depression in opiate addicts can be appreciated by the following findings: Among patients using illicit narcotics, the reported percentage of depressed patients has varied from 25–35 (Rounsaville et al. 1982a), to 80 (Woody and Blaine 1979). Among patients maintained on methadone, the incidence of depression at a given time has varied from 15–17 percent (Rounsaville et al. 1983; Rounsaville et al. 1982b), to 30 percent (after two weeks of treatment) (Woody and Blaine 1979), and 33 percent (moderate to severe) (Weissman et al. 1976). Two to three weeks after methadone detoxification, 35 percent of patients were found to have manifestations of major depression—although not necessarily major depressive illness. Dackis and Gold (1983, 1984) conclude that "at present the time course of depressive syndromes in detoxified opiate addicts remains unclear and . . . unresearched." This becomes quite apparent when one observes the claim by Gold and colleagues (1979) that depression *worsens* after opiate detoxification in light of the 35 percent incidence they have found of *post*detoxification depression and the 33 percent incidence *during* opiate maintenance found by others (Gold et al. 1979; Rounsaville et al. 1982).

The *lifetime* prevalence of major depression in an opiate-maintained group of 149 patients (that showed a 17 percent prevalence at a given time) was 48 percent. However, the vast majority of these patients had their first depressive episode *after* the onset of opiate abuse, arguing against the notion that initial heroin use was motivated by the need to cope with depression. This depression was generally of short duration and remitted without the need for antidepressant medication (Rounsaville et al. 1982b). Of a group of 110 opiate addicts about to begin a new treatment episode of methadone maintenance, 74 percent showed criteria for lifetime diagnosis of affective disease (O'Brien et al. 1984).

The following conclusions have been reached pertaining to depressed opiate use disorder patients:

1. They have a poorer prognosis in treatment than nondepressed ones (Rounsaville et al. 1982b).
2. They may either be similar to nonopiate-using depressives (Weissman et al. 1977) or differ by having greater anxiety which they cannot differentiate from depression (Prusoff et al. 1977).
3. They show an association between life events and depressive manifestations (Kleber et al. 1983).
4. Those with recurrence may require lithium (Kleber and Gold 1978).
5. Antidepressant treatment, when needed, should not be employed prior to four to six weeks after admission (Kleber and Gold 1978; Woody 1981), bearing in mind that, although four controlled studies revealed that doxepin was significantly more effective than placebo in reversing depression in methadone-maintained patients (O'Brien et al. 1984b), desipramine (Woody 1981) and imipramine (Kleber et al. 1983) were not.
6. There is a high spontaneous-remission rate with methadone alone (O'Brien et al. 1984b).
7. The depression may indicate a bipolar major affective disorder to be followed by mania, which either may be methadone maintenance or, if manifest, should be treated with lithium (Kleber and Gold 1978).

Unlike the case of opiate use disorder patients, alcoholics have been found to have a low incidence of major depression (Weissman and Myers 1980), while displaying a greater incidence of bipolar disorder than do opiate abusers (perhaps because of possible genetic links between major affective disorder and alcoholism). Dackis and colleagues (1984) found only a 7 percent incidence of major depressive illness two to three weeks after detoxification among 70 consecutive alcoholic patients admitted to an alcohol rehabilitation unit (in spite of the depressed appearance of many on admission). They conclude:

> . . . alcoholics strive for euphoria and will usually continue to drink even after symptom relief has been attained . . . . The diagnosis of major depression is problematic . . . because many depressive symptoms are also associated with alcoholism and

disappear readily with sobriety. Insomnia, anergia, guilty or suicidal thoughts, poor concentration and depressed mood may be caused by cerebral toxicity, withdrawal, intoxication, or the addictive lifestyle. . . . [A] two-week 'wash out' period with observation is sufficient to identify those alcoholics with alcohol-induced organic affective syndromes. Persistence of depressive syndromes beyond this period is consistent with the diagnosis of major depression. . . . (Dackis and Stuckey, 1984)

Although a manic episode often results in relapse to drinking (Dackis and Stuckey 1984), and patients in this affective state often drink heavily (Estroff et al. 1984), the diagnosis of alcoholism cannot be made in a manic patient (Dackis and Stuckey 1984).

In an attempt to study biochemical and neurotransmitter concomitants of affective disease found in SUD patients, Mirin and Weiss (1984a) studied a group of 160 nonpsychotic SUD patients, participating in a four-week program that involved detoxification (if necessary). Analysis of the group revealed that: 74 percent were male, mean age was 30 years; average duration of drug use was 10 years; and SUD breakdown included 57 percent opiate abusers, 22 percent stimulant abusers, and 21 percent depressant abusers. Affective disease was found in 29 percent of all patients (21 percent unipolar, 8 percent bipolar), and in 18 percent of opiate abusers, 18 percent of depressant abusers, and 31 percent of stimulant abusers. Platelet MAO activity was obtained in 88 patients (who were drug free for at least seven days). Urinary MHPG levels were also obtained. The study found that:

1. Opiate abusers had significantly less nondrug-related psychopathology than other abusers.
2. Approximately 20 percent of patients had continued depression with persistent bipolar features after detoxification.
3. Stimulant abusers showed a statistically significant increased incidence of affective disorder, particularly bipolar, compared to opiate abusers, and the former usually presented with either hypomania or retarded depression (which continued after four weeks of abstinence).
4. Depressant substance abusers showed a trend toward increased affective disorder compared to opiate abusers.
5. Stimulant abusers with retarded depression showed low or normal urinary MHPG levels and low platelet MAO activity, suggesting use of noradrenergic drugs as a self-treatment attempt (although the low MAO activity could indicate chronic stimulant abuse or a biological marker of primary affective disease).
6. A subgroup of opiate abusers was observed with underlying primary depressive disorder, usually presenting as agitated depression and showing increased urinary MHPG levels, indicating self-

treatment attempts (there is uncertainty as to the cause of low MHPG).

To further elucidate neurotransmitter function plasma cortisol levels (both resting and in response to ACTH stimulation), dexamethasone suppression tests, and effects of clonidine, naloxone, and naltrexone were studied. The findings included: They found: locus coeruleus hyperactivity and hypoactivity during acute withdrawal and acute opiate administration, respectively (Gold et al. 1982b); efficacy of clonidine to block withdrawal (Gold et al. 1982b); low cortisol levels in methadone-maintained patients, together with blunted cortisol response to ACTH stimulation, suggesting chronic low ACTH and possibly low beta-endorphin levels (Pheterson et al. 1983; Dackis et al. 1982); elevated cortisol levels in methadone-maintained patients, together with inadequate naloxone-induced ACTH release, suggesting functional endorphin deficiency during opiate dependence and rebound ACTH and cortisol hyperactivity after detoxification (Pheterson et al. 1983; Gold et al. 1981); in 42 consecutive opiate-dependent patients, two weeks after detoxification, dexamethasone suppression test (DST) nonsuppression was present in 33 percent, with a statistically significant correlation between DST abnormality and major depressive disorder (80 percent of patients with and 7 percent of patients without major depressive disorder had abnormal DST, although it is unclear whether the abnormal DST indicates opiate-induced neuroendocrine dysfunction, per se, or major depressive disorder) (Dackis et al. 1983). Dackis and Gold (1984) conclude:

> Extensive disruption of norepinephrine and hypothalamic–pituitary–adrenal axis function characteristic of opiate addiction are related to extraordinary prevalence rates of major depression seen in these patients post-detoxification. . . . [In this light], the close relationship between ACTH and beta-endorphin systems in the brain . . . [makes it] conceivable that both the DST abnormality and depressive syndrome are opiate induced. If this were true it would indicate that depression in the context of opiate addiction may represent an organic affective syndrome rather than a major depressive illness. . . . Given the probable involvement of norepinephrine neurons in the mechanism of depressive disorders and the profound disruption of norepinephrine homeostasis by exogenous opiate administration, opiate-induced norepinephrine effects could contribute to the high rates of depression in opiate addicts. . . . The issue of causality, however, remains unsolved. . . . Although depressions in methadone maintained patients may clear spontaneously, depression in detoxified opiate addicts may persist. . . . The self-medication of depressed states in postdetoxified opiate addicts may contribute significantly to their high recidivism rates and abysmal prog-

nosis. (This pattern may be especially prominent in patients detoxified from methadone maintenance.) . . . To the extent that it does, its successful management should improve the prognosis of drug rehabilitation. . . . We believe . . . there is a great risk in not treating depressive syndromes in detoxified addicts . . . [and] have considered pharmacotherapy to constitute an important part of recovery in many of our detoxified addicts.

In conclusion, although the actual prevalence of psychopathology among SUD patients is unclear, it does appear that there is a direct relationship between the socioeconomic class of the patient and the degree of discernible psychopathology (Kaufman 1974). Kissin (1977) calls this the "psychosocial equation"—an inverse relationship between the prevalence of drug dependence in a given sex or subculture and the degree of psychopathology in an addicted individual of the same sex or subculture. Thus:

- female alcoholics show greater psychopathology than male alcoholics;
- Jewish alcoholics show greater psychopathology than Irish alcoholics;
- female heroin addicts show greater psychopathology than male heroin addicts;
- white, middle-class heroin addicts show greater psychopathology than black, "ghetto" heroin addicts.

VOCATIONAL REHABILITATION AS A TREATMENT MODALITY

The treatment of SUD-related psychiatric disorders and SUD itself, as well as the use of a methadone program to treat opiate use disorder, are beyond the scope of this chapter and have been discussed exhaustively elsewhere (Salzman 1981; Wurmser 1978; Uhde et al. 1982; Kleber and Gold 1978; Woody et al. 1983; O'Brien et al. 1984b; Gold et al. 1982b; Rounsaville et al. 1983; Woody et al. 1984; Stimmel et al. 1983; Gerston et al. 1977; Schooff et al. 1984; Cohen 1986; Kleber et al. 1983; Woody 1981; Cohen and Stimmel 1978; Stimmel et al. 1978; Stimmel et al. 1981; Stimmel et al. 1982; Dupont et al. 1979; Lowinson and Ruiz 1981; Allison et al. 1985). What will be discussed is the use of the most specific treatment modality (although not the only one) utilized in the context of SUD-induced psychiatric disability—vocational rehabilitation (VR). In many cases, VR will be necessary but not sufficient to facilitate rehabilitation, especially where chemotherapy and/or counseling for the SUD or psychiatric care for other syndromes, or both, are required. However, VR is considered an essential and basic ingredient for most drug rehabilitation programs (Hanbury et al. 1973; Ross 1972; Sackstein 1981) and the earlier introduced, the better (Burros and Bozzone 1978). Most of

PSYCHIATRIC DISABILITY

the information on VR comes from studying opiate addicts, and most
of that from methadone-maintenance programs.

Rehabilitation services for SUD patients have become available
only recently, presumably because of the stigma attached to this
disorder. State offices or divisions of VR have been in existence under
federal law since 1920. Mental disorders were added only in 1943,
and drug/alcohol abuse only in the 1954 revisions to the Rehabilitation Act (Black et al. 1981).

According to Wolkstein and Hastings-Black (1979); "Vocational
rehabilitation is a process in which the client is helped to understand
his/her problems and strengths, and is provided with services which
will help him/her become employable and obtain and hold a job."
Platt and Metzger (1985) believe that "understanding is less important than the provision of job-related skills—namely, interpersonal
skills required to obtain and retain employment." They cite reports
that suggest "the value of acquiring specific job-seeking behaviors
such as asking relevant questions, responding appropriately to questions about oneself, and otherwise demonstrating effective interpersonal behavior" (Platt and Metzger 1985). This view is confirmed by a
report that working patients on a methadone program felt work was
made most difficult by their fear, shyness, and lack of confidence
(Wolkstein et al. 1973). Yet another research group (Tucker et al. 1975)
advanced this concept further by stating that the vocational aim
should be to avoid "subprofessionalism and dead-end training" and
aim for "full professionalism and occupational flexibility." This was
to be achieved by assuring that treatment not only results in "pur-
poseful, rewarding, nonself-destructive, self-constructive life styles,"
but, also in "coping skills that will increase . . . competence and
personal potency."

Vocational rehabilitation can be conceptualized in a number of
ways. One version (Presnall 1975) considers it as a "three-way traffic
junction," involving: a positive-seeking person who was formerly a
drug user; a helping agency or therapeutic program with which the
ex-user is involved; an employer, or prospective employer. Another
view (Laskin and Lissner 1973) centers on a "survival center," consisting of six facets: (1) job-readiness assessment; (2) social-economic
understanding; (3) job training; (4) job placement; (5) mandatory
follow-up meetings; (6) optional follow-up meetings for which the
importance of attendance has been stressed.

One possible explanation for SUD patients needing VR may be
that narcotics use is one of several interrelated social responses to
labor-market failure (Helmer and Vietorisz 1974). Whether or not this
is true, SUD patients clearly show characteristics which prevent
them from fitting into the job market (Wolkstein and Hastings-Black
1979). These involve poor self-esteem, impulsiveness, rebelliousness,
impaired ability to tolerate frustration or delay gratification, difficulty conceptualizing needs, and, often, affect intolerance, alex-

ithymia, anhedonia, and paralytic ambivalence with regard to drug taking (Krystal 1985). They often possess poor survival and language skills (Presnall 1975). Work and educational backgrounds are poor, and vocational and cognitive skills are deficient. Legal difficulty and prison records are not uncommon. Social skills are often poorly developed (Caplovitz 1978). Finally, the stigma of addiction creates a great obstacle, although ironically it may be used by nonworking patients to rationalize their inactivity and defend against awareness of their lack of credentials (Wolkstein et al. 1973).

In addition to these factors, the inability of some methadone-maintenance programs to increase the rate of patient employment may be explained by the absence of VR services, the failure to define who provides the services and what they are, the inadequacy of therapy offered to render the patient job-ready, and the absence of community-based vocational and educational services (Wolkstein and Hastings-Black 1979; Wright 1973).

Employment definitely correlates with rehabilitative success (Stimmel et al. 1982; Lowinson and Ruiz 1981; Vaillant 1966; Dole and Joseph 1978). In terms of antecedent factors, employability is associated with the completion of high school (Fisch et al. 1973), a shorter period of addiction (presumably because of less involvement with the drug subculture) (Dole and Joseph 1978), and the presence of a stable work history and higher earnings on admission to the treatment facility (Koenigsberg and Royster 1975). While in treatment, employment correlates with reduced criminal activity, increased retention in treatment, stable mood, improved neuropsychological functioning, better coping skills, and the ability to remain abstinent from mood-altering drugs (Stimmel et al. 1982; Platt and Metzger 1985; Bass and Woodward 1978; Braunstein et al. 1983). Once rehabilitated (working), patients with personal problems tend to have lower-paying jobs, which tend to fill voids created by the abandonment of the addict life style. Methadone patients, in corporate employment, do as well with respect to performance, and better in the areas of punctuality and attendance, than non-SUD employees (Randell 1973; Jones et al. 1972; Yankowitz and Randell 1978).

Wolkstein and Hastings-Black (1979) summarize types of vocational services: developing a vocational plan; assessing the patient's motivation, expectations, self-appraisal, goals, and obstacles; determining short- and long-term goals; providing ongoing vocational counseling; providing training to remedy education or vocational deficits; establishing referral procedures to secure needed services; providing readiness assessment to prevent premature referral; providing job development; providing job placement; establishing follow-up interventions if problems arise. Richman (1966) considers that the success of such a VR service package depends on the "degree of identification with and conformity to conventional modes of behavior and the degree of criminality. . . . Work requires at least two attributes, namely the skill and ability to perform the task required and the social ability to be part of the social matrix which is the job environment." Others agree that VR success depends on personal qualities of the individual (Katzker et al. 1974), and Bass and Woodward (1978) have documented that recipients of VR show increases in employment rate, legitimate income, and positive attitude toward society, and decreases in time incarcerated.

Because a SUD patient's compliance with any treatment plan is often poor, various techniques have been suggested to increase and improve participation in VR. Direct involvement of the community and maximizing the use of the community in the rehabilitative process have been recommended (Milkman et al. 1978; Sackstein 1981). SUD has been treated, in the context of an Employee Assistance Program (Jackson 1983) and other job-based substance abuse programs, according to a "constructive-confrontation" strategy with employees whose job performance has been deteriorating (Trice 1979). This technique "is most effective when repeated discussions balance both constructive and confrontational elements, and when the presence of the alcoholism policy encouraged supervisors to take more actions with problem drinkers, legitimized those actions, and made the threat of discipline more credible" (Trice and Beyer 1984).

In a study of 77 patients (39 alcohol-abusing, 38 drug-abusing) discharged from a residential treatment program (Waldo and Gardiner 1984), the investigators found that the first three months after discharge constituted a "vocational crisis period." Those patients who participated in outpatient treatment following discharge had significantly higher levels of employment at three months.

VR groups have been utilized with some success, and have included vocational groups (various activities), personal adjustment groups (women, adolescents, assertiveness training, shared deficiencies), and ongoing, in-depth vocational development groups (Horn et al. 1978).

Milkman et al. (1978) summarized different strategies and models to increase compliance, as follows:

1. The use of a central intake, counseling, and referral unit, which focuses on VR, leaving other aspects of treatment to the drug/alcohol abuse program is beneficial. The VR unit staff accepts referrals and performs assessment, counseling, and referral.
2. Create a mobile team of vocational specialists which serves as an adjunct to the drug treatment community, sharing responsibility for VR with program staff. Vocational specialists visit programs, consult with patients and staff, and make referrals and recommendations.
3. Implement institutional linkages providing drug-treatment programs with direct institutional access to available and appropriate vocational resources.

4. Effect a community-education effort, in addition to or in place of one of the above, to improve the relationship of a community's drug-treatment programs with vocational programs and area employers.

Black et al. (1981) conclude: "We are dealing with a younger population generally without manifest physical handicaps and with disabilities that seem mainly to be educational, social, cultural, and that seem as though they might be overcome. The outlook for VR of substance abusers, therefore, should be optimistic. . . . Within the (different) categories (of patients) sight must not be lost of the many individual and unique differences in lifestyle, native intellectual endowment, drug-related organic cerebral damage, concomitant sociopathy, histories of work achievement, marital status, etc.

Platt and Metzger (1985) summarize the ideal VR program as follows:

1. It should meet an important need of a large proportion of the SUD population.
2. It is of brief duration—8 to 10 sessions—because of the difficulty in holding patients in treatment.
3. It is located in the clinic itself to maximize compliance.
4. It is not isolated from other treatment elements, but rather is integrated with the rest of the program.
5. Treatment staff need not possess advanced degrees, since such persons "may be too closely allied with a clinical philosophy and therapeutic style inconsistent with the problem-solving training approach (required). Also individuals highly familiar with the practical aspects of employment difficulties for addicts should be used."

CONCLUSION

In recent years, a number of modalities of treatment have been established for this population, each with its own goals and philosophy. The basic modalities in use are detoxification, drug-free treatment, therapeutic communities, narcotic antagonists, methadone maintenance, and vocational rehabilitation.

There is a body, a personality, and an external world. When a person suffers a SUD-related psychiatric disability, each of these areas of functioning is affected. The complex nature of SUD as a psychiatric disability highlights the need for a complete and thorough assessment of each individual, so appropriate care and treatment can be provided. Every case of disability presents unique challenges, but systematic approaches to identifying, understanding, and treating these problems are possible.

REFERENCES
Adriani J: Drug dependence in hospitalized patients, in Acute Drug Abuse Emergencies: A Treatment Manual. Edited by Bourne PG. New York, Academic Press, 1976

Allison M. Hubbard RL, Rachal JV: Treatment Process in Methadone, Residential and Outpatient Drug-Free Programs. Rockville, MD, National Institute on Drug Abuse, 1985

American Medical Association: Guide to the Evaluation of Permanent Impairment, second edition. Chicago, IL, American Medical Association, 1984

American Psychiatric Association: Diagnostic and Statistical Manual of Mental Disorders, third edition. Washington, DC, American Psychiatric Association, 1980

American Psychiatric Association: Diagnostic and Statistical Manual of Mental Disorders, third edition, revised. Washington, DC, American Psychiatric Association, 1987

Balter M: Drug abuse: a conceptual analysis and overview of the current situation, in Drug Use: Epidemiological and Sociological Approaches. Edited by Josephson E, Carroll E. New York, Wiley, 1974

Bass UF, Woodward JA: Skills Training and Employment for Ex:Addicts in Washington D.C. National Institute on Drug Abuse Treatment Services Report. Washington DC, U.S. Government Printing Office, 1978

Black BJ, Kase HM, Benney C: Vocational rehabilitation, in Substance Abuse: Clinical Problems and Perspectives. Edited by Lowinson JR, Ruiz P. Baltimore, Williams & Wilkins, 1981

Bluestone H, McGahee CL, Klein NR: Training and education, in Substance Abuse: Clinical Problems and Perspectives. Edited by Lowinson JH, Ruiz P. Baltimore, Williams & Wilkins, 1981

Blumer D, Heilbron M: Antidepressant treatment for chronic pain. Psychiatric Annals 14:796–800, 1984

Braunstein WB, Powell BJ, McGowan JP, et al: Employment factors in outpatient recovery of alcoholics: a multivariate study. Addictive Behavior 8:345–351, 1983

Burros MG, Bozzone S: Early vocational rehabilitation of alcoholic outpatients, in Critical Concerns in the Field of Drug Abuse; Proceedings of the Third National Drug Abuse Conference. Edited by Schecter A, Alksne H, Kaufman E. new York, Marcel Dekker, 1978

Caplovitz D: The working addict, in Critical Concerns in the Field of Drug Abuse; Proceedings of the Third National Drug Abuse Conference. Edited by Schecter A, Alksne EH, Kaufman E. New York, Marcel Dekker, 1978

Casper RC, Eckart ED, Halmi KA: Bulimia: its incidence and clinical importance in patients with anorexia nervosa. Arch Gen Psychiatry 37:1030–1035, 1980

Childress AR, McLellan AT, O'Brien CP: Assessment and extinction of conditioned withdrawal-like responses in an integrated treatment for opiate dependence, in Problems of Drug Dependence. Proceedings of the 46th Annual Scientific Meeting, the Committee on Problems of Drug Dependence, NIDA Research Monograph 55. Edited by Harris LS. Rockville, MD, National Institute on Drug Abuse, 1985

Cloninger CR: The link between hysteria and sociopathy: an integrative model of pathogenesis based on clinical, genetic and neurophysiological observations, in Psychiatric Diagnosis: Exploration of Biological Predictors. Edited by Akiskal HSA, Webb WL. New York, Spectrum Publications, 1978

Cohen M, Klein D: Posthospital adjustment of psychiatrically hospitalized drug users. Arch Gen Psychiatry 31:221–227, 1974

Cohen M, Korts D, Hanbury R, et al: The effect of alcoholism in methadone-maintained persons on productive activity: a randomized control trial. Alcoholism: Clinical and Experimental Research 6:358–361, 1982

Cohen MJ: Treatment aspects of substance abuse, in The Providers Guide to Hospital-Based Psychiatric Services. Edited by Collins AH, Krause HH. Rockville, MD, Aspen Systems Corp., 1986

Cohen MJ, Stimmel B: The use of methadone in narcotic dependency, in Treatment Aspects of Drug Dependence. Edited by Schecter A. West Palm Beach, FL, CRC Press, 1978, pp. 1–33

Cohen MJ, Hanbury R, Stimmel B: Abuse of amitriptyline. JAMA 240:1372–1373, 1978

Cohen S: Cocaine anonymous. Drug Abuse and Alcoholism Newsletter 13:3, April 1984a

Cohen S: Drugs in the workplace. J Clin Psychiatry 12:4–8, 1984b

Cohen S: The chronic intractable benign pain patient. Drug Abuse and Alcoholism Newsletter 13, May 1984c

Cranshaw JA, Mullen PE: A study of benzhexol abuse. Br J Psychiatry 145:300–303, 1984

Dackis CA, Gold MS: Opiate addiction and depression: cause or effect? Drug Alcohol Depend 11:105–109, 1983

Dackis CA, Gold MS: Depression in opiate addicts, in Substance Abuse and Psychopathology. Edited by Mirin SM. Washington DC, American Psychiatric Press, 1984

Dackis CA, Stuckey RFL: Psychopharmacologic treatment of the alcoholic. Fair Oaks Hospital Psychiatry Letter 2, July 1984

Dackis CA, Gurpegui M, Pottash ALC, et al: Methadone induced hypoadrenalism. Lancet 2:1167, 1982

Dackis CA, Pottash ALC, Annitto W, et al: DST specificity for depression in opiate addicts. Paper presented at the 136th Annual Meeting of the American Psychiatric Association, New York, May 1983

Dackis CA, Bailey J, Pottash ALC, et al: Specificity of the DST and the TRH test for major depression in alcoholics. Am J Psychiatry 141:680–683, 1984

Dole VP, Joseph H: Long-term outcome of patients treated with methadone maintenance. Ann NY Acad Sci 311:181–189, 1978

Dupont RI, Goldstein A, O'Donnell J (Eds): Handbook on Drug Abuse. Washington, DC, U.S. Department of Health, Education and Welfare, 1979

Emrick CD, Lassen CL, Edwards MT: Nonprofessional peers as therapeutic agents, in Effective Psychotherapy: A Handbook of Research. Edited by Gurman AS, Razin AM. Oxford, Pergamon Press, 1977

Estroff TW, Dackis CA, Sweeney DR, et al: Drug abuse and coexistent bipolar disorder. Presented at the 137th Annual Meeting of the American Psychiatric Association, Los Angeles, May 5–11, 1984

Fisch A, Boudreau D, et al: Vocational rehabilitation—a treatment stumbling block. Proceedings of the Fifth National Conference on Methadone Treatment. New York, National Association for the Prevention of Addiction to Narcotics, 1973

Freud A: The Ego and the Mechanisms of Defense. New York, International Universities Press, 1946

Garfinkel PE, Moldofsky H, Garner H: The heterogeneity of anorexia nervosa. Arch Gen Psychiatry 37:1036–1038, 1980

Gawin FH, Kleber HD: Cocaine abuse treatment. Arch Gen Psychiatry 41:903–908, 1984

Gerston A, Cohen MJ, Stimmel B: Alcoholism, heroin dependency and methadone maintenance: alternatives and aids to conventional methods of therapy. Am J Drug Alcohol Abuse 4:517–531, 1977

Gleaton TJ, Goren S: The adolescent drug epidemic and the chronic young adult patient: is there a link? Fair Oaks Hospital Psychiatry Letter 3:2, 1985

Gold MS: 800-COCAINE. New York, Bantam Books, 1984

Gold MS, Pottash ALC: Endorphins, locus coeruleus, clonidine and lofexidine: a mechanism for opiate withdrawal and new nonopiate treatments. Alcohol Subst Abuse 1:33–52, 1981

Gold MS, Pottash ALC, Sweeney DR, et al: Rapid opiate detoxification: clinical evidence of antidepressant and anti-panic effects of opiates. Am J Psychiatry 136:982–983, 1979

Gold MS, Pottash ALC, Extein I, et al: Anti-endorphin effects of methadone. Lancet 2:973–974, 1980a

Gold MS, Pottash ALC, Sweeney DR, et al: Clonidine decreases opiate withdrawal-related anxiety: possible opiate noradrenergic interaction in anxiety and panic. Subst Alcohol Actions Misuse 1:239–246, 1980b

Gold MS, Pottash ALC, Extein I, et al: Evidence for an endorphin dysfunction in methadone addicts: lack of an ACTH response to naloxone. Drug Alcohol Depend 8:257–262, 1981

Gold MS, Pottash ALC, Extein I: Clonidine: Inpatient studies from 1978 to 1981. J Clin Psychiatry 43:35–38, 1982a

Gold MS, Dackis CA, Pottash ALC, et al: Naltrexone, opiate addiction, and endorphins. Med Res Rev 2:211–246, 1982b

Goodwin DW: Studies of familial alcoholism: a review. J Clin Psychiatry 45:14–17, 1984

Haertzen CH, Hooks NT: Changes in personality and subjective experience associated with the chronic administration and withdrawal of opiates. J Nerv Ment Dis 148:606–613, 1969

Haglund R, Schuckit M: The epidemiology of alcoholism, in Alcoholism: Development, Consequences and Interventions. Edited by Estes N, Heineman ME. St. Louis, C.V. Mosby, 1977

Halmi KA, Falk JR: Anorexia nervosa: a study of outcome discriminators in exclusive dieters and bulimics. J Am Acad Child Psychiatry 21:4–8, 1982

Hanbury R, Sturiano V, Stimmel B: The role of vocational rehabilitation in methadone maintenance: problems establishing criteria for success. Proceedings of the Fifth National Conference on Methadone Treatment. New York, National Association for the Prevention of Addiction to Narcotics, 1973

Hanlon JJ: Principles of Public Health Administration. St. Louis, C.V. Mosby, 1963

Helmer J, Vietorisz T: Drug Use, the Labor Market and Class Conflict. Washington, DC, The Drug Abuse Council, 1974

Ho AKS, Allen JP: Alcohol and the opiate receptor: interactions with the endogenous opiates. Adv Alcohol Subst Abuse 1:53–75, 1981

Horn R, Cetrangal M, Randell J, et al: Facilitating vocational development: use of vocational rehabilitation groups in methadone maintenance treatment, in Critical Concerns in the Field of Drug Abuse. Proceedings of the Third National Drug Abuse Conference. Edited by Schecter A, Alksne H, Kaufman E. New York, Marcel Dekker, 1978

Jackson GW: Prevention and alcoholism: the employee assistance program in health care institutions. Bull NY Acad Med 59:245–249, 1983

Jasinski DR: Opiate withdrawal syndrome: acute and protracted aspects. Ann NY Acad Sci 362:183–186, 1981

Johnston LD, O'Malley PM, Backman JG: Use of Licit and Illicit Drugs by America's High School Students 1975–1984. Rockville, MD, National Institute on Drug Abuse, 1985

Jones SW, Flowers E, Weldon CL, et al: Job counseling for the unskilled methadone maintenance patient. Proceedings of the Fourth National Conference on Methadone Treatment. New York, National Association for the Prevention of Addiction to Narcotics, 1972

Katzker E, Steer RA, Schut J: Differentiation of long-term methadone patients from their admission cohorts. Int J Addict 14:281–287, 1974

Kaufman E: The psychodynamics of opiate dependence: a new look. Am J Drug Alcohol Abuse 1:349–370, 1974

Khantzian EJ: Self selection and progression in drug dependence. Psychiatry Digest 36:19–22, 1975

Khantzian EJ: On the psychological predisposition for opiate and stimulant dependence. Fair Oaks Hospital Psychiatry Letter 3:1, 1985

Khantzian EJ, Khantzian NJ: Cocaine addiction: is there a psychological predisposition? Psychiatric Annals 14:753–759, 1984

Khantzian EJ, Treece CJ: Psychodynamics of drug dependence, in Psychodynamics of Drug Dependence. NIDA Research Monograph 12. Edited by Blaine JD, Julius DA. Rockville, MD, National Institute on Drug Abuse, 1977

Khantzian EJ, Mack JE, Schatzberg AF: Heroin use as an attempt to cope: clinical observations. Am J Psychiatry 131:160–164, 1974

Kissin B: Alcoholism and drug dependence, in Understanding Human Behavior in Health and Disease. Edited by Simon RC, Pardes H. Baltimore, Williams & Wilkins, 1977

Kleber HD, Gold MS: The use of psychotropic drugs in the treatment of methadone maintained narcotic addicts. Ann NY Acad Sci 311:81–98, 1978

Kleber HD, Weissman MM, Rounsaville BJ, et al: Imipramine as treatment for depression in addicts. Arch Gen Psychiatry 40:649–653, 1983

Koenigsberg L, Royster E: Jobs for Drug Abuse Treatment Program Clients. Rockville, MD, National Institute on Drug Abuse, 1975

Kreek MJ: Opioid interactions with alcohol. Adv Alcohol Subst Abuse 3:35–46, 1984

Krystal H: Some problems encountered in attempting psychoanalytic psychotherapy with substance dependent individuals. Drug Abuse and Alcoholism Newsletter 14(1), February 1985

Laskin J, Lissner A: Survival skills: the ex-addict's only hope. Vol. 4 of the monograph based upon State of the Art Editorial Seminar, Mills College, 1973

Lerner J: Evaluation of disability resulting from psychiatric conditions, in Compensation in Psychiatric Disability and Rehabilitation. Edited by Leedy J. Springfield, IL, Charles C Thomas, 1971

Lowinson JH, Ruiz P (Eds): Substance Abuse: Clinical Problems and Perspectives. Baltimore, MD, Williams & Wilkins, 1981

Ludwig AM: Principles of Clinical Psychiatry. New York, Macmillan, 1980

McLellan AT, Woody, G, O'Brien CP: Development of psychiatric illness in drug abusers. N Engl J Med 301:1310–1314, 1979

Mendelson JF, Mello NK: Experimental analysis of drinking behavior of chronic alcoholics. Ann NY Acad Sci 133:828–845, 1966

Milkman H, Frosch WA: On the preferential abuse of heroin and amphetamine. J Nerv Ment Dis 165:242–248, 1973

Milkman RH, Center LJ, Toborg MA: Ex-addict re-entry: strategies for maximizing the use of community services, in Critical Concerns in the Field of Drug Abuse. Proceedings of the Third National Drug Abuse Conference. Edited by Schecter A, Alksne H, Kaufman E. New York, Marcel Dekker, 1978

Mintz J, O'Brien C, Woody G, et al: Depression in treated narcotic addicts, ex-addicts, and suicide attempters. Am J Drug Alcohol Abuse 6:385–396, 1979

Mirin SM: Introduction, in Substance Abuse and Psychopathology. Edited by Mirin SM. Washington, DC, American Psychiatric Press, 1984

Mirin SM, Meyer RE, McNamee HB: Psychopathology and mood during heroin use: acute vs. chronic effects. Arch Gen Psychiatry 33:1503–1508, 1976

Mirin SM, Weiss RD, Sollogub A, et al: Affective illness in substance abusers, in Substance Abuse and Psychopathology. Edited by Mirin SM. Washington, DC, American Psychiatric Press, 1984a

Mirin SM, Weiss RD, Sollogub A, et al: Psychopathology in the families of drug abusers, in Substance Abuse and Psychopathology. Edited by Mirin SM. Washington, DC, American Psychiatric Press, 1984b

Morton DA: Medical proof of Social Security Disability. St. Paul, West Publishing Co, 1983

Mullaney JA, Trippett CJ: Alcohol dependence and phobias: clinical description and relevance. Br J Psychiatry 135:565–573, 1979

Nurco D, Lerner M: Occupational skills and life-styles of narcotic addicts, in Sociological Aspects of Drug Dependence. Edited by Winick C. Cleveland, CRC Press, 1974

O'Brien CP, Chadock B, Woody G, et al: Systematic extinction of narcotic drug use using narcotic antagonists, in Committee on Problems of Drug Dependency. Washington, DC, National Academy of Sciences/National Research Council, Academy Press, 1974

O'Brien CP, Childress AR, McLellan T, et al: Use of naltrexone to extinguish opioid-conditioned responses. J Clin Psychiatry 45:39–41, 1984a

O'Brien CP, Woody GE, McLellan AT: Psychiatric disorders in opioid-dependent patients. J Clin Psychiatry 45:9–13, 1984b

O'Donnell J: Narcotic Addicts in Kentucky. Washington, DC, National Institute of Mental Health, 1969

Parry S: The undertreatment for pain. Psychiatric Annals 14:808-811, 1984

Pfeffer AZ, Ruble DC: Chronic psychoses and addiction to morphine. Archives of Neurology and Psychiatry 56:665, 1948

Pheterson A, Dackis CA, Gold MS, et al: Plasma cortisol levels in opite addicts before and after detoxification. Proceedings of the Society for Neuroscience, Abstract 123.11, 1983

Pinsker H: Addicted patients in hospital psychiatric units. Psychiatric Annals 13:619–623, 1983

Platt JJ, Metzger D: The role of employment in the rehabilitation of heroin addicts, in Progress in the Development of Cost-Effective Treatment for Drug Abusers. NIDA Research Monograph 58. Edited by Ashery PS. Rockville, MD, National Institute on Drug Abuse, 1985

Porter J, Jick H. Addiction rare in patients treated with narcotics. N Engl J Med 302:123, 1980

Presnall LF: The employment and training of ex-drug users: a three-way interaction, in Developments in the Field of Drug Abuse. Proceedings of the First National Drug Abuse Conference. Edited by Senay E, Shorty V, Alksne H. Cambridge, MA, Schenkman, 1975

Prusoff BA, Thompson DW, Sholomskas D, et al: Psychosocial stressors and depression among former heroin dependent patients maintained on methadone. J Nerv Ment Dis 165:57–63, 1977

Pullen GP, Best NR, Maguire J: Anticholinergic drug abuse: a common problem? Br Med J 289:612–613, 1984

Quitkin FM, Rifkin A, Kaplan J, et al: Phobic anxiety syndrome complicated by drug dependence and addiction. Arch Gen Psychiatry 27:159–162, 1972

Randell J: Employment discrimination of the methadone patient. Proceedings of the Fifth National Conference on Methadone Treatment. New York, National Association for the Prevention of Addiction to Narcotics, 1973

Richman S: Return to productive community living: reflections on the twenty-year program experience of the New York State Vocational Rehabilitation Agency. Washington, DC, U.S. Department of Health, Education and Welfare, 1966

Ross S: The function of job rehabilitation in a methadone maintenance program: an examination of the interaction of treatment and job rehabilitation. Proceedings of the Fourth National Conference on Methadone Treatment. New York, National Association for the Prevention of Addiction to Narcotics, 1972

Rounsaville BJ, Weissman MM, Rosenberger PH, et al: Detecting depressive disorders in drug abusers: a comparison of screening instruments. J Affective Disord 1:255–267, 1979

Rounsaville BJ, Weissman MM, Wilber CH, et al: The heterogeneity of psychiatric diagnosis in treated opiate addicts. Arch Gen Psychiatry 39:161–166, 1982a

Rounsaville BJ, Weissman MM, Crits-Cristoph C, et al: Diagnosis and symptoms of depression in opiate addicts. Arch Gen Psychiatry 39:151–156, 1982b

Rounsaville Bj, Glazer WQ, Wilber CH et al: Short-term interpersonal psychotherapy in methadone-maintained opiate addicts. Arch Gen Psychiatry 40:629–636, 1983

Rubinstein J: Abuse of antiparkinsonism drugs. JAMA 239:2365–2366, 1978

Sackstein E: Drugs and youth: an international perspective on vocational and social reintegration. Bull Narc 33:33–45, 1981

Salzman B: Substance abusers with psychiatric problems, in Substance Abuse: Clinical Problems and Perspectives. Edited by Lowinson JH, Ruiz P. Baltimore, Williams & Wilkins, 1981

Schooff KG, Buck R, West P: Psychiatric consultation for the chronic pain patient who abuses drugs. Psychiatric Annals 14:801–807, 1984

Shopsin B, Kline NS: Monoamine oxidase inhibitors: potential for drug abuse. Biol Psychiatry 11:451–456, 1976

Siever LJ, Insel TR, Uhde TW: Biogenetic factors in personalities, in Current Perspectives on Personality Disorders. Edited by Frosch JP. Washington, DC, American Psychiatric Press, 1983

Snyder SH: Catecholamines in the brain as mediators of amphetamine psychosis. Arch Gen Psychiatry 27:169–179, 1972

Stabenou JR, Hesselblock VM: Psychopathology in alcoholics and their families and vulnerability to alcoholism: a review and new findings, in Substance Abuse and Psychopathology. Edited by Mirin SM. Washington, DC, American Psychiatric Press, 1984

Stimmel B, Cohen M, Hanbury R: Alcoholism and polydrug abuse in persons on methadone maintenance. Ann NY Acad Sci 311:99–109, 1978a

Stimmel B, Goldberg J, Cohen M: Detoxification from methadone maintenance: risk factors associated with relapse to narcotic use. Ann NY Acad Sci 311:173–180,1978b

Stimmel B, Korts D, Cohen M, et al: Opiate addiction and alcoholism: the feasibility of combined treatment approaches. Ann NY Acad Sci 362:50–56, 1981

Stimmel B, Hanbury R, Cohen M: Factors affecting detoxification from methadone. Journal of Psychiatric Treatment Evaluation 4:377–381, 1982

Stimmel B, Cohen M, Sturiano V, et al: Is treatment for alcoholism effective in persons on methadone maintenance? Am J Psychiatry 140:862–866, 1983

Tennant FS, Day CM, Ungeleider JT: Screening for drugs and alcohol abuse in the general medical population. JAMA 242:533–535, 1979

Tolis G, Dent R, Guyda H: Opiates, prolactin and the dopamine receptor. J Clin Endocrinol Metab 57:200–203, 1978

Trice HM: Job based alcohol and drug abuse programs: recent program developments and research, in Handbook on Drug Abuse. Edited by Dupont RI, Goldstein A, O'Donnell J. Washington, DC, U.S. Department of Health, Education and Welfare, 1979

Trice HM, Beyer JM: Work-related outcomes of the constructive-confrontation strategy in a job-based alcoholism program. J Stud Alcohol 45:393–404, 1984

Tucker RC, Bryant J, Bryant R, et al: Career development as an adjunct for the rehabilitative process, in Developments in the Field of Drug Abuse. Proceedings of the First National Drug Abuse Conference. Edited by Senay E, Shorty V, Alksne H. Cambridge, MA, Schenkman, 1975, pp. 383–391

Uhde TW, Redmond DE, Kleber HD: Psychosis in the opioid addicted patient: assessment and treatment. J Clin Psychiatry 43:240–247, 1982

U.S. Department of Health, Education, and Welfare, National Institute on Alcohol Abuse and Alcoholism: First Special Report to the U.S. Congress on Alcohol and Health. DHEW Publication No. HSM 72–9099, Wshington, DC, U.S. Government Printing Office, 1971

Vaillant GE: A twelve-year follow-up of New York narcotic addicts, IV: some characteristics and determinants of abstinence. Am J Psychiatry 125:573–586, 1966

Vaillant GE: Dangers of psychotherapy in the treatment of alcoholism, in Dynamic Approaches to the Understanding and Treatment of Alcoholism. Edited by Bean M, Zinberg N. New York, Free Press, 1981

Verebey K: Opioids and psychological disorders. Advances in Alcohol and Substance Abuse 1:101–123, 1981

Waldo M, Gardiner J: Vocational adjustment patterns of alcohol and drug misusers following treatment. J Stud Alcohol 45:547–549, 1984

Weissman MM, Myers JK: Clinical depression in alcoholism. Am J Psychiatry 137:372–373, 1980

Weissman MM, Slobetz F, Prusoff BB, et al: Clinical depression among narcotic addicts on methadone in the community. Am J Psychiatry 133:1434–1438, 1976

Weissman MM, Pottanger M, Kleber HD, et al: Symptom pattern in primary and secondary depression: a comparison of primary depressives with depressed opiate addicts, alcoholics and schizophrenics. Arch Gen Psychiatry 34:854–862, 1977

Whitehead CC: Methadone pseudowithdrawal syndrome: paradigm for a psychopharmacological model of opiate addiction. Psychosom Med 36:189–198, 1974

Wikler A: Psychodynamic study of a patient during experimental self-regulated readdiction of morphine. Psychiatry Q 26:270–293, 1952

Wikler A: Opioid Dependence: Mechanism and Treatment. New York, Plenum Press, 1980

Winick C: Epidemiology of substance abuse, in Substance Abuse—Clinical Problems and Perspectives. Edited by Lowinson JH, Ruiz P. Baltimore, Williams & Wilkins, 1981

Winokur A, et al: Withdrawal reaction from long term, low dosage administration of diazepam. Arch Gen Psychiatry 37:101–105, 1980

Wolkstein EJ, Hastings-Black D: Vocational rehabilitation, in Handbook on Drug Abuse. Edited by Dupont RI, Goldstein A, O'Donnell J. Washington, DC, U.S. Department of Health, Education, and Welfare, 1979

Wolkstein E, Balsam M, Cetrangal M, et al: Work: what difference does it make? Proceedings of the Fifth National Conference on Methadone Treatment. New York, National Association for the Prevention of Addiction to Narcotics, 1973

Woody GE: Use of antidepressants along with methadone in maintenance patients. Paper presented at the Conference on Opioids in Mental Illness: Theories, Clinical Observations and Treatment Possibilities. New York, October 29, 1981

Woody GE, Blaine J: Depression in narcotic addicts: quite possibly more than a chance association, in Handbook on Drug Abuse. Edited by Dupont RI, Goldstein A, O'Donnell J. Washington DC, National Institute on Drug Abuse, 1979

Woody GE, Luborsky L, McLellan AT, et al: Psychotherapy for opiate addicts: does it help? Arch Gen Psychiatry 40:639–645, 1983

Woody GE, McLellan AT, Luborsky L, et al: Severity of psychiatric symptoms as a predictor of benefits from psychotherapy. Am J Psychiatry 141:1172–1177, 1984

Wright M: Vocational rehabilitation: an intimate part of treatment. Vol 4 of the monograph based upon State of the Art Editorial Seminar, Mills College, 1973

Wurmser L: Psychoanalytic considerations of the etiology of compulsive drug use. J Am Psychoanal Assoc 22:820–843, 1974

Wurmser L: The Hidden Dimension. New York, Jason Aronson, 1978

Yankowitz RB, Randell J: Corporate employment and the methadone patient, in Critical Concerns in the Field of Drug Abuse. Proceedings of the Third National Drug Abuse Conference. Edited by Schecter A, Alksne H, Kaufman E. New York, Marcel Dekker, 1978

Zinberg NE: Addiction and ego function. Psychoanal Study Child 30:507–588, 1975

7

Psychiatric Disability in Children and Adolescents: Problems in Services and Financing

Nancy C. A. Roeske, M.D.*
Mary P. Crosby

T he problem in financing child and adolescent mental illness treatment has its roots in three facts: the historical societal attitudes toward parental rights and responsibilities; World War II's profound effect on the federal government's attitude toward health care; and the number and complexity of illnesses of children and adolescents that require psychiatric intervention.

It is only within this century that parents' absolute right to make decisions about their child's needs and contributions to the family has been overruled by laws governing the best interests of the child. The 1980s have seen a reemergence of legal disputes over the parents'

---

* Nancy C.A. Roeske, M.D., died on April 21, 1986. This chapter is an excellent representation of her professional concern about the lack of adequate financing for child mental illness services. Dr. Roeske accepted any assignment that would allow her to educate peers and the public to the difficulties and injustices in securing help for mentally ill children and adolescents. She was a member of the APA Committee on Professional Liability Insurance, and the APA delegate to the National Consortium for Child Mental Health Services (1983–1986). As a member of the American Academy of

rights to decide what is best for their child. The American ethos of individual self-determination ambivalently supports parental power. This national attitude has had other forms of expression since World War II in government decisions about health care. In the 1950s and 1960s, two premises guided government health policy: (1) Americans need more care, and (2) medical professionals and private voluntary institutions are best equipped to decide how to organize those services.

However, in the area of mental health care, the civil rights movement, reinforced by the availability of psychotropic medication and the beginning of concern about cost containment, resulted both in deinstitutionalization of patients from large public institutions, and the federal mandate to establish care of the mentally ill within the community. From its inception, the community mental health center movement has had an umbrella function, recognizing the interrelationship among education, vocational training, social experiences, medication, and mental health. Unfortunately, the complexity of needs of the mentally ill has served also to help undermine the recognition of the physicianhood of psychiatrists, especially child psychiatrists. Furthermore, the past decade's emphasis upon cost containment has fueled other questions about the medical basis of treatment recommendations. It is easier to delineate and assess procedures than it is services. The problems involved in the evaluation and treatment of mentally ill children and adolescents are among the most complex examples of all of these issues. Adequate treatment usually involves family members. If hospitalization is required, it may extend over several years, as will outpatient care. The child or adolescent may live in a group home or attend a boarding school since many emotionally disturbed children do not need hospitalization. Instead, these children need an opportunity to grow in a structured environment with appropriate mental health interventions away from families which destructively undermine their psychological development (Roeske 1984).

On the one hand, the medical care of children and adolescents, like adults, is financed, for the most part, by the major insurers; unfortunately, children receive the same coverage for their psychiatric care as adults, depending on the benefit package. On the other hand, in addition to the major insurers, children have opportunities to receive publicly provided services and treatment that adults do not. It is difficult to find data that show the unique treatment, utilization, and reimbursement needs of children and adolescents. Much of

Child and Adolescent Psychiatry and its chairperson of the Work Group on Consumer Issues, she was unyielding in her efforts to heighten awareness of the serious damage caused by inadequate or unavailable treatment for emotionally disturbed children and adolescents. Dr. Roeske was a child psychiatrist dedicated to the well-being of her patients, to the growth of her specialty, and to the advocacy for public policies that recognize children in their own rights.

the unevenness and uncertainty about financing child mental illness treatment reflects this lack of data, as well as the issues of ethos about parenting and the determination of a medical reason for insurance reimbursement, or the state of public support. It is difficult to find statistics that distinguish between the payments for children and adolescents and adults. Contributing to the problem of reimbursement is the lack of information about how many children there are who should be receiving treatment by a mental health professional, but who are not now in care. In recent months, the question of overutilization of psychiatric care for children and adolescents has been raised in the United States Congress in connection with the increased treatment of adolescents at long-term care facilities. Inadequate comprehension about the years of underutilization, about determination of diagnoses and appropriate treatment, and about inadequate reimbursement have generated questions that could damage existing and future care systems for impaired adolescents (Egan 1985).

In summary, the treatment needs of children and adolescents are not the same as those of adults. Yet, as this brief introduction outlines, the interplay among political, economic, and social factors impedes the investigation of needs and the development of a national policy on child and adolescent mental illness care.

SCOPE OF CHILDREN'S PSYCHIATRIC DISABILITIES

In 1969, the Joint Commission on the Mental Health of Children found that approximately 10 percent of the then 55–60 million American children were in need of mental health services (Joint Commission 1969). By 1978, the President's Commission on Mental Health had moved the estimate to as high as 15 percent (President's Commission 1978). More recent review of the past reports have now calculated that the 7–10 million children in need of services include approximately 3 million who are seriously emotionally disturbed (Knitzer 1982).

Children suffering from schizophrenic disorders, infantile autism, major affective disorders, pervasive developmental disorders, mental retardation, and alcohol and substance abuse often have the highest severity of illness rating. This means treatment needs are long term and expensive in terms of the hours of care needed from child psychiatrists and other mental health professionals (American Academy of Child Psychiatry 1982). The severely ill and the chronically ill are more easily assessed, but there are also millions of children at risk for emotional illness which can increase in severity if left untreated. Many of these at-risk children are those lacking access to both existing, less-than-adequate services or to a means of reimbursement for what is available.

In 1978, the American Academy of Pediatrics' Task Force on Pediatric Education identified several groups of children at high risk

(American Academy of Pediatrics 1982); using criteria integrating the impact of stress or illness and the child's living situation, the task force selection included children of low-income families, children with physical handicaps, foster children, institutionalized mentally retarded children, criminally detained youths, children of mothers who have had inadequate or no prenatal care or who are malnourished, children of a single parent, children of racial minorities, and children of migrant workers (American Academy of Child Psychiatry 1982). A major mental illness for which these children are at risk is depression. For two decades, child psychiatrists have called attention to the fact that depression exists in children (American Academy of Child Psychiatry 1982; Malmquist 1971a, 1971b). Yet, convincing insurance companies and policy makers that childhood depression is a serious, growing problem which warrants investigation continues to be problematic. We must know why increasing numbers of children and adolescents commit suicide or make repeated suicide attempts, or turn to drugs and alcohol or become mothers and fathers when they are still children themselves (Poznanski 1985). In addition, there is the question of the relationship between depression and the soaring rates of violent behavior in adolescents.

Reimbursement policies and politics have not yet begun to match the changing and expanding needs of children and adolescents in today's world. Reimbursement for their emotional care often gets caught up in the controversies of modern life; of runaway or throwaway children; of overindulgence or underprivilege; of disconnected networks of federal, state, and local agencies; and of insurance companies scrambling to keep up with the changes in their own industry as well as in the children their policies may or may not serve.

The American Academy of Child Psychiatry in its 1982 book on the future of child psychiatry, a three-year project of the association, commented on reimbursement policies now being used:

> Unfortunately, many clinicians are now confronted with a situation in which the fiscal tail wags the therapeutic dog. Instead of being able to make decisions concerning the most appropriate intervention for a given child on the basis of clinical needs, they may have to base their decisions on policies determined by individuals, whether in the public or private sector, who have no clinical background and are assigning automatic dollar values to certain units of care regardless of the nature of the case. . . . Often, these arbitrary limitations are applied simply because no adjustments are made for developmental issues, standards for adults thus being used for the delivery of care to children. (American Academy of Child Psychiatry 1982, p. 61)

As noted earlier, the cost of long-term inpatient treatment of children and adolescents has been a major stumbling block in developing reimbursement plans. Long-term treatment often could be abbreviated by adequate community support services; however, the critical shortage of such services has been well documented (American Psychiatric Association 1984). Few communities enjoy the types of aftercare services that provide secure, quality treatment reinforcement. A federal program, the Child and Adolescent Service System Program (CASSP), is an attempt to help states and communities improve the network between service agencies so that child and adolescent inpatient or residential care can be reduced, but this effort is still in its infancy (Isaacs 1984).

Another recent innovation in health care economics has been the Medicare Prospective Payment System (PPS) which began in 1983. Reimbursement under PPS is made prospectively by assigning inpatient length of stay (LOS) according to diagnosis. The lengths of stay were developed by a Yale study and are known as Diagnosis-Related Groups (DRGs). If patients are hospitalized longer than the assigned DRG, the hospital must make up the cost differential, and if the patient is discharged earlier than the DRG extends, the hospital still receives payment for the approved full number of days. Physicians' fees are not included in the DRGs.

Psychiatric hospitalization has been exempted from the Medicare PPS because the original study did not adequately test psychiatric DRGs. However, there is a possibility that the government will eventually require the use of DRGs for all inpatient care as well as for physicians' fees. Several studies have analyzed psychiatric hospitalization data and recommended that DRGs are not appropriate for inpatient treatment of psychiatric illnesses. Children and adolescents are distinguishable for their high use of hospital resources, which could have a negative effect, should DRGs ever be adopted for psychiatric hospitalization. One of the studies examining the use of the DRG system for psychiatric care is being done by the Neuropsychiatric Institute in Los Angeles. Dr. Susan Essock-Vitale has commented on the early findings for children and DRGs (in a presentation sponsored by the National Institute of Mental Health, in 1985):

> We must ask whether the average costs of treating a psychotic child and a psychotic adult are likely to be the same. The NPI data clearly suggest that they are not. . . . Another depressing thought is that children, identified by NPI data as high-cost patients, may become targets for discriminatory admission policies unless age is incorporated into psychiatric DRGs.

Since children are being shown to have longer lengths of stay and greater use of hospital resources, this new information can be a good or bad harbinger, depending on how it is used. Instead of the data being used to justify increasing the reimbursement for certain age groups, there is the threat that children will be perceived as such money losers for hospitals that they will be curtailed or excluded from care.

It must follow that the rise of for-profit hospitals places greater emphasis on the profits earned from treating patients. When there is one segment of the population not providing any profit and even causing a loss, that segment may be funneled into a very small number of facilities. Optimistically, there is the possibility the studies could result in more specialized care and treatment, with separate coverage being written for children and adolescents. This outcome could be one response to the advocacy efforts of many child psychiatrists and child mental health supporters.

REIMBURSEMENT NOW
For those children and adolescents currently being treated, the financing, other than private, out-of-pocket reimbursement is usually drawn from one of the four major types of insurer: (1) Blue Cross/Blue Shield; (2) Medicaid, including the Early and Periodic Screening, Diagnosis, and Treatment (EPSDT) program; (3) health maintenance organizations (HMOs), both traditional HMOs and the newer independent-practice HMOs (IPA/HMO); and (4) preferred-provider organizations (PPO) (Roeske 1984; American Society of Internal Medicine 1984; Sharfstein et al. 1984).

Not all of the financing methods adequately cover the continuum of services needed for treating child and adolescent mental illnesses. Reimbursement is needed, and should be provided for psychiatric treatments, which include behavioral assessment and other evaluations, inpatient hospitalization, outpatient visits, partial hospitalization, work with families; collaboration with teachers and others closely involved with the child; consultations in hospitals, schools, correctional institutions, and with other state and community agencies; and, last but not least in importance, individual and group therapy (American Academy of Child Psychiatry 1982). If this range of coverage were provided by public and private insurers, the diverse needs of children and adolescents could be met. Unfortunately, mental illness insurance benefits have been curtailed in recent years in an attempt to control health care costs. Children and adolescents, more than any other group, suffer when inadequate coverage results in incomplete treatment and delayed development (American Academy of Child Psychiatry 1982).

For example, when the federal government removed unlimited inpatient coverage for federal employees in 1981 and instituted a cap of 60 days of inpatient care and 50 outpatient visits, no consideration was given to the unique needs of children and adolescents. Emotionally ill children of federal workers were lumped into the same capped coverage for all age groups. The Civilian Health and Medical Services of the Uniformed Services (CHAMPUS) also limits inpatient coverage for all ages to 60 days, however, outpatient coverage remains unlimited. CHAMPUS regulations allow waivers for hospitalization beyond 60 days, but the criteria for approval are severely restricted.

At the state and local government levels, almost two-thirds of the mental illness care costs, as contrasted to one-third of overall health care costs, are paid through the public sector (Sharfstein et al. 1984). Systems vary in each state, but changes in federal financing already have had some effect on each state's mental health care system for children, as will be described later.

GROUP HEALTH OR INDIVIDUAL/FAMILY PLANS

Most children and adolescents covered by nonfederal insurance plans are covered through their parents' or guardians' group health insurance (American Society of Internal Medical 1984). This insurance is available through employers, labor unions, private insurance companies, or other professional associations. Mental health coverage in some form is found in 86.8 percent of the policies of the privately insured, with commercial insurers writing almost 7 million family/individual plans (under age 65) in 1983 (conversation with Consumer Office, Health Insurance Association of America). Adults may be covered by individual plans, but unless a child is employed in the entertainment industry or some other unique situation, such plans are not available to anyone under age 18 (depending on state laws). Family plans can be contracted for specific lengths of time directly from insurers and have greater options than group health insurance, which is usually written by the employer or the organization. Group plans, for the most part, are standardized with no difference between adult and child coverage. The option of "cafeteria coverage" for employees in group plans is gaining popularity, and this popularity could result in positive change for child and adolescent mental illness coverage.

If benefits are not mandated, parents and guardians are more likely to choose extra pediatric services or dental care before considering that their children may need treatment for an emotional disorder. For both group and family plan insurance, the likelihood or ability of anyone to choose the fullest coverage for mental illness is slim. Yet, data from the Employee's Assistance Society of North America indicate that approximately 40 percent of employees are seeking assistance for the emotional problems of their children or family. The Employee Assistance Program (EAP) staff within a business, industry, or other organization is in a pivotal position to determine to whom an employee or family member is referred for evaluation and treatment. Unfortunately, the percentage of employees seeking guidance who are directed toward psychiatrists is unknown (Gaeta et al. 1981–1982).

Insurance companies have been slow to appreciate the preventive health care benefits associated with the availability of full psychiatric coverage for children. Therefore, they often promote their packages in this manner: "Full coverage for office visits, medical, surgical and hospital care . . . no co-pays or deductibles, except for mental health services" (CapitalCare 1985). The provision of full coverage for all but mental health services reinforces the belief that adults *and children* are responsible for their own mental health and must pay extra to have mental illness treated. Although this requirement supports parental rights, it also conveys a punitive attitude toward the mentally ill child or adolescent and his or her parents. Parents choosing health care insurance for their families usually have to decide between plans that offer full coverage or require co-payments and/or deductibles. However, when it comes to the option of payment for mental illness, both types of plan require parents to contribute to part of the treatment required for an emotionally ill child. This requirement can only reinforce the parents' desire to avoid self-blame and the potential stigma of being parents of a psychiatrically disabled child or teenager.

HEALTH MAINTENANCE ORGANIZATIONS AND OTHER PREPAID PLANS

Children and adolescents now represent up to 25 percent of health maintenance organization members, with HMO national membership reaching 12.5 million in mid-1980 (from an unpublished abstract by Drs. Ackerman and Graffagnino 1985). Ackerman and Graffagnino note that a psychosocial diagnosis is found in 5 to 15 percent of children seen in HMOs. Another 8 to 10 percent have psychosomatic diagnoses. As was the case in the 1982 American Academy of Child Psychiatry Report, both innate and acquired psychosocial factors have a significant influence on the quality and nature of childhood morbidity.

Prepaid health plans (PHPs) often offer a combination of 20 individual mental health sessions per year and 40 group therapy sessions, with wide variation in the inpatient benefits. The nonprofit PHPs have the greatest difficulty financing increased services of any kind. Those mental health programs most often requested, for example, for treatment of depression, stress, anxiety, and childhood emergencies, cannot be implemented.

Parents and guardians enrolled in HMOs may now have the newer option of joining an independent practice association/health maintenance organization. This innovation allows members to continue going to their regular family physicians if that physician is a member of the IPA/HMO. The attractiveness of the prepaid premium coupled with the move away from the single-site requirement could bring more families (i.e., more children) into a situation where psychiatric care can be provided on a regular prepaid basis.

Children and adolescents, like adults, can receive psychiatric care through preferred provider organizations (PPOs), particularly since more and more psychiatrists are becoming involved in PPOs

(Gurevitz 1984). Figures are imprecise as to how many patients are involved in this system, whether psychiatrists are part of a contract involving a discounted rate for services, and a guaranteed patient load. Like IPA/HMOs, the family does not have to travel to a specific site or lose the ability to choose a specific physician for particular services.

FEDERAL REIMBURSEMENT FOR CHILD AND ADOLESCENT PSYCHIATRIC DISABILITIES

Reimbursement for the treatment of a mental illness by federal and state governments to the physician is sometimes directly contracted with third-party payors (Medicare, Medicaid, CHAMPUS) and sometimes indirectly paid through income supplements (Supplemental Security Income, Social Security Disability Insurance). Other federal programs provide states with assistance for developing services for mental health treatment where they are not available (Childhood and Adolescent Service System Program (CASSP); Alcohol, Drug Abuse, and Mental Health Block Grant; Education for All Handicapped Children Act).

Supplemental Security Income (SSI)

The Supplemental Security Income (SSI) program provides federal support to people in financial need who are either over 65 years of age, blind, or disabled. The program includes children. Children disabled by a serious emotional illness and who meet stringent income and resource limitations are eligible for the monthly stipend. Some states supplement the federal payments and, in most states, SSI recipients are automatically eligible for Medicaid insurance. Before 1974, when SSI became a part of the Social Security Act, disabled children in low-income families were not eligible in their own right for assistance under any federal program. The SSI program ended this discrimination, and by 1982, 220,000 children, or about 10 percent of all disabled beneficiaries, were receiving SSI benefits (from a memorandum by Jane Yohalem 1984). Efforts are now underway to review the criteria for children's mental illness disability with the hope that revisions updating the original criteria will bring more disabled children under the program. Reimbursement for the needs of the disabled child goes to the family under SSI, rather than to the physician, such as occurs with Medicaid, a program for which families receiving SSI are automatically eligible (in most states) (Select Committee Print 1984).

Medicaid

Medicaid is a federal/state insurance program which provides health care reimbursement to eligible low-income persons, including families with dependent children. Each state creates its own Medicaid program within relatively broad federal guidelines and adds federally permitted options as desired. Some mental illness coverage is required; other services are optional, giving states the opportunity to cover services in community mental health centers, to reimburse for day-treatment services, or to participate in an inpatient psychiatric program for persons under 20 years of age (Knitzer 1982). As a part of the Omnibus Budget Reconciliation Act of 1981 (P.L. 97-35, August 13, 1981), states were given the option of funding community-based services for a patient instead of placement in institutional care. This option could lead to a drop in medically supervised services (Knitzer 1982). Furthermore, states may be forced to relinquish all of their options if the Medicaid funding continues to be frozen or reduced. In view of other governmental actions, it is likely that reimbursement for treatment of child and adolescent mental illnesses could be dropped in the early round of curtailment decisions.

Early and Periodic Screening, Diagnosis, and Treatment Program

A federal program specifically directed at children's health care, offering treatment for emotional disorders as an option, is the Early and Periodic Screening, Diagnosis, and Treatment (EPSDT) program. Authorized as a part of the Medicaid program in 1967, this federal effort is a preventive health care initiative. EPSDT offers to Medicaid-eligible children under age 18 a program which identifies, diagnoses, and treats health problems, including developmental difficulties. States provide or purchase services using a reimbursement structure like Medicaid. Unfortunately, EPSDT has been slow to be implemented. First it was delayed until 1972 when regulations were finally published. Then it was involved in a controversy about the inclusion of mental health coverage until, in 1984, mental disorders were added to the regulations, but only for evaluation and diagnosis, not for treatment (Knitzer 1982).

Only 1,813,000 children were served by EPSDT in 1982 for all dental, medical, and development problems, as contrasted to 9,656,000 eligible Medicaid children (under age 21). Yet the EPSDT program is still the largest federally funded program for child health care, with $73 million appropriated in fiscal year 1982 (Select Committee Print 1984). One recent change in the program has not been evaluated yet as to its effect on the number of children served; in 1981, the Budget Reconciliation Act amended EPSDT to remove penalties to states which did not inform low-income families with dependent children of their eligibility for this preventive program.

Medicaid Inpatient Coverage

Some states have generously adopted the Medicaid option to provide coverage for inpatient psychiatric services to children under age 21. The regulations on this service require the assessment of other less restrictive alternatives before inpatient care is approved. This option is now offered by 34 states to those under 21; 22 states provide optional psychiatric services to both categorically needy (eligible because of limited income and resources) and medically needy (eligible because of special medical need without regard to income); and 12 states provide to categorically needy only (Muszynski et al. 1984).

CHAMPUS

The Civilian Health and Medical Program of the Uniformed Services (CHAMPUS) is a program providing medical benefits to individuals who qualify as dependents to active-duty armed-forces personnel. CHAMPUS provides for the treatment of mental illness for adults, adolescents, and children. Although limited to dependents, the CHAMPUS criteria for providing health care have been assessed as allowing the best range of services of any benefit plan (Department of Defense 1977). CHAMPUS is *not* an insurance program which contracts directly with the dependent families; instead, its contracts are with third-party payors such as Blue Cross/Blue Shield claims processing for a wide range of health care including inpatient, outpatient, and residential treatment for children and adolescents (CHAMPUS Cost and Workload Regionalization Report 01-10-83–03-09-84, 1984). In 1984, CHAMPUS approved inpatient psychiatric care payments of approximately $130 million, with 64 percent for patients under age 19.

The payment for mental illness under the CHAMPUS program traditionally has been unrestricted by standards set on other benefit programs. However, in recent years, the mental health regulations have been altered to match the federal employees' benefit program. As a result, the inpatient limitation is set at 60 days (both for adults and children) with 50 outpatient visits per year. CHAMPUS has a waiver policy for extending treatment beyond 60 days, and until 1983, the policy included several criteria for waiver approval. In 1983, waivers were severely restricted to those patients showing significant risk to self or danger to others, with the qualification that the waiver not be allowable even with either of those criteria if the treatment could be carried out in an alternative, less expensive setting. In 1983, 517 waiver requests were subject to peer review, with 383 for individuals under age 20 (Altman 1984).

In September 1984, CHAMPUS issued a series of rules further altering the payment for treatment of mental illness. While CHAMPUS has always allowed payment for all types of professionally recognized individual psychotherapy, allowance then was made for family therapy, which would include more children and adolescents. Also, allowances were made for therapeutic absences from inpatient facilities for more than 72 hours under certain conditions. CHAMPUS will not reimburse any mental health care ordered by a court unless the treatment is medically or psychologically necessary without the court order. Peer review is used for all CHAMPUS-paid treatment if it is requested (CHAMPUS News 1984a).

Payment for residential treatment has always been a part of the CHAMPUS program, and there are approximately 70 authorized residential treatment centers (RTCs) serving 400 to 500 CHAMPUS patients each year. The overall number of admissions for children under age 18 served annually in all RTCs is about 15,000 (Redick and Witkin 1983). In 1984, CHAMPUS also adjusted the RTC rules, tightening admission standards for children with mental disorders. This type of treatment is one of the most costly because it is long-term, 24-hour treatment. In order to curtail costs, CHAMPUS specified that only the severely emotionally ill be covered. This rule excludes children with "social environment" problems. This CHAMPUS policy also requires a medical justification as well as a treatment program aimed toward functioning outside the center (CHAMPUS News 1984b). Residential treatment centers were not covered by the 60-day limitation, which prompted the tightening of the RTC criteria to those patients who are severely ill.

In 1981, costs for 500 children in RTC care were $15 million ($30,000 per child). In that year, CHAMPUS attempted to eliminate altogether RTC reimbursement. However, a united mental health community built a strong and winning case for the continuation of coverage. One of the primary arguments was the fact that children and adolescents would be using the waiver procedure to extend hospitalization rather than using the less expensive RTC (American Academy of Child Psychiatry 1981).

CHAMPUS does not reimburse for partial hospitalization, which has been requested by many child psychiatrists. The use of partial hospitalization would respond to both the 60-day inpatient limit and the tightening of the RTC reimbursement requirements.

A presentation by Rhona Fisher, Ph.D. of the Center for Health Policy Studies to the National Consortium for Child Mental Health Services described a recently completed study that has implications for reimbursement alternatives for CHAMPUS residential treatment. She noted three designs for alternative payment: prospective (facility-specific rates), prospective (uniform rates), and redesigned retrospective payments. In addition, a model program utilizing the health maintenance organization structure has been developed by CHAMPUS. The results of these innovations in reimbursement options would be to place CHAMPUS closer to the private insurance industry's models addressing the issues of costs and care alternatives.

The Alcohol, Drug Abuse, and Mental Health Block Grant

The Alcohol, Drug Abuse, and Mental Health Block Grant (ADM) provides funds to states for grants to community mental health centers for mental health services, which can include the identification and assessment of severely mentally disturbed children and adolescents. The ADM block grant, as a part of the 1984 reauthorization for this program, mandates that at least 10 percent of the mental health dollars for services be for seriously disturbed children and adolescents or for other underserved or unserved populations. This mandate is a faint shadow of what was intended to be a major effort for child mental health services that began in 1972 with the Community Mental Health Centers Act, Part F (specialized services for children). By 1974, this program had been repealed and replaced briefly by the minimally funded "most in need" (MIN) program. Next, in 1978, children's services were written into the Mental Health Systems Act, but never enacted before being repealed and replaced by the ADM block grant in 1981 (Knitzer 1982).

Other Related Federal Programs
Other federal programs support interventions on behalf of mentally ill children and adolescents. They are supplemental programs that work primarily to prevent the onset of serious emotional disorders, or that provide developmental assessment. The Preventive Health and Health Services Block Grant provides grants to states for programs that could include emergency medical services, health education, and risk reduction including activities designed to deter smoking and the use of alcoholic beverages among children and adolescents (Select Committee Print 1984).

P.L. 94-142, the Education for All Handicapped Children Act (1975) is an example of federal, state, and local monies being pooled and made available for the evaluation and treatment of a special group of children and adolescents. The purpose of the act is to ensure that all handicapped children have available to them a free, appropriate public education including special education and related services. Medical services are included in the definition of related services for diagnostic and evaluation purposes only (P.L. 94-142 1975).

P.L. 94-142 can be viewed as a paradigm for the relationship among federal laws and regulations, state guidelines of compliance, and local efforts of implementation with varying degrees of ability and interest. This law establishes the federal regulations for the enactment of individual state laws. Federal monies are available to states which comply with federal standards through the U.S. Department of Education. Over the years, the amount of federal support has markedly declined as questions regarding implementation escalated to include an amendment mandating a study by the Office of Special Education to examine changing the term "seriously emotionally disturbed" to "behaviorally disordered." A significant structural problem is the lack of uniformity with regard to jurisdiction. In some states, the responsibility for education of the handicapped is under the Department of Education, in others it is under the Department of Health or the Department of Mental Health. Obviously, no matter where the ultimate responsibility lies, cooperation between state and local educational institutions must take place.

All handicapped children and their families are at risk for emotional illnesses and social problems including parental separation and divorce (Grossman and Stubblefield 1980). Thus, this population has a great need for at least psychiatric consultation and liaison work. The original act recognized the seriously emotionally disturbed child as a handicapped child. The definition of the term met psychiatric criteria. It included an inability to learn which cannot be explained by intellectual, sensory or health factors; an inability to build or maintain satisfactory interpersonal relationships with peers and teachers; inappropriate feelings or behavior under normal circumstances; a general, pervasive mood of unhappiness; and a tendency to develop physical symptoms or fears associated with personal or school problems. The term included schizophrenic and autistic children. Unfortunately, the terminology amendment has focused on changing this term to "behavior disorder." Although the majority of states' regulations have either "seriously emotionally disturbed" or "seriously emotionally disturbed and behavior disorder" as terminology, the argument is advanced that parents and teachers are distressed by the former term alone.

The original act had excellent potential for meeting the needs of emotionally disturbed children. As had been the case with other legislation, the proposed changes dilute or negate the original intent. They tend to support a superficial approach with an emphasis upon behavior rather than a concern for its origin; the possibility of missing the severely emotionally disturbed child who is extraordinarily good or quiet, thereby causing no behavioral disturbance in the classroom; and the word "behavioral" has come to be associated with specific training and responsibilities idiosyncratically defined by widely diverse groups of professionals. In the final analysis, altering the definition could change the population served and the providers of those services.

Probably a critical stimulant for the reassessment of programs and reimbursement mechanisms is the *cost* of providing adequate services and the decisions at a local, school, and community level regarding allocation of monies and resources. P.L. 94-142 is an example of this dilemma. Currently, if a school recommends evaluation of a child, the school must pay the bill.

CONCLUSION

This review of the current status of psychiatric services and financing of child and adolescent mental illness care highlights the wide and innovative variety of available programs; the constricting effects on mental illness care of a cost-containment policy; the necessity of understanding the issues and working within professional organizations and with other groups of similar intent to originate and monitor financial coverage; and the crucial responsibility of psychiatry to dispel the myths about mental illnesses and to educate the public about the unique needs of children and adolescents for care.

Hippocrates's comment, 2,400 years ago, about medicine sums up the current status and the importance for the country of adequate child and adolescent mental illness care—

> Life is short
> And the art long
> The occasion instant
> Experiment perilous
> Decision difficult
>
> —Hippocrates, *Aphorisms*

REFERENCES

Altman H: Inpatient psychiatric care under CHAMPUS (Statement of the American Psychiatric Association). Subcommittee on Defense, U.S. House of Representatives. Washington, DC, U.S. Government Printing Office, 1984

American Academy of Child Psychiatry: CHAMPUS Benefits for Residential Treatment (fact sheet). Washington DC, American Academy of Child Psychiatry, 1981

American Academy of Child Psychiatry: Child Psychiatry: A Plan for the Coming Decades. Washington, DC, American Academy of Child Psychiatry, 1982

American Society of Internal Medicine: Understanding and Choosing Your Health Insurance. Washington, DC, American Society of Internal Medicine, 1984

CapitalCare advertisement. The Washington Post, July 23, 1985

CHAMPUS: Cost and Workload Regionalization Report. 01-10-83–03-09-84, CHAMPUS, Denver, CO 1984

CHAMPUS News: CHAMPUS Streamlines Mental Health Rules (press release). 84-18, 1984a

CHAMPUS News: CHAMPUS Streamlines Rules on Residential Treatment Centers (press release). 84-19, 1984b

CHAMPUS News: CHAMPUS Claims Processor Chosen for Southwestern Region (press release). 85-8/P5, 1985

Crosby M: Government affairs update. American Academy of Child Psychiatry Newsletter. Washington, DC, American Academy of Child Psychiatry, Fall, 1984

Crosby M: Government affairs update. American Academy of Child Psychiatry Newsletter, Washington, DC, American Academy of Child Psychiatry, Fall 1985

Department of Defense, Department of Health, Education and Welfare: Civilian Health and Medical Program of the Uniformed Services (CHAMPUS). DOD, Washington, DC, 1977

Department of Defense: CHAMPUS solicitation for grant proposal #MDA 906-83-0012, 1983

Education for All Handicapped Children Act of 1975 (P.L. 94–142). Washington, DC, U.S. Government Printing Office, 1975

Egan J: Emerging trends in mental health care of adolescents. Committee Print Select Committee on Children, Youth and Families. Washington, DC, U.S. Government Printing Office, 1985

Gaeta E, Lynn R, Grey L: AT&T looks at program evaluation. EAP Digest Annual, 112-120, 1981–1982

Grossman HJ, Stubblefield RL (Eds): The Physician and the Mental Health of the Child, II. The Psychological Concomitants of Illness. Chicago, American Medical Association Press, 1980

Gurevitz H: Psychiatry and preferred provider organizations. Psychiatric Annals 14:342-349, 1984

House Select Committee on Children and Youth: Federal Programs Affecting Children: Select Committee Print. Washington, DC, U.S. Government Printing Office, 1984

Isaacs M: Technical Assistance Package for the Child and Adolescent Service System Program. Rockville, MD, National Institute of Mental Health, 1984

Joint Commission on the Mental Health of Children: Crisis in Mental Health: Challenges for the 1970s. New York, Harper and Row, 1969

Knitzer J: Unclaimed Children: The Failure of Public Responsibility to Children and Adolescents in Need of Mental Health Services. Washington, DC, Children's Defense Fund, 1982

Malmquist C: Depression in childhood and adolescence, part I. N Engl J Med 284:887-893, 1971a

Malmquist C: Depression in childhood and adolescence, part II. N Engl J Med 284:955-961, 1971b

Muszynski S, Brady J, Sharfstein S: Paying for psychiatric care. Psychiatric Annals 14:865-869, 1984

Poznanski E: Childhood Depression and Youth Suicide: Current Research and Policy Implications. Research Resources for Children, Youth and Families. Washington, DC, Society for Research in Child Development, 1985

President's Commission on Mental Health: Report to the President of the President's Commission on Mental Health, vol. 1. Washington, DC, U.S. Government Printing Office, 1978

Roeske NCA: The business of psychiatry. Psychiatric Annals 14:5, 1984

Sharfstein SS, Muszynski S, Myers E: Health Insurance and Psychiatric Care: Update and Appraisal. Washington, DC, American Psychiatric Press, Inc., 1984

Task Force on Pediatric Education: The Future of Pediatric Education. Evanston, IL, American Academy of Pediatrics, 1978

8

Aging and Disability

Robert N. Butler, M.D.

I ndustrialized societies are growing older. With the unprecedented increase in average life expectancy and reduced birth rates, the proportion and absolute number of older persons (defined by social convention as age 60 or 65 and above) have been increasing. The public and public-policy makers have become increasingly attentive to the consequences of "population aging" (sometimes called "societal aging").

There are at least two issues that arise immediately when considering the fast-growing numbers of older persons in our society: how to maintain the productive potential of such persons in an "aging society," and how to provide both care and income support for those no longer able to provide for themselves, those who become the disabled aged.

This chapter will limit itself to these two topics, placing emphasis on two recent developments: the Age Discrimination in Employment Act and the national focus on Alzheimer's disease, among the most disabling of conditions affecting the aged and near-aged. These topics clearly do not exhaust the many concerns created by the new and changing demography, but are illustrative and, it's to be hoped, provocative of the further research, study, and public-policy decision making that is required as we consider the aging of our society.

FRAMEWORK

There is a new, changing demography worldwide, characterized by unprecedented daily increases in the absolute number and relative proportion of older persons. Within the next 20 years, the number of persons over age 60 in the world will double; 60 percent of them will live in the developing world. The greatest percentage increase of older persons will occur in industrialized nations. Indeed, the fastest growing age cohort in the United States includes the "old-old," those over age 85. This remarkable increase in survivorship is a function of the substantial decrease in maternal, childhood, and infant mortality rates, and, over the last 20 years, decreases in mortality rates from heart disease and stroke. In industrialized nations, since the turn of the century, there has been a gain in average life expectancy of 25 years.

There has also been an overall increase in the health of older persons and, therefore, a concomitant increase in the quality of their lives. Instances of remarkable robustness in the later years are frequently seen. At the same time, however, there has been an increase in disability at all ages (Feldman 1983).

Although there is a relationship between increased survivorship and increased work ability (Butler 1983b), in the aggregate this relationship is not predictable at the level of the individual. (Cohen, for example, has described how individual factors—the influence of cognitive, affective, and behavioral problems of the individual—affect the person's capacity to maintain an independent level of functioning.) (Cohen, unpublished papers).

Based in large measure upon the public perception that work remains a central focus into older age, the Congress has moved up the age of eligibility for Social Security to 67—to be phased in incrementally between now and the year 2011. Since employment in the later years is difficult to obtain because of age prejudice in an era of continuing high unemployment, the change in eligibility is likely to subject significant numbers of older persons to poverty.

Income support of older people will continue to be a major challenge to society—whether through the provision of jobs, through federal and state income maintenance programs, or through other mechanisms not yet in existence. The economic survival of older persons must be considered within the context of a purpose for living, reflected usually in paid or unpaid employment. Without purpose, without meaning, increased physical and emotional difficulties begin to take their toll; physical health and mental acuity suffer, leading toward the downward spiral of disability in old age. Thus, the relationship between aging and increased disability must be evaluated in preventive and rehabilitative terms.

One of the greatest fears of growing old is the loss of intellectual capacity and independence, the fear of institutionalization. Since the mid-1970s, the American population has come to understand more about "senility," a popular, but not strictly medical, term. Senility is not inevitable with aging, but is due to a variety of diseases which have been better defined and classified recently. Some senility—perhaps as much as 20 percent—actually may be treatable, reversible mental illness (President's Commission on Mental Health 1978). Dementias, particularly Alzheimer's disease and multi-infarct dementia, are also culprits. Because of the rising number of older persons, Alzheimer's disease, in particular, has been called the "disease of the century" (Thomas 1981). Alzheimer's disease is, in fact, one of the key reasons for increasing disability with age.

Despite the clarifications of the nature of dementia and Alzheimer's disease, victims of these disorders and their families until very recently have not been afforded adequate health insurance, home care, and social services, or many of the benefits of Social Security Disability payments. In part, this is due to the structure of the benefit system. It is also due to the variable, even political, basis upon which evaluations have been conducted.

THE WORK LIFE AND OLD AGE

Until the twentieth century, retirement tended to be determined by functional criteria. Individual workers, whether in agriculture or in crafts in preindustrial economies, reduced the workload or switched its character as they aged, but, nonetheless, they worked until the end of life itself. For example, an aging sailor might become a sail maker. With industrialization, however, retirement became more common and specific, with an arbitrary age selected as the cut-off date. In this country, that age, until recently, has been set at 65. Many employers and policy makers felt that a mandated retirement age simplified the process of retirement in contrast to the previous history of individualized, flexible retirement. But in the 1960s and 1970s, criticism of this arbitrary approach grew (Butler 1975), and, under the leadership of Congressman Claude Pepper and others, the Age Discrimination in Employment Act was enacted in 1967 and further amended in 1978. The latter moved the mandatory retirement age to 70 in the private sector and ended it altogether in the federal civil service, the nation's largest single employer. Certain exceptions were retained for seemingly high-risk professions, or those that involved a significant potential of danger for other citizens in their conduct. For example, airline pilots were forced to retire at age 60.

Philosophy and political dynamics motivated various court cases and legislative efforts such as the Experienced Pilots Act to overcome such exceptions. In that instance, the Gray Eagles, a lobby of pilots who resented early retirement, led the struggle. From their perspective, they felt as capable of flying at 60 years of age as they did at 59. The Experienced Pilots Act of 1979, enacted by Congress, posed five questions, paraphrased below, in a mandated study to be conducted by the National Institute on Aging:

1. Is the mandatory retirement age of 60 medically justified?
2. Is any chronological age for retirement medically justified?
3. Are present examinations adequate in content?
4. Is the frequency of examination appropriate?
5. What is the impact of aging on human performance?

The legislation reflected the need for data to assist in regulation. The resulting study indicated the severe limitations of present knowledge.

At this time, knowledge of human aging and of human performance is not adequate to answer the questions posed, nor can it help us replace the contemporary retirement age in *all* occupations, especially where public safety is an issue. The technology for assessment that would permit flexible, individualized retirement programs in all occupations is not available. The questions raised, however, do point to the critical factor that age, in and of itself, is not disabling.

CONCEPT OF DISABILITY-FREE LIFE EXPECTANCY

Obviously, few want to live long if they will only experience burdensome disease and disability. There is more to life than average life expectancy. Needed are measures of healthy life status. The National Center for Health Statistics (NCHS) introduced the concept of disability-free life expectancy. In discussing the relationship between average life expectancy and work ability, Butler used the term "average health expectancy" (1983a, 1983b). Sidney Katz introduced the valuable concept of "active life expectancy" (Katz et al. 1983). Active life expectancy is important from both the social and individual perspectives. If the average life expectancy is 74 years in the United States, is the average active life expectancy about 72? What proportion of our lives is spent in illness and disability? These are essentially unanswered questions, but the methodology to help answer them is being built. We would also like to know the relationship of socioeconomic status to active life expectancy. We do know that socioeconomic status is highly related to average life expectancy. What are the policy implications of these findings? We may find answers in programs for assistance in daily living, for home health services, for hospital care, for those who may be able to continue an active life with a modicum of assistance.

Katz's 1983 study was designed to show the feasibility of forecasting functional health for the elderly. The authors used life table techniques and a measure of the activities of daily living (ADL) as a reflection of life expectancy (Katz and Akpom 1976). They found a decrease in active life expectancy from 10 years for persons between 65 and 70 to 2.9 years for those 85 years of age or older (as noted, the fastest growing age group in industrialized nations). The classification of disability represented in ADL derived from the work of the Commission on Chronic Illness of the early 1950s. This conceptual contribution was built into an index, developed by Katz and his colleagues, to assess active life expectancy (Katz and Akpon 1976).

SOCIAL SECURITY DISABILITY PROGRAM

The Social Security Disability program provides some protection for persons disabled before they are eligible for Social Security benefits. It has paid monthly benefits to 3.8 million people in 1985, costing $19.1 million.

Disability reviews are carried out by 54 state agencies, more than 800 federal reviewers and nearly 800 administrative law judges. It is a cumbersome, if necessary, process. The Social Security Administration has national responsibility for the administration of both the Social Security Disability program (SSDI, Title II of the Social Security Act) and the newer Supplemental Security Income program (SSI, Title XVI of the same Act). Title II provides coverage for cash benefits to those disabled workers and their dependents who have contributed to the Social Security trust fund through the FICA tax on earnings. Disabled workers have earned the right to disability benefits. Title XVI also provides a minimum income level for the needy aged, blind, and disabled who qualify because of financial need rather than as an earned right.

DEMENTIA AND DISABILITY

The epidemiology of dementia remains a difficult area for study. Screening techniques for measuring intellectual disability, such as memory decline, are not precise. The diagnosis of Alzheimer's disease per se is a presumptive diagnosis. It is usually "left over" after all other possible causes of dementias of old age are excluded. Ordinarily, we do not have the resources to provide detailed, comprehensive diagnostic assessment.

Nonetheless, we do have some data, albeit meager, on disability and aging, including psychiatric disability. Weissman et al. (1985) report upon prevalence rates of psychiatric disorders in 2,500 non-institutionalized persons aged 65 or over, drawn from a probability sample, in New Haven and 12 nearby Connecticut towns. Based upon the diagnostic categories of the American Psychiatric Association's *Diagnostic and Statistical Manual of Mental Disorders, Third Edition (DSM-III)* they found that 6.7 percent had psychiatric diagnoses. Using the Mini-Mental Status Exam, they found that 3.4 percent had severe cognitive impairments during the preceding six-month period, leaving a total of about 10 percent with some form of difficulty.

The rate of severe cognitive impairment did not increase until after age 79. The rate was higher in women, but this may be accounted for by the differential survival rate between the sexes. Note that about 6 percent of the 65-and-older age group are in institutions, and, therefore, were not included in the Weissman study.

Since those 85 and above constitute the fastest growing age group, attention is being focused upon them. They are referred to as the "oldest old" (Cornoni-Huntley et al. 1985). One report revealed an extraordinarily high rate, 38 percent, of cognitive impairment in this age group (Frank Williams, personal communication).

A World Health Organization study (1982) in Mannhein, Federal Republic of Germany, found a higher percentage of psychiatric disorders in the over-65 population than did the Weissman study. They found the incidence even higher after age 85 in women (and they believed this was not due to gender discrepancy in survival). "Organic psycho-syndromes were heavily concentrated in the lower socioeconomic strata" (p. 11). The Mannhein study, however, used a different methodology than the Weissman study.

There are some data available related to other disabilities in the aging which, in turn, may be associated with the occurrence of mental disorders. There are positive associations between mental and physical disorders, especially impairments of vision, hearing, and mobility.

However, the task of the disability-determination process is not only to establish the presence of impairment, but also to assess its severity. In fact, federal regulations specify that "dementia involves the loss of measured intellectual ability of at least 15 IQ points from premorbid levels or overall impaired range on the Luria–Nebraska or Halstead–Reitan" (*Federal Register*, February 4, 1985). Documentation thus becomes an important part of the process.

Inadequate documentation has created the problem of erratic benefits policies. The Alzheimer's Disease and Related Disorder Association (ADRDA) notes: "Since an Alzheimer's disease victim is unable to perform his/her well-earned accustomed work, it follows that he/she will be unable to learn another job, no matter how simple it may appear." The ADRDA further states that "the use of work evaluation facilities, and the various criteria proposed, do not effectively address the special needs of the Alzheimer's victim, as outlined in the notice [of proposed rule making]." This was expressed in a letter to the Acting Commissioner of Social Security on April 22, 1985. "We envision the necessity for an education program directed at both your examiners and our family members," the ADRDA continued. Until quite recently, some patients were approved for benefits in some states and, in others, they were repeatedly denied benefits. The statute-authorized disability benefits do not preclude benefit payments to individuals suffering from Alzheimer's disease. However, the guidelines used by claims examiners to determine eligibility had been somewhat vague when it came to Alzheimer's disease and other related disorders. The disease, until recently, was not listed among those brain disorders specifically identified in the guidelines. Obviously, the discovery of an antemortem marker of the disease and quantified precise measures of severity would help move toward yet greater clarification of the regulations on this subject.

HUMAN PERFORMANCE THROUGH THE LIFE SPAN
There is very little in-depth data related to human performance throughout the life span. This is largely a function of minimal commitment of funds to longitudinal studies which provide repeated measures of the same phenomena, the same variables, over extended periods of time. The longitudinal studies now available (Migdal et al. 1981) have been limited in scope, sampling accuracy, and duration.

Nonetheless, longitudinal studies have been invaluable sources of information, in particular the Framingham Heart Study, the Duke Longitudinal Studies, the National Institute of Mental Health Human Aging Study (Birren et al. 1963) and the National Institute on Aging's Baltimore Longitudinal Study on Aging (Shock et al. 1984). However, we do not yet have a successful measure of biological aging, an adequate profile of aging, or human biomarkers of aging (Reff and Schneider 1982). Chronological age per se is not a useful measure of biological aging. The National Institute on Aging has mounted a major long-term effort to ascertain such nonlethal biomarkers of aging.

Until the results of further research are available, policy makers must still rely upon arbitrary retirement ages and arbitrary criteria for disability evaluations, however imperfect, to assist early retirement. They must also find ways to keep those older persons whose skills and knowledge are of critical importance active in the work place. Society must provide adequate financial protection in periods of austerity. So far, efforts have not been totally satisfactory, although there has been progress. The most disadvantaged of older people are women and minority groups. One factor is that these groups have often been excluded from the work place.

Several new strategies have been adopted. These are reflected in the gerontological literature and are understood by many policy makers. The first is a political strategy to (a) increase pressure to elevate the mandatory retirement age or end it, to ensure that those who have the capability and desire to do so can continue to work and will not be eliminated from the work force on the basis of chronological age alone; (b) maintain, strengthen, and refine the Social Security Disability program and protect disabled workers; and, (c) maintain and increase Social Security payments in accordance with the cost-of-living adjustment (COLA) and basic floor assured by Supplemental Security Income (SSI). The second is a scientific strategy designed to develop a more effective means of evaluating individual performance of aging workers through interview, testing, and the identification of human biomarkers. For example, in response to the Experienced Pilots Act, the National Institute on Aging proposed to the Congress and the Federal Aviation Administration the introduction of a modified retirement strategy that would require and utilize short-term longitudinal data. This would give fliers who desire to do so a chance to fly beyond age 60 to age 65. To qualify, they would participate in rigorous examinations, beginning at age 55. Aircraft cockpit technology provides the opportunity for simulation to test flier capability.

CONCLUSION

The age structure of a population is a function of birth rate, death rate, and migration. Population aging in Europe, the United States, and Japan is largely a consequence of declining birth and death rates. What is happening is increased survivorship.

Since increased survivorship of the population should continue, as improved methods of intervention in disease are found, there will be individual and social advantages to the maintenance of productivity into later life (Butler and Gleason 1985). The "baby boomer" generation, born between 1946 and 1964, and the largest generation in United States history, will be working to later ages. The post-World War II baby boom generation's first members will turn 65 in the year 2011. In about 2020, this generation will reach its zenith in the over-65 age group. It is anticipated that perhaps 20 percent of the population will be over 65—1 out of every 5 Americans, in contrast to 1 in 11 today.

It is obvious that societies will have to change dramatically to help sustain the increasing number of survivors. Interestingly, it is likely that worldwide productivity will increase independently of population change or labor. Therefore, there may be increasingly widespread worldwide unemployment. The issue of productivity of the aged may be generalized across the life cycle. Public policy will require new social and economic arrangements for sharing work and income generated by societal productivity.

The aging of society and, specifically, the aging work force constitute a major challenge. Developing techniques of evaluation of disability and measures of productivity, as well as new social arrangements to facilitate paid and unpaid productivity, will constitute major tasks for societies not only in the immediate decades ahead, but in the twenty-first century, when there will be great waves of older persons, representing the triumph of survival due to medical and social progress.

REFERENCES

Alzheimer's Disease and Related Disorders Association: National Program to Conquer Alzheimer's Disease. Chicago, IL, ADRDA, 1985

Birren JR, Butler RN, Greenhouse SW et al: Human Aging: A Biological and Behavioral Study. Washington, DC, Public Health Publication No. 986, 1963

Butler RN: Why Survive: Being Old in America. New York, Harper and Row, 1975

Butler RN: An overview of research on aging and the status of gerontology. Milbank Memorial Fund Quarterly 61:351-361, 1983a

Butler RN: The relation of extended life to extended employment since the passage of social security in 1935. Milbank Memorial Fund Quarterly 61:420-429, 1983b

Butler RN, Gleason H: Productive Aging. New York, Springer, 1985

Cornoni-Huntley JC, Foley DJ, White LE, et al: Epidemiology of disability in the oldest old: methodological issues and preliminary findings. Milbank Memorial Fund Quarterly 63:350-376, 1985

Federal Register: Proposed Rules Federal Old Age, Survivors and Disability Insurance. Vol. 50, no 23, February 4, 1985. Washington, DC, U.S. Government Printing Office, 1985

Feldman JJ: Work ability of the aged under conditions of improving mortality. Milbank Memorial Fund Quarterly 61:430-444, 1983

Katz S, Akpom CA: A measure of primary sociobiological functions. Int J Health Serv 6:493-508, 1976

Katz S, Branch LG, Branson MH et al: Active life expectancy. N Engl J Med 17:1218-1224, 1983

Migdal S, Abeles RP, Sherrod LR: An Inventory of Longitudinal Studies of Middle and Old Age. New York, Social Science Research Council, 1981

Pear R: U.S. in shift, plans to follow courts on benefit claims: won't ignore precedent. New York Times, June 4, 1984

President's Commission on Mental Health: Report to the President on the President's Commission on Mental Health, vol. 1. Washington, DC, U.S. Government Printing Office, 1978

Reff M, Schneider EL: Biological Markers of Aging. NIH Publication No. 82-222. Washington, DC, U.S. Government Printing Office, 1982

Shock NW: Normal Human Aging, The Baltimore Longitudinal Study of Aging. NIH Publication No. 84-2450. Washington, DC, U.S. Government Printing Office, 1984

Thomas L: Problems of dementia. Discover Magazine, p. 34, August 1981.

Wiessman MM, Myers JK, Tischler GL, et al: Psychiatric disorders (DSM-III) and cognitive impairment among the elderly in a U.S. urban community. Acta Psychiatr Scand 71:366-379, 1985

World Health Organization Working Group: Preventing Disability in the Elderly. World Health Organization, Euro Reports and Studies 65, Copenhagen, Denmark, 1982

9

Psychiatric Rehabilitation and Chronic Physical Illness

Roland M. Gallagher, M.D.
Frances Stewart, M.D.

A person stricken with catastrophic illness or injury faces a long, arduous, and complex rehabilitation to achieve a satisfactory life style. A person suffering with a chronic medical illness must adapt to repeated losses and to restriction of function and life style. The discipline of psychiatry offers much to these persons, their families, and the medical teams caring for them. Consider the array of physical, psychological, and social difficulties implied by the following sketches of six very different but representative illnesses:

> An internist advises Michael I., a 30-year-old, married construction worker, to lose weight, to quit smoking, to reduce cholesterol intake, and to take bloodpressure medicine. Michael only sporadically complies. Five years later, still smoking, overweight, and hypertensive, he suffers a myocardial infarction during a drunken brawl with his wife. She depends on diazepam (Valium) to endure chronic anxiety while she tries to cope with three adolescent children from a previous marriage.

> Rita A., a 40-year-old, divorced accountant, has suffered with rheumatoid arthritis since the age of 14. After a total hip replacement, she is able to ambulate without pain for the first time in 5 years. However, she is depressed and dependent on narcotics to control pain. Her illness is worsened by competitive horseback

143

riding, a hobby that has sustained her self-esteem for almost 20 years.

Diane M., a 35-year-old, single receptionist at a doctor's office, lives alone in a small house on a family compound in the country. She manages her diabetes mellitis of 15 years quite well; but over the past 3 years she has tended to avoid social encounters outside the family and recently has considered quitting her job.

Leonard B., a 35-year-old, married father of two, suffers a back injury rupturing two intervertebral discs. His pain continues unabated despite two back surgeries. He has been unemployed for 3 years and workers' compensation recently stopped his disability pension.

Steve C., a 21-year-old college dropout, fractures his cervical spine in an auto accident and is left permanently quadraplegic. After a long and tumultuous rehabilitation, 5 years later he maintains an apartment with the help of a part-time attendant and holds a full-time job.

Mrs. D., a 60-year-old, married woman with chronic obstructive pulmonary disease, is admitted to the hospital intensive care unit during an acute episode of respiratory failure. She suffers terrifying panic attacks when the hospital first attempts to wean her off the respirator.

These people all have serious medical illness. Ironically, only Steve C., quadraplegic and perhaps the most physiologically disabled, has received psychiatric care. Similarly, to enable the other patients to resume or to maintain an optimally functional life style, given the constraints of their own physical disabilities, the medical team must integrate psychiatric concepts and skills into an individualized rehabilitation plan.

This chapter builds a psychiatric rehabilitation model for use with persons with catastrophic or chronic medical illness, a model based on research and successful clinical practice. This chapter briefly explores the rationale for psychiatry's interest in the rehabilitation and care of the medically ill; discusses the concepts underlying present clinical models of chronic illness; reviews psychosocial and behavioral patterns in chronic illness; using the dilemmas posed by the care of Michael I., presents how to apply the biopsychosocial medical model to the understanding and care of a representative chronic illness—myocardial infarction; discusses opportunities for future research, education, and clinical practice in psychiatric intervention and rehabilitation for medical illness; provides a list of references for background reading.

THE NEED FOR PSYCHIATRY IN THE REHABILITATION AND CARE OF THE CHRONICALLY ILL

The Incidence and Cost of Chronic Illness

The care of persons with chronic medical illness is a subject of increasing importance to our society. Approximately 10 percent of our population suffers from a chronic disorder or disability that limits activity. Moreover, there is some indication that this incidence is rising (Cataldo et al. 1980). These authors cite heart disease, arthritis, hypertension, and musculoskeletal disorders as the major causes of chronic illness. The elderly have a higher incidence: 43 percent of persons over age 65 are chronically ill. Of people 44–65 years old, 21 percent are also considered limited by chronic conditions. These medical problems cause pain, loss, suffering, and emotional problems for patients. They also create a major economic burden on our society. For example, 433 million workdays were lost due to disability, costing the United States economy $9.2 billion in 1975.

There are several reasons for these escalating numbers. Rapid advances in biomedical science have improved medical technology to the point that the mortality rate for such illnesses as myocardial infarction or end-stage renal disease have declined. Persons with these illnesses leave the hospital alive but chronically ill and disabled. Through superior technology, they often survive complications or exacerbations of their illness. Further, as the average age of our population continues to rise, a larger percentage of persons become susceptible to chronic illness. These persons must learn to cope with disability, lost income, depression, poor services, loss of hobbies, loss of relationships, and pain. With their families and health care providers, they must also develop strategies to cope with demanding and complex medical regimens that maintain their lives and provide an acceptable level of function.

Thus, chronic illness not only challenges those intimately involved—the patient, family, and physician—but presents an economic and social challenge to our society.

Psychosocial Risk Factors in Chronic Illness

The influence of psychosocial risk factors on the incidence and prevalence of chronic illness has been well established. The Institute of Medicine (Hamburg et al. 1982) recently concluded:

> The heaviest burdens of illness in the United States today are related to aspects of individual behavior, especially long-term patterns of behavior often referred to as "lifestyle." As much as 50% of the mortality from the 10 leading causes of death in the United States can be traced to lifestyle. Behavioral risk factors include cigarette smoking, excessive consumption of alcoholic beverages, use of illicit drugs, dietary habits, reckless driving,

nonadherence to effective medical regimens, and maladaptive responses to social pressures. (p. 3)

These authors cite only the known risk factors for the development of costly disease; most likely there are others yet undiscovered.

Psychiatric Disorders in Chronic Illness

Depression, anxiety, psychosis, delirium, family problems, and alcohol and drug abuse frequently accompany chronic illness. Mood changes are ubiquitous and take many forms. Almost all medically ill persons experience transient episodes of depressed mood, which are usually considered to be reactions to one or a combination of several factors, including physical discomfort; loss of function; concern about health and survival; changes in self-image; and loss of capacity in jobs, hobbies, and personal relationships.

Physical illness can be associated with more serious affective syndromes, such as profound demoralization, major depression, chronic depression, and manic episodes. These distinct states can present separately, in sequence, or in combination. For example, Cushing's disease or drugs such as reserpine or methyl-dopa can affect the neurophysiologic systems that regulate mood. Progressive illness, such as cancer; disabling illness, such as rheumatoid arthritis; disfiguring illness, such as psoriasis; or disfiguring cancer drugs, such as methotrexate, may precipitate a variety of different circumstances in which a patient repeatedly experiences loss and frustration—ultimately, demoralization and hopelessness. In fact, any disease or illness can be experienced as loss—of vitality, of beauty, of mobility, or of potential. A subliminal or suppressed awareness of a change in physical status or a subtle loss of normal function may precipitate depression before other symptoms of illness declare themselves. Depression may herald occult illness, such as pancreatic cancer. A depressed mood may temporarily alter a person's normal coping mechanisms, interfering with compliance behavior. Several of the cases presented earlier illustrate the interaction between mood states and illness.

> While shopping, Leonard B., the 35-year-old, disabled man with chronic lower back pain secondary to spondylolisthesis, encounters an old friend who inquires about his back and wonders aloud why he is not better and back at work. The patient's initial rage at a suggestion that he is a malingerer turns to despair. At home, he decides to split wood to relieve his frustration, knowing his doctor advises against wood-splitting. He tells his concerned wife "To hell with the damned back. No doctor is going to tell me what to do." He splits wood for 30 minutes, and is rehospitalized the next day with acute exacerbation of pain and spasms of his back muscles.

Rita A., the 40-year-old woman with rheumatoid arthritis and a hip replacement, experiences painfully depressed moods after work in the evening, when she sits in her parents' home longing to be able to resume competitive riding. To relieve these moods, she jogs for three miles, despite sore and swollen knees and feet, which she self-medicates with prednisone and narcotics she has stored over the years. Finally, on 50 mg prednisone daily, her depressed mood progresses to major depression and she requires hospitalization. The damage to her joints is significant.

Michael I., the 35-year-old postcoronary patient, walks past a bar where his work cronies are enjoying a beer after a day on the job. Missing his friends, he joins them for a drink. Their ribbing about his disability makes him despondent about not working and he proceeds to get drunk. Later, at home, he vents his frustration at being unemployed and unmanly. Exasperated by this now-familiar scene, his wife threatens to leave. That evening, she rushes him to the hospital with chest pain.

These cases are just a sampling of the many ways that mood can influence the course of illness.

Psychiatric Symptoms Manifesting Somatic Disorder
Psychiatric symptoms may be the first manifestation of serious physical disorder. Hall's review (1980) identifies 75 nonpsychiatric disorders that can present with depression, including categories such as infectious disease, hepatic disorder, pancreatic disorder, nutritional deficiency, electrolyte imbalance, cancer, and drug-induced disorder. Moreover, depression, also a serious complication of serious and chronic illness, is thought to increase morbidity in several chronic conditions such as spinal cord injury, arthritis, myocardial infarction, cancer, chronic pain, headache, diabetes, among others.

Hall (1980) lists 50 somatic causes of anxiety, categorized as neurologic, endocrine, infectious, autonomic, and circulatory. Common cases are drug abuse (including caffeine abuse), drug withdrawal, hyperthyroidism, fasting hypoglycemia, and hypercortisolism. Rare causes are brain tumor of the third ventrical and diencephalic epilepsy.

Intermittent psychotic episodes may be a manifestation of such diverse conditions as endocrinopathy, multiple sclerosis, alcoholism with intermittent hepatic failure, delirium tremens or hallucinosis, systemic lupus erythematosus, acute intermittent porphyria, herpes simplex encephalitis, temporal lobe epilepsy, and the use and abuse of prescription and illicit drugs. Delirium is estimated to occur in up to 30 percent of hospitalized patients (Cavanaugh 1983).

The effects of psychiatric complications on the course of any of these illnesses can be profound. Unfortunately, in the clinical process health practitioners often misdiagnose or overlook these problems and minimize how the complex interaction of physiologic, psychologic, and sociocultural factors influence the patient's illness. This situation calls for better training and supervision of those not accustomed to utilizing a biopsychosocial model, such as nonmedical mental health workers and nonpsychiatric physicians. Psychiatrists need to watch for somatic causes underlying psychological symptoms, and other physicians should watch for psychosocial factors or psychiatric disorders that complicate or contribute to nonpsychiatric medical illness. In one study of psychiatric clinic patients, the referring psychiatrist overlooked about one-half, and the referring nonpsychiatric physician about one-third, of the existing somatic conditions (Koranyi 1979).

Conclusions
Chronic illness not only challenges the patient, family, and physician, but presents a major economic challenge to society, with political ramifications. The staggering costs alone justify intensive research of new ways to reduce disability. Part of this effort must aim to reduce the psychiatric morbidity associated with chronic illness and to reduce the effects of psychiatric disorders, psychosocial factors, behavior, and life style on the incidence and outcome of chronic illness. Medicine urgently needs new clinical models to help prevent chronic illness and provide more cost-effective care.

CONCEPTS IN THE PSYCHIATRIC REHABILITATION OF THE PHYSICALLY ILL
Several key concepts contribute to our understanding of how emotions, behavior, and psychiatric disorder may interact with and influence the course of disease, the recovery process in acute illness, and the management of chronic illness. The evolution of these concepts reflects the history of how different but overlapping intellectual disciplines have struggled—sometimes in concert, sometimes in parallel, sometimes sequentially—to understand disease, illness, and illness behavior. Strict categorization, while heuristically useful, is somewhat forced because of the overlap inherent to disciplines converging on the same subject matter. These disciplines include: psychophysiology and psychosomatic medicine; learning theory and behavioral medicine; medical sociology and social anthropology; family theory; biological, psychological, and social aspects of stress and adaptation; psychobiology and neurobiology, including neurohumoral mechanisms, neurotransmitters, and psychopharmacology; and, finally, systems theory, the "new psychosomatics," and biopsychosocial medicine. The last enables a convergence of each of the aforementioned concepts into a unified theory of illness with practical application to clinical medicine.

Psychophysiology and Psychosomatic Medicine

Psychosomatic medicine is as old as the history of medicine. Until the advent of modern biomedical research, much of medical practice throughout the world relied upon psychosomatic techniques. Reiser (1975) describes how, in the twentieth century, theoretical investigations in psychosomatic medicine have been pursued along essentially two different lines. First, combined medical and psychological investigations of selected medical patients elucidate the role of psychological conflict and emotional arousal in the pathogenesis, precipitation, and course of medical illness. Second, researchers have measured physiologic variables during various states of stress. Following the reductionistic approach of infectious disease, these investigators tried to discover what psychological constructs caused physical disorder. Not surprisingly, few firm conclusions were reached. But four schemes were suggested: (1) no relationship between stress and organ systems; (2) a somatopsychic sequence, with organ systems provoking emotional and cognitive responses; (3) a psychosomatic sequence, with emotional changes causing physiologic changes; (4) a genetic predisposition, with an underlying constitutional factor related to genes and/or environment affecting both mind and body.

Reiser identifies several problems with this research. It relies on covariant data, deriving from the inherent differences between the social and biological sciences in their concepts, techniques, languages, complexity, and levels of abstraction. The research assumes that different events occurring within a specified time interval were causally related. While this model did not provide causality in the sense of the linear, reductionistic model of disease, it did provide an opportunity to examine the interplay of feedback loops within a matrix of factors, and how these factors influence the temporal relationship of events in predisposition, precipitation, and perpetuation, that suggest causality in the evolution of an illness. For example, in reviewing the case of Michael I., the 35-year-old man with heart disease, the history suggests several interacting mechanisms for his acute episode of chest pain after returning home from the bar:

Psychodynamic: emotional arousal during the fight with his wife caused anxiety, fear of abandonment, and pain, through a conversion mechanism which enables him to retain the sick role and thus her sympathy.

Psychophysiologic: emotional arousal during the fight with his wife increased cardiac load, producing myocardial ischemia and chest pain.

Psychophysiologic: emotional arousal during the fight with his wife increased circulating adrenaline, provoking arrhythmia, ischemia, and pain.

Psychophysiologic: emotional arousal stimulated chest wall muscle spasm and chest pain.

Behavioral–somatopsychic: increased physical activity when drunk provoked a sequence of angina, anxiety about another heart attack, irritability at his wife, and psychosomatic chest pain, perpetuating the initial pain of ischemic origin.

As demonstrated in these examples, psychophysiologic concepts were integrated into psychosomatic theory by involving the nervous system as a mediating factor.

Learning Theory and Behavioral Medicine

Pavlov's concept of classical conditioning and Skinner's concept of operant conditioning, further developed in the discipline of behavioral psychology, have been applied to problems of health and illness in the discipline of behavioral medicine. More recently, the definition of this term has been broadened to include the knowledge and skills of all the behavioral sciences as applied to the understanding and treatment of health and illness (Schwartz and Weiss, 1978). This enlargement of scope has been paralleled by a growing awareness that the major problems of health relate to aspects of individual or group behavior. Some examples of the scope of this work include: developing educational programs and environmental manipulations to change the smoking habits of large groups, such as teenagers in schools or employees in a company; biofeedback and relaxation interventions for reducing hypertension or headache; behavioral techniques in eating disorders; biofeedback to assist seizure control in persons with epilepsy; and behavioral modification for chronic pain patients. Elucidation of the neurobiology of learning has promoted a convergence of behavioral medicine with psychopharmacology and the neurosciences in the discipline of behavioral pharmacology.

Medical Sociology and Social Anthropology

These disciplines have contributed to our understanding of how patients behave in the context of medical illness, or their *illness behavior.* Parsons (1951) presented the concept of the *sick role,* to which all social groups assign a member who is unable to function normally. In our society the sick role is defined by exemption from normal duties, exemption from responsibility for sickness, the desire to get better, and an attempt to seek treatment and to cooperate with those who provide it. In chronic medical illness, the sick role is less well defined, because patients must continue to seek treatment for chronic illness, but also be functional and maintain responsibility to the degree that their illness will permit. Problems occur when a patient does not accept the sick role and his or her illness behavior becomes abnormal, for example, when the patient does not cooperate in treatment or appears to prefer the sick role to recovery; where there is the possibility that the patient has deliberately assumed the sick role for ulterior purposes; or when a disease can be regarded as self-inflicted.

Understanding where a patient fits on the continuum from optimal health to total disability and the appropriate degree of dependency and self-reliance is one of the most difficult challenges for the physician, patient, family, and employer when attempting to manage a person's chronic illness.

Pilowsky (1978) has described diverse patterns of "abnormal illness behavior," such as the denial of illness, the exaggeration of physical complaints, hypochondriasis, psychogenic pain, somatization disorder, conversion disorder, factitious disorder, and malingering. This classification scheme is descriptive and does not assume a particular etiology for these illness behavior patterns. All persons with chronic medical illness develop patterns of behavior to cope, some of which will be described later under the section on chronic illness. It is the physician's job to try to describe those patterns and help the patient develop the most adaptive behavioral patterns possible. For a thorough review of "illness behavior" see Nurcombe and Gallagher (1986a).

Family Theory and Therapy
Physicians have known from clinical experience over many years the importance of families in maintaining patients' health, but it has not been until relatively recently that this has received much research attention. The family has been studied in both illnesses usually thought of as psychosomatic and in other illnesses as well. For example, Medalie et al. (1973) in a five-year, prospective study of 10,000 men, found that reported family problems were a strong predictor of the development of angina pectoris. Men who reported the most family problems had almost three times the incidence as men who reported the fewest problems. End-stage renal disease and maintenance hemodialysis cause significant chronic distress for families, accompanied by a number of unexpected crises (Friedman 1970). Family adjustment varies widely in reports from different centers. As home dialysis has become more widespread, the special problems of these families have become more apparent (Levenberg et al. 1978–79).

Family therapy would be expected to be helpful in the case of several groups of physically ill patients (Stewart 1985):

1. Patients with psychosomatic or stress-related illnesses; even if problems are not apparent, families are a major source of social support and are important in dealing with stress.
2. Patients with chronic or life-threatening illnesses
3. Patients who are noncompliant with medications, diet, etc.; family support is a major factor in compliance. Doherty et al. (1983) showed that men whose wives were highly supportive had a 96 percent compliance with taking cholesterol-lowering medications,

while those whose wives' support was low were only 70 percent compliant.
4. Patients who have physical illnesses secondary to a psychiatric disorder; considerable success has been achieved with family therapy in disorders such as anorexia nervosa (Minuchin et al. 1978), drug abuse (Stanton 1982), and alcoholism (Steinglass 1976).

Research in family therapy of the physically ill obviously is in a very early phase and much work is needed. All the problems of psychotherapy outcome research—selecting a relatively homogenous group of patients, standardizing diagnoses, adequately specifying the nature of the therapy and therapists, finding adequate control groups, specifying outcome measures, and assuring adequate follow-up—are shared by family-therapy research. Since family therapy deals generally with families rather than with individuals, the issues of diagnosis and homogeneity are even more difficult. It also is more difficult to determine the appropriate outcome measures.

Since it is unlikely that large quantities of excellent research on this topic will be available soon, where does this leave the clinician? The evidence that family therapy is beneficial is primarily anecdotal, but does show considerable promise. Haggerty (1983) has suggested that until more research is done, the selection criteria for family therapy in psychosomatic patients should be the same as those Clarkin (1979) suggested for family therapy in general. These guidelines are also valid for other physically ill patients. They include exacerbations of illness related to family problems, stress caused by family developmental milestones, unresponsiveness to other forms of psychotherapy, symptoms in multiple family members, and distress in a child or adolescent.

Stress and Adaptation
Beginning in the nineteenth century, "stress and strain" began to be considered a cause of illness, but it was not until the 1920s that the concept of stress was used in medical research (Hinkle 1975). A complete review of this vast experimental literature is beyond the scope of this chapter, but the important findings are summarized:

- Cannon (1934) used the term stress when describing conditions, such as cold, excitement, or low blood sugar, that provoked a fight-or-flight response.
- Selye (1950) argued that stress was nonspecific and that any stress would elicit the *general adaptation syndrome*, which consists of three stages: alarm, resistance, and exhaustion. Evidence suggests that this response is psychologically mediated: Animals who sustain injuries while unconscious do not show the characteristic endocrine responses; and humans conscious during the final stages of terminal illness or injury do show these changes, whereas those unconscious do not.

- Lazarus (1975) and Hinkel (1975) promote the concept that, for any individual, each stressor produces a specific pattern of somatic response.
- Different psychological responses to similar stressors can cause different physiological responses. For example, the same stressor, a leukemic child, produced different physiologic responses in parents. Those with the least denial showed a significantly greater response (Friedman et al. 1963).
- Personality and cognitive factors may explain many of the idiosyncratic responses to stressors that are associated with many illnesses, such as hypertension (Roessler and Engel 1975).
- Life changes are stressful according to the amount of readjustment required by the individual (Holmes and Rahe 1967).
- Frequent stressful life events are associated with an increase in the incidence of disease (Kiritz and Moos 1974).
- The stress associated with specific events, while generally agreed upon, varies among cultural groups and with individual circumstances, such as how desirable or how controllable the event is for the individual (Hutner and Locke 1984).
- Social environments have physiologic effects (Kiritz and Moos 1974). Cohesion produces physiological co-variance. For example, female college friends in the same dormitory tend to synchronize their menstrual cycles. Group cohesion also decreases stress responses in group members. High stress responses, at least temporarily, are associated with other social factors, including high degree of involvement with others, high responsibility, and low clarity of environment.
- Social support has been shown to modify stress and prevent illness and to protect people from such diverse problems as low birth weight, tuburculosis, and myocardial infarction (Kiritz and Moos 1974; Cobb 1976).
- Individual factors, such as cognitive appraisal of a situation and coping skills, interact with these environmental factors to influence how a person may respond, emotionally and behaviorally, to any one situation (Lazarus 1975).

The adaptiveness of these behaviors in decreasing stress and problem solving plays a key role in maintaining health.

Physiologic mechanisms mediate the relationships among psychosocial factors, stress, and health. The central nervous system influences every physiologic process directly through the autonomic or peripheral nervous system, or indirectly through endocrine–metabolic processes. The reticular activating system, the limbic system, and the hypothalamus are particularly important in adapting to internal and external changes through their communication with the neocortex, the seat of the thought process.

Kiely (1975) presents the concept of the ergotropic and trophotropic systems. The former, which prepares the individual for

positive action, is subserved by the neurotransmitters norepinephrine and dopamine. Its activity is characterized by increased arousal,
sympathetic activity, and muscle tone. The trophotropic system, concerned with conservation and withdrawal, is subserved by seratonin
and acetylcholine. Its activity is characterized by an increased barrier to peripheral stimuli, increased parasympathetic tone, and decreased muscle tone. These systems work reciprocally in situations of
low stimulation, but both may be active in situations of high stimulation, accounting for a mixture of symptoms.

Neuroendocrine mechanisms play a key role in regulating physiologic processes. Henry (1982) has suggested that neuroendocrine
responses should be considered along three axes:

1. The sympathetic adrenal medullary axis, involved in the flight-or-
   fight response, served by the hormones norepinephrine and epinephrine and regulated by the amygdala and the lateral hypothalamus
2. The pituitary adrenal cortical axis, served by ACTH and cortisol
   and thought to be related to the general adaptation response or the
   functions of distress or helplessness that seem to activate this
   system
3. The hypothalamic–pituitary–sex-steroid axis, using sex hormones
   such as testosterone and functioning in aggression and to influence social interactions

These efforts integrating biological systems into functional behavioral repertoires are theoretically interesting and important, but not
of practical clinical significance.

Psychoimmunology, Psychoendocrinology, and Developmental Psychobiology

Recent studies have demonstrated a connection between a variety of
stresses (e.g., space flight, sleep deprivation) and different indices of
immune function. Other studies have demonstrated an interaction
among stress, coping abilities, and immune response. The neurohumoral consequences of stress are conveyed by the hypothalamus
through the pituitary, adrenal medulla, and other glands. While Cannon (1934) emphasized the unity of the stress response, research
increasingly has supported the concept's complexity and the diversity of the nature, intensity, and duration of stressors and individual
endocrine responses to stress. Lymphocytes have receptor sites for a
number of stress hormones, which indicates a mechanism for the
influence of stress on immune function (Locke 1978; Borysenko and
Borysenko 1982). Thus, the stresses inherent in having chronic medical illness may themselves influence the body's own capacity to fight
disease.

Certain neurophysiologic systems, subserved by neurotransmitters, are implicated in the genesis of disease and the modulation of

symptoms associated with chronic medical illness. Mrs. Rita A., the accountant with rheumatoid arthritis and major depression provides an example. Depression may have influenced the course of her illness in several ways: by altering the function of the immune system which mediates her disease; by reducing her capacity to modify pain perception through the influence of ascending and descending noradrenergic and serotonergic fibers originating in the brainstem on pain-modulating systems in the spinal cord and brain; by reducing her capacity to participate in and comply with rigorous physical therapy and a pain-management program, both of which require motivation and concentration; by increasing her use of drugs that provide immediate symptom relief, such as narcotics and steroids, but adversely affect her disease and prevent optimal management. Her physician believed that at least four and probably all five of these factors actually influenced her course.

Ader (1981) reviews the experimental evidence supporting the role of the brain in modulating the immune system. Here are some examples. Learning, through the respondent-conditioning model, can suppress the immune response (Ader and Cohen 1981). Communication between the brain and organs of the immune system include the presence of neurohumoral receptors, such as adrenergic and cholinergic receptors, or lymphocytes, and autonomic innervation of lymphoid tissue, such as the thymus. A feedback loop also seems to be part of the communication, as the immune system has been shown experimentally to influence the hypothalamus. Certain studies show that patterns of stress may influence an organism's capacity to resist infection (Plaut, Friedman 1981) or invasion by implanted neoplasms (Riley et al. 1981) and may also influence indices of immune function according to a person's coping abilities (Locke et al. 1984). Possible mechanisms mediating these effects have been reviewed by Borysenko and Borysenko (1982) as well as by Locke (1982).

Endocrine responses to stress appear to play a major role in immune modulation. Many of the hormones secreted as part of the stress response have effects on the immune system, including: corticosteroids, sex steroids, histamine, somatotropin, insulin, antidiuretic hormone, parathyroid hormone, beta adrenergic agonists, endorphins (Borysenko and Borysenko 1982; Locke 1982).

It should be noted that these endocrine responses do show simple variation. Coping styles that protect individuals from becoming particularly aroused or distressed reduce hormone responses (Moldofsky 1984). It appears likely that endocrine responses are involved in disease in ways other than mediating immune function, but these mechanisms are not yet clear.

Psychobiologic factors in disease susceptibility have also been looked at developmentally. This area has been reviewed by Ader (1975) and Moldofsky (1984). Most of these studies have been carried out with animals. Premature separation from mother has been shown to cause a predisposition to later pathology in animals. Also, exposure of a young animal to various noxious stimuli, such as electric shocks or handling, can predispose it to later infection, cancer, and gastric lesions. The timing and nature of these stimuli are quite important, however. A stimulus such as electric shock which, at a certain age, increases an animal's vulnerability to cancer, may actually decrease vulnerability if administered at a later age. Early experience appears to cause long-term changes in psychophysiology and disease susceptibility. These experiments are intriguingly similar to the psychoanalytic concept that trauma in certain vulnerable periods of childhood may influence the healthy development of the personality.

Proponents exclusively espousing any one of these conceptual models are being forced by accumulated evidence to accept that a complex field of perceptual, cognitive, and physiologic influences, interacting at many levels, mediates the relationship between the brain and the body, between events, illness, and disease. Neurobiological research is bridging ideological chasms amongst theories of neurobiology and analytic, cognitive, and behavioral psychology. Kandell's meticulous experiments on snail neurons provide a theoretical molecular mechanism that, through the concept of chronic sensitization, links psychodynamic and behavioral models of anxiety (Kandell 1983).

Biopsychosocial Medicine and the New Psychosomatics
Recent concepts have attempted to integrate the rapidly expanding knowledge in neuroscience and behavioral medicine with older psychosomatic theories in a systems approach, based on the theories of von Bertalanffy (1968) and Miller (1978). Engle (1977) has called for a new approach to the clinical care of patients, the biopsychosocial medical model, that emphasizes the need to conceptualize the patient and his/her illness as a system influenced by multiple factors from physical, psychological, and social dimensions. Reiser (1975) presents a theory of the *biopsychosocial field*, in which all illness and disease can be conceptualized as occurring in three phases: Phase 1 includes programing organ and tissue function for patterns that are related to genetically determined, mind–brain–body linkages. Phase 2 involves the concepts of developmental physiology, the sensitizing, by experience at critical periods of development, of regulatory mechanisms for mind–brain–body linkages. This sensitization process establishes vulnerability for the precipitation of actual disease by psychosocial stressors. Phase 3, once disease has been established, involves the perpetuation of disease by biopsychosocial factors.

Several authors have presented clinical models useful in teaching and practicing the biopsychosocial medical model. Leigh and Reiser (1980) present a clinical approach to patients based upon this model using a Patient-Evaluation Grid in a systems-contextual framework that describes the interaction of the disease, the person, and the environment. Nurcombe and Gallagher (1986b) describe the evolution of an illness in terms of how the biopsychosocial or systemic dimension transects the predisposition, precipitation, pattern, and perpetuation of an illness, or the temporal dimension. They use algorithms of the clinical reasoning process, a *diagnostic net*, and a protocol for management planning, resulting in a systematic approach to clinical decision making and patient care in psychiatric and primary care settings.

Future work will follow three broad tracks of endeavor. Neuroscience increasingly will elucidate mechanisms linking mind, brain, and behavior. Psychopharmacology, behavioral pharmacology, and behavioral medicine will discover new techniques to modify the negative effects of emotions and behavior on illness and predisposing risks. Practitioners will develop new clinical models that integrate this knowledge into cost-effective clinical care.

CHRONIC ILLNESS

The Mental Health of the Chronically Ill
Many studies have been done on various chronic illnesses looking at them as individual entities. Cassileth and associates (1974) noted the similarity of the various descriptions of personalities of patients with many different diseases. They administered the Mental Health Index to 758 outpatient and specialty clinic patients, suffering from such conditions as arthritis, diabetes mellitus, renal disease, cancer, nonmelanotic skin disorders, and chronic depression. The physically ill patients were clearly different from the chronically depressed patients but not from the general population. The Mental Health Index did not differentiate among the various groups of physically ill patients. It was noted that recently diagnosed patients and those more physically ill reported poorer mental health. Older patients reported better mental health.

Although reasons for this were unclear, the authors offered several interesting possible explanations: Chronic illness may offer social advantages, such as increased social activity (because of more involvement with others), more care, and more attention, all of which may be less available to healthy elderly people. Older patients may have developed more effective skills in managing stressful life events. Older patients may have a biological evolutionary advantage that enables them to adapt to illnesses more common with advancing years. As the authors point out, this study was intended to show global psychological patterns in patients with various illnesses, not to look specifically at issues significant to any one group. Further, the study did not seek to identify psychiatric illness or coping patterns. It did show that psychological adaptation in chronically ill patients was effective, but not disease specific. They did point out, however, that significant numbers of chronically ill patients do have mental health problems which require intervention.

Differences among Illness Groups

Mason et al. (1983) had similar results in their study comparing patients with rheumatoid arthritis with patients with other chronic diseases. Their study included patients with rheumatoid arthritis, hypertension, cancer, diabetes mellitus, heart disease, and pulmonary diseases, using the Arthritis Impact Measurement scales. They demonstrated significant differences among patient groups in pain and physical function but not in psychological status. Viney and Westbrook (1981) had similar results in an interview study of a group of chronically ill, hospitalized patients. There was no pattern of psychological reaction based on the type of disability. More severely disabled patients were noted to have increased anxiety, depression, and anger and less "good feelings." Depression was noted to be more common in younger patients and in patients of lower educational status, but also in patients with higher occupational status. There was no pattern based on sex differences.

Coping with Chronic Illness

Forsythe et al. (1984) studied the management style of chronically ill, hospitalized patients, using an interview technique. They studied patients with arthritis, chronic obstructive pulmonary disease and a variety of neurological disorders, emphasizing the patients' efforts to win over their diseases. They described patients as seeing themselves as normal by periodically redefining what is normal for them. As disease progressed and manifestations became more severe, patients would redefine their status in order to maintain normality. The authors emphasize that patients need to maintain control despite the unpredictability of chronic illness. To do this, patients must become active participants in their own care, becoming expert in various techniques to manage their illness and their personal reactions to various medications and treatments. Chronically ill patients assess the risks and benefits of treatment and make their decisions on that basis, a pattern which the authors do not consider an issue of compliance. Rather, they see this as part of an on-going effort to develop coping strategies. In this effort, a major role of health care professionals is to provide practical information on problems, and to help patients maintain hope and perceive themselves as winning over the disease.

Lipowski (1983b) describes a model of psychosocial reactions to chronic illness. Although this model can be used to describe reactions to acute illness, it is more applicable to patients with more chronic and more severe illness. He described three core components: personal meaning, coping style, and emotional response.

Personal meaning obviously is subjective and somewhat idiosyncratic, but there are several common issues. One is whether the patient perceives the situation as a challenge or a threat. Patients who see the situation as a challenge tend to react more positively and adaptively. A second major issue relating to meaning is that of loss. Chronically ill patients have multiple, on-going losses. Grief is an appropriate reaction to these losses, but there is no clear dividing line between normal grief and clinical depression. This is based partly on social norms regarding grief. A third major issue relating to meaning is whether the patient sees the illness as a gain or a relief. Many patients find that their illness relieves them from unpleasant responsibilities or provides other benefits. These gains can be an obstacle to recovery. A final issue related to meaning is whether or not the patient sees the illness as a punishment. Patients who do see the illness as punishment may see it as justified or unjustified. Patients who see the illness as unjustified punishment may become quite angry and even frankly paranoic. Patients who see the illness as a justified punishment may, in some cases, simply give up and perhaps die, notwithstanding adequate treatment. Some of these patients, however, may see a redemptive value in their suffering and may even have periods of elation.

A number of things determine the meaning that patients give to their illness. Some of these are intrapersonal factors. Intrapersonal factors most important appear to be the patients' cognitive perceptual style, their psychodynamic configuration, and their emotional state at the onset of illness. Interpersonal factors are also very important. Family support and the doctor–patient relationship in particular are major influences. There are also illness-related factors. These are related to the personal value the patient places on the various affected body parts or functions. Sociocultural and economic factors also play a role. Attitudes about various chronic illnesses vary markedly in this society. Patients with diseases such as cancer or seizure disorders may find themselves stigmatized. This is even more often a problem for the patient with AIDS.

The *emotional response* to chronic illness again shows no sharp boundary between normal and abnormal reactions. Anxiety, grief, anger, and guilt are often prominent.

Coping styles can be divided into *cognitive* and *behavioral* styles. The two most common cognitive styles are minimalization and vigilant focusing, both of which can be adaptive or maladaptive depending on their intensity and the context. A minimizing patient tends to play down his pain and other problems and to pay less attention to the seriousness of his illness. The vigilant focusing patient tends to be much more aware of body sensations and of possible problems. This can be adaptive; causing the patient to seek information and to cope actively, but can also lead to excessive anxiety and pain. Behavioral coping styles can be divided into three main types: tackling, capitulating, and avoiding. Again, these may be adaptive or maladaptive depending on the context.

Felton et al. (1984) studied the effect of individual *coping strategies* in chronically ill adults. They studied patients with diabetes mellitus, hypertension, rheumatoid arthritis, chronic lymphocytic leukemia, lymphoma, and multiple myeloma. They classified the various coping strategies used by patients into six groups. These were: cognitive restructuring, information seeking, emotional expression, wish-fulfilling fantasy, self-blame, and threat minimalization. They also found that the use of emotional expression, wish-fulfilling fantasy, and self-blame were associated with poorer adjustment. Coping strategies were found to be similar in all illnesses. Cancer and rheumatoid arthritis patients were noted to have lower self-esteem and illness acceptance than patients with hypertension or diabetes mellitus. This was thought to be due to the higher level of disability in the former patients. The authors noted that the effects of coping were rather modest. Social support and the use of interpersonal coping strategies were not considered in the study, and the authors suggested that these are probably major factors.

Illness Behavior in Chronic Illness

Wooley et al. (1978) describes what they call a syndrome of chronic illness behavior, described as a disability disproportionate to disease, a life style that revolves around the illness role, and a perpetual search for new and better medical care. They related this to the "psychosomatic V" seen on the MMPI, a pattern of hypochondriasis, depression, and hysteria often seen in patients with physical or pain disorders. They note that these behaviors are not seen in most patients with chronic illnesses, but are common in patients referred for psychiatric treatment after the failure of conventional medical treatment. These chronic illness behaviors elicit the care or attention of others and relieve the patient of responsibility. The authors offered a learning-theory explanation for the development of this pattern. They believe that there are three important factors. The first of these is *vicarious learning*, from watching the illness behavior of others. The second major factor is direct *social reinforcement* of illness behavior by family, friends, physicians, and others. The third factor is *avoidance learning*. The illness of many of these patients enabled them to avoid a variety of circumstances. They pointed out that most patients with this pattern have a background of failure in ordinary pursuits and a marked lack of social competence.

APPLICATIONS OF PSYCHIATRY TO CHRONIC ILLNESS MANAGEMENT: PRACTICE MODELS

Thus far, this chapter has reviewed the theoretical bases for the psychiatric rehabilitation of the medically ill. This section reviews the effectiveness of these theories when applied to the practice of medicine. Overall, most work describes successful educational and clinical programs or interventions for individual patients—outcome studies are scanty. Four basic models characterize this work, each differentiated by the way the psychiatrist functions in the clinical process. In the *consultation psychiatry model* the psychiatrist examines the patient and makes suggestions to the staff about management. The consultant may provide limited treatment in the context of the consultee's own clinical setting. In the *liaison psychiatry model* the psychiatrist does not work directly with the patient, but rather educates other professionals to use psychiatric knowledge and skills in the treatment of the patient. In the *integrated health center model* the psychiatrist provides liaison, consultative, and direct care services in conjunction with other medical specialists, particularly primary care physicians. In the *psychiatric practice model* the psychiatrist provides part of the care, or functions as the primary physician, for patients with medical illness in a medical model psychiatric practice.

Consultation Psychiatry Model
Consultation psychiatry developed as an outgrowth of general hospital psychiatry units, beginning with service at Albany Hospital in 1902. The development of psychosomatic medicine in the 1920s further encouraged the model (Lipowski 1974). Initially, services operated on the model of traditional medical consultation, such as the one at Massachusetts General Hospital described by Weisman and Hackett (1960). As the field has developed, new models have been introduced. Caplan (1970) described four types of mental health consultation. Two types, client-centered case consultation and consultee-centered case consultation, apply to patient care consultations. Schiff and Pilot (1959) described an approach to consultee-oriented consultations in the general hospital setting. They emphasized examining the manner in which consultations were requested and the background of the situation. The assumption was that every psychiatric consultation comes from physician concern, and that the most important frequently are not explicit. Myer and Mendelson (1961) describe a situation-oriented approach, in many ways an extension of the consultee-oriented approach, which emphasizes understanding interpersonal transactions among team members as a means of understanding patient behavior and the concerns of the consultee.

Despite differences in approach, psychiatric consultants must perform certain functions to meet the needs of patients and consultees. Generally, these functions include diagnostic evaluation, management advice, as well as psychotherapeutic interventions. The consultant may be involved in resolving conflicts between patients and staff and in teaching, but these latter functions are emphasized more in liaison approaches.

The Liaison Psychiatry Model

The term liaison psychiatry—possibly first used by Billings in 1939 when describing the program at the University of Colorado (Billings 1939)—was derived from a concept developed by Henry in his work at Cornell Medical School (Lipowski, 1979). In 1929, he suggested that every general hospital should have a psychiatrist who would make "regular visits to the wards, who would direct the psychiatric out-patient clinic, who would continue the instruction and organize the psychiatric work of interns and who would attend staff conferences so that there might be a mutual exchange of medical experience and frank discussion of the more complicated cases" (p. 4). A number of psychiatric liaison programs have developed. In most, the work is carried out by psychiatrists. An interesting exception is at the University of Rochester, where internists with "psychological training" carry out medical liaison (Engel et al. 1957).

Definitions of liaison psychiatry have varied. Lipowski (1967) emphasized the role of liaison psychiatrists in conflict resolution and in interpreting patient behavior to the staff. He also emphasized the importance of teaching and making the connection between biological and psychosocial factors. Strain and Grossman (1975) define liaison psychiatry as involving primary prevention, active treatment role, case detection, educational activities, and systems-oriented intervention. They see the liaison psychiatrist as a full member of the medical team. Mohl (1979) described consultation and liaison functions as extreme ends of a continuum, but distinguished them on the basis of the different social roles involved. He pointed out that the consultant is in the role of an outsider to the medical team who obtains temporary admission to the team under particular circumstances at the request of a team member. The liaison psychiatrist, on the other hand, must become a full member of the team, with the high status that allows him to be an intervenor rather than merely a reactor.

The relative importance of consultation and liaison functions has been a matter of much recent debate (Lipowski 1983a). Liaison functions appear to have advantages in preventing patient and staff problems, in providing services to patients who otherwise would be overlooked, and in teaching nonpsychiatric staff members about psychiatric aspects of patient care. Relatively little research has been done, however, to document these suggested advantages. Liaison approaches can be quite resource intensive. In some programs, a psychiatrist is assigned full time to a medical unit. Because of this heavy demand on resources, Lipowski has suggested that intensive liaison be used predominantly in areas of the hospital that have high levels of stress and frequent serious psychosocial and psychiatric problems among the patients, such as critical care units, oncology services, and rehabilitation services. He also suggested that the liaison aspect of each consultation be emphasized. To do this, the consultant takes care to discuss the patient with the consultee and other members of the team and to provide regular follow-up. He also suggested the use of liaison nurses to work with medical and surgical nurses.

The Integrated Health Team Model

Most experience in providing integrated health care has occurred in the hospital setting where the consultation–liaison psychiatrist, social workers, and medical psychologists are at hand to work collaboratively with other medical professionals. The hospital rehabilitation unit is a natural place for the psychiatrist and other mental health professionals to apply their knowledge and skills to the complex issues of the rehabilitation of the physically and mentally impaired (Bishop 1980; McKegney 1968). Here, perhaps more than anywhere in the health care system, mind–brain–body interactions require the consummate skills of multidisciplinary professionals working as a team. Most units aim to maintain a therapeutic rehabilitative milieu while the team develops specific plans, using principles of behavioral modification, to help patients achieve a higher level of physical, mental, and vocational function. However the best-laid plans can go astray when the patient's psychology or neurobiology do not permit full cooperation. In these circumstances, the consultation psychiatrist can, with the team, assess the entire matrix of biopsychosocial factors that influence this behavior. Ultimately, the setting and its patients challenge the psychiatrist's capacity to integrate his or her unique training in clinical psychiatry, neurology and medicine, in neurobiology, and in group dynamics and human behavior. On many rehabilitation units, the psychiatrist functions only as a peripheral consultant, advising about diagnosis and management of difficult behavior, or of psychiatric disorder, that have defied the interventions of the regular staff. Status as outsider and late entry into an already deteriorated situation render the psychiatrist less effective. The most effective units consist of a multidisciplinary team of psychiatrists, psychologists, physical therapists, nurses, occupational therapists, vocational therapists, and a psychiatrist who is not a stranger but a part of the team. The psychiatrist should be particularly skilled in managing the group dynamics of the system. She or he needs to provide critical expertise without threatening the overlapping roles of other key staff, such as the physiatrist, social worker, or psychologist. Because success on this ward depends to a great extent on a coordinated team effort, any group tension will translate inevitably into lower quality care.

Consultation–liaison psychiatrists have worked with other medical specialists to provide integrated hospital treatment for patients with many serious illnesses. McKegney and Gallagher (1985) describe the psychiatric aspects of caring for three serious illnesses: spinal cord injury, cancer, and end-stage kidney disease. Together, these illnesses represent a spectrum of problems common to rehabilitation and care of all chronic illness, but each presents its unique profile of problems:

- spinal cord injury, characterized initially by catastrophic loss and heroic rehabilitation, and eventually by persistent, usually stable, and often overwhelming disability;
- recurrent or progressive cancer, characterized initially by fear but often little disability, then by progressive pain and loss of function, and finally by the specter of death; and
- end-stage renal disease, characterized initially by physical sickness, then by dependence upon life-saving machinery or by dramatic surgery, and always by chronic uncertainty about outcome.

Team care of other illnesses has been described, including burns (Andreasen et al. 1972), arthritis (Rogers et al. 1980), and myocardial infarction (Cassem 1981).

This work is largely hospital based because that is the setting in which consultation–liaison (C–L) psychiatry programs first developed, with funding from federal training grants. The literature about integrated health care programs in ambulatory settings has been less prolific for several reasons. First, most academic departments of psychiatry are university-hospital based, so that C–L psychiatrists have not had much exposure to nonpsychiatric ambulatory settings. Second, only recently, in part due to the impact of chronic illness on health costs, has the research enterprise been interested in a large-scale effort in primary care and ambulatory care settings. Third, even when integrated clinical and teaching programs have been developed, they usually have been in primary care settings which do not easily lend themselves to the methodology of traditional disease-oriented research.

Ambulatory care settings provide the best opportunity for integrating psychiatric skills into the care of those recovering from serious illness or trying to cope with chronic illness. Here, the psychiatrist and mental health professional, working closely with other medical colleagues, can observe, describe, and research the psychiatric problems and psychosocial issues of recovery and disability in the context of the person's life style and life cycle. For it is the person's own community and family that must adjust to the accumulation of losses, the altered family and occupational roles, the pain and suffering associated with chronic illness. The patient and primary physician must establish a working relationship that enables the patient to accept a responsible amount of dependency—enough to achieve treatment and health-maintenance objectives—but autonomy and independence as well, enough to feel self-worth and some control of his or her own destiny. This objective is based on the assumption that the physician will systematically acquire a data base that reflects the physical, psychological, and social needs of the rehabilitating or chronically ill patient.

Nurcombe and Gallagher (1986b) propose a method of comprehensive biopsychosocial assessment and formulation which lends itself to this task. Data is recorded on a grid defined by two axes: the temporal axis, describing an illness in terms of its predisposition, precipitation, pattern, and perpetuation; and the systemic axis, describing the illness in terms of the physical, psychological, and social factors that influence its formulation. (See Figure 1.) As data are gathered over time by interview, physical, or laboratory examination, they are recorded on a Diagnostic Net in the appropriate category (e.g., predisposing social factor). The advantage of this system is that it forces the physician to consider systematically the psychological and social factors, not just the biomedical ones, that might influence the course of a person's illness. The method of recording data also lends itself to the systematic management planning, so critical to achieving the objectives of rehabilitation and to providing effective care of chronic illness.

Borus and Casserly (1979) have described the different models of integration of mental health workers into primary care centers. Integrated, flexible health care delivery systems are described by Adams et al. (1978) in an urban area and by McMahon et al. (1983) in a rural area. These practices utilize primary care and mental health personnel as appropriate to provide a range of psychiatric services that extends from the primary care setting into secondary and tertiary care settings. This design to some degree ensures patients the technical expertise of tertiary care while maintaining the continuity of therapeutic relationships and the smooth flow of critical information among various ambulatory and hospital settings.

Figure 1.

The diagnostic net: biopsychosocial and temporal dimensions.

		Temporal axis			
		Predisposition	Precipitation	Perpetuation	Pattern of response
	Physical				
Biopsychosocial	Psychological				
	Social				

The Psychiatric Practice Model

The loss of federal funding for C–L training programs, limited reimbursement for consultation and liaison activities, and the failure of present models of practice to have a positive impact on the course of the chronically ill patient have prompted medicine to search for new practice models that integrate psychiatric concepts and skills into the rehabilitation and care of the chronically ill. Specialty units in general hospitals have attempted to provide integrated approaches but, generally, these have been fiscally unsuccessful. Kimball (1985) describes the Continuing Care Unit at Yale–New Haven Medical Center, which provides integrated multidisciplinary care for patients recovering from severe illnesses such as stroke or myocardial infarction, so-called "psychosomatic illnesses", and eating disorders. Morgan, Kremer, and Gaylor (1979) describe the development and function of an inpatient behavioral medicine unit in a general hospital. Lipowski (1984) describes a psychosomatic hospital unit at Toronto that focuses on integrating psychotherapeutic and biomedical approaches to psychosomatic patients. Houpt, Keefe, and Snipes (1984) describe the structure and function of a hospital ward at Duke Medical Center that is designed specifically for the evaluation and treatment of chronic pain. Here, the psychiatrist is the primary physician on a multidisciplinary team that includes nurses, psychologists, physical therapists, social workers, and medical consultants from anesthesiology, neurosurgery, and orthopedics.

The Behavioral Medicine Service at the University of Vermont has extended this concept into the outpatient setting, establishing specialty clinics in pain evaluation and management, chronic medical illness management, pediatric stress-related disorders, anxiety and stress-related disorders, eating disorders, and alcohol and drug abuse disorders. Each program has a multidisciplinary staff headed by a behavioral medicine psychiatrist as primary physician, with designated consultants from other medical specialties. The service provides continuity of programs and care for patients in four settings: outpatient clinic, general hospital, inpatient behavioral medicine speciality unit, and home. The clinical model (McKegney and Gallagher 1983) is based upon experiences in family practice (McMahon et al. 1983), consultation psychiatry, and behavioral medicine (Morgan et al. 1980) and upon a conviction that a truly integrated biopsychosocial practice model could be better achieved in a setting where the psychiatrist is not a consultant but the primary physician.

The goals of this clinical model service include: to provide traditional psychiatric treatments, such as psychopharmacology and psychotherapy, to patients who initially do not accept the influence of psychosocial factors on illness; to provide people with symptom relief, often using medication, while enhancing learning and coping skills and self-reliance; to help people feel less isolated by their struggles with disease and illness; to use different biopsychosocial therapeutic modalities, fitted specifically to the patient's needs and level of acceptance, in an integrated, coordinated treatment plan provided by an interdisciplinary team. Below are listed some principles of practice for the service:

1. Start where the patient is: Many patients need an integrated approach, but few accept psychiatry and psychological concepts. Provide patients with an illness model that is close to their experience and acceptable to their value system. Patients who will not come to a psychiatric clinic might accept referral to a behavioral medicine service or a pain clinic to have their somatic symptoms initially reduced by medication, biofeedback, and physical therapy.
2. Assessment is comprehensive, both biomedical and psychosocial, following the model described by Nurcombe and Gallagher (1986b).
3. Treatment is individualized and multimodal, addressing the entire biopsychosocial matrix of factors influencing the patient's illness, not just the disease or disorder itself.
4. Care is rehabilitative, aiming to restore the patient to an optimal level of health and function.
5. Care is coordinated and collaborative, relying on patient, family, and clinical team working together.
6. Treatment is based on the latest research, changing as new methods are developed.

Fundamental clinical tactics include:

1. Reduce symptoms, establish therapeutic contracts, and engage the patient in record keeping to foster a trusting, therapeutic, and collaborative working alliance.
2. Educate the patient in the biopsychosocial model of symptom formation.
3. Diagnose and remediate physical factors that might hinder learning new coping skills.
4. Start with a cognitive–behavioral paradigm. All patients can be trained to change their maladaptive response patterns to stressors.
5. Train in relaxation, which is physiologically incompatible with anxiety and, to a lesser degree, pain, and provide the patient a degree of personal control over symptoms.
6. Foster an appropriate level of dependency and regression that will not interfere with critical function but facilitate the capacity to work with the team to achieve therapeutic goals.
7. Provide continuity of therapeutic relationships between clinical settings; outpatient, home, general hospital, hospital specialty unit.

8. Tolerate dependency and understand the psychodynamic factors that will influence the therapeutic alliance and the patient's progress toward achieving therapeutic objectives.
9. Provide for the support, dependency, and growth needs of the professionals on the service, who require a supportive, invigorating group process to tolerate the dependency of these complex patients.

These strategies have been successful in enabling the service to help manage the problems of patients with all the chronic illnesses listed in this chapter. The service also conducts clinical research, provides employee-assistance programs to improve health management, and educates medical students, psychiatric fellows, psychology graduate students, and residents in psychiatry and primary care specialties. The application of this service model to a clinical case of myocardial infarction, Michael I., will be described later in this chapter.

CORONARY ARTERY DISEASE (CAD)
To catalog the many psychiatric interventions useful in different chronic disorders and to illustrate each with examples from clinical experience is beyond the scope of this chapter. Much has been written about psychiatric intervention in chronic obstructive pulmonary disease (COPD), spinal cord injury, rheumatoid arthritis, lower back pain, headache, cancer, end-stage renal disease, diabetes, and other illnesses. This section will review pertinent knowledge about one illness, myocardial infarction, and will provide a case example of how psychiatric and behavioral medicine treatments can affect the outcome of this illness. This case will illustrate the general principles of an approach applicable to all chronic illness.

Coronary artery disease is now the leading cause of morbidity and death in the United States. Physicians have realized for many years that psychiatric problems critically influence the outcome of many patients. Over the past 20–30 years, the study of myocardial infarction and cardiac arrhythmias, two acute illnesses that complicate coronary artery disease, have shown that psychosocial and life style factors predispose to, precipitate, and perpetuate illness, and that psychiatric problems and disorders, such as major depression or dementia, affect recovery.

The Review Panel on Coronary-Prone Behavior and Coronary Heart Disease (1981) of the National Heart, Lung, and Blood Institute of the National Institutes of Health examined the research into the Type A or coronary-prone behavior pattern. They concluded that this pattern, characterized by extreme aggressiveness, competitiveness, ambition, and sense of time urgency (Friedman and Rosenman 1959) is an independent coronary-risk factor similar in magnitude to other accepted factors such as obesity, smoking, hypertension, and family history. The interesting research findings related to this conclusion as well as other biopsychosocial factors related to the several concepts discussed earlier in this chapter, are discussed below.

Type A persons, identified by structured interview, have greater elevations in systolic and diastolic blood pressure than Type B patients. Those identified by a questionnaire, the Jenkins Activity Survey, showed elevations in work settings but not in laboratory settings. In Type A persons, high hostility increases the risk for CAD (Thoresen et al. 1982) and predicts the extent of coronary disease (Williams et al. 1980). Suppressed hostility appears to be predictive of CAD and mortality, as well as being correlated with low social support, which may be the operative factor in increased mortality (Williams 1983). Work pressure encourages the sense of time urgency that is characteristic of Type A behavior, and also seems to be correlated with other risk factors for CAD, such as elevated serum cholesterol and hypertension. Work responsibility is not related to Type A, but is to CAD. Although CAD is more prevalent in blue-collar workers, Type A pattern is only a risk factor in white-collar workers, in whom it is prevalent, suggesting that both occupational status and work environment may influence the development of coronary-prone behavior (McQueen and Siegrist 1982). Among poorly educated persons, the higher morbidity and mortality from myocardial infarction appear to be a function of the higher levels of life stress associated with this group (Rubeman 1984). In fact, patients with high levels of stress and isolation were four times more likely to die than patients with lower levels. Life-change events in general seem to be associated with high mortality (McQueen and Siegrist 1982). Sudden death caused by ventricular arrythmias in the absence of overt myocardial infarction has been reported to be associated with psychosocial stress (Lown et al. 1976, 1980; Donlon et al. 1979; Reich and Gold 1983). The mechanisms seem to be the lowering of the threshold for arrhythmia by psychological stress, mediated by sympathetic beta-adrenergic stimulation, in predisposed individuals. Interestingly, serotonergic agents, which reduce sympathetic outflow from the brain, have been shown to increase the threshold for ventricular fibrillation. Endorphins and GABA may also be involved. The parasympathetic nervous system exerts a protective effect by reducing the effects of sympathetic activity. Lown et al. conclude that three factors are involved in the sudden death of many patients: (1) an electrically unstable ventricle; (2) a burdensome psychological state; and (3) a proximate psychological trigger.

Myocardial infarction, like sudden death, is usually an unexpected crisis in a patient's life; coronary artery bypass surgery to relieve angina or prevent infarction, while predictable, always occurs in the context of severe disease. The way in which patients and their families cope in these two circumstances may influence recovery, as outlined below.

Although denial can reduce anxiety and even mortality in the coronary care unit of a hospital, high levels during convalescence can contribute to noncompliance with treatment and rehabilitation programs (Soloff 1977). Delirium, a major complication of cardiac surgery, is multifactoral in origin. Its incidence can be lowered by preoperative preparation by nurses and by changes in ICU procedures to reduce the sensory monotony and sleep deprivation that contribute to the incidence of delirium (Milano and Kornfeld 1984). Depression and delirium are associated with a higher incidence of morbidity and mortality in recovering cardiac surgery patients (Kennedy et al. 1985). After cardiac surgery, patients report increased pleasure and satisfaction with surgical results and decreased angina, anxiety, and depression. However, problems with sexual function tend to persist. The low rate of return to work shown in American studies seems to be related more to premorbid psychological, social, and economic factors than to biomedical factors.

Psychiatric interventions for patients with or at risk for cardiac illness have been described in both hospital and outpatient settings.

Gruen (1975) reports a randomized, controlled trial of psychotherapy for hospitalized patients with myocardial infarction. Those who received psychotherapy showed the following advantages over controls: fewer days in the CCU and in hospital; reduced incidence of congestive heart failure, supraventricular arrhythmias, nurse observation of weakness, physician reports of depression, self-report of urgency, presence of extreme anxiety or lack of anxiety (indicating denial), and more social affection and vigor. At four months, they showed less residual fear and were more able to return to usual activities.

A comprehensive review of psychotherapeutic interventions with patients having surgery or myocardial infarction showed that a variety of interventions were both beneficial and cost effective. Educational interventions were effective, psychotherapeutic interventions more effective, and the two approaches combined most effective (Mumford et al. 1982).

The Recurrent Coronary-Prevention Project (Thoresen et al. 1982; Friedman et al. 1984), in a randomized, controlled trial involving postmyocardial infarction patients, tested the effectiveness of group counseling to reduce Type A behavior. The intervention effectively reduced the behavior as well as the incidence of angina and nonfatal infarction, but did not reduce mortality. Other reports indicate that early psychotherapeutic interventions are more helpful. Rahe et al. (1975, 1979) reported, in a four-year follow-up, that a randomized, controlled trial of brief group psychotherapy demonstrated that group patients had lower mortality and morbidity and were more likely to return to work. While group patients altered selected Type A behaviors, neither group nor control altered other risk factors for CAD.

The case of Michael I., the 35-year-old construction worker who sustained a myocardial infarction, illustrates the complexity of the management and treatment of CAD.

Michael was raised in a tumultuous household, the third and the oldest male of seven siblings, by an alcoholic father and hard-working but overwhelmed mother who had to ship him out to relatives several times during childhood. His father, never stead-ily employed, suffered a myocardial infarction at age 55 and became an invalid. Michael began drinking in early adolescence, and dropped out of high school to get a job to help support his family. His first marriage lasted five years and produced three children. He frequently clashed with the law, always while intox-icated, and in his early twenties spent several months in jail because of repeated violations of driving laws and his abusive behavior when accosted. Generally good natured, he became angry and impulsively violent when on one of his frequent drink-ing binges. Between sentences and binges lasting weeks at a time, he was a steady worker who prided himself on his work perform-ance.

When 30 years old, based upon his strong family history of CAD, he was advised by his doctor to alter some of his risk factors: hypertension, smoking, obesity, and chronic stress, and told him to stop drinking. He changed little, but two years later, he fell in love and married again, with the promise to his bride that he would reform. A year later, he stopped drinking after she threatened to leave, and settled down to a steady job. He con-tinued his sedentary ways, his smoking, and his overeating, and his hypertension was only sporadically lowered, because of his noncompliance and his difficulty sustaining a relationship with a doctor. His wife was vaguely aware of his risks, but was rebuffed when she tried to discuss these problems or his father's illness.

The events surrounding his myocardial infarction and subse-quent coronary artery bypass graft (CABG) are outlined in Table 1.

Table 1

Evolution of Coronary Artery Disease, Michael I.

1949	Born
1974	Father had myocardial infarction at age 55
1979	Married
1979	Michael told of hyperlipidemia and advised about hypertension, smoking, and obesity
8/03/83	Went to community hospital ER—diagnosis: indi-gestion; sent home from ER

8/04/83	More chest pain; returned to hospital and admitted overnight; no EKG; discharge
8/05/83	More chest pain, back to ER; cardiac arrest in ER
8/05/83	Transferred to tertiary hospital ER, second cardiac arrest; admitted to ICU
8/10/83	Transferred to hospital floor
8/25–10/10/83	15 admissions to ER and hospital with chest pain
10/10/83	Coronary artery bypass graft (CABG)
10/15/83–5/10/84	3 admissions with chest pain
5/10/84	Sudden return of chest pain; catheterization reveals final CABG; many trips to ER; increase in chest pain, drinking behavior, aggression, depression, and marital strife
6/01/84	Referral to Behavioral Medicine Service (BMS)

Clinical Process, on Behavioral Medicine Service

6/15/84	Initial evaluation; pain/anxiety-management training
6/28/84	Admitted to BMS hospital psychiatry unit; discharged AMA; pain; ETOH; fights; suicidal; multiple ER visits
7/13/84	Antidepressants begun
7/30/84	Admitted to BMS hospital psychiatry unit
8/06/86	Cardiac rehabilitation, phase II, begun Alcoholics Anonymous begun
8/24/84	Discharged from hospital AMA; antidepressants stopped; regressive behavior resumed
9/07/84	Couples therapy and treatment contract; antidepressants, Antabuse started
10/05/84	Admission contract, hospital psychiatry unit; continued marital therapy, anxiety management and Antabuse
12/20/84	Disability granted
1/23/85	Continued the following: anxiety management social skills training couples therapy Antabuse antidepressants Alcoholics Anonymous cardiac rehab phase III
4/01/85	Health maintenance visits every two to six months; volunteer jobs

Explanation of abbreviations—CABG = coronary artery bypass graft; BMS = Behavioral Medicine Service; AMA = Against Medical Advice; ETOH = alcohol

He was referred to the Behavioral Medicine Service after the cardiac surgery team considered doing a second CABG, even though indications were marginal.

His actual treatment progress following referral is outlined in Table 2. Note that he required three hospitalizations, each in a different circumstance, and a highly integrated treatment approach by a multidisciplinary team, including a consultation–liaison psychiatrist leading a behavioral medicine team, a psychologist specializing in cognitive–behavioral approaches to stress management and behavioral change, a psychologist specializing in couples therapy for chronically ill patients, and numerous house staff and nurses. Management planning, including his prioritized problem list, therapeutic goal statements, and treatment plans, are outlined in Table 2.

Table 2

Problem List, Goal Statements, and Clinical Plans

	Goal Statements	Plans and Tactics
Immediate Problem		
Somatic		
sleep disturbance; episodes of chest pain	sedation reduce pain reduce acute anxiety	sedating tricyclic nitroglycerine; IV lorazepam, as needed
Psychological		
acutely depressed mood;	stabilize mood	tricyclic; cognitive and interpersonal therapy
suicidal ideation	reduce intensity	mobilize support, instill hope
	decrease risks	remove guns, pills; decrease alcohol and sedative use
drinking behavior	avoid ETOH	antabuse; AA referral; stabilize mood
percodan overuse	reduce	ibuprofin; pain-management training
acute anxiety	control panic	tricyclic; relaxation training
Social		
marital chaos	stabilize	support wife; instill hope and responsibility
Pivotal Problems		
Somatic		
multiple medications	rationalize pharmacology	reduce medications
diazepam dependency	discontinue	relaxation training and gradual withdrawal

Table 2 (cont.)

	Goal Statements	Plans and Tactics
Psychological		
patient's and wife's fear of MI;	clarify diagnostic formulation	conjoint educational sessions
diagnosis of aggressive behavior	control	decrease alcohol, diazepam; reduce threats; increase trust
Social		
loss of family role;	clarify roles; improve adjustment	family therapy
chronic marital discord;		family therapy
no clear diagnosis and poor doctor–patient relationship	clarify formulation with physicians	medical conference and family education
Background Problems		
Somatic		
ASCVD	change risk factors	cardiac rehabilitation program
smoking	stop	smoking-cessation program
obesity	lose weight	weight/exercise program
Psychological		
personality traits;	reduce impact on rehabilitation	therapeutic tactics
type A behavior;	change	cognitive–behavioral psychotherapy
low self-esteem;	improve	cognitive–behavioral psychotherapy
unresolved anger at and distrust of authorities	resolve anger; improve trust	cognitive–behavioral psychotherapy
Social		
unemployment	employ	vocational rehabilitation plan
wife's alcoholism	reduce impact	AA, Alanon

Explanation of abbreviations—MI = myocardial infarction; ETOH = alcohol; ASCVD = arteriosclerotic cardiovascular disease

Clinical outcome can be measured in a number of ways: He was participating fully in cardiac rehabilitation; was working as a volunteer in the hospital. His self-esteem was restored; he was no longer running to the hospital. He was sober; he had lost some weight; his social supports were intact, if relatively fragile. He was no longer dependent on psychotropic drugs; he was compliant with medical regimens. He had stable therapeutic alliances with health care providers and he had little chest pain.

His medical costs are interesting. Table 3 outlines the costs of various phases of his care. What is striking is that the intense, multi-

Table 3

The High Cost of Catastrophic and Chronic Illness

Charges	Doctors	Hospital	Total	Cost per Week
Treatment Phase				
8/1/83–6/15/84 (cardiology and cardiac rehabilitation)	$12,354.00	13,015.53	25,639.53	539.78
6/16/84–11/30/84 (behavioral medicine and cardiac rehabilitation)	$ 6,440.20	18,345.22	24,785.42	1,032.73
12/1/84–12/1/85 (maintenance treatment, behavioral medicine)	$ 370.00	70.25	440.25	8.47

disciplinary specialty care provided by behavioral medicine and psychiatry, all necessary in a patient with this degree and complexity of problems, was very expensive, almost as costly as his medical/surgical care to that point. What is also striking is the absence of medical costs after treatment, but, consistent with the data for blue-collar workers locally and nationally, the continued difficulty in getting him back into the work place despite his strong work ethic. Michael's problems, their complexity shared by many ill persons, suggest the need for more sophisticated vocational rehabilitation programs that integrate principles and strategies of biopsychosocial medicine.

This case has demonstrated the complex treatment of a patient with almost all of the various psychosocial and behavioral risk factors and many of the psychiatric complications in CAD. As discussed above, most cases are not as extreme, and almost everyone with CAD can use help, as the following sketches of patients from the Behavioral Medicine Service illustrate:

Mrs. R., a 50-year-old woman who, one year ago, lost her husband in a car accident, suffers a myocardial infarction. Following an uncomplicated course in the hospital, she enrolls in a cardiac-rehabilitation program. After a stress-management training session by a psychiatrist, she asks the cardiologist questions about depression. She accepts a referral to the psychiatrist for evaluation and treatment of depression which is interfering with her ability to comply with the program. Evaluation reveals Type A characteristics, sedative dependency, and heavy smoking. Her depressed mood is diagnosed as secondary to a combination of factors, including anger at her loss of hobbies, particularly physical exercise; her loss of relationships at her old job, to which she may not be able to return; and the threat to a new relationship with a male; sedative dependency; unresolved grief over the death of her husband, for which she felt partially responsible;

guilt, on the verge of marriage, about the new relationship, since she had sworn on her first husband's deathbed that she would never marry again. Treatment by a team consisting of a behavioral psychologist and psychiatrist, over about six months, included individual psychotherapy to resolve the loss of her husband and to move on to the new relationship without guilt, stress, and anxiety; stress-management training to reduce dependency on benzodiazepines and to change Type A behaviors; smoking cessation; gradual and safe withdrawal from benzodiazepines; and gradual reintroduction to the work place. One year later, she was happily remarried and working part time in her new husband's business.

Mr. T., a 55-year-old engineer, suffers severe angina while at work. Any challenging task or interpersonal event that emotionally stimulates him provokes angina. He is despondent about his inability to be productive at work, and worried about premature retirement and its reduced income, when his children have financial problems. For several years, he worked with the chest pain before reporting it to his physician. Now, to avoid the humiliation of not functioning at the level of his peers, he stays home "sick" all the time, and is about to be fired. Assessment reveals major depression in a man with a Type A behavior pattern who has a strong and supportive wife. He is treated with antidepressants until he can concentrate better and his motivation improves. He learns how to control his arousal and reduce angina in stimulating circumstances, using biofeedback-assisted relaxation training, and works in psychotherapy to help him accept a temporary change in job status until physically he can no longer tolerate work. He then readily accepts a disability plan that enables him to maintain both his financial solvency and his self-esteem.

THE FUTURE OF PSYCHIATRIC INTERVENTION AND REHABILITATION FOR PHYSICAL ILLNESS

The relationships among mind, brain, and body discussed in the section on conceptual models and throughout this chapter are the research focus of two converging, often overlapping, disciplines—psychosomatic medicine and behavioral medicine—that link the concepts, knowledge, and skills of the behavioral sciences, the neurosciences, clinical psychiatry, and the rest of medicine. These disciplines, traditionally focused on the predisposition and precipitation of disease, are now turning their interest toward understanding perpetuating factors that determine outcome once a disease becomes chronic. Jenkins (1985), in his Presidential Address to the American Psychosomatic Society, calls for "greater attention to the psychoso-

matics of other phases of the natural history of illness, such as rehabilitation, recovery and long-term maintenance." He believes that all
illness must be defined in a matrix describing the interaction of
personal characteristics and environment with the temporal dimension of illness, and that practical applications of this knowledge in
clinical medicine must be developed.

The Institute of Medicine (Hamburg et al. 1982) decries the lack
of research funds, which are disproportionately low, relative to the
societal costs of the problems described in this chapter. McKegney
and Beckhardt (1982) voice similar concern about the lack of funding
for clinical research and training programs in key disciplines such as
consultation–liaison psychiatry. Medicine needs to develop skilled
clinician–researchers to work at the interface of medicine and this
complex matrix of ideas and facts. And these clinician–researchers,
in collaboration with their colleagues in other medical specialties
and in other health care disciplines, further need to develop innovative and cost-effective models of biopsychosocial health care for
rehabilitation and chronic illness. Specifically, more studies are
needed showing the impact of psychiatric and psychosocial factors
on the outcome of particular illnesses, for example, the studies by
Kennedy et al. (1985), showing depression and delirium as predictive
of poor outcome in patients recovering from cardiac surgery, and by
Gallagher et al. (1986), showing that psychosocial factors, more than
physical ones, predict return to work in lower back pain. The effectiveness of psychiatric interventions such as the ones described in
this chapter can be contrasted prospectively with standard approaches in at-risk patients.

Finally, a plea: Medical educators and scientists must strive to
communicate the importance of these ideas, and the effectiveness of
clinical interventions based on them, to those individuals and groups
responsible for funding relevant clinical training and basic and clinical research. Only then will society begin to benefit, on a large scale,
from the better health and increased productivity of its citizens.

REFERENCES

Adams GL, Brochstein JR, Cheney CC, et al: Primary care mental health training and
    services model. Am J Psychiatry 135:121-122, 1978
Ader R: The role of developmental factors in susceptibility to disease, in Psychosomatic
    Medicine. Edited by Lipowski ZJ. New York, Oxford University Press, 1975
Ader R: Psychoneuroimmunology. New York, Academic Press, 1981
Ader R, Cohen N: Conditioned immunopharmacologic responses, in Psychoneuroim-
    munology. Edited by Ader R. New York, Academic Press, 1981
Adsett CA, Bruhn JG: Short-term group psychotherapy for post-myocardial infarction
    patients and their wives. Can Med Assoc J 99:577-584, 1968
Andreasen NC, Nerris AS, Hartford CE, et al: Management of emotional reaction in
    severely burned adults. N Engl J Med 286:65, 1972
Barefoot JC, Dahlstrom G, Williams RB: Hostility, CHD incidence and total mortality:
    a 25-year follow up study of 255 physicians. Psychosom Med 45:59-63, 1983

Benson H, Alexander S, Feldman CL: Decreased premature ventricular contractions through use of the relaxation response in patients with stable ischemic heart disease. Lancet 2:380-382, 1975

Billings EG: Liaison psychiatry and intern instruction. Journal of American Medical Colleges 14:375-385, 1939

Bishop D (Ed): Behavioral Problems in the Disabled. Baltimore, Williams & Wilkins, 1980

Block AR, Kremer EF, Gaylor M: Behavioral treatment of chronic pain: the spouse as discriminate cue for pain behavior. Pain 9:243-252, 1980

Borus JF, Casserly MK: Psychiatrists and primary physicians: collaborative learning experiences in delivering primary care. Hosp Community Psychiatry 30:686-689, 1979

Borysenko JZ: Behavioral-psychological factors in the development and management of cancer. Gen Hosp Psychiatry 4:69-74, 1982

Cannon EB: Bodily Changes in Pain, Hunger, Fear and Race. New York, Appleton, 1934

Caplan G: Theory and Practice of Mental Health Consultation. New York, Basic Books, 1970

Cassem NH: Psychiatric problems in patients with acute myocardial infarction, in Coronary Care. Edited by Karlinger JS, Gregoratis G. New York, Churchill Livingstone, 1981

Cassileth BR, Lusk EJ, Strouse TB, et al: Psychosocial status in chronic illness: a comparative analysis of six diagnostic groups. N Engl J Med 311:506-511, 1984

Cataldo MF, Russo DC, Bird BL, et al: Assessment and management of chronic disorders, in The Comprehensive Handbook of Behavioral Medicine, vol. 3. Edited by Ferguson JM, Taylor CB. New York, Spectrum Publications, 1980

Cavanaugh S: The prevalence of emotional and cognitive dysfunction in a general medical population: using the MMSe, GHQ and BDI. Gen Hosp Psychiatry 5:142-148, 1983

Clarkin JF, Frances AJ, Moodie JL, et al: Selection criteria for family therapy. Fam Process 18:291-303, 1979

Cobb S: Social support as a moderator of life stress. Psychosom Med 38:300-313, 1976

Corse CD, Manuck SD, Cantwell JD, et al: Coronary-prone behavior pattern and cardiovascular response in persons with and without coronary heart disease. Psychosom Med 44:449-459, 1982

Cox T, MacKay C: Psychosocial factors and psychophysiological mechanisms in the aetiology and development of cancers. Soc Sci Med 16:381-396, 1982

Doherty WJ, Baird MA: Family Therapy and Family Medicine: Toward the Primary Care of Families. New York, Guilford Press, 1983

Donlon PT, Meadow A, Amsterdam E: Emotional stress as a factor in ventricular arrythmias. Psychosomatics 20:233-240, 1979

Dudley DL, Pitts-Poarch AR: Psychophysiologic aspects of respiratory control. Clin Chest Med 1:131-143, 1980

Dudley DL, Glaser EM, Jorgensen BN, et al: Psychosocial concomitants to rehabilitation in chronic obstructive pulmonary disease, part I: psychosocial and psychological considerations. Chest 77:413-420, 1980

Engel GL, Greene WJ, Reichsman F, et al: A graduate and undergraduate teaching program on the psychological aspects of medicine. J Med Educ 32:859-870, 1957

Engel GL: The need for a new medical model: A challenge for biomedicine. Science 196:129-136, 1977

Feiguine RJ, Johnson FA: Alexithymia and chronic respiratory disease. Psychother Psychosom 43:77-89, 1983

Felton BJ, Revenson TA, Hinrichsen GA: Stress and coping in the explanation of psychological adjustment among chronically ill adults. Soc Sci Med 10:889-898, 1984

Fielding R: A note on behavioral treatment in the rehabilitation of myocardial infarction patients. British Journal of Social and Clinical Psychiatry 19:157-161, 1980

Forsyth GL, Delaney KD, Gresham ML: Vying for a winning position: management style of the chronically ill. Res Nurs Health 7:181-188, 1984

Friedman EA: Psychosocial adjustment of the family to maintenance hemodialysis. New York Journal of Medicine 70:767-774, 1970

Friedman F, Mason J, Hamburg DA: Urinary 17-hydroxycortice-steriod levels in parents of children with neoplastic disease. Psychosom Med 25:364-376, 1963

Friedman M, Rosenman RH: Association of specific overt behavior pattern with blood and cardiovascular findings. JAMA 169:1286-1296, 1959

Friedman M, Thoresen CE, Gill JJ, et al: Alteration of type A behavior and reduction in cardiac recurrences in post-myocardial infarction patients. Am Heart J 108:237-248, 1984

Gallagher RM: The spinal cord unit, in Manual of Psychiatric Consultations and Emergency Care. Edited by Guggenheim FG, Weiner MF. Northvale, NJ, Jason Aronson, 1984

Gallagher RM, Rauh V: Psychosocial, not physical, factors predict return to work in low back pain. Psychosom Med 48:296, 1986 (abstract)

Gallagher RM, McCann W, Jerman A, et al: The development and operation of a behavioral medicine service: a multidisciplinary team approach to biopsychosocial medicine. Paper presented at the Annual Meeting of the Vermont Psychological Association, 1984

Gottlieb HV, Strite C, Koller R, et al: Comprehensive rehabilitation of patients having low back pain. Arch Phys Med Rehab 58:101-108, 1977

Grant I, Heaton RK, McSweeney AJ, et al: Brain dysfunction in COPD. Chest 77:308-309 (Suppl), 1980

Gruen W: Effects of brief psychotherapy during the hospitalization period on the recovery process in heart attacks. J Consult Clin Psychol 43:223-232, 1975

Haggerty JJ: The psychosomatic family: an overview. Psychosomatics 24:615-618, 1983

Hall RCW: Depression, in Psychiatric Presentation of Medical Illness. Edited by Hall RCW. New York, Spectrum, 1980

Hamburg DA, Elliot GR, Parron DL (Eds.) Health and Behavior: Frontiers of Research in the Biobehavioral Sciences. Washington DC, National Academy Press, 1982

Henry GW: Some modern aspects of psychiatry in general hospital practice. Am J Psychiatry 9:481-499, 1929-30

Henry JP: The relation of social to biological processes in disease. Social Sci Med 16:369-380, 1982

Hinckle LJ: The concept of "stress" in the biological and social sciences, in Psychosomatic Medicine. Edited by Lipowski ZJ. New York, Oxford University Press, 1975

Holmes TH, Rahe RH: The social readjustment rating scale. J Psychosom Res 11:213-218, 1967

Hornig-Rohan M, Locke SE: Psychological and Behavioral Treatments for Disorders of the Heart and Blood Vessels: An Annotated Bibliography. New York, Institute for the Advancement of Health, 1985

Houpt JL, Keefe FJ, Snipes MT: The clinical specialty units: the use of the psychiatric inpatient unit to treat chronic pain syndromes. Gen Hosp Psychiatry 6:1, 65-70, 1984

Hutner NL, Locke SE: Health locus of control: a potential moderator variable for the relationship between life stress and psychopathology. Psychother Psychosom 41:186-194, 1984

Inbahim MA, Feldman JG, Sultz HA, et al: Management after myocardial infarction: a controlled trial of the effect of group psychotherapy. Int J Psychiatry Med 5:253-268, 1974

Jacobsen A: Psychological issues in diabetes mellitus. Psychosomatics 25:1-154, 1984

Jenkins CDJ: Recent evidence supporting psychologic and social risk factors for coronary disease. N Engl J Med 294:1033, 1976

Jenkins CDJ: New horizons for psychosomatic medicine. Psychosom Med 47:3-25, 1985

Jensen PS: Risk, protective factors, and supportive interventions in chronic airways obstruction. Arch Gen Psychiatry 40:1203-1207, 1983

Johnston DW: The effects of cardiovascular feedback and relaxation on angina pectoris. Behavioral Psychotherapy 11:257-264

Kandell ER: From metapsychology to molecular biology: explorations into the nature of anxiety. Am J Psychiatry 140:1277-1293, 1983

Kennedy G, et al: Significance of depression and dementia in patients at risk for sudden death. Psychosom Med 47:90-91, 1985

Khouri-Haddad SE: Psychiatric consultation in a headache unit. Headache 24:32-38, 1984

Kiely WF: From the symbolic stimulus to the pathophysiological response: neurophysiological mechanisms, in Psychosomatic Medicine. Edited by Lipowski ZJ. New York, Oxford University Press, 1974

Kimball CP: Psychosomatic medicine, in Psychiatry. Edited by Michels R, Cavenar JO, Brodie HKH, et al. Philadelphia, Lippincott, 1985

Kiritz S, Moos RF: Physiological effects of social environments. Psychosom Med 36:96-114, 1974

Koranyi EK: Morbidity and rate of undiagnosed physical illness in a psychiatric clinic population. Arch Gen Psychiatry 36:414-419, 1979

Krantz DS: Cognitive processes and recovery from heart attack: review and theoretical analysis. J Human Stress 6:27-38, 1980

Lazarus RL: Psychological stress and coping in adaptation and illness, in Psychosomatic Medicine. Edited by Lipowski ZJ. New York, Oxford University Press, 1975

Leigh H, Reiser MF: The Patient. New York, Plenum Press, 1980

Levenberg SB, Jenkins C, Wendorf DJ, et al: Studies in family-oriented crisis intervention in dialysis patients. Int J Psychiatry Med 9:83-92, 1978-79

Lewis FM, Bloom JR: Psychosocial adjustment to breast cancer: a review of selected literature. Int J Psychiatry Med 9:1-18, 1978-79

Lipowski ZJ: Review of consultation psychiatry and psychosomatic medicine, I: General principles. Psychosom Med 29:153-171, 1967

Lipowski ZJ: Consultation-liaison psychiatry: an overview. Am J Psychiatry 131:623-630, 1974

Lipowski ZJ: Consultation-liaison psychiatry: past failures and new opportunities. Gen Hosp Psychiatry 1:3-10, 1979

Lipowski ZJ: Current trends in consultation-liaison psychiatry. Can J Psychiatry 28:329-339, 1983a

Lipowski ZJ: Psychosocial reaction to physical illness. Can Med Assoc J 128:1069-1072, 1983b

Lipowski ZJ: The psychosomatic medicine unit. Ontario Med Sept. 1984

Locke SE: Stress, adaptation and immunity: studies in humans. Gen Hosp Psychiatry 4:49-58, 1982

Locke SE, Kraus L, Lesserman J, et al: Life change stress, psychiatric symptoms and natural killer cell activity. Psychosom Med 46:441-453, 1984

Lown B, Temte JV, Reich P, et al: Basis for recurring ventricular fibrillation in the absence of coronary heart disease and its management. N Engl J Med 294:623-629, 1976

Lown B, Desilva RA, Reich P, et al: Psychophysiologic factors in sudden cardiac death. Am J Psychiatry 137:1325-1335, 1980

Mason JF: Health status in chronic disease: a comparable study of rheumatoid arthritis. J Rheumatol 10:678-763, 1983

Massie MJ, Holland JC: Psychiatry and oncology, in Psychiatry Update: The American Psychiatric Association Annual Review, vol. III. Edited by Grinspoon L. Washington, DC, American Psychiatric Press, 1984

McKegney FP: Emotional and interpersonal aspects of rehabilitation, in Rehabilitation and Medicine. Edited by Licht S, Licht E. New Haven, Yale University Press, 1968

McKegney FP, Beckhardt RM: Evaluation research in consultation-liaison psychiatry: review of the literature. Gen Hosp Psychiatry 4:197-218, 1982

McKegney FP, Gallagher RM: Consultation-liaison psychiatry in subspecialty medicine, in Psychiatry, vol. 2. Edited by Michels R, Cavenar JO, Brodie HKH, et al. Philadelphia, Lippincott, 1985

McMahon T, Gallagher RM, Little D: Psychiatry-family practice liaison: a collaborative approach to clinical training. Gen Hosp Psychiatry 5:1-6, 1983

McQueen DV, Siegrist J: Social factors in the etiology of chronic disease: an overview. Soc Sci Med 16:353-367, 1982

McSweeny AJ, Grant I, Heaton RK, et al: Life quality of patients with chronic obstructive pulmonary disease. Arch Intern Med 142:473-478, 1982

Medalie JH, Snyder M, Groen JJ, et al: Angina pectoris among 10,000 men: five year incidence and univariated analysis. Am J Med 55:583-594, 1973

Milano MR, Kornfeld DS: Psychiatry and surgery, in Psychiatry Update: The American Psychiatric Association Annual Review, vol III. Edited by Grinspoon L. Washington, DC, American Psychiatric Press, 1984

Miller JG: The Living System. New York, McGraw/Hill, 1978

Minuchin S, Rosman BL, Baker L: Psychosomatic Families: Anorexia Nervosa in Context. Cambridge, Harvard University Press, 1978

Mohl PC: The liaison psychiatrist: social role and status. Psychosomatics 20:19-23, 1979

Moldofsky H: Clinical research at the interface of medicine and psychiatry, in Psychiatric Update: The American Psychiatric Association Annual Review, vol III. Edited by Grinspoon L. Washington, DC, American Psychiatric Press, 1984

Morgan CD, Kremer E, Gaylor M: The behavioral medicine unit: a new facility. Compr Psychiatry 20:79-89, 1979

Mumford E, Schlesinger HJ, Glass GV: The effects of psychological intervention on recovery from surgery and heart attacks: an analysis of the literature. Am J Public Health 72:141-151, 1982

Myer E, Mendelson M: Psychiatric consultations with patients on medical and surgical wards: patterns and processes. Psychiatry 24:197-220, 1961

Nurcombe B, Gallagher RM (Eds): The comprehensive diagnostic formulation, in The Clinical Process in Psychiatry. New York, Cambridge University Press, 1986a

Nurcombe B, Gallagher RM (Eds): Illness behavior, in The Clinical Process in Psychiatry. New York, Cambridge University Press, 1986b

Ornish D, Scherwitz LW, Doody RS, et al: Effects of stress management training and dietary changes in treating ischemic heart disease. JAMA 249:54-59, 1983

Parsons T: Illness in the role of the physician: a sociological perspective. Am J Orthopsychiatry 221:452-460, 1951

Pilowsky I: A general classification of abnormal illness behaviors. Br J Med Psychol 51:131-137, 1978

Plaut SM, Friedman SB: Psychosocial factors in infectious disease, in Psychoneuroimmunology. Edited by Ader R. New York, Academic Press, 1981

Post L, Collins C: The poorly coping COPD patient: a psychotherapeutic perspective. Int J Psychiatry Med 11:173-182, 1981-1982

Rahe RH, O'Neil T, Hogan A, et al: Brief group therapy following myocardial infarction: eighteen month follow-up of a controlled trial. Int J Psychiatry Med 6:349-358, 1975

Rahe RH, Ward HW, Hayes V: Brief group therapy in myocardial infarction rehabilitation: three to four year follow-up of a controlled trial. Psychosom Med 41:229-242, 1979

Reich P, Gold PW: Interruption of recurrent ventricular fibrillation by psychiatric intervention. Gen Hosp Psychiatry 5:255-257, 1983

Reiser MF: Changing theoretical concepts in psychosomatic medicine, in American Handbook of Psychiatry (vol 4). Edited by Reiser M. New York, Basic Books, 1975

The Review Panel on Coronary-Prone Behavior and Coronary Heart Disease: A critical review. Circulation 63:1199-1215, 1981

Riley VA: Psychoneuroendocrine influences on immuno-competence and neoplasia. Science 212:1100-1109, 1981

Riley VA, Fitzmaurice MA, Speckman DH: Psychoneuroimmunologic factors in neoplasia: studies in animals, in Psychoneuroimmunology. Edited by Ader R. New York, Academic Press, 1981

Roessler R, Engel BT: The current status of the concepts of physiological response specificity and activation, in Psychosomatic Medicine. Edited by Lipowski ZJ. New York, Oxford University Press, 1975

Rogers MP, Regh P, Kelly MJ, et al: Psychiatric consultation among hospitalized arthritis patients. Gen Hosp Psychiatry 2:1, 89-94, 1980

Ruberman W, Weinblatt E, Goldberg J, et al: Psychosocial influences on mortality after myocardial infarction. N Engl J Med 311:552-559

Schiff SK, Pilot ML: An approach to psychiatric consultation in the general hospital. Arch Gen Psychiatry 1:349-357, 1959

Schwartz GE, Weiss SM: Yale conference on behavioral medicine: a proposed definition and statement of goals. J Behav Med 1:3-12, 1978

Selye H: The physiology and pathology of exposure to stress. Acta Montreal, 1950

Sexton DL: Wives of COPD patients: cast in the role of caretaker. Conn Med 48:37-40, 1984

Soloff PH: Denial and rehabilitation of the post-infarction patient. Int J Psychiatry Med 8:125-132, 1977

Stanton BA, Jenkins CD, Denlinger P, et al: Predictors of employment status after cardiac surgery. JAMA 239:907-911, 1983

Stanton MD: Family treatment approaches to drug abuse problems: review. Fam Process 18:251-280, 1982

Steinglass P: Experimenting with family treatment approaches to alcoholism 1950-1975: a review. Fam Process 15:94-123, 1976

Stern MJ, Gorman PA, Kaslow L: The group counseling vs. exercise therapy study: a controlled intervention with subjects following myocardial infarction. Arch Intern Med 143:1719-1725, 1983

Stewart FI: Family therapy in the treatment of medically ill adults. Paper presented at Research Day, Charleston Area Medical Center, Charleston WV, March 20, 1985

Strain JJ, Grossman S: Psychological Care of the Mentally Ill: A Primer in Liaison Psychiatry. New York, Appleton-Century-Crofts, 1975

Thoresen CE, Friedman M, Gill JJ, et al: The recurrent coronary prevention project: some preliminary findings. Acta Med Scand [Suppl] 660:172-192, 1982

Toevs CD, Kapln RM, Atkins CJ: The costs and effects of behavioral programs in chronic obstructive pulmonary disease. Med Care 22:1088-1098, 1984

Udelman HD, Udelman DL: Current explorations in psychoimmunology. Am J Psychother 38:210-221, 1983

Verrier RL, Lown B: Behavioral stress and cardiac arrythmias. Annual Review of Physiology 46:155-176, 1984

Viney LL, Westbrook MT: Psychological reactions to chronic illness-related disability as a function of its severity and type. J Psychosom Res 25:513-523, 1981

von Bertalanffy L: General Systems Theory. New York, Braziller, 1968

Weisman AD, Hackett TP: Organization and function of a psychiatric consultation service. International Record of Medicine 173:306-311, 1960

Wilkinson DG: Psychiatric aspects of diabetes mellitus. Br J Psychiatry 138:1-9, 1981

Williams R, Haney TL, Lee KL, et al: Type A behavior, mortality and coronary heart disease. Psychosom Med 42:539-549, 1980

Williams RB: Biobehavioral factors in cardiovascular disease, in Psychiatry, vol 2. Edited by Michels R, Cavenar JO, Brodie HKH, et al. Philadelphia, Lippincott, 1985

Wooley SC, Blackwell B, Wignet C: A learning theory model of chronic illness behavior: theory, treatment and research. Psychosom Med 40:379-401, 1978

10

Disability Among the Homeless Mentally Ill

Leona L. Bachrach, Ph.D.

A mong the mentally ill, those who are homeless stand out as uniquely affected by diverse and accumulated disabilities. This chapter examines the dimensions of disability among the homeless mentally ill and comments on service planning for that population. For purposes of this article, the homeless mentally ill include those individuals who, simultaneously, are homeless and exhibit the severe psychopathologies that are typically associated with chronic mental illnesses.

DEFINING THE HOMELESS MENTALLY ILL POPULATION

The population of homeless mentally ill individuals is difficult to define—and even more difficult to count and classify—as the result of a complex of factors (Bachrach 1984b). There is, first of all, no universally accepted definition of homelessness. Although the condition of homelessness is generally accompanied by a lack of shelter and a degree of isolation or social disaffiliation, both of these circumstances are themselves open to a variety of definitions.

Yet, even if consensus could be achieved concerning the precise meaning of homelessness, it would still be difficult to differentiate those persons in the homeless population who are chronically mentally ill from those who are not. That the definition of chronic mental illness is itself fraught with uncertainty (Goldman et al. 1981) is only part of the problem. There are, beyond this, certain distinctive problems associated with establishing the presence of psychopathology among individuals who are frequently shy and frightened and whose basic subsistence needs are typically unmet.

The extreme diversity that characterizes the homeless mentally ill increases definitional uncertainty even more. The homeless mentally ill population consists of members of both sexes, and of all ages. They possess a variety of functional levels and treatment histories. Some in the population have had many years of institutional residence; others, as the result of so-called admission diversion policies, have never received any inpatient care. Some are passive; others appear demanding, volatile, and, in patient-care settings, essentially noncompliant. Many have problems of substance abuse superimposed on their primary psychiatric illnesses.

A portion of this diversity is captured in descriptions of two contrasting subpopulations of the homeless mentally ill in New York City. Project HELP (1983), an outreach program with a mandate to serve the most severely psychiatrically disabled among the homeless, describes its target population in the following manner:

> The primary visual indicators include: extremely dirty and dishevelled appearance; obvious lice infestation; torn, dirty and/or layered clothing; weather-inappropriate clothing (especially heavy coats and woolen hats in mid-summer); and a cache of belongings in bags, boxes, shopping carts, etc. The primary behavioral indicators include: walking in traffic, urinating and/or defecating in public, remaining mute and withdrawn (p. 4).

This rather prototypical description of "bag ladies" or "grate gentlemen" may be contrasted with a description by Reich and Siegel (1978) of a different subgroup of homeless mentally ill individuals, almost exclusively male, who live on the Bowery:

> Most of these men are intelligent and have better than the usual education found on the Bowery. They present a fairly intact appearance even when undergoing severe inner disturbance and thus can avoid unwanted hospitalization even when their situation destabilizes and there is a threat of erupting violence (pp. 195–196).

Arce (1983) and his colleagues (Arce et al. 1983) provide data that underscore the diversity within the homeless mentally ill population. They differentiate between "street people" and "episodically homeless" individuals in a shelter setting in Philadelphia. Mentally ill street people in their study population tend to be floridly psychotic individuals with diagnoses of schizophrenia, sometimes with substance abuse, a history of mental hospitalization, and a variety of health problems. By contrast, the episodically homeless mentally ill in their population are generally younger and more often carry diagnoses of personality disorder, affective disorder, or substance abuse. They alternate between being domiciled and undomiciled and tend to utilize a wide variety of mental health and social services sporadically. They are likely to be regarded as "difficult" patients. A third category of homeless individuals described by Arce (1983), the "situationally homeless," are identified more by situational stress than by psychopathology. For these individuals, the lack of shelter is generally temporary, and the disaffiliation less pronounced.

A study by Goldfinger and his colleagues (1984) confirms a heavy concentration of episodically homeless individuals among admissions to emergency and inpatient psychiatric services at the San Francisco General Hospital. These "acute care recidivists" also utilize the full range of outpatient, residential, and day-treatment services. Chafetz and Goldfinger (1984) have found that 46 percent of a sample of admissions to psychiatric emergency services at the San Francisco General Hospital are, or at some very recent time have been, without stable housing.

These San Francisco study findings suggest strongly that the boundary between populations of domiciled and undomiciled chronically mentally ill individuals is a permeable one, and that these are probably not two separate populations. Instead, they probably constitute one large population with some rather loose and shifting components—a circumstance that certainly adds to definitional confusion (Bachrach 1984c). "Revolving door" patients (Geller 1982), "difficult" patients (Robbins et al. 1978; White 1981), "treatment-resistant" patients (Goldfinger et al. 1984), "chronic-crisis" patients (Bassuk and Gerson 1980), and, most recently, "young adult chronic" patients (Pepper et al. 1981; Bachrach 1982)—all at times overlap with the homeless mentally ill population. Indeed, there is a core who simultaneously fit all of these labels.

A remaining impediment to precise definition of the homeless mentally ill population resides in its geographic variability. Although homeless mentally ill individuals are often associated with inner-city residence; they are also found in small cities and in suburban and rural areas (Bachrach 1983; Fishman 1984; Melton 1984). It has been suggested, though not documented, that homeless mentally ill individuals adopt different behavioral patterns to match these geographic settings—a potentially researchable question.

Not only do the homeless mentally ill vary in where they are, they also differ in how long they have been there. Some comprise an essentially static population that is relatively fixed within defined geographic limits, sometimes as small as a few city blocks; others are very mobile over substantial areas. Some years ago, the Travelers Aid Society (TAS) began to notice, throughout the United States, an upsurge of clients in what they referred to as "psychological flight" (New Tasks 1969). A number of TAS studies have in fact addressed problems associated with identifying and serving travelers with severe psychiatric disabilities (Goldberg 1972; Green 1978; Health and Welfare 1983; Lewis 1978; Smith 1980; Travelers Aid 1976). One particularly noteworthy contribution describes a sample of severely mentally ill TAS clients identified in New Orleans. Of this population 54 percent were seen at a TAS facility in at least one other city, 45 percent in at least three other cities, and 22 percent in at least six other cities in addition to new Orleans (Travelers Aid 1976).

The foregoing discussion of the problems inherent in identifying, counting, and classifying the homeless mentally ill is more than an academic exercise. It has profound implications for the treatment of homeless mentally ill individuals. Difficulties in definition sometimes create, and almost invariably exacerbate, service-delivery problems for members of this population. These definitional issues are intimately related to the barriers to care which will be described below.

DISABILITY AMONG THE HOMELESS MENTALLY ILL

The concept of disability, as it has been developed by Wing and Morris (1981) and Shepherd (1984) in Great Britain is very helpful in understanding the service needs of homeless mentally ill persons in the United States. There are three essential varieties of disability that may be noted.

Primary disabilities consist of psychiatric impairments or dysfunctions that are otherwise described as the symptoms of psychiatric illness. These may include such conditions as lethargy, odd and unacceptable behavior, lack of awareness of handicaps, and disturbances in social relationships. It is typically the appearance of such symptoms that leads to diagnosis and, for many (though not all) of the homeless mentally ill, culminates in attempts at treatment.

Secondary disabilities stem from handicaps that are associated with the experience of psychiatric illness rather than from the illness per se. They are an individual's idiosyncratic responses to his or her illness. Shepherd (1984) aptly writes that "a major psychiatric episode is a frightening and disturbing experience and its effects may persist long after the primary symptoms have disappeared" (p. 5). The specific manifestations of secondary disability are varied and may range from responses of wariness, avoidance, and withdrawal, to a refusal to accept the limits of illness and persistent clinging to unrealistic goals. In any case, these "adverse personal reactions," as they are called by Wing and Morris (1981), which are so evident in the homeless mentally ill population, may present as much of a problem for successful engagement and treatment as do any primary symptoms of psychiatric illness.

Tertiary disabilities or handicaps are associated with what Wing and Morris (1981) call "social disablement." They are derivative from societal responses to illness and disability and include such circumstances as improverished social relationships, diminished social networks, stigma, poverty, unemployment, and a general lack of belonging. Wing and Morris specifically point to homelessness as one possible kind of tertiary disability. Although there are often preventable conditions that intensify such handicaps, tertiary disabilities, once established, tend to persist over time. What is more, the resultant social disadvantage tends to be cumulative.

It is difficult, both in theory and in actual contact with homeless mentally ill individuals, to sort out the manifestations of these various levels of disability; they are inextricably bound together. Thus, it is no easy task to determine how much of the variance in an individual's social withdrawal is the specific result of primary, secondary, or tertiary disability.

This uncertainty gives rise to a very thorny conceptual concern regarding the homeless mentally ill. In conducting research on this population should we seek out the homeless among the chronically mentally ill? Or, alternatively, should we focus on the chronically mentally ill in the homeless population (Bachrach, 1984c)? These two approaches suggest different sets of dependent and independent variables, and selection of one over the other should be determined by the level of disability that is being investigated. Thus, for example, for some chronically mentally ill individuals, homelessness may be an expression of a secondary disability; for others it may be a response to a tertiary disability resulting from urban gentrification. However, for most homeless mentally ill individuals, the condition of homelessness probably reflects multiple disabilities at all levels that are cumulative and mutually reinforcing.

DISABILITY AND BARRIERS TO CARE

Obstacles to care for the homeless mentally ill are clearly related to all three levels of disability. One major barrier is the existence of preclusive admission policies that serve to deny them admission to programs within the system of care. Even when care for homeless mentally ill individuals has been mandated, they are frequently excluded from facilities.

Preclusive admission policies may in fact reflect a variety of concerns on the part of the service system. Some of the symptoms and disabilities exhibited by the homeless mentally ill, such as poor or nonexistent personal hygiene and grossly antisocial behaviors, render them singularly unattractive in patient-care environments. In addition, their prolonged secondary and tertiary disabilities are often associated with a marked imperviousness to traditional treatment interventions. To the extent that service providers measure their programs' effectiveness in terms of "cures" (Stern and Minkoff 1979), the homeless mentally ill serve as constant reminders of the limits of our technology.

An additional source of barriers to care for the homeless mentally ill derives from their unique treatment needs. Even if facilities' doors were open to them, the members of this population would probably have a hard time finding what they need inside. Precisely because of their special disabilities, these individuals tend to have service requirements that are extraordinary in both number and content. Barrow and Lovell (1982), two investigators in New York City, have identified some 70 separate and individual services that homeless mentally ill individuals tend to need, and these include some not very traditional items, like the provision of mailboxes where SSI checks can be delivered, shower facilities, and delousing areas. Providers may be hard pressed to ensure that these special kinds of services will be delivered in their facilities, since psychiatric programs are generally not prepared to deal with patients' basic subsistence and sanitary needs. Unfortunately, however, until these needs have been met, clinical and rehabilitative interventions will probably have little discernible effect.

Not only are the number and the content of their service needs unique, homeless mentally ill individuals are often additionally deterred by their multiple disabilities from complying with the time constraints that prevail in many psychiatric service settings. Studies currently being completed at the New York State Psychiatric Institute document the fact that it may take months of protracted initial contact before a service provider is able to establish enough trust with a homeless mentally ill individual to begin to engage him or her in actual treatment (Bachrach 1984e).

Geographic mobility among the homeless mentally ill poses still another set of barriers to care. At times, mobility may be understood as an extreme manifestation of secondary disability. At other times, however, it may be associated with some primary and tertiary disabilities. That homeless mentally ill individuals often suffer painful and confusing symptoms, and that they generally lack access to treatment and residential facilities, may generate within them a longing and a search that is eloquently described in a single sentence by Streltzer (1979), who has written about homeless mentally ill in-migrants to Hawaii: "Those who were attempting to escape psychosis continued to be psychotic in Hawaii" (p. 468).

Geographic mobility may in fact reflect a response to certain policy initiatives that have guided service delivery in many psychiatric service settings. Historically, one of the major philosophical underpinnings of the community mental health movement involved fixing responsibility for chronic mental patients within defined geographic limits (Group for the Advancement of Psychiatry 1983). Although such "catchmenting" is no longer discussed extensively in the literature, its original intent, to force service providers to assume responsibility for the care of individuals within circumscribed boundaries so that no one would be overlooked (Panzetta 1971), continues to influence service provision (Marcos and Gil 1984).

However, for the homeless mentally ill, geographically determined responsibility has backfired seriously. In order to qualify for care in many service settings, patients must meet an array of residential requirements. Obviously, such a policy imposes severe barriers to care for people who have no home and no fixed address. Residence-based requirements often also affect the ability of many homeless individuals to qualify for various kinds of entitlements. Segal and his colleagues (1977) note that the lack of a permanent address "greatly increases the likelihood that an individual's SSI application will not be processed" (p. 398). Even if the application should be processed, the individual may still experience difficulty in receiving entitlements, because "notification of psychiatric appointments, requests for additional information or release forms, and all other communications from the Social Security Office are routinely conducted by mail" (p. 398).

The disabilities of the homeless mentally ill on all levels—primary, secondary, and tertiary—are so marked and so severe that they are often difficult for service providers to appreciate. This lack of understanding creates still another barrier to care, for it generates unrealistic expectations on the part of many service providers. The current controversy over whether individuals are homeless by "choice" (Williams 1984) reflects a naive expectation that the homeless mentally ill share the same expectations and the same prospects as other members of society. However, illness, itself, and its derivative disabilities often intervene to limit the choices of the homeless mentally ill in a definitive way (McCarthy 1984; Baxter and Hopper 1982; Schanberg 1984).

OVERCOMING THE BARRIERS

The difficulties inherent in overcoming barriers to care for the homeless mentally ill must not be minimized. These individuals are typically severely ill and multiply disabled, and proposed solutions that overlook these basic circumstances are bound to meet with failure. Thus, it must be said initially and emphatically that our technology is limited. We are still in the process of learning how to conceptualize the dimensions and needs of the homeless mentally ill population. More often than not, overcoming barriers to the care of these individuals puzzles us, bewilders us, frustrates us. They are, by and large, not responsive to traditional treatment modes. They reject our interventions, and they reject us, and this makes it very difficult for service providers to engage them in treatment. Planning services for this population often requires more dedication, and more imagination, than the service system has at its disposal. Yet, many efforts to reach these individuals are naive and simplistic. Often they are either imbued with religious evangelism, or else they are geared toward a level of rehabilitative competence that is simply out of range for many members of the population (Larew 1980).

But in spite of widespread difficulties in service delivery, it is possible to point to several positive developments in planning for this population. Our very ability to summarize and analyze service-delivery issues (Lamb 1984) underscores the emergence and growth of a body of relevant knowledge. Thus, even though our service structures for the homeless mentally ill are generally inadequate, and even though our efforts to reach individuals in that population may often be misdirected, we are beginning to gain an understanding of some of the requisites of relevant service development.

It appears that certain basic social and psychological circumstances must exist before barriers to care for the homeless mentally ill can be overcome. There must, first of all, be a prevailing climate that supports the care of this population as a proper pursuit and that reinforces the legitimacy of our directing scarce resources to them. This includes the provision of income supports as well as psychiatric and medical services and a range of housing alternatives. Programmatic efforts for the homeless mentally ill that seem to be "working" appear, almost invariably, to exist in climates where these individuals are perceived as sick and deserving and not as lazy and worthless. It is undoubtedly the accepting attitude of many religious groups that accounts for their frequent ability to reach homeless mentally ill individuals.

Beyond the presence of a favorable social climate, we must be prepared, in serving the homeless mentally ill, to apply the same kinds of planning principles that we now use in developing services for the domiciled chronically mentally ill. Those principles are widely discussed in the literature (Bachrach 1980, 1984d), and they deal with very basic matters—like providing flexible and multifaceted program formats, offering individualized but culturally relevant treatments, and facilitating communication within and between service-delivery agencies. In other words, they have to do with providing individualized care, comprehensive care, and continuity of care.

What specifically, then, might be involved in applying these principles to populations that, in addition to being chronically mentally ill, are also homeless?

First, there is a need for service planners and service providers to assign unambiguous priority to homeless mentally ill people in the service system—that is, if they really mean to serve the population at all. Because these individuals cannot advocate effectively on their own behalf, and because they are often shunned and their very existence is denied, they do not fare well when they must compete for resources with other individuals who are less severely impaired and much more attractive. Thus, any program that purports to serve the homeless mentally ill must back that intention up by aggressively enhancing their access to care.

This is not to imply that every psychiatric service agency should drop its other responsibilities and concentrate exclusively on the needs of the homeless mentally ill. Rather, it is a recognition of the fact that, when the homeless mentally ill have been mandated or designated as the recipients of services within an agency, special efforts must be taken to ensure that they are not somehow pushed aside. Their disabilities are such that the service system must back its intentions up with unambiguous and aggressive action.

Second, it appears at this time that we must reassess the possible role that institutional care can play in the spectrum of services for some members of this population—at least until such time as adequate alternatives have been provided in the community. Many homeless mentally ill individuals, precisely because of their complex disabilities, require asylum or safe haven simply in order to remain alive. Although, theoretically, the function of asylum may be separated from an institutional setting and provided in the community (Bachrach 1984a)—and although community-based asylum is regarded by many as more humane and less stigmatizing than state hospital care—the fact is that it is currently very difficult to find community-based facilities that can, or will, perform this special function. It is difficult enough to locate community residences for the homeless mentally ill, let alone the kind of total care that is implied in the concept of asylum.

Third, it is necessary to provide a complete array of services for this population in order to meet the needs generated by their complex and multiple disabilities. Housing is not enough, for, by itself, it creates a treatment vacuum from which the supportive effects of medical and psychiatric care are absent. Similarly, medical and psychiatric care should not be provided in a residential vacuum, for these interventions have little lasting effect when the patient finds himself or herself on the streets once again at their conclusion.

In fact, the notion of comprehensive care is an extremely critical one for meeting the needs of this population. However, it must be understood that comprehensive care, a concept very much in vogue in service planning today, actually has unique connotations for the homeless mentally ill, who generally have nothing and need everything. Thus, the cornerstone of planning for this population must be services that will meet basic survival needs first. Until these have been met, therapy and rehabilitative efforts will not have much positive effect.

Finally, a basic step in removing barriers to care for the homeless mentally ill is a working acknowledgement of the diversity of that population. Agencies must be prepared to plan services on an individualized basis and not to seek instant answers that will somehow magically meet the needs of all homeless mentally ill people. Recognition of the specific constellation of primary, secondary, and tertiary disabilities for each homeless mentally ill individual must be incorporated into treatment planning. Indeed, individualized planning is particularly critical for members of this population, because of their frequent fearfulness, their resistance, and their general inaccessibility. Each individual must be approached and, if possible, separately reassured.

The importance of individualized planning is largely accepted with respect to residential settings. There is a growing appreciation of the fact that no single kind of residential setting equally fills the needs of all homeless mentally ill people: Different members of the population have different kinds of housing requirements, and they need residential settings that range from places where they may live in relative independence to places with a great deal of structure. In addition, there must be both short- and long-term housing alternatives.

But providing a range of housing opportunities is only a starting point. Individualized treatment planning is required as well. In fact, offering differentiated treatment settings to the members of this population—settings that range from intensive inpatient care facilities, to drop-in centers, to outreach programs that actually go out on the streets to engage patients—is consistent with the principles of both effective case management and good medical care.

CONCLUSION

An understanding of disability among homeless mentally ill individuals begins with the acknowledgement that the members of this population are generally characterized by complexity, diversity, elusiveness, helplessness, and a need for a wide array of basic services. This population presents a major service-delivery challenge for the 1980s. Some service agencies may welcome that challenge as being within the province of their legitimate responsibilities; others may not. In any case, psychiatry now finds itself charged with having to care for these individuals and so must enhance its efforts to reach them (Bachrach 1984b).

Applying accepted principles of program planning to service development for the homeless mentally ill means making special adaptations and accommodations. It requires that we understand the unique consequences of the interaction of chronicity and homelessness, as well as the full range of serious disabilities that follow from this interaction. It is thus well, in summary, to recall the words of the Director of Policy Studies of the Health and Welfare Council of Central Maryland who noted, in a recent public television interview, that the homeless mentally ill "didn't get sick in a day, and they won't get well in a day" (No Place 1983). The challenges presented by this population are likely to continue well into the future.

REFERENCES

Arce AA: Statement before the Committee on Appropriations, in U.S. Senate Special Hearing on Street People. Washington DC, U.S. Government Printing Office, 1983

Arce AA, Tadlock M, Vergare MH, et al: A psychiatric profile of street people admitted to an emergency shelter. Hosp Community Psychiatry 34:812–817, 1983

Bachrach LL: Overview: model programs for chronic mental patients. Am J Psychiatry 137:1023–1031, 1980

Bachrach LL: Young adult chronic patients: an analytical review of the literature. Hosp Community Psychiatry 33:189–197, 1982

Bachrach LL: Psychiatric services in rural areas: a sociological overview. Hosp Community Psychiatry 34:215–226, 1983

Bachrach LL: Asylum and chronically ill psychiatric patients. Am J Psychiatry 141:975–978, 1984a

Bachrach LL: The homeless mentally ill and mental health services: an analytical review of the literature, in The Homeless Mentally Ill. Edited by Lamb HR. Washington, DC, American Psychiatric Association, 1984b

Bachrach LL: Interpreting research on the homeless mentally ill: some caveats. Hosp Community Psychiatry 35:914–917, 1984c

Bachrach LL: Principles of planning for chronic psychiatric patients: a synthesis, in The Chronic Mental Patient: Five Years Later. Edited by Talbott JA. Orlando FL, Grune & Stratton, 1984d

Bachrach LL: Research on services for the homeless mentally ill. Hosp Community Psychiatry 35:910–913, 1984e

Barrow S, Lovell M: Evaluation of Project Reach Out, 1981-82. New York, New York State Psychiatric Institute, June 30, 1982

Bassuk E, Gerson S: Chronic crisis patients: a discrete clinical group. Am J Psychiatry 137:1513–1517, 1980

Baxter E, Hopper K: The new mendicancy: homeless in New York City. Am J Orthopsychiatry 54:393–408, 1984

Chafetz L, Goldfinger SM: Residential instability in a psychiatric emergency setting. Psychiatry Q 56:20–34, 1984

Fishman C: Homeless in Fairfax lose shelter. Washington Post, pp. 81, 84, Apr 1, 1984

Geller MP: The "revolving door": a trap or a life style? Hosp Community Psychiatry 33:388–399, 1982

Goldberg M: The runaway Americans. Mental Hygiene 56:13–21, 1972

Goldfinger SM, Hopkin JT, Surber RW: Treatment resisters or system resisters? Toward a better service system for acute care recidivists, in New Directions for Mental Health Services: Advances in Treating the Young Adult Chronic Patient. Edited by Pepper B, Ryglewicz H. San Francisco, Jossey-Bass, 1984

Goldman HH, Gattozzi AA, Taube CA: Defining and counting the chronically mentally ill. Hosp Community Psychiatry 32:21–27, 1981

Group for the Advancement of Psychiatry: Community Psychiatry: A Reappraisal. New York, Group for the Advancement of Psychiatry, 1983

Green C: The transient mentally disabled: a new challenge to Travelers Aid Services. San Francisco CA, Travelers Aid Society, 1978

Health and Welfare Council of Central Maryland: A Report to the Greater Baltimore Shelter Network on Homelessness in Central Maryland. Baltimore, June 1983

Lamb HR (Ed.): The Homeless Mentally Ill. Washington, DC, American Psychiatric Association, 1984

Larew BI: Strange strangers: serving transients. Social Casework 63:107–113, 1980

Lewis N: Community Intake Services for the Transient Mentally Disabled (TMD). San Francisco, Travelers Aid Society, 1978

Marcos LR, Gil RM: Psychiatric catchment areas in an urban center: a policy in disarray. Am J Psychiatry 141:875–878, 1984

McCarthy C: Reagan's grate society. Washington Post p. A23, Feb 11, 1984

Melton RH: Shelter gives life to down and out. Washington Post, pp. C1, C7, Dec 23, 1984

New tasks faced by Travelers Aid. New York Times, p. 53, May 4, 1969

No Place Like Home. Aired on State Line Series, Maryland Public Television, Channel 22, Annapolis, MD, Dec 25, 1983

Panzetta A: Community Mental Health: Myth and Reality. Philadelphia, Lea and Febiger, 1971

Pepper B, Kirshner MC, Ryglewicz H: The young adult chronic patient: overview of a population. Hosp Community Psychiatry 32:463–469, 1981

Project HELP Summary, October 30, 1982-August 31, 1983. New York State Community Support Services, Governeur Hospital, New York City, 1983

Reich R, Siegel L: The emergency of the Bowery as a psychiatric dumping ground. Psychiatry Q 50:191–201, 1978

Robbins E, Stern M, Robbins L, et al: Unwelcome patients: where can they find asylum? Hosp Community Psychiatry 29:44–46, 1978

Schanberg SH: Reagan's homeless. New York Times, p. 23, Feb 4, 1984

Segal SP, Baumohl J, Johnson E: Falling through the cracks: mental disorder and social margin in a young vagrant population. Social Problems 24:387–400, 1977

Shepherd G: Institutional Care and Rehabilitation. London, Longmans, 1984

Smith HA: Psychosocial development of flight-chronic patients. New Orleans, Travelers Aid Society, 1980

Stern R, Minkoff K: Paradoxes in programming for chronic patients in a community clinic. Hosp Community Psychiatry 30:613–617, 1979

Streltzer J: Psychiatric emergencies in travelers to Hawaii. Compr Psychiatry 20:463–468, 1979

Travelers Aid Society of Greater New Orleans: Summary of Study of Wandering Mentally Ill, 1976

White HS: Managing the difficult patient in the community residence, in New Directions for Mental Health Services: Issues in Community Residential Care. Edited by Budson R. San Francisco, Jossey-Bass, 1981

Williams J: Homeless chose to be, Reagan says. Washington Post, pp. 1, 13, Feb 1, 1984

Wing JK, Morris B: Clinical basis of rehabilitation, in Handbook of Psychiatric Rehabilitation Practice. Edited by Wing JK, Morris B. Oxford, Oxford University Press, 1981

Section III

PSYCHIATRIC REHABILITATION

11

The Psychosocial Rehabilitation Movement in the United States

Irvin D. Rutman, Ph.D.

T his chapter presents a review and discussion of psychosocial rehabilitation as it exists today. It examines the field's historical origins and development, its essential characteristics and thrust, the scope of its services and programs, several major "schools" or orientations within the overall approach, and the effectiveness and significance of psychosocial rehabilitation for clients within the mental health system.

Since "psychosocial rehabilitation" programs encompass many methods and components, and since the term itself sometimes refers to a philosophy of care, and sometimes to a professional movement, the overall parameters of the field are quite extensive. As a result, it is possible that some noteworthy features, programs, or findings may not have been given the emphasis they merit. Such oversight, unfortunately, is a built-in limitation of any discussion which attempts to offer a state-of-the-art assessment. With this in mind, the following is a useful review of the salient issues and emerging directions in the field of psychosocial rehabilitation.

BACKGROUND

An estimated minimum of 2 million men and women in the United States can be characterized as chronically mentally ill (Goldman et al. 1981; Minkoff 1978; President's Commission on Mental Health 1978). This group is highly heterogeneous. It includes individuals who have spent major portions of their adult lives in mental institutions; persons who have experienced repeated short-term hospitalizations or other treatment episodes; those who, following one or two psychiatric hospitalizations, continue to function marginally in the community; elderly persons whose psychiatric difficulties are compounded by the effects of the aging process; and individuals between 18–30 (often referred to as "new chronic" clients) who resist formal involvement in the mental health system and whose behavior problems frequently bring them into contact with the criminal justice system and/or agencies dealing with substance abuse (Pepper et al. 1981; Talbott 1980).

These men and women are beset by an extensive range of personal, social, psychiatric, vocational, and financial needs. Several writers have described these needs at some length (Glasscote et al. 1971; Petersen 1978; Talbott 1978), summarized as follows: to secure the material resources such as food, shelter, clothing, and medical care necessary to support living in the community; to learn and to use the coping skills needed to meet the demands of daily living; to be freed of pathologically dependent relationships; to be helped to grow toward greater personal autonomy; and to establish and utilize a support system which assists individuals in accomplishing the above aims. Broader social needs are also present: to safeguard clients' personal dignity and rights to confidentiality, civil rights, and liberties; and to help reduce the destructive effects of stigma and societal rejection.

Until relatively recently, to a large degree, these needs were discounted or neglected by mental health planners, agencies, and professionals. There are many reasons for this, as discussed amply in the literature (Bachrach 1983; Scull 1977; Committee on Psychiatry and the Community 1978). Briefly, chronic mental patients first were dispersed from hospitals in massive numbers through poorly planned and executed deinstitutionalization procedures that frustrated efforts to link patients with community-based mental health care (Lamb and Goertzel 1971; Perlman 1980). Community mental health programs, which had been recently established, were neither geared nor motivated to offer rehabilitation services to this group. Further, mental health professionals—trained and oriented to provide treatment services to more responsive, less disabled clients through the use of traditional therapeutic methods—tended to regard serving the chronically mentally ill negatively, viewing them as an undesirable, low-prestige group which showed progress slowly if at all (Schofield 1964; Wolkon and Peterson 1986). Finally, the chronic mental patients themselves often displayed personal and behavioral characteristics which acted to discourage mental health agencies and staff from directing more than token services to them. These individuals were often unattractive, overly dependent, less than articulate, emotionally flat, and, as a group, difficult with which to work.

These conditions generally prevailed from the early 1960s, when deinstitutionalization policies began to accelerate throughout the nation, through the mid-1970s. By the latter period, tens of thousands of former mental hospital patients had been discharged into communities which typically were neither prepared to receive them nor sensitive to their needs. In short order, professional, advocacy, and family groups increasingly began to voice protest regarding the lack of continuity between hospital and community-based services and the dearth of adequate rehabilitation resources within the community. Further aggravating the situation were numerous newspaper and broadcast exposés which focused on the plight of chronically disabled people in the community and decried the presence of a growing number of "street people" in many cities and towns—a considerable portion of whom were assumed to be former mental hospital patients (Allen 1974; Anthony et al. 1978; Committee on Psychiatry and the Community 1983).

As these concerns mounted, federal and state mental health authorities began to come to grips with the need to resolve the problem of the chronically mentally ill. This response was sharply spurred by a 1977 report of the General Accounting Office which scrutinized deinstitutionalization policies and practices in several states, confirmed the inadequacies of planning and program-development efforts, and strongly recommended that government agencies needed to intensify their efforts on behalf of this target group (U.S. General Accounting Office 1977). In the succeeding months and years, a series of significant remedies began to take form: Federal agencies (and their state-level counterparts) developed and executed various cooperative agreements designed to improve coordination among human-service systems involved with helping this population; new programs were developed and resources found, making public funds available to stimulate expanded housing opportunities and vocational rehabilitation services (Bachrach 1981; Steering Committee on the Chronically Mentally Ill 1980). The National Institute of Mental Health initiated two important efforts in its own right: (a) the creation of the Community Support Program which encouraged states and communities both to engage in systems planning targeted to the unique needs of the chronically mentally ill, and to develop and replicate model programs serving these individuals (National Institute of Mental Health 1981); (b) amended legislation and funding criteria governing support of Community Mental Health Centers requiring centers to provide a range of community-oriented rehabilitation services.

Since the mid-1970s, a notable and still growing surge in priority—and resources—has been directed to the needs of severely disabled clients living in the community. Scores of state and local mental health authorities have initiated new residential services, expanded aftercare and socialization programs, and provided support for innovative vocational rehabilitation programs. Publicly funded mental hospitals have both dramatically reduced patients' average length of stay and redirected treatment programs to emphasize preparation of the patient for return to the community (Talbott 1981; Committee on Psychiatry and the Community 1978). Hundreds of mental health provider organizations have reshaped their operations substantially and in ways which strengthened the scope and quality of community rehabilitation services available to this group.

Clearly, many social, political, and professional forces interacted over the years to produce these major developments in the mental health delivery system. A unifying conceptual and programmatic orientation can be identified around which many of these planning and programmatic changes have been organized. This orientation increasingly is referred to as psychosocial rehabilitation.

THE NATURE OF PSYCHOSOCIAL REHABILITATION: CHARACTERISTICS AND DEFINITIONS

The term *psychosocial rehabilitation* is used today with increasing frequency, popularity, and, concomitantly, elasticity. As with many innovative programs or approaches that surface from time to time in human services, it has been applied to a wide range of programs offering services to a variety of socially, psychologically, and vocationally disabled populations. It therefore is of interest to consider some of the factors that underlie the term's rather loose and imprecise use.

First, psychosocial rehabilitation—meaning here the systematic use of a combination of specific modalities to assist in the rehabilitation of the mentally ill—is a relatively new movement. Its major origins in this country date to the 1950s with the formation of the first handful of agencies established expressly to work with chronically mentally ill persons. From that time until about the mid-1970s, the psychosocial movement expanded gradually, but at a generally slow rate and with rather modest effect on mental health systems. Only recently has the impact of the psychosocial approach increased to its current substantial level and, in the process, become firmly incorporated into state and local administrative plans, funding streams, and programmatic designs.

Second, even among those agencies totally engaged in providing psychosocial rehabilitation services for the chronically mentally ill, there is a lack of consensus regarding the "best" program components, modalities, and values of this approach. As these agencies came into being (in many different locales and under varying auspices), they found it desirable for a variety of reasons to emphasize distinctive methods and areas. As a result, there is currently no single psychosocial rehabilitation program model upon which all proponents would agree. Rather, a number of major identifiable psychosocial rehabilitation models (e.g., clubhouse model, high-expectancy model, intensive care management model, described below) have emerged, each with its adherents and each influencing other providers throughout the nation in the design of their programs (Beard 1976; Dincin 1975; Stein and Test 1983).

Because the term psychosocial rehabilitation is often used to refer to an attitude or philosophy rather than to the provision of specific programmatic interventions, service providers and practitioners who agree with the values imbedded in the psychosocial approach respond favorably to the concept. In turn, they identify their programs as psychosocially oriented even though, on closer examination, these programs may be quite different in structure and style from those generally classified as psychosocial.

Undoubtedly, there are still other factors which have contributed to the generally indistinct boundaries surrounding the term psychosocial rehabilitation. Yet, despite the lack of precision, most observers familiar with the field would readily agree upon a number of key qualities characterizing these services. It is an approach which stresses providing opportunities, to those being served, to participate as fully as possible in normalizing roles and relationships. These include the opportunity for enriched social and personal relationships, for preparing for and finding meaningful employment or related productive activities, for residing in attractive and minimally restrictive residential settings, for assuming responsibility for decisions affecting as many aspects as possible for their daily routines, for feeling respected and valued as individuals. Rudyard Probst and James Schmidt, long-time colleagues of John Beard (who directed Fountain House in New York City and was, for some 28 years, a leading pioneer in the psychosocial rehabilitation field) touched on this quality as part of their Remembrance to Beard following his death in 1982: " . . . [Such a facility provides] an ideal environment in which . . . people could feel that they were wanted, that they were needed, that they were welcomed, and within which they could make a contribution that would allow them to gain or regain their sense of vocational confidence and social independence."

A second feature of the psychosocial rehabilitation approach is its commitment to dealing with the practical, realistic elements of an individual's adjustment needs. Psychosocial rehabilitation programs, perhaps more than any other mental health treatment approach, are targeted to the requirements and basic conditions of community living that face all persons in society. Programs thus focus on helping the individual acquire appropriate residential arrangements; on assisting him or her with essential coping skills such as money management, transportation, hygiene and grooming, etc.; and on preparing the person to enter or reenter productive vocational activity. In addition, programs are offered which help clients improve the quality of family relationships and address their needs for additional education. These basic and tangible needs comprise the primary concerns of the psychosocial movement (Glasscote et al. 1971; Petersen 1978).

Next, psychosocial rehabilitation programs share an emphasis on facilitating social learning and behavioral change through experiential activities. In so doing, the psychosocial proponents reflect their disenchantment with the efficacy of individual, talking-therapy methods, conducted on some periodic basis in a professional office, that deal mainly with intrapsychic processes. It is not unusual for psychosocial services users to visit their programs every day, and to spend as many as 20–39 hours a week taking part in 8 to 10 different kinds of activities. This process, it is held, serves to strengthen the individual's ability to perform numerous practical tasks; to both observe and at times serve as a positive role model; and to gain skills in achieving appropriate relationships with peers, volunteers, and staff. Further, the ongoing participation in experimental learning acts to increase the individual's commitment to and involvement in the rehabilitation process and, at the same time, provides frequent opportunities through which appropriate social reinforcement can take place.

Finally, psychosocial rehabilitation programs and practitioners attempt to minimize differences in role, authority, and status between the disabled individual and the helping professional. Unlike traditional treatment approaches which ordinarily ascribe to the professional a superior level of knowledge regarding the client's problems and the methods that should be employed to bring about their amelioration, psychosocial approaches are organized along more balanced, egalitarian lines. The staff member is neither required nor presumed to have all the answers, but rather encourages frequent, active, and informal give-and-take which may lead to mutually developed approaches to problem resolution. Two noteworthy by-products of this quality may be seen in the names adopted by psychosocial rehabilitation programs and the terms used to describe individuals who utilize program services. Psychosocial facilities strongly tend to avoid using organization names that suggest formal mental health treatment services and therefore eschew identifying themselves as the "ABC Mental Health Clinic" or the "XYZ Rehabilitation Center." Instead, they adopt names that conjure up positive, uplifting images and sentiments, such as Independence House, Thresholds, Horizon House, Step-by-Step, Fountain House, Rainbow House, Forward House, etc. Similarly, the men and women who are served by these programs rarely are referred to as "patients." Traditionally, they were called "clients" but, in recent years, this term has also come to be regarded as possibly demeaning, and is gradually being replaced by "member" or "associate."

Several other qualities characterize the psychosocial rehabilitation approach and distinguish it from other treatment methods. In an earlier publication (1981), the author suggested the following additional dimensions along which the psychosocial rehabilitation approach is oriented: utilization of program settings that are deliberately housed in nonclinical, "normal" locations such as townhouses, church basements, or storefronts; assessment of the client's functional strengths and limitations in conjunction with highlighting his or her existing competencies; limited use of diagnostic studies and labels; utilization of staff members whose backgrounds tend to be varied and whose roles within the program are flexible and at times even unorthodox; and a program environment characterized by realistic expectations designed to convey to and reinforce for the client that the goal of social competency and personal independence is shared, valued, and reachable. A somewhat similar set of qualities describing psychosocial rehabilitation programs has been presented by Anthony et al. (1982), who suggest that psychosocial programs also can be characterized by the use of individual client rehabilitation plans, a team approach to the rehabilitation process, and the readiness to evaluate observable outcomes.

Definitions

Given the developments discussed above, and the wide range of programs which are psychosocially oriented, it should not be surprising that the field has found it difficult to agree on a formal definition. Through most of the 1970s and 1980s, no official definitions were formulated, nor did any appear in federal legislation, regulation, or planning documents. In 1985, in connection with proposed legislation then being formulated, the author developed the following definition at the request of the National Institute of Mental Health:

> Psychosocial rehabilitation refers to a spectrum of programs for persons with long-term mental illness. The programs are designed to strengthen individuals' abilities and skills necessary to meet their needs for housing, employment, socialization, and personal growth. The goal of psychosocial rehabilitation is to improve the quality of life of psychiatrically disabled individuals by assisting them to assume as much responsibility over their lives and to function as actively and independently in society as possible.
>
> Major psychosocial rehabilitation services, which are offered on a continuum, include socialization, recreational, vocational, residential, training in the skills of daily community living, and case management. In addition, psychosocial rehabilitation facilities may also provide client assessment and goal planning activities, educational programs, advocacy training and personal and family support.
>
> The individual may need to use these programs on a short-term basis or indefinitely. The programs are offered in the context of a supportive, non-stigmatizing environment in the community, and in a manner that emphasizes the "personhood" rather than the "patienthood" of the individual, maximizes the

individual's feelings of responsibility and self-worth, and encourages ownership in the rehabilitation process. The services are coordinated with those offered by other mental health and human services agencies.

This definition was adopted with minor revision, and incorporated into the legislative draft.

Other definitions have also been suggested by several writers. Tanaka (1983) suggests that psychosocial rehabilitation is:

> a goal-oriented program for the mentally ill which provides coping experiences toward improved living in the community. The program emphasizes common sense and practical needs and usually includes services of vocational, recreational, socialization, education, personal adjustment, and the prevention of unnecessary hospitalization. The psychosocial rehabilitation setting is purposefully normal to reduce the psychological distance between staff and member, and consciously engages the member as an active participant in program planning, development, policymaking, implementation and evaluation. (p. 10)

Beard, Probst, and Malamud, discussing Fountain House, a leading psychosocial rehabilitation organization, describe its program as providing "an intentional community designed to create a restorative environment within which individuals who have been socially and vocationally disabled by mental illness can be helped to achieve or regain the confidence and skills necessary to lead vocationally productive and socially satisfying lives" (Beard et al. 1983, p. 48). In the same vein, Anthony, Cohen, and Cohen (1983) suggest the goal of psychiatric rehabilitation is "to assure that the person with a psychiatric disability possesses those physical, emotional and intellectual skills needed to live, learn and work in his or her own particular environment. The major interventions by which this goal is accomplished involve either developing in clients the particular skills that they need to function in their environment, and/or developing the environmental resources needed to support or strengthen the clients' present level of functioning." (p. 70)

Finally, the International Association of Psychosocial Rehabilitation Services (1985), in connection with the preparation of a directory of organizations providing such services in the United States, suggests the following definition:

> [Psychosocial rehabilitation services involve] the process of facilitating an individual's restoration to an optimal level of independent functioning in the community . . . . While the nature of the process and the methods used differ in different settings, psychosocial rehabilitation programs invariably encourage persons to

participate actively with others in the attainment of mental health and social competence goals. In many settings, participants are called members. The process emphasizes the wholeness and wellness of the individual and seeks a comprehensive approach to the provision of vocational, residential, social/recreational, educational, and personal adjustment services. (p. iii)

PSYCHOSOCIAL REHABILITATION SERVICES AND PROGRAMS

Historically, most of the agencies providing psychosocially oriented services began by offering a single type of program. For many organizations, this was a socialization program, usually conducted in the context of an informal, homey group meeting and providing the individual with the opportunity to meet others, develop friendships, participate in activities, and simply feel accepted in a supportive climate. In other instances, the facility's first program was residential in nature, designed to assist a number of clients to obtain supervised housing either in a halfway house, group home, or supervised apartment. Still other agencies initially offered vocationally oriented services: a sheltered workshop, perhaps, or a job club formed to ease the transition into competitive employment. As these facilities matured, they sought to enrich and expand their program offerings: Drop-in socialization centers which, at the start, were open a few afternoons a week gradually grew to daily, full-time programs; facilities which offered a halfway house undertook to establish a second one or perhaps a satellite group of apartments. This growth occurred slowly for the most part, usually limited by the inadequacies of available funding.

Over time, however, an interesting development began to be observed. Agencies that initially offered a single-focus program increasingly became aware of the need to provide at least one and frequently several additional areas of service. This occurred mainly in response to the agency's growing recognition of the interrelated, deeply ingrained nature of the needs faced by their members. It thus became apparent that to offer, say, socialization activities alone left untouched the individual's need for either vocational training or for adequate living arrangements.

A pattern thus evolved—which continues to the present—such that most psychosocial rehabilitation facilities gear their offerings to include combinations of two, three, or more program modalities, in an effort to meet their clients' total needs as fully as possible. The most frequently utilized combinations offer some elements of residential, socialization, or vocational programs, and in many cases include all three. Further, many facilities also make additional services available for their members, including recreational activities, self-development courses, crisis intervention and crisis stabilization, family counseling and support, literacy and educational training, and advocacy.

The practice of providing combinations of program components has become so much a part of the psychosocial rehabilitation field that organizations seeking membership into the International Association of Psychosocial Rehabilitation Services are required to demonstrate that they offer at least two separate yet coordinated areas of service from among the following: vocational, residential, social/recreational, educational, personal adjustment, partial hospitalization, or other. This organization, in preparing its National Directory of Agency Resources (1985), identifies nine broad categories of service as comprising the range of psychosocial rehabilitation activities (several of which have already been noted):

- *vocational services*, for example, prevocational training, transitional employment programs, client-owned and -operated businesses, sheltered workshops, supported work, placement programs;
- *residential services*, for example, halfway houses, family foster-care homes, board and care homes, private houses or apartments with support, emergency shelters, group homes, cooperative apartments, crisis housing;
- *social/recreational services*, for example, daily independent-living skills training, member self-government, goal-oriented social club activities, goal-oriented sports, and cultural activities;
- *educational services*, for example, basic education courses, special education courses, GED classes, precollege preparation;
- *personal adjustment services*, for example, case management, goal-oriented evaluations, personal counseling, monitoring of medications;
- *natural support system services*, for example, consultation and education with families, friends, or landlords; facilitating self-help groups; helping clients connect with community institutions;
- *client-outreach and linkage services*, for example, relating to other agencies, arranging needed transportation, taking services to clients, keeping track of current and former members;
- *basic, need-oriented services*, for example, assisting members to procure needed food, clothing, shelter; assisting in procurement of income benefits; assisting in procurement of health care; assisting with arrangements for personal safety; and
- *larger system-oriented services*, for example, advocacy for needed system change; participating in health, human services, or other community planning.

The Variety of Program Modalities

Each of the above categories identifies a number of methods or interventions that may be employed to achieve the underlying aim of that category. Thus, a psychosocial rehabilitation agency offering residential services may provide any one style (or several) of eight residential arrangements which provide the member with suitable housing. A similar variety of modalities is found in each of the other categories. This means that there are not only numerous combinations of services and components that a given psychosocial rehabilitation provider may elect to utilize, but also that relatively few providers are likely to make available program offerings containing exactly the same mix of services and components to their clientele.

Two observations may be made regarding this extensive array of programs offered. First, the diversity has probably come about as a function of both structural and clinical factors. The former include the age, auspices, and financial resources of the provider agency; the urban or rural nature of the community; the prevailing local social and economic conditions; the size and training of the staff; the degree to which other mental health programs are available; and the organizational structure of mental health and rehabilitation services at the state and local levels. The clinical factors relate to the extreme heterogeneity of the chronically mentally ill served by these programs; the corollary is that the types of needs presented by these individuals are similarly heterogeneous, requiring providers to design and test many program components and combinations in an effort to respond to their clients' unique needs.

The second point deals with the ability of practitioners to predict which types of intervention will work best (or at all) for which clients. This is a complex question that is as yet unresolved. (A discussion of the effectiveness of psychosocial rehabilitation methods follows.) On the positive side, however, is the viewpoint which has been forwarded that this group of agencies should be commended for having developed and implemented such a large array of modalities through which to serve their clients. Seen from this perspective, the diversity of program methods reflects practitioners' unusual commitment to a long-neglected population, as well as their innovativeness and flexibility in attempting to respond to their members' individual adjustment difficulties.

MAJOR ORIENTATIONS WITHIN THE FIELD

Although the majority of facilities providing psychosocial rehabilitation services would readily agree with nearly all of the characteristics and values presented above, in recent years several differently styled psychosocial approaches have emerged. At least four such approaches can be identified, each with its own philosophical orientation and preferred program elements.

The Clubhouse Model

This approach emphasizes the importance of making available a fully supportive continuum of services that the member may participate in for as long as he or she wishes. It views the program as representing a symbolic surrogate family for the individual while recognizing that the member's need for and involvement in the program will likely fluctuate considerably over time. It nevertheless believes strongly that the person should have the right and opportunity to remain a member at whatever level is appropriate for an unlimited length of time.

This model views four program components as central: an accepting climate that establishes an unwavering sense of welcome; help in developing job-related skills that can lead to placement in regular jobs in business and industry, either through one or more transitional employment placements or in regular competitive employment; provision for those who need housing with an appropriate, normalized place to live (usually located in an apartment setting); and a milieu which stimulates active and meaningful participation on the part of all members in all phases of the program, from performing housekeeping chores, through assisting in the cafeteria or at the reception desk, to maintaining the agency's fiscal and clinical records.

The emphasis is on achieving an interactive, cooperating community. Roles and relationships among members and staff are balanced and remarkably interchangeable, so that it is often difficult to be sure to which group any given individual belongs. Conspicuously absent in most such facilities are individual offices for staff members to provide counseling or therapy.

Agencies following the clubhouse model tend to have strong leanings toward particular program modalities. Wanting their members to have opportunities for living and working experiences that are as nonstigmatizing and normalizing as possible, such agencies favor developing work assignments with regular business concerns paying minimum wages, rather than with sheltered-workshop programs. Similarly, they view apartment settings as more desirable for the individual than group homes or halfway houses; and they assist in arranging apartment leases in which two or three members share in the rent payment. In this model, as in most others, members and staff are on a first-name basis with each other and often work side by side in various chores or assignments.

The leading proponent of the clubhouse model is Fountain House. Established in the late 1940s, it now occupies several large adjoining buildings in Manhattan. It is open every day of the year and offers services to several hundred men and women daily. Fountain House pioneered the development of transitional employment approaches and the use of apartments for its members needing living arrangements. With the support of several federal grants over the years, it developed an extensive training program which has enabled hundreds of mental health workers across the country to observe and experience this well-established approach. Resulting from this training has been the formation of some 150 agencies throughout the United States which have modeled their programs along generally similar lines. These agencies maintain regular communications and participate in joint program-evaluation activities. In addition to this network, Fountain House has helped establish similar programs in several foreign countries including Poland, Pakistan, and Sweden. Several descriptions of Fountain House/clubhouse models, providing more detailed information about program and philosophy, have been published (Beard et al. 1983; Beard 1976; Beard 1975). Other leading agencies which employ the clubhouse model include Fellowship House in Miami, Florida, and Independence House in St. Louis, Missouri.

The High-Expectancy Model
Agencies organized around this model attempt to create a more structured, less open-ended environment than exists in the clubhouse approach. Program components tend to be made available in sequential segments, usually with suggested time limits. Members progress from one level or phase of an activity to successively higher ones, somewhat in the same way they would in a high school or college. Expectations for the individual's utilization and progress in the program are established at the outset of his or her participation and reviewed regularly thereafter. If difficulties occur in a given activity that slow or halt progress, these are discussed by the member and a staff worker.

This approach places strong reliance on the use of joint goal planning and the development of contracts between the individual and his or her workers. If problematic situations arise, they are reviewed in relation to the goals and contracts agreed to, with new goals and expectations usually being formed. Members frequently are involved in establishing house rules and procedures, suggesting new program activities, preparing a monthly newsletter, and in similar responsibilities that underscore their active participation in ongoing program operations.

Instead of the surrogate-family model, this approach is geared more along an educational model. A variety of classes, training programs, self-development activities, etc. are available to the member from which to choose. Having made his or her selection, the individual is expected to maintain appropriate progress consistent with the goals and agreements that had been set previously. An underlying expectation is that the member need not remain indefinitely in the program, but rather will, at the end of an agreed-upon period of time, "graduate" and make the transition into society.

Because agencies using this model emphasize the importance of planned sequences of activities, they are inclined to use some modalities that the clubhouse model would find unattractive. Thus, individuals interested in finding a job might be started in a sheltered workshop to learn basic work behavior and punctuality habits. After some time there, they would move to a job-training program or volunteer assignment, followed by assignment to transitional employment and/or to a regular competitive job. In a similar vein, the member in need of housing may first be placed in a group home or halfway house, after which he or she would be helped to locate an apartment supervised by the agency, and, at a later time, plan to move into an independent residence. Other program elements tend to be offered in the same general framework.

The high-expectancy model has not developed a formal network of agencies across the country. Instead, various aspects of this approach are used by a number of facilities which have adapted these methods to their own program style. It is used, too, by many facilities whose major services offering is residential care. In such programs, the notion of a time-limited period in the residence followed by a move into a less-supervised setting is commonly employed. The Thresholds program in Chicago, Illinois, which incorporates various elements of this approach has been described by Dincin (1981, 1975). Other established psychosocial agencies whose programs reflect the influence of this orientation include Portals House in Los Angeles, California; Stairways in Erie, Pennsylvania; Hill House in Cleveland, Ohio; and Horizon House in Philadelphia, Pennsylvania.

The Intensive Case Management Model

A quite different approach to psychosocial rehabilitation programming has recently come into prominence with the development of what may be termed the intensive case management program model. Here, the key concern is not to provide a range of services at a specific facility located in the community, but rather to assure that the chronically mentally ill individual receives close, ongoing assistance that is carefully attuned to his or her individual condition. It uses the client's own neighborhood as the training context.

Under this arrangement, each client works with members of a helping team. The entire team is updated daily on the individual's psychiatric condition, problems with family or living situation, medication needs, changes in functioning level, etc. Team members meet with the individual on an as-needed and where-needed basis. The staff worker may go to the client's home—perhaps to monitor whether the individual is taking medication or to make sure he or she is planning to keep an appointment at the welfare or Social Security office. If needed, the worker may accompany the client to the appointment, after which the two may do some shopping or have a snack together at a nearby restaurant. Evening contacts are made if necessary, as are weekend visits, to meet the goal of 24-hour coverage.

Contact between the team member and the individual may take place on a daily basis or less frequently, depending upon the client's observed moods and behavior. Occasionally the client may be asked to come to the program office for a special meeting or counseling session, but this is not the usual practice. Typically the contacts are held within the client's community—whether at the apartment or boardinghouse, the parents' home, a sheltered workshop, a volunteer assignment, or a nearby coffee shop.

This model relies on a team approach, rather than assigning a specific case manager, which lessens the client's dependency on a particular staff member. The team members operate interchangeably so any one of several staff may make contact with the individual over the course of a week or 10 days.

The approach has been described by one proponent as "psychosocial rehabilitation without walls" (personal communication). The clients typically served by this model are among the most seriously disabled of all persons who use psychosocial programs. The first objective is to maintain these men and women in the community and, using the heroic efforts described above, to prevent regression or return to the hospital. As a reasonable level of stability seems to be achieved, the team attempts to connect the client with appropriate mental health or human-service agencies in the community, such as vocational rehabilitation programs or drop-in centers, while gradually lessening their own contacts.

The model was initially developed as part of a federally supported demonstration program that tested the feasibility of a novel alternative-to-hospitalization community-treatment program. Located in Madison, Wisconsin, and termed Training in Community Living (TCL), the original program worked with patients of Mendota State Hospital in a carefully controlled experimental design. At the close of the demonstration period, the program was incorporated into the Wisconsin mental health system and in time was renamed the Program for Assertive Community Training (PACT). Over the past several years, it has been adopted, with some local modification, in several states throughout the nation.

The original TCL demonstration project was developed and conducted by Stein and Test, who have described its operations and outcomes (Stein and Test 1983; Stein and Test 1975). The ongoing PACT program in Madison is headed by William Knoedler and Deborah Allness.

The Consumer-Guided Models
The most recent additions to the scene are consumer-guided services which place emphasis on consumer leadership and, in many cases, direct sponsorship of the psychosocial program. Their development largely grew out of a mix of attitudes of some former patients: that the mental health establishment has been insensitive and ineffective in dealing with the needs of the severely mentally ill; that many individuals' civil rights and liberties have been compromised by their having been involuntarily committed to and given treatment in mental hospitals; or that persons who have experienced the anguish of psychiatric breakdown are in the best position (better, at least, than

mental health professionals) to plan and operate programs for other former patients and themselves.

Although these sentiments are dismissed, if not resented, by many mental health workers (who regard such feelings as indicative of denial or distortion of reality), support for the rights of consumers to develop and operate their own programs is gaining strength. The Community Support Program at the federal and state levels has been especially supportive of the need to create opportunities through which expatients can design their own program activities in keeping with their needs and experience.

Programs of the consumer-guided type are more diversified in their methods and modalities than those in the models discussed above. Further, since they are fewer in number as well as newer, their approach tends to be less consistently developed or documented. Some of them were initiated with the help of mental health facilities or advocacy organizations, while others came into existence through the efforts of consumers themselves.

The Lodge program, pioneered by Fairweather and his associates (1969), was an early forerunner of the consumer-guided approach. This program provided specialized training to a group of chronic mental hospital patients, then discharged them as a group into a communal residence in the community. Once in the Lodge residence, the expatients operated the program, which later also included a small business venture, with minimal or no staff involvement. To date, the Lodge program has been adapted and replicated in some 25 states.

Another program, operated mainly by consumers but originated by a mental health agency, is Project Return. Here, the focus is on creating expanded opportunities for social interaction and support among chronically disabled persons, achieved by creating neighborhood-based social clubs which meet regularly and conduct gatherings, outings, cultural and sporting events, picnics, etc. The activities and finances of the clubs are the responsibility of the members, with coordination and special assistance supplied by Project Return staff, some of whom are former patients. The program originated in the late 1970s in the Los Angeles area, and under the sponsorship of the Mental Health Association, is gradually expanding to other California communities. A similar program has recently been established by Rhoda Zusman in the Tampa, Florida, area as well as others in locales on the East coast.

However, the major thrust of this approach is in the programs which are the direct products of the consumer's own efforts. A growing network of consumer-designed and -led organizations is gradually beginning to take form throughout the nation. Their activities are varied, ranging from the operation of drop-in centers, through public education projects, to helping shape legislation involving the mentally ill.

Exemplifying the self-help movement are the Brighter Day Self-Help Group in Cumberland County, New Jersey, which operates a telephone help line seven days a week; the On Our Own group in Baltimore, Maryland, which developed a bill of rights for persons in psychiatric facilities in that state and also operates a drop-in center; the Mental Patients' Liberation Front of Boston, Massachusetts, which, with funding from the Massachusetts Department of Mental Health, is forming a series of expatient-run social clubs; and Project Share in Philadelphia, Pennsylvania, which organizes self-help groups throughout the state.

One of the most comprehensive self-help programs is the Mental Patients' Association (MPA) in Vancouver, Canada, which operates five community residences as well as a seven-day-a-week drop-in center. According to Judi Chamberlin (1984), a leading patient advocate:

> Anyone can become a member of MPA and take part in whatever combination of its programs and activities he/she chooses. And the organization is run by its members, who elect salaried coordinators to the various jobs for 6-month terms. Decision-making power is in the hands of the membership, exercised in weekly business meetings and in a general meeting every third week. (p. 57)

Descriptions of the programs and developments in the national ex-mental patient movement can be found in the quarterly publication *Madness Network News,* and a guide for mental health workers who deal with self-help groups has been published by the National Institute of Mental Health.

The Scope of Services in the United States

In 1971, Glasscote et al. authored a book reviewing the psychosocial rehabilitation field as exemplified by the methods and orientations used by six leading agencies. In describing the procedures for selecting the agencies to be included, the writers stated, "We anticipated that there would be few such comprehensive programs and that we would have difficulty in identifying them. . . . Eventually, we had developed a list of thirteen more or less comprehensive centers. There may be others that fit the definition, but if so, they are not known to any of the thirteen we dealt with" (Glasscote et al. 1971, p. 9).

A very different picture exists now, 15 years later. There are currently many hundreds of facilities providing some or all of the key services which comprise the psychosocial approach, many of which offer an array of services comparable to the 13 programs that Glasscote was able to locate. More specifically, the National Directory of Organizations Providing Psychosocial Services (International Association of Psychosocial Rehabilitation Services, 1985) identifies 985 facilities which describe themselves as offering, to long-term mentally ill adults, at least three of the following service categories: vocational, residential, social/recreational, educational, or personal adjustment. This number includes free-standing agencies (predominantly not for profit) as well as subunits of larger organizations such as community mental health centers, hospitals, or vocational rehabilitation facilities. Such agencies are found in each of the 50 states and the District of Columbia, and similar programs are also located in several provinces of Canada.

For the past 12 years, the International Association of Psychosocial Rehabilitation Services (IAPSRS) has sponsored an annual professional conference which attracts as many as 700–800 participants from North America and abroad. Some 200 psychosocial facilities are organizational members of the IAPSRS, as are some 400 individuals working in the field.

Some Closing Points
Before turning to other topics, a few concluding points regarding program models should be noted. First, the categorization of current psychosocial services into the four approaches described above should not be taken to suggest that (a) all agencies offering psychosocial services clearly fall into one or another model; (b) agencies which favor a particular approach utilize faithfully all the principles or methods of that approach; or (c) there are no other program methods that provide a planned, helpful orientation toward serving the chronically mentally ill.

Many psychosocial facilities, particularly those that offer only one or two areas of service, operate either along pragmatic lines that reflect no particular philosophical approach or are eclectic in their methods and use a mixture of values and techniques drawn from other models. There is a strong flavor of "we'll use what seems to work best for our clients" among these agencies, and as a result, a considerable degree of heterogeneity is found among provider organizations, even as it is among the clients they serve.

Next, among facilities that do closely identify with or adopt elements of a particular model, significant variation often is found. These may be evident in any of the major program modalities or in the facilities' ongoing operating procedures, use of staff, or relationships to other agencies. There are few if any formal program requirements, monitoring systems, or sanctions governing the field exercised either by mental health authorities or by professional organizations, and variations among agencies' programs are considerable. As Bachrach has noted (1981), exemplary program models developed in one facility under specified local conditions by highly committed, innovative practitioners tend not to transpose well to new agencies and locations.

Finally, it should be clear that there are a considerable number of other methods and approaches that have emerged in the past decade or that have been developed by leading workers in the field and are utilized by or otherwise influence programs throughout the country. There are numerous examples of such distinctive approaches: Mosher and Menn (1978) designed and tested a new technique for providing a community-based, medication-free residential program for persons diagnosed as schizophrenic which has shown positive results; Polak introduced a method whereby mentally disabled persons in crisis received short-term care and support while placed in a foster-home-like arrangement with families in the community and Anthony (1980) has fashioned an approach involving careful assessment of clients' deficits and strengths which is used in designing individual goals to assist the client to acquire needed skills in living, learning, and working relationships. These programs—and many others like them that might also have been cited—underscore again the diversity of approach and the vitality which has characterized the psycho-social rehabilitation movement in this country.

THE EFFECTIVENESS OF PSYCHOSOCIAL REHABILITATION SERVICES

The remaining basic question is, "How well do these programs work and for whom?" The answer unfortunately is neither simple nor yet decided. Numerous procedural and definitional questions obscure our reaching reliable conclusions regarding this issue. What criteria, for example, shall be used to measure the individual's degree of adjustment and productivity: return to hospital, employment, independent living, control of symptomatology, quality of life, some of the above, or all of the above? For many years, recidivism rate and employment status were used as the major criteria by which to measure program success. More recently, however, it has been argued that reliance on these measures alone is inadequate (partly because they are subject to errors of definition and interpretation, partly because they do not deal with a sufficient range of factors relevant to the individual's status and satisfaction as a member of society). Several writers have discussed the need for other, improved criteria.

Many additional inconsistencies and ambiguities also confound the challenge of evaluating psychosocial rehabilitation program effectiveness. As already discussed, clients, staff, program approaches, and modalities vary widely. What passes for a socialization program, a halfway house, or a transitional employment placement in one facility may be very different from programs called by the same name in another. The psychotropic medications prescribed for the disabled person and his or her compliance with them constitute another source of inconsistency, as do, obviously, the nature and duration of the client's psychiatric illness, his or her family and social supports, and related demographic, social, and clinical factors.

For all these reasons, the psychosocial field has not been successful in producing a large number of systematically planned, carefully controlled evaluation studies over most of its history. Although numerous reports describing program techniques and apparent results have appeared, these have been of uneven quality, with many failing to include adequate methodological controls that would justify the conclusions reached or permit replication. Nevertheless, a gradually accumulating body of evidence is beginning to appear that suggests that certain types and aspects of psychosocial rehabilitation are indeed of value, either in their own right or in combination with other treatment methods.

Several helpful reviews on the topic of evaluating the effectiveness of this group of services have been conducted. Anthony (1978, 1983), Bachrach (1982), Test and Stein (1978), Barofsky (1983), Liberman and Rueger (1984), and Meyerson and Herman (1983) are among those who have presented critical assessments of the issues, problems, and findings of evaluative studies in this field. A few highlights of these reviews point to the following conclusions:

- Aftercare services, regardless of their specific nature, lead to longer community survival for ex-hospital patients than does no aftercare (Barofsky 1983).
- Outcome studies on psychosocial rehabilitation centers show encouraging results, particularly for those members who regularly attend. However, a limitation of these programs is a high no-show and dropout rate (Test and Stein 1978).
- Community-based programs that show positive results typically employ high staff-to-patient ratios and have stable funding patterns (Bachrach 1982).
- Psychosocial treatment programs should be planned as long term—certainly one to two years, if not longer—and should be offered as early as possible as the client begins to reestablish his or her community relationships and activities (Bond et al. 1984).
- Psychosocial rehabilitation services when offered together with appropriate neuroleptics combine to offer greater protection against relapse and promote higher levels of social adjustment than drugs or psychosocial treatment alone (Liberman and Rueger 1984).

Several studies examining specific programs or modalities have yielded additional positive findings. As noted briefly earlier, the Training in Community Living program developed at Mendota State Hospital by Stein and Test as well as Fairweather's Lodge Program were both, upon careful analysis, found to be successful and cost effective. The same outcome was the case with Mosher's Soteria

House model (Mosher and Menn 1978). A national evaluation by Rutman (1984) of transitional employment programs concluded that psychosocial agency members who utilized such programs were two to three times more successful in finding full-time or part-time competitive employment (approximately 41 percent) than the general population of chronically mentally ill persons.

A recent evaluation of the Fountain House clubhouse model, based on over 600 members who participated in the Fountain House program over a 42-month period, was prepared by Malamud. The results show that for these men and women, all of whom participated in transitional employment programs, length of hospitalizations was significantly reduced, community isolation lowered, and that about one-third of the group succeeded in gaining regular competitive employment. Bond and Dincin (1984) recently reported on evaluations conducted at the Thresholds program in Chicago over the past eight years. They conclude that participation in the program reduced recidivism among several subpopulations differing in degree of disability by amounts ranging from about 40–63 percent; that between about 37–41 percent of active Thresholds clients were able to find and maintain competitive employment, either in transitional employment placements or in their own jobs; that regarding independent living status in the community, the percentages of members living independently increased from 24 to 39 percent in one substudy, and from 18 to 28 percent in a second; and finally, that members who attended Thresholds more regularly and for longer periods of time demonstrated more successful outcomes than those who came less frequently over shorter durations.

What do these reports tell us of the effectiveness of psychosocial rehabilitation services? Are such services of demonstrable value in assisting chronically mentally ill individuals to achieve and maintain productive roles and adjustment levels in society? The weight of evidence would suggest that the answer, in an overall sense, is almost surely in the affirmative. That is, the research findings strongly tend to support the conclusion that psychosocial programs which are used by the disabled individual for a long enough period of time, which employ a consistent approach to providing services and interventions, and which provide these services in the climate of mutual respect that characterizes the field, can expect to see favorable outcomes for a significant number of their clients.

What the data cannot tell us is the optimal combination of program activities, environmental supports, and expectancies that, in conjunction with specified psychotropic medication regimens and other psychiatric treatments, produce successful outcomes for an identified individual. Nor can we reliably predict, for a given client or group, which frequency, intensity, and timing of particular psychosocial interventions stand the best chance of achieving desired behavioral change. However, since studies currently are being planned and conducted that begin to examine these types of interactions, there is a reasonable likelihood that useful findings relevant to these issues will be forthcoming in the not-too-distant future.

For mental health professionals not familiar with the principles and methods of the psychosocial rehabilitation approach, the positive findings that are beginning to accumulate may be something of an eye-opener. For those who have been involved in the field for some time and have been party to its steady development and to the ingenuity of its practitioners, such findings are hardly surprising. For the latter group, the positive evaluative reports serve to confirm the feelings of confidence and commitment to psychosocial methods that they have shared for many years.

REFERENCES

Allen P: A consumer's view of California's mental health care system. Psychiatry Q 48:1-13, 1974

Anthony WA: The Principles of Psychiatric Rehabilitation. Baltimore, University Park Press, 1980

Anthony WA: A client outcome model for assessing psychiatric rehabilitation interventions. Schizophr Bull 8:12-38, 1982

Anthony WA, Cohen MR, Farkas M: A psychiatric rehabilitation treatment program: can I recognize one if I see one? Community Ment Health J 18:83-96, 1982

Anthony WA, Cohen MR, Cohen BF: Philosophy, treatment process, and principles of the psychiatric rehabilitation approach. New Directions for Mental Health Services 67-79, March 17, 1983

Bachrach LL: Overview: model programs for chronic mental patients. Am J Psychiatry 127:1023-1031, 1980

Bachrach LL: Deinstitutionalization: developments and theoretical perspective, in Planning for Deinstitutionalization. Project Share Human Services Monograph Series. Edited by Rutman ID. Washington, D.C., Department of Health and Human Services, 1981

Bachrach LL: Assessment of outcomes in community support systems: results, problems and limitations. Schizophr Bull 8:39-60, 1982

Bachrach LL: Concepts and issues in deinstitutionalization, in The Chronic Mental Patient in the Community. Edited by Barofsky I, Budson RD. New York, Spectrum, 1983

Barofsky I: Community survival of the chronic psychiatric patient, in The Chronic Psychiatric Patient in the Community. Edited by Barofsky I, Budson RD. New York, SP Medical and Scientific Books, 1983

Beard JH: The rehabilitation services of Fountain House, in Alternatives to Mental Hospital Treatment. Edited by Stein LI, Test MA. New York, Plenum Press, 1975

Beard JH: Psychiatric rehabilitation at Fountain House, in Rehabilitation Medicine and Psychiatry. Edited by Meislin J. Springfield, IL, Charles C Thomas, 1976

Beard J, Propst RV, Malamud T: The Fountain House model of psychiatric rehabilitation. Psychosocial Rehabilitation Journal 5:47-53, 1983

Bond GR, Dincin J, Setze PJ, et al: The effectiveness of psychiatric rehabilitation: a summary of research at Thresholds. Psychosocial Rehabilitation Journal 4:6-23, 1984

Braun P, Kochansky G, Shapiro R, et al: Overview: deinstitutionalization of psychiatric patients. Am J Psychiatry 138:736-749, 1981

Chamberlin J: Speaking out for ourselves: An overview of the ex-psychiatric inmates' movement. Psychosocial Rehabilitation Journal 2:57, 1984

Committee on Psychiatry and the Community: The Chronic Mental Patient in the Community (Monograph). New York, Group for the Advancement of Psychiatry, 1978

Committee on Psychiatry and the Community: Community Psychiatry: A Reappraisal (Monograph). New York, Group for the Advancement of Psychiatry, 1983

Dincin J: Psychiatric rehabilitation. Schizophr Bull 13:131–147, 1975

Dincin J: A community agency model, in The Chronically Mentally Ill: Treatment, Programs and Systems. Edited by Talbott JA. New York, Human Sciences Press, 1981

Fairweather GW, Sanders DH, Maynard H: Community Life for the Mentally Ill. Chicago, Aldine, 1969

Glasscote RM, Cumings E, Rutman ID, et al: Rehabilitating the Mentally Ill in the Community. Washington, DC, Joint Information Service of the American Psychiatric Association and the National Association for Mental Health, 1971

Goldman HH, Gattozzi AA, Taube C: Defining and counting the chronically mentally ill. Hosp Community Psychiatry 32:21–27, 1981

International Association of Psychosocial Rehabilitation Services: Organizations Providing Psychosocial Rehabilitation and Related Community Support Services in the United States: 1985. McLean, VA, IAPRS, 1985

Lamb HR: Treating the Long-Term Mentally Ill. San Francisco, Jossey-Bass, 1982

Lamb HR, Goertzel V: Discharged mental patients: are they really in the community? Arch Gen Psychiatry 24:28–34, 1971

Liberman RP, Rueger DB: Drug-psychosocial treatment interactions: comprehensive rehabilitation for chronic schizophrenics. Psychosocial Rehabilitation Journal 3:3–15, 1984

Madness Network News, A quarterly publication. P.O. Box 684, San Francisco, CA

Malamud T: Community adjustment: evaluation of the clubhouse model for psychiatric rehabilitation. Research Brief Vol IX, No. 2. Washington, DC, National Institute of Handicapped Research, Department of Education

Meyerson, AT, Herman GS: What's new in aftercare? a review of recent literature. Hosp Community Psychiatry 43:333–343, 1983

Minkoff R: A map of the chronic mental patient, in The Chronic Mental Patient. Edited by Talbott JA. Washington, DC, American Psychiatric Association, 1978

Mosher LR, Keith ST: Psychosocial treatment: individual, group, family and community support approaches. Schizophr Bull 6:10–40, 1980

Mosher LR, Menn AZ: Covered barriers in the community: the Soteria model, in Alternatives to Mental Hospital Treatment. Edited by Stein LI, Test MA. New York, Plenum, 1978

National Institute of Mental Health: A Network of Caring. The Community Support Program of the National Institute of Mental Health. Proceedings of the Fifth National Conference. Rockville, MD, U.S. Department of Health and Human Services, 1981

National Institute of Mental Health: Mutual Help Groups: A Guide for Mental Health Workers. Publication #ADMBO-646. Rockville, MD, National Clearinghouse for Mental Health Information, 1980

Paul G: The implementation of treatment programs for chronic mental patients: obstacles and recommendations, in The Chronic Mental Patient. Edited by Talbott JA. Washington, DC, American Psychiatric Association, 1978

Pepper B, Kirshner M, Ryglewicz H: The young adult chronic patient: overview of a population. Hosp Community Psychiatry 32:463–469, 1981

Perlman LG (Ed.): Rehabilitation of the Mentally Ill in the 1980s: A Report of the Fourth Mary E. Switzer Memorial Seminar. Washington, DC, National Rehabilitation Association, 1980

Petersen R: What are the needs of chronic mental patients? in The Chronic Mental Patient. Edited by Talbott JA. Washington, DC, American Psychiatric Association, 1978

Polak P: A comprehensive system of alternatives to psychiatric hospitals, in Alternative to Mental Hospital Treatment. Edited by Stein LI, Test MA. New York, Plenum Press, 1978

President's Commission on Mental Health: Report to the President from the President's Commission on Mental Health, vol. 1. Washington, DC, U.S. Government Printing Office, 1978

Propst RV, Schmidt JR: In remembrance: John Henderson Beard. Psychosocial Rehabilitation Journal 4:2, 1983

Rutman ID: Community-based services: characteristics, principles and program models, in Planning for Deinstitutionalization. Project Share, Human Services Monograph Series. Edited by Rutman ID. Washington, DC, Department of Health and Human Services, 1981

Rutman ID: A Comprehensive Evaluation of Transitional Employment Programs in the Rehabilitation of Chronically Mentally Disabled Clients. Washington, DC, National Institute of Handicapped Research, Department of Education, 1984

Schofield W: Psychotherapy: The Purchase of Friendship. Englewood Cliffs, NJ, Prentice-Hall, 1964

Scull AT: Decarceration: Community Treatment and the Deviant—A Radical View. Englewood Cliffs, NJ, Prentice-Hall, 1977

Smith CA, Smith CJ: Evaluating outcome measures for deinstitutionalization programs. Social Work Research and Abstracts 15:23–30, 1979

Steering Committee on the Chronically Mentally Ill: Toward a National Plan for the Chronically Mentally Ill: Report to the Secretary. Washington, DC, Department of Health and Human Services, 1980

Stein LI, Test MA: Training in community living: research design and results, in Alternatives to Mental Hospital Treatment. Edited by Stein LI, Test MA. New York, Plenum Press, 1975

Stein LI, Test MA: The community as the treatment arena in caring for the chronic psychiatric patient, in The Chronic Psychiatric Patient in the Community. Edited by Barofsky I, Budson RD. New York, SP Medical and Scientific Books, 1983

Talbott JA: What are the problems of the chronic mental patient?, in The Chronic Mental Patient. Edited by Talbott JA. Washington, DC, American Psychiatric Association, 1978

Talbott JA: Toward a public policy on the chronically mentally ill patient. Am J Orthopsychiatry 50:43–53, 1980

Talbott JA (Ed.): The Chronically Mentally Ill: Treatment, Programs, Systems. New York, Human Sciences Press, 1981

Tanaka HT: Psychosocial rehabilitation: future trends and directions. Psychosocial Rehabilitation Journal 4:7–12, 1983

Tessler RC, Goldman HH: The Chronically Mentally Ill: Assessing Community Support Systems. Cambridge, MA, Ballinger, 1982

Test MA, Stein LI: The clinical rationale for community treatment: a review of the literature, in Alternatives to Mental Hospital Treatment. Edited by Stein LI, Test MA. New York, Plenum Press, 1978

Thompson CM: Characteristics associated with outcome in a community mental health partial hospitalization program. Community Ment Health J 21:179—188, 1985

U.S. General Accounting Office: Returning the Mentally Disabled to the Community: Government Needs to Do More. HRD 76–152. Washington, DC, U.S. Government Printing Office, 1977

Wolkon GH, Peterson CL: A conceptual framework for the psychosocial rehabilitation of the chronic mental patient. Psychosocial Rehabilitation Journal 3:43–55, 1986

12

Overcoming Psychiatric Disability Through Skills Training

Robert Paul Liberman, M.D.
Harvey E. Jacobs, Ph.D.
Gayla A. Blackwell, R.N., M.S.W.
Alan Simpson, Ph.D.
H. Keith Massel, Ph.D.

T reatment and rehabilitation strategies for individuals suffering from schizophrenia can now be designed from a conceptual blueprint that explains and predicts the course and outcome of this major mental disorder. The variables comprising this blueprint are biobehavioral vulnerability; environmental protectors, potentiators, and stressors; and personal protectors. Schizophrenia is viewed as a biomedical stress-linked disorder that is moderated by coping and competence of the individual and supportiveness of the environment.

This framework for understanding the variability in schizophrenic disorders, both across individuals and over time within an individual, emphasizes a dynamic and homeostatic interaction among determinants at the biological, environmental, and behavioral levels. Depending upon the balance of factors at any one time, transient, intermediate states of psychobiological overload and hyperarousal can develop and lead to prodromal symptoms or even to florid symptoms characteristic of the disorder. This multilevel and interactional model of schizophrenia is graphically represented in Figure 1. It should be noted that the symptoms of schizophrenia, with their associated social and occupational impairments, may manifest for varying durations and in varying degrees of severity. Also, depend-

221

Figure 1.

A multilevel, interactional model of schizophrenia.

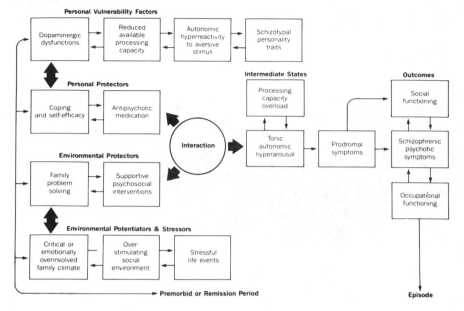

ing upon the interplay among vulnerability, stress, protective, and potentiating factors, the correlation between psychopathology and psychosocial functioning may range from high to low.

The symptoms and impairments in social functioning that characterize schizophrenic disorders can be viewed as being in equilibrium with influences converging from the biological, behavioral, and environmental levels. For example, the appearance or exacerbation of schizophrenic symptoms may occur in a psychobiologically vulnerable individual when:

1. Stressful events, such as drug abuse or loss of a job, overwhelm the individual's coping skills
2. Potentiating factors, such as high levels of intrafamilial tension or an overstimulating treatment environment, evoke hyperarousal and deficiency in the processing of information in an already compromised cognitive apparatus
3. The individual cannot meet the behavioral demands of everyday life because the protective effects of medication have been lost through noncompliance
4. Social problem-solving skills have withered through disuse and withdrawal or, alternatively, have never been learned in the first place
5. The individual's social support network weakens or collapses

The interactional, multilevel model of schizophrenia is a bidirectional one, and does not consign the patient to a passive role. Thus, appropriate use of neuroleptic drugs can abort a relapse; or social skills can be strengthened through training. Family intervention or participation in a psychosocial self-help club can bolster social support and buffer the noxious effects of both environmental tension and stressors, and of heightened biological diathesis.

Instead of viewing the pathogenesis of schizophrenia as arising mechanistically from biological and environmental determinants, it is useful to view individuals as active participants in the management and outcome of their disorders. The onset and course of a schizophrenic disorder is a reciprocal of the actions and behavioral repertoire of the individual, on the one hand, and of biological and environmental processes on the other. A model of schizophrenia that encompasses stress–vulnerability–coping–competence highlights the ability of the individual to exercise behavioral competencies that can have an effect on the social environment and on brain function.

For example, a person with good social and assertiveness skills can galvanize assistance and support from friends and relatives that, in turn, will aid in coping efforts, community survival, and instrumental problem solving. Repeated many times over the course of months or years, these mastery experiences may also favorably affect neurotransmitters or other aspects of central nervous system function. The intriguing work of Kandel (1983) with simple neuronal systems in sea snails has documented that classical conditioning procedures produce both functional and structural changes in nerve cells; for example, environmental stimulation increases vesicles in the active zones of neurotransmitter release on the presynaptic neuron.

After the onset of a schizophrenic disorder, the affected individual is presented with an enormous range of possibilities for action or inaction and for choice among many available options. While it is true that persons with schizophrenic vulnerability have a reduced capacity to act effectively on their own behalf because of impairments in cognitive, emotional, and behavioral functions, they can exercise personal choices which affect their adaptation or failure. Thus, the widely shared view that the schizophrenic's status is wholly determined by past history, psychobiological impairments, and premorbid behavioral repertoires should be supplanted by the view of such patients as capable of acting directly upon their environments, their personalities, and indeed their biological substrates—and by doing so, altering the trajectory of their future status.

As mental health professionals, we can help our patients to improve their own contributions to their life-span development. A vulnerability–stress—coping–competence model of mental disorder points us in useful directions for designing and implementing therapeutic interventions. Vulnerability can be compensated for by reducing environmental stressors, and by strengthening coping and competence in dealing with the stress that inevitably accompanies life outside the cloistered institution. Psychotropic drugs, at doses that are optimal for restoring cognitive capacities but which do not produce interfering side effects, can eliminate or suppress symptoms that undercut efforts at coping and learning from one's environment.

OVERCOMING IMPAIRMENT, DISABILITY, AND HANDICAP

In the lexicon of the rehabilitation practitioner are terms such as impairment, disability, and handicap. In major mental disorders, it is presumed that underlying, biological vulnerability, combined with inadequate protection by an individual's social support network and social competence, lead to abnormalities in central nervous system function which appear as *impairments* in cognitive information processing, psychophysiological states, and symptom formation. In turn, these psychobiological *impairments* lead to *disabilities* in the affected person's social and occupational functioning. (For example, the individual may withdraw from friends and family and may not be able to continue to work because of distractibility, loss of concentration and interest in the job, and the intrusion of delusions and hallucinations.) Finally, if these disabilities persist and there is no accommodation by the person's social and vocational environments, *handicaps* develop. For example, if the family and work systems are mystified by the person's disabilities, do not view them as part of a bona fide illness, and are unyielding in expectations for normal social and job performance, it is likely that the disabled person will be *handicapped* in his or her roles as a participating family member and worker.

Rehabilitation and treatment strategies can be directed at one or more of these points in the chain leading to handicap. Rationally prescribed and reliably used psychotropic medication can reduce *impairment:* For example, drugs such as lithium and the neuroleptics have potent effects on the positive symptoms of severe mental disorder. They also improve cognitive processes, attentional and arousal mechanisms, and learning capacities. Social and vocational skills training can remediate a patient's *disabilities:* Thus, an individual who has learned to establish and maintain peer relationships can improve his or her social adaptation; a person who develops greater work tolerance can obtain a job and experience improved quality of life. Supportive home and work environments that make allowances for the individual's impairments and disabilities, and compensate for them, can prevent or reverse *handicaps:* For example, a sheltered workshop or transitional employment program that includes initially lowered, and then gradually increased, expectations of performance with supportive supervisors and counselors can enable even a markedly disabled person with a mental disorder to function as a worker. Similarly, through family therapy that educates relatives about mental disorders and that helps them to lower, at least temporarily, their expectations of the patient's social ability and functioning, the family system can acquire coping skills to respond more flexibly to the patient's needs and disabilities which, in turn, enables the patient to sustain respect and integrity as a family member.

With chronic mental disorders that produce severe impairments, complex disabilities, and handicaps, it is understandable that a wide range of interventions will be necessary to achieve rehabilitation goals. Medication alone is rarely sufficient and psychosocial methods have little chance of success if isolated from the judicious use of psychotropic drugs. Thus, pharmacotherapy and psychosocial treatment should play complementary, not competing, roles in the comprehensive management of schizophrenic patients. Most experienced clinicians view neuroleptic therapy as achieving reconstitutive and prophylactic goals. In ameliorating the cognitive disorganization and disabling symptoms of psychosis, drugs enable the patient to make more effective contact with the environment and engage in a therapeutic alliance with a therapist or psychosocial program. Continuity of care that integrates both maintenance medication and the pursuit of personal, social, and instrumental role goals has the best chance of restoring the individual with schizophrenia to a functional existence and a reasonable quality of life.

Psychiatric rehabilitation can encompass three interlocking strategies for professional intervention:

1. Providing appropriate types, doses, and schedules of psychotropic medication;
2. Teaching the patient to develop or reacquire social and instrumental role skills;
3. Modifying the patient's social and physical environments to support whatever skills are in his or her repertoire or to compensate for continuing disabilities and handicaps.

Most chronically and severely mentally ill persons will require all three strategies for rehabilitation. A minority—such as those who are highly responsive to the benefits of antipsychotic drugs and who have high levels of premorbid adjustment—may only need pharmacotherapy and time-limited assistance in reestablishing their family, occupational, and residential connections. Despite the best efforts at drug therapy and skills training, some chronically disabled patients may be unable to achieve symptom stabilization and remission, or to learn and generalize social and independent-living skills. For such refractory patients, alternate compensatory skills and prosthetic environments—such as functioning in a long-term sheltered-workshop and supervised, residential facility—might be the preferred focus of rehabilitative efforts.

With chronic psychiatric disorders, some amount of continuing symptoms and residual impairment make necessary the acceptance of disability and the identification of lower, attainable goals. Learn-

226

ing how to cope with symptoms, manage medication, and utilize professional resources when necessary become important targets for rehabilitation. When deficits preclude gainful employment, the patient and family need assistance in generating alternative types of meaningful activity, social contact, and daily structure. While persisting symptoms may limit the level of functional engagement, the reciprocal also holds: Namely, the more that rehabilitation improves the patient's social and role performance, the more likely his or her symptoms will be held in check. The rehabilitation professional is guided by the optimism that desirable change is possible by harnessing the principles of human learning to the needs of the patient; that motivation for change can come from special arrangement of the patient's rehabilitation and natural environments, as well as from within the patient; that, building from the patient's assets and interests (including a supportive family environment), even small improvements can lead to significant functional changes which uplift the patient's quality of life.

The rest of this chapter will describe three methods of behavioral rehabilitation, emphasizing the training of functional skills related to social, family, and occupational aspects of community living. Imbedded in each of these methods are principles and techniques derived from social learning theory and operant conditioning, harnessing as much as possible what is known about the systematic process of behavior change.

SOCIAL SKILLS TRAINING
The literature suggests that social skills training is an effective means for improving patients' competence and ability to cope with stressors. The importance of premorbid and postmorbid social competence as a predictor of outcome in major psychiatric disorders has been well documented (Liberman 1982; Presly et al. 1982). This suggests that social skills training might improve the long-term prognosis of chronic patients by upgrading their social competence. Additionally, the extent of deficits in social and living skills has been established in chronic psychiatric patients. For example, Sylph and his associates (1978) found major functional deficits in social and personal areas in over 50 percent of a sample of chronic psychiatric patients. A multisite study of schizophrenic patients who were placed in foster homes after relatively brief hospitalizations found that relapse rates at one year after discharge were significantly higher among those patients who had existing deficiencies in social skills (Linn et al. 1980).

Methods of Social Skills Training
Social skills training involves the teaching of specific interpersonal skills, following the principles of human learning. Methods to promote the generalization and maintenance of trained skills are an important aspect of most training programs. A set of behavioral

procedures which have been developed to train interpersonal skills have been empirically tested and "packaged" for ready access by practitioners. While many psychosocial programs are described as social skills training, it is important to distinguish between non-specific, "resocialization" group activities and methods which consistently and systematically utilize behavioral procedures in a structured approach to skills building. Nonspecific socialization training can lead to acquisition of skills through incidental learning during spontaneous social interactions (Test and Stein 1977). In this chapter, however, the discussion of social skills training is limited to those procedures which deliberately and systematically utilize the principles of human learning to promote the acquisition, generalization, and maintenance of skills required in interpersonal situations (Liberman et al. 1975).

Highly directive behavioral techniques are required to train social skills to many chronic psychiatric patients, in that most of these patients have attentional, memory, and information-processing deficits. Typically, they display either hyperarousal or underarousal during psychophysiological testing, and they experience overstimulation from emotional stressors, or even from therapy sessions that are not tightly structured. In addition, they usually lack the ability to converse, a basic facet of social competence. Chronic schizophrenics have particular deficiencies in social perception and have difficulties in generating alternatives for coping with everyday situations, such as the side effects of drugs, grocery shopping, or arranging for transportation. They tend to use gestures inappropriately, make less eye contact, and have difficulty with vocal modulation, all factors which may impair social learning.

There are alternative ways to train social skills, depending on the social abilities and deficiencies of the individual patient. A standard treatment "package" for training social skills, generally featuring modeling and role playing, is appropriate for many patients. Training utilizing an information-processing framework has been found to be effective for those patients capable of learning problem-solving strategies (Foy et al. 1983). Patients are taught to improve their perceptions in interpersonal situations, process that information to choose a response, and send a response back to the other person. These approaches are ineffective, however, for patients with severe attentional deficiencies. A model using attention-focusing procedures, which minimizes distractibility, has been effective in training conversational skills to treatment-refractory chronic schizophrenic patients. The problem-solving and attention-focusing models will be presented in more detail below.

The Problem-Solving Model for Training Social Skills
Deficits in cognitive problem-solving abilities, which may lead to ineffective performances in social situations, have been found in

many chronic psychiatric patients (Edelstein et al. 1980; Platt and Spivack 1972). A method of teaching social skills, focusing on training components of problem solving, views interpersonal communication as a three-stage process, requiring:

1. Receiving skills—accurately perceiving cues and contextual elements of interpersonal situations
2. Processing skills—generating response options, assessing the consequences of each alternative, and selecting the most feasible option
3. Sending skills—integrating both verbal and nonverbal skills in implementing the chosen option for an appropriate social response

In this training model, an interpersonal scene is role played and videotaped. After the role play, the therapist asks questions to assess the patient's *receiving* skills, exemplified in the following dialogue:

> James is a 43-year-old male, diagnosed as a chronic schizophrenic. He is currently an outpatient, following several hospitalizations. James is a member of a therapy group, which centers on training heterosocial, or dating, skills. A role-play conversation between James and Martha, another patient, has just been completed and the therapist (T) is assessing James's (J) *receiving skills*.
>
> T: Very good, James. You were more active in your conversation with Martha. Let's go over a few points, though. James, what was Martha talking about?
> J: She was talking about relaxing and going to movies.
> T: What kind of mood was she in?
> J: I think she felt good. It was a friendly conversation.
> T: Very good. What was your goal in this interaction?
> J: Just to get to know Martha better.
> T: That's right, James. You are doing very well. You are paying attention and you have a good idea of the areas in which you need to work.

The therapist asked specific questions to determine James's perception of the situation. The next step in the training process is the assessment and, if necessary, the training of *processing* skills. This stage involves generating response options and identifying consequences, both positive and negative, of these options. Role-play conversations are then conducted. In our example, James has just had a conversation with Martha, in which he asked her for a date. The therapist assesses James's *processing skills*:

T: That was a good conversation, James. You seemed to be more relaxed this time. What could you have done when Martha told you she didn't want to go skating?

J: I don't know. She probably didn't want to go out.

T: You may not be right, James. How could you have checked it out?

J: I guess I could have asked her to go to a movie or something.

T: Very good. You already found out that Martha likes to go to movies. Do you think she would have agreed to go to a movie with you?

J: I don't know. Maybe she doesn't like me.

T: Possibly, but she might be really interested in going out with you. How could you have achieved your goal of making a date with her?

J: By suggesting more places to go, and not feeling rejected when she said she didn't like skating.

T: Excellent, James. You are doing well, now.

Specific questions were asked to gauge James's ability to process information, and the therapist prompted alternative responses, which were within James's skill level. The next stage of training involves *sending* skills. Following a role-play conversation, the patient is asked to assess his or her performance.

T: I want to ask you a few questions now about the conversation you just had with Martha. How was your eye contact?

J: It was okay, but I think I looked away too much.

T: Right. I think you could have made a little better eye contact. We can work on that later. How was the tone of your voice?

J: I thought it was fine.

T: Well, maybe it was just a little flat. If you were more enthusiastic, it would show that you were interested in her. Basically, you are doing very well, James. You are starting to have a good idea of your strengths and weaknesses. Let's continue working.

Specific questions were again asked to determine the subject's perception of his sending skills. In all three stages of this model, the therapist may prompt or model correct responses, or ask that the scene be role played again. When *sending* skills are performed at an acceptable level, assessment and training continue with a new interpersonal situation.

The scope of this problem-solving model has been expanded to areas of social and independent living other than conversational skills (Foy et al. 1983). Training "modules" are being developed in the areas of leisure and relaxation, medication management, and grooming skills, among others. The modules are designed to teach specific functional skills, to train the patient to solve problems which may be encountered while attempting to employ these new skills, and for practicing the skills *in vivo*.

The structure of a module, focused on the domain of medication self-management, is depicted in Figure 2. This particular module contains skill areas in (a) obtaining information and learning about the benefits of psychotropic medication, (b) acquiring the skills of self-administration and self-assessment of medication; and (c) identifying and coping with the side effects of medication. Patients can enroll in one or more of these modules depending on the extensiveness of their deficits and the nature of the goals established for their treatment.

This model of social skills training offers considerable promise for those patients who have the cognitive capacity for learning social skills in hour-long small groups. Each module is divided into separate skill areas; each area has specific behaviors taught to achieve personal effectiveness and competence, as shown in Figure 2. Patients proceed through each module in sequence, starting with an introduc-

Figure 2.

Each module is divided into separate *skill* areas, with each area having specific behaviors that are taught for personal effectiveness.

Module: **Medication self-management**

Skill area: **Negotiating medication issues**

Requisite behaviors:

Pleasant greeting
Describe problem specifically
Tell length of occurrence
Describe extent of discomfort
Specifically request action
Repeat/clarify advice/orders
Ask about expected time for effect
Thank for assistance
Good eye contact
Good posture
Clear audible speech

Table 1.

Learning Activities in Each Skill Area

1. Introduction to skill area	Introducing the topic and component skills with a rationale; and motivating the patients to participate
2. Videotape and questions/ answers	Viewing the skills being modeled in the videotape scene, which demonstrates skill usage with question/answer review
3. Role play	Practicing the skills
4. Resource management	Discussing the resources needed to perform the skills
5. Outcome problems	Solving problems associated with using the skill
6. In vivo exercises	Performing exercises in real-life situations with healthcare providers, in settings outside the training class
7. Homework assignments	Completing assignments autonomously

tion that highlights the values and advantages of the module, to motivate subsequent participation. After acquiring the skills in the training phase, patients learn how to gather the tangible and social resources required to put the skills to use. For example, in order to negotiate medication side-effects or dosage issues with the prescribing physician, a patient must be able to use a telephone to make an appointment to see the doctor, and to find transport to take him or her to the doctor. After solving resource-management problems, patients anticipate outcome problems, which might interfere with the successful implementation of their skills in the natural environment. Thus, patients learn how to deal with disappointing events such as the lateness or unpredicted absence of the physician at the appointment. The learning activities in this modular approach to training problem-solving skills are shown in Table 1.

The Attention-Focusing Model for Training Social Skills
The problem-solving training model, as well as the basic approach, depends on the patients' ability to attend to relatively complex training situations, which last from 30 to 90 minutes. A sizable number of chronic psychiatric patients are characterized by such severe impairments in the cognitive and attentional realms, however, that they are unable to benefit from these training models. A method for training social skills to these patients, which minimizes demands on cognitive

abilities, has been developed recently (Liberman et al. 1985). The Attention-Focusing Procedure (AFP) is characterized by multiple, controlled training trials, the sequential presentation of training material, and graduated and systematic prompting following incorrect responses. This procedure has been utilized to train conversational skills to highly distractible, institutionalized, chronic schizophrenics.

A trainer initiates a training trial with a patient by making a statement. If the patient makes a response which is consistent with training, he or she is praised and the response is sometimes reinforced with something to eat or drink. If a correct response is made, the trainer implements a prompt sequence. The patient is praised if he or she responds appropriately following the prompts. The same statement is presented by the trainer until the patient responds correctly several times in succession. Then, responses to other conversational statements are trained.

The following is an example of the Attention-Focusing Procedure with a patient named Sam, a chronic schizophrenic hospitalized for 18 years. Sam is withdrawn and he is highly distractible. The first goal of training is to teach Sam to ask relevant questions of other people. Sam (s) is being trained on asking questions by a therapist (t) and co-therapist, Bill (b).

Trial 1
B: I went to a movie last night.
s: (no response)
T: Sam, ask Bill a question.
s: (no response)
T: One question you can ask is, "What movie did you see?"
s: (no response)

Trial 2
B: I went to a movie last night.
s: (no responses)
T: Sam, ask Bill a question.
s: (no response)
T: One question you can ask is, "What movie did you see?"
s: What movie did you see?
B: I saw *Back to School.*
T: Very good Sam, that was a fine question.

Trial 3
B: I went to a movie last night.
s: Who was in the movie?
B: Rodney Dangerfield was the star.
T: Bill, that was an excellent question. You are really catching on now. Let's try it again.

If patients are unable to deliver an acceptable response on a trial, the trainer models a response; however, any appropriate response made by the patient is accepted as correct. Typically, patients are trained on 8 to 12 alternative exemplars in each of three domains of conversational skills.

Effectiveness of Social Skills Training
Reviews of empirical studies done on social skills training with schizophrenics have shown that a wide range of skills can be learned and maintained over short-term follow-up periods (Wallace et al. 1980). In one controlled clinical trial, 28 male schizophrenic patients, diagnosed by Present State Examination (PSE) and Catego criteria, were randomly assigned to either intensive social skills problem-solving training or to holistic health therapy. A multidimensional evaluation was conducted before and after 9 weeks of inpatient treatment and for 24 months in the community. Patients exposed to social skills training evidenced significantly greater acquisition, generalization, and durability of social skills; their social adjustment in the community was rated as better by relatives; and they experienced fewer relapses and rehospitalizations (Liberman and Wallace in press). Similar results have been obtained from skills-training programs in Italy (DeIsabella and Meneghelli 1983) and in Bern, Switzerland, by Brenner (1986).

While social skills training has made considerable progress in enhancing skill levels of psychiatric patients, more work is needed in assessing and promoting generalization and long-term change.

Generalization from trained to untrained items and situations has been found in many clinical studies (Bellack et al. 1976; Goldsmith and McFall 1975; Kelly et al. 1980; Liberman et al. 1984b). A number of different role-play scenes and responses are practiced during training sessions, resulting in various forms of the target skill being prompted and reinforced. For instance, an unassertive client might practice standing up to his or her spouse, asking for a raise, and taking faulty merchandise back to a store, among other scenes. Inadvertently, this method of training "multiple exemplars" may have the effect of increasing generalized responding of a particular skill.

With chronic psychiatric patients, generalization usually is limited if efforts are not made to promote the transfer of trained skills to nontherapy settings. Even though a patient may have mastered the targeted skills in training sessions, generalization may not occur because certain elements present in the training environment may be different in more natural settings. For instance, the conversant in the role plays may be more attentive and respond more positively than persons in other settings and the therapist may provide consistent reinforcement to the patient for making appropriate responses, while other people typically are more inconsistent.

A link between the training and extratherapy settings may be established by issuing homework assignments. Assignments to use trained skills in other settings have been utilized effectively by several clinical researchers (Finch and Wallace 1977; Liberman et al. 1984b). Recent studies have shown this tactic to be more effective when accompanied by prompts and reinforcement in the other setting (Martinez-Diaz et al. 1983; Massel et al. 1985). Family members, nursing staff personnel, and peers can assist by prompting and reinforcing new social behaviors until they are well established, at which point prompts and reinforcements may be withdrawn gradually.

While behavior skills training has been extremely effective in improving social competence, the data are not convincing that this actually reduces the probability of relapse or symptom exacerbation. Skills training imbedded within a family-therapy context may prove to have greater impact on long-term clinical status of chronic patients, such as in preventing relapse (Falloon et al. 1984; Liberman et al. 1984a). Much more outcome research must be done to document the extent to which social skills training benefits schizophrenic patients' long-term clinical and symptomatic outcomes, over and above the judicious use of antipsychotic medication. Since many patients have limited potential for acquiring and generalizing functional skills sufficient for fully independent living, there is continued value in developing rehabilitation approaches that emphasize environmental prosthesis and social support.

BEHAVIORAL FAMILY MANAGEMENT

Employing the same learning principles and techniques as are used in social skills training, a three-pronged module was developed to enhance the communication and problem-solving skills of families with a schizophrenic member (Falloon and Liberman 1983). Despite the development of community mental health programs and the widespread use of neuroleptic drugs, families continue to serve as the principal caregivers and primary resources for those suffering from schizophrenia. The burden of providing emotional, social, and instrumental support for schizophrenics has always fallen mainly on the patient's relatives. This burden has become even greater since the inception of the deinstitutionalization movement over 20 years ago. Based upon intensive interviews with 80 relatives of schizophrenics, a report, "Schizophrenia at Home," which summarized the problems described by relatives, was issued (Creer 1978). Problems fell into three major categories: (1) distress caused by the patients' symptomatic and socially impaired behavior; (2) anxiety and "burnout" experienced by the relatives; and (3) disturbances in the relatives' own social networks.

From the families' perspective, schizophrenic members living at home display two types of behavior that are distressing and with which coping is difficult. Social withdrawal and solitary patterns, on the one hand, and aggressive, bizarre, and disruptive behavior, on the other, are found in varying degrees at different points in time during the course of the illness. Social isolation, to the point of rarely exchanging conversation, is the more common pattern; it generates helpless frustration in relatives whose sustained social support requires a modicum of responsiveness. Another facet of isolated behavior is the apathy and indolence of the chronic schizophrenic, which galls relatives who view the patient as physically able, and do not understand such absence of constructive activity.

Relatives speak of being "constantly on a knife edge," "living on your nerves," or "feeling in constant dread of relapse and flare-ups of symptoms." Guilt, exhaustion, depression, anxiety, and anger are frequent experiences of relatives that, in combination with the patients' deviance, do much to explain the high "expressed emotion," (EE) in families—a factor found to predict relapse (Brown et al. 1972; Vaughn and Leff 1976; Vaughn et al. 1972, 1984). Expressed emotion, consisting of criticism, hostility, and emotional overinvolvement, is an understandable reaction of concerned family members who are at a loss to know how to help their schizophrenic relatives. Overinvolvement can lead a family to give up attachments to the outside community and to spend inordinate amounts of time at home with the patient. Criticism and hostility can lead to rejection of the patient and, ultimately, to a breach of the relationships within the family.

The behavioral family-management module was designed for use with individual families and with multiple-family groups and can be adapted for use with families of patients with other major mental disorders. It has been offered over 16 weekly, one-hour sessions. Alternatively, it has been provided for over a two-year period for more definitive skill-building, with weekly sessions for three months, biweekly sessions for six months, then monthly maintenance sessions. In three empirical evaluations and controlled studies, it has been shown to reduce family tensions, conflicts, and expressed emotion; markedly reduce relapse rates and rehospitalization; enhance problem solving and coping; improve social adjustment of patients; and lessen family burdens (Snyder and Liberman 1981; Falloon et al. 1984). Cost-effectiveness analysis indicates that a home-based version of behavioral family management is more effective and less costly than comparison clinic-based treatment of individuals.

Elements of Behavioral Family Management

The three facets of behavioral family management include in-depth analysis of each family member and of the family as a functional, interdependent unit; education about schizophrenia and its treatment; training in communication skills; and training in a stepwise and systematic problem-solving process. Following the in-depth assessments, the initial educational sessions are used to inform relatives and patients about schizophrenia—its causes, course, and management. Detailed information is presented, and patients and families are invited to discuss their own experiences and to express their own feelings and concerns. These sessions function to relieve some of the guilt, confusion, and helplessness experienced by family members, as well as to foster realistic expectations about treatment outcome and to emphasize the importance of continued maintenance medication. The impact of schizophrenia on each family member, and problems of management are discussed. The educational seminars are presented in a semididactic style, with visual aids and written materials. The patient is encouraged to take the role of "expert" and to describe his or her experiences to the family.

John is a 24-year-old schizophrenic living at home with his retired parents. He has been an outpatient for 8 months in spite of medication noncompliance. His father, frightened at times by John's bizarre behavior, does not relate to him except to take him to the hospital when John becomes upset. John's mother says, "He doesn't want to do anything for himself; he just wants a lot of sympathy. I wish he could get involved in school or something and make a better effort to be independent." John states, "I wish my parents would try to understand me more. I do try, but most of the time I just can't seem to finish anything. They don't seem to realize how scared I feel all the time."

As the therapist guides this family through the educational material on schizophrenia and its treatment, specifically regarding psychotropic medication, the parents become aware of the difficulties John experiences as the result of his illness. John becomes more aware of the impact of his illness on the lives of his family. Using a variety of empathic techniques, the therapist succeeds in creating a forum which allows each of the family members to air his or her concerns, fears, and doubts without recrimination. Toward the end of the discussions about schizophrenia and the importance of proper medication maintenance, John's father tells him, "I guess I could talk with you more when you get upset. But you'll have to let me know when something is bothering you. I don't really like taking you to the hospital all the time but I didn't know what else to do. Your mother and I don't want to see you hurt or unhappy. We just want you to do the best you can." His mother says, "I guess I've learned that you're not just faking and do need help. I just hope that you'll keep taking that medicine so that you'll be calm and can talk to us. We just want to be able to get along with you better." Thus, John learns that his parents are willing to try to understand, but that they need him to help.

Following these information-giving sessions, the objective is to train communication and problem-solving skills. Early sessions are devoted to assessment of the current communication pattern of the entire family to identify areas of communications-skills deficits. Initially, the therapist has family members demonstrate their current communication skills in brief role plays. This is followed by training and guided practice with feedback to teach four types of communication:

1. Using active listening skills, to learn the needs and emotions of others.
2. Expressing positive feelings and giving positive feedback.
3. Making requests of others; expressing expectations and setting rules.
4. Expressing negative emotions directly, such as feelings of anger and disapproval.

The initial phase of enhancing communication skills of family members focuses on improving family members' abilities to listen to each other, and moves on to the expression of positive feelings through prompting mutually rewarding behavior and empathic listening. The goal of the therapist during the early stages of family therapy is to create and maintain a warm milieu where family members are able to recognize and reinforce specific positive behavior in one another. In addition, they learn to identify areas of specific behavior they would like others to change, as well as to make appropriate requests for such changes. Finally, they develop the ability to sit down and discuss problems in an empathic, nonjudgmental way. Expression of strong negative feelings is taken up after positive communication and interaction have been established. Effective communication skills are important precursors of successful problem-solving discussion. The therapist uses a variety of behavioral techniques, such as shaping, modeling, and positive reinforcement to help each family member acquire these new skills. Family members are given written homework assignments at the end of each session, to encourage them to practice their newly acquired skills and to document the results of their use.

> She can be very helpful when she wants to be but, most of the time, she just lays around doing nothing. She can cook very well and sometimes she will try to help me do some of the things I have to do, but not if you ask her; she won't do anything you ask her, especially if mom asks her.
>
> This was 18-year-old Sandra's answer when the therapist asked her to give an example of something Barbara, her 25-year-old schizophrenic sister, had said or done to please her or to make her feel proud. Her response is not atypical of how family members sometimes describe the behavior of their ill relatives. The therapist helped Sandra identify three positive thoughts in

her statement about Barbara: "She can be very helpful"; "She can cook very well"; "She sometimes will try to help with things I have to do." The therapist then trained Sandra and the entire family to share positive things with each other without adding negative or qualifying statements. Mrs. Smith, Barbara's mother, was trained how to use the skill of making a positive request to get Barbara's cooperation with tasks around the house.

Once families have developed adequate communication skills, they are then in a position to learn techniques to improve problem solving. The ability to specify a problem and to discuss it in detail can only be carried out by families that have competent communication skills. Patients and their families are taught to solve problems using the step-by-step technique that follows:

1. Pinpoint, specify, and agree on one problem at a time.
2. Engage in "brainstorming" to develop several alternate or possible solutions.
3. Evaluate each alternative in terms of its possible consequences (advantages and disadvantages).
4. Choose alternative(s) that maximize(s) satisfaction and seem(s) reasonable.
5. Plan how to implement that alternative (or those alternatives) as a family.
6. Rehearse implementation of the selected solution and set a firm date for implementation.
7. Provide mutual support for each other in the implementation, including positive feedback for each family member for his or her participatory efforts.
8. Review the problem after the selected alternative solution has been implemented.
9. Return to Step 1 if the selected solution is unsuccessful.

These problem-solving steps are used repeatedly to analyze and focus on a wide range of family problems, especially those associated with tension and conflict. The repetitive practice of problem solving, together with repeated practice of the four basic communication skills, is aimed at inculcating durable and general problem-solving strategies.

Families are provided with work sheets that outline the steps of problem solving. Particular importance is attached to the detailed planning of the problem solution, with all anticipated difficulties discussed fully. Each family member takes a turn at chairing the family problems-solving sessions and recording details of the problem, all suggesting alternative solutions, the advantages and disadvantages of each, as well as step-by-step plans to carry out the "best" solution. A folder is kept in an accessible place at home so that any family members may refer to it at any time. Sometimes problem-solving plans may be displayed on the family notice board or on the refrigerator door to prompt family members on the tasks they have agreed to undertake to assist in the implementation of the selected problem solution.

The Jones family incorporated the problem-solving process into their ongoing family life. Bob Jones, 36 years old, had been living in a board-and-care home immediately following his sixth hospitalization for schizophrenia. He was unhappy and uncooperative in that setting, so his parents agreed to let him move back home. He lived with his parents and his two sisters, Susan, aged 14 and Annette, aged 20. They learned to achieve mastery of the problem-solving process through resolution of nonthreatening, low-key problems. Guided by the therapist, they then began to grapple with the more highly charged problems illuminated in the individual assessments.

During the individual assessments, Bob revealed that he had difficulty concentrating on anything for any length of time, and that he couldn't develop an interest in anything. He also stated that he would like to earn his own money. His parents complained that Bob's grooming was poor despite their repeatedly asking him to be neat and to shower more often. They also stated that he wouldn't go anywhere or do anything. His mother declared that she found it very difficult to communicate with him. Bob's sisters stated they did not know how to relate to him because of the differences in their ages and because he would do mean things to tease them. Without revealing who had stated which problems, the therapist enabled them to define all the problems as follows: Bob's difficulty concentrating; Bob's inability to earn his own money; Bob's inability to develop a hobby or social interest; Mrs. Jones' inability to communicate with Bob; Bob's teasing behavior with his sisters.

The therapist then polled the family to determine which problem was to be given priority and encouraged them to work on it during their weekly family conferences. They chose Bob's difficulty concentrating and began to develop alternatives in the session to help him improve in this area. At the following session, Bob reported on their progress. "We discussed my not trying to do too many things at one time, to write things down, and to do things a little at a time." His mother added, "We were never aware that he'd been having the kind of difficulties he told us about in the meeting. We gave him the best suggestion we had. George, Bob's dad, said he would try to avoid telling him to do too many things at one time. He went on to say that they liked the logical approach to discussing things and that they had agreed to meet every Thursday evening. The therapist encouraged them to continue to use the step-by-step process and to be as specific as possible in their discussions. She reinforced their use of communication skills and had them practice expressing themselves at every opportunity in the sessions.

In addition to the structured problem-solving approach, families are trained in the use of a range of behavioral strategies for dealing with specific problems that arise. These may include contingency contracting for parental discord, which is a method for clarifying what each parent expects from the other and what he or she is willing to give to get their needs met; and token-economy programs, which are based on a reward system to reinforce desired behaviors, as negotiated within the family, to enhance constructive daily activity of the patient. Family members can also participate in social skills training or behavioral management strategies for anxiety or depression. In these instances, *all family members* are usually involved in the execution of the specific strategy. Behavioral family management can be most effective when it is part of a patient's comprehensive treatment and rehabilitation plan. It is not intended to supplant but rather to supplement other forms of treatment that have been shown to be helpful in the rehabilitation of the chronically mentally ill.

JOB-FINDING CLUB

The ability to work and be productive affects almost every aspect of daily life. Unless accidents or illness produce disabilities, most people can expect to work for 40 to 45 years. Thus one's personal identity and self-image are inextricably interwoven with one's occupation. Work provides money for self and family support, sustenance, and adds to the quality of our lives. Work provides status; self-respect and esteem from others; a functional role within the work place, our community, and society; the opportunity to make friends and socialize with others. This, in turn, can affect health and psychiatric status. Historically, during periods of economic downturn, when unemployment rates zoom upward, the incidence of mental disorders and rate of psychiatric hospitalization also rise (Brenner 1973). Clinically oriented studies have found correlations between unemployment and suicide rates, depressed mood, and other physical and psychological symptoms (Hagen 1983).

Work is perceived as important by individuals suffering from major mental disorders. In a survey of 500 chronic mental patients residing in Los Angeles board-and-care homes, Lehman and his colleagues (1983) found that lack of work was one of the greatest complaints related to poor quality of life. Even persons with chronic disabilities who were supported by Social Security pensions had not relinquished their aspirations for a job—their dissatisfactions with unemployment and excess leisure time were significantly greater than a cross section of the normal population. Despite their desire for work, unemployment among this population has remained high. In a review of 1980 census data derived from working-age, disabled people, 65.5 percent of the men and 80.6 percent of the women were not working. Moreover, their average income was less than $5,000 (Lehman 1983).

Being able to work may also compensate for the social stigma attached to mental illness. Our society places a high premium on productivity and family. Friends and acquaintances are often willing to tolerate an individual's deviant behavior in direct proportion to his or her ability to be a productive and contributing member. We are all familiar with the character of the eccentric genius who is slovenly and cannot negotiate his way out of a parking lot, but who is valued by society because of his unique understanding of particle physics. In the same way, persons with psychiatric disabilities who are able to contribute to their communities and families may also receive such supportive treatment.

Another way to appreciate the functional connection between psychopathology and work is to view it from the vantage point of individuals who have mental illnesses and are working. In addition to providing a source of income for community sustenance, many individuals indicate that the ability to work can also help them control their symptoms. For example, one such individual described the impact of work on his symptoms in the following manner: "Work helps me organize my thoughts, makes me feel less crazy. It keeps me busy so I don't get bored, then depressed. I think better and concentrate more when I'm not depressed. When I'm bored, my thoughts go wild" (Strauss and Hafez 1981).

Finally, the economic benefits of helping disabled persons return to work are substantial to all of us. It has been estimated conservatively that society regains five times as many dollars in productive employment as are invested in rehabilitation. This is in addition to the personal gains and increase in self-worth that individual patients obtain by being able to return to work (Michigan Division of Vocational Rehabilitation 1970; Reagles and Wright 1971).

Despite these many benefits there is no denying that persons with psychiatric disability have difficulty locating employment. Reviews of vocational rehabilitation programs among this population indicate that approximately 30 percent may return to work following discharge, with less than 20 percent of those who find jobs still employed one year later (Anthony et al. 1978). The lack of financial and social resources that results from unemployment also jeopardizes each person's ability to remain in the community. With neither the money nor personal contacts generated by a job, it becomes very difficult to live independently and make a positive social contribution to society.

Not all mentally disabled persons are able to go back to work and there are few jobs awaiting even those who are capable of assuming full-time, competitive employment. As a result, job placement becomes a crucial linchpin for those who are ready to meet the challenge of work. Successful job placement is not simply a matter of telling patients to find a job. To successfully place rehabilitation patients requires specific knowledge in a number of areas. The vocational specialist must be knowledgeable about the local job market, labor unions, workers' compensation, and wage and hour regulations. He or she also must have an in-depth knowledge of the client (Newman 1973). Many people who have competent vocational skills still require training in job-seeking skills in order to find the job (Jacobs et al. 1984). This includes training on how to participate in employment interviews, locate effective sources of job contacts, fill out application forms, present job histories, and maintain the motivation and persistence necessary for a potentially long and frustrating job search. Poor job-seeking skills rather than poor vocational skills preclude employment for many disabled persons (Jacobs et al. 1984).

Elements of the Job Club

Over the past decade, one of the most successful programs to help people find work is the job club model (Azrin and Bessel 1980). Developed for mixed populations, the job club represents an integrated package of training, support, and management modules designed to help people conduct an effective job search. Key elements of the program include: (1) the use of an environment conducive to motivating patients in their job search; (2) the use of reinforcement strategies to make the search less demanding; (3) a breakdown of tasks involved in finding a job, in order to make the search more manageable; and (4) the training of skills needed to find a job. In this manner, the original job club program combined earlier recommendations about how to improve individual components of the job-placement process into an effective whole. Results of early job club studies indicated that between 70 and 85 percent of all participants located employment in half the time of other job-placement programs and at one-tenth the cost (Azrin 1978; Azrin et al. 1975; Azrin and Phillip 1979).

More recently, Jacobs et al. (1984) adapted a three-segment model of the job club to meet the needs of the psychiatrically disabled. In addition to the original design, it was necessary to increase the daily structure of the program by including daily goal-setting activities, remedial training in job-seeking skills, and providing staff support and counseling as required to help patients manage personal stressors and potentiators that could affect their employment potential. Each of these additions was developed and retained because it helped patients find jobs more effectively. The program is also under constant evaluation and revision as the vocational climate changes or patients present different needs. Table 2 depicts the methods that are used in each of the program's segments.

Table 2.

Job Club Methods

Teaching Job-Seeking Skills
Finding job leads
Contacting employers
Using the telephone
Completing applications
Writing resumés
Job interviews
Using transport
Appropriate grooming

Sustaining the Job Search
Daily goal setting
Frequent counselor–patient contact
Incentives
Prompting
Generous praise for effort
Peer support
Liaison with other treatment personnel

Training in Job-Seeking Skills
During the first week of the program, patients participate in an intensive, 20-hour workshop designed to assess and train basic job-finding skills. The curriculum includes identifying sources of job leads, contacting employers, filling out employment applications, developing resumés, participating in job interviews, learning how to set both long-term and daily goals, and how to use public transportation. Instruction is competency based, with trainers using programmed materials, didactic instruction, role playing, and in vivo training exercises. Wherever possible, the program uses materials and situations that the client will face during the job search. For example, patients practice completing bona fide job applications and contacting actual sources for job leads. In situations where real life assessments are not possible, such as job-interview training, role plays are substituted. Patients' progress is continually monitored, and additional instruction is provided to those who fall behind or present special training needs.

Job Search
After completing the job-seeking skills workshop, patients begin the job search. The program provides work areas, secretarial support, and current job leads and counselors to provide assistance with the job search. Job leads are gleaned from newspaper ads, Yellow Pages,

employment notices, civil service announcements, and weekly visits by state job-placement counselors from two different agencies. The patients, in turn, are expected to attend the program daily and approach the job search with the same effort and responsibility as a full-time job.

One protocol developed was a daily, individualized goal-setting session to help each client plan job-search activities. Initially, many patients had good intentions about finding a job but organized their daily searches poorly. Now, each morning, before beginning the day's search, each client meets with program staff to identify the most advantageous options for the day's search, develop outcome expectations for each activity and a time line for completion, and to problem solve, in advance, any stumbling blocks that may be encountered during the day. Patients are expected to keep a daily log of their job-seeking activities and account for their time.

A second procedure involves teaching patients how to manage the daily problems and stresses associated with looking for employment. In addition to helping patients develop realistic expectations and daily goals, supportive and goal-directed counseling is also provided as needed. This includes not only issues directly related to the job search, but other areas that could impede job-finding success, such as finding reliable housing in the community, adjusting to work hours, and learning how to interact with others.

Evaluation of the Club

An initial study of program effectiveness (Jacobs et al. 1984) reported that 57 percent of the 97 patients who participated in the program secured employment, and another 10 percent entered full-time, job-training programs; 12 percent voluntarily dropped out of the program during the first week of job-seeking skills training, before they had actually begun to job search, and another 10 percent dropped out after the first week of job-searching itself. An additional 11 percent of the patients were returned to their wards by program staff while engaged in the program because of reappearing symptoms that interfered with their participation.

Participants spent an average of 24 working days in the program, with a range of 1 to 140 days. The average program stay for patients finding jobs was 12 days longer than for those who left the program unemployed. Approximately 60 percent of all jobs secured were in clerical, sales, and service occupations; 11 percent were in professional occupations, and 12 percent were in factories or construction. Patients reported that the most effective job leads (those resulting in jobs) came from newspaper ads (39 percent), rehabilitation counselors (22 percent), and friends and relatives (14 percent). There was no relationship between the type of job obtained and the source of the job lead.

Six months of follow-up data were collected on 74 percent of the patients who entered jobs or job-training from the program. The percentage of people employed 30, 60, 90, and 180 days after leaving the program was 80 percent, 75 percent, 80 percent, and 68 percent respectively. Not all patients remained at the same job; 10 patients switched jobs during this six-month period; 6 of the 10 returned to the job club for assistance. Patients switched jobs for a variety of reasons including being fired or laid off (two persons), finding a better position (five persons), having to find a new job following symptom relapse (two persons), or moving to a new location (one person).

Of the 12 persons who had left the program employed, but who were unemployed at six-months' follow-up, four lost their jobs due to symptom exacerbation, four quit their positions because of job dissatisfaction, three were fired, and one required hospitalization due to physical illness. None of the 25 patients who had left the program without a successful placement had found a job six months later.

Three years and 300 patients later, program outcome has remained stable. Approximately 65 percent of all program participants have located jobs through the program, of whom 65 percent were still employed six months later. Analyses of demographic trends, job histories, and psychiatric treatment indicated that age and absence of positive psychiatric symptoms correlated with ability to find and maintain jobs. Older patients and individuals with positive symptoms were less likely to obtain jobs. Previous work history and education did not predict the likelihood of finding employment, but did affect the type of job secured. New program efforts are being developed in the areas of job maintenance, to help those who find jobs stay employed.

Case Study in Vocational Skills Training
Tony was a 37-year-old, never-married male with a long history of chronic major depression, who was readmitted for the fifth time to the Brendwood VA Medical Center. Although he held a bachelor's degree in liberal arts and a certificate in bookkeeping, he worked only sporadically and never in his areas of training. The inpatient staff viewed his prognosis favorably because of his obvious intelligence and easygoing manner, yet felt frustrated because of his repeated hospitalizations and inability to harness his skills in a constructive manner. It was their consensus that if he could obtain proper employment, his persisting depressive symptoms and hospitalizations would decrease. An initial evaluation by the rehabilitation counselor revealed that Tony's ambivalence about work was fueled by his fear of rejection by an employer, coupled with his insecurity in his own field of bookkeeping: "I don't know if I can do it; the field has changed so much."

The first step in the rehabilitation process was to arrange for an assignment for Tony to demonstrate what his skills were, as well as to help him build confidence in a semicompetitive (volunteer) setting. As he had typing and secretarial skills, he was assigned to work in a small office where typing, filing, and some bookkeeping were done. At the same time, he was administered the General Aptitude Test Battery (GATB), the Strong–Campbell Vocational Interest Inventory, and the Kuder Occupational Interest Survey Test which indicated high verbal and numerical ability, and an interest in the clerical and bookkeeping fields. Tony's supervisor was requested to start slowly, gradually increasing his duties, and finally exposing him to light bookkeeping tasks. With this supervision and encouragement, it was felt that, after three months in the assignment, he was ready for competitive employment. He enrolled in the job club.

It was discovered that Tony had a great deal of difficulty filling out application forms, particularly in efforts to explain his lack of work experience. Help was provided in both areas by job club staff and a decent (although brief) resumé was developed. Much effort was devoted to mock employer-interview techniques, and training in telephone employer contact. In canvassing the community for possible employment, Tony decided to find work in a finance company as it would allow him to begin in a lower-level clerical capacity and graduate to bookkeeping as he gained self-confidence.

Despite the fact that he was listing employer calls and visits on his goal sheet, Tony was not, in fact, calling or visiting these prospective employers for interviews. The rehabilitation counselor therefore decided to accompany Tony to the job-interview sites, offering encouragement on the way. This low-level intervention—utilizing coaching of skills previously acquired in the job club—enabled Tony to be hired on the first interview. He worked for the company for a full year, the longest period of time he had ever been employed, with marked reduction in his depression and reduced need for maintenance antidepressant drugs.

SUMMARY

The goal of rehabilitation is not to cure disease, but to enhance an individuals' functioning level of adaptation, and quality of life. The necessary design and validation of fully effective technology for skills training in social, family, and vocational domains will require tools from a variety of disciplines—psychopharmacology, social and cognitive psychology, developmental psychology, behavior analysis, psychodynamics, systems theory, and environmental psychology. For example, it is already demonstrated that patient's learn social problem-solving skills better when they are taking optimal doses of neuroleptics; when their families are involved in educational activities aimed at improving family emotional climates; when they are exposed to repeated practice with slow and gradual steps; when visual as well as auditory cues and instructions are used; when positive feedback and corrective feedback are liberally provided; when social modeling is provided that uses peers as well as therapists; and when skills training is personalized and overlearned.

Beyond the drug and social therapies available to schizophrenic patients, a new force for maintaining patients in the community with satisfactory quality of life has emerged that involves advocacy, self-help, and nonprofessional intervention. Community-support programs, psychosocial rehabilitation programs (e.g., Fountain House and its analogues), and family advocacy groups (e.g., National Alliance for the Mentally Ill in the United States, Schizophrenia Fellowship in Great Britain) have become popular and effective methods to enable patients to live in dignity and with less threat to their community survival. Just as neuroleptic drugs require consistent and indefinite use to maintain their therapeutic and prophylactic effects, so psychosocial treatments require consistency and long-term application. Remediating psychological and social deficits in patients with schizophrenic disorders involves the same persistent application of the environment as does remedying the patient's neurochemical disturbances with medication.

REFERENCES

Anthony WA, Cohen MR, Vitalo R: The measurement of rehabilitation outcome. Schizophr Bull 4:365–383, 1978

Azrin NH: The job finding club as a method for obtaining eligible clients: demonstration, evaluation, and counselor training. (Final Report #51-17-76104). Washington, DC, Department of Labor, 1978

Azrin NH, Bessel V: Job Club Counselors Manual: A Behavioral Approach to Vocational Counseling. Baltimore, University Park Press, 1980

Azrin NH, Phillip RA: The job club method for the job handicapped: a comparative outcome study. Rehabilitation Counseling Bulletin 23:144–155, 1979

Azrin NH, Flores T, Kaplan SJ: Job finding club: a group assisted program for obtaining employment. Behav Res Ther 13:17–27, 1975

Bellack A, Hersen M, Turner V: Generalization effects of social skills training in chronic schizophrenics: an experimental analysis. Behav Res Ther 14:391–398, 1976

Boker W, Brenner HD: Management of Schizophrenia. Bern, Switzerland, H. Huber, 1986

Brenner MH: Mental Illness and the Economy. Cambridge, MA, Harvard University Press, 1973

Brown G, Birley JLT, Wing JK: Influence of family life on the course of schizophrenia. Br J Psychiatry 121:241–258, 1972

Creer C: Social work with patients and their families, in Schizophrenia: Towards a New Synthesis. Edited by Wing JK. London, Academic Press, 1978

DeIsabella G, Meneghelli A: Un training di abilita sociali per la rehabilitazione di pazient paicotici cronici. Rivista Sperimentale di Frenia-tria 5:1194–1204, 1983

Edelstein BA, Couture E, Cray M, et al: Group training of problem solving with psychiatric patients, in Group Therapy: An Annual Review, vol. 2. Edited by Upper D, Ross SM, Champaign, IL, Research Press, 1980

Falloon IRH, Liberman RP: Behavioral family interventions in the management of chronic schizophrenia, in Family Therapy of Schizophrenia. Edited by McFarlane W. New York, Guilford Press, 1983

Falloon IRII, Buyd J, McGill CW: Family Care of Schizophrenia. New York, Guilford Press, 1984

Finch B, Wallace CJ: Successful interpersonal skills training with schizophrenic inpatients. J Consult Clin Psychol 45:885–890, 1977

Foy DW, Wallace CJ, Liberman RP: Advances in social skills training for chronic mental patients, in Advances in Clinical Behavior Therapy. Edited by Craig KD, McMahon RJ. New York, Brunner/Mazel, 1983

Goldsmith JC, McFall RM: Development and evolution of an interpersonal skill training program for psychiatric inpatients. J Abnorm Psychol 84:51–58, 1975

Hagen DQ: The relationship between job loss and physical and mental illness. Hosp Community Psychiatry 34:438–441, 1983

Jacobs H, Kardashian S, Krienbring RK, et al: A skills-oriented model for facilitating employment among psychiatrically disabled persons. Rehabilitation Counseling Bulletin 28:87–96, 1984

Kandel FR: From metapsychology to molecular biology: explorations into the nature of anxiety. Am J Psychiatry 140:1277–1293, 1983

Kazdin AE: Behavior Modification in Applied Settings. Homewood IL, Dorsey Press, 1984

Kelly JA, Urey JR, Patterson JT: Improving heterosocial conversational skills of male psychiatric patients through a small group training procedure. Behav Ther 11:179–183, 1983

Lehman AF, Ward NC, Linn LS: Chronic mental patients: the quality of life issue. Am J Psychiatry 133:796–823, 1983

Liberman RP: Social factors in schizophrenia, in Psychiatry Update: The American Psychiatric Association Annual Review, vol. 1. Edited by Grinspoon L. Washington, DC, American Psychiatric Press, 1982

Liberman RP, Wallace CJ: Social skills training for schizophrenics: a controlled clinical trial. Psychiatry Res (in press)

Liberman RP, King LW, DeRisi WJ, et al: Personal Effectiveness: Guiding People to Express Their Feelings and Improve Their Social Skills. Champaign, IL, Research Press, 1975

Liberman RP, Falloon IRH, Wallace CJ: Drug-psychosocial interactions in the treatment of schizophrenia, in The Chronically Mentally Ill: Research and Services. Edited by Mirabi M. New York, SP Medical and Scientific Books, 1984a

Liberman RP, Lillie F, Falloon IRH, et al: Social skills training for relapsing schizophrenics: an experimental analysis. Behav Mod 8:155–179, 1984b

Liberman RP, Massel HK, Mosk M, et al: Social skills training for chronic mental patients. Hosp Community Psychiatry 36:396–403, 1985

Linn MW, Klett J, Caffey FM: Foster home characteristics and psychiatric patient outcome. Arch Gen Psychiatry 37:129–132, 1980

Martinez-Diaz JA, Massel HK, Wong SE, et al: Training and generalization of conversational skills in chronic schizophrenics. Paper presented at the World Congress on Behavior Therapy, Washington, DC, 1983

Massel HK, Bowen L, Wong SE, et al: The development of a discrete-trials procedure for training social skills to chronic schizophrenics: acquisition and generalization effects. Paper presented at the meeting of the Association for the Advancement of Behavior Therapy, Houston, Texas 1985

Platt JJ, Spivack G: Problem solving thinking of psychiatric patients. J Consult Clin Psychol 28:3–5, 1972

Presly AS, Grubb AB, Semple D: Predictors of successful rehabilitation in long-stay patients. Acta Psychiatr Scand 66:83–88, 1982

Snyder KS, Liberman RP: Family assessment and intervention with schizophrenics at risk for relapse, in New Directions for Mental Health Services (No. 12). Edited by Goldstein MJ. San Francisco, Jossey-Bass, 1981

Stokes TF, Baer DM: An implicit technology of generalization. J Applied Behav Analysis 10:349–369, 1977

Strauss JS, Hafez H: Clinical questions and "real" research. Am J Psychiatry 138:1592–1597, 1981

Sylph JA, Ross HE, Kedward HB: Social disability in chronic psychiatric patients. Am J Psychiatry 134:1391–1394, 1978

Test MA, Stein LI: Special living arrangements: a model for decision-making. Hosp Community Psychiatry 28:608–610, 1977

Vaughn CE, Leff JP: The influence of family and social factors on the course of psychiatric illness. Br J Psychiatry 129:125–137, 1976

Vaughn CE, Snyder KS, Liberman RP, et al: Family factors in schizophrenic relapse: a California replication. Schizophr Bull 8:425–426, 1982

Vaughn CE, Snyder KS, Freeman W, et al: Family factors in schizophrenic relapse: a California replication. Arch Gen Psychiatry 41:1169–1177, 1984

Wallace CJ, Nelson C, Liberman RP, et al: A review and critique of social skills training with chronic schizophrenics. Schizophr Bull 6:42–63, 1980

13

Training and Technical Assistance in Psychiatric Rehabilitation

William A. Anthony, Ph.D.
Mikal R. Cohen, Ph.D.
Marianne D. Farkas, Sc.D.

P sychiatric rehabilitation is designed to develop skills and to maximize community support for psychiatrically disabled persons. The practice of psychiatric rehabilitation requires unique practitioner skills and innovative agency programs. Psychiatric rehabilitation training and program consultation technology is being developed to ensure that agencies are equipped with skilled rehabilitation practitioners and relevant programs. This technology provides the field with the capacity to change both its personnel and its programs to meet the needs of those they serve.

A TRAINEE'S PERSPECTIVE

The following describes a psychiatric rehabilitation training experience through the eyes of a trainee:

> My extensive psychosocial background led me to believe that I was as psychosocial as one could get. Then came psychiatric rehabilitation skills training! Doing it, however, involves a much harder task than the initial material indicates. Quickly, one learns that "simple" does not necessarily mean "easy."
>
> There were three grueling weeks of training, audiotapes of sessions of clients and me to be critiqued by our trainers, teach-

ing sessions with my staff on material I was still struggling to learn (52 hours of teaching since April), study groups, critiquing my staff's tapes, etc., etc.! The results from all this, I am finding to be tremendous.

Psychiatric rehabilitation offers great value to our clients and helps us put into action what conceptually we all know, believe, and even think we are doing: In actuality we have just scratched the surface. The model forces us to carry our psychosocial philosophy to its fullest extent by creating a process for optimal client involvement. The client, finding our services individualized and personalized, discovers greater benefits, thereby becoming more receptive and participatory in the entire process. The client becomes "the captain of his/her rehabilitation effort.". . . Implementation of this model is very challenging. It involves extensive training for staff, and program development for application of the model in individualized programs. (Hillhouse-Jones, 1984)

Becoming an expert in the practice of psychiatric rehabilitation is *not* something one does overnight. It is *not* something one automatically acquires when hired to "do rehabilitation."

In the past, most people were not formally educated or trained in psychiatric rehabilitation. They experienced it firsthand in psychosocial rehabilitation settings from the leaders in the field such as Beard, Grob, Dincin, Rutman, and others. However, as the popularity of the psychiatric rehabilitation concept increased and more and more people became involved, the need for technical assistance (i.e., training and program consultation) became more apparent. In 1977, Anthony facetiously characterized the present state of psychiatric rehabilitation as "the development of nontraditional psychiatric settings for the purpose of using traditional psychiatric teachings by traditionally trained personnel." (Anthony 1977, p. 660) Clearly, psychiatric rehabilitation practitioner training and program consultation were needed.

The acceptance of the concept of psychiatric rehabilitation and the creation of psychosocial rehabilitation settings have laid the foundation for an emerging consensus about the philosophy and principles underlying the field. In addition, a number of research studies have shown that the two major interventions of psychiatric rehabilitation—teaching skills to clients and developing environmental supports for clients—have been found to be related to various types of client rehabilitation outcome (e.g., more frequent and higher levels of client independent living and vocational functioning.) Dozens of studies have reported on a positive correlation between client skills and client rehabilitation outcome (reviewed most recently in Anthony et al. 1984; Anthony and Jansen 1984). In essence, the articulation of the philosophy and principles of psychiatric rehabilitation, the empirical studies of rehabilitation, and the nationwide development of psychosocial rehabilitation settings have resulted in further definition of the psychiatric rehabilitation approach.

THE PSYCHIATRIC REHABILITATION APPROACH

The psychiatric rehabilitation approach, on which training and consultation can now be provided, integrates the philosophy and principles of physical rehabilitation with various techniques of the psychotherapeutic approach. The "rehabilitation model," as practiced with severely physically disabled persons (e.g., person with quadraplegia, blindness, etc.) serves as a conceptual model for the basic goals and treatment process of psychiatric rehabilitation (Anthony 1982).

The basic philosophy of rehabilitation provides direction to the psychiatric rehabilitation process (i.e., disabled people need skills and support to function in the living, learning, and working environments of their choice). There obviously are vast differences between a severe psychiatric disability and a severe physical disability, but there are sufficient similarities to allow the physical rehabilitation approach to be used as a conceptual model for psychiatric rehabilitation. For example, both groups of service recipients need a wide range of services, exhibit impairment of role performance, may be receiving these services for a long period of time, and often do not experience complete recovery from their disabilities. Physically disabled clients are less stigmatized than the psychiatrically disabled. A physical disability seems more understandable than "mental illness," and the treatment of physical disorders appears more credible and recognizable to the layperson than does the treatment of psychiatric disorders. By showing how the psychiatric rehabilitation approach is modeled on the philosophy of physical rehabilitation, the concept of psychiatric rehabilitation can be made more clear, legitimate, and acceptable.

The practice of psychiatric rehabilitation consists of three phases: the diagnostic phase, the planning phase, and the intervention phase. The *diagnostic phase* lays the groundwork for the development of the rehabilitation plan. In contrast to the traditional psychiatric diagnosis which describes symptomatology, the rehabilitation diagnosis yields a behavioral description of the psychiatrically disabled person's current skill functioning in the living, learning, social, and/or working environments in which he or she chooses to function. The diagnostic information enables the rehabilitation practitioner to work with the client in the *planning phase* to develop a rehabilitation plan. A rehabilitation plan specifies how to change the person and/or the person's environment to achieve the person's rehabilitation goals. The plan is similar to an individualized service plan with the major difference being its identification of skill and resource development objectives and interventions rather than service providers. In the *intervention phase,* the rehabilitation plan is implemented to increase the person's skills and/or to make the environment more supportive of the person's functioning.

The articulation of a psychiatric rehabilitation approach has made it possible to specify the practitioner skills and program characteristics required for psychiatric rehabilitation to occur. These practitioner skills and program characteristics have been defined by the Center for Rehabilitation Research and Training (1984). A training technology to teach practitioners these skills and a consultation technology to assist programs in developing these characteristics is being developed.

ESSENTIAL SKILLS OF A PSYCHIATRIC REHABILITATION PRACTITIONER

Psychiatric rehabilitation practitioners need certain knowledge, attitudes, and skills to guide a client effectively through the three phases of the rehabilitation process—diagnosis, planning, and intervention. The knowledge required includes knowledge about the client population, psychiatric disabilities, psychiatric rehabilitation research, psychiatric rehabilitation practice, and the perspectives of other disciplines involved with the client group. Psychiatric rehabilitation practitioners also need to know about community resources and their functional requirements (Farkas and Anthony 1980). Attitudinally, practitioners need to be positive about the severely psychiatrically disabled client and the potential for improvement, as well as to believe in their own ability to facilitate client rehabilitation through the use of psychiatric rehabilitation skills.

In addition to the basic knowledge and attitudes, the rehabilitation practitioner needs a comprehensive repertoire of skills to increase client success in the environment of choice. The critical skills a practitioner needs to assist through the three phases of rehabilitation have been described (Center for Rehabilitation Research and Training 1984). Table 1 provides a summary of these skills.

Rehabilitation Diagnosis

Practitioners conducting a rehabilitation diagnosis attempt to involve clients in coming to an agreement about the environments in which they intend to function in the next 6 to 18 months (i.e., setting the client's overall rehabilitation goals). For example, Grace Jones and her practitioner may come to an agreement that she will work on the overall rehabilitation goal of "living in the Green Street Group Home until October of next year." This overall rehabilitation goal is the basis for a subsequent skill and resource assessment.

By means of a functional assessment, the practitioner and client develop an understanding of those skills which the client can and cannot perform related to achieving the client's overall rehabilitation

Table 1.

Skills of Psychiatric Rehabilitation

Rehabilitation Diagnosis
Setting an overall rehabilitation goal
Functional assessment
Resource assessment

Rehabilitation Planning
Selecting high-priority objectives
Assigning interventions
Monitoring the plan

Rehabilitation Interventions
Direct skills teaching
Skills programming
Resource coordination
Resource modification

goal. Practitioners work with clients to generate a list of unique skills based on the behavioral requirements of the chosen environment as well as from the behaviors personally important to enhance the client's satisfaction in the particular environment he or she has chosen. For example, one of the skills needed by Grace to live successfully at Green Street is "demonstrating understanding." Grace and her practitioner describe the use of this skill as "the percentage of times per week Grace restates the feelings of other residents, and the reasons for those feelings, when negotiating the house chores during community meetings." Once use of the skill is described, Grace and her practitioner evaluate Grace's present and needed use of this skill at Green Street House.

A resource assessment evaluates the presence or absence of supports critical to the client's achieving the overall rehabilitation goal. By means of a resource assessment, the practitioner involves the client in listing those persons, places, or things which are necessary for the client to be successful in the chosen environment. Again, the resources listed are based on both environmental requirements and personal needs. For example, the Green Street Group Home may require clients to attend a minimum of four hours of day programming. The resource assessment might then evaluate the present and needed "number of days per week a day program provides at least four hours of structured activities for Grace." Table 2 presents a sample portion of a completed functional assessment, and Table 3 presents a sample portion of a resource assessment.

Table 2.

Functional Assessment Example: Overall Rehabilitation Goal—Grace Intends to Live at Green Street House until October, 1986

Strengths/ Deficits	Critical Skills	Skill Use Descriptions	Skill Evaluations[1]					
			Utilization		Application		Acquisition	
			Present	Need	Yes	No	Yes	No
−	Following directions	The percentage of times per week Grace performs the steps of a task as described when the house manager gives her instructions	0	90%		✓	✓	
−	Demonstrating understanding	The percentage of times per week Grace restates the feelings of other residents, and the reasons for those feelings, when negotiating house chores during community meetings	0	70%		✓		✓
−	Meal planning	The number of days per week Grace writes a dinner menu before 5:00 P.M.	0	5	✓			
+	Making the bed	The number of days per week Grace tucks in the sheets and blankets on her bed at the house within an hour of getting up in the morning	7	7				

[1] The client's skill level is evaluated in the three different ways. The utilization column indicates the client's highest present level of spontaneous use of the skill in the target environment as compared to the needed level of skill use. The application column indicates whether the client can (Yes) or cannot (No) perform the skill at least once in the target environment. The acquisition column indicates whether the client can (Yes) or cannot (No) perform the skill in an assessment or learning environment. If the client's present level of skill use is zero, then skill application is evaluated. Similarly, if the client has been evaluated as unable to apply (No) the skill, then skill acquisition is evaluated.

Table 3.

Resource Assessment Example: Overall Rehabilitation Goal—Grace Intends to Live at Green Street House until October, 1986

Strengths/ Deficits	Critical Resources	Resource Use Description	Present	Needed
Neighborhood contacts	–	Number of times per week next-door neighbors telephone Grace when she is home for the weekend	0	2
Spending money	+	Number of weeks per month Grace's parents give her $25.00 for her own personal expenses	4	4
Day programming	–	Number of days per week a day program provides at least four hours of structured activities for Grace	3	5

Rehabilitation Planning
Based on the diagnosis, priorities are assigned to the skill and re-source-development objectives which will be the initial focus of the intervention phase. The practitioner identifies a specific intervention for each skill or resource objective in the plan and organizes the responsibilities for carrying out the intervention selected for each objective. The client and the practitioner sign the rehabilitation plan to indicate agreement. Table 4 presents a sample portion of a com-pleted rehabilitation plan.

Rehabilitation Interventions
The rehabilitation practitioner uses two major types of intervention: skill development and resource development. These interventions improve the client's use of skills or resources. There are two ways to develop such skills. The first is direct skills teaching. This interven-tion is used when the functional assessment indicates the client has not acquired the skill. Direct skills teaching involves leading the client through a systematic series of instructional activities resulting in the client's use of new behaviors. Direct skills teaching is unique in its use of comprehensive teaching methods which result in the client's learning to use the skill when needed. The second way to develop skills is skills programming, which prescribes a step-by-step proce-dure to prepare the client to use an existing skill as needed. Skills programming is designed to help clients overcome barriers to using a skill they *can* do. Skills programming prepares the client to use a skill as frequently as needed in a particular environment.

For example, the practitioner would help Grace develop the skill of "demonstrating understanding" by first teaching her how to "re-state another person's feelings and the reasons for that feeling" in simulated situations in the teaching setting. Then the practitioner, together with Grace, would generate a series of action steps to over-come the barriers that prevent Grace from using this skill outside the teaching setting in the chosen environment as frequently as needed (i.e., 70 percent of the times per week with other residents when negotiating household chores during community meetings at Green Street House).

In contrast to skill-development interventions, resource-develop-ment interventions are designed to link the client with a resource that presently exists (resource coordination), or to develop resources that do not exist in the particular way needed by the client (resource modification). Resource coordination involves selecting a preferred resource, arranging for its use, and supporting the client in using the resource. For example, for Grace's resource objective of "day pro-gramming," Grace and her practitioner would work to clarify the important values in making a choice about where she would go for day programming (e.g., cost, location, type of program). Once the

Table 4.

Rehabilitation Plan Example: Overall Rehabilitation Goal—Grace Intends to Live at Green Street House until October, 1986

Priority Skill/ Resource Development Objectives	Intervention	Person(s) Responsible (Name)	Starting Date	Completion Date	Essential Signatures
Following directions	Direct skills teaching	Writing content outline and lesson plan: oc-cupational therapist	Oct. 15	Jan. 1	
		Teaching resi-dence staff programming skill use: residence staff			
Day programming	Resource coordination	Case manager	Dec. 1	Jan. 1	

I helped prepare this plan. Client's Signature: _____

Practitioner's Signature: _____

resource was selected, Grace would be assisted in connecting with the program. The practitioner would work with both the day program and Grace to overcome any barriers that might prevent Grace from successfully using the day program.

Resource modification is the technique of adapting an existing resource to better fit the needs of the client. For example, Grace's preferred day program might be a volunteer program at a local church. The volunteer program may fit most of her needs except that the volunteer positions are for three days per week rather than the needed four. The practitioner might work with the church program to modify the program to allow Grace to take on more than one volunteer position. The skills of resource modification involve negotiating with community resources to achieve a particular client's resource objective.

In summary, the rehabilitation practitioner has a set of skills which engage clients and significant others in diagnosing, planning, and developing the skills and resources required by the client to be successful in a particular environment. The practitioner's ability to involve the client is facilitated by the ability to explain the rehabilitation process to the client and by the practitioner's level of interpersonal skills. Rehabilitation is done *with* clients and not *to* them (Anthony 1980) and, to that extent, they must understand the process and be encouraged to participate.

A TRAINING TECHNOLOGY TO TRAIN PRACTITIONERS

As just described, the essential skills of a psychiatric rehabilitation practitioner have been articulated in a way that makes them capable of being observed and measured. As a result, it has become possible to develop a technology to teach practitioners those skills. Six books have been developed for the purpose of teaching some of the previously identified skills of psychiatric rehabilitation to practitioners (Anthony et al. 1980). The training program was evaluated in a 150-hour pilot training program for rehabilitation-counseling student interns and mental health and vocational rehabilitation practitioners. The training was built around the skills presented in the six manuals. The evaluation of the training indicated that the skills of psychiatric rehabilitation can be learned and measured, and that trainees considered these skills to be important in the performance of their jobs. Furthermore, the results suggested that clients of practitioners who scored high on written assessments of these skills were more apt to report feeling involved, understood, and taught new skills (Rehabilitation Research Brief 1980). Hundreds of practitioners have been trained in psychiatric rehabilitation (Center for Rehabilitation Research and Training in Mental Health Final Report 1984) and the training has been incorporated into master's and doctoral degree programs.

Development of a Psychiatric Rehabilitation Training Dissemination Strategy

Although the training was documented to be both needed and effective, there was no mechanism for large-scale dissemination of the training to mental health practitioners. A training/dissemination strategy was needed. The dissemination and utilization literature has been reviewed (e.g., Caplan 1980; Fairweather 1971; Glaser and Taylor 1969; Hamilton and Muthard 1975; Havelock 1971; Havelock and Benne 1969; Muthard 1980; Pelz and Munson 1980; Soloff 1972; Switzer 1965) and suggests that training dissemination ideally should be built into an organization's system as an ongoing process. Preferably, it is viewed by all those affected as crucial to the maintenance and growth of the organization. The active involvement of key personnel is vital to smooth dissemination. In training dissemination, key personnel, including administrators and practitioners, are involved from the beginning whenever possible (Muthard 1980). Such initial involvement creates a sense of ownership, identification, and purpose. This situation is enhanced when the persons involved are aware of a "felt need" for the training (Glaser and Taylor 1969; Pelz and Munson 1980).

Based on the literature as well as on training experience, a training-of-trainers strategy has been developed to disseminate psychiatric rehabilitation skills. The strategy incorporates three key ingredients based on the dissemination/utilization literature review:

1. Careful selection of service settings in which to disseminate the training, and careful selection of the personnel who are to be trainers;
2. Training trainers in the clinical practice of the skills of psychiatric rehabilitation, as well as in how to teach these skills to others;
3. On-site assistance to trainers on the planning and implementation of the training in their service settings.

In 1981, NIMH funded an evaluation of the training dissemination strategy with mental health agencies. Of 100 from around the country which volunteered to be training sites, 9 were selected. Representatives from these agencies were trained in the psychiatric rehabilitation skills and in how to teach these skills to others. These new trainers then trained their agency staffs in psychiatric rehabilitation skills, and the agency staff used the skills with their clients. Data analysis indicated the viability of the strategy for facilitating practitioner training and utilization of the psychiatric rehabilitation skills (Center for Rehabilitation Research and Training in Mental Health 1984). Since the development of the training-of-trainers strategy, more than 60 trainers have been trained, representing over 40 service settings. The trainers work for state departments of mental health, state psychiatric hospitals, psychosocial rehabilitation centers, and private hospitals.

Training Materials That Support the Training-Dissemination Strategy

The training of trainers, as well as the training of practitioners, requires special expertise and materials. The materials needed to support the training-dissemination strategy are practitioner books, trainer packages, and master trainer guides. The practitioner books (Anthony et al. 1980; Cohen et al. 1985a; Cohen et al. 1985b) introduce the practitioner to the skills of psychiatric rehabilitation. After training, the books are used by practitioners to review their new knowledge and skills.

Trainer packages (Cohen et al. 1985a, 1985b) should contain detailed lesson plans and training aids for use during training sessions. The packages are important because they save trainer preparation time and provide a tested program with attractive training aids. The master trainer guides (Cohen and Nemec 1985) should provide master trainers (i.e., current center staff) with information about "how to" develop trainers. These guides are important because they allow new master trainers to be developed.

The psychiatric rehabilitation training technology is similar to a ladder that builds upward from a firm foundation. The foundation of the technology is the psychiatric rehabilitation approach. Next, the training program teaches the essential psychiatric rehabilitation skills to psychiatric rehabilitation practitioners. Last comes the dissemination of the training program, which involves a training-of-trainers strategy which prepares trainers and mater trainers to use training materials to teach practitioners and trainers.

ESSENTIAL CHARACTERISTICS OF A PSYCHIATRIC REHABILITATION PROGRAM

The implementation of psychiatric rehabilitation depends upon the practitioners' ability to utilize their competencies effectively on a regular basis. A rehabilitation program provides the organizational support to practitioners in diagnosing, planning, and intervening with their clients. Three major characteristics of a program have been defined which affect the practitioner's ability to utilize psychiatric rehabilitation (Anthony et al. 1982; Farkas et al., in press). These are the program mission, the program structure for delivering diagnosis planning and intervention, and the network of environments in which programming occurs.

The Program Mission

The statement of the program mission gives overall direction and purpose to the program. The psychiatric rehabilitation mission is "to increase a person's ability to function in the environment of that person's choice, given the least amount of intervention necessary" (Anthony 1979). The mission is demonstrated by written statements of program purpose and by verbal statements by program leaders and administrators. An ideal psychiatric rehabilitation mission statement includes four key concepts: *functioning, client choice, environmental specificity,* and *independence.*

The first key mission concept addresses the program's focus on client functioning. This orientation directs program activities toward the development of client competencies, rather than the reduction of symptoms. The second concept critical to the process of psychiatric rehabilitation underlines a belief in the importance of client choice. To the degree possible, the client is seen as a partner in the rehabilitation process, with the right to obtain practitioner assistance in becoming successful in an environment of choice, rather than one in which they are placed. Client involvement is the cornerstone of psychiatric rehabilitation and the program which supports it. The third concept, environmental specificity, emphasizes the need to view the person's functioning in relation to the demands of a particular living, learning, social, or working environment. The last concept is independence. The mission of the program is to increase the client's independence rather than maintenance. The psychiatric rehabilitation mission defines increased independence as the "least amount of intervention." While the mission puts forth the value of independence, there also is recognition that some intervention may always be needed. In psychiatric rehabilitation, relative dependency is expected. The goal is to increase client functioning while decreasing professional support.

The Program Structure
The psychiatric rehabilitation program's policies, procedures, record keeping, and activities reflect the program's mission. Program activities are designed to facilitate the client's movement through the rehabilitation process of diagnosis, planning, and intervention. The program structure begins with an opportunity to explore the client's overall rehabilitation goal. For instance, a program may organize visits to various work sites or residences to allow clients to begin to clarify for themselves what they like and do not like. Classes may be held to teach clients how to choose settings, if they do not know how to make choices in a systematic fashion. Program activities are also organized to facilitate an assessment of the clients' skills and supports, involve clients in developing an overall plan, and participate in the skills teaching designed for them to learn skills they do not have and practice skills they need to improve. Such a process requires a flexible program that designs skills-teaching activities based on the needs of the current clients. For instance, Grace would need a class to learn the skill of "demonstrating understanding." She would not need to attend a standard class on "assertiveness," simply because that

was what was offered in the program's activities. The program structure would also allow time for a practitioner to develop a skill-use program with Grace to help her overcome specific barriers to her "demonstrating understanding at Green Street House." In addition to skill-development interventions, the program structure also assists the clients in obtaining the resources they lack.

Program records based on the psychiatric rehabilitation approach require the practitioner to document evidence for each portion of the rehabilitation process. For instance, the records ask for an overall rehabilitation goal chosen by the clients during the rehabilitation diagnosis. A section of the record asks for an evaluation of the client's functioning on described skills.

Practitioners' job descriptions, based on the rehabilitation approach, include the diagnosis, planning, or intervention tasks which are appropriate for them. The intake worker, for instance, may be designated as the staff person who has the task of setting the overall rehabilitation goal. Day-treatment unit supervisors may conduct functional assessments on skills related to their specific settings. A curriculum developer may develop content outlines and lesson plans, while life-skills teachers conduct the classes. The assignment of staff varies greatly from program to program. The total job descriptions reflect the entire process of diagnosis, planning, and intervention.

The Network of Environments

A rehabilitation program is only complete to the extent that it has access to a continuum of residential, vocational, social, or educational/treatment environments. A comprehensive program has access to all four types of setting. A continuum of environments means an integrated range of settings with increasing skill requirements and decreasing amounts of support. These environments are integrated in that the exit criteria of one setting match the entry criteria in the next most demanding environment. In this way, the continuum does not necessarily include a standard set of residential facilities. A program with access to a halfway house, a group home, and a supervised apartment does not necessarily have a continuum of residences. The functional requirements of each setting have to be incrementally greater, with an incrementally reduced amount of staff support to constitute a continuum. Mechanisms of linking one environment with the next, such as interagency agreements and liaisons are present as well. An adequate network of environments includes a range of settings whose functional requirements match the functional levels of the clients seen by the program. The availability of group homes whose requirements are minimal is obviously not useful if most of the program's client population demonstrate the residential skills required to live in a nonsupervised apartment. An ideal network of environments allows clients a range of options that match their values as well as their functional requirements. Some clients prefer to live alone. Some clients prefer to share housing. Some clients enjoy the routine assembly tasks of most sheltered workshops. Some clients' vocational interests involve working with ideas or people. An ideal rehabilitation program has access to a sufficient variety of residential, social, vocational, and educational settings that the client does not have to "fit" or be placed in environments simply because they are available.

In summary, the essential ingredients of a psychiatric rehabilitation program involve a *mission* which focuses the program on increasing client functioning in an environment of choice, while decreasing the amount of long-term professional support; a *structure* which is designed to involve clients in rehabilitation diagnosis, rehabilitation planning, and rehabilitation intervention; and a *network of environments* which allow the client to choose a setting which matches his or her abilities and preferences.

A CONSULTATION TECHNOLOGY TO CHANGE PROGRAMS

Even though there is increased knowledge about the characteristics of a psychiatric rehabilitation program, creating a new psychiatric rehabilitation program or changing a traditional program into a rehabilitation program is very difficult for service settings. The development of a psychiatric rehabilitation program usually requires change in the physical environment, funding, daily operation, staffing, mission, program structure, and record keeping, as well as the creation of new rehabilitation environments. Often, staff assigned the responsibility of program development lack the knowledge and skills necessary to make these changes. An historical way of helping agencies to develop or change is through the provision of technical assistance.

Technical assistance involves the transfer of "technical" knowledge and skills (Donergue 1968; Havari 1974; Sufrin 1966) from a "donor" (i.e., technical expert) to a "recipient" (i.e., technical nonexpert). Nemec (1983) provides an excellent discussion of the distinction between technical assistance and other forms of assistance (e.g., financial assistance, technical cooperation). In essence, technical assistance involves both consultation and training.

Psychiatric rehabilitation consultation is defined as the transfer of technical knowledge focused on program development, while psychiatric rehabilitation training is the teaching of attitudes, knowledge, and/or skills for the purpose of personnel development. The format for program consultation is usually a one-to-one, on-site relationship, while training is often delivered in group meetings, off-site. In the mental health field, there are unlimited examples of on-site consultation. In fact, an important focus of the National Institute of Mental Health has been on provision of consultation around new program developments (e.g., development of community mental health center programs and community-support programs).

A psychiatric rehabilitation program consultant has unique knowledge (i.e., knows the elements of a psychiatric rehabilitation program) and unique consultant skills (i.e., how to create a psychiatric rehabilitation program). The consultant uses a four-step consultation process of (1) determining readiness, (2) assessing the program, (3) proposing program change, and (4) creating the program change (Center for Rehabilitation Research and Training 1985). The process emphasizes a careful diagnosis of the program (e.g., its mission, structure, and network of environments) to evaluate the program's compatibility with the psychiatric rehabilitation approach and its potential for change.

Based on the determination of readiness and the assessment of program strengths and deficiencies, the consultant proposes a plan for change. The plan specifies the consultation interventions, and time lines for achieving the goals. Next, the interventions are delivered to create program change. These interventions include developing a mission statement, writing new policy statements, designing a new program structure, revising record keeping, modifying job descriptions, and starting new living, learning, social, or working environments.

Unfortunately, there are only a minimal number of psychiatric rehabilitation program consultants (Center for Rehabilitation Research and Training 1984). In response to this lack of psychiatric rehabilitation consultants, a strategy for training program consultants has been developed after consideration of alternative strategies, and the principles derived from the literature on planned change (Bennis et al. 1976; Jung and Spaniol 1981; Zaltman and Duncan 1977). The strategy includes a description of *who* ideally is a program consultant, *where* ideally a program consultant is located, and *how* ideally program consultation is conducted.

The New Jersey Division of Mental Health and Hospitals funded a technical assistance project to "help the State's 54 partial care agencies deal with the multitude of service issues encountered in rehabilitating the chronically mentally ill." Four consultants and a project supervisor were selected because of their experience in psychiatric rehabilitation programs, their technical knowledge, and their consultation skills. The consultants were located at a psychosocial rehabilitation center that was also funded by the state. The project supervisor received technical assistance from the Center for Rehabilitation Research and Training in Mental Health on the development of the program-consultation process. The program-consultation process included three phases: (a) assessment of partial care programs; (b) development of an individual technical assistance plan; and (c) provision of technical assistance interventions such as common-issue training and on-site consultation. Initial evaluation of the consultation process has indicated positive results (Borys and Fishbein 1983; Kelner 1984).

FACTORS INCREASING THE PROBABILITY OF PRACTITIONER AND PROGRAM CHANGE

The following factors are considered critical to the success of technical assistance (i.e., training and consultation) in psychiatric rehabilitation:

1. Change in practice is facilitated by readiness for change (e.g., a felt need for change).
2. Change in practice is facilitated by new technology that is credible, observable, relevant, compatible, understandable, and accessible.
3. Change in practice is facilitated by the teaching of new skills and/ or programming the use of existing skills.
4. Change in practice is facilitated by peer models in the service setting.
5. Change in practice is facilitated by a supportive internal (i.e., agency) environment including supportive management and program (i.e., mission, structure, network of environments).
6. Change in practice is facilitated by on-site transfer of knowledge about program developments.
7. Change in practice is facilitated by interpersonal exchange between the change agent and the target of change.
8. Change in practice is facilitated by a supportive external (i.e., system) environment including supportive funding requirements, monitoring criteria, and provision of adequate financial resources.
9. Change in practice is developmental and takes sufficient time (e.g., usually two or more years).

In summary, there is burgeoning knowledge about psychiatric rehabilitation. No longer must someone learn to do psychiatric rehabilitation by trial and error—often at the expense of one's clients. A psychiatric rehabilitation technology, in which practitioners can become expert and which guides the development of programs, is being articulated. The practitioner training and program consultation needed to disseminate the psychiatric rehabilitation technology are being developed. The growth of a psychiatric rehabilitation technology, along with the means to train practitioners and develop programs, will give power to the psychiatric rehabilitation field's good intentions and substance to its hopes.

REFERENCES

Anthony WA: Psychological rehabilitation: a concept in need of method. Am Psychol 32:658:662, 1977
Anthony WA: Principles of Psychiatric Rehabilitation. Baltimore, University Park Press, 1979
Anthony WA (Ed): Rehabilitation on the person with a psychiatric disability: the state of the art. Rehabilitation Counseling Bulletin 24: 6-21, 1980

Anthony WA: Explaining psychiatric rehabilitation by an analogy to physical rehabilitation. Psychosocial Rehabilitation Journal 5:61-65, 1982

Anthony WA, Jansen M: Predicting the vocational capacity of the chronically mentally ill: research and policy implications. Am Psychol 39:537-544, 1984

Anthony WA, Cohen M, Vatalo R: The measurement of rehabilitation outcome. Schizophr Bull 4:365-383, 1978

Anthony WA, Cohen M, Pierce R, et al: Psychiatric Rehabilitation Practice Series: Books 1–6. Baltimore, University Park Press, 1980

Anthony WA, Cohen M, Farkas M: A psychiatric rehabilitation treatment program: can I recognize one if I see one? Community Mental Health J 18:83-96, 1982

Anthony WA, Cohen M, Cohen B: Psychiatric rehabilitation, in The Chronic Mental Patient: Five Years Later. Edited by Talbott JA. New York, Grune & Stratton, 1984

Bennis WG, Benne KD, Chin R, et al: The Planning of Change, third edition. (New York, Holt, Rinehart and Winston, 1976

Borys S, Fishbein S: Partial Care Technical Assistance Project: Pretest Results (MS). Trenton, New Jersey Division of Mental Health and Hospitals, 1983

Caplan N: What do we know about knowledge utilization? in New Directions for Program Evaluation, No. 5. Edited by Braskamp LA, Brown RD. San Francisco, Jossey-Bass, 1980

Center for Rehabilitation Research and Training in Mental Health: Research Brief. Boston, Boston University, 1980

Center for Rehabilitation Research and Training in Mental Health: Final Report. Boston, Boston University, 1984

Center for Rehabilitation Research and Training in Mental Health: Annual Report. Boston, Boston University, 1985

Cohen M, Nemec P: Psychiatric Rehabilitation Trainer Packages: Trainer Orientation. Boston, Center for Rehabilitation Research and Training in Mental Health, 1985

Cohen M, Danley K, Nemec P: Psychiatric Rehabilitation Trainer Packages: Direct Skills Teaching. Boston, Center for Rehabilitation Research and Training in Mental Health, 1985a

Cohen M, Farkas M, Cohen B: Psychiatric Rehabilitation Trainer Packages: Functional Assessment. Boston, Center for Rehabilitation Research and Training in Mental Health, 1985b

Donergue M: Technical Assistance: Theory, Practice and Politics. New York, Praeger, 1968

Fairweather GW: Methods of Changing Mental Hospital Programs: Progress Report to NIMH, Grant #R12-178887. East Lansing, Michigan State University, 1971

Farkas M, Anthony WA: Training rehabilitation counselors to work in state agencies, rehabilitation and mental health facilities. Rehabilitation Counseling Bulletin 24:129-144, 1980

Farkas M, Cohen M, Nemec P: Psychiatric rehabilitation programs: the gap between orientation and implementation. Boston, Center for Psychosocial Rehabilitation, 1986

Glaser EM, Taylor S: Factors Influencing the Success of Applied Research: Final Report on Contract #43-67-1365, NIMH. Washington, DC Department of Health, Education and Welfare, 1969

Hamilton LS, Muthard JE: Research Utilization Specialists in Vocational Rehabilitation. Gainesville, Florida Research Institute, 1975

Havari D: The Role of the Technical Assistance Expert. Paris, Organization for Economic Co-operation and Development, 1974

Havelock RG: Planning for Innovation through Dissemination and Utilization of Knowledge. Ann Arbor, Institute for Social Research, 1971

Havelock RG, Benne KD: An exploratory study of knowledge utilization, in The Planning of Change, second edition. Edited by Bennis WG, Benne KD, Chin R. New York, Holt, Rinehart and Winston, 1969

Hillhouse-Jones L: Psychiatric rehabilitation training: a trainee's perspective. Florida Community Support Network Newsletter, August 1 and 8, 1984

Jung H, Spaniol L: Planning the Utilization of New Knowledge and Skills: Some Basic Principles for Researchers, Administrators, and Practitioners. Unpublished manuscript. Center for Rehabilitation Research and Training in Mental Health, Boston University, 1981

Kelner FB: A rehabilitation approach to program diagnosis in technical assistance. Psychosocial Rehabilitation Journal 7:32-43, 1984

Muthard JE: Putting rehabilitation knowledge to use. Rehabilitation Monograph II. Gainesville, Rehabilitation Research Institute, 1980

Nemec P: Technical assistance. Unpublished paper. Center for Rehabilitation Research and Training in Mental Health. Boston University, 1983

Pelz DC, Munson RC: A framework for organizational innovating. Unpublished paper. University of Michigan, 1980

Soloff A: The utilization of research. Rehabilitation Literature 33:66-72, 1972

Sufrin SC: Technical Assistance: Theory and Guidelines. Syracuse, Syracuse University Press, 1966

Switzer ME: Forward, in Research and Demonstration Grant Program (revised). Washington, DC, Vocational Rehabilitation Administration, U.S. Department of Health, Education and Welfare, 1965

Zaltman G, Duncan R: Strategies for Planned Change. New York, John Wiley & Sons, 1977

14

Training Psychiatrists in the Treatment of Chronically Disabled Patients

Leonard I. Stein, M.D.
Robert M. Factor, M.D., Ph.D.
Ronald J. Diamond, M.D.

Over the past 15 years there has been an explosion in knowledge in treating the chronically disabled patient. If we were to put into practice what we now know, the vast majority of these patients could be helped to live relatively stable lives in the community. To do this requires both the development of a variety of specific clinical programs and a staff trained to work in those programs. Unfortunately, there is a terrible shortage of both. The shortages of programs and staff are directly related. If more programs were available, more staff would be trained to work in them; and if more staff were trained, more programs would be established. This chapter focuses on the staff side of this equation, and more specifically on psychiatric staff.

The training of psychiatrists in this new technology has been primarily through postresidency, continuing medical education (CME). This has taken the form of CME courses and symposia at the annual meetings of the American Psychiatric Association and the Institute of Hospital and Community Psychiatry; workshops by the Community Support Program branch of the NIMH; and a host of state and regional workshops and conferences, on the chronic patient. However, commensurate activity in residency training programs has been lacking. There are literally just a handful of programs in the

271

country that give their trainees sufficient exposure to the psychosocial aspects of treating the chronically impaired psychiatric patient (White and Bennett 1981; Cutler et al. 1981; Faulkner et al. 1982; Nielson et al. 1981). As a result, the vast majority of psychiatrists graduating from residency training are ill equipped to play a full role in community programs treating these patients. If they work in these programs at all, they usually operate on the periphery of the program as "prescription writers," who have little impact on other aspects of the treatment process; the better psychiatrists leave as quickly as they can get a "more stimulating" practice started. The victims in this scenario are the patients, who do not receive the benefits of comprehensive psychiatric involvement in their total treatment program.

Why have medical educators not incorporated the advances in treatment for the chronic patient into medical school or residency curricula? The two most important reasons are money and the new image that psychiatry is trying to assume.

For academia, money is in very short supply. Departments of psychiatry wishing to expand must do so by moving into areas that will generate money to pay for the expansion, generally by obtaining funds from third-party payors or grants. Most health insurance, including public entitlement programs, will pay for expensive hospitalization, but not for the kind of services required to rehabilitate chronically mentally ill and disabled persons. Since these services are provided by multidisciplinary teams, their activities fall between the cracks of federal granting agencies, which are usually divided along professional boundaries. Thus, the sources of money for expansion—third-party payors and granting agencies—provide little financial incentive for departments of psychiatry to move into this area.

Furthermore, psychiatry is on the march to "remedicalize" its image. There is a tension within departments between the "biologic types," as a new force for change, and the "dynamic types," trying to preserve some of their "turf." While this conflict itself has its own destructive effects, both sides view psychosocial rehabilitation as foreign to psychiatric practice. Because psychosocial rehabilitation combines biological, psychological, and social factors, it does not appear "organic" enough for the biologists nor "psychological" enough for the psychotherapists. Indeed, the way in which psychiatrists doing psychosocial rehabilitation treat social workers, nurses, occupational therapists, et al. as co-workers is sufficient to convince some of their psychiatric colleagues that they are endangering the profession. After all, in medicine, one relates to these other professions as ancillary personnel rather than as co-workers.

Is there a way to overcome these barriers and develop training programs in our medical schools and psychiatric residencies for the treatment of chronically disabled psychiatric patients? We believe the answer is yes. State commissioners of mental health, who are responsible for the public care of the chronic patient, recognize that if community-based rehabilitation services are not expanded to reduce hospital use, state mental health budgets will face a severe crisis. The cost of hospital care is rising at such a rapid rate that within a few years it "may capsize other essential components of the public mental health system" (Goodrick 1984). Some of these commissioners recognize that psychiatry is a key element in the success of community programs, and would be willing to subsidize training of psychiatrists who would work in the public sector with chronic patients. In return, however, departments of psychiatry would need to become involved with public-sector service agencies.

Another even more readily available source of training funds is the already budgeted salaries for psychiatrists in community mental health centers. This money can be spent on salaries for faculty and stipends for psychiatric residents, to the advantage of both the centers and the departments of psychiatry. The faculty and residents will enrich the centers' programming and improve the quality of psychiatric care. Psychiatric residents will learn much clinically and organizationally about the delivery of services to seriously ill psychiatric patients, especially about the advantages of teamwork with nonmedical mental health professionals.

The training program described in this chapter is funded, in part, by the latter method. The psychiatric staff of the Dane County Mental Health Center are full-time faculty in the University of Wisconsin Medical School Department of Psychiatry. Their salaries are paid in part by the center's budget, as are the stipends for the residents, thus giving the department a vested interest in maintaining a collaborative relationship with the center.

THE RESIDENCY TRAINING PROGRAM AT THE UNIVERSITY OF WISCONSIN MEDICAL SCHOOL

The community psychiatry training program at the University of Wisconsin Medical School has implemented a curriculum that successfully teaches residents the necessary skills for working with severely disabled, chronically mentally ill patients living in the community. In addition, the training program demonstrates to residents that they can be effective in treating severely ill patients, and that the experience can be professionally rewarding.

The key elements of the training program include:

1. a set of clearly articulated learning goals for the program
2. an experience with an effective service delivery system that enables residents to be effective; this experience involves the resident in the total care of the patient, a wide variety of professional skills can be utilized, not simply the prescription of medication
3. staff psychiatrists who work alongside the residents and serve as role models

4. quality supervision provided by psychiatrists who are knowledge-able about both clinical issues in working with severely ill patients in a community setting and the service-delivery system where the residents are working
5. a didactic program conceptually grounded in research findings, and closely tied to the residents' clinical experience

The Key Elements, in Detail

Learning goals for the clinical rotation in community psychiatry
Psychiatry residents at the University of Wisconsin start their re-quired six-month, 20-hours/week, community psychiatry rotation in their second year of training, after finishing a first year of inpatient rotations on acute care wards. Inpatient wards have a clear, hier-archical administrative structure and clear, short-range treatment goals. In the second year, residents are then plunged into the more complex and less structured world of the outpatient programs at the mental health center. There, the treatment goal is the less well-defined task of helping patients make a life-long adjustment to the community.

Residents and other professional staff have much less control over patients than they had in the hospital. Not only are patients under less supervisory control but so are the residents. During their first-year inpatient rotations, virtually every decision made by resi-dents was supervised and reviewed. During their second year outpa-tient rotations, residents function more autonomously, commensu-rate with their increased experience. Even with close supervision, however, this new autonomy increases their sense of vulnerability and their feeling of anxiety.

Clear expectations for the rotation help the residents decrease their anxiety, provide a focus for their experience, and help provide a structure to ease the transition from the hospital to the community environment. We discuss these educational goals with the residents at the beginning of the community psychiatry rotation, and we moni-tor the success of both the trainees and the training program in meeting these goals as the rotation progresses. The goals of the com-munity psychiatry rotation include:

Assessment
1. learning how to establish rapport and interview seriously ill out-patients, including those who are psychotic
2. learning how to make a comprehensive psychosocial assessment of a patient, including identifying specific needs that must be met in order for the patient to live stably in the community
3. learning how to make accurate psychiatric and other medical diagnoses

4. learning how to assess the underlying psychodynamic factors influencing the behavior of severely ill patients
5. learning how to assess a patient's disability, both for treatment-planning purposes and to help the patient obtain needed financial entitlements

Treatment planning
1. learning how to develop comprehensive treatment plans that address pharmacological, psychological, and psychosocial issues
2. learning how to distinguish the goals, strategies, and tactics of both short- and long-term plans

Intervention
1. learning how to work with chronically disabled patients utilizing both traditional and nontraditional approaches, individually, with families, and with groups
2. learning crisis intervention: how to stabilize and treat acutely disturbed patients in an outpatient setting
3. learning to deal with countertransference issues in themselves and other staff

Psychopharmacology
1. learning the indications and side effects of psychotropic medications, with emphasis on effective use in an outpatient setting
2. learning about interactions of drugs with each other and with medical illness
3. learning how to influence patients to take medications reliably and to stimulate their active participation in the overall treatment plan
4. learning how to integrate psychotropic medications with other parts of a comprehensive treatment program

Knowledge of the system
1. learning how to work effectively with families and other parts of patients' natural support systems
2. learning how to work with parts of the mental health system outside of the mental health center
3. learning how to mobilize resources and services outside of the mental health system

Working with nonmedical mental health professionals
1. learning how to work cooperatively with, and use the expertise of, nonmedical mental health professionals within the complex environment of a multidisciplinary team
2. learning how to function effectively as a consultant to non-medical mental health professionals

Attitudes
1. learning how to set realistic treatment goals for chronically disabled patients
2. learning to help maintain patients when we do not know how to cure
3. understanding patients within the context of their entire lives, rather than in the narrow setting of the inpatient ward or the outpatient clinic

Our fundamental goal is to have residents adopt a comprehensive approach to the care of these difficult and demanding patients. Individual treatment elements that might seem mundane or of low priority in their own right often take on a new significance when viewed within a larger context. For example, residents often dismiss the work of preparing a well-written report for a disability determination as "bureaucratic paperwork" (American Psychiatric Association, 1983; Goldman 1985). In reality, the disability determination and the consequent ability of the patient to receive entitlement benefits such as SSI/SSDI might be as important as psychotropic medication in helping the patient achieve stability in the community.

Working in an effective treatment system
The community psychiatry training program at the University of Wisconsin utilizes the Dane County Mental Health Center as its clinical site. This center has been recognized nationally as a model in the community treatment of the chronically mentally ill, and it has been selected by the NIMH as a National Resource Training Center for community-support programs. The Dane County Mental Health Center includes a number of different program elements that address the differing needs of patients.

In addition to the program elements described below, the system of care for the chronically mentally ill in Dane County also includes a number of agencies outside the center with which the residents must learn to work. The system of care involves coordination with housing and vocational agencies, police departments, welfare offices, and individuals, such as local landlords, who are important in the lives of patients but who are outside of the formal mental health system.

With this system of care, patients can be provided with whatever supports that are needed to allow them to live in the community, usually in their own homes and apartments. The support to a patient can be as infrequent as occasional contacts for supportive psychotherapy and medical monitoring, or as intensive as contact with staff seven days a week to ensure that the patient has eaten and has taken necessary medications. It can be as simple as going with a patient to the laundromat or the grocery store to ensure that his clothes are clean and that food is in his apartment; or as sophisticated as conducting family therapy or negotiating with a patient who is decompensating because she refuses to take needed medication. While psychiatric residents do not need to make many laundromat visits, they need to understand the practical and therapeutic value of this activity for the patient.

The result of this comprehensive system of care is that even severely ill, chronically disabled patients can be treated successfully in the community with a clear improvement in their quality of life (Stein and Diamond 1985; Stein and Test 1980). The cost of high-quality, community-based care for the chronically mentally ill is no greater than the alternative, revolving-door care that has these patients rotating in and out of the hospital (Gilman and Diamond 1985; Weisbrod et al. 1980).

Psychiatric residents working in this comprehensive system experience firsthand that treatment can be effective and that their own interventions do make a difference in the quality of their patients' lives. It becomes obvious to the residents that many of the patients they are treating in this system would spend much of their lives in the hospital if the treatment were not available. Furthermore, the residents learn firsthand that even "treatment-resistant" patients often can be treated successfully, if approached in the right way.

Role models
All too often, residents are sent to work with chronically mentally ill patients while their faculty remain back at the university. While residents might be told that they are doing important work, the nonverbal message is clear. A key part of the University of Wisconsin training program is that full-time academic faculty work alongside the residents, treating the same patients and working with the same multidisciplinary teams. While there are many benefits of having faculty on-site in terms of improving the quality of supervision, a major benefit is that it gives legitimacy and status to working in this setting with this population. The absence of role models and good clinical training sites may explain why many young psychiatrists do not find the chronically mentally ill "an attractive population to treat" (Mirabi 1985; Eichler 1982), and may leave jobs in the public sector at the first opportunity.

Three full-time academic faculty members (the authors) are on the staff at the center. One of them is the medical director of the center, while two of them function as medical directors of two of the program elements. Each is involved in other aspects of the residency training program. All provide general resident supervision and lead seminars for residents; currently, one is the residency training director, and another is head of the curriculum committee. Residents view the rotation at the center as a core part of the residency training program, taught by core faculty. Even those who do not choose a career in community psychiatry still view it as a valid area for research and for seeking professional positions following residency.

Supervision

Supervision is a critical element in making the community psychiatry rotation an effective training experience. At the beginning of the rotation, the residents are often overwhelmed by the difference between the mental health center and the more familiar hospital. They are intimidated by working with severely ill patients outside the hospital. They are also confused about their role amidst all the other professionals who work with the same patients.

Approximately half of the supervision time is spent dealing with clinical problems presented by patients. The other half is spent discussing the role the residents play in working effectively with the rest of the team. We believe it is important to focus supervision on both of these areas.

We have found that group supervision is a useful adjunct to more traditional individual supervision. Once a week, the four residents on the center rotation meet with the faculty supervisors, all of whom also work at the center. Discussions about particularly difficult patients often turn out to involve questions of who is responsible for what, how to deal with different professional orientations, how to set limits, or how to deal with countertransference issues. Many of these issues are common to all of the residents, and dealing with them in a group allows each individual to see more easily the influence of the system on his or her own experience.

Didactic teaching

All four residents participate in a weekly seminar for the entire six months of their rotation. The goal of the seminar is to connect the clinical experience to a broader academic understanding of some of the main issues in community psychiatry and the treatment of chronically disabled psychiatric patients. We mingle discussion of assigned readings with discussion of clinical cases that bear on the topic. At times, the seminar becomes a focused extension of the group supervision. Consistent with our view that community psychiatry is an exciting career option following residency, we include the subject of how to negotiate a job in a community setting that both meets the service needs of the agency and is professionally and personally rewarding for the psychiatrist. The broad topics covered are as follows:

1. The role of the psychiatrist in community mental health
   (3 sessions)
2. Treatment of the chronically mentally ill in the community
   (4 sessions)
3. Assessment of disability and criteria for entitlement
   (1 session)
4. Economic considerations in mental health treatment
   (3 sessions)

5. Psychotherapy with the chronically ill (including families) (2 sessions)
6. Issues of social control: labeling theory, whose agent is the psychiatrist?; confidentiality, dangerousness and its prediction, criminal behavior among the chronically mentally ill, and involuntary and coercive treatment (5 sessions)
7. Chronic mental illness as a life style (3 sessions)
8. Transcultural psychiatry (1 session)
9. Alcohol and drug abuse (1 session)

Other topics germane to community psychiatry, such as management of patients who are acutely psychotic, violent, intoxicated, etc., are covered in a seminar on emergency psychiatry.

Clinical Experiences
As already noted, all residents take a six-month, half-time rotation in community psychiatry at the Dane County Mental Health Center. (During this rotation, the other half of their time is spent at the university hospital seeing outpatients, covering the emergency service, and attending seminars and supervision.) In the center, they work in the units devoted in large part to delivering a program of titred care to the chronically severely mentally ill (see Stein and Diamond 1985, for a detailed description of these units). Four residents are on the rotation at a time. Each works in both the Adult Clinical Services Unit (ACS) and the Crisis-Intervention Services Unit (CIS); in addition, two work in the support network day-treatment unit (SN), while the other two work in the mobile community-treatment unit (MCT). The hours spent per week by each resident in each unit are shown below:

	ACS	CIS	SN	MCT
2 residents	4.5	10.5	5	
2 residents	4.5	5.5		10

As an indication of the high level involvement of residents in the rotation, most continue to follow a small number of patients at the center during their final two years of residency.

Crisis-Intervention Services (CIS)
This unit provides 24-hour, seven-day/week crisis-intervention and crisis-resolution services. It has a mobile team of professional crisis workers who can see individual patients and families in the community as well as at the center; and, in addition, operates a 24-hour crisis telephone line. Most initial contacts with the unit are through this crisis line. The unit's staff provides emergency coverage for other center clinicians whose patients are in crisis and also serves a large number of people who are not regular center patients. The staff

screens all psychiatric hospital admissions in Dane County that are paid for by public funds. When hospitalization is not appropriate, they help provide or arrange for alternative treatment. This gatekeeping function is successful in providing treatment in the community for 75 percent of patients who typically would be hospitalized without such treatment.

Residents in this unit act as both crisis workers and as medical consultants. Nearly always, they see patients along with another crisis worker, and occasionally along with a faculty supervisor. In addition to learning to prescribe medications to patients in crisis, they learn to treat these patients using a variety of psychological and social interventions. Depending on their own interests, they may focus some of their time on working with families, consulting to the county jail, acting as the attending psychiatrist for center patients admitted to the psychiatry ward at the community hospital, and consulting to other community agencies.

Faculty supervisors also see patients and act as consultants to this unit. Faculty thus have ongoing side-by-side experience with the residents. Residents may call on faculty for immediate consultation when necessary and discuss less emergent problems with them during regular supervision. Residents can also observe faculty doing the same kinds of work they are learning to do, as well as doing cotherapy with faculty.

Mobile Community Treatment (MCT)
This unit is modeled after the Training in Community Living Program (Stein and Test 1980). It was designed to provide intensive, assertive treatment for the most difficult chronically ill patients in the community, most of whom would otherwise be hospitalized, longterm. It serves approximately 100 patients and operates seven days per week with a clinical staff (not counting the psychiatrists) of eight nurses and social workers. They provide aggressive case management, close monitoring of clinical status and medications (on a daily basis, if necessary), assistance with tasks of community living (such as help with maintaining an apartment, shopping, laundry, etc.), and daily socialization activities. Most of these patients are too disturbed to be able to participate in extensive group activity, and much of the work done by this unit is done in the field. Case-management responsibilities are shared by the staff as a whole, operating as a team. The team discusses each patient, at least very briefly, on a daily basis and all the staff, including the residents and the medical director (a faculty member), meet one afternoon per week for more extensive clinical discussions.

Two residents each spend 10 hours per week at MCT. They have an opportunity to observe and participate in a unit that is highly effective in helping severely ill patients live in the community. They spend about one-third of their time working with the staff doing outreach visits with patients, working with their families, and intervening in crises. As this activity closely parallels some of the experience in the CIS unit, the two residents who work at MCT spend less time in the CIS unit than do the residents who work at SN. A third of their time is spent doing medical evaluations. They almost always see patients with one of the nurses or social workers in the unit, and occasionally also with the medical director. The final third of their time is spent in staff meetings and informal consultations to the staff. The residents assigned here have an opportunity to work alongside both psychiatric faculty and nonmedical staff. They function as part of the treatment team and develop relationships with the members of the team and the patients over an extended period.

Support Network (SN)
This unit is a psychosocial rehabilitation center serving, five days per week, approximately 200 adults with diagnoses of schizophrenia, major affective disorders, and severe personality disorders. It has a clinical staff of 10 (not counting the psychiatrists), who have backgrounds in social work, vocational rehabilitation, and psychiatric nursing. The program works with patients who have at least some motivation to participate in treatment and who can tolerate group activities, though they are not as functionally intact as those served by ACS. The staff provides case-management services; vocational support, and a daily schedule of activities for recreation, skills training, group therapy, and supportive counseling. About 90 percent of the patients in the program take medication at some time. Of these, about 40 percent see private psychiatrists in the community, and the other 60 percent have their medications prescribed at SN by the medical director (a faculty member) or one of the two residents. All staff participate in overall monitoring of patients. Each patient has a case manager and a primary psychiatric nurse.

Two residents each spend one five-hour day per week at SN. The residents have an opportunity to observe and participate in various facets of the operation of an effective program that helps chronically severely ill adults live in the community. They also get experience and supervision in doing evaluations, managing medications, and working closely with both psychiatric nurses and with nonmedical mental health professionals in a consultative capacity over an extended period. On his or her day at SN, each resident and the medical director begin with a one-hour group supervisory session, along with the nurse clinicians who regularly work with that resident. Together, they discuss the patients who were seen by the nurses the previous week and the patients who will be seen in the coming week. The resident then sees several patients, along with each patient's nurse. These appointments are scheduled by the patient's nurse at intervals determined in the group supervision and are used to do initial evaluations of new patients, to change medications, to provide periodic monitoring by a physician, and to treat crises. Like the residents, the medical director also sees patients along with the primary nurse, and frequently sees a patient with a resident.

Each resident and the medical director attend a twice-weekly staff meeting. They participate in the general clinical and administrative discussions, as well as in discussions of clinical issues concerning specific patients. One of the residents co-leads a medication group with the medical director (for a further description of this group, see Wilson, Diamond, and Factor 1985). Depending on the particular interests of the resident, he or she may co-lead another group or see an individual patient or family, usually along with another staff member.

Adult Clinical Services (ACS)

This unit is an outpatient clinic where patients can see a psychotherapist for individual or group therapy or supportive counseling, and can see a psychiatrist for medications. It serves many schizophrenic patients who are relatively stable, who are functional enough to be able to attend appointments on a scheduled basis, and who need little service other than the above. The residents spend approximately four and a half hours per week in this unit in scheduled appointments. They evaluate and follow patients for medication who have been referred by a center psychotherapist. They also consult to center psychotherapists on difficult clinical problems. They learn to do brief and effective evaluations, develop consultative relationships with nonmedical therapists, and become skilled at prescribing a wide range of medications to outpatients.

As in CIS, faculty supervisors also work in this unit and thus are familiar with its operation. Faculty supervisors are available for consultation to the residents, for face-to-face evaluation of patients with residents, and for co-therapy.

CONCLUSION

Learning to work with chronically disabled psychiatric patients involves acquiring a broad base of knowledge and a complex range of skills. The training must be incorporated into basic residency training programs for general psychiatrists. In this chapter, we have described the key elements of the training program in community psychiatry at the University of Wisconsin Medical School Department of Psychiatry. The residency training program and supervising faculty are affiliated with and partially funded by the Dane County Mental Health Center to the benefit of both. This marriage between the public mental health care provider and the academic psychiatric training program has produced a happy extended family and a fertile environment for training future generations of psychiatrists.

REFERENCES
American Psychiatric Association, Committee on Rehabilitation: Guidelines for psychiatric evaluation of social security disability claimants. Hosp Community Psychiatry 34:1044–1051, 1983

American Psychiatric Association, Division of Government Relations: Testimony presented before the Subcommittee on Social Security, Ways and Means Committee, U.S. House of Representatives (unpublished reproduction). Washington, DC, American Psychiatric Association, 1983

Cutler DL, Bloom JD, Shore JH: Training psychiatrists to work with community support systems for chronically mentally ill persons. Am J Psychiatry 138:98–191, 1981

Eichler S: Why young psychiatrists choose not to work with chronic patients. Hosp Community Psychiatry 33:1023–1024, 1982

Faulkner LR, Eaton JS Jr, Bloom JD, et al: The CMHC as a setting for residency education. Community Ment Health J 18:3–10, 1982

Gilman SR, Diamond RJ: Economic analysis in community treatment of the chronically mentally ill, in The Training in Community Living Model: A Decade of Experience; The New Direction for Mental Health Services, no. 26. Edited by Stein LI, Test MA. San Francisco, Jossey-Bass, 1985

Goldman HH, Runck B: Social Security Administration revises mental disability rules. Hosp Community Psychiatry 36:343–345, 1985

Goodrick D: Survival of public inpatient mental health systems: strategies for constructive change. Presented at the National Conference of State Legislatures Program, Boston, July 25, 1984

Mirabi M, Weinman ML, Magnetti MS, et al: Professional attitudes toward the chronic mentally ill. Hosp Community Psychiatry 36:404–405, 1985

Nielson AC, Stein LI, Talbott JA, et al: Encouraging psychiatrists to work with chronic patients: opportunities and limitations of residency education. Hosp Community Psychiatry 32:767–775, 1981

Stein LI, Diamond RJ: A program for difficult-to-treat patients, in The Training in Community Living Model: A Decade of Experience, New Directions for Mental Health Services, no. 26. San Francisco, Jossey-Bass, 1985

Stein LI, Test MA: Alternative to mental hospital treatment, I: conceptual model, treatment program, and clinical evaluation. Arch Gen Psychiatry 37:392–397, 1980

Weisbrod BA, Test MA, Stein LI: Alternative to mental hospital treatment, II: economic benefit-cost analysis. Arch Gen Psychiatry 37:400–405, 1980

White HS, Bennett MB: Training psychiatric residents in chronic care. Hosp Community Psychiatry 32:339–343, 1981

Wilson WH, Diamond RJ, Factor RM: An approach to group therapy with severely disturbed patients. Yale J Biol Med 58:363–372, 1985

Section IV

ADMINISTRATIVE AND LEGAL ISSUES: THE CLINICAL PERSPECTIVE

15

The Psychiatric Consultation for Social Security Disability Insurance

James Krajeski, M.D.*
Melvin Lipsett, M.D.

I n this chapter, we address the relationship between pathology and disability and the way this relationship influences how and what kinds of reports are prepared by clinicians for the Social Security Disability Insurance (SSDI) program. Since psychiatrists are called upon to perform evaluations and render reports to the Social Security Administration (SSA), it is important to be familiar with the system's statutory, regulatory, and policy requirements to ensure that the patient receives a fair decision.

The SSDI system has legal as well as medical parameters, and reports developed and submitted by treating or consulting physicians are processed in accord with the rules and regulations governing the SSA disability determination process. In the Social Security Disability Insurance system, the disability evaluation report is utilized by both claims examiners and Social Security medical reviewers to determine whether the claimant is capable of work or not.

---

* The views contained in this chapter are those of the authors, and do not represent those of the Social Security Administration.

Unfortunately, unless one specializes in a practice directed specifically at disability examinations, a clinician may have little opportunity to learn how best to provide the data that are necessary for a complete disability report. Certainly, the topic of how to prepare specialized clinical reports is not often seen in curricula of residency or continuing medical education programs. Rarely does one obtain feedback from agencies about the usefulness of prior reports, a procedure which could result in the preparation of better reports for the requesting agency.

Preparing a useful clinical report will depend on the psychiatrist knowing for whom the report is being prepared and the factors upon which the disability determination is based. In this way, the report may be tailored to provide specific data which will lead to an equitable, correct decision.

Psychiatrists are trained to examine, to evaluate pathology, and to arrive at a differential diagnosis utilizing criteria contained in the *Diagnostic and Statistical Manual of Mental Disorders, Third Edition, Revised (DSM-III-R)*. This process is important for any disability system and forms the basis upon which the psychiatrist documents the extent of an individual's impairment. Documentation of disability may require a new frame of reference for the psychiatrist because pathology does not necessarily equate to disability. For example, an individual diagnosed with "severe paranoid schizophrenia" may be able to function very well in a particular job setting and so may not be disabled under the agency's criteria. This chapter provides a suggested approach to preparing a report for the Social Security Disability Insurance program.

THE PSYCHIATRIC CONSULTATION FOR DISABILITY IN THE SOCIAL SECURITY SYSTEM

Three basic concepts underlie the determination of disability by the Social Security Administration:

1. There must be a medically determinable impairment (a mental disorder, in this case).
2. The medically determinable impairment must result in an inability to work. To receive benefits, the claimant must be unable to perform any work available in substantial numbers in the national economy. For most categories of workers, consideration is given to factors such as age, education, and prior work experience in addition to medical factors in determining whether there is work that the claimant can do.
3. The inability to work resulting from the medically determinable impairment must last or be expected to last for at least 12 months, or the impairment can be expected to result in death. (However, this latter provision would rarely, if ever, apply in mental disorder cases.)

Therefore, the disability report is expected to document that: (1) a mental disorder exists, and (2) that it interferes with the individual's ability to work over a period of time.

Establishing the Existence of a Mental Disorder

The Social Security criterion that there must be a medically determinable *impairment* implies that one must establish the existence of a mental disorder. The SSA disability-determination process necessitates that the data provided be sufficient to enable a physician who has not seen the claimant to review the evidence and make a determination based solely on reported findings. The SSA physician–reviewer is not to make decision(s) based solely on conclusions of providers' reports without the objective data to support the conclusions.

New disability regulations for cases involving mental disorders were promulgated in 1985 (see Appendix). These regulations, which are commonly referred to as "the Listings," have updated Social Security terminology to be consistent with *DSM-III-R*. The guidelines for adjudication of cases involving mental disorders have been divided into eight broad categories, including:

1. organic mental disorders
2. schizophrenic, paranoid, and other psychotic disorders
3. affective disorders
4. mental retardation and autism
5. anxiety-related disorders
6. somatoform disorders
7. personality disorders
8. substance addiction disorders

Reports should clearly indicate the specific *DSM-III-R* diagnosis. The diagnosis or diagnoses of the mental disorder should be accompanied by the specific findings (signs, symptoms, and laboratory findings) which the clinician has used in determining the appropriate diagnosis. Though it is preferable to have an exact diagnosis, cases can still be adjudicated properly by SSA if the existence of a mental disorder can be established without an exact diagnosis. In cases in which there is uncertainty about the exact diagnosis, the actual medical findings should be included and a differential diagnosis discussed.

In addition to the psychiatric history, a thorough mental status examination is essential in establishing the existence of a mental disorder. The specific findings, both positive and negative, of the mental status examination should be included. In the disability report, it is inappropriate to report only conclusions drawn from the examination. For example, it is not sufficient to state only, "There is no evidence of organicity," or, "The claimant exhibited mild organicity." Instead, the specific findings should be detailed; for example, "The claimant was able to subtract serial 7s very slowly with several errors, as follows: 93, 86, 81, 74, 64, 56, 64, 55, 48, 41, 37, 30, 23, 14, 7, 0"; or, "The claimant was able to remember 3 objects after 10 minutes, recall 7 digits forward and 3 backward."

Establishing the Restriction of Function Due to a Mental Disorder
Once the existence of a mental disorder has been established, then the Social Security medical reviewer determines to what degree the claimant's ability to function is limited. This determination is based on a number of factors. The 1985 changes in the mental impairment regulations for evaluating severity of impairment incorporated four areas to be evaluated: (1) activities of daily living; (2) difficulties in maintaining social functioning; (3) deficiencies of concentration, persistence, or pace resulting in frequent failure to complete tasks in a timely manner (in work settings or elsewhere); (4) episodes of deterioration or decompensation in work or worklike settings which cause the individual to withdraw from that situation and/or to experience exacerbation of signs and symptoms (which include deterioration of adaptive behaviors). Therefore, the psychiatric report should delineate the ways in which a claimant is either capable or incapable of functioning, with particular attention to the above areas. Each of these areas is considered in more detail below. (See Appendix, also.)

Activities of daily living
The psychiatric report should focus on how the claimant is limited in his or her ability to perform activities commonly encountered in daily life, such as grooming, cooking, driving, paying bills, etc. The limitations should be clearly related to the claimant's mental disorder, rather than other factors. For example, some individuals may have significant limitations in their activities due to a lack of money, or a need to remain at home to care for a family member. Such limitations would not be considered in determining an individual's capacity to work. There should be a specific description of activities rather than such global conclusions as, "The claimant is not capable of caring for his or her personal needs," or "The claimant doesn't do anything with his or her time." Instead, such specific data should be provided as, "Due to a persistent preoccupation with hallucinations, the claimant customarily neglects his personal hygiene. He does not brush his teeth, bathes infrequently, and rarely combs or washes his hair."

Ability to maintain appropriate social functioning
To document this section of the psychiatric report, the psychiatrist should provide specific data regarding the claimant's ability to get along with other people. For example, does the claimant have any

difficulty relating to other individuals? Are there specific circumstances or specific times when the claimant has difficulty in maintaining appropriate relationships? How does any difficulty in maintaining relationships manifest itself? Specific examples should be cited to document the difficulties.

Deficiencies of concentration, persistence, or pace
This criterion was added in the 1985 disability regulations to focus attention on those individuals who have difficulty sustaining activities. Many individuals may have the ability to perform tasks, but may be unable to sustain the activities over a normal workday or workweek, or perform activities in a timely manner. Documentation of this particular facet of the claimant's history should be based on both the psychiatric examination and on history. From the clinical examination, one may note difficulty in sustained concentration. An awareness of the claimant's day-to-day functioning, prior work attempts, or of the claimant's functioning in such structured settings as day-treatment centers, etc., may also permit the clinician to make observations about the claimant's ability to concentrate adequately, persist in activities, or perform at a reasonable pace. All observations should include actual examples derived from the clinical examination and history, or other relevant data available to the consultant such as psychological testing or work-evaluation reports.

Deterioration in work or worklike settings
Documentation of this characteristic should include any evidence which indicates that the claimant has difficulty functioning adequately under the "stress" of work. This might include episodes of deterioration or decompensation under any circumstances which the claimant experiences as stressful. The criterion would apply not only to actual failed work attempts, but also would apply to decompensation under conditions which may mimic work situations. Examples of these might include school, rehabilitation programs, or other structured settings where the claimant is required to make decisions, complete tasks, keep to a schedule, interact with supervisors or peers, etc.

Cases in which the clinician is concerned about the ability of the claimant to withstand the pressures of the work situation should be documented with actual examples. These examples should include an account of the precipitants which lead to decompensation or deterioration. The extent of decompensation should be documented clearly as should the period of time and recovery. If a claimant is capable of functioning adequately in some kinds of work situations or worklike situations, that should also be documented. Such conclusions as, "The patient decompensates under the slightest stress" are of no value unless the supporting documentation for the conclusion is included.

Residual Functional Capacity

In the adjudication of Social Security disability claims, the Social Security medical reviewer must determine if the claimant has limitations in the four areas described above. In cases in which it is evident that the claimant has some limitations in his or her ability to function, but does not have the precise findings described in the Listings, the Social Security medical reviewer ordinarily determines the claimant's residual functional capacity (RFC). RFC may be defined as a multidimensional description of the work-related abilities which an individual retains in spite of medical impairment. In other words, it is a description of the abilities which the claimant retains. Depending upon the claimant's actual abilities, a decision will be made by SSA regarding the claimant's ability to perform actual work. Because the clinician has no way of knowing in advance whether a particular patient will require an assessment of RFC, reports should contain material that will permit the SSA medical reviewer to make such an assessment. RFC assessments sometimes may require more precise data than it is possible to obtain from a standard psychiatric examination. However, insofar as possible, the psychiatrist should provide data which will assist in evaluating RFC.

The RFC determination addresses four primary areas which enlarge upon or are derived from the functional criteria already discussed: (1) understanding and memory; (2) sustained concentration and persistence; (3) social interaction; and (4) adaptation. In completing this assessment, the SSA medical reviewer is guided by the following items under each heading:

Understanding and memory
1. the ability to remember locations and worklike procedures
2. the ability to understand and remember very short and simple instructions
3. the ability to understand and remember detailed instructions

Sustained concentration and persistence
1. the ability to carry out very short and simple instructions
2. the ability to carry out detailed instructions
3. the ability to maintain attention and concentration for extended periods
4. the ability to perform activities within a schedule, maintain regular attendance, and be punctual within customary tolerances
5. the ability to sustain an ordinary routine without special supervision
6. the ability to work in coordination or proximity to others without being distracted by them
7. the ability to make simple work-related decisions
8. the ability to complete a normal workday and workweek without interruptions from psychologically based symptoms and to per-

form at a consistent pace without an unreasonable number and length of rest periods

Social interaction
1. the ability to interact appropriately with the general public
2. the ability to ask simple questions or request assistance
3. the ability to accept instructions and respond appropriately to criticism from supervisors
4. the ability to get along with co-workers or peers without distracting them or exhibiting behavior extremes
5. the ability to maintain socially appropriate behavior and adhere to basic standards of neatness and cleanliness

Adaptation
1. the ability to respond appropriately to changes in the work setting
2. the ability to be aware of normal hazards and take appropriate precautions
3. the ability to travel in unfamiliar places or use public transportation
4. the ability to set realistic goals or make plans independent of others

It will be obvious that making the above determinations is sometimes very difficult and may require refined evaluations, such as work sampling evaluations or psychological testing. However, by keeping in mind the very detailed kind of conclusions which must be drawn, the psychiatrist can attempt to provide sound data upon which such conclusions can be based. If the clinician is aware of any additional restrictions which specifically may prohibit the claimant from performing certain types of duties or occupations, these should also be detailed. For example, a claimant who has a fixed delusional system that involves telephones may be prohibited from working in situations which involve answering telephones, but may be capable of work which customarily involves no telephone contact.

Establishing the Extent of Impairment over Time
The Social Security law essentially requires that a claimant be disabled or expect to be disabled for a period of not less than 12 months. This does not mean that the claimant has to be found incapable of working every day of the 12 months. However, it does mean that SSA must determine that the claimant is not expected to be able to function in a work setting, even though there are some periods of time during the 12-month period when the claimant may function rather well. Making this determination requires that there be an adequate history of the claimant's functioning over a period of time. Therefore, the evidence provider should detail the variability of the claimant's condition over time. This should be quite specific, with descriptions

of the claimant during times of exacerbation and during times of remission. The relative length and frequency of exacerbations and remissions should be indicated, thereby adequately describing the course of illness.

Problems to Avoid in Preparing Disability Reports

A number of inadequacies can be avoided if the clinician remembers that the reviewers are to make decisions based on objective clinical data, rather than solely on conclusions of the disability report. Unfortunately, reports sometimes fail to provide the supporting data necessary to establish the existence of a mental disorder. This may result from an inadequate history or mental status examination. Diagnoses which are not part of the current *Diagnostic and Statistical Manual* should be avoided. For example, diagnoses such as "borderline schizophrenia" or "pseudoneurotic schizophrenia" are likely to be confusing because they do not have a universally accepted meaning. The use of terms which are not part of the current official nomenclature may also bring into question the expertise of the provider.

In attempting to establish the extent of functional restrictions experienced by the claimant, it is important to avoid making conclusions without providing data which support the conclusions. Generalizations or overly broad conclusions may also bring into question the validity of reports. For example, such statements as, "The claimant doesn't do anything all day" or "The claimant spends all his time sleeping," may be intended to convey very limited ability to function but, in fact, are so global and extreme that they cannot be taken seriously. A reviewer can only guess at the meaning of the statement.

Reports also may fail to make a "connection" between the functional restrictions and the existence of a mental disorder. An individual may be unconventional in appearance or behavior. Such lack of conformity may interfere with the individual's ability to relate to other people. However, if the lack of conventional behavior is due to a life-style choice, it may be disregarded; while, if it is due to a mental illness, it would have to be considered in the disability determination. Reports should indicate clearly whether restrictions in functioning are due to a mental disorder or due to other factors.

In some cases, reports may make the claimant appear to function more adequately than is actually the case. The use of the term *in remission* should be qualified carefully. It may be interpreted to mean that the claimant no longer has a mental disorder and, therefore, would not be considered disabled. On the other hand, it may be used to apply to individuals who continue to demonstrate residual symptoms or signs of illness and who may be functionally restricted. Therefore, terms such as *in remission* need to be explained carefully. Also, descriptions of individuals indicating that they participate in a wide range of activities may suggest that a claimant is not restricted in his or her functioning when, in fact, the claimant can be quite restricted if one considers the independence, appropriateness, and effectiveness of the claimant's actions. For example, individuals who live in structured settings may participate in a wide range of activities only because they are assisted and encouraged to do so. In such cases, reports should indicate these facts clearly.

WRITING THE REPORT

It is useful to follow a standard format in preparing the disability-evaluation report. The following outline has been adapted from Social Security guidelines and incorporates the 1985 regulation changes. The outline can be used by both psychiatrists performing consultative examinations and by those providing medical reports on patients they are treating.

Identification Data

This section should contain the claimant's name, age, sex, Social Security number, date first seen, frequency of contacts, and date of most recent exam.

History of the Present Illness

The history should establish a longitudinal picture of the claimant's illness. The source of the history should be indicated and there should be an estimate of the reliability of the history.

Present illness: Be as detailed and specific as possible.

1. Onset: Indicate the date and nature of the onset of the illness. Include data which indicate when the claimant stopped working or alleged that he or she could not work, as well as the reasons for being unable to work.
2. Claimant's complaint: Describe the claimant's symptoms and the manner in which they interfere with the claimant's ability to function.
3. Course of the illness: Describe the variability of the illness over time.
4. Hospitalizations: Provide dates, locations, durations, and other relevant data, such as admission and discharge summaries, if available.
5. Outpatient treatment: Describe previous treatment, including treating sources, dates, duration, medications, response, etc.
6. Laboratory findings: Include psychological testing results (with subtest scores), blood and radiographic studies, EEG findings, etc., if they have been performed. Provide a copy of the actual laboratory report if available.
7. Ability to function: Describe in detail and with examples, the claimant's abilities or limitations in the following areas:
   - activities of daily living;

- social functioning (ability to interact appropriately and communicate effectively with others);
- concentration, persistence, and pace in completing tasks;
- deterioration in work or worklike settings, causing the individual either to withdraw from that situation and/or to experience exacerbations of signs and symptoms (be specific regarding dates, precipitating stress, the nature and duration of the
  decompensation, and the extent and time of recovery).

Past history: Describe educational, social, military, marital, and occupational history relevant to:

1. establishing the existence of a mental disorder;
2. establishing the level of functioning during the time of the alleged
   disability; and
3. establishing a prognosis.

In many cases, early family history may have little relevance to the
disability report. This section should also establish a baseline level
for the claimant's functioning prior to the onset of the mental disorder.

History of physical illness: Include any significant history of physical
illness which may have some bearing on the claimant's ability to
function.

Mental status examination: Describe in detail! Do not use conclusions
without the findings which support the conclusions.

1. general appearance, attitude and behavior;
2. nature of thinking and content of speech;
3. mood and affect;
4. orientation, memory, ability to abstract and calculate, general
   knowledge;
5. judgment and insight.

Diagnosis
Use current American Psychiatric Association nomenclature. Be cer-
tain that the report provides the data to support the diagnosis. Use all
DSM-III-R axes.

Prognosis/Medical Assessment
Provide an estimate of the future course of the illness. Include recommendations for treatment and the expected result of treatment. Provide a rationale for the prognosis given. Give your opinions regarding
the claimant's ability to reason or make occupational, personal, or
social adjustments. (Review of the various parameters in the section

of the text on RFC may be useful in guiding the examiner's opinions. All opinions should be supported clearly by data contained in the report.)

Claimant's Ability to Manage Own Benefits
Provide an opinion regarding the claimant's ability to handle his or her own funds.

Report Limitations
Provide any data which may limit the usefulness or validity of the reported findings. This might include factors such as the necessity of conducting the examination through an interpreter, inability to obtain a reliable history, evidence of malingering, or failure to cooperate with the examination.

CONCLUSION
The decisions that SSA must make regarding a claimant's ability to work are obviously complex ones. Because of this complexity, the need for an adequate data base upon which decisions can be based is evident. The foregoing chapter presents the evaluating psychiatrist with a suggested format for reports. At the heart of the disability report is the need to document the existence of an impairment and how it interferes with an individual's functioning. Reports must emphasize the clinical findings so independent reviewers can arrive at a reasonable and fair decision.

REFERENCES
Committee on Rehabilitation of the American Psychiatric Association: Guidelines for psychiatric evaluation of Social Security Disability claimants. Hosp Community Psychiatry 34:1044-1051, 1983

Social Security Administration: Disability Evaluation under Social Security. SSA Publication No. 0510089. Washington, DC, U. S. Department of Health and Human Services, February, 1986a

Social Security Administration: Social Security Regulations: Rules for Determining Disability and Blindness Including Regulations No. 4, Subpart P (Title II) and Regulations No. 16, Subpart I (Title XVI). SSA Publication No. 64014. Washington, DC, U.S. Department of Health and Human Services, Social Security Administration, Office of Disability, April, 1986b

APPENDIX

Social Security Regulations No. 4, Subpart P, Appendix 1 (Listing of Impairments), Section 12.00 (Mental Disorders)

The mental disorders listings in 12.00 of the Listing of Impairments will only be effective for 3 years unless extended by the Secretary or revised and promulgated again. Consequently, these listings will no longer be effective on August 28, 1988.

A. Introduction:
The evaluation of disability on the basis of mental disorders requires the documentation of a medically determinable impairment(s) as well as consideration of the degree of limitation such impairment(s) may impose on the individual's ability to work and whether these limitations have lasted or are expected to last for a continuous period of at least 12 months. The listings for mental disorders are arranged in eight diagnostic categories: organic mental disorders (12.02); schizophrenic, paranoid and other psychotic disorders (12.03); affective disorders (12.04); mental retardation and autism (12.05); anxiety related disorders (12.06); somatoform disorders (12.07); personality disorders (12.08); and substance addiction disorders (12.09). Each diagnostic group, except listings 12.05 and 12.09, consists of a set of clinical findings (paragraph A criteria), one or more of which must be met, and which, if met, lead to a test of functional restrictions (paragraph B criteria), two or three of which must also be met. There are additional considerations (paragraph C criteria) in listings 12.03 and 12.06, discussed therein.

The purpose of including the criteria in paragraph A of the listings for mental disorders is to medically substantiate the presence of a mental disorder. Specific signs and symptoms under any of the listings 12.02 through 12.09 cannot be considered in isolation from the description of the mental disorder contained at the beginning of each listing category. Impairments should be analyzed or reviewed under the mental category(ies) which is supported by the individual's clinical findings.

The purpose of including the criteria in paragraphs B and C of the listings for mental disorders is to describe those functional limitations associated with mental disorders which are incompatible with the ability to work. The restrictions listed in paragraphs B and C must be the result of the mental disorder which is manifested by the clinical findings outlined in paragraph A. The criteria included in paragraphs B and C of the listings for mental disorders have been chosen because they represent functional areas deemed essential to work. An individual who is severely limited in these areas as the result of an impairment identified in paragraph A is presumed to be unable to work.

The structure of the listing for substance addiction disorders, listing 12.09, is different from that for the other mental disorder listings. Listing 12.09 is structured as a reference listing; that is, it will only serve to indicate which of the other listed mental or physical impairments must be used to evaluate the behavioral or physical changes resulting from regular use of addictive substances.

The listings for mental disorders are so constructed that an individual meeting or equaling the criteria could not reasonably be expected to engage in gainful work activity.

Individuals who have an impairment with a level of severity which does not meet the criteria of the listings for mental disorders may or may not have the residual functional capacity (RFC) which would enable them to engage in substantial gainful work activity. The determination of mental RFC is crucial to the evaluation of an individual's capacity to engage in substantial gainful work activity when the criteria of the listings for mental disorders are not met or equaled but the impairment is nevertheless severe.

RFC may be defined as a multidimensional description of the work-related abilities which an individual retains in spite of medical impairments. RFC complements the criteria in paragraphs B and C of the listings for mental disorders by requiring consideration of an expanded list of work-related capacities which may be impaired by mental disorder when the impairment is severe but does not meet or equal a listed mental disorder. (While RFC may be applicable in most claims, the law specifies that it does not apply to the following special claims categories: disabled title XVI children below age 18, widows, widowers and surviving divorced wives. The impairment(s) of these categories must meet or equal a listed impairment for the individual to be eligible for benefits based on disability.)

B. Need for Medical Evidence:

The existence of a medically determinable impairment of the required duration must be established by medical evidence consisting of clinical signs, symptoms and/or laboratory or psychological test findings. These findings may be intermittent or persistent depending on the nature of the disorder. Clinical signs are medically demonstrable phenomena which reflected specific abnormalities of behavior, affect, thought, memory, orientation, or contact with reality. These signs are typically assessed by a psychiatrist or psychologist and/or documented by psychological tests. Symptoms are complaints presented by the individual. Signs and symptoms generally cluster together to constitute recognizable clinical syndromes (mental disorders). Both symptoms and signs which are part of any diagnosed mental disorder must be considered in evaluating severity.

C. Assessment of Severity:

For mental disorders, severity is assessed in terms of the functional limitations imposed by the impairment. Functional limitations are assessed using the criteria in paragraph B of the listings for mental disorders (descriptions of restrictions of activities of daily living; social functioning; concentration, persistence, or pace; and ability to tolerate increased mental demands associated with competitive work). Where "marked" is used as a standard for measuring the degree of limitation, it means more than moderate, but less than extreme. A marked limitation may arise when several activities or functions are impaired or even when only one is impaired, so long as the degree of limitation is such as to seriously interfere with the ability to function independently, appropriately and effectively. Four areas are considered.

1. *Activities of daily living* including adaptive activities such as cleaning, shopping, cooking, taking public transportation, paying bills, maintaining a residence, caring appropriately for one's grooming and hygiene, using telephones and directories, using a post office, etc. In the context of the individual's overall situation, the quality of these activities is judged by their independence, appropriateness and effectiveness. It is necessary to define the extent to which the individual is capable of initiating and participating in activities independent of supervision or direction.

"Marked" is not the number of activities which are restricted but the overall degree of restriction or combination of restrictions which must be judged. For example, a person who is able to cook and clean might still have marked restrictions of daily activities if the person were too fearful to leave the immediate environment of home and neighborhood, hampering the person's ability to obtain treatment or to travel away from the immediate living environment.

2. *Social functioning* refers to an individual's capacity to interact appropriately and communicate effectively with other individuals. Social functioning includes the ability to get along with others, e.g., family members, friends, neighbors, grocery clerks, landlords, bus drivers, etc. Impaired social functioning may be demonstrated by a history of altercations, evictions, firings, fear of strangers, avoidance of interpersonal relationships, social isolation, etc. Strength in social functioning may be documented by an individual's ability to initiate social contacts with others, communicate clearly with others, interact and actively participate in group activities, etc. Cooperative behaviors, consideration for others, awareness of others' feelings, and social maturity also need to be considered. Social functioning in work situations may involve interactions with the public, responding appropriately to persons in authority, e.g., supervisors, or cooperative behaviors involving coworkers.

"Marked" is not the number of areas in which social functioning is impaired, but the overall degree of interference in a particular area or combination of areas of functioning. For example, a person who is highly antagonistic, uncooperative or hostile but is tolerated by local storekeepers may nevertheless have marked restrictions in social functioning because that behavior is not acceptable in other social contexts.

3. *Concentration, persistence and pace* refer to the ability to sustain focused attention sufficiently long to permit the timely completion of tasks commonly found in work settings. In activities of daily living, concentration may be reflected in terms of ability to complete tasks in everyday household routines. Deficiencies in concentration, persistence and pace are best observed in work and work-like settings. Major impairment in this area can often be assessed through direct psychiatric examination and/or psychological testing, although mental status examination or psychological test data alone should not be used to accurately describe concentration and sustained ability to adequately perform work-like tasks. On mental status examinations, concentration is assessed by tasks such as having the individual subtract serial sevens from 100. In psychological tests of intelligence or memory, concentration is assessed through tasks requiring short-term memory or through tasks that must be completed within established time limits. In work evaluations, concentration, persistence, and pace are assessed through such tasks as filing index cards, locating telephone numbers, or disassembling and reassembling objects. Strengths and weaknesses in areas of concentration can be discussed in terms of frequency of errors, time it takes to complete the task, and extent to which assistance is required to complete the task.

4. *Deterioration or decompensation in work or worklike settings* refers to repeated failure to adapt to stressful circumstances which cause the individual either to withdraw from that situation or to experience exacerbation of signs and symptoms (i.e., decompensation) with an accompanying difficulty in maintaining activities of daily living, social relationships, and/or maintaining concentration, persistence, or pace (i.e., deterioration which may include deterioration of adaptive behaviors). Stresses common to the work environment include decisions, attendance, schedules, completing tasks, interactions with supervisors, interactions with peers, etc.

D. Documentation

The presence of a mental disorder should be documented primarily on the basis of reports from individual providers, such as psychiatrists and psychologists, and facilities such as hospitals and clinics. Adequate descriptions of functional limitations must be obtained from these or other sources which may include programs and facilities where the individual has been observed over a considerable period of time.

302
PSYCHIATRIC DISABILITY

Information from both medical and nonmedical sources may be used to obtain detailed descriptions of the individual's activities of daily living; social functioning; concentration, persistence and pace; or ability to tolerate increased mental demands (stress). This information can be provided by programs such as community mental health centers, day care centers, sheltered workshops, etc. It can also be provided by others, including family members, who have knowledge of the individual's functioning. In some cases descriptions of activities of daily living or social functioning given by individuals or treating sources may be insufficiently detailed and/or may be in conflict with the clinical picture otherwise observed or described in the examinations or reports. It is necessary to resolve any inconsistencies or gaps that may exist in order to obtain a proper understanding of the individual's functional restrictions.

An individual's level of functioning may vary considerably over time. The level of functioning at a specific time may seem relatively adequate or, conversely, rather poor. Proper evaluation of the impairment must take any variations in level of functioning into account in arriving at a determination of impairment severity over time. Thus, it is vital to obtain evidence from relevant sources over a sufficiently long period prior to the date of adjudication in order to establish the individual's impairment severity. This evidence should include treatment notes, hospital discharge summaries, and work evaluation or rehabilitation progress notes if these are available.

Some individuals may have attempted to work or may actually have worked during the period of time pertinent to the determination of disability. This may have been an independent attempt at work, or it may have been in conjunction with a community mental health or other sheltered program which may have been of either short or long duration. Information concerning the individual's behavior during any attempt to work and the circumstances surrounding termination of the work effort are particularly useful in determining the individual's ability or inability to function in a work setting.

The results of well-standardized psychological tests such as the Wechsler Adult Intelligence Scale (WAIS), the Minnesota Multiphasic Personality Inventory (MMPI), the Roschach, and the Thematic Apperception Test (TAT), may be useful in establishing the existence of a mental disorder. For example, the WAIS is useful in establishing mental retardation, and the MMPI, Rorschach, and TAT may provide data supporting several other diagnoses. Broad-based neuropsychological assessments using, for example, the Halstead–Reitan or the Luria-Nebraska batteries may be useful in determining brain function deficiencies, particularly in cases involving subtle findings such as may be seen in traumatic brain injury. In addition, the process of taking a standardized test requires concentration, persistence and pace; performance on such tests may provide useful data. Test results should, therefore, include both the objective data and a narrative description of clinical findings. Narrative reports of intellectual assessment should include a discussion of whether or not obtained IQ scores are considered valid and consistent with the individual's developmental history and degree of functional restriction.

In cases involving impaired intellectual functioning, a standardized intelligence test, e.g., the WAIS, should be administered and interpreted by a psychologist or psychiatrist qualified by training and experience to perform such an evaluation. In special circumstances, nonverbal measures, such as the Raven Progressive Matrices, the Leiter international scale, or the Arthur adaption of the Leiter may be substituted.

Identical IQ scores obtained from different tests do not always reflect a similar degree of intellectual functioning. In this connection, it must be noted that on the WAIS, for example, IQs of 69 and below are characteristic of approximately the lowest 2 percent of the general population. In instances where other tests are administered, it would be necessary to convert the IQ to the corresponding percentile rank in the general population in order to determine the actual degree of impairment reflected by those IQ scores.

In cases where more than one IQ is customarily derived from the test administered, i.e., where verbal, performance, and full-scale IQs are provided as on the WAIS, the lowest of these is used in conjunction with listing 12.05.

In cases where the nature of the individual's intellectual impairment is such that standard intelligence tests, as described above, are precluded, medical reports specifically describing the level of intellectual, social, and physical function should be obtained. Actual observations by Social Security Administration or State agency personnel, reports from educational institutions and information furnished by public welfare agencies or other reliable objective sources should be considered as additional evidence.

E. Chronic Mental Impairments:

Particular problems are often involved in evaluating mental impairments in individuals who have long histories of repeated hospitalizations or prolonged outpatient care with supportive therapy and medication. Individuals with chronic psychotic disorders commonly have their lives structured in such a way as to minimize stress and reduce their signs and symptoms. Such individuals may be much more impaired for work than their signs and symptoms would indicate. The results of a single examination may not adequately describe these individuals' sustained ability to function. It is, therefore, vital to review all pertinent information relative to the individual's condition, especially at times of increased stress. It is mandatory to attempt to obtain adequate descriptive information from all sources which have treated the individual either currently or in the time period relevant to the decision.

F. Effects of Structural Settings:

Particularly in cases involving chronic mental disorders, overt symptomatology may be controlled or attenuated by psychosocial factors such as placement in a hospital board and care facility or other environment that provides similar structure. Highly structured and supportive settings may greatly reduce the mental demands placed on an individual. With lowered mental demands, overt signs and symptoms of the underlying mental disorder may be minimized. At the same time, however, the individual's ability to function outside of such a structured and/or supportive setting may not have changed. An evaluation of individuals whose symptomatology is controlled or attenuated by psychosocial factors must consider the ability of the individual to function outside of such highly structured settings. (For these reasons the paragraph C criteria were added to Listings 12.03 and 12.06.)

G. Effects of Medication:

Attention must be given to the effect of medication on the individual's signs, symptoms and ability to function. While psychotropic medications may control certain primary manifestations of a mental disorder, e.g., hallucinations, such treatment may or may not affect the functional limitations imposed by the mental disorder. In cases where overt symptomatology is attenuated by the psychotropic medications, particular attention must be focused on the functional restrictions which may persist. These functional restrictions are also to be used as the measure of impairments severity. (See the paragraph C criteria in Listings 12.03 and 12.06.)

Neuroleptics, the medicines used in the treatment of some mental illness, may cause drowsiness, blunted affect, or other side effects involving other body systems. Such side effects must be considered in evaluating overall impairment severity. Where adverse effects of medications contribute to the impairment severity and the impairment does not meet or equal the listings but is nonetheless severe, such adverse effects must be considered in the assessment of the mental residual functional capacity.

H. Effect of Treatment:

It must be remembered that with adequate treatment some individuals suffering with chronic mental disorders not only have their symptoms and signs ameliorated but also return to a level of function close to that of their premorbid status. Our discussion here in 12.00H has been designed to reflect the fact that present day treatment of a mentally impaired individual may or may not assist in the achievement of an adequate level of adaptation required in the work place. (See the paragraph C criteria in Listings 12.03 and 12.06.)

I. Techniques for Reviewing the Evidence in Mental Disorders Claims to Determine Level of Impairment Severity:

A special technique has been developed to ensure that all evidence needed for the evaluation of impairment severity in claims involving mental impairment is obtained, considered and properly evaluated. This technique, which is used in connection with the sequential evaluation process, is explained in § 404.1520a and § 416.920a.

12.01 Category of Impairments—Mental

12.02 Organic Mental Disorders:

Psychological or behavioral abnormalities associated with a dysfunction of the brain. History and physical examination or laboratory tests demonstrate the presence of a specific organic factor judged to be etiologically related to the abnormal mental state and loss of previously acquired functional abilities.

The required level of severity for these disorders is met when the requirements in both A and B are satisfied.

A. Demonstration of a loss of specific cognitive abilities or affective changes and the medically documented persistence of at least one of the following:

1. Disorientation to time and place; or

2. Memory impairment, either short-term (inability to learn new information), intermediate, or long-term (inability to remember information that was known some time in the past); or

3. Perceptual or thinking disturbances (e.g., hallucinations, delusions); or

4. Change in personality; or

5. Disturbance in mood; or

6. Emotional lability (e.g., explosive temper outbursts, sudden crying, etc.) and impairment in impulse control; or

7. Loss of measured intellectual ability of at least 15 I.Q. points from premorbid levels or overall impairment index clearly within the severely impaired range on neuropsychological testing, e.g., the Luria–Nebraska, Halstead–Reitan, etc.;
AND

B. Resulting in at least two of the following:

1. Marked restriction of activities of daily living; or

2. Marked difficulties in maintaining social functioning; or

3. Deficiencies of concentration, persistence or pace resulting in frequent failure to complete tasks in a timely manner (in work settings or elsewhere); or

4. Repeated episodes of deterioration or decompensation in work or work-like settings which cause the individual to withdraw from that situation or to experience exacerbation of signs and symptoms (which may include deterioration of adaptive behaviors).

12.03 Schizophrenic, Paranoid and Other Psychotic Disorders:
Characterized by the onset of psychotic features with deterioration from a previous level of functioning.

The required level of severity for these disorders is met when the requirements in both A and B are satisfied, or when the requirements in C are satisfied.

A. Medically documented persistence, either continuous or intermittent, of one or more of the following:

1. Delusions or hallucinations; or
2. Catatonic or other grossly disorganized behavior; or
3. Incoherence, loosening of associations, illogical thinking, or poverty of content of speech if associated with one of the following:

a. Blunt affect; or
b. Flat affect; or
c. Inappropriate affect;

OR

4. Emotional withdrawal and/or isolation:

AND

B. Resulting in at least two of the following:

1. Marked restriction of activities of daily living; or
2. Marked difficulties in maintaining social functioning; or
3. Deficiencies of concentration, persistence or pace resulting in frequent failure to complete tasks in a timely manner (in work settings or elsewhere); or
4. Repeated episodes of deterioration or decompensation in work or work-like settings which cause the individual to withdraw from that situation or to experience exacerbation of signs and symptoms (which may include deterioration of adaptive behaviors);

OR

C. Medically documented history of one or more episodes of acute symptoms, signs and functional limitations which at the time met the requirements in A and B of this listing, although these symptoms or signs are currently attenuated by medication or psychosocial support, and one of the following:

1. Repeated episodes of deterioration or decompensation in situations which cause the individual to withdraw from that situation or to experience exacerbation of signs or symptoms (which may include deterioration of adaptive behaviors); or
2. Documented current history of two or more years of inability to function outside of a highly supportive living situation.

12.04 Affective Disorders:

Characterized by a disturbance of mood, accompanied by a full or partial manic or depressive syndrome. Mood refers to a prolonged emotion that colors the whole psychic life; it generally involves either depression or elation.

The required level of severity for these disorders is met when the requirements in both A and B are satisfied.

A. Medically documented persistence, either continuous or intermittent, of one of the following:

1. Depressive syndrome characterized by at least four of the following:

    a. Anhedonia or pervasive loss of interest in almost all activities; or

    b. Appetite disturbance with change in weight; or

    c. Sleep disturbance; or

    d. Psychomotor agitation or retardation; or

    e. Decreased energy; or

    f. Feelings of guilt or worthlessness; or

    g. Difficulty concentrating or thinking; or

    h. Thoughts of suicide; or

    i. Hallucinations, delusions or paranoid thinking; or

2. Manic syndrome characterized by at least three of the following:

    a. Hyperactivity; or

    b. Pressure of speech; or

    c. Flight of ideas; or

    d. Inflated self-esteem; or

    e. Decreased need for sleep; or

    f. Easy distractability; or

    g. Involvement in activities that have a high probability of painful consequences which are not recognized; or

    h. Hallucinations, delusions or paranoid thinking;

OR

3. Bipolar syndrome with a history of episodic periods manifested by the full symptomatic picture of both manic and depressive syndromes (and currently characterized by either or both syndromes);

AND

B. Resulting in at least two of the following:

1. Marked restriction of activities of daily living; or

2. Marked difficulties in maintaining social functioning; or

3. Deficiencies of concentration, persistence or pace resulting in frequent failure to complete tasks in a timely manner (in work settings or elsewhere); or

4. Repeated episodes of deterioration or decompensation in work or work-like settings which cause the individual to withdraw from

that situation or to experience exacerbation of signs and symptoms (which may include deterioration of adaptive behaviors).

12.05 Mental Retardation and Autism:

Mental retardation refers to a significantly subaverage general intellectual functioning with deficits in adaptive behavior initially manifested during the developmental period (before age 22). (Note: The scores specified below refer to those obtained on the WAIS, and are used only for reference purposes. Scores obtained on other standardized and individually administered tests are acceptable, but the numerical values obtained must indicate a similar level of intellectual functioning.) Autism is a pervasive developmental disorder characterized by social and significant communication deficits originating in the developmental period.

The required level of severity for this disorder is met when the requirements in A, B, C, or D are satisfied.

A. Mental incapacity evidenced by dependence upon others for personal needs (e.g., toileting, eating, dressing, or bathing) and inability to follow directions, such that the use of standardized measures of intellectual functioning is precluded;
OR

B. A valid verbal, performance, or full scale IQ of 59 or less;
OR

C. A valid verbal, performance, or full scale IQ of 60 to 69 inclusive and a physical or other mental impairment imposing additional and significant work-related limitation of function;
OR

D. A valid verbal, performance, or full scale IQ of 60 to 69 inclusive or in the case of autism, gross deficits of social and communicative skills with two of the following:

1. Marked restriction of activities of daily living; or
2. Marked difficulties in maintaining social functioning; or
3. Deficiencies of concentration, persistence or pace resulting in frequent failure to complete tasks in a timely manner (in work settings or elsewhere); or
4. Repeated episodes of deterioration or decompensation in work or work-like settings which cause the individual to withdraw from that situation or to experience exacerbation of signs and symptoms (which may include deterioration of adaptive behaviors).

12.06 Anxiety Related Disorders:

In these disorders anxiety is either the predominant disturbance or it is experienced if the individual attempts to master symptoms; for example, confronting the dreaded object or situation in a phobic disorder or resisting the obsessions or compulsions in obsessive compulsive disorders.

The required level of severity for these disorders is met when the requirements in both A and B are satisfied, or when the requirements in both A and C are satisfied.

A. Medically documented findings of at least one of the following:

1. Generalized persistent anxiety accompanied by three out of four of the following signs or symptoms:
a. Motor tension; or
b. Autonomic hyperactivity; or
c. Apprehensive expectation; or
d. Vigilance and scanning;

or

2. A persistent irrational fear of a specific object, activity, or situation which results in a compelling desire to avoid the dreaded object, activity, or situation; or

3. Recurrent severe panic attacks manifested by a sudden unpredictable onset of intense apprehension, fear, terror and sense of impending doom occurring on the average of at least once a week; or

4. Recurrent obsessions or compulsions which are a source of marked distress; or

5. Recurrent and intrusive recollections of a traumatic experience, which are a source of marked distress;

AND

B. Resulting in at least two of the following:
1. Marked restriction of activities of daily living; or
2. Marked difficulties in maintaining social functioning; or
3. Deficiencies of concentration, persistence or pace resulting in frequent failure to complete tasks in a timely manner (in work settings or elsewhere); or
4. Repeated episodes of deterioration or decompensation in work or work-like settings which cause the individual to withdraw from the situation or to experience exacerbation of signs and symptoms (which may include deterioration of adaptive behaviors);

OR

C. Resulting in complete inability to function independently outside the area of one's home.

12.07 Somatoform Disorders:

Physical symptoms for which there are no demonstrable organic findings or known physiological mechanisms.

The required level of severity for these disorders is met when the requirements in both A and B are satisfied.

A. Medically documented by evidence of one of the following:

1. A history of multiple physical symptoms of several years duration, beginning before age 30, that have caused the individual to take medicine frequently, see a physician often and alter life patterns significantly; or

2. Persistent nonorganic disturbance of one of the following:

a. Vision; or

b. Speech; or

c. Hearing; or

d. Use of a limb; or

e. Movement and its control (e.g., coordination disturbance, psychogenic seizures, akinesia, dyskinesia; or

f. Sensation (e.g., diminished or heightened).

3. Unrealistic interpretation of physical signs or sensations associated with the preoccupation or belief that one has a serious disease or injury;

AND

B. Resulting in three of the following:

1. Marked restriction of activities of daily living; or

2. Marked difficulties in maintaining social functioning; or

3. Deficiencies of concentration, persistence or pace resulting in frequent failure to complete tasks in a timely manner (in work settings or elsewhere); or

4. Repeated episodes of deterioration or decompensation in work or work-like settings which cause the individual to withdraw from that situation or to experience exacerbation of signs and symptoms (which may include deterioration of adaptive behavior).

12.08 Personality Disorders:

A personality disorder exists when personality traits are inflexible and maladaptive and cause either significant impairment in social or occupational functioning or subjective distress. Characteristic features are typical of the individual's long-term functioning and are not limited to discrete episodes of illness.

The required level of severity for these disorders is met when the requirements in both A and B are satisfied.

A. Deeply ingrained, maladaptive patterns of behavior associated with one of the following:

1. Seclusiveness or autistic thinking; or

2. Pathologically inappropriate suspiciousness or hostility; or

3. Oddities of thought, perception, speech and behavior; or

4. Persistent disturbances of mood or affect; or

5. Pathological dependence, passivity, or aggressivity; or

6. Intense and unstable interpersonal relationships and impulsive and damaging behavior;

AND

B. Resulting in three of the following:

1. Marked restriction of activities of daily living; or

2. Marked difficulties in maintaining social functioning; or

3. Deficiencies of concentration, persistence or pace resulting in frequent failure to complete tasks in a timely manner (in work settings or elsewhere); or

4. Repeated episodes of deterioration or decompensation in work or work-like settings which cause the individual to withdraw from that situation or to experience exacerbation of signs and symptoms (which may include deterioration of adaptive behaviors).

12.09 Substance Addiction Disorders:
Behavioral change or physical changes associated with the regular use of substances that affect the central nervous system.

The required level of severity for these disorders is met when the requirements in any of the following (A through I) are satisfied.

A. Organic mental disorders. Evaluate under 12.02.
B. Depressive syndrome. Evaluate under 12.04.
C. Anxiety disorders. Evaluate under 12.06.
D. Personality disorders. Evaluate under 12.08.
E. Peripheral neuropathies. Evaluate under 11.14.
F. Liver damage. Evaluate under 5.05.
G. Gastritis. Evaluate under 5.04.
H. Pancreatitis. Evaluate under 5.08.
I. Seizures. Evaluate under 11.02 or 11.03.

16

The Psychiatric Evaluation in Workers' Compensation

Carroll M. Brodsky, M.D., Ph.D.

Workers' compensation systems are no-fault insurance programs designed to provide medical treatment, disability benefits, and, if necessary, rehabilitation services for workers who have suffered an injury or illness arising out of work or in the course of work. The "no-fault" component indicates only that negligence generally is not an issue, not that all other aspects of the case may not be disputed and litigated (Halleck 1980; Larson 1978).

Although each *jurisdiction* sets its own eligibility requirements, benefit levels, and claims procedures, most workers' compensation laws are generally similar. Demonstrating eligibility for workers' compensation usually requires medical documentation of the claimant's injury or illness and its effects. The determination of compensability is not entirely medical and involves consideration of the worker's ability to compete in the open labor market (Greenwood 1984).

If any part of the worker's claim alleges emotional stress or the presence of a mental disorder, the claimant is commonly referred for evaluation to a mental health professional. Many psychiatric examinations are requested as the result of disputes regarding the legitimacy of the claimant's complaint, with both sides in the dispute recruiting their own experts. Sometimes the applicant's attorney will refer the claimant to one mental health professional and the defense attorney to another, and the professionals may reach differing conclusions.

Whether the claim is disputed or not, the psychiatrist is asked to conduct the examination in order to determine a number of facts and issues:

- if the applicant has a mental disorder;
- the duration and the patterns of any mental disorder found;
- the cause of the disorder(s), and, specifically, its relation to work;
- the need for psychiatric treatment and, if the need is due to a work-incurred disorder, the length of time during which treatment will be needed;
- if, in the future, different psychiatric treatment will be needed (e.g., residential care), and the likelihood that the applicant will get better, stay the same, or get worse;
- if the applicant is deemed able to return to the former job or a similar one, on what date he or she will be able to do so, and what residual disability there might be in doing that job, or other work;
- if the applicant is not considered able to return to his or her former job or occupation, whether rehabilitation is indicated and feasible and the likely impact of the psychiatric impairment(s) on rehabilitation;
- what the applicant would have been like without the work-incurred impairment;
- whether the applicant's condition is now stable or if it is likely to improve or deteriorate.

Each, or several, of the above categories may be disputed (Harter 1983–84). Although most workers' compensation claims are not litigated (*California Workers' Compensation Reporter* 1985), as many as 39 percent of permanent–partial and 52 percent of permanent–total disability claims are litigated (Mussoff 1981). For example, the employer may argue that no illness, impairment, or disability exists or that, if it did, it has long since resolved; that it was not caused or aggravated by the work, but rather was the result of trauma or other conditions unrelated to work, such as preexisting personality structure or nonwork sources of stress.

Some cases deal only with cause, for example, cases in which the applicant committed suicide and the psychiatrist is asked to render an opinion about the relationship between the suicide and work conditions and/or a work-incurred illness or injury (Brodsky 1977b).

In most instances, the referring source specifically presents the above questions in the referral letter, with variations, depending upon the nature of the claim and the structure of the workers' compensation system in which it is being processed.

RECORDS AVAILABLE BEFORE EXAMINATION

If the claim is a recent one, the psychiatrist may be presented with nothing more than a letter referring the patient and describing the injury. If the claim was filed two or three years earlier, the psychiatrist may receive a footlocker full of records. Among the data usually forwarded are:

- records of examinations and treatment pertaining to the work-incurred illness or injury in question;
- medical contacts, examinations, and treatment prior to the work-related event, sometimes including records reaching back to child-hood or even birth;
- school, military, and prior work records;
- records of legal involvement, civil and criminal;
- reports of investigations and statements from co-workers, supervisors, subordinates, former employers and co-workers, and even neighbors;
- depositions taken of the applicant, physicians, co-workers, and employers involved in this claim or who were involved with the applicant in earlier legal actions.

The psychiatrist should review these records before examining the applicant to gain an overall view of the issues and to note any contradictions found and questions evoked by the records which need to be addressed with the applicant. The examiner should not pre-judge the issues on the basis of the records alone and should suspend judgment on the credibility of persons presenting conflicting information until the examination is completed and all the data are studied.

INITIAL CONTACT WITH APPLICANT

The initial contact with the applicant may be on the telephone or in person. Applicants may call to inquire, "What kind of a doctor are you?" or to ask for directions to the examination site. At the time of the first meeting, the examiner should inform the applicant:

- that the examiner is a psychiatrist;
- that the examination is being conducted in the context of the workers' compensation claim;
- who referred the applicant to the examiner (e.g., the applicant's attorney, the defense attorney, or the insurance company), or whether the examiner was selected by both sides as an Agreed Medical Examiner;
- that there is no confidentiality in the communications between the examiner and applicant, and that the examiner would prefer not to hear "off the record" comments;
- that the examiner will be sending a written report to the referring source;
- that the examiner will provide no treatment and will not refer the applicant directly to other physicians for treatment;

- that the examiner will provide no conclusive opinion or recommend treatment by others directly to the applicant. The examiner must avoid the role of the treating psychiatrist in order not to establish a physician–patient relationship which makes the examiner subject to accusations of malpractice (Heiman and Shanfield 1978).

EXAMINATION TECHNIQUES

Describe the sequence of your examination to the applicant so he or she can know what areas will be covered, and so as to reduce apprehension about "psychiatric" questions. Direct questions elicit the information necessary to complete the report, but tend to exclude responses that provide important but unpredicted data. Therefore, a style that combines direct and open-ended questions which encourage elaborated responses is preferable. If answers are unresponsive to the questions, the examiner should keep asking the question until a full answer is elicited. If the answer is responsive but continues in greater detail than is necessary, the examiner should interrupt at a pause and ask the next question.

The examination is designed to elicit the information needed rather than to permit the applicant to ventilate, although occasionally the latter will happen. It is not designed to make the applicant feel better, as in forms of crisis intervention, although applicants sometimes report spontaneously that they feel relieved upon having the opportunity to discuss their situation. The examination is not structured to be the first step in a therapeutic relationship, and there is good reason to avoid the conflict of interest between the roles of independent evaluator and treating physician.

TAPE-RECORDING THE INTERVIEW

Frequently, applicants, fearing that they will be misquoted or that their statements will be distorted, bring tape recorders to the examination and request or even demand permission to record the examination. In my experience, tape-recording does not interfere with the examination and, if anything, reduces the applicant's suspicions. The examiner should also make a tape-recording, if the applicant is doing so. The applicant's permission should be obtained, and the recording should occur openly. Tape-recording may actually facilitate an examination in which the applicant talks so fast or is so excited while reporting experiences that the examiner has difficulty taking notes.

PRESENCE OF THIRD PARTIES

Occasionally, relatives or attorneys seek to be present during the examination. In my experience, conducting an examination with interested third parties present limits the applicant's spontaneity. The applicant may turn to a spouse or lawyer and ask about dates or medications or may become embarrassed when asked about social history or sexual matters. Third parties interrupt to add or correct the applicant's version. When possible, the psychiatrist should insist on examining the applicant alone.

After the applicant's examination, the examiner should permit family members to report their experiences when they ask to do so or when the applicant requests it, and, at that time, the examiner can meet with family members alone or, if they so request, in the presence of the applicant. Family members can provide, and indeed may be the only source of, useful information about the applicant's symptoms, level of functioning, and changes in function, if the applicant is incapable of providing this information to the examiner.

In cases where the subject of the claim is deceased, the examiner conducts the equivalent of a "psychological autopsy," in which family members and records are the primary informants. The evaluation can proceed as if the applicant were being examined, while recognizing that much of the information from family members is second hand and may have many gaps that must be filled from other sources.

INTERPRETERS

An interpreter is necessary when the psychiatrist and applicant do not share a common language. The psychiatrist should arrange for an independent interpreter experienced in working in medicolegal settings in which exact, rather than approximate, translation is required. Relatives and friends are unacceptable as interpreters because they may edit the applicant's statements or because they may have heard the applicant's story so many times that they have developed their own versions. Unless the psychiatrist has worked with the interpreter before and is satisfied with the interpreter's language skills and techniques of interpreting, the psychiatrist should instruct the interpreter carefully:

1. to make exact translations in the applicant's own style and to leave a sentence unfinished if the applicant has done so;
2. to inform the psychiatrist if the applicant says things that the interpreter does not understand; and
3. that, as is true with an applicant with whom the psychiatrist shares a common language, the object of the examination is not merely to disclose what happened, but to hear the applicant's version of the history.

Before the examination begins, the psychiatrist should describe the process of a mental status examination to the interpreter and ask the interpreter to find common proverbs in the applicant's language and culture that would be equivalent to those used in the examination with applicants who grew up in the U.S. society and culture. The psychiatrist and interpreter should agree upon those to be used during the course of the mental status examination.

THE PSYCHIATRIC EVALUATION

The standard psychiatric examination format is as described in standard textbooks (MacKinnon 1980a, 1980b; Ginsberg 1985), with a special focus on answering the questions asked by the referring source.

In Chapter 4 of this volume, I describe some of the elements that constitute the system that results in an individual's being labeled as having a work-related psychiatric disability. These elements can be categorized under rubrics such as mental impairment, genetic endowment, acquired knowledge and skills, and capacities for adapting to social interactions, including work, motivation to work, and factors affecting motivation to work. A study of these elements will help explain why an individual who has a profound mental or physical impairment continues to work in spite of medical consensus that he or she is disabled, while a person who has no discoverable impairment claims to be disabled. Each case has its own configuration of elements. Intuitive preexamination predictions are often proven to be incorrect once data are available.

I am suggesting that the following questions be asked and that the following areas be covered because it is likely that the explanation for specific disability behavior will be found among them and that these will range from impairment due to organic mental disorder to claimed disability due to disincentives to work.

Age and birth date: The examiner needs to know the true age in order to assess disability more accurately. Occasionally, the records of another person with the same name are inserted into the files unintentionally. Having the birth date helps the examiner determine not only if the correct records are included but also the applicant's veracity, as some individuals lower their ages to help obtain employment.

Occupation: Attending to the response to the question, "What is your occupation?" can be enlightening, as the answer of "welder," "former policeman," or "disabled" reflects how the applicant sees him- or herself. Also determine the amount of time working in that occupation, and any other occupations for which the applicant is qualified.

Present job: When the applicant is currently employed, ask in what position and for how long. The present job may or may not be the index job, the subject of the applicant's current workers' compensation claim. Obtain a complete description of the job, the hours worked in a day or week, changes in duties, shift or shift changes, pay, and a description of how well the applicant is performing, as measured by applicant's subjective evaluation and by performance reports by supervisors.

Last job: If the applicant is not working at present, then inquire when the applicant last worked and why he or she stopped working. Most often, if the applicant is not working at present, the last job is likely to be the subject of the workers' compensation claim and, therefore, as much data as possible should be obtained about this job. The applicant should be asked to provide a detailed description of the job, including the hours, the shifts, pay, variety of tasks, and the ease with which the applicant was able to perform those jobs prior to the time of injury or illness. The applicant should be asked if he or she liked the job; got along well with co-workers, superiors and subordinates; and about special areas of satisfaction and dissatisfaction on the job. In addition, the examiner should learn if the applicant was employed in other jobs simultaneously—if he or she was "moonlighting"—and obtain the same information about those jobs, because the cumulative effect of both jobs might explain reactions not understandable in light of either job alone. Inquire specifically whether the applicant had any job-related problems and/or filed any workers' compensation claims in reference to this job.

Index injury or illness: Ask the date of onset of the illness or injury. If the claim is the result of an injury, determine the applicant's mental and physical state just prior to the injury. One can ask, "How were you on the day before this injury occurred? Were you under the care of a physician and, if so, for what? What treatment were you receiving? What medications were you taking?" Obtain a full description of the event or events to which the applicant attributes the onset of the injury or illness (e.g., an accident; exposures to substances, noise, or temperature; psychological interactions; stress; etc.).

Immediate medical care: Obtain a detailed description of the events that occurred immediately after the injury or the onset of the illness. To whom did the applicant report on the job; to what health care provider did he or she go or was he or she sent for examination or treatment; and how was he or she treated by that person, clinic, or hospital? Leggo (1953), Miller et al. (1961), and Brodsky (1977a), have all observed that perceived dismissal of the worker's complaints or inadequate initial evaluation or diagnosis produce strong resentments that may contribute to prolonged disability.

Subsequent medical care: Ask the applicant to describe the subsequent medical treatment. Ask about the course of the symptoms as they related to the treatment. Obtain a detailed description of the medications and dosages which were prescribed and used. Specifically ask the applicant if his or her condition has changed with treatment and time. Is the applicant better, worse, or has the condition remained the same?

Current condition: Obtain a complete list of physical and mental symptoms and conditions of which the applicant is complaining at present. One way of obtaining that information is to ask, "Tell me everything that is wrong with you at present," and then to ask, "Anything else?" until the applicant reports that there are no other symptoms or conditions considered to be present. Ask the applicant which of these conditions are attributable to work-related causes and which to other causes. Obtain a complete list of the medications which the applicant is taking as of the day of the examination. Ask what medications the applicant actually took in the 24 hours before the examination and on the day of the examination itself. Again, inquire specifically about any psychotropic medications. Also determine whether the applicant is or has felt suicidal.

An individual may be followed by several specialists and in more than one institution. Ascertain the names of all current treating health care professionals and the duration of treatment and the medication each prescribes.

Return to work: Did the applicant at any time attempt to return to the index job; under what conditions (full or part time or "light duty"), for how long, and what was the outcome? What was the perceived response of management and co-workers? Was the individual able to do the job or did residual symptoms or medication effects interfere with his or her performance? If the applicant is still working at the index job, have there been periods of disability, and for how long? If the applicant is not working at the index job, but is working elsewhere, how long was he or she off work?

Work plans: If the applicant is not working, does he or she think that finding another job is feasible/desirable? What kinds of work has the applicant considered, and what job-seeking activities (preparing or distributing a resumé, reading the want ads, completing job applications) has he or she accomplished? Once again, how applicants see themselves and their situations will be reflected in such statements as, "Who's going to hire a 58-year-old man?" "My husband's retired and likes me at home," "I hurt so much, there's nothing I could do," or "When I applied, I was told that the company would be concerned that I'd have another heart attack."

Has rehabilitation been considered or implemented? Sometimes applicants impose conditions for returning to work (e.g., the job would have to pay as much as the old job or would have to be close to home or would have to be stress-free). Other requirements, as stated by applicants, are that the job would have to permit them to lie or sit down or stand up every few minutes. Sometimes they report that they want jobs where they could "help people" or jobs at which they would not be involved with other people. The psychiatrist will match these requirements with the realities of the job market, as he or she knows it or learns of it from rehabilitation counselors who have studied the applicant's situation, and will take into account the person's educational qualifications and social skills. The psychiatrist will make a judgment about the likelihood of successful reemployment or rehabilitation by analyzing and integrating these data.

Current income: Is the applicant earning a salary, or what are the public (e.g., workers' compensation, welfare, Social Security) benefits or private (savings, insurance policies, investments) funds that are sources of the applicant's income? What is the applicant's total income? What was the applicant's income before the injury (illness)? How does the applicant's present net income compare with his or her previous income? How long will benefits continue? Is there a spouse who works for pay? Were there any changes in the spouse's working hours because of the applicant's disability, thereby resulting in a change in family income?

Current mental state: How are the applicant's spirits? Have interpersonal relationships been affected by irritability, pain, etc.? How is the individual's memory? Has the applicant been suicidal? Inquire about eating, including weight gain or loss over time, weight patterns in childhood and adolescence, and present eating habits, sleeping (bedtime, sleep patterns, times up during the night, time of arising, average hours of sleep, dreams and content), and sexual activity (present and past function, arousal, and satisfaction).

Substance abuse: Does the applicant smoke—quantity, changes, duration? Does the applicant drink—quantity, changes, duration, ever in trouble over drinking (driving, working), health effects? Does the applicant use street drugs—present and past use, which, how long, and what effects?

Family status: Marital status, children, health of spouse, health of children; does the applicant support children living with him or her, or living elsewhere? Does support continue in spite of disability? Is there a recently born child who requires care, and how has that care been provided? Is the applicant receiving or paying child support?

Living situation: What is the location and type of residence, is it owned or rented, length of time there, and monthly payments. Of persons living with applicant, relationships, ages, health, employment status? Does the applicant have other residences? Does the applicant live on a farm/ranch on which he or she works?

Typical daily/weekly activities: Does he or she drive an auto? What are the typical household and family activities (cooking, cleaning, shopping); what does he or she watch on TV and/or read; what exercise, hobbies, trips, school, or sports activities are engaged in? What and with whom are the applicant's usual social interactions (relatives, personal friends, spouse's friends; civic, fraternal, community or professional formal organizations, churches)? Are their social interactions satisfying? Which are during the day and which at night? How much time is devoted to health care? As in all functions, inquire if there have been changes over time and the reasons therefor.

Plans for the future: A simple question, like, "What are your plans for the future?" may elicit the applicant's own evaluation of his or her personal and occupational future. Not infrequently one hears, "I don't have any." Other responses may include such statements as, "Play with my grandchildren," "Buy a motor home," "Go back to school," "Just hang on 'til retirement," or "I can't do anything until this case is settled." Sometimes the question, "What do you think would help you most?" will elicit more comments that may be helpful to the evaluation.

Past medical history: The complete review of past illnesses during childhood, adolescence, and adulthood is best done by asking the applicant if he or she has had any of the illnesses on a standard list, system by system. Frequently, applicants forget about previous illnesses or medical conditions until they are asked specifically about them. Inquire about nonwork-related accidents and injuries, with associated periods of disability, treatment, and the outcome; all previous hospitalizations, and operations. Also elicit information about earlier emotional disorders, contacts with any mental health professionals (including pastoral counselors, school psychologists, and the like), and psychiatric hospitalizations. Ask about reasons for contacts with other health care providers, such as chiropractors and acupuncturists.

Legal difficulties: One should ask specifically about previous or current difficulties with the law, the nature and outcome of such difficulties, periods of incarceration, if any, and the conditions under which problems arose. Also ask if the applicant is or has been involved in any other civil actions related to injuries or disabilities.

Military service: Has the applicant ever served in the military forces of any country? Was the applicant ever rejected for military service? If he or she served, was he or she drafted or a volunteer? What were the years of service, special training, assignments (location and function), promotions, disciplinary actions (demotion, transfer, brig, court martial), and rank at discharge. Specifically ask if the applicant had any medical, physical, or behavioral/adjustment problems while in the service, has any residual disability, and was ever treated at a Veterans' Administration hospital after discharge. What was the applicant's discharge status (honorable, dishonorable, general, medical)? How does the applicant describe his or her service experience?

Social history: Elicit information regarding the applicant's birthplace, parental birthplaces, and national heritage; parents' ages, occupations, physical and mental health status, location, and age at and cause of deaths (if appropriate); number of siblings, applicant's birth rank, and siblings' ages, locations, occupations, and mental and physical health status. Was the parents' marriage intact while applicant was growing up? If not, how old was applicant at time of separation/divorce/remarriage/death? Where did the applicant grow up? If an immigrant, age at entry and length of time in current area. What language was spoken at home? Ask for descriptions of the parents, significant early memories, and feeling tone of childhood. Did the applicant have friends while growing up? Did the applicant have any neuropathic traits (enuresis, thumbsucking, sleepwalking, temper tantrums) or particular fears during childhood?

Education: What were the age at school entry, and the type of school system (public, private, parochial, alternative, or "special") throughout primary and secondary grades? Did the applicant have any problems when starting school (e.g., school phobia, non-English speaking)? Ask the number of different schools attended and their locations. Were there any learning or behavioral difficulties? Was he or she ever suspended or expelled? What were the applicant's grades in school?

The examiner should not settle for answers like, "Average," or "O.K.," when the question is, "How did you do in school?" Instead, one should inquire about how well the individual learned to read, write, spell, and do arithmetic. Many who have high school diplomas can barely read, and some will report that they had difficulty in reading from the beginning of school to the present. Was the applicant ever referred to school counselors for any reason?

Was the applicant athletic or socially active? Ask the applicant to describe his or her personality during high school. Did he or she receive special honors? Did the applicant work during high school? If yes, did the applicant work by choice or by necessity? Did the applicant graduate, and at what age? Information about postsecondary education should be elicited in great detail. If, for example, the applicant reports, "I had two years of college," the examiner should inquire about the name of the school, what courses were taken, grades in those courses, and how many credits were accumulated during those "two years." If the responses indicate that the applicant dropped out of school, one should learn the reasons. If the applicant has a bachelor's degree or beyond, inquire where and when the applicant went to school, major and minor courses of study, and grades. Did the applicant have any vocational or technical training—where, when, grades, and what certificates? Is the applicant mono- or multilingual, reading and/or speaking?

Prior employment: A detailed employment history should be obtained that should contain information about the "first real job," and the duration of time on each job, job duties and performance, relationships with co-workers and superiors, reasons for leaving, and periods of unemployment between jobs. Occasionally, the applicant reports that he or she spent two or three years "traveling" or "bumming around" and, in such instances, the examiner should inquire about the specifics of those experiences and about the sources of support during those times. Specific inquiry should be made regarding any previous work-related injuries or illnesses, previous experience with workers' compensation claims, and periods of disability, if such information has not already come to the fore.

Marital history: The examiner should take a detailed marital history and learn the reasons for separations or divorces. If the applicant has never been married, inquire about significant relationships. Similarly, one should explore the quality of the person's present marital and other significant relationships, as well as other aspects of family life, including problems with children or other family members. Are there any nonwork relationships that are sources of stress in the individual's life, now and/or that were present at the time of onset of the occupational injury or illness? How have the spouse, partner, or children reacted to the applicant's disability?

MENTAL STATUS EXAMINATION

A mental status examination should be conducted according to standard formats in textbooks, which provide detailed protocols. The psychiatrist is, of course, conducting a mental status examination throughout the entire course of this evaluation. However, in psychiatric evaluations of workers' compensation applicants, it is important to administer those tests that measure cognitive capacities, memory, and the ability to convert verbal directions into visual–motor work, in addition to assessing affect and contact with reality. From the results of these tests, the examiner might discover that the applicant is much more intelligent and knows more than would be indicated by his or her education or that the applicant is less knowledgeable and less intelligent than would be indicated by his or her background, education, or job level. Simple screening tests, such as having the applicant draw a clock, may indicate evidence of an organic mental disorder. The examiner will better understand why high school teaching is stressful for an individual if he or she cannot answer the simple informational items on the mental status examination, cannot do comparisons, or cannot provide abstract interpretations of proverbs.

ENDING THE EXAMINATION

At the end of the interview, the examiner should ask the applicant about any notations in the medical or other records that require description or elaboration. Applicants often have read some or all of the medical reports in their files and may take issue with certain parts of other examiners' histories or conclusions. Some applicants will have "forgotten" some past illnesses or life events, about which the examiner can inquire. Before ending the examination, the examiner should ask the applicant if there is anything he or she would like to add or change, or if there was anything that was overlooked that would be helpful for the examiner to know.

INDICATIONS FOR PSYCHOLOGICAL TESTING

If the examiner finds evidence of or suspects the presence of an organic mental disorder, the applicant should be referred for detailed neuropsychological testing in order to determine the degree of the impairment and the special functions that may be affected. In addition, the psychologist can determine how easily the applicant is distracted and under what conditions the applicant functions optimally. Any previous psychological test results should be obtained, for use as base-line data to determine any differences between pre-injury or early postinjury status and present function.

Many psychiatrists have all applicants complete the Minnesota Multiphasic Personality Inventory (MMPI) questionnaire which may then be interpreted by a computerized scoring service. A recorded version and a Spanish-language version of the MMPI also exist. In most instances, the psychiatrist who conducts the lengthy and detailed examination described above will have formed impressions that correlate highly with the MMPI interpretations. Some orthopedic surgeons administer the MMPI in order to determine if the applicant's profile matches those of persons who recovered from back surgery versus those who did not. Although the MMPI will show differences between groups of work-injured patients who recovered from surgery and those who remained disabled, those differences say nothing about the presence of orthopedic pathology in the individual tested.

Psychologic testing is also indicated when the employer or applicant suggests that the applicant was incompetent on the job or has become less competent over time. Frequently, after matching the results of the tests with the requirements of the job, the psychiatrist can understand why an applicant might not have been able to do the job.

Psychological tests are useful but should not be glorified as any more "objective" than the psychiatrist's examination, including the mental status examination. A test battery is only a tool and is only as good as the examiner administering and interpreting it. The *Handbook of Psychological Assessment* (Groth-Marnat 1984) is an excellent text describing the assets, liabilities, reliability and validity of the more common tests currently in use. Repki and Cooper (1983) and Snibbe et al. (1980) discuss the use of the MMPI in workers' compensation applicants.

THE REPORT
The report should contain all of the data described above. At the beginning, the examiner should note that he or she reported his or her professional identity to the applicant, warned the applicant that there was no confidentiality, and any other conditions under which the examination was conducted. *Reporting of details might seem tedious both to the person writing the report and the reader, but omitting those details will invite further inquiry and possibly critical cross-examination.* The psychiatrist should expect that there will be further inquiry about the report, requests for supplemental reports based on additional records or on reports by other physicians, that a deposition might be taken, and that he or she might be subpoenaed to appear at hearings or trials. Therefore, the detailed report will serve the psychiatrist, as well as the referring source and judges, as a

repository of the data on which the conclusions of the report were based.

Some psychiatrists present the summary of the records before the description of findings in the course of the examination, while others prefer to describe the records after analysis of the mental status examination. I prefer the latter approach because the presentation of the reasons why the applicant filed the claim and the events that have occurred since the onset of the injury or illness present a context in which the records can be compared to the events as presented by the applicant and to the records that were made following the onset of injury or illness.

Following the presentation of this material, the psychiatrist concludes the report with a section in which all the questions asked by the referring source are answered to the best of the examiner's ability, and, when the questions cannot be answered, the examiner explains why. It is well to begin such a section (entitled Summary and Conclusions) by presenting a very brief summary of the reasons for the claim, the applicant's preclaim health and occupational status, and the applicant's statements about his or her present level of disability. This provides the reader with the contextual framework in which the examination was undertaken and the conclusions drawn.

The examiner should then answer *all* of the questions that were expressed in the referral letter or that are implicit in most workers' compensation referrals. Sometimes the questions are easy to answer, and sometimes they cannot be answered given the data available. If the latter is so, the psychiatrists should report that to the referring source. Psychiatrists who report their own thinking or speculations, while ignoring the questions asked, do not serve the needs of the system.

The psychiatric examination in the workers' compensation system is designed to provide information that the system can translate into benefits (i.e., medical care, wage replacements, rehabilitation, and payments for permanent loss-of-earning capacity). The information communicated to the workers' compensation system must be in terms that can be converted into quantitative benefits (Rosner 1982). Data that are qualitative and not readily convertible to those quantitative terms are sometimes useless to the referring sources and to the court. Hedging, when a reasonable medical approximation could be offered, imposes the burden of judgment on those who, by referring the patient to the psychiatrists, have admitted that their own professional qualifications are inadequate to make the medical judgment. The psychiatrist who consults for the system must satisfy its needs, even though its terms and requirements for quantification are frequently foreign to psychiatrists who have not engaged in forensic practices (Danner and Sagall 1977).

Not only must psychiatrists answer questions put to them and state their conclusions in quantitative terms when necessary, but they must also give the reasoning through which their conclusions are reached. It is not enough to state that an individual suffered an industrial injury or is temporarily disabled or needs treatment or that the condition has become "permanent and stationary." The data relied upon and the reasoning, medical or otherwise, that was applied to the data that led to the conclusions must be stated. If such reasoning is not convincing, the referring source will ask for clarification or the applicant will be sent to another psychiatrist for a report that does provide the reasoning that led to the quantitative and qualitative conclusions. In disputed claims, judges will rely on the opinion in which the case facts conform most closely to the data in the record, and they will rely on the psychiatrist whose reasoning is most persuasive in integrating those facts with psychiatric knowledge (Bazelton 1974; Diamond 1973; Gorman 1983; Halleck 1980; Weinberger and Gross 1982).

Each workers' compensation system has its own labels for approximating the degree of disability. Usually, they have quite specific percentages that are attached to those labels, and amounts of money that are paid based on those categories. A psychiatrist indicating that a patient has a "slight" disability might mean that he or she has practically no disability, whereas the rating scale might attach an approximate 20 percent disability to this "slight" rating. Therefore, the psychiatrist is well advised to be familiar with the classification system used in his or her jurisdiction.

Among the questions asked are those related to "diagnosis," and some workers' compensation judges have become attached to *DSM-III* diagnostic axes (American Psychiatric Association 1980; Beohm 1978). This is not the place to critique the *DSM-III*, but those who are going to use the terms for medicolegal purposes should be aware of such critiques, especially if they are made by lawyers (Mussoff 1981). *DSM-III* (1980) states clearly in its opening pages:

> **CAUTIONS:** The purpose of *DSM-III* is to provide clear descriptions of diagnostic categories in order to enable clinicians and investigators to diagnose, communicate about, study, and treat various mental disorders. The use of this manual for non-clinical purposes, such as determination of legal responsibility, competency or insanity, or justification for third-party payment, must be critically examined in each instance within the appropriate institutional context.

Whenever possible, the report should contain the diagnostic categories that most accurately describe the applicant's present mental state. The examiner should not make a forced choice; and, if more than one label seems to apply, they should be stated, and the examiner should explain why the applicant cannot be placed in a single diagnostic category. Further, the psychiatrist should go beyond the labeling process and explain to the reader what the label means in the context of the applicant's work and nonwork life, and in what way it might be disabling or not disabling, if that was the conclusion. Further, when possible, the psychiatrist should note what diagnostic labels might have been applied *before* the onset of the symptoms that led to the claim. Psychiatrists in clinical practice know that many of their patients, who are working and functioning effectively at high levels in business and government or professionally, have symptoms and behavior that conform to mental disorders described in the *DSM-III*.

FACTORS LEADING TO BIAS

Applicants are referred to a psychiatrist:

- by the applicant's representative or by the defense;
- when both sides agree to select a single examiner;
- when a hearing officer or judge asks a medical bureau to name a psychiatrist from its list of Independent Medical Examiners.

In all instances, opinions of such psychiatrists can be affected by:

- tendency to identify with referring sources;
- pressure for a favorable opinion from referring sources;
- examiner's philosophic identification with workers or employers generally;
- examiner's taking over the role of trier-of-fact, a dispenser of justice;
- examiner's responding to the forensic challenge of countering another psychiatrist's report;
- the examiner's wish to appear evenhanded and unbiased to the point where he or she can't render a definite opinion;
- personal feelings, favorable or unfavorable, engendered by the applicant or someone associated with the applicant.

Psychiatrists recognize that they have biases and that they must be aware of them in order to minimize them. Examiners should review their reports with an eye to detecting these biases in any of their stated opinions.

The psychiatrist functions most effectively by recognizing that the workers' compensation systems are structures designed by legislators and lawyers. The concepts of causation applied are legal and not medical, and the mechanisms of justice are implemented by judges. Lawyers, not physicians, are the gladiators and the physician should not try to do the lawyers' work by joining them in the battle.

MALINGERING

In clinical medicine, we assume that patients are telling the truth, and we respond to what patients tell us by engaging in extensive diagnostic testing or by treating their symptoms directly. Patients are hospitalized on the basis of their symptoms and surgeons operate on them on the basis of symptoms because they believe that the patients are credible. Rosenhan (1973) demonstrated that psychiatric patients, too, are hospitalized and retained on the basis of their symptoms. The medical literature is replete with reports of the astounding lengths to which "dishonest" patients will go to gain or maintain the patient role by inducing factitious disorders (Aduan et al. 1979; Reich and Gottfried 1983). Individuals with factitious disorders are distinguished from malingerers who feign or fabricate illness to gain a specific end—evading the draft, escaping punishment, or, in the present context, obtaining benefits fraudulently.

DSM-III (American Psychiatric Association 1980; Hyler and Sussman 1984) contains the category of somatoform disorders to describe those individuals who have physical symptoms in the absence of physical findings that explain them. *DSM-III* also presents a category of malingering, in which there is a "voluntary" production and presentation of false or grossly exaggerated physical or psychological symptoms. It notes that the symptoms are produced in pursuit of a goal that can be recognized if one knows the individual's circumstances. It suggests a high index of suspicion when the examination is conducted in the medicolegal context if marked discrepancy was found between the person's claimed distress or disability and the physical findings. Suspicion should be raised if the patient does not cooperate with diagnostic evaluation and prescribed treatment regimens. Further, it suggests that an antisocial personality disorder might be present. *DSM-III* notes that, under some circumstances, malingering could be adaptive (e.g., feigning illness while a captive of the enemy during wartime). In fact, one cannot understand malingering in the context of workers' compensation unless one recognizes that it is an adaptive effort and, frequently, a successful one. The workers' compensation system does not compensate for pain and suffering, but compensates only for residual disability and the need for medical treatment and rehabilitation. Therefore, there are times when it is to the applicant's advantage to appear to be disabled and to require future medical treatment for the cause of the disability (Pollack et al. 1982a).

It is difficult to detect malingering that exaggerates symptoms slightly, even when those symptoms are not maintained consistently. More often, the malingerer presents symptoms and claims disability that are so extreme and so inconsistent with any known physical syndrome that any experienced observer will likely conclude that the explanation is malingering. In addition to applying the criteria of *DSM-III* in order to "diagnose" malingering, the psychiatrist will review reports of orthopedists, neurologists, and neurosurgeons because in those reports detailed evidences of inconsistencies may further heighten suspicions of malingering.

From time to time, the detection of malingering is made by subrosa motion picture films that show an applicant engaged in activities that he or she denied were possible. One should consider the possibility of malingering when examining an applicant who had a previous prolonged disability with recovery after settlement and who, in the context of the present examination, minimizes or dismisses that earlier disability.

From a medical perspective, those who are later demonstrated to be malingering are frequently histrionic in the presentation of their symptoms and are hostile and uncooperative in the psychiatric examination, as if trying to intimidate or confuse the examiner.

Some researchers have found psychometric approaches to malingering to be helpful. Bash and Alpert (1980) have employed the WAIS, Bender-Gestalt, and Rorschach to diagnose malingering in hospital settings. In a forensic setting, Repki and Cooper (1983) utilized the validity indicator of an elevated F-K index on the MMPI to distinguish between malingerers and nonmalingerers, and found that 7 percent of their sample qualified for the former category.

Psychiatrists who examine workers' compensation applicants would do well to assume that the applicants are telling the truth, and that the data they provide are accurate, unless proved otherwise. Examiners frequently assume that all applicants have the capacity for accurate and total recall and that distortions, inaccuracies, and inconsistencies in their presentation of past events are indicative of malingering, while, in fact, they may also be the result of forgetting, the need "to make psychological sense" of earlier events, or the result of organic mental disorders (Rogers and Cavanaugh 1983). The author's opinion is that, in most cases, the applicants are reporting the symptoms and the events that occurred as they perceive them and as honestly as they can. However, in any situation in which there is gain from being ill or disabled, the examiner must at least consider the applicant's credibility and the validity of the data presented.

SUMMARY

The psychiatric examination of workers' compensation applicants is similar to those described in standard texts and those that first-year psychiatric residents are taught to conduct. I have presented some special areas of emphasis that are required in order to make the usual psychiatric examination responsive to the referring sources' questions and useful to those who make decisions in the workers' compensation systems.

The elemental components of the questions put to psychiatrists by referring sources in the workers' compensation system were presented and special data needed to answer those questions were discussed. Some matters of procedure and technique for conducting a psychiatric examination of workers' compensation applicants were described and the specific elements of the report are discussed. The author urges psychiatrists to present the reasoning behind their conclusions. Presentation of such reasoning will help the applicant get fair treatment and will minimize the costs. In many cases, another psychiatrist will examine the same patients and will write a report which might present a somewhat different picture and conclusions (Zusman and Simon 1983). The reasoning and the use of the data available will weigh heavily in determining which way the trier-of-fact decides (Pollack et al. 1982b).

REFERENCES

Aduan RP, Fauci AS, Dale DC, et al: Factitious fever and self-induced infection: a report of 32 cases and review of the literature. Ann Intern Med 90:230–242, 1979

American Psychiatric Association: Diagnostic and Statistical Manual of Mental Disorders, third edition. Washington, DC, American Psychiatric Association, 1980

Bash IY, Alpert M: The determination of malingering. Ann NY Acad Sci 347:86–99, 1980

Bazelton DL: Psychiatrists and the adversary process. Sci Am 230:18–23, 1974

Beohm DO: DSM-III and the legal system. Bull Am Acad Psychiatry Law 6:31–35, 1978

Brodsky CM: Genesis of a problem population, in, Communication and Social Interaction. Edited by Ostwald, PF. New York, Grune & Stratton, 1977a

Brodsky CM: Suicide attributed to work. Suicide and Life-Threatening Behavior 7:216–229, 1977b

California Workers' Compensation Reporter. 13:85–112, 1985

Danner D, Sagall EL: Medicolegal causation: a source of professional misunderstanding. Am J Law Med 3:303–308, 1977

Diamond BL: The psychiatrist as advocate. Journal of Psychiatry and the Law 1:5–21, 1973

Ginsberg GL: Psychiatric history and mental status examination, in Comprehensive Textbook of Psychiatry/IV. Edited by Kaplan HI, Sadock BJ. Baltimore, Williams & Wilkins, 1985

Gorman WF: Are there impartial expert psychiatric witnesses? Bull Am Acad Psychiatry Law 11:379–382, 1983

Greenwood JG: Intervention in work-related disability: the need for an integrated approach. Soc Sci Med 19:595–601, 1984

Groth-Marnat G: Handbook of Psychological Assessment. New York, Van Nostrand Reinhold, 1984

Halleck SL: The psychiatrist's role in evaluating psychic injury, in Law in the Practice of Psychiatry: A Handbook. Edited by Halleck SL. New York, Plenum, 1980

Harter PJ: Dispute resolution and administrative law: the history, needs and future of a complex relationship. Villanova Law Review 29:1393–1419, 1983–84

Heiman EM, Shanfield SB: Psychiatric disability assessment: clarification of problems. Compr Psychiatry 19:449–454, 1978

Hyler SE, Sussman N: Somatoform disorders: before and after DSM-III. Hosp Community Psychiatry 35:469–478, 1984

Larson A: The Laws of Workers' Compensation. New York, Matthew Bender, 1978

Lasky H: Psychiatry and California workers' compensation laws: a threat and a challenge. California West Law Review 17:1–25, 1980

Leggo C: Resentment—an obstacle to recovery. Industrial Medicine and Surgery 22:241–245, 1953

MacKinnon RA: Diagnosis and psychiatry: examination of the psychiatric patient, in Comprehensive Textbook of Psychiatry/III, vol. 1. Edited by Kaplan HI, Freedman AM, Sadock BJ. Baltimore, Williams & Wilkins, 1980a

MacKinnon RA: Psychiatric history and mental status examination, in Comprehensive Textbook of Psychiatry/III, vol. 1. Edited by Kaplan HI, Freedman AM, Sadock BJ. Baltimore, Williams & Wilkins, 1980b

Marcus EH: Causation in psychiatry: realities and speculations. Medical Trial Techniques Quarterly 424–433, 1983

Marcus EH: Psychiatric disability litigation: definitions and problems. Medical Trial Techniques Quarterly 137–146, 1984

Miller MF, Watkins C, Davis CL: Some attitudes commonly found in patients injured on the job. Industrial Medicine and Surgery 30:135–137, 1961

Mussoff J: Determining the compensability of mental disorders under workers' compensation. Southern California Law Review 55:193–253, 1981

Pollack S, Gross BH, Weinberger LE: Dimensions of malingering, in The Mental Health Professional and the Legal System. San Francisco, Jossey-Bass, 1982a

Pollack S, Gross BH, Weinberger LE: Principles of forensic psychiatry for reaching psychiatric-legal opinions: application, in The Mental Health Professional and the Legal System. San Francisco, Jossey-Bass, 1982b

Reich P, Gottfried LA: Factitious disorders in a teaching hospital. Ann Intern Med 99:240–247, 1983

Repki GR, Cooper R: A study of the average workers' compensation case. J Clin Psychol 39:287–295, 1983

Robertson AJ: Malingering, occupational medicine and the law. Lancet 2:828–831, 1978

Rogers R, Cavanaugh JL Jr: "Nothing but the truth" . . . a reexamination of malingering. Journal of Psychiatry and the Law 11:1–17, 1983

Rosenhan DL: On being sane in insane place. Science 179:250–258, 1973

Rosner R: Medical disability compensation: a practicum, in Critical Issues in American Psychiatry and the Law. Edited by Rosner R. Springfield IL, Charles C Thomas, 1982

Rothstein MA: Legal issues in the medical assessment of physical impairment by third-party physicians. J Leg Med 5:503–548, 1984

Snibbe JR, Peterson PJ, Sosner B: Study of psychological characteristics of a workers' compensation sample using the MMPI and Millon Clinical Multiaxial Inventory. Psychol Reports 47:959–966, 1980

Weinberger LE, Gross BH: The mental health-legal report, in The Mental Health Professional and the Legal System. Edited by Gross BH, Weinberger LE, San Francisco, Jossey-Bass, 1982

Zusman J, Simon J: Differences in repeated psychiatric examinations of litigants to a lawsuit. Am J Psychiatry 14:1300–1304, 1983

17

Psychiatric Disability: The Veterans' Administration

John O. Lipkin, M.D.

Throughout history, nations have sought to settle disputes between them by fighting. The foot soldiers, archers, sailors, cavalry, and other combatants were exposed to a unique range of human experience which often changed their lives in permanent ways. Some were triumphant and reaped large benefits as spoils of war, grants of land, powerful positions in their societies, or the positive sense of having overcome terrifying odds. Others had more complex experiences characterized by mixtures of terror and triumph, pain, survival, and uncertainty about the meaning and importance of both national policy and their own lives. No one lives through a war without being changed by the experience.

After a war, nations have always been faced with groups of soldiers whose combat skills cannot be used readily in a peaceful setting. In addition, for the wounded and disabled, the need for a societal response has been recognized for centuries. The development of career military service for the former and veterans' benefits for the latter represent an approach to each of these issues.

THE VETERANS' ADMINISTRATION DISABILITY SYSTEM: A CASE APPROACH

The development of psychiatric symptoms or illnesses occurs in 20 percent of men and women who serve in combat settings. Some of the illnesses derive simply from the psychological stresses of war. Other illnesses must be understood in more complex terms. Schizophrenia, the etiology of which has genetic, biologic, and environmental factors, occurs in young adults of military age, but may not afflict a particular individual without exposure to the deprivation, fear, and danger produced by military service. The development of anxiety disorders, affective illness, and organic brain syndromes can be understood easily in some cases, but may be very difficult to sort out in others. Determination of psychiatric disability, in general, and determination of its relationship to military service, in particular, poses an assortment of clinical questions which can be exceedingly complex. These determinations are often critically important to veterans because of the sweeping impact on veterans' benefits which follow from them.

The Veterans' Administration (VA) manages a variety of programs for veterans, including health care, financial awards, educational benefits, mortgage insurance, and burial benefits. Access to these benefits in some instances depends on the presence or absence of a disability as determined by the VA. For many people, the process of disability determination seems mysterious and time consuming. Because nearly two-thirds of the VA budget is spent on compensation, pension, or survivor benefits for veterans and/or their families, the legislative and executive branches of government have struggled to provide a system which is both responsive and cautious. The 1985 VA budget approaches 30 billion dollars. A decision to provide service-connected disability to a young veteran can provide benefits to that individual and cost the government as much as a million dollars during a lifetime.

In high school, Joe was an excellent student who played varsity basketball and worked on the school newspaper. He dated occasionally and seemed well liked. After graduation, he enlisted in the Navy, hoping to see some of the world and earn enough money to go to college. His first two years of active service apparently were successful, but he began to come to the infirmary for occasional symptoms like ringing in the ears and headaches. His early evaluations described him as consistently cooperative, efficient, and reliable. Toward the end of the second year, he was not accepted for a special training course because a superior described him as somewhat isolated and occasionally suspicious of others' motives. Within a few weeks he asked to see the commanding officer to appeal this rejection. During the discussion he indicated that he knew he had been rejected because people were accusing him of homosexuality. He indicated that he had heard these accusations on his radio and showed the officer a copy of his latest evaluation in which his name had been spelled "Jo." He said that leaving off the "e" in Joe was proof that people were lying about him. Psychiatric consultation found him to have delusions, auditory hallucinations, ideas of reference, and a fear of being controlled. After a month of intensive outpatient psychotherapy and a low dose of trifluoperazine, he seemed improved and was able to complete four years in the Navy with monthly follow-up care. Following discharge from the Navy, he enrolled in college. He sought outpatient care from the college health service, but received no medication. His therapist described him as pleasant, socially isolated, and occasionally suspicious of others. The diagnostic impression was schizotypal personality disorder. During final exams at the end of the first year, he walked out of an examination, shouting that he could not answer the questions when everyone was looking at him and accusing him of being a homosexual, communist punk. He was so agitated that the campus police brought him to a local hospital where he was heavily medicated with chlorpromazine. Within a few days, he was transferred to a VA medical center where he seemed subdued, inappropriate, suspicious, and referential. He left after two days and took his remaining exams with passing grades. Three months later (14 months after discharge from service) he was hospitalized again, with hallucinations, delusions of control, thought insertion, flat affect, and agitation. Extensive observation without medication revealed severe psychosis. Given neuroleptics, he cleared rapidly, and after a month confided that the voices seemed to diminish with medication, but had been present since his third year in the Navy. The diagnosis was paranoid schizophrenia. A VA contact officer (VA employee who counsels hospitalized patients about their benefits) encouraged him to apply for service-connected disability benefits.

The process of obtaining service-connected disability can follow a variety of paths. The fictional case history provided will be used to illustrate many of the steps involved.

Service-connected disability means that a particular injury or illness resulting in disability occurred while the individual was on active duty in the military. In some situations, a condition which existed prior to enlistment in the military may be aggravated by events during the period of military service and be considered service-connected. The underlying principle is that the individual was carefully screened before entering service and had been considered "sound" before he or she was accepted for military duty.

If Joe had been severely psychotic while in the service, he would have received a medical discharge which would have established that his illness began during the service period. He would have been placed on the Temporary Disability Retired List (TDRL) and reexamined every 18 months for five years. There would be no question about the service-connected status of his illness, and the only subject for further deliberation would be the degree of disability present.

In order to pursue his application for service-connected disability, Joe filled out forms provided by the contact officer and sent them to the nearest Veterans' Administration Regional Office (VARD) where the material was reviewed by the Department of Veterans Benefits (DVB). During the next few months, his military records, including medical records and the records of his treatment in college and at the community hospital were compiled and reviewed.

The application for service-connected disability was denied because his first formal diagnosis of psychosis occurred 14 months after discharge from the service. (One year is the presumptive period allowed for psychiatric illness, except in prisoners of war and in cases of post-traumatic stress disorder, delayed type.) The military record did not make a definitive diagnosis, and the first diagnosis rendered was schizotypal personality disorder. Since personality disorders are considered lifelong response patterns, a personality disorder diagnosis cannot be classified as service-connected.

During the next three years, Joe paid no attention to the question of disability. He struggled to complete college, but had increasing difficulty and lower grades each semester. Because his disorder was not service-connected, his eligibility for outpatient care stopped one year after his discharge from the hospital. He occasionally took some trifluoperazine, which he had leftover from his year of outpatient treatment. During his last year of college he had another hospitalization which lasted three months. He was again advised to apply for service-connected status. He was briefly examined at the VA regional office where he denied delusions and hallucinations, but also did not inform the examiner of his past history or current medications.

The application was denied for the second time, again because the diagnosis was schizotypal personality disorder.

He completed college after five years, but could not find a job. After a month of unsuccessful interviews in which his marginal college record and withdrawn personal style worked against him, he sought inpatient treatment because he thought that his hallucinations were so loud that the job interviewers could hear them. He met all *DSM-III* criteria for schizophrenia. On the advice of another patient, he contacted a representative of one of the veterans' service organizations (American Legion, AMVETS, Disabled American Veterans, Veterans of Foreign Wars, Vietnam Veterans of America, etc.), who reviewed the case and recommended that he initiate an appeal to the Board of Veterans' Appeals (BVA).

The Board of Veterans Appeals provides final review of all claims which have been rejected by the Department of Veterans Benefits and are appealed by the veteran or his or her authorized representative. The decisions of the Board are final except in cases where new information has been found.

The Board of Veterans' Appeals received all of Joe's records and reviewed them. The members of the Board (two lawyers and a physician) determined that an outside evaluation should be done and sent the records to an outside expert in psychiatry. The outside examiner reviewed all the information and summarized the case as follows:

> This 28-year-old veteran enlisted in the Navy at 18 after an apparently excellent high school career. He successfully completed boot camp and two years of active duty with excellent ratings. In his second year he began to have vague physical complaints and his evaluations began to indicate, for the first time, some social isolation and suspiciousness. Following a rejection for advanced training, he expressed delusions, ideas of reference, and paranoid thinking. Psychiatric consultation described him as having hallucinations, delusions, and the fear of being controlled. Although no formal diagnosis was made, he was treated with major tranquilizers as if he had a psychotic illness. In all probability, a definite diagnosis was avoided in order to allow him to complete his service if at all possible. He appeared to respond promptly to medication. The most likely diagnosis would have been schizophrenia, although not enough time had elapsed to permit a definite diagnosis. He was maintained on medication for the last two years of his military service. Following discharge from the service, he was hospitalized within a year with an illness requiring medication and hospitalization, but left before it was possible to separate his clinical condition from medication effects. After a short interval, he was rehospitalized and carefully studied. A clear diagnosis of schizophrenia which meets *DSM-III-R* criteria was made. Despite his completion of college, his performance appears to have declined gradually, and he has residual symptoms of schizophrenia. His difficulty getting a job is consistent with the course of many people who have schizophrenia.
>
> "The VA examiner who saw him as a schizotypal personality was misled by both medication effects and the patient's unwillingness to trust him with essential clinical information. Based on the information provided, the diagnosis of schizotypal personality is understandable, but mistaken.

"This veteran's diagnosis is paranoid schizophrenia as described in *DSM-III-R* and it began during his second year in the Navy. His subsequent clinical course is fully consistent with this diagnosis and is not consistent with a diagnosis of personality disorder.

Based on this careful review and analysis of the case, the Board of Veterans' Appeals awarded service-connected disability for schizophrenia. This award guaranteed eligibility for treatment of his illness, and for compensation depending on the degree of his disability.

CONDUCTING THE DISABILITY EVALUATION OF A VETERAN

In examining a veteran to determine whether a psychiatric disability is present, psychiatrists should obtain and evaluate all available information. In addition to the usual careful history, special attention must be paid to the history of military service, both because it is directly relevant to the question of service-connection and because it may provide clear information about the veteran's adaptability, response to stress, and early adult development. Veterans who have been in combat situations are at risk to develop post-traumatic stress disorder (PTSD), which is often missed if details about specific events, injuries, and losses are not elicited.

Clinical record review often will provide hints about sudden or subtle changes in personality. Caution must be exercised to place a patient's longitudinal history in a logical perspective. Since these patients have often been examined by different clinicians at different stages of their lives, they may have received different diagnoses. Some clinicians place great emphasis on previous diagnosis while others focus entirely on current signs and symptoms. Neither approach alone will do justice to the patient in some situations. In general, it is most practical to seek a single framework to explain the range of difficulties which may be found in a lengthy clinical record. *DSM-III* stresses the importance of listing multiple Axis I diagnoses when the necessary diagnostic criteria have been met. However, when evaluating patients for the purpose of disability, it is essential to remember the complex, nonclinical, social issues which will be addressed on the basis of the evaluation, and provide a clarifying explanatory discussion. For example, in the clinical case used above, an effective disability evaluation will explain the relationship between schizotypal personality disorder, medication effects, and prodromal or residual signs of schizophrenia.

During the interview, attention must be paid to all of the subtleties of the mental status examination. Questions raised during the review of previous examinations and records should be resolved whenever possible. Once service-connection has been established, the VA determines the degree of disability by using a rating schedule which assesses the average impairment of earning capacity in civilian occupations. For this reason, the psychiatric examiner must make special efforts to determine what findings on the mental status examination may have clear impact on the person's ability to seek, obtain, and keep a job. Although this task may be complex, it is central to the disability examination for veterans.

For a veteran with a service-connected illness or injury, severe disability in which gainful employment is not feasible will be rated as 100 percent. This disability may be the result of an impairment of mind or body. The rating schedules range from 0-percent disability, which maintains permanent eligibility for treatment, to 100-percent disability, which pays an unmarried veteran over $1,000 per month.

Specifics of the veteran's current functioning ability, obtained directly or with the assistance of family members' reports and social work surveys, also will provide essential information to be used in the determination of the extent of an individual's disability.

Essential Information for Psychiatric Disability Examinations of Veterans

Records of previous examination and treatment: The *Claims File* is the record of information maintained by the Department of Veterans' Benefits. It usually contains military medical records and records of other treatment received by the veteran and often contains statements by the military, the veteran, and the veteran's family about the development of the illness.

Military records: Particularly for prisoners of war and patients with possible post-traumatic stress disorders, military records may be critically important in clarifying the nature of the conditions experienced by the veteran. These may be obtained from the National Personnel Records Center (GSA) (Military Personnel Records), 8700 Page Blvd., St. Louis, Missouri 63132.

Thorough clinical evaluation with emphasis on:
1. Longitudinal history—childhood, adolescence, military, and subsequent developments which pertain to the diagnosis and its evolution through the life cycle
2. Past and present specific signs and symptoms of psychiatric illness with recognition of their impact on educational, vocational, and social life (See *Physician's Guide for Disability Evaluation Examinations,* Veterans' Administration, March 1, 1985, and available at VA Medical Centers and Clinics.)
3. Pertinent physical examination and laboratory studies including psychological testing when necessary. The subtle deficits associated with organic mental syndromes require careful description in disability evaluations.

Certain veteran disability evaluations pose complex problems, for both the evaluating physician and the rating boards, which make final determinations concerning service-connection and level of disability particularly difficult. Faced with these cases, it is often prudent to seek consultation or supervision from a clinician who has substantial experience with the disability process of the Veterans' Administration.

Occasionally, an individual who has had psychiatric treatment as an adolescent is accepted for military service. If a psychiatric illness emerges during the period of active duty, its relationship to the previously treated condition will be of critical concern for the Veterans' Administration. As long as the person's condition is either entirely different from the prior illness or unquestionably has been aggravated by military duty, the individual may be awarded a service-connected disability. In cases of anxiety disorder, depressive disorder, and substance abuse, these determinations can be extraordinarily difficult. Careful review of previous medical records, school performance, and other early data are most helpful in making these evaluations.

Another issue for disability examiners involves alcohol abuse and related problems. The military and the Veterans' Administration view alcoholism as the result of "willful misconduct" and will not grant service-connection for it. However, the sequelae of alcoholism, such as liver disease, organic mental syndromes, and traumatic injuries secondary to motor vehicle accidents may be service-connected. Of particular interest in some patients with anxiety disorder, affective disorder, and post-traumatic stress disorder is the question of whether the alcoholism is a secondary effect of another major disorder. When the clinical history spans many years, this can be a difficult determination to make, but has important implications for the patient.

Finally, in the case of individuals seeking award of service-connected disability benefits for post-traumatic stress disorder, particular attention must be paid to the issue of the precipitating stress. Combat can be easily understood as a life-threatening stressor, but many veterans of Vietnam, Korea, and World War II do not find it easy to discuss their experiences. An exceptionally careful military history must be developed and studied for its relevance to present symptoms. For Vietnam veterans, the general conditions of a guerrilla war may have provided a stressor. Familiarity with military conditions can be of value to examiners who have not previously worked with this condition. The VA requires careful documentation of both the stressor and its relationship to current difficulties, and may also verify the military records by contacting the Military Records Center in St. Louis. Any details and corroborative materials which can be provided during the examination will facilitate this determination.

DOES THE VA COMPENSATION AND PENSION PROGRAM HELP VETERANS?

The existence of a compensation and pension program for psychiatrically impaired veterans has made the long-term treatment of these men and women more manageable by guaranteeing them minimal levels of financial support. (Compensation payments are made to veterans with service-connected illness. Pension payments are made to veterans who are totally disabled by psychiatric illness which is not the result of a service-connected condition.) This support provides for basic living arrangements, facilitates maintenance of family units, and enables many veterans to remain in the community.

Unfortunately, there is a widespread belief that this system promotes illness. Despite the absence of evidence for this assertion, many clinicians apparently believe that these payments encourage patients to remain disabled.

Walker and McCourt studied 211 patients discharged from a Veterans' Administration facility who had diagnoses of schizophrenia and had been hospitalized for a median length of stay of seven months. Patients were evaluated in terms of their in-hospital work activity and their work activity during the six months after discharge. Walker and McCourt observed that 53 percent participated in some form of work during the last one to two months of hospitalization, while only 23 percent were employed in the community after discharge. In addition, they report that service-connected status had no relationship to work status either in the hospital or in the community. The authors were particularly impressed by the difficulty experienced by patients with schizophrenia in obtaining jobs (Walker and McCourt 1965).

Veterans rated less than 100-percent disabled for service-connected psychiatric illness receive a temporary increase in their disability rating (and compensation) if they are hospitalized for that illness longer than 21 days. During the period of hospital treatment, they receive compensation as if 100-percent disabled. Pokorny and Moore studied 100 consecutive psychiatric admissions to a Veterans' Administration hospital, making subjective estimates of the relationship of compensation issues to the admission. They estimated that there was no connection in 70 percent of the admissions (Pokorny and Moore 1975). Carlton (1966) studied 97 patients with a diagnosis of schizophrenia whose level of disability and compensation were reduced over a 10-year period. Rehospitalizations were examined, looking for relationships to compensation reduction. To the author's surprise, veterans whose compensation was reduced stayed out of the hospital longer than those whose compensation was not decreased. In addition, veterans who appealed these reductions stayed out of the hospital longer than those who did not appeal.

These small-scale explorations of the relationships between illness and remuneration are not sufficient to dismiss the question of a detrimental impact of compensation on the health of veterans. The available information consistently denies the hypothesis that veterans' benefits promote psychiatric illness. More important, perhaps, for clinicians making these evaluations, there is no question that service-connection provides eligibility for treatment on a sustained basis.

There are 455,648 veterans whose psychiatric or neurologic diseases are service-connected; 28 percent of this group were rated as 10-percent disabled or less, receiving compensation of less than $100; 65 percent were rated as 50-percent disabled or less; only 21 percent of these veterans were viewed as 100-percent disabled. It is also interesting to note that two and one-half times as many veterans are rated as 100-percent disabled for psychiatric or neurologic reasons as for medical or surgical ones (Veterans' Administration 1984).

CONCLUSION

The Veterans' Administration compensation and pension system provides a useful financial support system for a significant number of disabled veterans. Despite folklore to the contrary, there is no evidence that these benefits hamper veterans' recovery.

Careful scrutiny of relevant clinical and historical facts is essential to the development of a coherent analysis of each veteran's situation and needs.

REFERENCES

Carlton MG: Relation of reduction in compensation to rehospitalization. Psychol Rep 19:835-841, 1966
Pokorny AD, Moore FJ: Neurosis and compensation II. Archives of Industrial Health 15:284-292, 1957
Veterans' Administration: Annual Report. Washington, DC, U.S. Government Printing Office, 1984
Walker R, McCourt J: Employment experience among 200 schizophrenic patients in hospital and after discharge. Am J Psychiatry 122:316-319, 1965

18

Incentives and Disincentives of Disability Insurance for the Chronically Mentally Ill

H. Richard Lamb, M.D.

D isability-insurance programs for the chronically mentally ill are now takcn for granted in the United States. The discussion here will focus on the federal programs, Social Security Disability Insurance (SSDI) and Supplemental Security Income (SSI), and, in particular, on SSI. Theoretically, there is a distinction between SSDI and SSI. SSDI is a form of insurance (earned and paid for by those who receive benefits) and is linked to Medicare entitlement, while SSI is a form of welfare (Liebman 1976) and is linked to Medicaid. In fact, there tends to be a blurring of these two income-maintenance programs; the longer a person receives benefits, the more blurred the distinction becomes in the minds of the recipients and in the perceptions of others. SSI is by far the larger program, and will be used here to illustrate the advantages and problems of income-maintenance programs for the psychiatrically disabled.

The extension of eligibility for Aid to the Totally Disabled (ATD—now, SSI) to the mentally ill in 1963 had a major impact on psychiatry. What have been the benefits and what have been the adverse effects of this eligibility? What can be done to ensure that the large population of the long-term mentally ill who require SSI are initially

343

approved to receive it and then are successful in retaining their eligibility?

BENEFITS OF THE SHIFT FROM AID TO SSI

The beneficial consequences have been impressive. Above all, a source of funding became available that made it possible for the mentally ill who are unable to support themselves through work or private funds to move out of state hospitals and to be maintained in the community. Previously, state governments had been willing to bear the cost of state hospitals, making only feeble and scattered attempts to provide funding for community alternatives. Although the frequently adverse consequences of prolonged state hospitalization were evident and were made known to the public on occasion through newspaper exposés (Deutsch 1948), the fear of the mentally ill, and the public's apathy and desire to isolate them in locked and usually distant institutions, prevailed. The advent of psychoactive medications and the community mental health movement made it feasible for the mentally ill to live outside the massive, impersonal institutions, but only the availability of ATD funds enabled those without resources, who would have been destined to spend their lives in state hospitals, to actually be placed in a variety of community-living arrangements. These settings ranged from good to poor, from independent living to single-occupancy hotel rooms. In some cases, ATD payments made these patients more acceptable to their own families; before this financial support was made available, the patients sometimes had been regarded as an economic and emotional burden. Although there were many indignities to be suffered in the process of being approved for ATD, the end result was a dependable source of income for the mentally ill. I am convinced that thousands of patients could have been discharged from state hospitals years earlier had ATD been available to them. Furthermore, the extension of welfare and income maintenance to the mentally ill meant that their needs were at last recognized; prior to this, ATD was available only for the physically disabled.

From the beginning, there were concerns about potential problems with this process—particularly with regard to officially labeling this group "totally disabled" and "mentally ill" and thereby stigmatizing them. Because of this danger, Aid to the Totally Disabled was changed to Aid to the Disabled. The program was, however, still called AID. To indicate the possibility of recovery, a periodic review of eligibility was required by the regulations, although it was actually performed perfunctorily. While these changes were a step in the right direction, the term *disabled* was impressed on the minds of recipients, who generally continued to feel labeled and stigmatized.

The change from ATD to SSI in January 1975, and the shift in administration from welfare departments to the Social Security Administration, has lessened the stigma of ATD for some patients (Liebman 1976). One study (Lamb and Goertzel 1977) revealed some of these effects. Most of the subjects in this study referred to themselves as being "on Social Security" or "on Social Security insurance." Their financial support no longer clearly labeled them (in their own eyes at least) as psychiatrically disabled, and most no longer considered themselves to be on welfare. The term Social Security had a more normative sound to recipients. Thus, SSI had partially resolved some important problems for the mentally ill.

But Estroff (1981, p. 169) makes a strong argument that, for many others, "SSI represents one of the most permanent and visible labels the clients possess. It is the culmination of the chronic client-labeling process." She points out that patients have to reveal their source of income when applying for housing and some are turned down because of this. Moreover, they have to attest under oath on their SSI application forms that they are disabled and must specify this disability as mental disorder. Even in superficial conversations with strangers, the patient's lack of a job and means of income are usually revealed.

The advantages and disadvantages of SSI apply, of course, not only to those who have been deinstitutionalized, but also to the generation of chronically and severely mentally ill persons who have reached adulthood in this era of deinstitutionalization.

SECONDARY GAIN IN SSI

In recent years, interest has developed anew in treatment and rehabilitation programs for long-term severely ill patients (Lamb 1971). Components of such programs are usually social and vocational rehabilitation, designed to help these patients join in the mainstream of society to the extent to which they are able, and to experience the satisfactions of participation and even production.

To what extent does the aspect of secondary gain inherent in SSI interfere with such an approach? Although much has been written about compensation neurosis, little has been said publicly about the corresponding, although more subtle, problems inherent in the SSI program. Perhaps we do not mind paying for mental illness so long as it keeps patients quiet and out of sight. It is the thrust of this chapter that serious consideration should be given to all aspects of the impact of SSI on the psychiatrically disabled. Let us turn first to problems of vocational rehabilitation.

Ask a roomful of experienced clinicians how many psychiatric patients they have known who, once having gotten on SSI, have gotten off and returned to work. Only occasionally does one find a clinician who knows more than one or two.

An event in Missouri highlights the disincentive effects of SSI. When ATD was made readily available for psychiatric patients, one-third of those enrolled in sheltered workshops precipitously quit

(Hilary Sandall, personal communication, May 1976). Unfortunately, no follow-up study was done and we do not know how these patients fared in the long run. This event did make the problem clear, however. We talk of appropriating large sums of money for vocational rehabilitation for the mentally ill, but, at the same time, we undermine their already weakened resolve to overcome their apprehension and try to deal with the everyday demands of life, such as self-support and achievement of a measure of independence.

Frequently, although by no means always, the severely mentally ill have a reduced work capacity. For many, the routine demands of work and social relations are major stresses. So much effort goes into their struggle with illness that they have little energy left to deal with a work situation. Handling interpersonal relationships with supervisors and co-workers is a major stress. The very thought of work is frightening, for it carries the risk of yet another failure. A therapeutic or, at least, protective work setting and an adequate preparatory period of vocational rehabilitation should be made available for many of these precariously compensated people.

Those who believe in the value of vocational rehabilitation stress that heightened self-esteem issues from experiencing oneself as productive, making a contribution to society, and achieving at least partial self-support and independence. Work therapy is recognized as being fully as important as talking therapy. Having no reason to get up in the morning and no structured day to look forward to causes profound feelings of emptiness in the lives of most of the severely mentally ill. Rewarding and gratifying use of leisure time is equally important. A combination of work and play is both normative and restorative.

How does this square with a system in which continued financial support at a low standard of living is contingent upon the patient maintaining a sick status? When one includes Medicaid, food stamps, the supplement to the basic federal grant supplied by a number of states, exemption from income taxes, and the possibility of pooling one's resources and living together with another recipient, the standard of living may not be so low. It is not surprising that a large percentage of the mentally ill remain "disabled" and totally (or almost so) dependent on SSI. Most of these persons could be rehabilitated only into low-paying, sheltered employment or entry-level jobs at a minimum wage, even if they succeeded in overcoming their fear of losing one of the cornerstones of what little security they have: their SSI status (DeLott 1976). The secondary gain of illness, already a problem with many long-term psychiatric patients, is thus further reinforced.

Case Example

Mr. A, a 26-year-old man, has been hospitalized three times with a diagnosis of paranoid schizophrenia. His social worker suggested that he apply for SSI during his second hospitalization, and he has now been on SSI for two years. He has held a number of entry-level jobs, but none for more than six months and none in the last two years. He is now seeing a psychiatrist and takes antipsychotic medication regularly. He was referred to a vocational rehabilitation counselor who thought Mr. A could handle a low-pressure job, providing that he remain in treatment. The counselor arranged for him to be interviewed for a job as groundskeeper at a golf course. The foreman there handles his employees well and has supervised ex-mental patients in the past with good results.

The prospect of being a groundskeeper appealed to Mr. A. He liked outdoor work, and the job would involve minimal demands to interact with other people. He found staying home all day difficult and depressing; he did not know how to answer when people asked what he did. Mr. A was interviewed and hired, but later that day he called the boss and quit the job. Why? Later he talked with his counselor about his fear of failure. Despite reassurance from both his counselor and the Social Security office, he could not be convinced that he would not lose his SSI permanently if he accepted the job. He could not forget the red tape and interminable delays involved in getting SSI, both initially and later when he was discharged from the hospital and had to be reinstated. Besides, Mr. A told his counselor, his net pay from the job (at minimum wage) would be little more than his SSI check (which includes the California supplement) plus food stamps. He would be taking quite a chance, and he was frightened. Two years later, nothing has changed. Mr. A refuses to see his vocational counselor and is depressed and immobilized.

The message given to patients by the SSI system is fully as important as the financial remuneration. Essentially, they are told, "You are sick, disabled, and unable to work." Rehabilitation may be mentioned, but the patient is seldom convinced. Thus, the SSI system does not counteract the pull toward regression and dependency. Its purpose is income maintenance, not helping the person act or feel like a contributing or significant member of society. In terms of their source of income, patients perceive that society expects little of them. If recipients of SSI choose to do so, they have the means to live an undemanding life with family or in a board and care home. There is little incentive to participate in a treatment program, either social or vocational. For a significant proportion of the chronically mentally ill patients who have ego strength sufficient only to cope with modest demands and minimal social stimulation (Lamb 1979), this arrangement may be entirely appropriate. Nevertheless, such a system undermines the already reduced motivation of many mental patients who could benefit from rehabilitation programs.

FUNDING VOCATIONAL REHABILITATION

We are in an era of growing unpopularity of expansion or even retention of social programs. Whatever rehabilitation funding agencies may say, and even feel, about the desirability of vocational rehabilitation or work-activity programs that improve the quality of life without necessarily leading to paid employment, they must face certain realities. When one is justifying a budget to Congress or to a legislature, for instance, no argument is more persuasive than the potential of a program to rapidly place people in competitive employment—to "transform taxeaters into taxpayers." Such "rehabilitation" programs may seek patients who need little assistance to join the ranks of the employed.

Thus, there is a disinclination to provide the kinds of rehabilitation appropriate to the needs of long-term, severely disabled patients. This holds true not just for services to improve the quality of life, but also programs that, in the long run, are capable of placing individuals in sheltered employment and preparing them for entry-level jobs. These services may take years and are not cheap; funding sources often give lip service to them but when the final budget is made known, these services are funded in token amounts if they are funded at all. There is, then, a reluctance to provide adequate rehabilitation to the seriously disabled even if they are potentially capable of achieving increased independence through employment. Given the reluctance to fund rehabilitation appropriate to the needs of the severely disabled and the disincentives associated with income-maintenance programs, one might conclude, as some in government are starting to imply, that society has decided to "pay off" the mentally ill rather than rehabilitate them.

WHAT CAN BE DONE?

Steps should be taken to improve income-maintenance programs such as SSI. The first step would be to screen individuals carefully for entry into the SSI system and encourage them to apply only if they are truly disabled. A major problem is the pressure from local jurisdictions such as cities and counties to divert persons from general relief or general assistance (funded entirely by local money) to SSI (funded primarily by federal and state money). Since SSI usually provides more money than general relief, sometimes the pressure comes from a patient's case manager or therapist.

Mental health professionals often contribute to the problems: We are frequently reluctant to see our patients take low-status, minimum-wage jobs even though this is the present limit of their capabilities. Middle-class professionals need to guard against a tendency to view nonprofessional or nonintellectual work in terms of their own subjective reactions to it (Mackota 1976). Concentrating on the aspects of work they themselves find dull, monotonous, or even degrading, they often fail to see that others can achieve as great a sense of mastery and self-worth from success in whatever job is within their capabilities as professionals do in theirs.

Individuals who need general relief only for a temporary crisis may find themselves propelled into a system where, despite the required periodic SSI review, they remain for years or even life. At times in the past, the mere fact that a person was in psychotherapy seemed sufficient to a welfare department eligibility worker to initiate an SSI application, even though the person may have functioned well in the past and was only temporarily disabled. Such inappropriate entries into the SSI system need to be reevaluated; primary consideration should be given to the patient's *long-range* interests.

Another way to reduce the occurrence of chronic regression in the SSI system is to make SSI reevaluation more meaningful. Each patient should be evaluated carefully and sensitively by rehabilitation professionals, who would offer the opportunity of social and vocational rehabilitation suited to the individual patient. Patients who are not likely to withstand the stress of such activities should not be pressured or made to feel guilty about not participating in them. Further, the opportunity to receive rehabilitation should be seen both by the patient and the Social Security Administration as a benefit, like Medicaid, not as a requirement. The patient's participation—or nonparticipation—in rehabilitation programs should in no way affect his or her eligibility for SSI (or SSDI).

To minimize the disincentive effects of SSI and the sick role, the law now allows SSI recipients to keep a share of earnings from employment. This provision should not only be retained, but great care should be taken to ensure that recipients do not find their checks stopped rather than simply decreased. By the same token, there should be prompt restoration of SSI if the patient's effort to work is not successful. Fears of long delays in restoration of benefits deter many patients from even attempting to venture into the world of work.

Since it cannot be predicted which patients will benefit from a rehabilitation or habilitation program and which might react adversely, every person at the point of application and approval of SSI should be given every opportunity to participate in a comprehensive treatment and rehabilitation program. Whatever services are indicated should be made available: individual and group psychotherapy, social and vocational rehabilitation, training, sheltered work settings, employment assistance, day treatment, linkage to therapeutic housing programs, and social services. Patients should be monitored to ascertain how they respond to treatment and to inducements to greater social and occupational participation. If patients react adversely, manifest an exacerbation of symptoms, or seem refractory to active help, the professional should be able to reset their goals at any point in the process and accept the patients' limitations and possibly their needs for a passive, dependent life style that will make minimal demands on them. But professionals should leave the door open to treatment and rehabilitation opportunities in the future. In the meantime, they should offer patients services they can or will accept, including the option to call at times of crisis or great stress. Efforts must also be made to upgrade residential facilities and bring treatment and supportive services to patients who are not ready to come to them.

Mental health professionals also have an important role to play with that large proportion of the long-term mentally ill who require SSI on an ongoing basis. After helping them gain initial approval, the professional can help them retain their eligibility. The two main principles for professionals to remember in this regard are persistence and documentation of disability (Anderson 1982). Most mentally disabled persons need considerable assistance in finding their way through the SSI application procedure, and are especially prone to drop their claims after the first denial. It is at this point, as well as at the time of initial application, that the advocacy of mental health professionals on behalf of their patients is crucial. It should be remembered that there is considerable disagreement even among psychiatrists doing disability determinations on SSI claims and, moreover, that a large proportion of denials are reversed by Administrative Law Judges upon appeal (Anderson 1982).

A FINAL WORD

I urge discussion and reassessment of a social policy that was conceived in a humanitarian spirit but that has brought about some unintended and undesirable results. The topic is often avoided by professionals who fear that even the raising of questions will support the arguments of those who would abolish social programs because they consider any social dependency immoral, even that brought on by psychiatric disability.

REFERENCES

Anderson JR: Social Security and SSI benefits for the mentally disabled. Hosp Community Psychiatry 33:295-298, 1982

DeLott F: Societal income versus willingness to succeed. Paper presented at the National Conference of the International Association of Psycho-Social Rehabilitation Services, Chicago, October 14–17, 1976

Deutsch A: The Shame of the States. New York, Harcourt Brace Jovanovich, 1948

Estroff SE: Making It Crazy: An Ethnography of Psychiatric Clients in an American Community. Berkeley, University of California Press, 1981

Lamb HR: The new asylums in the community. Arch Gen Psychiatry 36:129-134, 1979

Lamb HR, Goertzel V: The long-term patient in the era of community treatment. Arch Gen Psychiatry 34:670-682, 1977

Lamb HR: Rehabilitation in Community Mental Health. San Francisco CA, Jossey-Bass, 1971

Liebman L: The definition of disability in Social Security and Supplemental Security Income: drawing the bounds of social welfare estates. Harvard Law Review 89:833-867, 1976

Mackota C: Using work therapeutically, in Community Survival for Long-Term Patients. Edited by Lamb HR. San Francisco, Jossey-Bass, 1976

19

A Cross-Cultural Perspective on Psychiatric Disability

Martin Gittelman, Ph.D.
Bertram Black, M.S.W.

Every society must decide how it will cope with those unable to care for themselves. Until the eighteenth century, with the advent of the asylum, the mentally ill were cared for by their families or were dependent on charity dispensed by religious organizations or individuals. In the twentieth century, the disabled slowly have begun to be integrated into the general society. First to win entitlement to special care and rehabilitation were soldiers wounded in World War I. Since then, other groups of disabled persons gradually have come to be recognized as needing attention and aid.

The mentally ill, perhaps the largest group among all the disabled—fewer than 10 percent escape long-term impairment (Ciompi 1980)—have had the greatest difficulty in winning acceptance by society. In fact, in the 1930s and 1940s, the mentally ill and mentally retarded were among those the Nazis deemed unfit to live, and tens of thousands of them perished in concentration camps or died of starvation in asylums. Even in our own time, hundreds of thousands of the mentally ill are homeless, wandering the streets, and finding shelter wherever they can.

World War II saw the largely serendipitous establishment of some of the earliest rehabilitation schemes for the mentally ill. England, faced with a struggle for survival, set up workshops in mental hospitals. In France, groups of mental patients were taken by physicians to work on farms in exchange for food. Drs. P. Palvet (personal

351

communication, 1979), J. Tosquelles (Palvet, personal communication, 1979), and J. Dury (personal communication, 1967) were among the first to engage in this work, and found that their patients markedly improved. In the 1960s, these psychiatrists became leaders in the movement to develop the sector system[1] of care in France.

From the standpoint of technique, European psychiatry differs little from that practiced in the United States. What is different is that, in the main, European psychiatry (defined more commonly as *social psychiatry*) is practiced within the framework of the community. It is part of a universal, comprehensive, publicly supported system of health services. Further differentiation is based on the European tendency to adopt what might be termed a "low-technology" approach. To be sure, medication, psychotherapy, and hospitalization are used in treating mental illness; but other types of care are likely to be accessible as well—types of care that are less common in the United States. For example, it is not unusual that at least half of all care provided the acutely mentally ill is rendered in the patients' homes. Moreover, long-term neuroleptic medication is much more likely to be used in Europe, where patients may be seen by the same physician regularly for years (personal communications, George Simpson; Stefanis et al., 1986).

Since World War II, most countries of Western Europe have become what is known as welfare states. Despite swings from left, to center, to right in political power, there has been a generally increasing movement toward providing health services, economic assistance, housing, and other necessities of life for the entire population. Although the course of service development has not been free of criticism or difficulty, the period since the war has been one of considerable progress in the care of the mentally ill.

With but few exceptions, there are no homeless mentally ill in Western Europe, nor is there widespread dissatisfaction with the service system. The exceptions are countries such as Ireland and England, where some support payments are time limited and may cease after 90 days or a year. This has begun to produce a growing number of homeless mentally ill people. The number, however, is still relatively small compared with the United States, presumably because other components of the "safety net"—the system of services, benefits, entitlements, and lodging schemes—are still in place.

Deinstitutionalization has proceeded at a slower pace in some European countries than it has in the United States. France and the Netherlands, for example, have reduced their psychiatric hospital bed capacities from the high census of the 1950s by little more than

---

[1] France has been divided, as have many European countries, into geographic regions, or *sectors*. Each sector has its psychiatric team which is responsible for the comprehensive care and rehabilitation of the mentally ill. Teams work both in psychiatric hospitals and in the community. (For further discussion, see Gittelman, 1975.)

20 percent (Gittelman 1983), and England, by 50 percent (Morris 1983). At the moment, further reduction in the number of beds for long-term care is the subject of debate. The emergence of the "new" chronically mentally ill—those who have not previously been hospitalized—in part has dispelled the notion that poor hospital conditions alone are responsible for chronicity. The impetus appears to be toward retaining the current number of beds for those patients requiring long-term care and reducing the number of beds for acute, short-term care, thereby prompting home or other types of community care as an alternative.

The hierarchy of services and benefits—the community-support system—that prevails in most Western European countries is important in such trends. Mental health professionals there have a considerable range of care options available.

CHARACTERISTICS OF WESTERN EUROPEAN SYSTEMS

Most Western European countries' mental health services are distinguished by:

Continuity in planning, policy, and administration: Unlike the United States, direction in planning and administration of services does not change following elections. Most systems are administered by career officials who have risen through the ranks, often having served first as district or sector psychiatrists. Such continuity fosters more accountability. Those who plan systems are usually still working within them and are present to be held responsible for any shortcomings which ultimately emerge (Gittelman 1975; Goldman 1982–83).

Publicly financed, comprehensive health and mental health care: Financing systems vary from nation to nation. In some, such as England and Ireland, health program funding is derived from progressive taxation; in the Scandinavian countries, from local taxation; and in Belgium, France, and West Germany, from a combination of payroll and employer taxes. In any case, all Western European countries through the years have moved toward a system which provides treatment, medication, and follow-up at little or no cost to the patient at the time of care (Gittelman 1975; Goldman 1982–83).

Organization of health care to minimize gaps and ensure continuity (e.g., through sectorization): Care is made available in community centers, psychiatric wards of general hospitals, outpatient facilities of various kinds, and even the patients' homes by teams of salaried professionals covering the population of a specified geographic area, or sector. Each team often is responsible for as many as 30,000 people (Gittelman 1975; Goldman 1982–83)

This arrangement is now common in many Western European countries. Team members get to know their long-term patients in their own environments; they help patients cope with bureaucratic eligibility requirements and prevent them from "falling between the cracks" of the system. Hospitalizations tend to be avoided through home care and aid of various kinds to patients' families. Some teams in France have demonstrated that it is possible to function without hospital beds at all—all treatment being provided in the home and/or through outpatient services.

Benefits or entitlements for the mentally ill and their families are also available, both in kind (home or office visits, hospital care, medication) or in cash benefits (cash support for those previously employed, never employed, or for families who elect to keep their mentally disabled members at home).

Benefits are widely diversified and often depend on the initiative of local mental health teams. For instance, a team may arrange for temporary hospital care of a patient so the patient's family may enjoy a vacation and much-needed respite from caring for its mentally disabled member. A group of mentally disabled patients may be taken on a trip, under the supervision and care of a mental health team; such vacations are a regular feature of Scandinavian programs. Further, there are such important, but often neglected items of care as dental treatment and the provision of eyeglasses. In a recent study (Roth 1985), it was found that most of the homeless mentally ill in Ohio in need of eyeglasses had none that were usable—eyeglasses that might have enabled them to read employment or housing advertisements. Eyeglasses and dental care are provided for the mentally ill throughout Europe.

Cash benefits generally are available to families who care for disabled members and to the disabled themselves. Such benefits may be time limited, or without time limit, as in the case of payments to the mentally ill in most of Scandinavia. In some instances, a distinction is made between those who have worked (as in the U.S. Social Security Disability Insurance system) and those who have not, but are nonetheless eligible for support, usually at a lower rate (Gittelman 1975; Goldman 1982–83).

Tax incentives for families who care for their mentally ill and/or for employers who arrange for sheltered or full employment for mentally disabled persons capable of work: In recent years, governments have increased the number of incentive programs for firms that employ the mentally disabled (Gittelman 1975; Goldman 1982–83).

Reserved jobs: Traditionally, a small percentage of jobs has been reserved for the war-wounded and the blind. More recently, in several countries, industry has been required to reserve a proportion of positions for the mentally disabled; the numbers, however, have never been great (Gittelman 1975; Goldman 1982–83).

Housing: Policy with regard to housing for the mentally disabled may include transitional arrangements, permanent residence, reservation of a fixed percentage of new housing for the mentally disabled, and tax incentives to promote housing for the disabled or for family associations to develop condominia for their children (Gittelman 1975; Goldman 1982–83).

Habilitation programs to prepare the mentally disabled to live in the community, either independently, with groups, or with families: Such programs include social skills training; independent-living skills (e.g., cooking, shopping, dressing, etc.); and family-support programs and groups. Begun in England and Scotland 15 years ago, such programs have become common throughout Western Europe (Morris 1983; Leff and Vaughn 1984). Medication, various forms of psychotherapy, and psychosocial interventions remain standard treatment for the seriously mentally ill; but the new approach— teaching competence in daily living—is rapidly becoming standard outpatient care practice. The aim is to assist the patient in adapting as comfortably as possible to community and/or family settings and to minimize handicaps.

Families of patients are often enrolled in related training and educational programs, organized either by mental health teams or by parent or family associations (e.g., the Schizophrenia Fellowship, the Union des Familles des Malades Mentales). They are instructed in how to deal with problems they may encounter as a consequence of their family member's illness. The orientation is somewhat similar to that used by programs dealing with other chronic disorders, such as epilepsy, diabetes, etc. Families learn about medications and their side effects, and how to detect signs of impending decompensation, manage aberrant behavior, and reduce stress and conflict—in general how to deal with the mentally ill person in their midst (Alpert et al. in press).

Rehabilitation, day-care centers, day and night hospitals, etc.; economic benefits for the mentally disabled (in the form of discounts on public transportation, on certain types of consumer items, and on admission to recreational facilities, movies and legitimate theaters, sports events, etc.); and *vocational rehabilitation* (discussed in detail below) are also available.

Such a vast array of social and health benefits is, of course, expensive. Yet, in no European country are expenditures on health greater in relation to the GNP than those in the United States (Aaron and Schwartz 1984; Himmelstein and Woolhandler 1986). The difference seems to stem from the greater use of costly hospital care and the fee-for-service system in the United States. In contrast, European mental health care, including planning, policy, and functioning, is provided largely by salaried physicians and is usually the responsibility of the central government.

SOCIAL AND VOCATIONAL REHABILITATION SERVICES

As noted above, rehabilitation services for the handicapped arose from concern for disabled World War I veterans (Black 1977). For example, the British Ex-Service Mental Welfare Society set up a sheltered work environment for shell-shocked veterans of World War I, under the name Thermega, Ltd., located just outside London. In the mid-1920s, the Netherlands opened Consultation Bureaux for the mentally ill that covered many aspects of aftercare and sociovocational therapies. Special vocational services were established in a number of settings for patients with tuberculosis, many of whom were reported to be emotionally disturbed as well.

The Legal Foundation
It was not until after World War II that laws and regulations were enacted which made explicit a range of services that truly could be called rehabilitative. While stimulated by the needs of disabled war veterans, such services gradually became available to all handicapped persons. Laws relating to the disabled generally did not specify the handicapping condition to which they were to apply (e.g., British Disabled Persons Employment Act of 1944, the Netherlands Act of 1947, the 1953 Act of the Federal Republic of Germany, and the Belgian Special Aid Fund of 1956), but the services made available were largely for the physically handicapped (Black 1970). It was not until the 1960s and 1970s that new legislation or amendments to previous laws were enacted making clear that the mentally disabled and mentally ill were to be included (e.g., in the Mental Health Acts of 1959, 1960, and 1961 in the United Kingdom; the General Special Sickness Insurance Act of 1967 in the Netherlands; an Act of 1961 in West Germany that extended the scope of earlier legislation; the Rehabilitation Act of 1968 in Belgium; expansion in 1972 of Denmark's Rehabilitation Act of 1960; a 1963 Royal Ordinance in Sweden; and the addition, in 1961, of the mentally disabled to Norway's Disabled Persons' Act of 1958—see Black 1970).

Significantly, the legal extension to the mentally ill of services for the handicapped came about as countries were beginning to ponder community approaches to psychiatric treatment. Even before neuroleptic drugs began to be used widely in mental hospitals, a number of European countries were experimenting with community mental health care (e.g., in Amsterdam and The Hague in the Netherlands; in Nottingham, England; at the Karolinska Hospital in Stockholm, Sweden; and in such programs as the Association pour l'Élan Retrouvée, in Paris, France).

The term *rehabilitation* was not necessarily used, but there were frequent references to *ergotherapy* and work adjustment. The Europeans put much less emphasis on the psychotherapies and much more on such strategies as creative-arts therapies (e.g., music, art, dance), occupational and recreational therapy, resocialization, psychomotor retraining, and work activities. (Indeed, farming on a large scale was part of the "therapy" in French asylums even in the nineteenth century.) Attempts were made to utilize services for the disabled, particularly those for employment and preparation for employment, on behalf of mental patients; but, initially, success was quite limited.

In many European countries, the relevant legislation deals with three major areas: extension of general social insurance provisions to the disabled, no matter the age at which the handicapping condition occurs; special training and/or special work settings for those unable to return to ordinary employment; and reservation for the handicapped of a certain proportion of jobs in regular business and industry.

The various disability insurance schemes are linked to the social welfare programs and national health insurance systems of their respective countries. They ensure basic economic support for the unemployed disabled. It is true that many rehabilitation specialists believe that all-embracing welfare schemes act as a disincentive to many handicapped people to become involved in occupational training or sheltered-work programs (which may actually be what they are intended to do, in times of high employment). However, in a country such as Sweden, which has as complete a welfare scheme as can be designed, there seems to be no dearth of interest on the part of the disabled, including the mentally disabled, in participating in rehabilitation efforts.

The United Kingdom

Over the past 20 years, the British have developed certain resources for the rehabilitation of the mentally disabled. While there is general agreement that work rehabilitation is useful, there is no great national pressure to give it high priority. Though there are some sheltered-work and industrial programs, the predominant focus is on housing and psychosocial rehabilitation. For example, the Richmond Fellowship, a private nonprofit organization, maintains group homes for the mentally disabled throughout England. Social support groups and social clubs for the mentally ill are common everywhere.

A recent report of the Royal College of Psychiatrists (1980) lists the following relevant types of facility: hospital rehabilitation units, including industrial therapy units, occupational therapy units, and hospital day units; Local Authority day centers; Local Authority rehabilitation and assessment centers; industrial therapy organizations; community-based industrial units; sheltered workshops, including Remploy factories (discussed below); sheltered industrial groups; employment-rehabilitation centers; skill centers; residential training colleges; and colleges of further education.

In reality, there are only two Local Authority rehabilitation centers, five industrial therapy organizations, and only about 200 places in sheltered industrial groups. In general, many of the facilities for rehabilitation of the disabled are better suited to, and more likely to be used by, the physically handicapped than the mentally disabled.

Nevertheless, three of the resources identified on the Royal College list warrant special mention. England was probably the first Western European country to introduce industrial therapy units into its mental hospitals. Industrial therapy programs were established in the 1960s at Banstead Hospital in Sutton and Netherne Hospital in Surrey (Black 1977). The units were transitional in nature, beginning with work on the wards and occupational therapy, progressing through sheltered industrial work and resettlement in the community, to living outside while performing sheltered or open employment.

During the 1960s, there was a series of such developments, but interest began to wane during the 1970s with the emergence of community-based programs. Both the cost required to launch what were really small businesses during a period of economic stringency, and the difficulties in finding capable management and interested psychiatrists also had their effect upon the trend. Yet another factor was deinstitutionalization which, though not carried out to the extent it was in the United States, left in the hospitals only those patients with little functional capacity.

Under the Disabled Persons Act of 1944, the British Ministry of Labour was empowered to establish a company called the Disabled Persons Employment Corporation, Ltd., which came to be known as Remploy. Today, Remploy operates nearly 90 factories, employing about 9,000 disabled people; only a minority are mentally disabled. The factories produce leather and textile goods and furniture and do assembling and packaging. Remploy enjoys preference in acquiring contracts for the manufacture and processing of goods for the government; it also bids for work in the open market. The wage rates are set by agreement with trade unions, which participate in establishing a standard minimum (Black 1977).

During the 1960s, partly because of Remploy's unwillingness to accept recent mental hospital dischargees, and partly as a logical extension of in-hospital industrial therapy units, some hospital superintendents and consulting psychiatrists developed their own community-based sheltered workshops. Most notable were those of the Mapperly Day Hospital, Nottingham, and the industrial therapy organizations (ITOs) in Bristol and London (Southall). In time, some of the ITOs became recognized as specialized, designated Remploy industries. This enabled the former mental patients employed in such workshops to receive the full social insurance benefits given to employees of regular Remploy factories. As in the regular Remploy facilities, government subsidies became available to cover operating deficits and capital outlays. There is now a British Industrial Therapy Association which provides advocacy and training for staff of the ITOs.

An innovative approach to vocational rehabilitation for the mentally ill, borrowed by certain psychosocial rehabilitation centers in the United States, is the use of transitional employment and work enclaves in regular business and industry. In the 1960s, the Bristol ITO tried placing expatients in selected entry-level positions in local industry; this gave the patients an opportunity to test their capabilities and to learn employment skills. Then the ITO placed groups of patients in normal factory settings, under the supervision of a nurse and a regular foreman. Wages were paid by the firms to the ITO, which in turn paid the patients/employees (Black 1970).

The British Manpower Service Commission has since expanded upon this idea for all handicapped persons. As a service for the mentally ill, these sheltered industrial groups (SIGs, as they have come to be called) offer a great advantage. The patient is prepared for regular employment in a realistic setting in which work conditions approximate those in the work-a-day world as closely as possible. For schizophrenic patients, this is particularly significant in alleviating their most serious difficulty, that of transposing experience from one setting to another.

England has led the way in establishing habilitation and assessment programs for the mentally ill. Social and independent-living skills are now routinely taught in most psychiatric day programs and acute care facilities, and families are given training in working with their mentally ill members.

The Netherlands

Traditionally, the Netherlands has depended largely on the family and mental hospitals for care of its mentally ill (DeJong 1984). Health care, in general, is free, and financial support in the form of disability pensions is not time limited. Financial benefits (social security and sick-fund pensions) ease the burden for families caring for mentally ill members. At about the age of 35–40, however, many of the chronically mentally ill enter hospitals, largely because their families (e.g., aging parents) are no longer able to care for them. There is a growing number of group homes and community residences to help solve such problems, but the family home is still the principal locus of care.

Recently there has been a move toward sectorization and provision of mental health services by catchment area. As noted above, deinstitutionalization is progressing slowly in the Netherlands, and hospital stays are longer than almost anywhere else in Europe (May 1976).

Efforts to decentralize care and to humanize hospitals have included the establishment of modern suburban-type group homes in Bakkum, where a single staff member supervises 8 to 10 patients in a family-type residence, which gives the units more of a family atmosphere. Day centers, clubs, and psychosocial rehabilitation centers are staffed largely by hospital-based mental health professionals, who work part time in the extramural settings.

The Dutch have developed a rehabilitation program, unique in its social welfare philosophy, which recognizes the tripartite nature of the country's religious and political system. The philosophy embraces two concepts: *verauiling*, which means mutual cooperation and mutual independence, and *subsidiarity*, which holds that a societal function should be the responsibility of the lowest social unit capable of fulfilling that function. This has led to the development of social and health services under the auspices of voluntary organizations, referred to as *particulier initiatief* (PI) (private initiative), rather than under government control. These PI agencies have become the main provider of services for the disabled. Their organization reflects the three "confessional" divisions of the population: Catholic, Protestant, and nondenominational. Until recent years, each of these divisions was represented in the major political parties as well. In the 1970s, the government began to consolidate the PI agencies, and the strictly political divisions began to blur. The government now owns and manages a number of social service programs, including mental hospitals, a few vocational training facilities, and many of the more than 200 sheltered workshops; but the PIs still own most of the programs for the handicapped, over half of which still have religious connection.

The Netherlands has been using sheltered workshops for the disabled longer than any other European country. Since the Social Employment Scheme for Manual Workers was enacted in 1949, the mentally ill, wherever possible, have been placed in sheltered workshops by the hospital aftercare services. Community-based sheltered workshops have also been established. By 1966, there were 185 sheltered workshops, located throughout the Netherlands, most of which were organized as nonprofit foundations or corporations. The boards of managers or trustees include municipal officials and representatives of industry. The national government has certified the shops, provided funds for capital and start-up, and, to a large extent, covered the deficits in operation. A training and oversight program for workshop directors has been set up under government control.

It is interesting to note that these work-for-pay facilities continue to draw clients despite the fact that the Netherlands has the most complete disability insurance and transfer payment coverage in the world (Reitsma 1984). By the 1970s, the coverage amounted to 80 percent of a disabled person's last wage. All costs of illness and incapacity are paid for through the social and health insurance systems (for a brief but inclusive description of these systems, see De-Jong 1984). A story on the Dutch in the *New York Times* (1985) stated:

> The earned wealth of hard work and the new riches of giant natural gas fields under the marshy land of the north have subsidized schemes that add up to guaranteed lifetime support for everyone, whether they work or not. Dutch egalitarianism is now

such that at great multinational corporations, such as Royal
Dutch/Shell and Phillips, average earnings of top management
are only five times the take-home pay of the lowest laborer. And
combined welfare, unemployment, and disability payments can
add up to much more than working people earn. "It's a bit
ridiculous, I know," said a clerk in an Amsterdam bookstore,
without any trace of resentment. "But, of course we must do it,
because it would be wrong not to."

France
The concept of rehabilitation is by no means a new one in France,
although it is still not accepted completely as an integral part of
psychiatric care.

All health and mental health care and medication are provided at
no cost to the patient (Dubuis and Gittelman 1986). Moreover, there
are now more than 300 psychosocial transitional housing units in
France (Jean Francois Reverzy, personal communication 1984). These
are primarily small units funded under contract to the social security
system. Clients who live in the community and are either unable to
work, or working in a sheltered setting, receive a stipend of the
equivalent of about 300 dollars per month (2,000 francs). Rent stipends are also available through social security. Continuity of care is
probably handled better in France than in most other countries
because of part-time rotation of sector staff in hospital and extra-
hospital settings. (For a fuller description, see Gittelman 1975,
Dubuis and Gittelman 1984, 1986).

Reference to ergotherapy as an approach to treatment for the
mentally ill appeared as early as the 1920s. The therapeutic pessi-
mism that prevailed in the 1930s changed after World War II, with
the drive to establish community-based care provided within localized sectors. A post–World War II pioneer in psychiatric rehabilitation was Dr. Paul Sivadon, who introduced work for pay at the Ville
Evrard Hospital outside Paris. Shortly thereafter, he was asked to
direct psychiatric treatment for the Teachers' Union of France (Mutuelle Generale de l'Education Nationale). In an unusual mental institution at the Chateau de la Verriere, near Versailles, Sivadon established workshops for occupational and work therapy. This program is
still functioning, but the Teachers' Union is now sectorized and cares
for all who live within the catchment areas in the Paris region and in
Trappes, Ruel, Rouen, Bordeaux, Toulouse, Grenoble, Lyon, and Lille
(Chanoit 1983). Paul Sivadon's greatest contribution to rehabilitation
in France was linking his *ateliers therapeutiques* (therapeutic workshops) to new hospital day programs, which provide a significant
extension of activity therapies (therapeutiques actives), including
recreational and occupational therapy.

When sectorization of mental health services (which had actually
begun in the 1950s) was given administrative sanction by the Minis-

try of Health in 1960, the way was clear for building in each of the sectors and regions rehabilitative services based on the Sivadon model. It is important to note, however, that this did not result in the development of sheltered workshops. It has been suggested that resistance to such a development may have stemmed in part from the French people's experience with concentration camps during the German occupation of World War II. At the entrance to such camps banners bore the slogan *Arbeit mach frei* (Work creates freedom). It has been only in recent years that what we would recognize as sheltered workshops have been established.

In the area near Grenoble, the Centre de Cotagon operates a large sheltered work and training program specifically dedicated to readaptation to agrarian trades. Workshops are organized as "teams" in four major areas: metalworking (iron work, mechanical work, plumbing); building (woodworking, masonry, painting); outdoor work (horticulture, gardening, lawn care, apprenticeship in use of agricultural implements, breeding rabbits and sheep); and cooking Dubuis and Gittelman 1984).

In Lyon and vicinity, L'Association des Industries Services, affiliated with the Centre Hospitalier General Lucien Hussel, now has a number of sheltered work sections. These include a shop for making tablecloths and napkins, a packaging and assembly plant, a metalwork shop, and units that undertake painting and wallpapering, maintenance of lawns and gardens, clerical services, laundry, and the operation of two restaurants (in Lyon and Caluire). These enterprises all bear the trade name *Messidor*.

The Scandinavian Countries
The Scandinavian countries have been characterized as "cradle-to-grave welfare states." Their national welfare schemes provide total unemployment and welfare insurance and complete health insurance coverage. Nationwide programs for all the disabled were written into law in the late 1950s and early 1960s, and complete vocational training and vocational rehabilitation are included (Dencker 1980; Lereim 1980; Schulman 1981).

In Denmark, Norway, and Sweden, there are examples of excellent rehabilitation services; but these are by no means distributed throughout these countries. Psychosocial rehabilitation, however, has become a regular component of care. Associations of parents of the mentally disabled are active throughout Scandinavia, and parents are encouraged to join such associations, which receive government support.

Denmark
Care of the mentally ill in Denmark, as in many northern European countries, is based on supporting the family's ability to care for its disabled member. Toward this end, families receive financial aid

when they accept care of their handicapped members. The disabled who are able to live independently receive stipends for both rent and living expenses. There are no homeless mentally disabled in Denmark.

Mental hospitals are used largely for long-stay, older patients for whom community placement or family care is unavailable or inappropriate. Community care generally is provided by family physicians; psychiatric consultation is provided where necessary. Day centers are found in most districts. They emphasize occupational and industrial therapy and, increasingly, psychosocial rehabilitation activities focusing on training in daily living and social skills (Dencker 1980; Schulman 1981).

Denmark has a number of sheltered workshops for the disabled, operated primarily by voluntary agencies. Labor unions participate in setting minimum wages. There is also a very worthwhile program in many factories which allows groups of disabled people to hold jobs in special enclaves, and be paid through the factory payrolls.

Redke has reported that despite the all-encompassing welfare insurance coverage, there seems to be little disincentive for disabled people to work in the sheltered shops or in the special work enclaves. One Danish expert has stated, however, that "In spite of good intentions . . . problems of sufficient staff, particularly of psychologists with clinical experience, training for staff, and high unemployment interfere with full realization of rehabilitation goals for all disabled persons" (Redke 1975).

Norway
In Norway, rehabilitation is the responsibility of a number of organizations, including the State Labor Exchange, state rehabilitation institutes, sociomedical departments of hospitals, vocational schools, sheltered workshops, private industry, and public employment. Rehabilitation is conceived of as more than vocational, and much emphasis is placed on skills training, socialization, and residential care (Lereim 1980; Ogar 1983).

Sweden
Rehabilitation in Sweden currently means efforts to help the disabled live in the community, rather than work rehabilitation (based, in large measure, upon the current economic situation).

Psychiatric care is essentially without cost to the patient at the time of treatment. (There is a charge of 40 kronen—five dollars—for the first eight visits, with care at no charge for the same illness thereafter.) Treatment teams are now sectorized, each team being responsible for a particular geographic area.

For many years, housing policy has been favorable for the handicapped, including the mentally disabled. In both public and private housing, units are allocated to the aged and the physically and mentally disabled. Tax incentives and legislative fiat have provided ample housing for the mentally ill, who have been helped to reside in the community in other ways as well. With ready access to treatment, home visits, and acute hospital care given largely in psychiatric units of general hospitals, the basic system works quite well (Schulman 1981; Holmberg, in press).

Psychosocial rehabilitation is practiced in most units before discharge. Patients requiring training in social or independent-living skills participate in lengthy habilitation programs.

There is no time limit on pension benefits; the mentally disabled receive funds as long as they are unable to work.

The Swedish National Labour Market Board administers all vocational rehabilitation and sheltered workshops. Regional evaluation centers undertake assessment of working ability and adjustment. Many industrial rehabilitation units are located near sheltered workshops.

Dencker (1980) has described an integrated psychosocial rehabilitation program at Lillhagen Hospital, Goteburg. Here, work is used as therapy at the top step of a system in which the mental patient moves to increasingly less-restrictive living as functional abilities increase. The patient then moves from the hospital to supervised community living. Sheltered work is available and leads to open employment for those who have made the necessary adjustment. The unique characteristic of this program is the way in which all facets of the rehabilitation services are integrated under one administration, and the patients receive continuous care practically throughout their lives.

Another well-known Swedish program for the mentally ill is at the Regional Hospital at Orebro. There, the Department of Psychiatric Rehabilitation conducts an integrated program from hospital to community, covering residential supervision, physiotherapy, occupational therapy, industrial occupational therapy, psychotherapy, and structured music and art therapy (Black 1977; Schulman 1981).

The International Labour Office has described Swedish vocational training centers, particularly one at Skovda, that provide 20 weeks of training in social and work coping skills.

The Vocational Rehabilitation Division of the National Labour Market Board gives grants to private enterprises that employ both disabled and nondisabled people. Particularly interesting is the Swedish Archivist Program, which puts disabled and other hard-to-place people to work in public institutions, such as museums. The government pays the full cost of many such white-collar projects; others are subsidized in part by municipalities (Black 1977; Schulman 1981).

Sweden, like Denmark, has enclave work for the disabled in open employment in factories. Sweden is known to be socially advanced and has experimented with wage subsidies and reduced working hours for disabled workers; local governments subsidize the wages. Recently, however, these practices have been abandoned.

Other Western European Countries
There are elements of rehabilitation programs in some of the other Western European countries. In general, they have begun to follow the patterns described for the United Kingdom, the Netherlands, France, and Scandinavia. A few points warrant particular mention.

Belgium
Belgium takes pride in being one of the first countries to establish community placement of the mentally ill. This is not hard to believe, since the first attempt took place in Gheel in the Middle Ages.

The social welfare law of 1958 set up a council to undertake and support training, rehabilitation, and resettlement of the handicapped. In 1963, additions to the act made it clear that it was applicable to the mentally as well as the physically disabled (Schulman 1981).

Belgium has developed a number of sheltered workshops, under private support, although there has been increasing government subsidy. As the years have passed, growing numbers of participants in the workshops are coming from among the mentally handicapped and mentally ill.

Health care in Belgium is sectorized and without cost to the patient.

Switzerland
The Swiss Federal Disability Act of 1960 made it clear that mental illness and disability were among the categories covered. The state provides subsidies to organizations serving the disabled, including costs of construction, establishment and renovation of institutions and workshops, and some help in covering operating deficits (Goldman 1982–83).

Federal Republic of Germany
Rehabilitation legislation was enacted in 1974 and 1976 in the Federal Republic of Germany (FRG). Rehabilitation, however, falls within the purview of five federal social insurance agencies, each of which contracts for services from public institutions and private nonprofit organizations. "In each system or agency, the responsibility for an individual's rehabilitation program is dependent on the cause of disability. Thus, a job-related disability is administered by the industrial accident program, whereas a disease-related disability is the obligation of the health insurance system" (Steinmeyer and Tracy 1985).

There are a number of sheltered workshops in the FRG that offer training for open and permanent employment for those whose disability is not too severe. Reports indicate that the workshops demand from the applicants a functional capability that excludes the very seriously disabled. Only a small number of disabled people make the transition from sheltered work to open employment.

Italy
In the one part of Italy that has moved precipitously to abolish mental institutions in favor of community-based care, Trieste, workers' cooperatives have been organized to meet the need for vocational rehabilitation.

The Workers' Cooperative in Trieste consists of 120 workers. The cooperative is administered by two committees: the assembly and the administrative counsel. The administrative council assists with getting contracts, negotiations with the union, public relations, and serves as an advisory group. All decisions affecting the cooperative are decided by the assembly (Crawford 1980; Mollica 1985). Crawford states that the cooperative has proved to be economically viable.

Greece
Formal rehabilitation came late to Greece. The first attempts to deal with the handicapped provided only for disabled veterans and mandated the assignment of newsstands and kiosks to them as private businesses. It was not until 1979 that legislation broadened government support and established the National Institute for the Rehabilitation of the Disabled and the Organization for Human Resources Development (OAED). The former certifies the disability; the latter provides training and employment opportunities (Coudroglou 1984; Stefanis et al., in press).

For the disabled unable to enter the competitive labor market, the OAED has set up centers for sheltered work, fabricating commercial products under contract to the government. The contract employers pay the wage at a competitive market rate; and the government supplies housing, health care, and other subsistence expenses. Rather liberal government subsidies are granted to employers willing to hire the disabled. The state also provides all insurance and fringe benefits during the first year of employment, but none thereafter. This works fine for the physically disabled (orthopedically handicapped), but poses problems for those with relapsing, exacerbating illnesses such as mental disorders.

CONCLUSION
Mention has been made of programs that provide wage subsides to regular employers as an incentive for them to employ the handicapped. England, the Federal Republic of Germany, Greece, and Sweden have all gone this route; the schemes differ in detail, but all seem, in theory, to be useful. Actual experience has not been good, however.

Perhaps the reasons are those suggested in a report of the British Department of Employment:

> . . . A disability, instead of being regarded as a handicap to overcome in the right job, would tend to be looked upon as qualifying for a special financial consideration. It would act as a constant suggestion to the disabled that they were less capable than their fellow workers . . . subsidies would suggest to an employer . . . that the employment of disabled people constituted a financial burden for employers . . . other workers might regard subsidized disabled workers as a form of cheap labor . . . the possibility of escalation would indeed be very real . . . it would be hard to define the category of disabled people who should benefit from subsidies and . . . there would be pressures to extend the arrangement to other disabled workers . . . and to other groups of disadvantaged people. Subsidies could in this way become immensely expensive. (Piercy Committee 1977)

In its social welfare legislation of 1944 and 1958, the United Kingdom set up a quota system requiring employers of firms of a certain size or greater to include at least a minimum number of handicapped people in their labor force. Such programs are also in operation in Belgium, the Federal Republic of Germany, France, and the Netherlands. But experience with quotas has been mixed. They have all of the disadvantages of the subsidy program, noted above, though they do keep before employers the needs of the disabled and make them likely to employ such people if they are otherwise eligible for jobs. In the United Kingdom, however, and to some extent in the FRG, the tendency has been for employers to find sufficient "disabilities" among their regular employees to fill the quotas, which usually are about 3 percent (Black 1977).

It is not always clear to what extent the programs and services in Western European countries actually meet the needs of the mentally ill. A comment made by Bennet (1973) more than a decade ago seems still to be largely true: "The greatest disadvantage in many European countries is that the psychiatrically disabled are still dependent on services designed for the physically disabled and therefore not particularly adapted for them."

REFERENCES

Aaron JH, Schwartz WB: The Painful Prescription: Rationing Hospital Care. Washington, DC, Brookings Institute, 1984

Akabas SH: Study of the Role of the Private Sector in Relation to the Rehabilitation of Physically and Emotionally Disabled Persons: The Experience in Canada and the United Kingdom. Final Report. New York, World Rehabilitation Fund, 1984

Alpert M, Tunnell G, Gittelman M: Schizophrenia: tertiary prevention approaches for negative symptomatology. International Journal of Mental Health (in press)

Bennett D: The European Program. International Conference on Productive Participation Programs for the Mentally Ill. Amsterdam, Exerpta Medica, 1973

Black BJ: Substitute permanent employment of the deinstitutionalized mentally ill. Journal of Rehabilitation 42:2, 1977

Chanoit PF: Analyse Instrumentale Des Hopitaux de Jour de la M.G.E.N. Paris, Mutuelle Generale de l'Educatrion Nationale, 1983

Ciompi L: The natural history of schizophrenia in the long term. Br J Psychiatry 136:413–420, 1980

Coudroglou A: Abilitating the Disabled: Policy Issues and Program Realities, the View from Greece. Fellowship Report. New York, World Rehabilitation Fund, 1984

Crawford JL: Mental Health Reform in Trieste. Italy Final Report. New York, World Rehabilitation Fund, 1980

DeJong G: Independent Living and Disability Policy in the Netherlands: Three Models of Residential Care and Independent Living. Monograph No. 27. New York, World Rehabilitation Fund, 1984

Dencker SJ: Hospital-based Community Support Services for Recovering Chronic Schizophrenics: The Experience at Lillhagen Hospital. New York, World Rehabilitation Fund, 1980

Dubuis J, Gittelman M: Rehabilitation for the mentally ill in France. Paper presented at the annual meeting of the American Public Health Association, Montreal, October 1984

Dubuis J, Gittelman M: Recent developments in French public mental health care. Paper represented at the annual meeting of the American Public Health Association, November, Las Vegas, 1986

Fraser RT, Smith WR: Adjustment to daily living, in Epilepsy: Handbook for the Mental Health Professional. Edited by Sands H. New York, Brunner/Mazel, 1982

Gillis LS, Keet M: Factors underlying the retention in the community of chronic undifferentiated schizophrenics. Br J Psychiatry 3:1057–1069, 1965

Gittelman M: Sectorization: The quiet revolution in European mental health care. Am J Orthopsychiatry 42:159–167, 1972

Gittelman M: Recent developments, european rehabilitation programs for mental patients, in Progress in Community Psychiatry, vol. 3. Edited by Bellak L, Barton H. New York, Brunner/Mazel 1975

Gittelman M: Psychosocial disability and the consumer movement, in Consumers in a Shrinking World. Proceedings, 10th International Congress of Consumers Union, The Hague, Netherlands, 1982

Gittelman M: Developments in foreign psychiatry: an introduction. Hosp Community Psychiatry 34:2, 1983

Gittelman M, Dubuis J, Gillet M: Recent developments in French public mental health. Psychiatr Q 47:4, 1973

Goldman HH: International perspectives on deinstitutionalization. International Journal of Mental Health 11:4, 1982–83

Himmelstein DV, Woolhandler S: Cost without Benefit. N Engl J Med 7:314, 1986

Holmberg G: Treatment, care and rehabilitation of the chronically mentally ill in Sweden. Hosp Community Psychiatry (in press)

Leff J, Vaughn C: Expressed Emotion in Families: Its Significance for Mental Illness. New York, Guilford, 1984

Lereim K: Norway, in International Rehabilitation. Edited by Cull JG, Hardy RE. San Antonio, Clinical Prediction Press, 1980

May A: Mental Health Services in Europe. WHO Offset Publication No. 23. Geneva, WHO, 1976

Miller GA, Couler EJ, Schoor LB, et al: The world economic crisis and children: U.S. case study. Int J Health Serv 15:95–134, 1985

Mollica R: The unfinished revolution in Italian psychiatry. International Journal of Mental Health 14:1–2, 1985

Morris B: Recent developments in the care, treatment and rehabilitation of the chronic mentally ill in Britain. Hosp Community Psychiatry 34:159, 1983

Neilson LJ: Development and Evolution of Vocational Rehabilitation and Its Service Delivery Systems in the United Kingdom: A Ten-element Examination. Final Report. New York, World Rehabilitation Fund, 1978

Ogar B: Treatment, care and rehabilitation of the mentally ill in Norway. Hosp Community Psychiatry 34:4, April 1983

Piercy Committee: Sheltered Employment for Disabled People: A Consultative Document. London, Department of Employment, Disabled Persons Branch, DPS, 1977

Redke H: Sheltered workshops abroad: what we might learn about sheltered employment. Rehabilitation World 1(2), October 1975

Reeves R: The Permissive Dutch. New York Times Magazine, October 20, 1985

Reitsma WH: Organization and administration of rehabilitation in Holland. Quarterly Bulletin. Association of Medical Rehabilitation Directors and Coordinators 23 (3), March 1984

Roth D, Bean J, Stefl ME, et al: Homelessness in Ohio: Findings from a statewide study. Paper presented at the annual meeting of the American Public Health Association, 1985

Royal College of Psychiatrists: Psychiatric Rehabilitation in the 1980s. Report of the Working Party on Rehabilitation of the Social and Community Section. London, Royal College of Psychiatrists, 1980

Schulman ED: Rehabilitation of the Mentally Ill: An International Perspective. The President's Committee on Employment of the Handicapped. Washington DC, U.S. Government Printing Office, 1981

Stefanis K, Mandianos M, Gittelman M: Treatment, care and rehabilitation of the chronically ill in Greece. Hosp Community Psychiatry 37:1041–1044, 1986

Steinmeyer H, Tracy MB: Rehabilitation program issues in the Federal Republic of Germany. Journal of Rehabilitation July-Sept, 1985

Wing J: Innovation in social psychiatry. Psychol Med 10:219–230, 1980

SECTION V

ADMINISTRATIVE AND LEGAL ISSUES: THE JUDICIAL PERSPECTIVE

20

Social Security Disability: Political Philosophy and History

Patricia Dilley, J.D.*

Throughout its 30-year history, the Social Security Disability Insurance program (SSDI) has been the focus of Congressional and bureaucratic concern, based on an ever-present threat of runaway benefit expension. Until recently, the program was relatively unknown to the general public, notwithstanding occasional newspaper articles in the late 1970s about the escalating costs of cash benefits for disability insurance.

However, beginning in 1981, with widespread newspaper and electronic media coverage of the continuing-disability review process begun in March of that year, the level of public knowledge of the program's labyrinthine eligibility requirements and adjudication procedures rose substantially. Unfortunately, media awareness of the program and its problems could do little to increase public or professional understanding of the internal dynamics underlying the disability policy-making process.

This chapter explores the political philosophy, or more accurately, philosophies, that have guided the program since its inception in 1954, as the disability freeze, to the current, post–1984 Disability Reform Act period. While I have not included a detailed legislative history of the program (several excellent ones are available, particu-

---

* The views expressed in this chapter are those of the author and do not represent or reflect the views of the Committee on Ways and Means or its members.

larly Deborah Stone's book, *The Disabled State* [1984]) selected incidents and legislative patterns are described in some depth to illustrate the themes and problems endemic to disability-benefit programs in the United States.

The chapter is divided into two main segments. Section one identifies and enlarges on the basic principles and inherent tensions of the Social Security Disability Insurance and Supplemental Security Income (SSI) disability programs. The major focus is the principal source of continuing controversy: the conflict of differing perceptions of the program's mission, and expectations about program performance, held by members of Congress, Social Security Administration personnel, the professional medical and legal communities, and the public (both as benefit applicants and as taxpayers), as a result of the way disability is defined in the law. Section two presents a selective analytic legislative history, illustrating the themes outlined in section one that are apparent in the administrative, legislative, and judicial development of the SSDI and SSI programs from the 1954 freeze to the passage of the 1984 Disability Reform Act. The goal of this analysis is to explain the apparent discontinuity the 1984 amendments represent in the historical pattern of congressional efforts to restrict program costs and eligibility in the face of judicial pressure for less stringent interpretation of the basic program definition of disability.

The realities of the legislative process, of course, inevitably have shaped the development of the disability program: the necessity for at least tentative consensus among the legislative actors on what changes are needed; the transformation of relatively clear legislative direction in various bills as originally considered into vague and general precepts at the end of House–Senate deliberations; and finally, the wide gap between congressional intent and administrative reality, a problem endemic to all congressionally mandated regulatory and benefits programs.

These forces have created a program which is now required to meet several completely contradictory expectations under its legislative mandate: Give benefits *only* to those completely unable to work, and yet rehabilitate these same people; give benefits to *all* those unable to work, and yet make sure no one even marginally capable of working retains benefits. These conflicting demands naturally give rise to extraordinary pressures on administrative interpretations of what are less-than-precise legislative definitions.

While the same phenomenon can be found in the realm of regulatory law, throughout the legislative development of the disability-insurance statute the same words are used by both sides in the legislative process to mean completely different things. When administrators transform these words into real operating rules governing benefit grants, one side or the other is disappointed, and the round of legislative oversight and re-examination of the program begins again.

This chapter seeks to shed light on recurring themes in this process, and to offer some suggestions for future development of the disability programs that may lead to a resolution of at least some of the current conflicts. It is clear, however, that as long as provision of public income support is made conditional upon the objective evaluation of a subjective condition, no administrative structure or legislative mandate will be completely satisfactory.

FUNDAMENTAL UNDERSTANDINGS AND CONTRADICTIONS

The Social Security system is this nation's principal mechanism for providing public support to categories of people we, as a society, do not expect to work: in general, the aged, the infirm, and their minor dependents. Providing for income maintenance through Social Security, rather than relying on haphazard or risk-laden individual savings, ensures a more efficient flow of resources from the working to the nonworking, according to socially determined priorities for redistribution of income from high-wage to low-wage families, and from single workers to workers with families.

The threshold test for Social Security eligibility is whether the applicant has worked and contributed long enough to the system to qualify for benefits. In contrast, the threshold test for directly needs-tested programs, such as Aid to Families with Dependent Children (AFDC) and SSI, is simply income assets (i.e., whether the applicant is poor enough to justify public income support).

Once one of these initial tests is satisfied, the more difficult eligibility question must be answered: Can this person be expected to work? The fundamental purpose of providing cash income assistance to any person is to support him or her because he or she is not expected to provide for him- or herself. Every public income-maintenance program contains some test, or set of tests, to determine who fits that description.

Inherent in these tests is a social judgment: to separate the "deserving" nonworking from the "undeserving" nonworking. The former are entitled to public support, either because they are too old, too young, or too infirm to work (or too busy caring for someone else who is too young to work). The latter are suspected of simple indolence, and of attempting to defraud the public into supporting their laziness by *appearing* unable to work when, in fact, they are just willing to do so. This suspicion that the indolent will attempt to slip into programs meant for the truly deserving greatly increases the pressure on eligibility tests to be clear and reliable in making very difficult distinctions.

The importance of the disability determination itself thus cannot be overstated. In essence, it embodies what this society views as an acceptable reason for not working. In the retirement and survivor programs, the eligibility decision serves the same end, but the line is much clearer—the person has reached a given age and has stopped working, or the wage earner of a family has died, and surviving children are automatically entitled until age 18.

Disability is not as easy to define and sometimes cannot even be seen. Moreover, it is a condition with which society as a whole is extremely uneasy. Old age and death are certainties; in contrast, while disability may befall anyone, we all hope to avoid it, and may be successful in doing so. In this culture, disabled people arouse in the nondisabled contradictory feelings of pity and contempt, sympathy and avoidance, and, perhaps most important, both relief that we are not so afflicted, and suspicion that the disabled could really overcome their handicaps if they only tried.

It is therefore hardly surprising that our major public expression of concern for the disabled—cash income assistance—embodies all of these conflicts. Three principal themes may be discerned in the development of the disability program:

- The inherent subjectivity of the concept of disability itself;
- The mistrust of self-reports of inability to work, leading to demand by the public and legislators for objective tests for a subjective phenomenon; and
- The insistence on an all-or-nothing category—disabled or not disabled—to prevent those with mere disadvantage, rather than real disability, from supplementing their lower incomes with scarce public funds. This attempt to draw a clear line, where in fact a substantial gray area of partial disability and handicap in need of support really exists, leads to great rigidity in the eligibility-determination process and great pressure on the concept of disability itself as a basis for income support.

Subjective Concept, Objective Ideal

The common description of Social Security Disability Insurance is that it is an impairment-based benefits program. While impairment is obviously an important part of the concept of disability, it represents only the beginning of the inquiry. In some cases (such as those suffering from pain), the existence of any impairment in the usual sense may be in doubt. In others, particularly in mental impairment cases, the untrained layperson (or member of Congress) may question whether the impairment is really a medical condition, rather than just a character flaw or moral deficiency.

The definition of disability used in the Social Security Act gives the appearance of objectivity and certainty: "inability to engage in substantial gainful activity by reason of a medically determinable impairment expected to last at least 12 months or to end in death." The key word here, however, is "inability," as contrasted, for example, with a standard which equates loss of a limb with a set percentage loss in capacity to perform certain tasks. (This latter standard exists in other public disability programs and serves to further confound understanding of the SSDI standard.)

Inability to perform is an inherently subjective concept, and is susceptible to measurement only in crude terms. The capacity to perform a variety of tasks varies from person to person, and each of us is likely to see our own ability differently from the way an outside observer would measure it. Two consequences important to the disability program flow from this subjective definition. First, each person's ability or inability to function will differ from every other person's, making uniform tests for disability virtually impossible to concoct. Second, it is difficult, if not impossible, for any individual to agree with another about his or her own ability or abilities.

Inability to work, of course, is not the only part of the definition open to subjective interpretation: *Substantial gainful activity* (SGA) is nearly as vague a concept. Regulations have defined the term as a given dollar amount of earnings per month (currently, $300). This attempt to quantify an abstract concept generally has led applicants and laypersons to believe that a person with an impairment who earns less than $300 a month is qualified for benefits.

However, the legislative history of the disability definition indicates that substantial gainful activity was intended to refer to any work activity capable of producing *any* earnings at all. The dollar limit was established for administrative reasons not reflected in the statute, which itself offers no guidance on how to determine SGA.

Disability, as defined in the Social Security Act, is therefore an essentially *internal* condition, with some external manifestations in the form of medically determinable impairments. However, it is clear that two people with the same set of disabling impairments, and similar age, education, and work experience, will not necessarily experience this internal condition—and loss of work ability—in the same way. This is both the fundamental dilemma of the SSDI program and the core principle on which the program is based.

Objective Tests of a Subjective Phenomenon
In theory, the disability program pays benefits to people who are unable to work. In practice, however, the program pays benefits to people who no longer are working and who are sufficiently impaired that they can be *presumed* to be unable to work. The legislative history of the program reveals a consistent conviction on the part of Congress that theory matches reality—that the disability program must pay benefits only to those who, in fact and objectively, are unable to work. The implication of years of committee-report language and statutory amendment is that the disability condition *can* be proven through objective means, usually left for administrators to establish.

However, because the disability determination is based on *inference* rather than demonstrable *fact*, the presumption of disability can be challenged easily and thus must be established based on the unique circumstances of each individual case. Moreover, the distinction between inability to work, as determined under the *presumptive* process, and unemployment due to a handicap is subtle and difficult to establish. As a result, almost since the inception of the program, and certainly since the Kerner decision in 1960 (see below), there has been constant conflict between the SSA and the courts, with Congress occasionally intervening to reiterate the stringency of the definition.

In response to this subjectivity, the Social Security Administration has developed a determination process consisting of an elaborate system of checks and balances designed to prevent individual judgment from outweighing administrative and legislative policies defining disability. The initial decision is made according to submitted clinical findings, a deliberate paper decision which avoids the personal influence of either the claimant or the physician.

The examiner's decision is then subjected to several further reviews, through the quality-assurance system and through a multi-layered appeals system. Deliberate second-guessing of initial decisions is the way in which the current structure attempts to ensure as much objectivity as possible in an inherently subjective decision-making process. This process consists first of the initial application for disability benefits, made at the federal Social Security District Office where the claimant is interviewed and the sources of medical evidence are recorded. After determining whether the applicant meets the insured-status requirements, the case is then sent to the state agency which, operating as an agent of the Social Security Administration, makes the initial determination of disability. If a claimant, or a beneficiary whose eligibility is terminated after review, is dissatisfied with an initial denial or termination of disability benefits by the state agency, he or she may request a reconsideration (also performed by the state agency) within 60 days of notice of denial. This traditionally has been a paper review of the record along with any additional evidence either the agency or the claimant wishes to add to the file. In certain cases, according to the requirements of the 1984 Disability Reform Act, a personal, or face-to-face interview between the agency examiner and the claimant may be required. If upon reconsideration, the claimant is again denied benefits, he or she will be given a hearing before an Administrative Law Judge (ALJ), providing a request is filed within 60 days of notice of denial. If the claim is denied by the ALJ, the claimant has 60 days to request review by the Appeals Council. The Appeals Council may also, on its own motion, review a decision within 90 days of the ALJ's decision. The claimant may appeal an adverse decision by the Appeals Council to the United States District Court.

Very little of this administrative process and structure is required by the statute, which simply states the definition (as presented above); states that it should be applied taking into account the person's age, education, and work experience; and that the existence of jobs in the national economy, not just the local region, must be the determining factor. Nearly all of the many steps required of the claimant and examiner have been established by the agency, at the direct behest of Congress to establish the objective standards that Congress itself has been reluctant to write into the law.

Bright Line in a Gray Area

In addition to insisting on objectively correct decisions, Congress also has mandated that benefits only be paid to those totally unable to work. This principle is among the least comprehensible aspects of the program, for disability and rehabilitation professionals and disabled people alike. The all-or-nothing character of the cash-benefit program seems to defy the realities of existence for people with severe impairments who want to work or at least *attempt* a productive existence.

The problem is particularly severe for the mentally disabled, who often can only reenter the mainstream of working life one step at a time, perhaps as part of a therapeutic community at first, and gradually work toward independent living. For SSI disability recipients—most of whom have never had any work history or who have had only minimal experience in the distant past—the law's nine-month trial work period (allowing work attempts without loss of benefits) is woefully inadequate.

Yet, since 1956, Congress has resisted almost all attempts to give disability beneficiaries a declining benefit, offset against earnings, similar to the earnings test in the retirement and survivors' program. The *earned income disregard* (the amount of earned income an SSI recipient may have each month before losing benefits—the first $65 of monthly earned income plus one-half of remaining earnings) for SSI recipients was not designed with the disabled in mind. In fact, it is directly countervened by the SGA limit under the disability definition discussed above. The reasons underlying this resistance are consistent with the ideology that has shaped congressional disability activity for 30 years.

The Title II SSDI program, onto which the SSI program was later grafted, has a very limited goal: to provide income maintenance for the relatively small number of people who are absolutely unable to work, and who have essentially no expectation of ever returning to work. The program was not designed to provide a support system for working handicapped persons, or to pay benefits for partial disabilities, as the veterans' system does.

Thus, suggestions that disability benefits be phased out gradually, in cases where the person becomes self-supporting over time, run directly counter to the base-line congressional assumption that anyone who can work at all should not receive benefits. Moreover, such proposals have prompted very high cost estimates which have prevented serious consideration. Along with most in the agency and in congress, the Social Security actuaries assume that an offset mechanism (e.g., reducing benefits by one dollar for every two earned) would only lead to permanent, limited work efforts by beneficiaries seeking to retain eligibility both for cash-income supplements and for Medicare benefits.

Given the resistance to providing benefits to those who may be able to work, it seems anomalous that so much emphasis has been placed on giving beneficiaries incentives to return to work. Indeed, the 1980 act seems designed to alternatively cajole and threaten beneficiaries into returning to work and removing themselves from the disability rolls, even though under the definition of program eligibility, they weren't supposed to be able to work at all in the first place.

Again, the answer probably lies in the uncertainties inherent in the administrative process on which Congress has placed so much reliance. While there has been general agreement that only those truly disabled should receive benefits, there is no agreement on how many people fall into that category. Program cost is for legislators the sole means of monitoring the general accuracy of the decision-making process. In the 1970s, as costs escalated far beyond actuarial projections, it was assumed that benefits were going to more people than the law allowed. Thus, far from expanding the program into the gray areas of partial and temporary disability, the historic response of Congress has been to require the administrators to draw the line that is only generally defined in statute.

CONGRESS AND THE DISABILITY PENDULUM

The previous section's themes are evident throughout the troubled legislative history of the disability program. A brief examination of three critical periods in the program's development—the mid-to-late 1960s, the late 1970s leading up to the 1980 amendments, and the 1981–1984 period which led to the 1984 amendments—reveals a fairly consistent pattern.

First, the agency attempts to administer the law according to published and unpublished standards: general principles stated in published regulations, and more exacting standards embedded in unpublished administrative guidelines. The courts intervene, usually in the direction of expanding program benefits, to take account of real unemployability in the absence of distinct regulations on the issue. Finally, Congress reacts, reasserting the stringency of the law with unkind words for both the agency and the courts, yet each time leaving considerable vagueness in the definition.

This pattern was broken by the 1984 amendments, where, for the first time in the history of the program, the administrators were on the defensive against criticism from both the courts and the Congress for drawing the line too harshly. This rare alliance between Congress and the judiciary (which congressional reports for years had lambasted for excessive activism and misinterpretation of the disability statute), against the agency, may signal the beginning of a new era in the program.

The 1960s—Kerner and Its Aftermath

A comparison of the original requirements for entitlement to disability benefits with the law after the 1967 amendments gives some indication of the struggle over the program during that period. In 1957, the definition of disability read: "inability to engage in any substantial gainful activity by reason of any medically determinable physical or mental impairment which can be expected to result in death or to be of a long continued and indefinite duration." In addition, workers under age 50 were not eligible to apply for benefits at all and, in order to be insured for benefits, a claimant must have worked 20 out of the last 40 quarters (10 of the last 20 years) and also 6 of the 13 quarters preceding disability. No dependents' benefits were payable.

In contrast, the definition in 1970 was both more liberal and less open to interpretation: The impairment needed only to last 12 months, but must be so severe that the individual could not only be unable to perform his or her previous work, but also could not, "considering his age, education and work experience, engage in any other kind of substantial gainful work which exists in the national economy, regardless of whether such work exists in the immediate area in which he lives, or whether a specific job exists for him, or whether he would be hired if he applied for work." The insured-status requirement had been reduced to only 20 out of 40 quarters preceding disability, with a special reduced requirement for workers becoming disabled under age 31. Benefits were now available to all workers under age 65, as were dependent benefits for children, for a spouse caring for minor children, and for adults disabled before age 22.

The original 1937–1938 Advisory Council, convened after the enactment of the Social Security Act in 1935 to examine the basis of the whole program and make recommendations to Congress on the changes needed, had strongly recommended that the Social Security program be expanded to cover disability, as one of the hazards of industrial society against which workers need protection. Nonetheless, Congress had created the disability program only after years of reluctance to enter an area in which private insurers had "lost their shirts" in the 1930s. The actual benefits program was preceded by two years of the disability "freeze," which held harmless for insured-status purposes for retirement benefits workers kept out of the work force because of disability. (The actual disability-benefit program was preceded by two years by the disability freeze which merely limited the loss of insured status because of the worker's disability and provided no actual benefit payments at all.)

Clearly, Congress was worried from the beginning that demand for benefits could overwhelm the bounds of the narrow, catastrophically oriented program envisioned in the statute. Thus, it is critical to an understanding of the later development of the program, and the pressures on the definition as the major standard of eligibility, to remember that in the beginning the definition itself was not the only screen that Congress established to keep demands on Social Security resources at a minimum.

First, the more stringent insured-status requirements of 6 out of 13 quarters meant that *any* absence from the work force of longer than two years would exclude a worker from coverage. This requirement was eliminated in 1958 after only two years in effect. Nonetheless, its revival in 1981, as part of the Administration's proposals for revising the financing of the Social Security program, indicates how powerful a mechanism the insured-status requirements are for limiting access to the program. It was estimated in 1981 that the 6-of-13 quarters requirement would disqualify almost 40 percent of those then insured under the 20-of-40 quarter requirement.

Equally important and more long-lasting was the provision of benefits only to workers aged 50 and older. This limit was not eliminated until 1960, and initially may have done much to persuade both the courts and the public that the disability program was really a form of disability–retirement insurance, rather than a catastrophic-impairment program. Nonetheless, the universe of applicants was restricted to older workers who, it must be remembered, had matured in a society that tolerated few excuses for not working, and were correspondingly less likely to apply for public benefits without good cause. As long as truly objective standards such as the insured-status requirement and the age-50-and-over limit existed, the pressures on the definition itself were less severe.

However, by 1959, sufficient problems had surfaced to lead the House Committee on Ways and Means to form the Harrison Subcommittee on the Administration of the Social Security Laws. The subcommittee issued a report a year later (March 1960), dealing with what it deemed to be the "problem areas" in disability, including ". . . the nature of the definition of disability and the lack of detailed regulations as to its application; and the confidentiality of certain substantive criteria established by the Department of HEW which are used in the determination of disability" (Ways and Means Committee, Harrison Subcommittee Report, 1960, p. iii).

The *Harrison Subcommittee Report*, developed after over a year of deliberation and several public hearings on a variety of issues, contained a detailed discussion of the definition of disability, and the problems inherent in its implementation. The report fully supported the medical criteria developed by the Bureau of Disability Insurance (BDI), and stated that the criteria should be refined over time to take advances in medicine into account. More concern was expressed about the use of nonmedical criteria and the fact that decisions were being made using unpublished rules to which the public had no access:

> The subcommittee recognizes the difficulty of developing and enunciating specific criteria for the weight to be given non-medical factors in the evaluation of disability and the extreme sensitivity of this area. But the subcommittee believes that the time has come, if it is not well overdue, to make a determined effort to develop and refine these criteria and make them available to the evaluators and to the public in the form of published regulations (Harrison Subcommittee Report, 1960, p. 18).

It is clear from this report that the committee fully expected the agency to make the statue's general definition workable by amplifying issues such as the nonmedical criteria for ability to work, even though the statutory definition itself was silent on those questions. Also, Congress saw medical criteria as much easier to pin down in regulations, more objective perhaps, despite much accumulated testimony from the medical profession that medical judgments as to disabling impairments were no more uniform or objective than any other evaluation (Stone 1984, pp. 107–117).

The subcommittee also reemphasized the stringency of the definition, and the critical difference between the disability program and unemployment insurance:

> The subcommittee takes note of the very real problem of employability in a disability program. Lack of ability to *engage* in a job is essential to a determination of disability as it is currently being interpreted. Lack of ability to *get* a job, however, is immaterial, or at least so in theory, under the law and the Bureau's practices (p. 19). [Emphasis added.]
>
> The subcommittee believes it is essential that there be a clear distinction between this program and one concerned with unemployment. It also believes it is desirable that disability determinations be carried out in as realistic a manner as possible, and that theoretical capacity in a severely impaired individual can be somewhat meaningless if it cannot be translated into an ability to compete in the open market. The subcommittee believes the Department should make a thorough study of this situation to see if criteria can be developed which retain the basic emphasis of the program on major medical impairment, but at the same time allow for a more realistic assessment where there are multiple bars to employment, e.g., age, employer bias in hiring, and other factors that limit job opportunity. (p. 20)

It should be noted that this discussion rests as much on then-current agency policy as on statutory interpretation. The Congress clearly seemed to believe that the agency must bear the burden of clarifying the real meaning of statutory terms such as substantial gainful activity. In fact, the Harrison report cited to that effect the 1949 Advisory Council report in which the original recommendation for a definition of disability was contained:

> The exact limits of what constitutes 'substantial gainful activity' should, in the early years of the program at least, be defined by regulation . . . administrative experience will doubtlessly indicate ways in which the definition can be improved. . . . The Council believes, however, that the regulations governing this definition should be strict. (p. 20)

While the agency did begin to publish its strictly medical criteria and even some nonmedical standards in minor and very general amendments to the regulations, no major changes in the pattern of administering through unpublished guidelines were made until the development of the vocational–educational "grid" guidelines in the 1970s. The federal courts stepped into this void with great regularity, most notably in the Kerner decision, which was handed down in 1960, after the Harrison report had been issued.

In *Kerner v. Flemming* (1960), Judge Friendly of the Court of Appeals for the Second Circuit wrote a very influential opinion interpreting the definition of disability in the case of a claimant who had proven that he could not perform his previous work and that he had few or no obvious skills for other jobs. Many lower courts had previously held that in such a case, it was the government's burden to prove that the claimant actually, rather than theoretically, was able to perform to prove that the claimant actually, rather than theoretically, was able to perform some type of work. In other cases, district courts had gone the opposite way, holding under the "substantial evidence rule" that the Secretary had to show only that substantial evidence supported the finding of ineligibility for benefits. In such cases, as in the district court finding in Kerner, the courts held that as long as it was clear from the evidence that the claimant could do some kind of work "[t]he fact that work which would be within his capacity may not be readily obtainable, cannot be substituted as standards of disability for the strict standards set forth in the act, namely, complete inability to do any substantial gainful work" (Ways and Means Committee Staff Report 1974, p. 46).

Judge Friendly dismissed this reasoning, stating that he did not have enough evidence to either affirm or reverse the district court finding in the absence of any substantial vocational evidence concerning the claimant's ability to work.

> The court concluded that the Secretary had offered nothing save speculation to warrant a finding that Kerner could perform light

or sedentary work. Judge Friendly declared that a disability determination 'requires resolution of two issues—(1) what can applicant do, and (2) what employment opportunities are there for a man who can do only what applicant can do. Mere theoretical ability to engage in substantial gainful activity is not enough if no reasonable opportunity for this is available.' (Ways and Means Committee 1974, pp. 46–47)

This opinion was widely followed in federal courts throughout the country, as cases were remanded to the Secretary for re-review on the basis of the Kerner guidelines. Although Congress might have been expected to oppose the introduction of direct "employability" concerns into the disability-determination process, it did not react with corrective legislation until 1967.

The discussion of the Kerner decision and its aftermath in the 1974 committee report is revealing. After detailing the Kerner decision, the report describes how the doctrine of a two-part decision—what can the applicant do, and what employment opportunities are there for someone who can do only what the applicant can do—had begun to slip into internal BDI policy guidance, without concomitant change in regulation. Similarly, the staff report describes how, throughout the mid-1960s, the courts intervened regarding the question of whether job availability was to be tested based on the nation as a whole or on the applicant's immediate area of residence, and in many cases required the Secretary to demonstrate job availability in the local area:

> In 1966 the Administration printed in the Social Security Rulings decisions of the 4th and 6th circuits with the notation that they did not "acquiesce in the decisions." On the other hand, the Administration did not clearly spell out what its policy was. . . . Moreover, the Government did not appeal the cases nor did the Administration amend the regulation. (Ways and Means Committee 1974, p. 48)

After roundly criticizing the Administration for failing to clarify its policies in regulations, the report cited a principal source of pressure for limiting the application of the unemployability concept in disability: "Developing contemporaneously with these developments was a substantial actuarial deficit in the Disability Insurance Trust Fund. . . . When legislation was being considered in 1967, there was an even more serious deficiency, but still the Administration did not suggest any substantive change in the disability definition" (Ways and Means Committee 1974, p. 49). In the absence of an Administration recommendation, the Congress augmented the statutory definition of disability with the "national economy test" (cited above), the paragraph now appearing at Section 223(d)(2)(A) of the act.

It is interesting to note that the agency was repeatedly criticized in congressional reports for failing to publish guidelines to clarify a definition which Congress itself declined to clarify. Moreover, Congress appeared to conclude that both a problem existed and that the problem was that the definition was being misinterpreted by the courts, solely from the increasing cost of the program. Since the tax rate for the program is set according to actuarial estimates on the basis of projected experience, the funding shortfall in the mid-1960s was simply the result of experience outrunning the estimates. Such an effort could easily have been the product of bad estimates or actuarial assumptions, on either the revenue or expenditure sides.

However, Congress translated the phenomenon into a problem, assuming that increased costs were attributable solely to liberalization of the definition by the courts. The House report on the 1967 disability amendments stated:

> Your committee has become concerned with the way [the] defini-
> tion has been interpreted by the courts and the effects their
> interpretations have had and might have on the future adminis-
> tration of the disability program by the Social Security Adminis-
> tration . . . [T]he committee observed that the last long-range
> projection prepared by the Social Security Administration
> showed a significant increase in the proportion of the population
> becoming disabled within the definition. . . . Over the last four
> years the number of disability allowances was larger than the
> number estimated. Because there is no evidence to indicate that
> the proportion of the disabled in the country is greater now than
> four years ago, the committee is forced to conclude that over a
> period of years a number of subtle changes may have occurred in
> the concept of the 'disabled worker' (p. 28).

While the 1967 report listed other factors which might have contributed to an increase in the incidence of disability—more knowledge of the program, improved evidentiary and assessment methods—it clearly focused on the impact of liberal court decisions which seemed to be moving the program in the direction of an occupational rather than a total disability program: "Your committee has also learned that there is a growing body of court interpretations of the statute which, if followed in the administration of the disability provisions, could result in substantial further increases in the costs in the future." After summarizing the liberalizing trends of court decisions, the report states: "As a remedy for the situation which has developed, your committee's bill would provide guidelines to re-emphasize the predominant importance of medical factors in the disability determination process" (p. 30).

It should be noted that the 1967 committee report gives no hint of exactly how the cross-pollination between court decision and agency policy might occur. The assumption here and elsewhere in the congressional responses over the 1960s and 1970s to perceived liberalization of the program appears to have been that outside forces, such as the courts and public opinion, would change actual adjudication standards significantly even in the absence of statutory or regulatory changes. This effect was viewed as resulting from the agency's failure to resist expansionist pressures on its unwritten, actual operating policy, making it necessary for Congress to step in with the 1967 act incorporating the unwritten guideline into statute.

While this adjustment may have settled the "national economy" question, and reemphasized the importance of medical criteria in the disability decision process, it by no means eliminated either the subjectivity of the core definition, or the difficulties of distinguishing *ability* to engage in work from *opportunity* or *willingness* to do so. Congress continued to leave to the administrators precisely the area in which lines are most difficult to draw, apparently on the theory that the area in which lines are most difficult to draw, apparently on the theory that "operational" standards are virtually impossible for Congress to codify in the abstract and are best developed incrementally through administrative experience.

An important and often overlooked theme in Social Security, which was touched on earlier, is the essentially private and defensive process through which SSA has regulated the disability program, at least up until the 1984 amendments. While the disability program, like all federal programs, is governed by regulations issued under the Administrative Procedures Act, these regulations usually have been used to state more general and basic policy precepts. Daily operating procedures have been produced on an ad hoc basis, through what are now called the Program Operating Manual System (POMS), in weekly, daily, or sometimes even more frequent communications between SSA's central office and the state agencies. An even less public area of policy communications has been the quality-assurance system, in which federal examiners review state decisions. Even after elimination of 100 percent federal review in the face of workload pressures in the mid-1970s, decisions returned to the state agencies for readjudication, after review in a federal sample process, served as the clearest direct indication to state personnel of what the federal administrators were looking for in disability decisions.

These "private," or at the least, nonpublic, avenues of communication between policymakers and adjudicators may be defended as necessary to preserve flexibility in a cumbersome administrative structure, probably the largest federal–state bureaucracy in existence. Some latitude for administrators to develop criteria based on "what works" at the day-to-day disability-examiner level is probably essential and unavoidable. However, the price paid for that latitude is the vulnerability of the decision-making process to informal influence, both from outside the system, such as public pressure and judicial interpretation, and from within the system, through the quality-assurance system and other sorts of informal communications.

In the 1970s, most critics of the system, whether correctly or not, attributed the significant inconsistency in program experience—wide swings in the numbers of people being awarded benefits from year to year, and wide variation in adjudication criteria from state to state, and from one level to the next—to informal public pressures on a flawed administrative structure too open to variation at the local state agency level. The inability to explain the growth of the disability program in this period, coupled with evidence of substantial variation in the way disability decisions were made from one adjudicator to the next, contributed to a rising sense of panic in the late 1970s, both within the agency and in Congress, over a program seemingly out of control.

The Crisis Years: 1974–1980

The first page of the 1974 Ways and Means Committee Staff Report on the Disability Insurance Program neatly summarizes the concerns that were to dominate discussion of the disability program over the next six years, culminating in the 1980 Disability Amendments. The first paragraph, in particular, identifies the central focus of congressional attention:

> Chronic actuarial deficiencies have developed in the Disability Insurance system over the last ten years. At present, social security disability awards are substantially greater than estimated and there is some reason to believe that elements in the new Supplemental Security Income (SSI) program may accelerate this trend.

Increasing cost was the principal reason for examining the disability program in this and later investigations both in Congress and in the executive branch. The primary suspects for this increase in costs were all identified on the same page of the 1974 report, a few of which were destined to be examined exhaustively over the next half-decade:

1. Expansionary pressures from the new SSI program, by implication because of the different "welfare" and mental disability applicant populations;
2. Workload pressures on the state agencies and Administrative Law Judges (ALJs) from the SSI and black lung programs, which was ". . . virtually monopolizing the services of the Social Security Administrative Law Judges."
3. The structure of the appeals process and the high reversal rates by ALJs, " . . . suggesting to applicants whose claims have been denied the wisdom of continued appeal."

4. The lack of uniformity in application of standards among the different appeals levels, in different state agencies, and among individual ALJs. The report particularly notes the elimination of federal review of state decisions, reducing " . . . what used to be a 100-percent check of State Agency decisions to a national 5-percent sample and a 7-percent sample of SSI cases . . . reviewed in regional offices after they are effectuated."

5. The continuing effect of court decisions on administrative standards. It is worth citing the staff report verbatim here:

> Final administrative denials are reviewed by the Courts under the substantial evidence rule which states that 'the findings of the Secretary as to any fact, if supported by substantial evidence, shall be conclusive. . . .' Despite this, the experience under the program is that many courts continue to review the facts de novo. Some have argued that the Courts have played a more substantive role in the development of the definition of disability than the Congress or the Social Security Administration. Others have maintained that the definition in the law is so subjective that it invites a variety of administrative interpretations and judicial interventions. (p. 1)

The report goes on for nearly 450 pages, detailing these concerns, and compiling statistical program information. More questions were raised than answered, but the agenda was set for the next six years, as Congress attempted to bring disability costs under control. A series of House reports in this period, as well as General Accounting Office (GAO) investigations and internal Administration studies, focused on the disability adjudication process, particularly on the problems of the federal–state relationship, as the primary source of increasing costs. Implicit in that assumption, of course, was the conviction that increasing numbers of ineligible people were being given benefits.

The numbers taken by themselves, particularly from 1965 to 1975, were striking indeed. In 1965, 533,000 workers applied for disability benefits, and total awards that year numbered 253,000, a disability incidence rate (number of disability awards per thousand insured workers) of 4.7. In 1975, in contrast, the number of applications had more than doubled to total 1,285,000, with total awards of 592,049 and a disability incidence rate of 7.1. The total benefit outlays of the program had more than doubled from $3.0 billion in 1970 to $8.0 billion in 1975, and a substantial shortfall in the SSDI trust fund was projected, with the trust fund becoming exhausted well in advance of the old-age and survivors' fund (Social Security Trustees' Report 1975).

It is not surprising that Congress eventually reacted to what appeared to be runaway cost increases in the absence of any major legislative change in the program. What is notable about the reaction—culminating in the 1980 amendments—is that increased costs alone appeared to be enough proof for most observers that ineligible people were being placed on the benefit rolls. In fact, the old-age and survivors' program was under even greater financial pressure through this period, as a result of a faulty benefit structure which resulted in unexpectedly high benefits for all beneficiaries, disabled workers included. Nonetheless, there was a widespread assumption that internal disability reform was needed to "bring the program under control." A comparison of two 1977 disability-reform packages—an early Ways and Means Subcommittee bill which did not advance (H.R. 8076) and an SSA disability package which similarly did not receive consideration outside the Department of Health and Human Services—is illuminating (Commissioner of Social Security 1977).

The SSA package focused directly on reducing costs by cutting disabled workers' benefits by 20 percent (by calculating benefits based on the formula for age-62 workers). In contrast, the subcommittee bill revised the definition of disability dramatically, making the definition for workers under age 50 more strict, based on medical criteria alone, disregarding vocational factors, while liberalizing the definition for workers aged 50 or older based on inability to perform work using comparable skills or abilities from the worker's previous job. Both packages required more extensive federal review of state decisions, extended the trial work period beyond nine months, and, significantly, severely limited federal court review of disability claims. The agency approach seemed to suggest that if costs were to be reduced, all beneficiaries should suffer, making no judgments about which of them might not be truly disabled. In contrast, the congressional approach seemed to assume that younger, less disabled workers posed the clearest threat to the continued financial security of the system. Their proposed definition would have moved the program significantly in the direction of a disability–retirement system, with severely restricted availability to younger workers. Neither package suggested broader review of current beneficiaries, beyond the existing "diary" procedure for those predicted to recover when benefits were granted.

By the time serious work began on the legislation that became the 1980 Disability Amendments, major legislation had been enacted in 1977 which at least temporarily restored the financing of all three Social Security trust funds. Indeed, the disability fund would not again be subject to adverse financial projections, in contrast to the continuing difficulties of the old-age fund, until the 1983 financing amendments. While the 1977 amendments, which reallocated the total old-age, survivors' and disability insurance tax rate to improve disability financing over the short term, made a major difference in SSDI trust fund stability, another trend, less noticed at the time, was also responsible for that stability. The growth of the SSDI program, far from continuing "out of control" through the 1970s, in fact had peaked in 1975, both in the number of awards and in the disability incidence rate. By 1978, the disability incidence rate stood at 5.2 percent. The number of awards had dropped to 464,415, over 20 percent lower than the figure for 1975. By 1980, before the new disability bill was even implemented, the disability incidence rate was 4.0, lower than in 1960, and the number of disability awards was less than 400,000, the lowest since 1970, and well below the mid-1970s average of 500,000 or more each year.

Since the financial crisis of the system was over, and the program apparently was not expanding significantly, there does not seem to have been much reason in 1980 for major disability reform. However, the momentum from years of staff work on administrative shortcomings in the federal–state system, coupled with continuing congressional concern that ineligible people were still getting benefits and had no incentive to return to work, propelled the legislative process toward reform anyway. The interest in work incentives stemmed from two sources. First, a decreasing number of people seemed to be leaving the benefit rolls to return to work—the rate of benefit terminations due to recovery or return to work fell from 32 persons per 1,000 beneficiaries in 1967 to 16 persons per 1,000 in 1975. Around 100,000 people per year were re-examined under the diary procedure, and the number losing benefits as a result jumped from 39 percent in 1977 to 46 percent in 1978, a percentage that was to remain roughly constant until 1984. There was some feeling in Congress that the agency should be expending more resources to re-examine more beneficiaries to determine if they were still eligible or if they had recovered.

A second source of concern about work incentives, and by far the strongest influence on the 1980 amendments, was data from a variety of sources showing that roughly one-quarter of new beneficiaries were receiving more in benefits for themselves and their families than they had earned while working. The conclusion was that the level of benefits was both inducing people to apply for benefits and discouraging them from attempting to leave the rolls. In the budget-cutting atmosphere of the late 1970s, when the Carter Administration produced several budgets advocating reductions in several kinds of Social Security benefits, the emphasis on reductions in expenditure even in the absence of a program-financing problem is not surprising.

Finally, even among those who took note of the change in disability experience, there was some distrust of the downturn in the numbers. Just as there was no satisfactory explanation for the growth in the program, there was no identifiable cause for the slowdown. In retrospect, it seems very likely that the contraction in the program resulted at least in part from internal reaction to outside pressure for reductions in program costs—the "adjudicative climate" which operated in that gray area of policy development at the state agency level and in communication between state and federal officials below the level of public regulatory action.

One set of statistics is revealing in this connection: In 1975, 44 percent of all initial state agency allowance decisions were based on a determination that the applicant's condition "equaled" the medical listing requirement, a type of decision which requires more individual judgment from the examiner and which was viewed by some as a less reliable basis for a finding of disability. Only 29 percent of allowances in 1975 were based on "meeting" the listing requirement exactly. By 1979, only 23 percent were based on "equals listing," while 55 percent were based on "meets listing." By 1982, the vast majority of all decisions were based on meeting the listings—73 percent—while less than 10 percent were based on equaling the listings.

The fact that such substantial changes in both disability experience and decision making could occur in the absence of any change in the law demonstrates the extreme sensitivity of the program to indirect influence. But while the agency and Congress seemed most to fear liberalizing judicial influence, clearly the strongest informal influence by 1980 was agency policy makers themselves, urged on by congressional scrutiny.

Provisions and Effects of the 1980 Amendments

The principal focus of the 1980 amendments, as finally enacted, was on work incentives to encourage beneficiaries to leave the benefit rolls, and on increased federal control over state agency decisions and ALJ decisions. The center of controversy over the bill at the time was the reduction in family benefit amounts and in the number of years of lowest earnings disabled workers could "drop out" of their benefit calculations, both designed to reduce benefits and thus the perceived financial incentive to become and remain a disability beneficiary. To balance these reductions, there were several provisions to encourage a return to work, primarily extending Medicare benefits for some period after benefit eligibility ceased, and lengthening the trial work period.

However, the legislation contained many more provisions aimed at the process of disability administration itself, and at the problem of variations in decisions from state to state among ALJs. The bill required a dramatic increase in the amount of management review and oversight of the program at all levels (House of Representatives, Conference Report, 1980):

1. Federal review ("pre-effectuation") of a percentage of state agency allowance decisions before the decision takes effect, beginning with 15 percent in 1981, 35 percent in 1982, and 65 percent in years thereafter;

2. Federal review at least once every three years of all beneficiaries not determined to be permanently disabled;

3. Reinstatement of SSA agency review of ALJ decisions ("own-motion" review); and

4. Requirement for disability determination procedures to be published in regulations or "other written guidelines of the Secretary" (p. 54) and specific provisions for the Secretary to take over the determination process in poorly performing states.

While the final agreement did not directly affect federal judicial review of disability decisions, the original Senate bill contained a provision which would have dramatically limited federal court review. The Senate provision modified the scope of federal review to make the Secretary's findings conclusive with respect to facts, unless found to be arbitrary and capricious. The substantial evidence rule would have been eliminated. The conference agreement deleted this provision because of uncertainty as to the implications and because of ". . . the concern that the administrative process is not operating with the degree of credibility which would justify elimination of the 'substantial evidence rule'" (p. 61).

The statement goes on to express grave concern about the number of court cases and the unevenness in adherence to the substantial evidence rule in courts across the country, concluding: ". . . the courts should interpret the substantial evidence rule with strict adherence to its principles since the practice of some courts in making de novo factual determinations could result in very serious problems for the Federal judiciary and the social security programs." This provision represents the outer limit of the congressional effort to insulate agency decisions and standards from the federal courts, prior to the 1984 Senate version of disability reform.

In summary, the 1980 Disability Amendments were designed to tighten administrative control over the adjudicative process, not to restructure the program or even to reduce its costs dramatically, other than through the direct benefit reduction for families of disabled workers. The earlier 1977 bill would have made it easier for older, less disabled workers to get benefits and much more difficult for younger applicants, by adding an additional objective screen—age—to the determination process and thus reducing some of the pressure on the more subjective elements of the definition itself. In contrast, the 1980 bill, at least by inference, seems to have accepted the program as structured, and to have laid the blame for whatever problems existed primarily at the door of lax administration.

Given later events, it is important to note here that the requirement for three-year re-examination of beneficiaries, or continuing-disability reviews (CDRs), was part of the re-emphasis on overall federal reviews. The savings estimate for this provision in the final conference report totalled only $218 million over the period 1982 to

1985; administrative costs of the review were estimated to exceed benefit savings for the first two years of operation. Moreover, the House report on the bill which contained the original provision, indicted that, given the heavy administrative impact of the re-exam, SSA should take three years after the effective date, already delayed until January 1982, or 18 months after enactment, to fully implement the reviews. It should also be noted that there was virtually no examination of what criteria should be applied to long-term beneficiaries. Notwithstanding evidence that internal pressures had led to significantly tighter operating standards despite the lack of more formal regulatory or statutory changes, the 1980 amendments were silent on criteria to be applied to current beneficiaries on review.

Moreover, the agency itself had reversed an internal policy followed followed from 1969 to 1976, under which the state agencies were not allowed to terminate benefits unless an improvement in the beneficiary's medical condition could be demonstrated (the LaBonte principle, after the ALJ who established it). It is unclear how aware members of Congress were of this policy reversal, and of the implications for the three-year re-exam requirement. Clearly, given the cost estimates, it was expected that some ineligible people would be found and would lose their benefits. However, if the slow start-up anticipated in the 1980 amendments had occurred, administrators might well have realized the morass of problems inherent in the re-exam, and the possible magnitude of benefits loss which could result if current standards were applied to old beneficiaries, in time to mitigate the ultimate public relations disaster of the CDR campaign.

The CDI Crisis and the 1984 Amendments
Through the late 1970s, during a Democratic administration, the pressure to reduce federal spending was strong, and Social Security was not exempted from the Administration's annual budget suggestions to Congress for ways to reduce expenditures (President's Budget, FY 1979). The three-year re-exam provision, however, was a congressional initiative, and was viewed at the time as simply one more federal check on the volatile disability-adjudication process. The House discussion of that provision was included in a broader discussion of all provisions dealing with increased program accountability and administrative uniformity: "Your committee is also concerned by the lack of followup on the medical condition and the possible work activity of individuals who have been on the rolls for years."

After describing the provision, and stating that the review should not be implemented fully until three years after the date of enactment, in order to give SSA adequate preparation time, the report states: "If periodic review at least every three years proves not to be cost-effective, the Secretary should report this to the committee" (Ways and Means Committee, House Report, 1979). Clearly, there were congressional doubts about whether the flame would be worth the candle; equally clearly, significant budget savings were not projected for several years after enactment.

In December 1980 and January 1981, the new Reagan Administration began formulating a budget message to Congress, due to be delivered by the president on February 18, 1981. The message would embody a stringent philosophy of reduced government expenditures in all domestic spending areas, including Social Security. While the public focus at the time was mainly on certain legislative proposals contained in the February message, notably elimination of the minimum Social Security benefit for those currently receiving it, the February proposals also contained a "management" proposal for disability insurance, described as "improved disability management."

This proposal was in effect an announcement of the Administration's intention to accelerate the three-year re-exam procedure, specifically to achieve budget savings estimated in documents submitted to Congress at $50 million in 1981, $200 million in 1982, $500 million in 1983, $700 million in 1984, and $900 million in 1985. The Office of Management and Budget's initial description of this proposal, contained in budget memoranda submitted to the president, described the proposal as follows:

> Unpublished SSA pilot quality control studies indicate a 15–20 percent SSDI error rate, with most of the misspent funds going to individuals misclassified as disabled. . . . A top-flight management team, starting immediately and operating under current law, could produce sizable savings starting in FY 82. Savings would be delayed [until then] since, for example, a no longer disabled individual could receive benefits for six months, while exhausting several levels of administrative appeals (unpublished OMB memorandum, January 1981, in possession of the author).

A detailed history of the Administration initiatives and congressional reactions that flowed from this OMB recommendation and the Administration's aggressive implementation of it from 1981 to 1983 cannot be included here. However, it is instructive to look at a few of the major events of the period between 1981 and 1983 to understand the genesis of the 1984 amendments.

Two questions are of primary importance: First, how did the 1984 amendments, which supported the federal courts against the agency and put into the statute a relatively more expansive rather than restrictive interpretation of the definition of disability for current beneficiaries, come about in light of the previous history of congressional reaction to federal court involvement in disability? Second, why were the 1984 amendments limited as they were to making the current program work rather than revamping its purpose and structure? The answer to the second question will set the stage for a final word on what the agenda for the next decade in disability may look like.

Administration Campaigns: 1981–1983

The development of disability legislation in 1983 and 1984 must be examined in the context of three major Administration initiatives over the 1981–1983 period. While the CDI acceleration obviously is the most clear direct reason for the eventual passage of the 1984 act, there were two other areas in which the Administration sought to restrict eligibility for and access to Social Security benefits: the abortive 1981 budget and "financing" packages, and the vigorous pursuit of overpayment recovery in all Social Security programs, including legislative attempts to expand greatly the use of computer matching of federal benefits records to find sources of income for beneficiaries that they may not have reported, and resulting offset of benefits against those other income sources. The latter two initiatives, while not specifically targeted on disability beneficiaries, did create an atmosphere in which the Administration's motives toward the Social Security program came to be deeply suspect on Capitol Hill, even among conservative Representatives who were inclined to give any Administration the benefit of the doubt in administering a complex program.

The May 1981 "financing" package, in particular, created a memorable firestorm on Capitol Hill: It was difficult for anyone to remember an Administration package being rejected so totally and swiftly by Congress, with the Republican-controlled Senate going on record as opposing the proposals 99 to 0 within a month of their announcement. Most of the furor surrounding that package centered on the proposal to reduce early retirement benefits by over 30 percent beginning in 8 months, which would have saved $17.6 billion over five years, and on the long-term reduction in the wage-indexing of benefits, which alone would have reduced the overall level of benefits by over 10 percent. However, the disability portion of these proposals would have dramatically reduced the size of the disability program by restricting eligibility in a variety of ways. First, two of the benefit reductions applied to SSDI as well—the wage-indexing restriction and a delay in the Costs of Living Adjustment (COLA). Second, four proposals specifically centered on disability:

1. Applying a "medical-only" definition of disability, with no consideration of age, education, and work experience (savings of $7.7 billion over 5 years);
2. Increasing the disability waiting period by one month (savings of $1.4 billion);
3. Requiring a prognosis of duration of impairment of 24 months instead of 12 months (savings of $2.8 billion); and

4. Requiring covered work in 30 out of the 40 quarters prior to disability, instead of 20 of 40 (savings of $10.0 billion).

The key to these proposals was the same as to the CDI acceleration, which was at its heart also a money-saving device. These proposals all reveal an overall perception that Social Security and disability in particular are nothing more than thinly disguised welfare programs, subject to infinite claims which must be restricted through a variety of objective means in order to preserve the federal budget's fiscal integrity. Of course, this attitude bears considerable resemblance to the traditional congressional perspective on the disability program, which stressed the importance of holding the line on program growth and restricting financial claims on the trust fund.

However, there were several significant differences in the new Administration's goals and methods. First, there was a strong commitment actually to reduce federal spending, not just to restrict its growth. Thus the Social Security packages and administrative initiatives went beyond limiting growth—they would have substantially *reduced* the size and benefits of the programs. Second, the method used to accomplish the goal of reduced spending was similar to that classically used to restrict welfare programs: First, try to change the legal requirements for eligibility and, if that won't work, restrict the access to the program by putting administrative hurdles in the way.

Thus, the proposal to increase insured-status requirements would have resulted in a loss of disability insurance for many millions of workers who would not really have been aware of their loss until they became disabled and sought their benefits. The proposals to increase the prognosis requirement and to require a medical-only definition of disability—especially in combination with the ongoing disability reviews in which the new standards presumably would have been applied to beneficiaries under review—would have drastically reduced the actual numbers of current and future beneficiaries, all under the rationale of making disability standards more objective.

These proposals were never accepted. However, the fact that they were seriously advanced by the Administration, at the precise moment the CDI campaign was being launched in the state agencies, reveals their assessment of what the disability program should be: a program limited to those with catastrophic medical conditions, admission to which should be limited not only through restrictive definition, but through additional, completely objective screens of stringent insured-status requirements. After it became clear that this view could not be implemented through legislative channels, the CDI process became the principal vehicle for restricting access to the program. Given the cumbersome and complex nature of the adjudicative process, once people were weeded out of the system through the eligibility review, it would be much more difficult for them to work their way back in.

The CDI acceleration, which began as an OMB initiative in January 1981, was strenuously objected to internally by SSA and departmental officials, and, of course, provoked the only real public relations problems for the Administration's first term, once the impact of terminating benefits for half-a-million people hit the press. However, the internal objections by career SSA and departmental staff to implementing OMB's proposal were quite different from the public and judicial objections to the campaign. The former group essentially objected to the speed and scope of the review because of the difficulties of doing the task in light of the restrictions on state agency resources and staffing. Government analysts also registered severe doubts about the size of the estimates for savings, which were viewed as greatly inflated.

The public reaction was more complex, based as much on public views toward entitlement to benefits and the nature of disability itself, and on impatience with bureaucratic red tape and obvious bungling, as on any focused response to the Administration's attempts to reduce government spending. Throughout the disability-review controversy, both the press and the public displayed the same attitude toward disability as a former Supreme Court Justice apparently had toward obscenity: They couldn't really define it, but they knew it when they saw it, and the Administration was clearly terminating benefits for obviously disabled people.

Whatever the merits in individual cases for either continuation or termination, the fact that state agencies called in over 400,000 people to be reviewed between March 1981, and April 1982, and terminated benefits for over 200,000 of them, was in itself a source of controversy. Added to the sheer number of people who clearly considered themselves to be disabled but who were now suddenly without benefits, were numerous stories in the press of people losing benefits and then dying, either as the result of their disability or through suicide. The mentally impaired were a particular focus of review, and were thus especially affected, given their inherent difficulties in pursuing the maze of the appeals process. [See *City of New York v. Heckler*, 578 F.Supp.1109 (E.D.N.Y. 1984) for Judge Weinstein's excellent summary of the facts in the major mental impairment class-action suit.]

Congressional Response and Counter-Response: 1982 and 1984

The congressional response to the CDI campaign took some time to develop, and was far from unified. Deep divisions in approach persisted down to the final House–Senate conference in the summer of 1984, a full year after the House Subcommittee on Social Security had approved a reform bill, and two years after the Ways and Means Committee had approved a bill diametrically opposite in effect and purpose from the 1984 reform effort. A complete discussion of the congressional reaction to the CDI campaign would include mention of the efforts of the House and Senate Aging Committees (non-legislative, advocacy committees) to force legislative action from both Ways and Means in the House and Finance in the Senate. However, rather than attempt a detailed chronological account of the various hearings and partial legislative remedies enacted during the period (notably payment of benefits through the appeals process for CDI cases, enacted at the end of 1982), this section will present some observations about the development of the bill that was finally enacted into law in 1984, notably its timing and its very substantial difference from the 1982 bill.

The first circumstance which should be noted in examining why it took three years for corrective legislation to be enacted is the Social Security financing debate which occupied center stage in Administration and congressional discussions from 1981 to March 1983, when the Social Security financing-reform act was approved. During the first two years of the CDI campaign, the legislative committees with responsibility for the disability program (House Ways and Means and Senate Finance Committees) were preoccupied with financing and budget debates, in which the dominant theme was the impending bankruptcy of the entire system. In such an atmosphere, it is hardly surprising that Administration efforts to reduce costs were met with neutrality, if not welcomed outright, by legislators facing the need to refinance the basic benefit structure itself.

Second, those outside Congress frequently overlook the fundamental reluctance of Congress to involve itself in day-to-day administrative issues, based on the assumption that the executive branch is in a better position to know how to run its programs. Even without the financing crisis, this pervasive disinterest in "interfering" with executive branch judgment would have presented major obstacles to those protesting the Administration's conduct of the CDI process. It was this set of assumptions that shaped the first disability bill in 1982, which never reached the House floor, despite approval by the Ways and Means Committee.

Finally, while press coverage of the disability crisis provoked considerable criticism of the program outside Congress, the real pressure for reform came from within the congressional process itself—from Representatives and their staffs, who were inundated with the complaints of disabled people who had had their benefits cut off. Through their letters and personal complaints, affected beneficiaries formed a powerful, if not completely organized lobby for reform, particularly after the staffs of individual Representatives, won over after dealing with scores of complaints, became convinced that the Administration had run amok. No amount of press coverage, which was by no means complete (particularly in the Washington area, where Representatives, after all, spend most of their time), could have generated the widespread bipartisan support in Congress for action which was apparent by 1983.

H.R. 6181: 1982 Ways and Means Bill

As pressure for some sort of action on disability began to mount in early 1982, the House Ways and Means Subcommittee on Social Security held hearings on the disability crisis in March. Shortly thereafter, the staff developed a series of disability proposals which, after consideration in subcommittee and full committee, eventually became H.R. 6181. As this bill never received consideration by the House and died in the Rules Committee, its significance is almost purely historical, as a contrast to the legislation developed by the same committee a year later. The basic outline of the 1982 bill, however, reveals the strength of traditional congressional views toward restraint of disability expenditures and toward court "interference."

The key provisions of the 1982 bill were on the one hand ameliorative, focused on the sometimes harsh effects of the continuing reviews, and, on the other hand restrictive, aimed at promoting "consistency and uniformity" of decision making. The first goal was met by providing interim payment of benefits to those beneficiaries, found ineligible on review by the state agency, who pursued an appeal through the ALJ level. These payments were subject to recovery as overpayments if the denial was upheld by the ALJ. The policy statement contained in this provision seems to be that although the process itself was not at fault, either in the grounds for denial of benefits or in the conduct of the review, the effect of losing benefits for many beneficiaries was too harsh and should be mitigated, if only temporarily.

The heart of this bill, however, was the reiteration of long-standing congressional concerns about the vulnerability of the decision-making process to varying interpretations of the law at the various adjudicative levels. In a subcommittee report issued in September 1982, after H.R. 6181 had stalled in committee, the staff summarized the purpose of the 1982 bill:

> On March 3, 1982, Mr. Pickle and Mr. Archer, chairman and ranking minority member of the Subcommittee . . . introduced H.R. 5700 which was designed to remedy some of the problems in the CDI process. . . . A number of provisions were included which were designed to strengthen the structure of the disability appeals process and make decisionmaking more uniform through all levels of the system. (Ways and Means Committee Print, 1982 p. 15)

The staff report also spells out in some detail the controversy over the two most important provisions designed to achieve that goal: closing the claimant's record at the reconsideration level of adjudication (before the ALJ hearing) and requiring ALJs to abide by the program-operating instructions sent to the state agencies, as well as regulations and Social Security rulings. In particular, the suggestion of closing the record, after a newly required face-to-face interview at reconsideration, raised so much controversy that the bill was amended in both subcommittee and full committee to allow some new evidence to be heard. Opposition was so strong that the committee's rule request (which governs how the measure will be debated in the House of Representatives) included the highly unusual provision for a separate vote on the closed-record provision.

> The various amendments did not mollify the opposition of the advocacy groups who appear to see any restrictions on the ALJs' ability to deal with the case on a de novo basis as injurious to the system. Underlying this argument is a distrust of the State agencies who they see as not being capable of making an "independent" adjudication of the cases. As stated earlier, the Committee on Ways and Means report, however, emphasizes their independence. (p. 18)

These amendments failed to defuse opposition to the bill, and the Rules Committee never acted on the motion for a rule. Thus, the bill died at the close of the 97th Congress.

While the bill did not specifically prohibit ALJs from abiding by federal circuit court interpretations of the Social Security Act, the intent of the provision clearly was to require ALJs to use the same criteria as the state agencies, which did not follow federal court interpretative opinions at all. The Subcommittee report cites the previous issued committee report on H.R. 6181 to the effect that the high reversal rate of state agency denials appealed to the ALJ level (58 percent reversed by ALJs in FY 1981) was principally due to the fact that " . . . State agencies and the ALJs have been making decisions on the basis of different criteria" (p. 19).

Clearly, H.R. 6181 followed the traditional pattern of legislative attempts to make the program less subject to federal court interference, both by restricting the kind of evidence the ALJ would hear (i.e., no new evidence, but simply a closed paper record from the reconsideration level), and by requiring ALJs to use only administratively generated criteria—POMs, rulings, and regulations—of which only the last were subject to public review. While both of these provisions were liberalized over the course of committee consideration, the thrust remained intact. The bill represented a general endorsement of the Administration's ongoing CDI efforts, with only a relatively minor attempt to mitigate the impact of benefit termination. As addressed by H.R. 6181, the source of the problems for the disability program was that the ALJs (and, by implication, the federal courts), not the state agencies, were out of control.

1983–1984: New Directions in H.R. 3755
After completing work on the 1983 Social Security Amendments in March 1983, the Subcommittee on Social Security of the House Ways

and Means Committee undertook a new effort to develop disability-reform legislation. Reform measures addressing the standards used in disability reviews had been introduced in both the House and Senate in 1982 and early 1983, but no action was taken on either the House or Senate side until, in the summer of 1983, the Ways and Means Subcommittee began serious work on a new bill, quite different from H.R. 6181.

The difference in subcommittee approach was signaled by a subcommittee document, issued June 28, 1983, in preparation for later disability hearings. After summarizing the budgetary origins of the Administration's CDI campaign, the report stated the problem:

> There is evidence of widespread terminations without good cause in only one region, in connection with mental impairments. However, many other beneficiaries who have been on the rolls for several years, who had no expectation of ever working again, and whose medical condition has not appreciably changed from when they were first given benefits, are having their benefits terminated, during a time of high unemployment even for the able-bodied. These people are angry and confused and in some cases desperate, since their level of impairments and long period of not working probably makes it impossible for most of them to find work now. (Staff background paper, 1983, p. 8)

The staff paper goes on to identify three major reasons for "the most controversial initial termination decisions":

> (1) Beneficiaries are being reevaluated as if they were first-time applicants, without regard to whether their current condition has changed since they were initially allowed. . . . (2) These reevaluations are based on current standards of medical criteria which are in many cases more clear-cut and exact than the standards on which benefits were initially based, and reflect improvements in medical technology and treatment. . . . (3) The overall 'adjudicative climate' has been tougher than in earlier years, so that reexamined beneficiaries, being looked at as if they are new applicants, will have tougher standards applied. (p. 9)

This summary of the problem of the adjudicative standards being used to conduct CDI reviews incorporates the problems dealt with in the final legislation: the medical improvement standard requiring a showing that the beneficiary's condition had improved since being granted benefits in order to support a finding that he or she was no longer disabled; the multiple-impairment provision requiring an evaluation of the combined effect of impairments in determining initial and continuing disability; a moratorium on mental impairment determinations pending the development of new mental impairment standards (required to be developed in conjunction with the American Psychiatric Association and others in the mental health community); and a study of how subjective evidence of pain could be used in determining disability.

An additional area which proved to be a major bone of contention in the final conference negotiations on the bill was highlighted at the Ways and Means Subcommittee hearing in June 1983: Administration "nonacquiescence" in federal court interpretations of the law. In several long and contentious exchanges between subcommittee members and Administration witnesses, the bitter, emerging conflict between the agency and the courts became evident. By 1983, almost all Circuit Courts of Appeals—the highest federal courts below the Supreme Court—had ruled that current law required state agencies to make a finding of improvement in the beneficiary's medical condition in order to terminate benefits on the grounds of renewed ability to work.

Ordinarily, a Circuit Court of Appeals interpretation of law is followed by all lower courts in that circuit, as the "law of the circuit," unless and until the interpretation is overturned by the Supreme Court on appeal by the losing party. Administrative Law Judges, as lawyers and adjudicators, in general feel bound to follow such circuit law. However, the Social Security Administration steadfastly refused to follow circuit court opinion as precedent, at either the state-agency or the ALJ level, even though they were forced to pay benefits in each individual case litigated at a circuit court level.

The agency defended this practice in the June hearing, by stating that the Internal Revenue Service also issued rulings of nonacquiescence which had never been held as invalid by the Supreme Court (Ways and Means Committee, June 1983, p. 64). This defense could charitably be termed somewhat disingenuous, as the IRS's policy of nonacquiescence is quite different from SSA's. First, it applies primarily to decisions of the Tax Court, an Article I administrative court, not an Article III judicial branch court; second, the IRS does follow federal circuit court decisions within the jurisdiction of the circuit deciding the case, and only issues nonacquiescence rulings where it has decided not to apply rulings of one circuit court to cases in other circuits.

In any event, the Administration's defense of its policy apparently was not convincing to the subcommittee, as the subcommittee bill, and the final House bill up until the last moment of conference negotiations in September 1984, would have required the Administration to acquiesce within the circuit. This provision marks a complete break with past congressional attempts to rebuff federal court influence over disability decision making, as in the 1967 amendments' clarification of the disability definition. Indeed, more than once, the conference negotiations nearly broke down completely because of the reluctance of the Senate to incorporate such federal court control over disability-program standards into the law. It is therefore worth citing the House report at some length, to clarify the reasons for such a complete change of heart both from the 1982 bill and from traditional concerns as they continued to be championed by Senators Dole and Long. After first pointing out the growing burden of disability cases in the federal district courts, and the fact that in many instances circuit courts had and continued to issue interpretive opinions which they intended to be binding on lower courts and the agency as the law of the circuit, the report stated that SSA does not follow circuit court rulings either within the circuit or nationwide:

> Moreover, the agency frequently does not appeal district court or circuit court opinions with which it disagrees. This practice insures that the Supreme Court will not have the opportunity to review the issue and render a decision with which the agency would be compelled to comply. Social Security ALJs are not able to follow court of appeals decisions as precedent. . . . SSA has been criticized for this policy, both by outside experts and Federal judges, on the grounds that it undermines the structure of Federal law, and in essence allows SSA to overrule the legal judgment of the Federal courts by administrative inaction.

The report cited a 1979 Administration brief for the Supreme Court in which HHS stated that the Secretary would either abide by or appeal an unfavorable circuit court ruling, and stated, "This statement is in marked contrast to the repeated instances brought to the committee's attention of SSA's non-acquiescence policy . . . " (House Report 1984, pp. 23–24).

The report summed up the House concerns as follows:

> The committee is concerned about the result of this non-acquiescence policy for claimants, the courts and SSA. First, while it is clearly of utmost importance that a Federal program be administered according to uniform, Federal standards, it is not clear that SSA's policy of non-acquiescence substantially achieves that end. In fact, under the current policy, distinctions exist within circuits between policies applied to those claimants who pursue their claims to the appeals court level and those who cannot.
>
> The committee is most concerned about the impact of this policy on beneficiaries and claimants, and on their relationship to the Social Security program. If a circuit court rules on a given issue such as medical improvement, it is a foregone conclusion that subsequent appeals to that court on that issue will be successful. By refusing to apply the circuit court ruling, SSA forces beneficiaries and applicants to re-litigate the same issue over and over again in the circuit, even though the agency is certain to lose each case.

The committee can find no reason grounded in sensible public policy to force beneficiaries to sue in order to obtain what has been declared by the Federal court as justice in a particular area. Such a policy creates a wholly undesirable distinction between those beneficiaries with the resources and fortitude to pursue their claims, and those who accept the government's original denial in good faith or because they lack the means to appeal their case. . . . The increasingly adversarial character of the process for becoming eligible for disability benefits, and especially for retaining eligibility, does immeasurable harm to the public's trust in the Social Security program and in government as a whole. . . . The committee sees no compelling reason why the Social Security Administration's interpretation of the statute, particularly in issues where the definitions are not specific or are completely silent on the issue, should be automatically considered superior to that of the Federal court. . . . If the Federal circuit courts hand down decisions that appear detrimental to the purposes or operation of the program, either the Supreme Court should be given the opportunity to make a determination that remedies the situation, or Congress may well have to clarify the law. . . . Short of legislative changes, however, the committee sees no reason to allow SSA to ignore the law as determined in each circuit by the highest Federal court simply because the administrators view the Federal court's decision as mistaken. (pp. 24–25)

The committee bill, approved originally in fall 1983, but not brought to the House floor until spring, 1984, reflected the changed perception of the problem with disability outlined above: The problem was with the standards being applied at the state agencies, not in the courts. In addition to the core provision on medical improvement, and the acquiescence requirement, the bill, for the first time, put SSA under the Administrative Procedures Act, to formally require Social Security regulations to be issued according to public notice and comment procedures. This provision, in one way, marked a departure from traditional attempts to insulate the agency from public pressures on adjudication standards, but in another, was a continuation of the tradition of pressuring the agency to put its standards in writing, rather than leaving essential elements of the process inchoate and unstated in public documents.

The House bill was generally greeted with enthusiasm by advocates, given the marked contrast with previous Ways and Means disability efforts. Nonetheless, the bill did not go very far in requiring extensive or longitudinal work evaluations of applicants, an issue of principal concern to mental disability advocates, nor did it really alter or substantially clarify the existing definition of disability. In fact, the new legislation did not constitute basic reform, but rather imposed a separate standard of review on top of the basic, unchanged standard of disability.

It is not difficult to understand why the House bill was as limited as it was, if two other factors are considered. First, an extremely high cost was estimated by the Administration for even the limited provisions of the Ways and Means-reported bill (about $2 to $5 billion over five years). Second, and more important, the House bill faced the intransigent opposition of some Senators, notably Senator Long, ranking Democrat and former Chairman of the Senate Finance Committee, and Senator Dole, then Chairman of the Senate Finance Committee, and of the Administration, notably the Justice Department, to any "liberalizations" of the review process and above all, to legitimation of federal court interpretations of the Social Security statute.

The Senate disability bill, approved in May 1984, in almost every respect was the diametric opposite of the House bill. The medical improvement standard was, in fact, a medical "nonimprovement" standard, in which the beneficiary had to demonstrate that his or her condition had deteriorated or stayed the same, in order to maintain benefits. Second, the agency practice of ignoring allegations of pain was codified in statute. Finally, the bill would have insulated the agency even further from the federal courts by codifying the current nonacquiescence practice, and by requiring federal courts to dismiss most, if not all, class-action suits brought in the previous three years on the medical improvement and other issues (e.g., both *MHA of Minnesota vs. Schwieker* and *City of New York vs. Heckler* on the subject of mental impairment) on the procedural grounds that the unnamed plaintiffs in the suits had not pursued their claims through the complete administrative appeals process before being included in the class action. It should be noted that the Supreme Court, in a June 1986, opinion in the *City of New York* case, unanimously ruled against the Justice Department's position that claimants in the class-action suit should have exhausted all administrative remedies before seeking judicial review of their claim.

There would have been no disability-reform bill in 1984, if not for the confluence of several factors. First, by March, the disability program itself was close to collapse. More than half of the state agencies had stopped administering the review, in many cases under court order, because of the nonacquiescence policy. Second, the House conferees, notably Chairman Pickle, persisted in efforts to compromise and reach agreement without sacrificing the core medical improvement provision completely. Finally, in an election year, with both a president running on his record and Republican control of the Senate at stake, the disability mess represented a public relations blot on the Administration's record which could easily be exploited by Democrats.

The final bill, although much closer to the House version than the Senate's, represented a classic legislative compromise, with the result that the much-needed clarification of disability standards is considerably more vague than anyone would have wanted. The new medical improvement standard, with its multiplicity of exceptions, has yet to be fully implemented, and continuing reviews, as of this writing, have barely been renewed. Finally, since the House gave up its insistence on a legislative acquiescence requirement, in order to reach a conference agreement, the Administration continues in its policy of non-acquiescence with only minor changes.

Nonetheless, the 1984 act represents both a traditional compromise approach to disability problems, with much of the hard decision making left to the agency, and a departure from tradition, in its attempt to bring the agency within the general authority of the federal courts. The question to be faced now is whether there is any possibility for still greater departure from tradition in the disability program—Is real reform in the foreseeable future?

CONCLUSION: PROSPECTS FOR REFORM

The fundamental dilemma of the disability program remains much as it was in 1967: How can we tell when someone is truly unable to work because of a disability, and when he or she is simply using impairment as an excuse to receive public support in lieu of working for a living? It should be clear from the previous discussion that in any close case, no matter how much medical evidence we gather, how many personal interviews with the applicant we conduct, or how stringently we apply written criteria, we simply cannot make such a determination with certainty. It may well be time for Congress and disability professionals to begin concentrating on questions for which there are concrete answers, instead of renewing attempts to impose an objective process on an inherently subjective decision.

The core issue is the all-or-nothing nature of the current disability program, to which most of the stresses on the disability-determination process must be attributed. If, for example, we were willing to restrict eligibility to workers over a certain age, or workers with no significant break in service in the period prior to disability, the disability definition itself could be considerably more objective *and* more liberal without significantly increasing the cost of the program. However, if as a society we want most workers in covered employment to be reasonably well insured against the loss of earning capacity as a result of disability, of necessity we must continue to place pressure on the only significant test of eligibility: the existence of disability itself.

Moreover, the increasing importance and difficulty of mental impairment determinations in the disability process poses an additional challenge to stereotypical thinking, both about "faking" eligibility, and about the possibility for return to productive life. If real improvement is to be made in the area of disability reform, we must begin to explore ways in which the program can become a transition, rather than a dead end.

The historic focus of disability legislation has been on making sure that only completely disabled people get benefits, and, more recently, on insuring that only those who *remain* completely disabled remain entitled to benefits. The disastrous CDR campaign, and the painful struggle for the 1984 bill, serve as warnings that overly narrow concentration on perfecting the process by which disability is determined will result in little progress, and can produce inhumane and irrational results.

Over the next decade, as improvements continue to be made in treatment of all sorts of disabilities, and control of disorders that were once completely disabling, it will be time for Congress to look more closely at what can loosely be called—for want of a better term—rehabilitation. What we need, however, is a much broader and more flexible approach to maintenance in the community and the work place for people with a whole range of disabling mental and physical impairments. The pressures to expand the current Snarrow income maintenance program into a full-scale rehabilitative or partial-disability program will only increase in the future and will probably be met with staunch resistance if such a change is billed as simply part of the current program's mission.

In order to create the kind of transitional support and employment programs that are necessary to allow disabled people to be truly part of mainstream life, a new kind of thinking about disability income support will be necessary. Instead of trying to expand the current program to cover payments to those who can work despite their impairments, we should begin to develop a new structure to provide transitional payments, partial payments on a longer term basis, immediate rehabilitation, employment, transportation and medical support, and a whole host of other support-network needs.

It must be admitted that the creation of a new social welfare program in an age of public retrenchment may not be an easy or obvious solution to the current problems of the older disability program. Nonetheless, those who advocate greater support and more creative responses to the needs of the disabled must recognize that the disability-insurance program cannot be stretched to accomplish those goals without breaking altogether. Once it is clear that new programs are needed to meet the real changing needs of a non-homogeneous disabled population, concrete solutions can be found, and the old barriers to expansion of the SSDI program can be avoided. It's a project worth doing.

REFERENCES

City of New York v. Heckler, 578 F.Supp. 1109 (E.D.N.Y., 1984), affd. 742 F.2d. 729 (2d Cir. 1984), affd. on reh. 755 F.2d 31 (1985), affd. *Bowen v. City of New York,* 476 U.S. ____ (1986)

Commissioner of Social Security: Internal Departmental Memorandum. August 19, 1977

Executive Office of the President: President's Budget for FY 1979. Washington, DC, U.S. Government Printing Office, 1979

Kerner v. Flemming, 283 F.2d, 918 (1960)

Mental Health Association of Minnesota v. Heckler, 554 F. Supp. 157 (D. Mn. 1982), aff'd. with mod. 720 F.2d 965 (8th Cir. 1984)

Social Security Administration: Report of the Social Security Trustees, 1975. Washington, DC, Government Printing Office, 1975

Stone D: The Disabled State. Philadelphia, Temple University Press, 1984

U.S. House of Representatives: Conference Report on 1980 Disability Amendments, H. Rpt. 96-944, Washington, DC, U.S. Government Printing Office, May 13, 1980

Subcommittee on Social Security: Staff Background Paper. Washington, DC, U.S. Government Printing Office, June 28, 1983

Ways and Means Committee: Harrison Subcommittee Report. Washington, DC, Committee Print/U.S. Government Printing Office, March 11, 1960

Ways and Means Committee: House Report, 1967 Disability Amendments. Washington, DC, U.S. Government Printing Office, 1967

Ways and Means Committee: Staff Report on Disability Amendments, Washington, DC, U.S. Government Printing Office, 1974

Ways and Means Committee: House Report 96-100, on H.R. 3236. Washington, DC, U.S. Government Printing Office, April 23, 1979

Ways and Means Committee: Committee Print 97-37. Washington, DC, U.S. Government Printing Office, September 20, 1982

Ways and Means Committee: Hearings on Disability Insurance, Serial 98-25. Washington, DC, U.S. Government Printing Office, June 1983

Ways and Means Committee: House Report 98-618. Washington, DC, U.S. Government Printing Office, March 1984

21

Social Security Disability Programs: How They Work for the Mentally Impaired

John M. Hamilton, M.D.

T he United States Congress first considered the establishment of a federal disability program in 1952, during its deliberations surrounding the Social Security Amendments of that year. While the substance of those disability-related provisions was never implemented,[1] they did rouse further congressional discussion of this act, leading to the Social Security Act Amendments of 1956. In adopting the 1956 act, the first cash benefits under the Social Security Disability Insurance (SSDI) program became a reality. This program was, and remains, funded through worker and employer

---

[1] The Social Security Amendments of 1952 included a measure providing for establishment of a "disability freeze." The disability-freeze provision was designed to protect the benefit rights of workers and their dependents by providing that the worker's period of disability would not be counted in determining insured status under the retirement-insurance program, or in determining the worker's average earnings for purposes of computing benefit amounts. Under the 1952 amendments, the disability-freeze provision was to become operative July 1, 1953, if Congress affirmed the measure before that time. Congress took no action, and the 1952 provision did not become operative. Its specific provisions, however, served as the basis for the disability freeze enacted in the Social Security Amendments of 1954.

contributions, just as the Old-Age Pension Fund is under the Social Security Act. It is intended to benefit those persons who have contributed to the fund through employment during a statutorily set minimum work period.

The statutory criterion for disability eligibility has remained essentially constant through the years, representing a rather strict construction of disability when contrasted with other government-sponsored systems and with private insurers. It requires an individual to have a "medically determinable impairment" (i.e., one which can be documented by signs, symptoms, laboratory, or psychological tests; and which is expected to last or has lasted 12 months, or which terminates in death). The program restricts itself to payments for "total" disability, which anticipates that anyone meeting its definition will be unable to work at *any* job. (In the case of children, a comparable level of severity is required, though work is not the standard.) It is important to note that the program distinguishes clearly between "total" and "permanent" disability, not requiring the latter as an even more stringent standard.

The Supplemental Security Income (SSI) program, which became federal law in 1972, sets basic federal standards and a federal matching payment for state benefit programs for the medically indigent, including among them a certain number of the disabled and blind. The program is a "needs" program, with eligibility dependent upon meeting a needs test against income. For the disabled, eligibility under SSI is not dependent upon having been a worker who contributed to a fund over a specified period of time as in the SSDI program. If a person meets the medical criteria (which are essentially the same as in the SSDI program, with the exception of some onset restrictions), and meets the income restrictions, he or she is eligible, without regard to other factors.

THE MEDICAL CRITERIA FOR DETERMINING ELIGIBILITY

In the early days of the disability program, the Social Security Administration (SSA) undertook the task of operationalizing the statutory eligibility definition. Many American physicians participated in advisory councils and through independent sources to establish the medical criteria upon which the decision-treelike structure which leads to a determination of disability has been based over the 30-year history of the program. Briefly, the medical criteria established were divided by body system (e.g., respiratory, cardiovascular, gastrointestinal, mental, musculoskeletal, etc.). Each body system has a set of listed impairments—physical and mental disorders—as well as characteristics of the disorders which impose functional restrictions of such severity as to lead to a presumption (based upon reasonable medical certainty) of disability. Thus, someone meeting the criteria of an impairment and its characteristics, as written, would be found incapable of engaging in *any* work activity.

Such an individual is said to "meet" the "Listings" (short-hand for "Listings of Impairments," the medical, body system-oriented document described above). An individual may "equal" the intent of the Listings if a mental or physical disorder, though not listed, can be demonstrated to be medically determinable, and has a level of severity comparable to a listed impairment. An individual may also equal the intent of the Listings if he or she is found to have a constellation of impairments which, combined, equal the severity of a comparable, listed disorder.

The medical portion of the determination process also may find a person to have a "severe" impairment, but not one which meets or equals the Listings of Impairments. In such cases, a nonmedical reviewer assesses whether adverse vocational factors, such as age, work experience, and education, in combination with the medically determined severe impairment, would preclude the person from engaging in work.[2]

THE DISABILITY-DETERMINATION PROCESS
The SSA has developed a complex, five-step process by which claims are received and evaluated for disability. As noted above, only a portion of that determination is medical and conducted by a physician.

Local SSA offices, called district offices (DOs), are located strategically throughout the country and staffed by federal employees who receive applications from potential SSDI claimants. These DOs represent the first intake position for the agency—acquiring general identification and administrative information about the claimant. A claimant's statements about entitlement are recorded, along with information about medical and lay sources who could document the claimant's case. DO interviewers also record personal observations about the claimant for use at later stages of the review and adjudication process.

District offices submit claims information to the Disability Determination Service (DDS), the state agency required under statute to conduct the adjudication process on behalf of the SSA. It is here that both initial and "reconsideration" (a second-chance review, if a claimant appeals a previously unfavorable decision) decisions are made, either allowing or denying benefits. The DDS staff gathers the medical and lay evidence which forms the basis for both the medical and nonmedical portions of the claim review. The DDS's medical staff reviews the medical evidence against the Listings: the nonmedical staff conducts additional reviews of vocational factors in cases which are not determinable based solely on the medical facts. Figure 1

---

[2] Children, widows, and widowers are excluded from this latter consideration and can qualify only by meeting or equaling the Listings.

Figure 1.

The flow of a claim through the SSA system

DO (Federal Office, SSA Employees)

Takes claimant's application (phone or in person)
Records: • Allegations

• Medical sources

• Lay sources

• Vocational background

• Observations

DDS (State Agency, State Employees)

Receives DO Information
Collects Medical and Lay Evidence
Adjudicates Claim:
• Allows claims (pays benefits)

• Denies claims

Processes Reconsideration of Denied Claims:
• Allows on reconsideration (pays benefits)

• Denies reconsideration

Processes Continuing Diability Reviews:
• Initial review

• CDR

RO (Regional Office Review)

Quality Assurance Sample (no fixed %)
(this is a post-adjudicative review)

Pre-effectuation Review (PER)
(a 65% sample of all allowances)

CO (Central Office Review)

Office of Disability Operations (ODO) does a PER for continuances
(a 65% sample)

Office of Assessment (DA) does review of regional performance
(no fixed %)

Special Studies

details the flow of a claim in its process through the SSA system, including regional and national supervisory levels beyond the DDS. Figure 2 provides a snapshot of the decision-tree approach to decision making.

The critical area, particularly for those individuals suffering from mental disorders, is the DDS adjudicative process. At that level, a team of adjudicators—traditionally an examiner (lay adjudicator) and a physician (ideally matched in specialty to the claimant's impaired organ system)—work hand-in-hand to make determinations in accordance with the Listings of Impairments and vocational measures of severity. They review the documentation submitted by the claimant, his or her physician, and other lay sources, and occasionally may supplement these data with agency-generated evidence from consultative examinations by SSA-contract physicians and, in the more rare case, from workshop evaluations. Based upon these data, and working against both the Listing of Impairments and the Procedures and Operations Manual System (the POMS, a 14-volume compilation of adjudication procedures which have operationalized the statute and regulations for day-to-day use), the medical–lay adjudication team renders a decision, either to deny or grant benefits. Unfavorable decisions may be appealed at the DDS level, to a higher level of the Administrative Law Judge corps, and yet higher to the Appeals Council of the SSA in Baltimore, Maryland. (A last recourse, which will not be discussed here, is appeal to the federal court system.)

Figure 2.

The decision-tree approach to decision-making.

A claim may be:

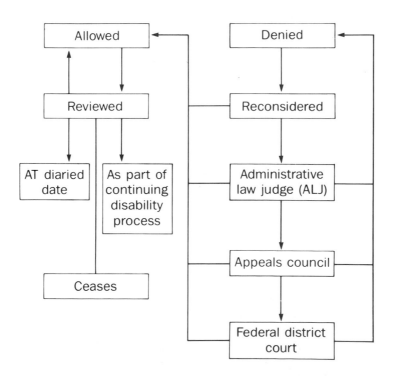

SSDI AND THE MENTALLY ILL: IMPACT OF THE 1980 AMENDMENTS

The Social Security Amendments of 1980, while applied across the entire SSDI system, held special import and impact for those potential and actual claimants and beneficiaries suffering from mental disorders. The 1980 amendments were intended to (1) strengthen the integrity of the disability programs; (2) offer greater assistance to those beneficiaries who were trying to return to work; and (3) improve program administration. These amendments included measures designed to strengthen incentives to engage in rehabilitation programs and to return to work. To enhance the likelihood of work attempts, the 9-month trial work period was extended by an additional 15 months to enable a beneficiary to test his or her ability to work while retaining disability status. Payments are not made for those months in which the disabled individual is able to perform "substantial gainful activity," but are automatically reinstated should the work attempt fail. These initiatives were of crucial significance to the rehabilitation process for the mentally disordered.

Perhaps the most important feature of the 1980 amendments, with the greatest impact upon the mentally impaired, was a provision requiring periodic review of all disability beneficiaries' records to redetermine continuing eligibility. Congress sought to ensure the fiscal integrity of the program by requiring that the status of beneficiaries be reviewed at least once every three years unless the beneficiary's disability was considered permanent. (Prior to these amendments, continuing reviews were conducted only in selected cases, for example, where the individual's condition was expected to improve, or where the individual had returned to work.) While Congress had built in an 18-month delay period before such reviews were to be undertaken (in the main, to enable the DDS offices to "gear up"), the new Administration embraced the reviews as a means of budget containment, and accelerated their enforcement, with the result that many obviously severely impaired beneficiaries—predominantly the mentally ill—were removed from the rolls.

In the wake of these activities, a consortium of consumers, providers of health services, law advocates, and a bipartisan cadre of Senators and Representatives sought to redress what was perceived to be unfair behavior on the part of the Social Security Administration. The end result of these activities was adoption in 1984 of the Social Security Disability Reform Act. Among other issues, the amendments mandated certain changes which would directly affect the mentally impaired. They included: (1) a medical improvement standard which required improvement before a beneficiary could be removed from the rolls; (2) consideration of the combined effect of multiple, nonsevere impairments in the disability-determination process; (3) the establishment of a commission to conduct a study of the evaluation of pain in determining disability; (4) the conduct of face-to-face reviews on a trial basis in several states; (5) the use of psychiatrists and psychologists in cases involving psychiatric impairment, particularly where denial is contemplated; and (6) perhaps most important, the imposition of a moratorium on review of mental impairment cases, pending the development and promulgation of revised medical criteria for evaluating psychiatric impairment.

REVISING THE MENTAL IMPAIRMENT MEDICAL CRITERIA: 1984

Immediately following enactment of the 1984 amendments, the Social Security Administration undertook a determined and apparently sincere effort to achieve public and professional involvement in the recodification of the mental impairment Listings. Literally, what had been a closed, internal government system to create and impose standards, became a more open, cooperative system where a world of expertise—psychiatric, psychological, rehabilitative—became part of the regulatory process. Because of the moratorium and congressional mandate, the mental impairment area became the first of the Listings to be tackled.

The use of a work-group approach became a cornerstone for enhancing the cooperation which SSA sought to weld between outside professional and clinical resources and internal program management and staff skills. A 25-member work group developed, over the course of 18 months, a new, revised listing of mental impairments which made sweeping changes in a medical determination process that had not been reviewed or altered for over 10 years.

The evolution of the Listings is an interesting bit of history which parallels the development of psychiatric nosology generally. The SSDI program had always been impairment-oriented, rather than diagnosis-oriented, though there had been an attempt to relate the severity of psychiatric signs and symptoms to the capacity or inability to work. Study and research in the area have not established such a direct relationship. The program had also relied to a greater-than-appropriate extent upon the ability to conduct activities of daily living as a predictor of capacity to perform work—another correlation not supported in the scientific literature. Each of these basic premises was assessed as a significant area for change in the revision of the criteria.

The "old" Listings were divided into four groups, reflecting certain disorder categories (organic brain syndrome, functional psychotic disorders, functional nonpsychotic disorders, and mental retardation). Within each, two sets of criteria—literally A criteria and B criteria—were designated. The A criteria described the signs, symptoms, and findings necessary to establish the existence of a medically determinable impairment. The B criteria set out characteristics designed to assess functional limitations which exist as the result of the impairment found to exist under the A criteria.

The work group undertook to (1) expand the number of categories, so appropriate descriptions could be tailored, thereby enhancing the accuracy and precision of each category; (2) revise the B criteria to better reflect functional limitations which are more clearly work-related; (3) construct a preface to the Listings to provide sufficient explanatory power to ensure greater reliability and consistency in the Listings' use in the field; (4) establish a valid and reliable instrument for assessing the residual functional capacity which better captured the B criteria; and (5) create additional functional criteria (C criteria) for those disorders which had routinely, and incorrectly, fallen through the previous SSDI screens.

In its final report to the SSA, the work group presented a radical departure from the previous Listings. Categories were expanded from the four cited above to eight categories (organic mental disorders; schizophrenic, paranoid, and other psychotic disorders; affective disorders; mental retardation; anxiety-related disorders; somatoform disorders; personality disorders; and substance abuse disorders). (It should be noted that the last category was deleted by the Office of Management and Budget just prior to promulgation of the Listings in the *Federal Register.*)

One of the most common criticisms of the past Listings had been that the B part was rather insensitive to the behaviors and attitudes essential to making a satisfactory adjustment in the work place. While the routine activities of daily living were retained by the work group as one of the B criteria, and social function is addressed as a second, two added criteria were structured to reflect exactly what is required in the work place if a mentally ill person is to make a reasonable adjustment to work. The ability to concentrate and persist at an assigned task was considered to be critically significant in this area, as was the capacity to withstand the mental demands of work without experiencing deterioration or decompensation.

New C criteria were added to two of the new Listings to clarify functional assessment in those categories. Throughout the adjudication process, there seemed to exist a previous insensitivity to the chronic schizophrenic whose signs and symptoms were attenuated by treatment interventions, but who, nevertheless, remained withdrawn, isolated, and subtly bizarre enough to preclude work. A C criterion addressed this specific problem. The other group—agoraphobics who, notwithstanding their inability to leave home, were unable to meet the old standard of markedly decreased activities of daily living, and were thus disallowed from the SSDI rolls—also fell through the cracks under the old Listings. A C criterion dealing with their inability to leave home as the direct result of their mental impairment was constructed, to ensure that such persons were evaluated more appropriately on the basis of their particular disease.

Last, and perhaps as important as any of the previously described alterations, the new Listings of mental impairments bear a strong relationship to current nomenclature. This has added clarity and specificity to the Listings without doing damage to the concept that the Listings remain "impairment driven" and not "diagnosis driven." It was intended to help adjudicators make better sense of medical records' relationship to the mental impairment Listings, by using similar language, rather than requiring "translation" from *Diagnostic and Statistical Manual of Mental Disorders* parlance to SSDI parlance as an integral part of the adjudication process.

CONCLUSION

While much of the process remains the same—the five-step adjudication is still in place, the use of lay and medical personnel still occurs, redress of decisions remains largely the same—there have been significant changes which will affect the conduct of the disability-review process for the mentally impaired. The system of adjudication of the claims of mentally impaired persons has undergone a complete revision,[3] and now has the use of modern, state-of-the-art science tools for the evaluation of level of impairment, severity, and capacity to engage in work activity. The regulations have been changed and DDS professionals have been trained in the use of the new tools. Greater care is being exercised in meeting the special needs and requirements of the mentally ill under the program at each step of the adjudication process—recognizing, perhaps for the first time, the special nature of mental illness and its effect upon program compliance. Internal and external quality-assurance mechanisms are in place to help protect an individual's right to a fair and equitable hearing at all levels of the SSDI determination process. With continued deliberate action, the difficulties which confronted mentally ill beneficiaries and claimants in the past should not again come to pass.

REFERENCES

Ashbaush JW, Manderscheid RW: A method for estimating the chronic mentally ill population in state and local areas. Hosp Community Psychiatry 36:389–393, 1985
Ballantyne HC: Actuarial status of the OASI and DI trust funds. Soc Secur Bull 46(10):3–8, 1983
Ballantyne HC: Actuarial status of the OASI and DI trust funds. Soc Secur Bull 47(5):3–8, 1984
Collins KP, Erfle A: Social Security Disability Benefits Reform Act of 1984: Legislative history and summary of provisions. Soc Secur Bull 48(4):5–32, 1985
Copeland LS: International trends in disability program growth. Soc Secur Bull 44(10):25–36, 1981
Hadler NM: Medical ramifications of the Federal regulation of the SSDI program: Social Security and medicine. Ann Intern Med 96:665–669, 1982
Lando ME, Farley AV, Brown MA: Recent trends in the SSDI program. Soc Secur Bull 45(8):75–79, 1982
Levy JM: Demographic factors in the disability determination process: a logistic approach. Soc Secur Bull 43(3):11–96, 1980

---

[3] The 1984 amendments continued the SSA policy that an individual's subjective complaints of pain alone are not sufficient to establish disability. There also must be medical signs and findings which show the existence of a medical impairment which could reasonably be expected to produce the pain or other symptoms alleged.

Lloyd DW, Tsuana MT: Disability and welfare—who wants it? J Clin Psychiatry 46:273–275, 1985

McManus LA: Evaluation of disability insurance savings due to beneficiary rehabilitation. Soc Secur Bull 44(2):19–26, 1981

Price DN: Workers compensation: Coverage, benefits and costs. Soc Secur Bull 47(12):7–13, 1984

Reno VP, Price DN: Relationship between the retirement, disability and unemployment insurance programs: the U.S. experience. Soc Secur Bull 48(5):24–37, 1985

Social Security Administration: Social Security Disability Amendments of 1980: Legislative history and summary of provisions. Soc Secur Bull 44(4):14–31, 1981

Social Security Administration: Actuarial cost estimates for OASDI and HI and for various possible changes in OASDI. Soc Secur Bull 46(3):14–51, 1983

Social Security Administration: Deficit Reduction Act of 1984: Provisions related to the OASDI and SSI programs. Soc Secur Bull 47(11):3–10, 1984

22

Legal Representation for the Psychiatrically Disabled: Administrative Procedures

Eric J. Fischer, J.D.

Many millions of Americans obtain their financial sustenance through federally funded disability programs, the
most significant of which will be highlighted in this chapter.

The various disability-related Social Security plans, for example,
provide benefits to some 4.5 million impaired individuals plus an
estimated 1.2 million of their dependents (Social Security Administration 1985). Although the agency is now in the midst of its first ever
calculation to determine the number of mentally disabled recipients
within the total, extrapolation from available data on new 1983
recipients would indicate the numbers are considerable. Of the
311,490 additions to the Social Security wage-earner disability rolls
that year, 50,633 were classified as mentally impaired (Social Security Administration 1983).

Similarly, the mentally impaired constitute the most significant
element of Veterans' Administration disability beneficiaries, under
both the service-connected and nonservice-connected programs. As of
March 1985, there were some 328,425 recipients of service-connected
benefits who were primarily impaired psychiatrically. This was the
largest single category among the 2,244,424 veteran beneficiaries
(Veterans' Administration 1985). The picture is the same in the non-

service-connected disability program, where 108,799 out of 704,802 beneficiaries were so characterized (Veterans' Administration 1985). These VA figures do not include dependents of veterans who are themselves in receipt of VA benefits.

In examining the various programs, it is important to keep in mind that these are *not* "unemployment" plans for people unable to find jobs. The initial burden of proof, rather, always rests with the claimant to prove that he or she would be unable to sustain employment (to some stipulated degree) due to impairment(s), even if such jobs were available.

The most immediate, pressing concern for the legal representative is to apply agency regulations, which in all cases require broad construction of the disability laws to effectuate the "beneficent" purpose of Congress, to satisfy the claimant's threshold burdens.

THE SOCIAL SECURITY PROGRAMS

The Social Security Act provides for disability benefits under two major classifications: (1) Title II, varied plans for qualifying former wage earners and their dependents—that is, contributors "insured" through FICA tax withholding (42 U.S.C. sections 401 et seq.); (2) Title XVI, essentially a federal "welfare" scheme providing relief for indigent disabled adults and children with limited resources, regardless of tax contribution—that is, Supplemental Security Income (42 U.S.C. sections 1381 et seq.).

Definition of Disability

The general definition of disability for both Title II and Title XVI programs is specifically applicable to psychiatric impairments by its own language:

> The law defines disability as the inability to do any substantial gainful activity by reason of any medically determinable physical *or mental* impairment which can be expected to result in death or which has lasted or can be expected to last for a continuous period of not less than 12 months. (20 C.F.R. sections 404.1505, 416.905 [emphasis added])

A stricter standard, however, is applied to the widows/widowers/ surviving divorced-wives program, requiring inability to engage in "any gainful activity," rather than "substantial gainful activity." (See, in this regard 20 C.F.R. sections 404.1572(b), 404,1577.) The widows' program, as well as that for child benefits, is further subject to other, more stringent regulatory criteria, to be discussed later in this chapter.

The Review Process

Applicants go through a multitiered review process, during which they may submit any expert or other supportive evidence, and the agency investigates and develops their claims (20 C.F.R. sections 404.1512–404.1518, 416.918). This process can result in a finding of disabled status, and the grant of benefits, at any point in the administrative evaluation (i.e., initial consideration, reconsideration, decision following hearing, and Appeals Council review in Washington, D.C.). The applicant always bears both the initial burden of proof[1] and the obligation to appeal disability denials, within the specified time limits, to the next stage of the review process.

In the event the claimant is ultimately unsuccessful before the administrative agency, further appeal into federal court is permitted (42 U.S.C. sections 405(g), 1383c(3)).

The Five-Step, Sequential Evaluation Process
In determining satisfaction of the section 404.1505/416.905 disability criteria, the agency utilizes a five-step, sequential evaluation process.

With the exception of Step 3, failure to satisfy the requirements of any particular step will necessarily require a finding of no disability at that point, precluding resort to later steps in the sequential evaluation process. This is a "refinement" process, each succeeding step presenting a stricter standard leading to the ultimate ascertainment of those applicants who are indeed "disabled."

The five-step, sequential evaluation process is stated as follows:

1. *"If you are working.* If you are working and the work you are doing is substantial gainful activity, we will find that you are not disabled regardless of your medical condition or your age, education, and work experience" (20 C.F.R. sections 404.1520(b), 416.920(b)).

2. *"You must have a severe impairment.* If you do not have any impairment(s) which significantly limits your physical or mental ability to do basic work activities, we will find that you do not have a severe impairment and are, therefore, not disabled. We will not consider your age, education, and work experience. However, it is possible for you to have a period of disability for a time in the past even though you do not now have a severe impairment" (20 C.F.R. sections 404.1520(c), 416.920(c)).

3. *"When your impairment meets or equals a listed impairment in Appendix 1.* If you have an impairment which meets the duration requirement and is listed in Appendix 1, or we determine that the impairment is equal to one of the listed impairments, we will find you disabled without considering your age, education and work experience" (20 C.F.R. sections 404.1520(d), 416.920(d)).

---

[1] See our subsequent discussion in this chapter.

4. *"Your impairment must prevent you from doing past relevant work.* If we cannot make a decision based on your current work activity or on medical facts alone, and you have a severe impairment, we then review your residual functional capacity and the physical and mental demands of the work you have done in the past. If you can still do this kind of work, we will find that you are not disabled" (20 C.F.R. sections 404.1520(e), 416.920(e)).

5. *"Your impairment must prevent you from doing any other work.*
(1) If you cannot do any work you have done in the past because you have a severe impairment, we will consider your residual functional capacity and your age, education, and past work experience to see if you can do other work. If you cannot, we will find you disabled.

(2) If you have only a marginal education, and long work experience (i.e., 35 years or more) where you only did arduous unskilled physical labor, and you can no longer do this kind of work, we use a different rule (see 404.1562)" (20 C.F.R. sections 404.1520(f), 416.920(f)).

The successful representation of disability applicants demands careful attention to agency and court interpretation and analysis of this five-step, sequential evaluation process.

If you are working
In practice, this is an easy hurdle to surmount: People generally apply for disability only after they have ceased employment activity. However, continued performance of some "gainful activity" will not bar disability entitlement unless such work is "substantial."[2] As a term, substantial gainful activity, although described in the regulations (20 C.F.R. sections 404.1510, 404.1572(a), 416.910, 416.972(a)), is somewhat of a gray area. Analysis of the relevant regulations, which also include 20 C.F.R. sections 404.1574 and 416.974, would indicate that, *for most purposes,* substantial gainful activity involves more than part-time but less than full-time employment.
Of special importance to the mentally impaired, substantial gainful activity requires the ability to perform competitively. Therefore, specially tailored or sheltered-workshop jobs *may* not disqualify the disability applicant (*DeRienzis v. Heckler,* 748 F.2d 352, 353–354 (2d Cir. 1984), citing *Markham v. Califano,* 601 F.2d 533, 534 (10th Cir. 1979); *Cornett v. Califano,* 590 F.2d 91, 94 (4th Cir. 1978); *Caffee v. Schweiker,* 752 F.2d 63, 67–68 (3d Cir. 1985)).

---

[2] Widows/widowers/surviving divorced wives are an exception, as discussed elsewhere in this chapter.

You must have a severe impairment
Congressional expectation seems to have been that disability denial at Step 2 of the sequential evaluation process was to be an infrequent occurrence (*Stone v. Heckler*, 752 F.2d 1099, 1102–1103 (5th Cir. 1985), citing H.R. 3755, 98th Cong., 2d Sess., 130 Cong. Rec. 9821–9839 (1984)). Evidence indicates that only applicants with "slight" abnormalities were intended to be eliminated from consideration at this phase of the determination procedure. In actual practice, the Social Security Administration has interpreted the term "severe" as creating a far more onerous evidentiary burden. Step 2 has thus emerged as a major stage for benefits denials, to the increasingly vocal dissatisfaction of the federal courts (*Stone*, supra, at 1101–1103, 1106 and cases cited therein). In the area of mental impairments, a major problem has been the agency's refusal to attach determinative weight to treating-psychiatrist's reports, which are frequently viewed as insufficiently "objective," without psychological test results, despite court interpretation to the contrary (*Cook v. Heckler*, 739 F.2d 396, 398–399 (8th Cir. 1984); *Van Horn v. Schweiker*, 717 F.2d 871, 874 (3d Cir. 1983)). At least some "objective verification of an applicant's underlying impairments is required by the Social Security Act (*Green v. Schweiker*, 749 F.2d 1066, 1071 (3d Cir. 1984)). The agency does not appear to concede that a mental status examination itself is necessarily a "medically accepted technique" (pursuant to Pub. L. 98–460, section 3(a)(1)) so as to render findings based thereon automatically "objective" under the Social Security Act. Since mere opinion (albeit expert) cannot be controlling, agency refusal to accede to court interpretation of the law can have a devastating impact on the mentally impaired claimant.

Recent developments have placed the Step 2 severity evaluation in legal limbo: It has been invalidated by at least four Courts of Appeals, as creating an onerous burden inconsistent with the authorizing Social Security Act. (See *Hansen v. Heckler*, 783 F.2d 170, 173–176 (10th Cir. 1986) and cases cited therein.)

When your impairment meets or equals a listed impairment
The administrative regulations provide two itemized Listings of Impairments—one for adults (Appendix 1, Part A, following 20 C.F.R. section 404.1599) and, generally more stringent, classifications for children under 18 (Appendix 1, Part B). These itemize various specific diseases and impairments with purportedly characteristic signs and symptoms. Satisfaction of the criteria within any subsection in the appropriate listing leads to an automatic "per se" entitlement to disability (*Heckler v. Campbell*, 461 U.S. 458, 460 (1983)). However, except for child disability and widows' cases,[3] failure to meet or equal

---

[3] Under both these programs, failure to show at least listing "equivalency" will result in benefit disqualification. See respectively, 20 C.F.R. sections 416.923 and 404.1578.

in severity the specified terms of any enunciated listing is not a disqualification from entitlement, merely moving the focus to consideration at the next step of the sequential evaluation process.[4]

The above does not preclude the entitlement of other, somewhat less seriously afflicted claimants, who can nonetheless demonstrate, through written and oral evidence, a realistic inability to perform any competitive, regular employment, pursuant to Steps 4 and 5 of the agency evaluation process. This we will refer to as *non–Listing disability*, which provides the same benefits as for that based upon listed criteria. See *City of New York v. Heckler*, 578 F. Supp 1109 (E.D.N.Y. 1984), discarding a "fixed clandestine [agency] policy against those with mental illness" (Id. at 1115). Said policy illegally presumed "that mentally disabled claimants who do not meet or equal the listings necessarily retain sufficient capacity to do at least 'unskilled work'" (Id). The district court decision has been affirmed (472 F.2d 729 (2d Cir. 1984), affd. on reh. 755 F.2d 31 (1985), affd. *Bowen v. City of New York*, 476 U.S.—(1986)).

The adult mental impairment listings had traditionally been divided into four categories: chronic brain syndromes, psychotic disorders, nonpsychotic disorders (psychophysiologic, neurotic, personality, and substance abuse disorders in adults), and mental retardation. The standard enunciated in those listings, with their reliance upon significant restriction of interests, activities, and social interaction, had been the subject of growing criticism, with charges that they did not conform with appropriate medical/vocational criteria determinative of ability to work (*Mental Health Assn. of Minnesota v. Heckler*, 544 F.Supp. 157, 162 (D. Mn. 1982), affd. with mod. 720 F.2d 965 (8th Cir. 1983)).

As a result of building public pressure, Congress enacted new legislation requiring review and modification of the mental impairment listings (Social Security Reform Act of 1984, Pub.L. 98–460, section 5(a)), resulting in agency promulgation of new, more empathic adult listing regulations. After being formally published (50 Fed. Reg. 4948–4955 (Feb. 4, 1985)), they have superseded the old four-part listing criteria. These regulations incorporate many of the broad indicia outlined by the *Diagnostic and Statistical Manual of Mental Disorders, Third Edition (DSM-III;* American Psychiatric Association 1980). Listed categories include organic mental disorders; schizophrenic, paranoid, and other psychotic disorders; affective disorders; mental retardation; anxiety-related disorders; somatoform disorders; and personality disorders. (See Appendix 1, Part A, section 12.01 et seq.)

---

[4] This is because the Listings are intended only to identify the most severely disabled class of claimants, given a level of documented seriousness that permits an *automatic* presumption of disability.

Significantly, the agency decided against adoption of a substantive substance abuse listing, pending further study, referring such claimants to the listings for associated and secondary conditions (i.e., personality disorders, liver dysfunction, etc.), instead. (See Id., section 12.09.)

The relevant children's listings are restricted, at least for the time being, to three mental impairment categories: chronic brain syndrome; psychosis of infancy and childhood; and functional non-psychotic disorders (Appendix 1, Part B, section 112.01 et. seq.).

Your impairment must prevent you from doing relevant work
"Past relevant work" is substantial gainful activity which a claimant has performed at some time during the last 15 years (20 C.F.R. sections 404.1565 and 416.965).

This has evolved into the most critical section of the five-step, sequential evaluation process since the Courts of Appeals have unanimously found a claimant's satisfaction of this part presents a prima facie case, shifting the burden of proof for the first time to the agency for rebuttal (*Ellis v. Schweiker,* 739 F.2d 245, 248 (6th Cir. 1984); *Parsons v. Heckler,* 739 F.2d 1334, 1339 (8th Cir. 1984); *Caffee v. Schweiker,* 752 F.2d 63, 64 (3d Cir. 1985); *Reeves v. Heckler,* 734 F.2d 519, 525 (11th Cir. 1984)). A claimant satisfies the section when his or her subjective testimony of inability to perform prior relevant work is verified by the expert medical evidence (Id.). Such expert evidence must be more than bare, unsupported conclusions (*Bloodsworth v. Heckler,* 703 F.2d 1233, 1240 (11th Cir. 1983); *Houston v. Secretary of Health and Human Services,* 736 F.2d 365, 367 (6th Cir. 1984)).

The agency does not appear to have adopted the above court rule (*Miller v. Heckler,* 747 F.2d 475, 477 (8th Cir. 1984)). See also (Heaney 1984, 11–12). As discussed previously, this has resulted primarily from the Administration's insistence that "objective" clinical and laboratory test results are needed to afford determinative weight to treating-physician reports, including psychiatric evidence.[5] Such a requirement, in itself, defies court precedent (*Green v. Schweiker,* 749 F.2d 1066, 1070–1071 (ed Cir. 1984); *Cook,* supra, pp. 398–399). It also flies in the face of the agency's own policy rulings which indicate, for example, that claimant responses, made during a psychiatric interview, which reveal a pathological aspect of disease, may qualify as "objective" for disability purposes (Social Security Ruling 83–17 (1980)). Other relevant factors, per the agency rulings, include: an emphasis on treating-physicians' reports over time, in preference to those of any one-time, agency-hired medical consultants; failed job attempts; adverse effects of drug therapy; the "quality" of daily ac-

---

[5] See cases cited, elsewhere in this chapter.

tivities; and lay testimony. [See, generally, Social Security Rulings 83–15, 83–17 (1980) and 85–7, 85–8 (1985).]

In practice, as opposed to theory, however, the agency continues to evince considerable confusion as to how to properly evaluate mental disability (*Smith v. Heckler*, 735 F.2d 312, 316–318 (8th Cir. 1984); *DeLeon v. Secty. of Health and Human Services*, 734 F.2d 930, 937–938 (2d Cir. 1984); *Wallace v. Secty. of Health and Human Services*, 722 F.2d 1150, 1153–1155 (3d Cir. 1983); *Suarez v. Secty. of Health and Human Services*, 740 F.2d 1 (1st Cir. 1984)). As a result, the courts continue to challenge the Secretary's repeated rejections of what is alleged to be inadequate, though uncontested, expert data supporting psychiatric disability (*Wallace*, supra, at pp. 1153–1154; *Suarez*, supra, at pp. 1–2; *McLain v. Schweiker*, 715 F.2d 866, 869 (4th Cir. 1983)).

In the area of substance abuse, unique problems have arisen concerning the proper non–Listing disability[6] standard to apply. A Social Security ruling dictates that a demonstration of chronic alcohol habituation, combined with a documented total lack of control over intake, merely justifies a diagnostic classification as an addict (Social Security Ruling 82–60 (1980)), rather than the inherent disability suggested by logic and judicial precedent (*Ferguson v. Heckler*, 750 F.2d 503, 505 (5th Cir. 1985); *McShea v. Schweiker*, 700 F.2d 117, 119 (3d Cir. 1983)).[7]

There is little doubt that defiance of court interpretation of "what the law is" (*Marbury v. Madison*, 5 U.S. (1 Cranch) 137, 177, 2 L.Ed 60 (1803)) violates common law; constitutional and statutory principles (*Lopez v. Heckler*, 725 F.2d 1489, 1493–1494, 1501 n. 9–10, 1502–1503 (9th Cir.), vac. and rem. on other grounds, 105 S.Ct. 583 (1984)); but, as a whole, the courts have been reticent in holding the agency and its Secretary in contempt.

Your impairment must prevent you from doing any other work
Once a claimant satisfies the prima facie threshold, the claimant should be found eligible for benefits, absent rebuttal medical and/or vocational evidence[8] indicating ability to perform specific regular

---

[6] See discussion at Footnote 4.

[7] It is important to make the distinction between *no* control of alcohol intake and mere impaired control. This seemed to have troubled the Third Circuit in a subsequent case, *Purter v. Heckler*, 771 F.2d 682, 698–99 (3d Cir. 1985). See especially Id., n. 18, conceding that alcoholism "alone" can be disabling. Thereafter, the *Purter* court proceeded to weigh various factors, including his failed detoxification effort, itself directly related to the issue of determining how much control had been lost. The Secretary was found to have violated the *McShea* standard.

[8] Vocational evidence alone may not be sufficient to rebut in the presence of overwhelming medical data to the contrary—*DeLeon v. Secretary of Health and Human Services*, 734 F.2d 930, 934–935 (2d Cir. 1984), citing *Yawitz v. Weinberger*, 498 F.2d 956, 961 (8th Cir. 1974).

competitive employment existing in the economy in substantial numbers.[9]

The Social Security Administration has promulgated vocational "grids" (appearing at Appendix 2—Medical–Vocational Guidelines, following 20 C.F.R. section 404.1598). These charts apply the applicant's age, education, and prior relevant work characteristics to his or her residual functional capacity so as to determine vocational ability (or inability) to perform substantial gainful activity.

The grids, however, can only be controlling in "exertional" impairment cases. Psychiatric disorders are nonexertional in nature. In the latter circumstance, the vocational grids *cannot* rebut a prima facie case. (See *Burgos Lopez v. Secty. of Health and Human Services*, 747 F.2d 37, 41 (1st Cir. 1984); *McClain v. Schweiker*, supra, 715 F.2d at 869 n.1; *Parsons v. Heckler*, 739 F.2d 1334, 1339 (8th Cir. 1984); *Falcon v. Heckler*, 732 F.2d 827, 830 (11th Cir. 1984); *Wallace v. Secty. of Health and Human Services*, 722 F.2d 1150, 1155 (3d Cir. 1983).) Individualized vocational *testimony* or evaluation is therefore required (*Clark v. Heckler*, 733 F.2d 65, 69 (8th Cir. 1984); *Burgos Lopez*, supra, at p. 42; *McClain*, supra, at pp. 869–870).

THE VETERANS' ADMINISTRATION PROGRAMS

Veterans' disability can be most conveniently divided into service-connected (i.e., disability *compensation*) and nonservice-connected (i.e., disability *pension*) programs.

The Service-Connected Scheme: Definition of Disability

The service-connected disability (compensation) scheme is itself divisable into "wartime" and "peacetime" plans. (See, respectively, 38 U.S.C. section 310 and section 331). The basic entitlement under both sections is identical:

> For disability resulting from personal injury suffered or disease contracted in line of duty, or for aggravation of a preexisting injury suffered or disease contracted in line of duty, in the active military, naval, or air service . . . , the United States will pay to any veteran thus disabled and who was discharged or released under condition other than dishonorable from the period of service in which said injury or disease was incurred, or preexisting injury or disease was aggravated, compensation as provided in this subchapter, but no compensation shall be paid if the disability is the result of the veteran's own willful misconduct. (id.)

---

[9] See cases cited herein.

In-service "aggravation" is represented by an increased disability of a pre-existing impairment during service, and unrelated to the natural progression of the disease process (38 U.S.C. S 353).

Unlike the various Social Security programs examined, disability *compensation* will be payable even when functional limitation from the service-connected impairment is not total—in fact, it may be as little as 10 percent. Monthly benefit payment amounts are graded upwards pursuant to a written schedule notating 10-percent disability increments to a 100-percent maximum rating of "total disability" (38 U.S.C. section 314, section 334).

These percentage ratings

> represent as far as can practicably be determined the average impairment in earning capacity resulting from such diseases and injuries and their residual conditions in civil occupations (38 C.F.R. section 4.1)

Thus, unemployability is *not* essential to qualify for service-connected benefits, although a realistic inability to perform substantial gainful employment due to service-connected impairments *may* result in payments at the level of total disability even though the schedule rating itself is less than 100 percent (38 C.F.R. section 4.16).

Service-connection can be demonstrated by affirmative evidence and/or application of presumptions (38 C.F.R. section 3.303(a))—the latter includes a "presumption of sound condition" as to diseases and impairments not diagnosed at induction (38 U.S.C. sections 311, 332), as well as presumption of service-connection related to certain specified diseases and disease types (38 U.S.C. sections 312, 333). A specific "wartime" presumption relates to psychiatric disability, to wit:

> Psychosis which became manifest to a degree of 10 percentum or more within two years from the date of separation from such service; shall be considered to have been incurred in or aggravated by such service, notwithstanding that there is no record of such disease during the period of service (38 U.S.C. section 312(c)(2)).

Note all presumptions are rebuttable (38 U.S.C. section 313; 38 C.F.R. section 3.304(b), (c)) but not by "medical *judgment* alone as distinguished from accepted medical *principles* . . ." (38 C.F.R. section 3.304(b)(1)) (emphasis added). Nor can written statements against interest, signed by the veteran in service and "conceding" impairment pre-existence, be controlling in their own right (10 U.S.C. section 1219; 38 C.F.R. section 3.304(b)(3)).

Further, the diagnosis of a disease process in service as chronic is sufficient to establish even a remote, postservice reemergence of such chronic disease as service-connected, despite lack of continuity, absent a clear-cut, intervening cause (38 C.F.R. section 3.303(b)).

The Nonservice-Connected Scheme: Definition of Disability
Nonservice-connected disability *pension*, on the other hand, is similar to SSI in that only total disability is remunerated (38 U.S.C. section 502) and restrictive resource/income maximums apply (38 U.S.C. sections 503, 522). However, the VA pension standard is further modified for the two veteran classes covered—the elderly and veterans who served during a period of war. Pursuant to 38 U.S.C. section 502(a)

> a person shall be considered to be *permanently* and totally disabled if such person is sixty-five years of age or older or became unemployable after age 65, or suffering from—
> (1) any disability which is sufficient to render it impossible for the average person to follow a substantially gainful occupation, but only if it is reasonably certain that such disability *will continue throughout the life* of the disabled person; or
> (2) any disease or disorder determined by the Administrator to be of such a nature or extent as to justify a determination that persons suffering therefrom are *permanently* and totally disabled (Id.) [emphasis added]

Section 521(a) states that

> The Administrator shall pay to each veteran of a period of war who meets the service requirements of this section (as prescribed in subsection (j) of this section) and who is *permanently* and totally disabled from nonservice-connected disability not the result of the veteran's willful conduct, pension at the rate prescribed by this section, as increased from time to time under section 3112 of this title (Id.) [emphasis added]

The Service and Nonservice-Connected Schemes:
The Review Process
Administratively, both service and nonservice-connected cases normally begin with the veteran making a formal claim for benefits at a Veterans' Administration regional office. As in parallel Social Security programs, the claimant and agency are expected to work jointly to develop the expert record (38 C.F.R. section 3.104(a), (b)). The veteran can *request* a hearing to present the testimony of witnesses (38 C.F.R. section 3.103(c)) and is entitled to representation, "of his choice . . . " (38 C.F.R. section 31103(d)). Note, however, that highly restrictive federal legislation, limiting private attorneys' fees before the VA to 10 dollars per legal count, substantially inhibits the latter course (38 U.S.C. section 3404(c)). The legitimacy of this law was recently upheld by the United States Supreme Court in *Walters v. National Association of Radiation Survivors,—U.S.–, 105* S.Ct. 3180, 87 L.Ed.2d 220 (1985).

Should this first stage of the review process result in benefit denial, appeal to the Board of Veterans' Appeals in Washington, D.C., can be effectuated by filing a written *notice of disagreement* thereto (38 U.S.C. section 4005; 38 C.F.R. sections 3.103(e) 19.117, 19.118), followed by issuance of a *statement of the case* by the authority entering the original denial decision (38 C.F.R. section 19.119). Thereafter a new hearing can be requested in front of the board (38 C.F.R. section 19.157), and additional evidence can be developed by the board and/or appellant (38 U.S.C. section 4009; 38 C.F.R. sections 19.174, 19.176, 19.177).

Final decision by the board on the merits of the claim is *not* appealable into federal court (38 U.C.C. section 211(a)), although reconsideration to the board may be requested (38 C.F.R. sections 19.185 et seq.). Although the bar to court review of the merits has been upheld as constitutional, the agency is *not* immune from in-court challenges to the constitutionality of legislation governing provision of such VA disability benefits (*Johnson v. Robison* 415 U.S. 361, 367, 94 S.Ct. 1160, 1165, 39 L.Ed. 2d 389, 389 (1974)). Additionally, in cases where VA benefit denial is premised on questionable conclusions of evidence in the underlying service (Army, Navy, or Air Force) records, correction may be sought through the appropriate military agency. If correction is granted, a revised service record (without the offending material) can then be presented anew to the VA for benefit evaluation. Note, importantly, that correction denials, unlike those for VA benefits themselves, *are* appealable into federal court. [See *Mozur v. Orr*, 600 F. Supp. 772 (E.D. Pa. 1985)]

Despite the inadequacy of agency statistics and the virtually total blackout of court review, the limited facts that have come to light indicate that the VA disability process is seriously skewed against the disability claimant as a result of (1) the complexity of procedural and substantive regulatory requirements; (2) the general inadequacy of available nonattorney representation; (3) a regular failure to develop the record properly through presentation of witness testimony and authorization of medical consultations; (4) failure to subpoena supportive documentation; and (5) discouraging claimants from seeking a hearing at the initial determination stage; (6) all of which contributes to establishing an "adversarial" environment, despite the contrary regulatory directive (*National Ass'n of Radiation Survivors v. Walters*, 589 F.Supp. 1302, 1319–1323 (N.D. Ca 1984)).

CONCLUSION: DEVELOPING A CASE

It is easy to decry an administrative agency that remains impassive in the face of judicial challenge and public outcry. But even in the best of economic times, elephantine bureaucracies are not known for their sensitivity and receptivity to change.

Under these circumstances, what should the legal representative do to best preserve a client's interests? One thing is for certain: It is rarely in the client's individual interest to "slug it out" for years in federal court, in an effort to chart the borderline between evidentiary adequacy and inadequacy. All the while, benefits will generally not be paid. In the short run, the legal representative is most often forced to play by the agency interpretation of the "rules," which may invoke standards far in excess of those prescribed by court or logic.

There are obviously exceptions to the above maxim. Where indigent claimants are involved, for example, harsh administrative interpretations may prove inordinately burdensome, or even impossible, to satisfy: The poor have less access to medical expertise and lack the financial wherewithal to readily compensate for this deficiency during case preparation. These resource inadequacies, paired with unreasonable agency standards, may make an ultimate court battle inevitable.

In the typical case, psychiatric evidence must be expeditiously tendered at the earliest possible stage of the administrative review process to verify a mental disability. A treating psychiatrist can expedite the adjudicative process by submitting a thorough medical history, all treatment notes and test results, along with a detailed explanatory report. This will almost always obviate the need for a personal appearance by the treating psychiatrist. Psychological tests should be tendered to lend "objective" support to the psychiatric diagnosis. If such tests are not available, practicable, or appropriate, and diagnosis is based upon a standard mental status evaluation, the significance of this evaluation should be explained (i.e., that it constitutes a "medically accepted technique" for diagnosing psychiatric impairments). If the claimant is in *remission*, the term should be explained, to indicate what factors contribute to the maintenance of such status (e.g., therapy, partial hospitalization, minimal stress, halfway house, etc.) and what would induce decompensation to an active state. The physician should always reach a bottom line, if possible—whether the claimant could *reasonably* be expected to withstand the pressures and strains of *competitive* gainful employment on a sustained basis.

The lawyer for his or her part, must: (1) Examine the agency evidentiary file at the earliest possible opportunity. (2) Object, in writing or at the hearing, to admission or to weight (whichever appropriate) of potentially adverse expert evidence that is inadequately qualified (no professional qualifications; not based upon expert examination; prepared by a resident; one-time examiner lacked evidence from treating physicians and hospitals, etc.). (3) Familiarize his- or herself with the *DSM-III-R* and the more detailed aspects of the medical criteria involved, through medical library research; these photocopied materials may be submitted into evidence at a hearing. (4) Submit any relevant listing of impairments to the treating psychiatrist for comparison with claimant's specific impairment—does the impairment meet *or equal* a regulatory listing? (5)

Submit all other medical evidence of record to the treating psychiatrist for evaluation and report. (6) Obtain all medical and hospitalization reports. Make sure social worker and other therapist evaluations are co-signed by supervising psychiatrist. (7) Request that evidence from recalcitrant experts be subpoenaed. (8) Get, or request, psychiatric/psychological consultations where appropriate. (9) With client's permission, interview friends, relatives, former employers, etc. with the intent of getting potential corroborative witnesses for hearing. Notarized affidavits can also be submitted. (10) Examine the case law, so as to cite appropriate controlling cases at administrative hearing. (11) Examine the statute, regulations, rulings, etc., and apply them at the hearing in a manner consistent with the case law and due-process rights. (12) At the hearing, testimentary evidence should be fully developed and detailed, replete with lengthy specific explanation and examples that dramatize the impairments, symptoms, social limitations, restricted level of activities and interests from onset, relative to preimpairment days. (13) Restrict the testimony of nonexamining medical *advisors* to their assigned narrow regulatory role of explaining technical terms and the like—they do not fulfill the role of medical *consultants*. (14) Object to vocational testimony based on hypothetical questions that fail to accurately reflect the complete residual functional setting as supported by the record. Frame hypotheticals for the vocational expert to consider. (15) Be creative.

BIBLIOGRAPHY
THE SOCIAL SECURITY PROGRAMS
Cases
Bloodsworth v. Heckler, 703 F.2d 1233 (11th Cir. 1983)
Burgos Lopez v. Secty. of Health and Human Services, 747 F.2d 37 (1st Cir. 1984)
Caffee v. Schweiker, 752 F.2d 63 (3d Cir. 1985)
City of New York v. Heckler, 678 F.Supp. 1109 (E.D.N.Y., affd. 742 F.2d 729 (2d Cir, 1984), affd. on reh, 755 F.2d 31 (1985), affd. Bowen v. City of New York, 476 U.S. _____ (1986)
Clark v. Heckler, 733 F.2d 65 (8th Cir. 1984)
Cook v. Heckler, 739 F.2d 396 (8th Cir. 1984)
Cornett v. Califano, 590 F.2d 91 (4th Cir. 1978)
DeLeon v. Secty. of Health and Human Services, 734 F.2d 930 (2d Cir. 1984)
De Rienzies v. Heckler, 748 F.2d 352(2d Cir. 1984)
Ellis v. Schweiker, 739 F.2d 245 (6th Cir. 1984)
Falcon v. Heckler, 732 F.2d 827 (11th Cir. 1984)
Ferguson v. Heckler, 750 F.2d 503 (5th Cir. 1985)
Green v. Schweiker, 749 F.2d 1066 (3d Cir. 1984)
Hansen v. Heckler, 783 F.2d 170 (10th Cir. 1986)
Heckler v. Campbell, 461 U.S. 458 (1983)
Houston v. Secty. of Health and Human Services, 736 F.2d 365 (6th Cir. 1984)
Lopez v. Heckler, 725 F.2d 1489 (9th Cir.), vac. and rem. on other grounds, 105 S. Ct, 583 (1984)
Marbury v. Madison, 5 U.S. (1 Cranch) 137, 2 L. Ed. 60 (1803)
Markham v. Califano, 601 F.2d 533 (10th Cir. 1979)
McLain v. Schweiker, 715 F.2d 866 (4th Cir. 1983)
McShea v. Schweiker, 700 F.2d 117 (3d Cir. 1983)

Mental Health Association of Minnesota v. Heckler, 554 F. Supp. 157 (D. Mn. 1982), aff'd.
with mod. 720 F.2d 965 (8th Cir. 1983)
Miller v. Heckler, 747 F.2d 475 (8th Cir. 1984)
Parsons v. Heckler, 739 F.2d 1334 (8th Cir. 1984)
Purter v. Heckler, 771 F.2d 682 (3d Cir. 1985)
Reeves v. Heckler, 734 F.2d 519 (11th Cir. 1984)
Smith v. Heckler, 735 F.2d 312 (8th Cir. 1984)
Stone v. Heckler, 752 F.2d 1099 (5th Cir. 1985)
Suarez v. Secty. of Health and Human Services, 740 F.2d 1 (1st Cir. 1984)
Van Horn v. Schweiker, 717 F.2d 1099 (5th Cir. 1985)
Wallace v. Secty. of Health and Human Services, 722 F.2d 1150 (3d Cir. 1983)
Yawitz v. Weinberger, 498 F.2d 956 (8th Cir. 1974)

Statutes
42 U.S.C. sections 401 et seq.
42 U.S.C. section 405(g)
42 U.S.C. sections 1381 et seq.
42 U.S.C. section 1383(c)(3)
PL 98–460, Social Security Reform Act of 1984

Regulations
Appendix I, Part A, Listing of Impairments, sections 12.01–12.09, following 20 C.F.R.
section 404.1599
Appendix I, Part B, Listing of Impairments, section 112.01–112.04, following 20 C.F.R.
section 404.1599
Appendix 2, Medical-Vocational Guidelines, following 20 C.F.R. section 404.1598; 20
C.F.R. sections 404.1505, 404.1510, 404.1512, 404.1518, 404.1520(b)–(f), 404.1562,
404.1565, 404.1572, 404.1574, 404.1577, 404.1578, 416.905, 416.910,
416.912–416.918, 416.920(b)–(f), 416.923, 416.965, 416.972, 416.974, 416.977,
416.978

Proposed Regulation
50 Fed. Reg. 4948–4955

Administrative Policy Rulings
Social Security Ruling 83–15
Social Security Ruling 83–17
Social Security Ruling 83–7
Social Security Ruling 83–8

Text
American Psychiatric Association: Diagnostic and Statistical Manual of Mental Disorders, third edition. Washington, DC, American Psychiatric Association, 1980

Article
Heaney: Why the high rate of reversals in Social Security Disability cases? 7 Hamline
Law Rev. 1 (Jan. 1984)

Statistics
Disability Compensation Data, RCS 20–0223 (Veterans Administration, Office of Infor-
mation Management and Statistics, March 1985)
Disability Pension Data, RCS 20–0225 (Veterans Administration, Office of Information
Management and Statistics, March 1985)
Monthly Benefits Statistics; Summary Program Data, Office of Policy, Social Security
Administration, Dept. of Health and Human Services (Jan. 1985), No. 1
Social Security Administration Continuous Disability History Sample of New DI
Allowances, Dept. of Health and Human Services (1983)

Miscellaneous
H.R. 3755, 98th Cong., 2d Sess., 130 Cong. Rec 9821–9839 (1984)

VETERANS' ADMINISTRATION PROGRAMS
Cases
Johnson v. Robison, 415 U.S. 361. 94 S. Ct. 1160, 39 L. Ed. 2d 389 (1974)
Mozur v. Orr, 600 F. Supp. 772 (E.D. Pa. 1985)
National Assn. of Radiation Survivors v. Walters, 589 F. Supp. 1302 (N.D.Ca. 1984)
Walters v. National Assn. of Radiation Survivors. —U.S—, 105 S. Ct. 3180, 87 L. Ed. 2d
(1985)

Statutes
10 U.S.C. section 1219
30 U.S.C. sections 2211, 310–314, 331–334, 353, 502, 503, 521, 522, 3404(c), 4005, 4009

Regulations
38 C.F.R. sections 3.103, 3.303–304, 4.1, 4.16, 19.117–19.119, 19.157, 19.174, 19.176,
19.177, 19.185 et seq.

23

The Courts and Psychiatric Disability

Leonard S. Rubenstein, J.D.
Jane Bloom Yohalem, J.D.

sychiatric disability is no longer a stranger to the courts. In the past two decades, the dramatic increase in litigation involving psychiatric disability has led to the creation of new journals exclusively devoted to legal issues in psychiatry. Notwithstanding this, the courts have barely touched upon what may be the most important issue in public-sector psychiatry today: the financing and development of a coordinated system of community services and housing to meet the needs of the chronically mentally ill.

Instead, the discussion of legal issues surrounding psychiatric disability has been moored in a continuing debate about society's responsibilities regarding compulsory treatment. Although an important issue, it cannot compare to the decisions (often made with little or no public debate) about what services—voluntary or not—society will provide to the psychiatrically disabled. A brief look at the phenomenon of homeless patients with simply no place to go for housing, social support, and treatment illustrates the critical need to develop legal and other necessary strategies to foster appropriate services.

Using the law effectively to help develop an adequate system of community care is no easy task. The courts are often unfamiliar with the complex of legal issues concerning community care, issues often plagued by substantial ambiguity and outright confusion about the extent and definition of legal rights. Moreover, a new conservatism about the role of the courts in such matters undeniably undercuts their ability to influence the issues at all (*Pennhurst State School v. Halderman* 1984; *Atascadero State Hospital v. Scanlon* 1985). Even after a decision is made and a legal right established, courts remain reluctant to involve themselves in the implementation of their decisions, a process that is tedious at best and fraught with political, administrative, and legal pitfalls. Limits on the judiciary's ability to resolve the nearly inevitable funding crises during the implementation process surely contribute to their reluctance to play an active role.

It would be a mistake, then, to deny that the legal system is limited in its ability to effect the systematic changes necessary to establish needed services for the psychiatrically disabled. However, it would be an equally great mistake to discount the law's and the courts' capacity to help resolve the current crisis in community psychiatric care. More than innovative judges and lawyers will be necessary to use the law and the courts effectively. A new alliance must be forged among lawyers, patients, and health professionals. This chapter discusses three areas in which progress may be made through the courts, despite substantial obstacles: provision of community-based services; equal access to employment, education, and government services; and enforcement of government-funding programs.

JUDICIAL INTERVENTION AS A CATALYST IN THE DEVELOPMENT OF A COMMUNITY-CARE SYSTEM

Any discussion of psychiatric disability and the courts must begin with the unprecedented wave of suits against mental institutions in the 1970s. Federal courts became a new and, briefly, dominant player in the struggle for better conditions in psychiatric and mental retardation institutions, predominantly state hospitals. Landmark lawsuits, like Wyatt v. Stickney (1974), *New York Association for Retarded Children v. Rockefeller (Willowbrook)* (1973), and *Pennhurst State School and Hospital v. Halderman* (1984), brought enormous change to these institutions. Whether viewed as a white knight or as an intruder, the federal court became a force in the history of the institutions (Rothman and Rothman 1984). The legacy of these cases has been a body of law regarding institutional treatment, which itself has spawned countless individual suits and numerous class actions.

This body of law, though, has not traveled well into the community, since the institutional cases, for the most part, were premised on a constitutional right to treatment. The legal theory was straightforward: When the state deprives a person of liberty for the purpose of treatment, it has an obligation to provide that treatment (Wyatt 1974). Other theories relating to constitutional rights, such as the right to protection from harm, are equally tied to the fact of institutionalization and the loss of liberty it entails (Youngberg v. Romeo 1982). Once the institution is left behind and the individual is in the community, the issues are not as neatly framed. Community-based psychiatrically disabled individuals are no longer either deprived of liberty or subjected to harm by custodians who control all aspects of their lives.

To the courts, the absence or inadequacy of community psychiatric treatment programs appears more as a deficiency in the welfare state than as a problem resulting from a denial of legal rights. More bluntly, they look like problems of poverty, not liberty. The Supreme Court has firmly rejected the proposition that the Constitution or federal law require government to intercede to alleviate poverty or otherwise to meet minimal human needs, such as providing a minimum level of welfare benefits (*Jefferson v. Hackney* 1972) or education (*San Antonio Independent School District v. Rodriquez* 1973). Therefore, it is not surprising that federal courts have been far less involved in issues surrounding community care than those regarding institutions. Only two federal cases, *Dixon v. Weinberger* (1975) and *Brewster v. Dukakis* (1978), were brought with the intent of developing a comprehensive system of community care for the psychiatrically disabled. Optimists predicted a wave of similar cases but, to date, none has developed.

Advocates' efforts to circumvent this body of constitutional law have focused principally on establishing a least-restrictive alternative to institutional care. Its premise is that if compulsory treatment is to be carried out, due process requires that it infringe as little as possible upon a person's liberty. While somewhat successful in civil commitment litigation (*Lessard v. Schmidt* 1972), it has proved more difficult to utilize the concept of least-restrictive alternative to build a community-care system than to prevent hospitalization in an individual case. After early victories in *Dixon* and *Brewster* (each of which established extensive standards for a community-care system relying upon the least-restrictive alternative theory), this approach has fared far less well than advocates hoped (*Society for Goodwill to Retarded Children v. Cuomo* 1984). One recent decision, summarizing the state of the law, flatly and probably correctly stated, "There is no constitutional right to community mental health treatment or mental health treatment in the least restrictive environment" (*MHA v. Deukmejian* 1985). Further, as greater numbers of people are treated outside institutions or hospitalized for only short periods, the underpinnings of the theory collapse: If little or no treatment is provided in any setting, the problem can no longer be framed as one of institution versus community—more-restrictive versus less-restrictive setting. The problem becomes the lack of services in any setting.

A second theory, related to the theory of least-restrictive alternative, is the right to freedom of unreasonable restraint under the due process clause of the 14th Amendment, a right articulated by the Supreme Court in *Youngberg v. Romeo* (1982). Some lower courts have held that when professionals concur that a community placement is appropriate, freedom from undue restraint entitles an institutionalized mentally disabled person to that community placement (Scott v. Plante 1982; *Thomas S. by Brooks v. Morrow* 1984; *Clark v. Cohen* 1985). The theory holds some promise: Two courts have held that where professional judgment so directs, the right must be fulfilled notwithstanding the absence of funds allocated for that purpose (*Thomas S. by Brooks v. Morrow* 1984; *Clark v. Cohen* 1985). This line of cases, while helpful, has limited applicability to the issue of mandated community services. In particular, it suffers from the same difficulty as the concept of least-restrictive alternative because it, too, is premised on restraint. It may force the creation of a community placement for a person inappropriately institutionalized, but, for the person who is abandoned within the community, there is no restraint and, hence, no violation.

This review paints a dismal picture of the value of litigation as a tool for the development and enhancement of community services, but it is an incomplete picture. Although prospects for constitutional claims may be dim, state laws offer reason to hope. When legal advocacy for the psychiatrically disabled began in the 1970s, advocates, in the main, looked to the federal Constitution and federal courts. State laws offered little help. Indeed, restrictive state laws themselves were often the subject of constitutional challenge. State courts were considered backwaters, hostile to civil rights plaintiffs and tied too closely to state and local government to provide a hospitable environment for these cases.

Since that time, however, fundamental changes have occurred. State mental health statutes have been thoroughly overhauled. Many states have enacted detailed requirements for community mental health care and have assigned responsibility for compliance to specific agencies. In some states, the provisions are mandatory. While the compulsory-treatment aspects of those statutes have been subject to detailed analysis, other aspects of such statutory reform, such as the requirements for community care, largely have been ignored.

At the same time, state courts have become both more sophisticated and willing to become involved in questions affecting the disabled. For example, the majority of the litigation challenging the use of zoning ordinances to exclude group homes for the mentally retarded has taken place in state courts. Indeed, the results have been largely favorable on such issues as whether a district zoned for single families may include group homes or whether state public policies encouraging deinstitutionalization preempt exclusionary zoning ordinances (Kanter 1984).

As a result, state courts now may be hospitable to suits challenging the failure to implement mandatory community programs. Such suits would ask state courts to hold that state law requiring specific services be considered a government obligation which cannot be short-circuited, even absent allocated funds for those services (*ARC v. Dept. of Developmental Services 1975*). In a recent case, *Arnold v. Sarn* (1985), a state court did just that. Relying on state statutes, an Arizona state court ordered that a comprehensive, community-based system of care for the chronically mentally ill be developed. This was the first state court to so rule.

The plaintiffs alleged that state and local agencies responsible for providing services to chronically mentally ill Phoenix residents failed utterly to fulfill their responsibilities. The court's decision is a primer on the deficiencies in community mental health care and the need for a comprehensive system of community-based care. The court found that medical treatment of residual phases of chronic mental illness requires services, including case management, residential services, day treatment, outreach, medication, counseling, crisis stabilization, mobile crises services, socialization, work adjustment, and transportation. It found that "deinstitutionalized individuals have high rehospitalization rates because the residual impairments of their illness interfere with successful adjustment to community life unless provided with adequate community mental health services."

The court assessed the precise service needs for Maricopa County, which encompasses the city of Phoenix. It then analyzed the particular deficiencies in that city's community mental health system, assessing the responsibilities of each level of government and of all components of the system, including the state psychiatric hospital. Finding that the deficiencies thus identified violated the Arizona state statutory requirements to provide a full continuum of care, the court ordered that the relevant agencies provide appropriate services. For example, the Arizona State Hospital has been required to ensure that housing arrangements and community health services are specified in each patient's discharge plan and that each patient actually receives those services upon discharge.

The initial dramatic success of this case inevitably raises questions about implementation. If advocates have learned anything from litigation against institutions, it is that the final court order neither ends the litigation nor solves the problem. Rather, it opens a new phase in which the lawsuit becomes an added player in the political effort to obtain the services mandated by the decision rendered in the lawsuit. Advocates who rely upon a court decree as if it transcended politics may lose not only the political battle, but elements of the court decree itself (Rothman and Rothman). Case history is again instructive. In *Brewster v. Dukakis*, the Massachusetts state legislature refused to appropriate sufficient funds to carry out the court decree, and the court of appeals did not compel the legislature to do so (*Brewster v. Dukakis* 1982). Instead of leading to collapse, however, the decree became the subject of political negotiation, resulting in the development of a successful community mental health program. The other case, *Dixon v. Weinberger* (1975), brought in the District of Columbia, has been a disappointment. Even after contempt proceedings, implementation by a local government disinterested in the issue has been sluggish. Nonetheless, the decree had political importance, particularly in the context of legislation transferring St. Elizabeths Hospital, the local public psychiatric facility, from the purview of the federal government to that of the District of Columbia. The legislation accomplishing this transfer specifically incorporated the *Dixon* decree, which may lead to its implementation in ways ultimately unforeseen by its drafters.

Other recent cases suggest a similarly complex interplay among judicial decisions, legislation, and executive action. Advocates cannot expect that by obtaining a court order they can ensure an adequately funded system of community-based care (*MHA v. Deukmejian* 1985). Indeed, it is likely that funding will be the singular element over which the courts can exercise only indirect, if any, authority. When dollars are not appropriated by the legislature to finance community programs to which state legislation creates a right, state courts are not likely to require the defendants to do more than actively seek funding from that legislature (*ARC v. Department of Social Services* 1975). But litigation can still act as a political catalyst to that funding, as it did in *Brewster* in Massachusetts, and as appears to be the case in New York with respect to the development of community residences for the chronically mentally ill (*Klostermann v. Cuomo* 1984).

These cases have a common thread: They each became part of the political process, which ultimately determined social policy. The sharp schism most people see between litigation and legislation, in fact, is bridged. The lesson to be learned from the litigation, then, is not whether the defendants find the resources and develop the system as a result of the court order. Rather, the lesson is that systemic litigation about community mental health should be viewed as part of the larger political process into which a new and powerful player— the courts—has entered.

Some critics of this so-called law-reform or system-change litigation have long contended, and with some justification, that one result of that litigation is to force states to allocate resources to the subject of the litigation, be it a prison, a state hospital, or a toxic-waste dump, which otherwise might have been spent elsewhere (Mills 1985). Rather than bemoan that fact, as interference with "normal" channels of political influence, advocates for community services should take advantage of the opportunity presented by these state laws to shift resources to the psychiatrically disabled. Psychiatrically disabled people are among the last to be provided resources by society. Using litigation to force these resources to be allocated to community programs to their benefit hardly seems to require further justification.

Those who claim the role of advocate for the mentally ill, then, must utilize this valuable and important tool, not be frightened by it. To be sure, courts often act within very constricted limits: In many states, mental health codes do not create concrete obligations; in others, the courts still defer to the other branches of state government; in yet others, procedural barriers prevent effective litigation. Nevertheless, courts still have the potential to become significant players in the effort to develop community care systems which provide decent conditions for psychiatrically disabled people in the community. It remains for patients, health professionals, and advocates to fulfill that potential.

JUDICIAL INTERVENTION TO ENSURE EQUAL ACCESS TO EMPLOYMENT, EDUCATION, AND GOVERNMENT SERVICES

An array of services for the psychiatrically disabled in the community is only the first requirement for full integration into the community. Psychiatrically disabled persons also need access to the building blocks of a normal life: jobs, housing, education, and medical care. For many other disadvantaged minorities in this society, the courts have played an active role in opening the doors to employment, education, and housing, through prohibitions against discriminations. For the psychiatrically disabled, however, the constitutional and statutory protections against discriminations have not yet developed sufficiently to address fully the needs of these individuals.

The antidiscrimination requirement of the equal-protection clause of the 14th Amendment to the Constitution has been a potent sword for disadvantaged groups. From *Brown v. Board of Education* (1954), racial minorities, then women, aliens, illegitimate children, and others have successfully relied upon the expansive concepts of equality embedded in that amendment. The courts have interpreted the equal-protection clause to require that, if discrimination is shown to exist against the victimized group, it must be justified (in the case of racial minorities) by a "compelling state interest" or (in the case of women, aliens, or illegitimates) by reasons "substantially related" to an "important government interest" (*McLaughlin v. Florida* (1964); *Mississippi University for Women v. Hogan* (1982); *Mills v. Habluetzel* (1982)).

Mentally disabled people sought this second level of protection as well. In a zoning case, the U.S. Court of Appeals for the Ninth Circuit held that because former mental patients are subject to "archaic and stereotypic notions" and to pervasive prejudice, local legislation concerning them should be subjected to detailed scrutiny of its legitimacy by the courts. The court applied the "intermediate" standard of review under the equal-protection clause (*J.W. v. City of Tacoma* 1984). However, in a more recent zoning case concerning mentally retarded people, the Supreme Court rejected that view. It held that discrimination against mentally retarded people will be sustained if it serves some "rational" government interest. The Court thus accorded the same deference to the wisdom of the local legislative body it applies when nothing more than discrimination in economic regulation is at issue (*City of Cleburne v. Cleburne Living Center, Inc.* 1985). The Court wrote: "(h)eightened scrutiny inevitably involves substantive judgments about legislative decisions, and we doubt that the predicate for such judicial oversight is present when the classification deals with mental retardation." In other words, courts will defer to the legislature, without bothering to examine closely the legislature's justification for its actions. As long as the reasons given appear "rational," that will satisfy the court. While *Cleburne* only concerns the mentally retarded, the Court left very little doubt that the ruling applies to the mentally ill and other disabled people as well. By refusing to recognize that mentally disabled people have been subject to a long history of mistreatment and prejudice, it renders permissible continued expressions of such prejudice.

To be sure, in *Cleburne* the Supreme Court did put some new teeth into the "rational basis" test. It found that governmental concerns, such as the negative attitude of nearby property owners and the fears of elderly residents in the neighborhood toward the home's establishment, were irrational: "government cannot give effect to private biases." Still, the fact that the psychiatrically disabled will have to rely on such a low level of court review means that a government's failure to provide needed services—failing to provide for the psychiatrically disabled when considering low-income housing or discriminating in the provision of medical care (e.g., the Medicare $250-per-year limitation on outpatient psychiatric care)—will remain constitutionally immune from challenge.

Section 504 of the Rehabilitation Act of 1973 has greater potential. It prohibits discriminatory actions taken by federal agencies or by programs or activities which receive federal funding. So far, however, it has not been interpreted in a manner particularly helpful to the mentally disabled.

Disabled people, unlike other victims of discrimination, often require more than equal treatment; some accommodation must be made to their disability. Hence, the Supreme Court has endorsed interpretive regulations which require "reasonable accommodation" of disabled people as part of the nondiscrimination obligation (*Consolidated Rail Corporation v. Darrone* 1985; *Alexander v. Choate* 1985). Still, this obligation is ambiguous. The line between "reasonable accommodation," required under the law, and "substantial accommodation or fundamental alteration in the nature of the program," which are not required, is blurry (*Southeastern Community College v. Davis* 1979). Although courts have nominally recognized that avoiding discrimination against the handicapped sometimes may require modification of the services offered, in fact, only the most insubstantial adjustments have been required of programs or employers.

This may be due to Congress's own failure to face the nature of required accommodations when crafting the law. Whatever the reason, the judicial track record where mental illness has been involved is particularly poor. Courts routinely allow employers and educational programs to take into account the risk of possible disruption or even the risk of distress to fellow employees occasioned by the possibility, however remote, that an individual with a psychiatric history may behave "bizarrely" while on the job (*Thomas v. General Services Administration* 1985).

The U.S. Court of Appeals for the Second Circuit has held that if there is an appreciable risk of harm from a possible return of the applicant's symptoms, nothing in Section 504 requires a university to "alter, dilute or bend" its standards to admit a handicapped applicant. Moreover, the court held this risk of harm can be weighed in deciding between the handicapped applicant and other qualified applicants for a limited number of places, even if the applicant meets minimum qualifications (*Doe v. New York University* 1981).

Doe, involving as it did an individual with a long history of a severe psychiatric condition who was applying to medical school, may not be perfectly representative of the courts' response in other situations where the perceived risk to society in making an error in admission is lower. Still, the successful cases have been few. Virtually the only successful claims of discrimination in employment brought by the mentally ill so far have been cases where a job was lost or admission to a program denied because of a history of mental illness without evidence of any continuing symptoms or difficulties. The successful cases involve relatively long-standing recoveries. The jobs sought often pose little likelihood of danger to others even if the illness were to recur, such as *Doe v. Syracuse School District* (1981), which held that refusal to hire a teacher's assistant because of a history of mental illness violates section 504, and *Davis v. Bucher* (1978), deciding that denial of employment to a former drug user solely on the basis of prior drug use violates section 504. The only appellate decision, which concerned former patients as to whom no current disability was alleged by the employer at all, while recognizing that the Rehabilitation Act views discrimination against the handicapped as "an evil on a par with racial, sexual and ethnic discrimination," nevertheless permits lower courts to take into account the "rapid change" in a recovered patient's condition [*Allen v. Heckler* (1985)].

The only notable exceptions to this trend are a series of cases involving alcoholics employed by the federal government. In several of these cases, courts have mandated extensive efforts at treatment, liberal leave policies, and liberal discounting of performance deficiencies and breaches of discipline attributable to alcoholism (*Whitlock v. Donovan* 1985; *Walker v. Weinberger* 1984). Similar employer "understanding" of chronic mental illness would go a long way toward helping psychiatric patients retain jobs. Unfortunately, although the cases cited here offer a glimmer of hope, they are of somewhat limited legal impact because they rely on a special federal alcoholism abuse prevention and treatment statute, not solely on section 504 of the Rehabilitation Act.

This somewhat pessimistic view needs to be tempered by the fact that only a few cases have been brought in employment, and even fewer in housing, and standards have just begun to emerge. Further, there is some reason for optimism. It is likely in the future that standards for reasonable accommodation will be based on new federal regulatory interpretations which represent a better balance between the needs of employers and reasonable accommodation to the employee than is reflected in recent court decisions. The new regulations require that a handicapped person with or without reasonable accommodation be able "to perform the essential functions of the position without endangering the health or safety of the individual or others" (United States Code of Federal Regulations 1985). This health-or-safety standard is certainly broader than a "disruptiveness" standard. Further, the regulations require that a number of accommodations be considered: job restructuring, modified work schedules, and modified examinations, among others. While no accommodation is required which would result in "undue hardship" to the employer, the requirements at least offer some guidance to courts on accommodations which should be required in appropriate cases.

In conclusion, then, court challenges based on claims of discrimination have not yet begun to fulfill their potential for the psychiatrically disabled. In the future, they can become a basis to ensure that lifelong stigma unrelated to qualifications for education or work will not stand in the way of reintegration into society.

JUDICIAL INTERVENTION TO ENFORCE FEDERAL STANDARDS

Using the power of the courts to ensure that state and federal agencies properly administer federal statutory programs is becoming increasing important to psychiatrically disabled individuals. For many years, advocates for the disabled focused nearly exclusively on civil rights issues. Increasingly, however, advocates' attention has shifted to the major federal programs which provide funds and basic services to the psychiatrically disabled.

The prime example of this new approach has been the joint effort by lawyers and mental health professionals to challenge unlawful standards used by the Social Security Administration in considering claims for disability benefits based on a mental impairment. Court decisions have held that the Social Security Administration improperly inferred that these claimants were able to work based on criteria which, legally and clinically, permitted no such inference (*Mental Health Association of Minnesota v. Schweiker* 1982; *City of New York v. Heckler* 1983). These cases, moreover, spearheaded a broad-based advocacy effort aimed at the Congress, the press, and the Social Security Administration itself (Rubenstein 1985; Koyanagi 1985). Ultimately, substantial changes were made by both the Congress and the Social Security Administration, changes which have made the program far more fair to the psychiatrically disabled.

Other federal funding programs, among them Medicaid, vocational rehabilitation, and housing programs, are of similar importance to the psychiatrically disabled, but have not been subject to similar challenge. Lawyers, professionals, and the courts can play an important role in ensuring that the psychiatrically disabled receive what they are entitled to under these programs as well. Without this vigilant oversight and the threat of court involvement, the psychiatrically disabled risk falling prey to governmental efforts to cut costs.

Although litigation focusing on government-funding programs is highly promising, there are limitations here as in other areas. These must be taken seriously if strategies in this area are to continue to prove successful. Careful selection of issues which offer real prospect for reform through the courts is as important here as in other areas of the law. Claims must be well grounded in statutory or regulatory requirements. General claims of discriminatory treatment or general allegations that a practice is unfair to the psychiatrically disabled simply will not prove adequate.

A comparison of successful Social Security litigation with an unsuccessful Medicaid claim is illustrative. The legal challenges to the Social Security Administration's evaluation of disability succeeded because the agency's policy—denying mentally disabled individuals benefits even thought they were clearly unable to work—violated specific statutory requirements which keyed benefits to ability to work.

By contrast, attempts to use general nondiscrimination obligations to challenge the government's allocation of funding and resources have not been particularly successful. In a case challenging limits on services by a state's Medicaid program, the Supreme Court has made clear that it will not use general nondiscrimination obligations to force the allocation of additional resources to the handicapped. The Court held that so long as no statutory requirement of the funding mechanism is violated, states are free to exercise discretion in allocating resources without meeting the special needs of the handicapped (*Alexander v. Choate* 1985). The Court, of course, acknowledged that excluding the disabled from "meaningful access" to a program, or singling them out for specifically poor treatment, may sometimes be challengeable.

In this area, procedural hurdles to court access also loom as potential obstacles to effective legal challenge. Despite obstacles to effective action, carefully crafted litigation designed to address particular problem areas remains an important strategy for advocates or professionals representing psychiatrically disabled individuals. Even limited statutory claims in this area have the potential for generating large amounts of funding and services. For example, the Social Security disability-reform effort is estimated to have put 5 billion dollars (over five years) into the hands of the psychiatrically disabled—money which buys food, clothing, shelter, and support services for thousands of disabled persons. The Medicaid program—a frontier virtually untouched by advocates—pays for 43 billion dollars in medical services annually. Thus, in sheer dollar terms, the importance of generating new strategies involving these programs cannot be overestimated.

CONCLUSION

Those who call themselves advocates for the mentally ill must take hold of the valuable and important tool offered by the law and the courts. To be sure, courts often act within very confined limits. Many times, mental health codes or federal statutes do not go far enough. Rather than acting forcefully, courts sometimes prevent effective litigation. Nevertheless, the courts have the potential to become significant players in the effort to develop community-care systems which provide decent conditions for psychiatrically disabled people. It remains for patients, health care professionals, and advocates to work together to fulfill that potential.

REFERENCES
Alexander v. Choate, 53 U.S.L.W. 4072 (1985)
Allen v. Heckler, 780 F.2d 64 (D.C. Cir 1985)
ARC v. Department of Development Services, 38 Cal.3d 384, 211 Cal. Rptr. 78, 696 P.2d 150 (1975)
Arnold v. Sarn, No. C4322355 (Super. Ct. Ariz. 1985)
Atascadero State Hospital v. Scanlon, 52 U.S.L.W. 4985 (1985)
Baxter E, Hopper K: Shelter and housing for the homeless mentally ill, in The Homeless Mentally Ill. Edited by Lamb HR. Washington, DC, Am Psych Press, 1984
Brewster v. Dukakis, No. 7-76-4423-F (D. Mass. 1978)
Brewster v. Dukakis, 675 F.2d 1 (1st Cir. 1982)
Brown v. Board of Education, 347 U.S. 483 (1954)
City of Cleburne v. Cleburne Living Center, 53 U.S.L.W. 5022 (1985)
City of New York v. Heckler, 578 F. Supp. 1109 (E.D.N.Y. 1983), *aff'd*, 742 F.2d 729 (2d Cir. 1984), *reh. den.*, 755 F.2d 31 (2d Cir. 1985), *aff'd* No. 84-1923 (U.S. June 2, 1986)
Clark v. Cohen, No. 84-3393 (E.D. Pa. 1985)
Consolidated Rail Corp. v. Darrone, 465 U.S. 624 (1985)
Davis v. Bucher, 1 MDLR 696 (M.D. Pa. 1978)
Dixon v. Weinberger, 405 F. Supp. 974 (D.D.C. 1975)
Doe v. New York University, 666 F.2d 761 (2d Cir. 1981)
Doe v. Syracuse School District, 5 MDLR 172 (N.D.N.Y. 1981)
Halderman v. Pennhurst State School, 477 F. Supp. 1295 (E.D. Pa. 1977)
Heckler v. Ringer, 104 S. Ct. 2013 (1984)
Jefferson v. Hackney, 406 U.S. 535 (1972)
J.W. v. City of Takoma, 720 F.2d 1126 (9th Cir. 1984)
Kanter AS: Recent zoning cases uphold establishment of group homes for the mentally disabled. Clearinghouse Review 18:515-518, 1984
Klostermann v. Cuomo, 463 N.E.2d 588 (N.Y. Ct. App. 1984), *on remand*, 481 N.Y.S.2d 850 (N.Y. Trial Term 1984)
Koyanagi C: Social Security Disability Reform Act of 1984: implications for those disabled by mental illness. Psychosocial Rehabilitation Journal 9:21-31, 1985
Lessard v. Schmidt, 349 F. Supp. 107B (E.D. Wisc. 1972)
McLaughlin v. Florida, 379 U.S. 184 (1964)
Mental Health Association v. Deukmejian, No. CA 000540 (Cal. Super. Ct., L.A. Co. 1985)
Mental Health Association of Minnesota v. Schweiker, 554 F. Supp. 157 (D. Minn. 1982), *aff'd*, 720 F.2d 965 (8th Cir. 1983)

Mills v. Habluetzel, 456 U.S. 91 (1982)

Mills MJ: The mental health commissionship: major changes over a decade. Hosp Community Psychiatry 36:363-368, 1985

Mississippi University for Women v. Hogan, 458 U.S. 718 (1982)

New York Association for Retarded Children v. Rockefeller, 357 F. Supp. 752 (E.D.N.Y. 1973)

Pennhurst State School and Hospital v. Halderman, 465 U.S. 89 (1984)

Rehabilitation Act of 1973, 29 U.S.C. SS 791 *et seq.*

Rothman D, Rothman S: The Willowbrook Wars. New York, Harper & Row, 1984

Rubenstein LS: Science, law and psychiatric disability. Psychosocial Rehabilitation Journal 9:7-14, 1985

San Antonio Independent School District v. Rodriguez, 411 U.S. 1 (1973)

Scott v. Plante, 691 F.2d 634 (3d Cir. 1982)

Society for Good Will to Retarded Children v. Cuomo, 737 F.2d 1239 (2d Cir. 1984)

Southeastern Community College v. Davis, 442 U.S. 397 (1979)

Thomas v. General Services Administration, 756 F.2d 86 (Fed. Cir. 1985)

Thomas S. by Brooks v. Morrow, 781 F.2d 367 (4th Cir. 1986)

United States Code of Federal Regulations. Title 29, Part 1613 (1985)

Walker v. Weinberger, 600 F. Supp. 757 (D.D.C. 1984)

Whitlock v. Donovan, 598 F. Supp. 126 (D.D.C. 1985)

Wyatt v. Stickney, 325 F. Supp. 781, 334 F. Supp. 1341 (M.D. Ala. 1974)

Youngberg v. Romeo, 457 U.S. 307 (1982)

Index

454 INDEX

Employment
  job-finding clubs and, 240–246
  psychosocial rehabilitation and, 217
  substance use disorder patients, 88, 107–108
  See also Work
Endocrine system, 155
Environmental resource development, 38–39
Environment continuums in psychiatric rehabilitation, 264–265
Equal access litigation, 443–446
Ergotherapy, 361
Experienced Pilots Act of 1979, 135

Family involvement, workers' compensation evaluations, 317
Family therapy
  behavioral family management, 234–240
  chronic physical illness, 151–152
  for schizophrenia, 78–79, 224–226
Federal government
  health insurance benefit cap, 122–123
  reimbursement for child and adolescent psychiatric disabilities, 125–127
Federal Republic of Germany disability services, 353, 365–366
Feighner system of diagnosis, 69, 76
Fellowship House, 209
Financing, treatment for children and adolescents, 118–119
Flexible System of diagnosis, 76
Fountain House (New York City), 201, 204, 208, 217, 247
Framingham Heart Study, 139
French disability services, 361–362
Functional assessment, 254–255

Gainful activity, 424
Gender, prevalence of mental disability and, 19

Gray Eagles, 135
Greek disability services, 366
Group health insurance, 123–124
Guides to the Evaluation of Permanent Impairment (AMA), 10

H.R. 3755, 401–407
H.R. 6181, 400–401
Habilitation programs, 355
Hallucinogenic drugs
  abuse by personality-constricted types, 100
  disabling effects, 94
Halstead-Reitan test, 138
Handicaps, World Health Organization classification, 7–8
Harrison Subcommittee on the Administration of the Social Security Laws, 382–384
Health insurance. See Reimbursement policies
Health maintenance organizations (HMOs), 124–125
Hill House (Cleveland), 210
Homeless mentally ill
  barriers to care, 187–192
  definition, 183–186
  disability among, 186–187
  diversity of, 184–185, 191–192
  geographic variability, 185, 188–189
  historical background, 199
  service delivery, 189–192
Horizon House (Philadelphia), 210
Hospital rehabilitation units, 163
Humpty-Dumpty syndrome, 55

Illness behavior syndrome, 150–151, 160
Immune system, 154–155
Impairment, World Health Organization classification, 7
Inadequacy syndrome, 55
Income maintenance programs. See Supplemental Security Income
Incompetence, disability and, 54
Independence House (St. Louis), 209